Cognition and Suicide

Cognition and Suicide
Theory, Research, and Therapy

Edited by Thomas E. Ellis

American Psychological Association • Washington, DC

Published by
American Psychological Association
750 First Street, NE
Washington, DC 20002
www.apa.org

To order
APA Order Department
P.O. Box 92984
Washington, DC 20090-2984
Tel: (800) 374-2721; Direct: (202) 336-5510
Fax: (202) 336-5502; TDD/TTY: (202) 336-6123
Online: www.apa.org/books/
E-mail: order@apa.org

In the U.K., Europe, Africa, and the Middle East, copies may be ordered from
American Psychological Association
3 Henrietta Street
Covent Garden, London
WC2E 8LU England

Typeset in Goudy by Stephen McDougal, Mechanicsville, MD

Printer: Data Reproductions, Auburn Hills, MI
Cover Designer: Naylor Design, Washington, DC
Technical/Production Editor: Tiffany L. Klaff

Library of Congress Cataloging-in-Publication Data

Cognition and suicide : theory, research, and therapy / Thomas E. Ellis, editor.
   p. cm.
  ISBN 1-59147-357-8
  1. Suicidal behavior—Treatment. 2. Suicidal behavior—Diagnosis. 3. Cognitive therapy.
I. Ellis, Thomas E.

  RC569.C55 2005
  362.28—DC22   2005020260

British Library Cataloguing-in-Publication Data
A CIP record is available from the British Library.

Printed in the United States of America
First Edition

I dedicate this book to my parents, Joe and Whibry Ellis, whose love, guidance, and support have provided the foundation for all that I do.

CONTENTS

CONTRIBUTORS

Thorsten Barnhofer, PhD, Department of Psychiatry, Warneford Hospital, University of Oxford, Oxford, England

Aaron T. Beck, MD, Department of Psychiatry, Center for Cognitive Therapy, University of Pennsylvania, Philadelphia

Max Birchwood, PhD, University of Birmingham, Birmingham, England

Gregory K. Brown, PhD, Center for Cognitive Therapy, University of Pennsylvania, Philadelphia

Milton Z. Brown, PhD, California School of Professional Psychology, Alliant International University, San Diego

Andrea B. Burns, MS, Department of Psychology, Florida State University, Tallahassee

Carmen Caelian, MA, Department of Psychology, University of British Columbia, Vancouver, Canada

Catherine Crane, DPhil, Department of Psychiatry, Warneford Hospital, University of Oxford, England

Danielle S. Duggan, PhD, Department of Psychiatry, Warneford Hospital, University of Oxford, England

Albert Ellis, PhD, Albert Ellis Institute, New York, NY

Thomas E. Ellis, PsyD, Department of Psychology, Marshall University, Huntington, WV

Lisa Firestone, PhD, Glendon Association, Santa Barbara, CA

Gordon L. Flett, PhD, Department of Psychology, York University, Toronto, Ontario, Canada

Kathryn H. Gordon, MS, Department of Psychology, Florida State University, Tallahassee

Gregg R. Henriques, PhD, Department of Graduate Psychology, James Madison University, Harrisonburg, VA

Paul L. Hewitt, PhD, Department of Psychology, University of British Columbia, Vancouver, Canada

Zaffer Iqbal, PhD, School of Psychology, University of Birmingham, Birmingham, England

Elizabeth Jeglic, PhD, Department of Psychiatry, University of Pennsylvania, Philadelphia

David A. Jobes, PhD, Department of Psychology, The Catholic University of America, Washington, DC

Thomas E. Joiner Jr., PhD, Department of Psychology, Florida State University, Tallahassee

Donald Meichenbaum, PhD, Department of Psychology, University of Waterloo, Ontario, Canada

Robert A. Neimeyer, PhD, Department of Psychology, University of Memphis, TN

Kathryn N. Nelson, MA, Department of Psychology, The Catholic University of America, Washington, DC

Israel Orbach, PhD, Department of Psychology, Bar-Ilan University, Ramat-Gan, Israel

Marisol Perez, PhD, Mexican American/Latino Research Center, Department of Psychology, Texas A & M University, College Station

Mark A. Reinecke, PhD, ABPP, Division of Psychology, Feinberg School of Medicine, Northwestern University, Chicago, IL

M. David Rudd, PhD, ABPP, Department of Psychology, Baylor University, Waco, TX

Simon B. Sherry, PhD, Department of Psychology, University of British Columbia, Vancouver, Canada

Barry M. Wagner, PhD, Department of Psychology, The Catholic University of America, Washington, DC

Rheeda L. Walker, PhD, Department of Psychology, University of South Carolina, Columbia

Foluso M. Williams, MS, Department of Psychology, Florida State University, Tallahassee

J. Mark G. Williams, PhD, Department of Psychiatry, Warneford Hospital, University of Oxford, England

LaRicka R. Wingate, MS, Department of Psychology, Florida State University, Tallahassee

David A. Winter, PhD, School of Psychology, University of Hertfordshire, Hatfield, Herts, England

Joanna H. Zimmerman, MA, Department of Psychology, The Catholic University of America, Washington, DC

FOREWORD

MARSHA M. LINEHAN

Suicidal behavior is a worldwide problem that has posed major challenges to efforts to understand and treat it. Around the world, suicide takes nearly 1 million lives each year, placing it among the top 10 leading causes of death. The incidence of suicide has changed little over the past century. Research on the treatment of suicidal behavior has proved notoriously difficult. Methodological problems exist at almost every level. Difficulties are encountered in the classification of suicidal behaviors, in the generalizability of data collected on individuals who have engaged in one category of suicidal behavior to individuals engaging in other categories, and in the applicability of findings collected after individuals have already engaged in suicidal behavior to the understanding of individuals before they engage in suicidal behavior. In addition, the relative infrequency of suicidal behavior, coupled with the ethical imperative to prevent suicidal acts when possible, precludes experimental analyses of factors inducing suicide.

Despite the prevalence of suicide, suicide attempts, and suicidal ideation, despite the associated suffering of suicide survivors, despite the cost to the health care system and to society at large from suicidal behavior, including the high therapist stress and legal liability associated with such behaviors, and despite the evident suffering of the individuals who ultimately kill themselves, attempt to do so, or wish to die, there is remarkably little research on whether therapeutic interventions aimed directly at reducing suicide risk and parasuicidal behaviors are effective in achieving these aims. There are many books, articles, professional workshops, and legal precedents dictating treatment of suicidal behaviors, but few of the recommended or required interventions have been subjected to controlled clinical trials. Thus, although there are standards of care for intervening with individuals at high risk for suicidal acts, there are little or no empirical data confirming that these standards of care are effective in preventing suicide or reducing the frequency or medical severity of suicide attempts. Fewer than 40 randomized clinical trials have been conducted evaluating treatments aimed specifically at treating individuals at high risk for suicide (see Linehan, 2000). This is in contrast to the thousands of studies on the various mental disorders presumed to underlie suicidal behavior.

Unfortunately, data are sparse regarding which treatments (if any) for primary mental disorders actually reduce the risk for suicide, suicide attempts, or suicidal ideation. The exclusion of highly suicidal individuals from most studies notwithstanding, investigators frequently include measures of suicidal behaviors in their outcome batteries. Because studies consistently find that affective disorders are the most common diagnoses related to suicide, the most attention has been given to the effect of treating depression on subsequent suicidal behaviors, the assumption being that effective treatment of depression will reduce the incidence of suicide. Although this assumption makes intuitive sense, no empirical data actually back up the assumption. Pharmacotherapy regimes that are more effective than placebo for reducing depression may or may not be more effective in reducing suicidal ideation (e.g., Beasley, Dornseif, & Bosomworth, 1992; Smith & Glaudin, 1992). To date, no data show that antidepressants reduce the incidence of either suicide attempts or suicide. For example, Buchholtz-Hansen, Wang, and Kragh-Sorensen (1993) followed 219 depressed inpatients who had previously been participants in psychopharmacological multicenter trials. Not only were suicide rates higher than expected at follow-up, but there was no association between response to the antidepressant treatment in the trial and the suicide risk during the first 3 years of observation. Meta-analyses of pooled data from 17 double-blind clinical trials comparing fluoxetine ($n = 1765$) with a tricyclic antidepressant ($n = 731$), placebo ($n = 569$), or both in the treatment of individuals with major depression have shown no significant reductions in suicidal acts as a result of taking antidepressants (Beasley, Saylor, & Bosomworth, 1991; Beasley et al., 1992).

In studies in which actively suicidal individuals were not enrolled, the failure to find significant treatment effects may be because of the low base rate of suicidal acts in a nonsuicidal population. That is, the treatment may not be powerful enough to make a large difference or our current statistics may not be powerful enough to detect a small difference. Findings reported by Beasley et al. (1991) of a pooled incidence of suicidal acts of 0.3% for fluoxetine, 0.2% for placebo, and 0.4% for tricyclic antidepressants suggest that power may not be the problem, on the one hand. Time of follow-up, on the other hand, might be an important factor. Results are reported for only the 5 or 6 weeks during which individuals were active in the treatment protocol; no follow-up data were reported. Even if reducing depression does reduce suicide and parasuicide risk, it is unlikely that effects would show up so quickly.

An absence of significant effects could also be due to equivalent efficacy across many interventions with low-severity patients. That is, any active treatment may be equally effective at suicide prevention within a population at low initial risk for suicide. Looking at the relationship of reducing depression to reducing suicidal behavior from the reverse direction, Linehan, Armstrong, Suarez, Allmon, and Heard (1991) showed that a cognitive–behavioral therapy that resulted in a significant reduction in suicide attempts and other intentional self-injury compared with treatment as usual did so despite being no more effective in reducing depression or hopelessness than the control condition (depression and hopelessness improved in both treatments). A similar finding was reported by Sakinofsky, Robin, Brown, Cumming, and James (1990), who found that improvement in depression, hostility, locus of control, powerlessness, self-esteem, sensitivity to criticism, and social adjustment measured at an index parasuicide was not related to reduced risk for repeated parasuicide over the next 3 months.

What can be done to improve our treatment of suicidal behaviors? As Tom Ellis notes in this volume, we need to reevaluate our theories of suicidal behavior and look to new approaches and thinking that might lead to new and effective treatments. We need to look at the basic research on mechanisms related to suicidal behaviors to mine them for ideas that will lead to effective interventions. Tom has brought together a team of outstanding experts in suicidal behaviors to do just this. The cognitive approaches to suicidal behavior described in this book include a huge range of theories, including those focusing on cognitive processing (chap. 7, by Neimeyer & Winter; chap. 8, by Williams, Barnhofer, Crane, & Duggan), those more focused on cognitive content—for example, theories of Beck (chap. 3, by G. K. Brown, Jeglic, Henriques, & Beck) and Albert Ellis (chap. 1, by T. E. Ellis; chap. 4, by A. Ellis & T. E. Ellis)—theories both more behavioral in focus (e.g., chap. 5, by M. Brown), and those more rooted in psychodynamic and developmental theories (e.g., chap. 6, by Firestone; chap. 9, by Orbach; chap. 13, by Wagner & Zimmerman). A particularly innovative social disconnection model is described in chapter 10 by Hewitt, Flett, Sherry, and Caelian. Taken together, these chapters are a gold mine of ideas for future treatment development research. If read closely, each offers a multitude of ideas for constructing innovative treatments that may be effective in the treatment and prevention of suicidal behavior. This book offers a wonderful opportunity to jump-start the field of suicide treatment research.

REFERENCES

Beasley, C. M., Dornseif, B. E., & Bosomworth, J. C. (1992). Fluoxetine and suicide: A meta-analysis of controlled trials of treatment for depression. *International Journal of Clinical Psychopharmacology, 6*, 35–57.

Beasley, C. M., Sayler, M. E., & Bosomworth, J. C. (1991). High-dose fluoxetine: Efficacy and activating-sedating effects in agitated and retarded depression. *Journal of Clinical Psychopharmacology, 11*, 166–174.

Buchholtz-Hansen, P. E., Wang, A. G., & Kragh-Sorensen, P. (1993). Mortality in major affective disorder: Relationship to subtype of depression. *Acta Psychiatrica Scandinavica, 87,* 329–335.

Linehan, M. M. (2000). Behavioral treatment of suicidal behaviors: Definitional obfuscations and treatment outcomes. In R. Maris, S. Canetto, J. McIntosh, & M. Silverman (Eds.), *Review of suicidology 2000* (pp. 84–111). New York: Guilford Press.

Linehan, M. M., Armstrong, H. E., Suarez, A., Allmon, D., & Heard, H. L. (1991). Cognitive–behavioral treatment of chronically parasuicidal borderline patients. *Archives of General Psychiatry, 48,* 1060–1064.

Sakinofsky, I., Robin, R. S., Brown, Y., Cumming, C., & James, P. (1990). Problem resolution and repetition of suicide: A prospective study. *British Journal of Psychiatry, 156,* 395–399.

Smith, W. T., & Glaudin, V. (1992). A placebo-controlled trial of paroxetine in the treatment of major depression. *Journal of Clinical Psychiatry, 53,* 36–39.

PREFACE

This book represents the overlap of two respected, interdisciplinary literatures in the behavioral sciences. I am therefore indebted to two "families" of pioneering theorists and researchers. I have been profoundly influenced by the cognitive–behavioral approach to describing, explaining, and treating psychopathology and, after 25-plus years as a practitioner, teacher, supervisor, and researcher, still regard myself as a student in some respects. My training at the Institute for Rational Emotive Therapy (now the Albert Ellis Institute) proved to be one of the best investments I could have made early in my career; as such, I am indebted to Albert Ellis and other teachers at the institute, notably Ray DiGiuseppe and Janet Wolfe. I have also benefited immeasurably from my exposure to the work of Aaron Beck and Judith Beck through their training, publications, and friendship through the years.

The other "stream" flowing into this book is *suicidology* (a neologism of Edwin Shneidman's now making its way into "mainstream" clinical and research lexicons). As a young clinician, I was mystified and intimidated by suicidal patients; I soon discovered that I was in the company of most clinicians in this regard, largely because the literature held little in the way of specific clinical guidance and even less rigorous research on intervening with this high-risk population. Attending a clinical suicidology workshop in 1983 turned out to be a defining moment for me, providing a focus for my research and a channel for my passion for cognitive–behavioral therapy (CBT). That workshop was led by Lanny Berman (now executive director of the American Association of Suicidology); no one has been more supportive through the years, and I will always be in his debt. Others within the suicidology community to whom I am indebted include David A. Jobes, M. David Rudd, Thomas E. Joiner Jr., Lisa Firestone, Sylvia Canetto, Steve Stack, David Lester, and many others. And right at the intersection of CBT and suicidology, where I am most at home, is Marsha M. Linehan, who welcomed me to Seattle for a few days in 1987 and dazzled me with many of the ideas that were eventually to set the standard for empirically based, comprehensive treatment of suicidal individuals, stretching the definition of CBT in the process.

Other people who have inspired me and served as role models and valued peers, I am thrilled to say, appear in the contributors list to this book. This list truly comprises a "dream team" of individuals who have shaped the field of cognition and suicide. I was amazed and immensely gratified at the number of accomplished individuals who accepted my invitation without hesitation (it is also exciting to see the number of younger colleagues who joined as coauthors, thus suggesting a promising future for further advances in theory and research).

A book of this scope is not produced without a strong supporting cast. I thank Susan Reynolds, acquisitions editor, and Emily Leonard, development editor, in the Books Department at the American Psychological Association, for their support, guidance, and flexibility during this, my first venture into book editorship. Thanks also to my colleagues at the West Virginia University School of Medicine, Charleston Division, where the foundation for this book was laid, and to Marshall University, which provided a Summer Research Award to support its completion. I have also greatly appreciated the help of two able graduate assistants, Pamela Tenney and Danielle Fridley, through whose cheerful and conscientious assistance this became a better book. Thanks also to my colleague, Professor Steven Mewaldt, for commentary on portions of the book and general cheerleading. Finally, I acknowledge my loving wife Clare, who has continually amazed me with her unwavering support for my career and projects like this, and my children, Taylor and Carter—reasons for living if ever there were any.

Cognition and Suicide

INTRODUCTION

THOMAS E. ELLIS

Cognitive–behavioral therapies (CBTs) have long since exited the ranks of "new" or "revolutionary" psychotherapies and are now solidly positioned in the front ranks of mainstream therapeutic approaches. This position has been earned through rigorous and systematic approaches to development by well-respected theorists, researchers, and clinicians worldwide. In a recent summary statement, Prochaska and Norcross (2003) described CBTs as "the fastest growing and most heavily researched orientations on the contemporary scene," commenting further that "if we were forced to purchase stock in any of the psychotherapy systems, Beck's cognitive therapy would be the blue-chip growth selection for the next five years" (p. 369).

Such enthusiasm has contributed to accelerating efforts to further actualize the promise of cognitively oriented approaches to a wide variety of problems, from psychological disorders to medical conditions. Unfortunately, one population that has not benefited equally from this growth is individuals with suicidal thoughts and behaviors. With few exceptions to the rule (e.g., Ellis, 1986; Linehan, 1993; Rudd, Joiner, & Rajab, 2000; Schotte & Clum, 1987), CBT has differed little from other therapies in its failure to articulate fully how therapy might be tailored to address the specific dysfunctions and vulnerabilities of suicidal individuals. Despite a large and growing research literature showing a variety of clinically significant cognitive differences between suicidal and nonsuicidal psychiatric patients (see especially Part III: "Cognitive Aspects of Suicidality," this volume), the field has seen only a few attempts to date to articulate specifically how to tailor CBT to suicidal individuals (e.g., Berk, Henriques, Warman, Brown, & Beck, 2004; Ellis & Newman, 1996; Freeman & Reinecke, 1993; Linehan, 1993; Rudd et al.,

2000). Controlled outcome research in the area is even more conspicuously lacking (see Linehan, 2000).

This is particularly striking in light of the enormity of suicide as a public health problem and the ubiquity of suicide in psychotherapeutic practice. In 1999, U.S. Surgeon General David Satcher issued a Call to Action, declaring suicide "a major public health problem," responsible for more deaths in the United States than homicide or AIDS (U.S. Public Health Service, 1999). Risk is particularly high among clinical populations: At least 90% of suicides involve some psychiatric disorder, with suicide rates among people with specific disorders many times that of nonpsychiatric populations (Institute of Medicine, 2002). For example, studies show that between 4% and 10% of people with schizophrenia die by suicide, a suicide rate 30 to 40 times that of the general population. (Institute of Medicine, 2002). (See chap. 14, this volume, for a discussion of suicidality in schizophrenia.) It is further recognized that the experience of the suicide of a patient is a relatively common—and profoundly troubling—occurrence among mental health professionals (e.g., Chemtob, Bauer, Hamada, Pelowski, & Muraoka, 1989).

Given the promise of CBTs and the urgency of the problem of suicide, one wonders why the field has not responded with a flurry of research activity and clinical development, comparable to that seen with anxiety disorders in the 1990s. One reason may be the lack of a definitive and integrated body of clinical research on the cognitive psychopathology of the population. CBT for panic disorder was shaped profoundly by the empirically derived construct of anxiety sensitivity, shown to distinguish panic disorder patients from those with other anxiety disorders (Barlow, 2002). The key role of safety behaviors among people with agoraphobia (Barlow, 2002), body dissatisfaction among eating disorder patients (Fairburn, 1997), and uncontrollable worry among patients with generalized anxiety disorder (Barlow, 2002) are other examples of psychopathology research driving the development of effective therapeutic techniques. With the possible exception of the construct of hopelessness (Beck, Brown, & Steer, 1989), however, CBT has not benefited to a comparable extent from research into the cognitive "ingredients" of suicidal ideation and behavior. As indicated earlier, this is not for lack of meaningful research. Rather (with the exception of hopelessness), there seems to be a sort of disconnect between this knowledge base and the development of intervention strategies.

The present volume is an attempt to bring together for the first time the work of leading theorists and researchers exploring various facets of cognition and their influence on the experience of suicidal individuals. The book's purpose is to form a basis for synthesizing this disparate body of work and to understand its implications for the development of CBT strategies, while also illuminating areas in which the research falls short and is in need of further expansion.

That suicidal thinking and behavior are related is, of course, obvious. One can scarcely imagine self-destructive behavior in the absence of suicidal fantasies, planning, rehearsal, rumination, and so forth—all cognitive processes. This self-evident association between thinking *about* suicide and the act itself was obviously not discovered by cognitive–behavior therapists or researchers. Nor are discussions of *attitudes and beliefs* about suicide anything new. Philosophers and theologians have discussed and debated these (cognitive) aspects of suicide for centuries: Is suicide acceptable? Is it sinful? Noble? Is suicide a reasonable solution to problems in living?

However, current theory and research, as presented in this volume, take place in a very different context from these earlier discussions. Descriptions of suicidal ideation (thinking about killing oneself), whether ancient or modern, are only that—descriptions. Although of great value in literary usage and in some clinical contexts (e.g., suicide risk assessments), mere descriptions lack explanatory value. Yet explanation is an essential prerequisite to effective treatment. In other words, descriptive accounts do not help us to understand *why* people become suicidal or *how* to help a person make changes through therapy. Similarly, attitudes and beliefs about suicide, including whether suicide is a desirable, acceptable, or effective solution to unhappiness may affect the threshold for suicidal acts, but they do not explain why one person experiences self-destructive urges in the first place, whereas another, similarly stressed individual does not. This question perhaps best reflects the various issues tackled in this book.

The book is organized into four parts: The first, "Overview and Historical Perspective," takes the reader through the chronology and theoretical developments starting with the first intersections of cognitive theory and the study of suicide, through the series of intellectual and empirical developments that set the stage for the present volume. In chapter 1, I summarize a series of developments that led up to what I would suggest is the crucial and most potentially valuable break with prior thinking in which cognition moves from a correlational to a causal relationship with suicidality and its modification. In chapter 2, David A. Jobes and Kathryn N. Nelson provide an illuminating, detailed account of Edwin Shneidman's seminal contributions to the understanding of the role of thought processes in suicidal phenomena.

Clinician readers will be most interested in the second part, "Theoretical Systems," which covers each of the major CBT perspectives, with contributors describing how each respective theory approaches suicide and suicidal behavior. Authors were specifically asked to (a) describe suicidal behavior from within their theoretical framework, (b) explain from a cognitive perspective why suicidality occurs in some individuals and not others, (c) show how specific cognitive characteristics might translate into specific cognitive–behavioral intervention strategies, and (d) describe research findings germane to the use of these interventions. The qualifications of these contributors are unimpeachable; I feel extremely fortunate that each chapter is authored either by the creator of the theory or by individuals who have worked closely with the originator. In chapter 3, Aaron T. Beck joins lead author Gregory K. Brown and colleagues to outline Beck's perspective on suicidal patients and outline their cutting-edge, manual-based therapy for working with them. In chapter 4, Albert Ellis and I (no relation, by the way) provide the first-ever detailed explication of rational–emotive behavior therapy's approach to explaining suicidality and how this theory translates into therapeutic intervention. Chapter 5 presents a well-documented synopsis of Marsha Linehan's influential dialectical behavior therapy (DBT) by Milton Z. Brown, who worked closely with Dr. Linehan at the University of Washington. DBT is noteworthy as the first therapy (and still one of the only therapies, cognitive or otherwise) to have been shown in randomized controlled studies to have an impact on suicidal behavior.

Chapters 6 and 7, although less recognizable as traditional cognitive therapies, nevertheless have important things to say about how and why people become suicidal and how we might best help them. I am pleased that Lisa Firestone agreed to contribute a chapter on voice therapy. Created by her father, Robert Firestone, voice therapy draws on psychodynamic and existential traditions; however, the therapeutic technique contains some unmistakable cognitive ingredients. What voice therapy adds is a vital expressive component, often missing in cognitive approaches, that enables access to the kinds of deep cognitive and affective processes that likely are activated during suicidal episodes. Robert A. Neimeyer and David A. Winter's contribution on constructivist therapy (chap. 7) covers yet another key area, eloquently reminding us of limitations to the information processing model of cognition and affect and coming full circle with George Kelly's early observation that to help suicidal individuals, we must help them to see that reality is, to a considerable extent, a product of our own constructive processes, which can victimize us or be harnessed to ameliorate our pain.

The book's third part, "Cognitive Aspects of Suicidality," will be of greatest interest to researchers, although it contains key insights for clinicians as well. It provides summaries of research programs investigating specific areas of cognitive functioning thought to serve as cognitive diatheses that place some individuals at elevated risk for becoming suicidal and may constitute appropriate foci for targeted interventions. Contributors were asked to summarize their own and related research in the area and to discuss associated treatment implications. Three of these chapters cover mainstay topics in the area of cognition and suicide: In chapter 8, J. Mark G. Williams and colleagues summarize their seminal work on overgeneral autobiographical memory; in chapter 10, Paul L. Hewitt, Gordon L. Flett, and colleagues discuss how perfectionism increases the likelihood of suicidality; and in chapter 11, Mark A. Reinecke provides an overview of one of the most consistent findings in the cognition and suicide literature: the association between ineffective problem solving and suicidal ideation and behavior. Also appearing are two contributions that may be less familiar to the informed reader but no less germane to the discussion. In chapter 9, Israel Orbach presents his compelling theoretical and research-based views on the importance of one's feelings and attitudes about one's body in relation to self-harm acts and impulses. In chapter 12, Thomas E. Joiner joins with lead author LaRicka R. Wingate and colleagues to demonstrate the relevance of positive psychology (optimism in particular) to the issue of suicide. As a collection, these chapters constitute the beginnings of a mosaic of the suicidal mind.

The final part, "Special Topics," provides summaries of other theoretical and empirical developments in the theory and research of cognition and suicide, including specific patient populations, developmental issues, and process issues important to the onset, maintenance, and recurrence of suicidal thinking and behavior. In a piece remarkable for its scope (chap. 13), Barry M. Wagner and Joanna H. Zimmerman explore developmental issues regarding suicidality in children and adolescents, including how a developmental gap in brain development might contribute to the development of cognitive characteristics that predispose young people to suicidality. Neurobiological considerations continue in Zaffer Iqbal and Max Birchwood's contribution (chap. 14) discussing suicidality in the context of schizophrenic illness and associated depression and psychotic processes (this chapter also suggests a significant reorientation in treating patients with schizophrenia to focus more on the emotional impact of experiencing this devastating illness). In chapter 15, CBT pioneer Donald Meichenbaum echoes constructivist principles from Neimeyer and Winter's chapter in his insightful discussion of addressing suicidality in the context of posttraumatic stress disorder. Finally, in chapter 16, M. David Rudd, drawing on many of the findings discussed in other chapters, presents a new and fascinating theoretical proposal (fluid vulnerability theory) that explains why and how individuals vary with respect to their threshold for activation of the "suicidal mode."

In closing, a disclaimer is in order: The concentration here on cognitive content and processes is offered in service of advancing cognitive therapeutic interventions and should not be viewed as denying or minimizing the multifactorial nature of suicide, including biological, developmental, social, and cultural influences. Recent advances have shown clearly that dichotomous thinking (e.g., nature vs. nurture) has no place in the study of suicide; an integrative approach is clearly more appropriate. For example, in an important contribution proposing a cognitive diathesis–stress model of suicidality, Yang and Clum (1996) presented evidence from the literature showing how cognitive factors were associated not only with suicidal outcomes but also with antecedent developmental events (e.g., child maltreatment). This proposed model is consistent with empirical findings by Lewinsohn and colleagues showing a cognitive pathway through which physical illness, psychopathology, environmental factors, and interpersonal problems were associated with suicidal behavior (Lewinsohn, Rohde, & Seeley,

1996). Refer to van Heeringen, Hawton, and Williams (2000) for another example of this perspective. The stage is clearly set for an integrative approach to the study of cognition and suicide.

REFERENCES

Barlow, D. H. (2002). *Anxiety and its disorders* (2nd ed.). New York: Guilford Press.

Beck, A. T., Brown, G., & Steer, R. A. (1989). Prediction of eventual suicide in psychiatric inpatients by clinical rating of hopelessness. *Journal of Consulting and Clinical Psychology, 57,* 309–310.

Berk, M. S., Henriques, G. R., Warman, D. M., Brown, G. K., & Beck, A. T. (2004). A cognitive therapy intervention for suicide attempters: An overview of the treatment and case examples. *Cognitive and Behavioral Practice, 11,* 265–277.

Chemtob, C. M., Bauer, G. B., Hamada, R. S., Pelowski, S. R., & Muraoka, M. Y. (1989). Patient suicide: Occupational hazard for psychologists and psychiatrists. *Professional Psychology: Research and Practice, 20,* 294–300.

Ellis, T. E. (1986). Toward a cognitive therapy for suicidal individuals. *Professional Psychology: Research and Practice, 17,* 125–130.

Ellis, T. E., & Newman, C. F. (1996). *Choosing to live: How to defeat suicide through cognitive therapy.* Oakland, CA: New Harbinger.

Fairburn, C. G. (1997). Eating disorders. In D. M. Clark & C. G. Fairburn (Eds.), *Science and practice of cognitive behavior therapy* (pp. 209–241). Oxford, England: Oxford University Press.

Freeman, A., & Reinecke, M. A. (1993). *Cognitive therapy of suicidal behavior: A manual for treatment.* New York: Springer.

Institute of Medicine. (2002). Psychiatric and psychological factors. In S. K. Goldsmith, T. C. Pellmar, A. M. Kleinman, & W. E. Bunney (Eds.), *Reducing suicide: A national imperative* (pp. 61–100). Washington, DC: National Academies Press.

Lewinsohn, P. M., Rohde, P., & Seeley, J. R. (1996). Adolescent suicidal ideation and attempts: Prevalence, risk factors, and clinical implications. *Clinical Psychology: Science and Practice, 3,* 25–46.

Linehan, M. M. (1993). *Cognitive–behavioral treatment of borderline personality disorder.* New York: Guilford Press.

Linehan, M. M. (2000). Behavioral treatments of suicidal behaviors: Definitional obfuscation and treatment outcomes. In R. W. Maris, S. S. Canetto, J. L. McIntosh, & M. M. Silverman (Eds.), *Review of suicidology, 2000* (pp. 84–111). New York: Guilford Press.

Prochaska, J. O., & Norcross, J. C. (Eds.). (2003). *Systems of psychotherapy: A transtheoretical analysis.* Belmont, CA: Brooks/Cole.

Rudd, M. D., Joiner, T. E., & Rajab, M. H. (2000). *Treating suicidal behavior: An effective, time-limited approach.* New York: Guilford.

Schotte, D. E., & Clum, G. A. (1987). Problem-solving skills in suicidal psychiatric patients. *Journal of Consulting and Clinical Psychology, 55,* 49–54.

U.S. Public Health Service. (1999). *The Surgeon General's call to action to prevent suicide*. Washington, DC: U.S. Department of Health and Human Services.

van Heeringen, K., Hawton, K., & Williams, J. M. (2000). Pathways to suicide: An integrative approach. In K. Hawton & K. van Heeringen (Eds.), *The international handbook of suicide and attempted suicide* (pp. 223–234). Chichester, England: Wiley.

Yang, B., & Clum, G. A. (1996). Effects of early negative life experiences on cognitive functioning and risk for suicide: A review. *Clinical Psychology Review, 16,* 177–195.

I

OVERVIEW AND HISTORICAL PERSPECTIVE

1

THE STUDY OF COGNITION AND SUICIDE: BEGINNINGS AND DEVELOPMENTAL MILESTONES

THOMAS E. ELLIS

The creation and empirical development of cognitive–behavioral therapies (CBTs) represent a milestone in the history of psychotherapy. CBT's rigorous empirical standards have effectively challenged other therapeutic approaches to follow suit, spurring an increase in research activity in therapy camps that once considered empiricism almost irrelevant (see, e.g., Leichsenring, Rabung, & Leibing, 2004). We are also seeing a shift from identification of CBT as an assemblage of therapeutic techniques to a framework for developing a variety of cognitively oriented interventions tailored for specific disorders according to research-based formulations for those disorders. In fact, CBT pioneer A. T. Beck's very definition of cognitive therapy now embraces this specificity.

> Although there have been many definitions of cognitive therapy, I have been most satisfied with the notion that cognitive therapy is best viewed as the application of the *cognitive model of a particular disorder* with the use of a variety of techniques designed to modify the dysfunctional beliefs and faulty information processing *characteristic of each disorder*. (Beck, 1993, p. 194, emphasis added)

Thus, we now see specific therapies for panic disorder, obsessive–compulsive disorder, depression, eating disorders, and many others that, although sharing cognitive–behavioral underpinnings, differ markedly in their formulations, foci, and intervention strategies.

Specifics of the relationship between cognition and suicide did not become clinically important until the introduction of cognitive therapy. Previously, suicidal thinking and behavior were viewed simply as going hand in hand, much as thinking was associated with any other behavior, from driving a car to proposing marriage. Suicidal ideation was variously conceptualized as (a) a component of a free, moral choice by an individual; (b) a concomitant aspect of suicidality; (c) a symptom of psychopathology (depression, schizophrenia, etc.); or (d) an epiphenomenon of underlying psychological processes (psychodynamics). In each case, the suicidal thinking itself was of less interest than what was thought to cause it, which became the primary target for change.

However, with the introduction of cognitive therapy in the second half of the last century, the significance of cognition itself changed. Fundamental to the cognitive–mediational model are the notions that (a) cognition exists in a *causal* relation to pathological affect and behavior and (b) interventions that modify dysfunctional attitudes, beliefs, attributions, logical errors, and so forth can be expected to produce therapeutic benefit. The significance of this shift to the treatment of suicidal individuals can hardly be overstated, for this marks *the first time in the history of theorizing about suicide that thought processes were viewed, not only as part of the problem of suicide, but also as a part of a potential solution.*

Thus, the focus on cognitive change as a central curative mechanism requires more than simple recognition of the self-evident; for before one can systematically change a psychological process, it first must be understood with a degree of specificity that allows the development of measurement methods and specific, targeted change strategies. This development carries significant implications not only for cognitive therapy with suicidal individuals, but also for the study of suicide in general. Through the years, suicide has variously been conceptualized as a matter of morals, spirituality, philosophy, unconscious processes, biological dysfunction, environmental forces, or a combination of these. The cognitive perspective brings with it important new implications for treatment and prevention, with an optimistic underlying message that human beings, with guidance when needed, are able to make choices about their perceptions of their circumstances that—without those circumstances necessarily changing—can change how they feel about the ultimate decision: whether "to be or not to be." Indeed, the implications of this body of work (assuming continued positive research findings) extend well beyond the psychotherapy arena to the very essence of what it means to be suicidal. I am hopeful that the full implications of this work will become clear as the reader digests the wide-ranging content of this volume.

THE STUDY OF COGNITION AND SUICIDE: A CHRONOLOGY

Before proceeding to the current state of the art and science of what we might refer to as "cognitive suicidology," let us first consider its roots. Although it would not be unreasonable to assume that the evolution of theory and research into the relationships between cognition and suicide coincided with the "cognitive revolution" impelled by Albert Ellis, Aaron T. Beck, and other CBT pioneers, we would be remiss not to recognize the influence of Edwin Shneidman (also see Jobes & Nelson, chap. 2, this volume). Widely known as "the father of suicidology," Shneidman throughout his career has emphasized psychological processes, more so than biological or environmental factors, as central to the understanding and prevention of suicide. In a groundbreaking research program at the Los Angeles Suicide Prevention Center, hundreds of suicide notes were analyzed for clues to the states of mind of suicide victims. In perhaps the first empirical study of cognitive processes and suicide, Shneidman and colleague Norman Farberow (1957) described several varieties of "illogic" manifested by suicidal individuals, notably in terms of confusing one's self as experienced subjectively with one's self as a person thinks he or she is experienced by others. Shneidman later introduced notions such as cognitive constriction and cognitive rigidity and was a major influence on an early researcher in this arena, Charles Neuringer (see interview in Appendix 1.1).

Although Shneidman clearly deserves credit as an influential figure in the early history of the study of cognition and suicide, some might question whether he should be identified with the cognitive camp. His model certainly gives cognition a prominent place in the phenomenology of suicide. For example, he observed that "the *idea* that 'I can stop this pain by killing myself' is the unique essence of suicide" (Shneidman, 1997, p. 8, emphasis added) and later commented that the word *only* (signifying cognitive constriction) is "the single most dangerous word in suicidology" (p. 59). It is also true, however, that Shneidman's explanatory model has a distinct psychodynamic inclination. Attributing suicide most basically to intractable emotional pain (for which he created the term *psychache*), his therapeutic approach focuses primarily on addressing the unmet needs thought to cause emotional distress and makes little reference to interventions to modify directly cognitive aspects of suicidality. In any event, there is no question that his contributions merit a prominent place in this discussion (hence the inclusion of a chapter on his contributions in this volume).

It is interesting to note that a chapter by George Kelly in a 1961 book edited by Shneidman and Farberow seems to qualify as the first explicitly cognitive conceptualization of suicide, complete with suggestions for a cognitively oriented approach to treatment (Kelly, 1961). In extending his personal construct theory to suicide, Kelly observed the following about a suicidal patient: "The events he described were important not because of what they did to him but because of *what he had made out of them*" (p. 257) and later observed, "none of the alternatives that beckon so clearly in our own minds was quite so visible in his" (p. 259). This is a signature statement of a cognitive theory of suicidal behavior, stating, in other words, not only that the individual had suicidal thinking but that one reason why he was thinking about suicide was the way that he was construing his situation. A different cognitive construal likely would have resulted in a different (perhaps nonsuicidal) outcome.

Kelly went further, anticipating later efforts to apply cognitive–behavioral functional analysis ("what it accomplishes from the point of view of the person who performs it" [p. 257]) not only to suicide but to nonlethal self-harm behavior as well. Observing that many nonlethal suicide attempts are actually efforts to enhance life rather than terminate it, he noted that two sets of cognition dictate when an individual will decide that death makes more sense than living.

> The first is when the course of events seems so obvious that there is no point in waiting around for the outcome. . . . The other is when every-thing seems so utterly unpredictable that the only definite thing one can do is abandon the scene altogether. (1961, p. 260)

Kelly's theories inspired further theorizing by later postmodern writers, leading to considerable empirical research and several varieties of constructivist therapies (Neimeyer & Raskin, 2001; Neimeyer & Winter, chap. 7, this volume).

Aside from the work of A. T. Beck and associates (discussed subsequently), the shift to empirical investigation of cognitive factors as causal factors in suicidality can be credited largely to Charles Neuringer of the University of Kansas (Dr. Neuringer was unable to accept my invitation to write a contribution for this book but was kind enough to agree to an interview, appended to this chapter). Strongly influenced by Shneidman's notions of dichotomous thinking and cognitive constriction, Neuringer pursued a systematic program of research throughout the 1960s and 1970s to elucidate the varieties of suicidal cognition.

In an increasingly sophisticated series of studies, Neuringer was the first to present empirical evidence that the thinking of suicidal individuals, relative to that of comparison groups, was characterized by dichotomous thinking (Neuringer, 1961, 1967, 1968), cognitive rigidity (Neuringer, 1964), and impaired problem solving (Levenson & Neuringer, 1971). In another important finding, Neuringer showed that highly suicidal individuals, relative to less severely suicidal and nonsuicidal individuals, not only evaluated life and death more extremely but were the only group actually to view death in a more favorable light than life (Neuringer & Lettieri, 1971). In the first published review of research on cognition and suicide, Neuringer (1976) concluded that there was, indeed, sufficient evidence to conclude that "there is a difference in the cognitive structures and activities of suicidal individuals" (p. 246) relative to other people. He presented the following specific notions as hypotheses for further research:

1. Suicidal individuals have difficulty in utilizing and relying on internal imaginative resources to a greater degree than nonsuicidal individuals.
2. Suicidal individuals polarize their value systems to a greater degree than normal people. . . .
3. Suicidal individuals are more rigid and constricted in their thinking than nonsuicidal persons. . . .
4. Suicidal individuals are much more present oriented as opposed to being past and future oriented than nonsuicidal individuals. They show a startling lack of ability to project or imagine themselves into the future. (p. 247)

Working concurrently with (although separately from) Neuringer during the 1960s, Aaron Beck took a somewhat different path to the study of cognition and suicide. Whereas Neuringer studied primarily cognitive processes, Beck looked more at the content of suicidal thinking. In asking the key question of why only a subset of depressed patients becomes suicidal, Beck and associates proposed the important construct of hopelessness. In a key definitional step, hopelessness was conceptualized not as an affective state but as a set of negative expectations about the future (Minkoff, Bergman, Beck, & Beck, 1973). Subsequent studies not only have shown hopelessness to be a measurable and reliable risk indicator for suicide but have also established it as a key mediational link between depression severity and suicidality (Weishaar, 2000).

An important recent addition to the hopelessness construct has been Beck's idea of "modes." Proposed as a means of addressing some of the limitations of the schema construct as a more or less linear processing model (Beck, 1996), modes consist of cognitive, affective, behavioral, and motivational processes that are activated under specific conditions (e.g., "fight–flight mode"). Rudd (2000) applied this model to suicidality by elaborating a specific "suicidal mode." The suicidal mode helps explain the dramatic temporal shifts often seen in suicidal individuals and describes in detail underlying components that may be subject to therapeutic intervention.

The past 2 decades have seen important elaborations and refinements to the foundational work of Shneidman, Neuringer, and Beck. Prominent among these have been the contributions of Marsha Linehan, notably the Reasons for Living (RFL) Inventory and dialectical behavior therapy (DBT). The RFL construct presented not only a novel means of discriminating suicidal from nonsuicidal individuals but also an intuitively appealing assessment instrument with valuable clues for helping suicidal individuals. DBT, although developed initially as a structured therapy for individuals with bor-

derline personality disorder (Linehan, 1993), is also one of the only therapeutic interventions with empirical evidence of efficacy specifically with
people who are suicidal (e.g., Verheul, van den Bosch, & Koeter, 2003).
Other important contributions to the study of cognition and suicide, such as
memory function, problem-solving deficits, and perfectionism, are described
in depth elsewhere in this volume.

In summary, the theorists and researchers described in this chapter set
the stage for later, potentially revolutionary, advances in understanding
suicidality through the lens of cognitive processes. Through this work, it became clear that, far from being merely reflective of the suicidal state, a variety of cognitive processes were deeply implicated in the genesis and maintenance of suicidal impulses, plans, and behaviors. Moreover, it was
demonstrated that these processes were observable (measurable) and potentially modifiable. What remained to be determined was further identification and explication of the nature and variety of cognitive processes involved
and the development of effective therapeutic procedures for modifying them.
These, of course, are ongoing agendas and constitute the substance for the
remainder of this volume.

APPENDIX 1.1:
AN INTERVIEW WITH CHARLES NEURINGER

Editor's Note: Because of his prominent place in the initial
conceptualization of and research into cognitive aspects of suicidality, Dr.
Charles Neuringer was at the top of my list of potential contributors to this
book. Indeed, not only did he conduct the seminal studies testing Shneidman's
ideas about cognitive characteristics of suicidality, he also wrote the first
review of the cognition and suicide literature (Neuringer, 1976). Because
the 30th anniversary of that review was approaching, it seemed more than
fitting that his perspective be tapped for a retrospective overview of the area
for this book. Unfortunately, because of ill health, he was unable to accept
my invitation. However, he was kind enough to allow me to conduct the
following telephone interview with him. Dr. Neuringer is professor emeritus
at the Department of Psychology, University of Kansas, Lawrence. The interview took place on March 20, 2003.

> TE: Dr. Neuringer, you began a pioneering career in the study of
> cognition and suicide over 40 years ago. What do you think of
> the idea of a book devoted to the topic?

> CN: It's about time!

> TE: It's about time?

> CN: It's about time! Yes, I always thought to myself that there ought
> to be a major symposium or a research push in this area, because

I think this is the key to dealing with suicide. I've said this before. You know there are lots of theories about suicide starting with Freud and others. I don't think that any of that has been helpful . . . the theory, the personality theory stuff is interesting. But I don't know that it really helps the caregiver or therapist.

TE: You had said in some of your early work that the motivational approach to suicide had been disappointing—obviously, you felt like an alternative was needed.

CN: Yes! As I said in terms of understanding what's happening or why the individual is committing suicide, I think the cognitive approach is best. As far as treatment goes, social engineering and a sort of retraining is most effective.

TE: We have seen research on cognition and suicide expand into many areas such as hopelessness, problem solving, perfectionism, and so forth. You were well ahead of your time in anticipating these developments.

CN: Thank you!

TE: How was it that you settled upon this, I think, as your dissertation topic, correct?

CN: Yes. It was in 1958. I had passed my preliminary examinations and was going to start on my internship, and I was, of course, looking for a dissertation topic. I happened to be at the APA which was held in New York that year, and I just wandered into a symposium on suicide and Dr. Shneidman was presenting on what he had learned from the analysis of suicide notes.

TE: And this was a revelation to you?

CN: Yes it was, and he offered some hypotheses that were very interesting.

TE: Can you say what in particular it was about his approach that appealed to you?

CN: Well, it was the linguistic analysis of suicide notes. He had used a lot of Osgoods's type analysis in which the words *never* and *always* appeared, and he drew a hypothesis about extreme thinking. And that's what interested me and I said to myself, you know I can evaluate that . . . I can test that. Which is what I did in my dissertation.

TE: Now, was this prior to your time at the Los Angeles Suicide Prevention Center?

CN: Oh yes. What happened was I was a VA trainee and—listen, in the middle of Kansas you don't find too many subjects! I asked if I could be transferred to the Los Angeles VA Hospital where

Dr. Shneidman was to do the research, and Shneidman was willing, the VA was willing, so I spent the year at the Los Angeles VA Hospital and the Los Angeles County Hospital gathering data for the dissertation.

TE: What was it like there during those years? Those were exciting times for the development of the study of suicide and suicide prevention.

CN: Yes, they had a working relationship with the county hospital, which is where I got most of my subjects. And also with the Los Angeles County Coroner and they did a lot of what they called psychological autopsies. When the coroner was not sure about the cause of death, he would call in his team of suicidologists and ask them to investigate. And I did some of those; in fact, you know when I finished up and got my degree, Shneidman asked me to join the group in Los Angeles and I said yes, so I worked in Los Angeles with the suicide prevention center for 2 years.

TE: There were some real pioneers there at the time, Shneidman, Norman Farberow, Robert Litman . . .

CN: Oh yes. Norman Tabachnik and a whole bunch of others.

TE: Did anyone in particular there affect your thinking about cognition and suicide?

CN: Well, Shneidman.

TE: It was mainly Shneidman?

CN: Yes—the man is a genius.

TE: High praise.

CN: Yes, he is, he is! I owe a great deal of my career in the area of suicide to him. He is a father figure for me.

TE: You published a paper in 1961 about dichotomous thinking. Was that your first study on cognition and suicide?

CN: I don't have my vita before me. I think that's right.

TE: This was using the semantic differential test . . . you were looking at extreme value judgments and so forth. But, if not your first, that was one of your early ones. Do you think that you were among the first to make a connection between suicidality and problem solving?

CN: Well, maybe explicitly. I wasn't the first to mention it. It's implied in the writings of many, many people. The suicidal individual doesn't know what to do or he doesn't see a future. So I think the relationship between the way a person thinks and his ability to solve problems has always been there. And I just stated it explicitly.

TE: A bit more clearly and looked at it empirically?

CN: Yes, but I can't really take credit for originating the idea.

TE: Your writings have focused mainly on empirical findings and relatively less on the origins of suicidal cognition. Can you speculate some on why you think certain people develop these kinds of cognitive vulnerabilities?

CN: You know, that's a million dollar question, because the answer to that question, if it can be answered, revolves around something that people have talked about, the so-called suicidal personality. That somebody is "born to die." You get a lot of that in literary writings, that there's something called the suicide personality. Now I'll tell you, I do not think that there is a suicidal destiny in an individual or that there's some gene that's linked to suicide. I don't think you're born suicidal, but I do think the early parental training or early parental treatment, especially if the superego is very strong or you have harsh parents who demand perfection from kids, punish them for transgression, or put an emphasis on honor—that kind of early training leads some children to see the world in a particular way.

TE: I see . . .

CN: Of which there is no charity, no forgiveness, no moderation. It instills impossibly high ideals in children. And I think that kind of early training is going to lead to a particular way of looking at the world, which is no good for them. So I do think it's something that's learned.

TE: Learned.

CN: Learned in early childhood. I don't think you just become suicidal later in life. I think the germ or the seeds are laid down in early childhood. Now, such a person may get through life if everything goes okay. So, there's no stress, but I think that basically if you are "educated" that way by your parents, by society, you are vulnerable to dealing with stress in a particularly lethal way.

TE: Might we also talk about what is *not* learned in childhood, namely, how to identify and define problems and approach them in a systematic way of problem solving?

CN: Yes, yes, obviously it's true that if you don't know how to roll with the punches or solve problems, you're going to be in trouble. So I don't think it's innate, I don't think it's genetic, I think it's the product of a certain kind of early training.

TE: Which I suppose is a more optimistic appraisal, since what's learned can be modified.

CN: Yes, but there's always one problem. What's learned early in life and constantly reinforced is, of course, harder to extinguish.

TE: I see.

CN: So, I think therapy with suicidal individuals is tough, because you're fighting a lifetime of seeing the world in a certain way.

TE: I'd like to come back to that point in a moment. Let me ask you first: You wrote in 1971 that suicidal people are not just more troubled but are "in a different world," in the sense that—and here we're talking particularly about severely suicidal people— . . . they actually step over and start to view life in a negative light and death in a positive light. Recently, researchers have been reporting a similar qualitative difference between people who are severely or repeatedly suicidal versus other people who may be suicidal but less often or severely. Do you see this as a significant issue in terms of this qualitative difference between severely suicidal people and others?

CN: The reason I'm sighing is when you say severely suicidal and less suicidal, you're getting into, of course, a methodological morass because, you know, we talk about suicide attempters and suicide committers, and there are lethality scales, and it's hard, it's hard to answer that question. But I certainly do agree with the research that the "serious" suicidal individuals are qualitatively different than the less serious. So it's not just a case of them being more or less suicidal . . . I think they are in a class by themselves and they have their own peculiar view of the world. You see, with the less serious you really never know if it's manipulation or whether it's emotional extortion and that dying is not really what they're after. But, like I say, I really do think there is a qualitative difference between the less and the very serious. Okay, does that answer your question?

TE: Yes it does, and it sounds like understanding this will be extremely important in terms of developing our interventions.

CN: Yes.

TE: Next question: An unresolved and rather complicated question is whether the cognitive characteristics of suicidal people are just correlates of the suicidal state that disappear after the crisis resolves or perhaps are more traitlike vulnerabilities that can be treated to reduce the future risk of suicide. Do you subscribe to one view or the other? I think you were sort of hinting at that earlier.

CN: As always, all the answers are complicated. I do think that those individuals who have what we call suicidal cognitive organization are constantly under bombardment. They may be better, you know, they may feel better when an environmental stress is removed, but they remain constantly vulnerable.

TE: We sometimes worry when we get differences in our studies that they are . . . the differences are only due to the crisis state that the individual might have been in at the time of the study.

CN: Yes.

TE: And I believe that you did follow some subjects over a period of weeks.

CN: Yes! They didn't change.

TE: No change?

CN: Didn't change, which is kind of horrifying in a sense.

TE: Well, and it's very important for those of us who may be doing crisis intervention to understand that just because a crisis has resolved and the patient feels better, this doesn't necessarily mean that their underlying vulnerability has been addressed.

CN: That's right, exactly. There's always another crisis around the corner waiting which, of course, is the way life is.

TE: Yes.

CN: That's the way life is.

TE: And we need to think about how to better equip people to deal with the next adversity.

CN: Yes, yes. That's why cognitive retraining is important and why social engineering . . . getting them out of environments or getting them out of bad relationships is probably the first line of defense.

TE: Shneidman has written on the psychological commonalties of suicide. Do you think that most suicidal people share the same basic cognitive vulnerabilities or possibly that we should think in terms of subtypes, different people with different specific vulnerabilities?

CN: I really don't know the answer to that. My feeling is that there is a common type. But the problem is with the term *suicide*. We use it to cover a multitude of behaviors. So, for example, an individual who will drink a bottle of iodine and tell their spouse that they've taken poison . . . that's characterized as suicidal. Now such a person I think is not the same type as the individual who gets a gun and blows his brains out. Yet both of these people are considered as suicidal, so when Shneidman talks about different types, I'm confused—I don't know whether he is talking about the whole variety of behaviors we call suicidal. So I can't, I personally believe we're talking about the serious individuals, the ones that die, I think that's a group in and of themselves. Other people that are also called suicidal, are, of course, different.

TE: You wrote a paper in the late 1980s about popular myths about suicide and why people tend to believe them. What prompted you to write that article?

CN: You want to know?

TE: Sure!

CN: Okay, the Popular Culture Society was having their annual meeting in Wichita and I wanted to go, and I wanted to be able to get some university support for the trip, so I submitted the so-called "Popular Myths About Suicide."

TE: I see.

CN: So that was basically the motivation. But, of course you know, my point in the paper was that the myths are self-serving.

TE: You certainly had some concern about the public's general conceptions of suicide, or we should say misconceptions.

CN: Yes, and these myths—just like all myths—serve a purpose. Let me give you an example: There is a popular myth about suicide that says, "If they have made up their mind to kill themselves, there is nothing that you can do to stop them." This belief is popular because it relieves you of any responsibility for intervening or stopping the death. The death is not your fault because there is nothing you could do to stop it.

TE: Related question. In general you devoted much of your career to putting common assumptions and folklore about suicidal people to the empirical test. You even challenged the usefulness of the Rorschach test as a suicide predictor.

CN: Yes!

TE: You must feel good about the move in recent years to evidenced-based medicine and empirically supported treatments.

CN: Well, I guess so. I've been really out of the suicide area or what you call the suicide game for a long time. Over the last 10 to 15 years, I've switched to an interest in the psychology of acting. So I have to admit to you I have not kept up with what's going on in the area of suicide.

TE: I see.

CN: It's depressing, it's depressing. One time at a party, somebody introduced me, and said, "Oh, Charlie Neuringer is here . . . he's interested in suicide, terminal illness, schizophrenia . . . he's just a fun guy." You know, and I thought about this, I said it's true. And I decided to change. I was interested in acting. I said, "I'm really going to do something in an area which is life-affirming instead of death oriented." And I was an amateur actor, so I switched to that. I really abandoned the area of suicide . . . you might call it burnout, because it is hard . . . it is hard.

TE: Well, I'm not sure that you could say that something that's life-affirming is unrelated to suicide. You might see it as the flip side of the coin.

CN: Yes. I wanted to flip the coin.

TE: Sure.

CN: I'm sorry I got off on that . . . repeat the question.

TE: Well, it was less a question than an invitation to comment. It's just that you have been very dedicated to empiricism in your career and challenging common assumptions and misconceptions or at least testing some of the theories to provide evidence, notably Shneidman's theories, and I was just observing that throughout your career empiricism seems to have been very important to you.

CN: Yes, okay, yes, I would say yes.

TE: What do you consider your most important or useful contribution to the study of suicide?

CN: Oh boy, that's a toughie. You know, I really am not sure. It's covered the range, you know, the stuff I've done, from visual perception to time perception. I guess it's the original dichotomous thinking . . . that's what I would say is the thing that I'm most proud of, but I also want you to remember that it was not really original with me.

TE: You give a lot of credit to Dr. Shneidman, obviously.

CN: Absolutely, he is the major figure in this area.

TE: Where would you hope to see the science of suicide go in the future? I mean we generally conclude our articles by saying, here are the limitations of our research and here's where the research needs to go in the future.

CN: I wrote a paper which was kind of a summation of all the research, and at the end I said something to the effect we should study suicidal children because they are still impressionable and vulnerable. We should open up the range of cognitive—although you know we've done that quite a bit in time perception . . . you know actually in perception in which we know that suicidal individuals don't seem to have much peripheral vision, which is interesting in and of itself. So I guess one would have to explore on a theoretical level a whole host of cognitive abilities. But, of course, I think where we should concentrate our research is in prevention; how do you deal with people to make sure that they are going to live.

TE: And, of course, we don't know a whole lot as yet about how to modify some of the characteristics that we've learned about, dichotomous thinking for one thing.

CN: Yes, yes.

TE: Or how to prevent its development in the first place.

CN: Yes.

TE: Looking toward the future, would you be willing to make any predictions about what we are likely to learn . . . what we are likely to see in the study of suicide?

CN: No, I really don't know. You know, I looked over the stuff you sent me, and I think all these people are really working on important areas. I don't know, I don't know, I hope that we go further in the prevention area.

TE: I gather you don't anticipate the discovery of a brain scan or a pill that's going to provide the answers?

CN: Oh, I would love it. I would love it. You never know. There are, of course, happiness pills, maybe there will be an antisuicidal pill, I doubt it, but I'm not against chemistry helping out people. If we do discover an antisuicidal pill, I'm all for it! Whether there will be any brain scan that will show up anything odd I doubt it, but I wouldn't mind if they did.

TE: It would sure solve a lot of problems for us, wouldn't it?

CN: Like I said, a happiness pill would be fine. I remember one of my colleagues making a joke, he said he came up with a way to deal with all suicidal people, and he called it money therapy.

TE: Money therapy?

CN: Money therapy. Just give them thousands and millions of dollars and that would cure them. He was, of course, kidding, but, listen, if it works . . . see our job, you know, all the research and all the speculation is for one reason and that is to save people's lives. That's why we are doing it, and if money therapy or hap-piness pills will do the job, that's alright with me.

TE: Well, just having listened to you, I think that you're probably on to a more likely alternative, which is life-affirming experi-ences, which is something that's separate and distinct from money, but certainly you have served as a role model, saying here's something . . . I've made my contribution in the suicide arena, and now I'm going to move on to something that's more life-affirming and I can't think of a better example to cite.

CN: Thank you! Thank you!

TE: Well, that's all my questions. I can't thank you enough for spend-ing this time with me.

CN: It's my pleasure and I wish the book much success.

TE: Thank you, Dr. Neuringer.

REFERENCES

Barlow, D. H. (2002). *Anxiety and its disorders* (2nd ed.). New York: Guilford Press.

Beck, A. T. (1996). Beyond belief: A theory of modes, personality, and psychopa-thology. In P. M. Salkovskis (Ed.), *Frontiers of cognitive therapy* (pp. 1–25). New York: Guilford Press.

Kelly, G. A. (1961). Suicide: The personal construct point of view. In N. L. Farberow & E. S. Shneidman (Eds.), *The cry for help* (pp. 255–280). New York: McGraw-Hill.

Leichsenring, F., Rabung, S., & Leibing, E. (2004). The efficacy of short-term psy-chodynamic psychotherapy in specific psychiatric disorders: A meta-analysis. *Archives of General Psychiatry, 61*, 1208–1216.

Levensen, M., & Neuringer, C. (1971). Problem-solving behavior in suicidal adoles-cents. *Journal of Consulting and Clinical Psychology, 37*, 433–436.

Linehan, M. M. (1993). *Cognitive–behavioral treatment of borderline personality disor-der*. New York: Guilford Press.

Minkoff, K., Bergman, E., Beck, A. T., & Beck, R. (1973). Hopelessness, depression, and attempted suicide. *American Journal of Psychiatry, 130*, 455–459.

Neimeyer, R. A., & Raskin, J. D. (2001). Varieties of constructivism in psycho-therapy. In K. S. Dobson (Ed.), *Handbook of cognitive–behavioral therapies* (2nd ed., pp. 393–430). New York: Guilford Press.

Neuringer, C. (1961). Dichotomous evaluations in suicidal individuals. *Journal of Consulting Psychology, 25*, 445–449.

Neuringer, C. (1964). Rigid thinking in suicidal individuals. *Journal of Consulting Psychology, 28*, 54–58.

Neuringer, C. (1967). The cognitive organization of meaning in suicidal individuals. *Journal of General Psychology*, *76*, 91–100.

Neuringer, C. (1968). Divergencies between attitudes towards life and death among suicidal, psychosomatic, and normal hospitalized patients. *Journal of Consulting and Clinical Psychology*, *32*, 59–63.

Neuringer, C. (1976). Current developments in the study of suicidal thinking. In E. S. Shneidman (Ed.), *Suicidology: Contemporary developments* (pp. 234–252). New York: Grune & Stratton.

Neuringer, C., & Lettieri, D. J. (1971). Cognition, attitude, and affect in suicidal individuals. *Life-Threatening Behavior*, *1*, 106–124.

Rudd, M. D. (2000). The suicidal mode: A cognitive–behavioral model of suicidality. *Suicide and Life-Threatening Behavior*, *30*, 18–33.

Shneidman, E. S., & Farberow, N. L. (1957). The logic of suicide. In E. Shneidman & N. Farberow (Eds.), *Clues to suicide*. New York: McGraw-Hill.

Verheul, R., van den Bosch, L. M., & Koeter, M. W. (2003). Dialectical behaviour therapy for women with borderline personality disorder: 12-month, randomised clinical trial in the Netherlands. *British Journal of Psychiatry*, *182*, 135–140.

Weishaar, M. E. (2000). Cognitive risk factors in suicide. In R. W. Maris, S. S. Canetto, J. L. McIntosh, & M. M. Silverman (Eds.), *Review of suicidology, 2000*. New York: Guilford Press.

2

SHNEIDMAN'S CONTRIBUTIONS TO THE UNDERSTANDING OF SUICIDAL THINKING

DAVID A. JOBES AND KATHRYN N. NELSON

In 1949, Edwin S. Shneidman, running a half-hour errand for his boss at the Veteran's Administration (VA) hospital, found himself in the vaults of the coroner's office in Los Angeles. At the relatively tender professional age of 31, young Shneidman's simple errand became a life-changing event—for him and for the larger pursuit of suicidology and suicide prevention as we have come to know it today. As Dr. Shneidman (1991) recalled,

> The fulcrum moment of my suicidological life was not when I came across several hundred suicide notes in a coroner's vault while on an errand for the director of the VA hospital, but rather a few minutes later, in the instant when I had a glimmering that their vast potential could be immeasurably increased if I did *not* read them, but compared them, in a controlled blind experiment, with simulated suicide notes that might be elicited from matched nonsuicidal persons. (p. 247)

Shneidman later ventured back to the vault in the coroner's office and received permission to use 721 suicide notes for research purposes. With his friend and colleague Norman Farberow, who had that year received his PhD from the University of California at Los Angeles, a line of seminal research in the study of suicide notes was launched; in that moment, contemporary suicidology was born.

Shneidman and Farberow's initial suicide note research collaboration would ultimately spawn much of what now defines and shapes suicidology and suicide prevention today. Drs. Shneidman, Farberow, and Robert Litman (along with key staff colleagues Tabachnick, Heilig, Klugman, Wold, and Peck) founded and created the fabled Los Angeles Suicide Prevention Center (LASPC), a veritable suicidology Garden of Eden. This group of innovators simultaneously initiated new lines of empirical suicide-related research, generated whole lines of new theory, and created a wealth of clinical wisdom pertaining to working with suicidal individuals.

In retrospect, it is difficult to appreciate the full impact and scope of Shneidman's various and considerable contributions. Indeed, much of the language that we commonly use in suicidology—the word *suicidology*, for example—was either directly coined by Shneidman or indirectly shaped by his thinking, intellectual influence, and scholarly contributions. Shneidman is well known, even infamous, for his many neologisms. Beyond the core term of suicidology, Shneidman is also credited with developing many additional words and terms in the field, including *psychological autopsy*, *postvention*, *subintentioned death*, *perturbation*, and *psychache*, among others. To complete the full picture of contributions and to contextualize his role in the field, it is important to further note that Shneidman was the founding president of the American Association of Suicidology in 1968 as well as the founding editor in chief of that organization's premier scientific journal *Suicide and Life-Threatening Behavior*.

When one considers Shneidman's historic contributions to the contemporary psychological understanding of suicide and the larger suicide prevention movement, it is obvious that an examination of his contributions to the area of suicidology is essential to the current text. To that end, Shneidman has said a great deal about the role of cognition and has many ideas regarding suicidal thinking.

Throughout his career in suicidology, Shneidman's theoretical work has consistently and directly addressed cognitive aspects of suicide. Furthermore, his research has unfailingly examined, either directly or indirectly, cognitive processes and the inherent nature of suicidal thinking. Moreover, much of his clinically oriented writing addresses cognitive aspects of the suicidal mind with insights about how one best approaches, assesses, and treats a patient who entertains thoughts of ending life.

We must observe, however, that Shneidman would never call himself a cognitivist, either in terms of theoretical approach or in terms of clinical practice. Unquestionably, he ardently represents himself as a passionate mentalist; he holds the fervent view that suicide exists as a phenomenon of the mind. In this regard, Shneidman is captivated by introspection and phenomenology and stresses the psychology of suicide as it exists in mentation. To this end, Shneidman (2001) said,

> My view [of suicide] is definitely mentalistic. I believe that suicide is a matter of the mind. The mind—that mysterious microtemporal substance-free "secretion,"—has a mind of its own; the main business of the mind is to mind its own business. When it comes to suicide—which is my main business—I am a 21st-century mentalist. (p. 201)

Certainly, cognition is implicated in Shneidman's psychology of suicide, but it is not a core feature in Shneidman's thinking. As we shall make plain in the course of this chapter, cognition in Shneidman's view is but a crucial piece of the whole mental pie of suicide and is deeply implicated in suicidal states. Yet without equivocation, in Shneidman's worldview of suicide, the sun, stars, and moon all rise and set on one central construct—*psychache*. As Shneidman (2001) put it,

> I believe that suicide is essentially a drama in the mind, where the suicidal drama is almost always driven by psychological pain, the pain of negative emotions—what I call *psychache*. Psychache is at the dark heart of suicide; no psychache, no suicide. (p. 200)

The reason for strongly emphasizing Shneidman's perspective as a passionate mentalist is not to minimize his work related to cognition and suicide—because it is considerable—but to represent, frame, and contextualize accurately this particular aspect of his work within the totality of his psychological approach to understanding suicide. In other words, even though Shneidman is not a self-defined cognitivist as such, he nevertheless has had a great appreciation for the key role that cognition plays in the total psychology of suicide.

In this chapter, we thus endeavor to present a balanced, thoughtful, and contextualized picture of Shneidman's contributions to our understanding of suicidal thinking, with a particular emphasis on his contributions that are most specific to cognition. At times we may take certain liberties when interpreting some of this work, as we endeavor to attend to the focus of the current text (i.e., cognition and suicide). For example, this chapter began with the story of a young Shneidman wandering through the vault of the coroner's office considering the potential importance of researching suicide notes. As noted, this fateful spark of a research idea ignited an entire field of study and spurred a larger movement in society—that we should earnestly, purposefully, and methodically endeavor to prevent the tragedy of suicide. Beyond this aspect, however, the importance of the Shneidman and Farberow studies of suicide notes cannot be overstated. For what are suicide notes if not the final psychological considerations, musings, feelings, requests, communications, thoughts—*cognitions*—of the suicidal person? As a written testament to an individual's tragic suicidal end, the study of suicide notes historically marked a significant beginning for the study of suicide as a larger field and, as we shall see, it also fundamentally shaped Shneidman's thinking and views on the topic of suicide. To that end, we explore some of Shneidman's key theoretical, empirical, and clinical contributions to historic as well as contemporary suicidology.

SHNEIDMAN'S THEORETICAL WORK RELATED TO COGNITION AND SUICIDE

Shneidman's theoretical contributions to our understanding of cognition and suicide are both direct and indirect. In terms of direct contributions, we are referring to those aspects of his work that speak specifically to and directly address the nature of suicidal cognitions. Our discussion of the so-called indirect contributions includes those aspects of Shneidman's theoretical work that have shifted and shaped new and different ways of psychologically understanding how suicide actually occurs. To this end, we emphasize here a few of these theoretical contributions including (a) the logic of suicide, (b) the 10 commonalities of suicide, (c) cognitive constriction and suicide, (d) the cubic model of suicide, and (e) aphorisms of suicide.

The Logic of Suicide

Shneidman was among the first to truly explore the thinking process of the suicidal individual, what he called the "logic" of suicide (Shneidman, 1959). This was to be an area of theoretical work that Shneidman would pursue throughout his career in suicidology. Writing about the logic of suicide, Shneidman (1985) asserted the following:

> Figuratively speaking and from the point of view of logic, the suicidal individual hangs himself from his major premise and makes an erroneous deductive leap into oblivion . . . reason is as much a part of suicide as emotion is. Just as emotions may feel "necessary" at the moment of their expression, so illogical conclusions may seem "sensible" when they occupy and sway the mind. (p. 136)

This particular quote marks the beginning of Shneidman's discussion of cognitive aspects of suicide in his important 1985 text, *Definition of Suicide* (Shneidman, 1985). What follows is a far-reaching discussion of the phenomenological nature of suicidal thinking and how an individual's style of reasoning, cognitive maneuvers, and beliefs fundamentally shape virtually every suicidal act. As Shneidman noted,

> There is no single suicidal logic; however, there are features of logical styles and ways of mentating that facilitate (even predispose) suicidal behavior. I call these kinds of reasoning catalogical because they are de-

structive; they are destructive not only in the sense that they abrogate the rules for logical and semantic clarity, but they also destroy the logician who thinks them. (p. 137)

In a synopsis such as this, it is critical to quote Shneidman's own words at length to highlight his unique and idiosyncratic way of considering the topic of suicide. It is plain to us that no one talks or writes about suicide quite the way Shneidman does. Sometimes overly complex and elliptical, his writing invariably challenges the reader to think and rethink what they thought they knew. In challenging his readers to think, Shneidman also compels them to consider their preexisting assumptions and open their minds to the potential worth of his ideas. Frankly, his writing is occasionally elusive and sometimes overly complicated; we find that some of his work requires multiple readings to really grasp the essential points. However, Shneidman's theorizing and writing is often clever and imaginative. For better or for worse, although many suicidologist scholars have said similar or related things as Shneidman, virtually no one in the field has synthesized and elaborated on the theory and perspective on suicide with quite the depth and scope as Shneidman. Thus, in discussing the logic of suicide to his readers, Shneidman customarily and characteristically endeavors to open new doors of theorizing, inspire new lines of empirical research, and challenge clinicians to consider, reconsider, and perhaps change how they clinically engage a person who entertains thoughts of suicide.

The 10 Commonalities of Suicide

In the previously mentioned text, *The Definition of Suicide*, Shneidman (1985) distilled and crystallized his thinking around the notion that completed suicides tend to share much in common. Specifically, Shneidman outlined what he calls the 10 commonalities of suicide. These common characteristics include the following:

1. The common stimulus in suicide is unendurable psychological pain.
2. The common stressor in suicide is frustrated psychological needs.
3. The common purpose of suicide is to seek a solution.
4. The common goal of suicide is the cessation of consciousness.
5. The common emotion in suicide is hopelessness–helplessness.
6. The common internal attitude toward suicide is ambivalence.
7. The common cognitive state in suicide is constriction.
8. The common interpersonal act in suicide is communication of intention.
9. The common action in suicide is egression.
10. The common consistency in suicide is with lifelong coping patterns.

The field of suicidology for many years has struggled to define the characteristics (e.g., risk factors) that are consistent across suicides while simultaneously working toward understanding individual differences in the pursuit of creating typologies, subtypes, or making sense of atypical suicides. In the midst of this struggle, Shneidman's 10 commonalities provide a relatively concise way to think about a coherent core of interrelated constructs that define, organize, and synthesize the essential psychology of virtually every suicidal act.

Among the 10 commonalities, the seventh specifically speaks to cognition as it pertains to the completion of suicide. Commenting on this particular commonality, Shneidman (1985) said,

> I am not one who believes that suicide is best understood as a psychosis, a neurosis, or a character disorder. I believe that it is much more accurately seen as a more or less transient psychological constriction of affect and intellect. Synonyms for constriction are a tunneling or focusing or narrowing of the range of options usually available to *that* individual's consciousness when the mind is not panicked into dichotomous thinking: either some specific (almost magical) total solution *or* cessation; all or nothing . . . the range of choices has narrowed to two—not very much of a range. The usual life-sustaining images of loved ones are not disregarded; worse, they are not even within the range of what is in the mind. (pp. 138–139)

Cognitive Constriction

Shneidman's theoretical work and elaborations on cognitive constriction are among his most enduring contributions. When Shneidman talks about the logic of suicide, the critical role of cognitive constriction is readily apparent. In many of his works, Shneidman endeavored to identify, describe, and portray the nature and processes of constricted suicidal thinking—a tunneling and narrowing of perspective, a dangerous reduction of the person's range of problem-solving options (e.g., Shneidman, 1993). In his description of "psychological myopia," Shneidman depicted an insidious process whereby constricted dichotomous thinking leads the suicidal person into a desperate psychological space. Closely connected to the dangerous psychological state of cognitive constriction is Shneidman's notion of *perturbation*. For Shneidman (1993), the concept of perturbation most directly and principally refers to a state of being emotionally upset, disturbed, and disquieted—often a state most notable for its proclivity for action. In relation to suicide, perturbation also implicates cognitive constriction wherein he argues that acute suicidal states are driven by this intense penchant for self-harm or ill-advised action. In this state of emotional upset, cognitive constriction often contributes to a rapid reduction and deconstruction of the patient's perceptual and cognitive range of problem solving, resulting in black-and-white dichotomous thinking (e.g., endless suffering vs. immediate and eternal relief).

Shneidman's Cubic Model of Suicide

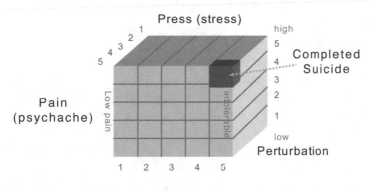

(Shneidman, 1987)

Figure 2.1. Shneidman's cubic model of pain–press–perturbation. From "A Psychological Approach to Suicide," by E. S. Shneidman, 1987, in G. R. Vandenbos and B. K. Bryant (Eds.), *Cataclysms, Crises, and Catastrophes: Psychology in Action.* Washington, DC: American Psychological Association. Copyright 1987 by the American Psychological Association.

The Cubic Model of Suicide

Shneidman's (1987) cubic model of suicide conceptualizes suicidal behaviors as occurring from a confluence of three psychological forces that exist on three axes. As shown in Figure 2.1, the first axis in this cubic model is unbearable psychological pain (the previously mentioned core notion of psychache) that can be rated from *low* (1) to *high* (5). The second axis is that of unrelenting psychological pressures (refer to Murray's 1938 notion of "presses") or stressors that can be rated from low to high (1–5). The third axis is the previously mentioned perturbation construct, also rated from low to high (1–5). Within this cubic model, Shneidman asserted that every suicidal person completes the act of suicide by being at the maximum levels of pain, press, and perturbation—the 5-5-5 corner cubelet of the model. He allowed that not every person who is in this cubelet will necessarily commit suicide but insisted that every person who commits suicide is psychologically in this cubelet at the time of the act.

One of the essential virtues of the cubic model is that it creates a three-dimensional method of conceptualizing suicidal behavioral events. This model makes clear that suicidal behaviors are fundamentally situation specific; there is always a synergy of events, circumstances, psychological suffering, and upset that come together at a critical point in time to create a lethal behavioral moment. Within a relatively simple three-dimensional model, Shneidman described what he believes creates the decisive suicidal act. In so doing, he moved us beyond exhaustive one-dimension lists of suicide risk factors that actually predict very little. Conceptually sophisticated, comprehensive, researchable, and clinically useful, the cubic model is emblematic of Shneidman's work.

Aphorisms of Suicide

Shneidman (1984) has offered a range of aphorisms pertaining to suicide that are noteworthy and provide further theoretical insight on his general views about suicide. Although we do not recount all 20 of his original aphorisms, a few are particularly notable as we round out our consideration of his theoretical contributions. For example, consider the following four aphorisms of suicide:

1. There are two basic, albeit contradictory, truths about suicide: (a) suicide should never be completed when one is depressed (or perturbed or constricted); and (b) almost every suicide is completed for reasons that make sense to the person who does it.
2. The primary thought disorder in suicide is that of a pathological narrowing of the mind's focus, called constriction, which takes the form of seeing only *two* choices: either something painfully unsatisfactory *or* cessation.
3. There is nothing intrinsically wrong (or aberrant) in thinking about suicide; it is abnormal only when one thinks that suicide is the *only* solution.
4. The chief shortcoming of suicide is that it unnecessarily answers a remediable challenge with a permanent negative solution. In contrast, living is a long-term set of resolutions with oftentimes only fleeting results.

SHNEIDMAN'S RESEARCH CONTRIBUTIONS RELATED TO COGNITION AND SUICIDE

Although Shneidman is perhaps best known for his theorizing and his contributions to clinical work with suicidal patients, he has been an active empirical researcher throughout his career. Indeed, his research contributions are considerable, and his research and theories have sparked additional empirical work among many other suicidologists as well. Although not all of Shneidman's research bears directly on the study of suicide and cognition, we have opted to present a broad overview of his research to contextualize the cognitive aspects of his work. As noted further on, Shneidman's first empirical research was in psychological assessment, but for our purposes we begin our discussion where we began this chapter, examining his initial empirical work with Norman Farberow in the study of suicide notes.

Suicide Note Research

As previously noted, Shneidman's formal work in suicidology began in 1949 when he discovered a trove of suicide notes in the Los Angeles County Coroner's Office. What he later called "a scientist's dream," Shneidman quickly realized that suicide notes held a wealth of extraordinarily useful information about the inherent nature of suicide in the precious final moments that preceded self-inflicted suicidal death.

In their first controlled studies of suicide notes, Shneidman and Farberow (1957a, 1957b) developed methodologies that uncovered critical early psychological knowledge about suicide. In their studies comparing genuine versus simulated suicide notes along with studies using other methodologies, these early pioneers in suicidology found that hate directed toward others and self-blame were both evident in the notes they studied. Their investigations of suicide notes showed that suicidal persons were deeply ambivalent. Moreover, within the context of this ambivalence, suicide could be understood as the turning of outward murderous impulses against the self. Wishes and needs that had previously been directed against a traumatic event or toward someone who had rejected the suicide completer were inverted and directed at the self. Thus, suicide was understood as a form of veiled or overt aggression against the self—"murder in the 180th degree" (Shneidman, 1985).

Shneidman and Farberow (1960) went on to further analyze 948 suicide notes obtained in a 3-year period in the Los Angeles area. They deduced that the reasons indicated for suicide vary with the type of area in which the person lived. In Area Type I (most advantaged suburbs), the suicide notes depicted people who were tired of life; in Area Type III (most advantaged apartment areas), the notes frequently noted illness as a reason for suicide; Area II was unremarkable. Shneidman and Farberow concluded that those from moderately advantaged areas expressed the most emotion in their notes and might have benefited most from psychotherapy. Those from the least advantaged areas seldom gave reasons for their suicide but usually gave instructions for disposition of their corpse or their estate. (A little-known anecdote: In the early 1990s, Shneidman returned to the Los Angeles County Coroner's Office to determine whether the contents of suicide notes had changed. He concluded that they essentially had not; Shneidman, 1996b.)

Shneidman also researched the actual writing of suicide notes and how they may or may not predict a completed suicide. In 1973, Shneidman described suicide notes as "dull and poignantly pedestrian" (p. 390). He suggested that a person who could write a meaningful suicide note would not be in the position of completing suicide. In a similar vein, Shneidman (1972) presented samples from 100 self-obituaries elicited from college students in 1969. He concluded that the young have difficulty in objectifying themselves or seeing themselves as dead, as evidenced by their difficulty in completing the task.

Descriptive–Risk Factor Studies

In 1966, Farberow, Shneidman, and Neuringer established that "suicide-significant" variables were found in the life history and hospital records of 218 male mental hospital patients who had completed suicide in comparison to 220 control patients. They determined that the following areas could discriminate between the two groups: population characteristics, diagnoses, early childhood, marital histories, educational achievements, military history, and prehospital and hospital difficulties. In 1955, Farberow and Shneidman reviewed anamnestic and psychiatric data for attempted, threatened, and completed suicide cases. They concluded that "the dangerous patient, suicidally speaking, is the one with a history of previous suicidal attempts or threats, and that the most dangerous period is when the patient appears to have recovered," a notion that foreshadowed solid empirical evidence that would appear decades later (e.g., Joiner, Rudd, Rouleau, & Wagner, 2000).

Eisenthal, Farberow, and Shneidman (1966) conducted a follow-up study of 912 patients in a VA Neuropsychiatric Hospital who had been placed on suicide observation status from 1954 to 1958. Complete data were obtained for 90% of the patients. Forty percent of these patients manifested further suicidal behavior, 6% completed suicide, 17% made nonlethal attempts, and 17% reported suicidal ideation. Suicide history, demographic information, and psychiatric hospitalization did not discriminate any of these groups. The researchers concluded that the ability to predict a suicide was a modest 8% to 13%, whereas the best predictors for an attempt ranged from 23% to 29%. They concluded that in this particular population, suicide is more likely to occur than in the psychiatric hospital or general population (Eisenthal et al., 1966).

Terman Longitudinal Data

Shneidman used a data set archived by the Murray Center originally collected by Terman (1922) and his collaborators (Terman, Sears, Cronbach, & Sears, 1922) to study suicide in the intellectually gifted. Using a methodology that included teacher nominations and intelligence testing, 1,470 children in California with an IQ of 135 or greater were selected for further study. From 1927 to 1928, 58 siblings of the participants were added as a comparison control group. Of the 1,528 participants in the study, 856 were boys and 672 were girls; the average date of birth for the sample was 1910. In 1922, parents filled out an extensive questionnaire describing the child's birth, previous health, education, social experiences, interests, and conduct. The children's teachers filled out a comparable questionnaire. The children took a battery of intelligence, achievement, and personality tests and answered questionnaires about their interests and their knowledge on a range of issues.

Comparable data were subsequently collected at 4-year intervals. In 1972, 1977, and 1982, the follow-up data collections were increasingly oriented to problems of aging—issues of life satisfactions, retirement, living arrangements, health, and vitality. The data collected in 1986 included questions about changes in well-being, time use, importance of religion, perspectives on life accomplishments, and changes in family relationships, concerns, and goals. Shneidman (1971) analyzed 30 cases from this data set for which longitudinal personality data were available from 1921 to 1960. All individuals studied were male Caucasians with high IQs. Five had died by suicide (all by gunshot), 10 (matched) individuals had died natural deaths from cancer or heart disease, and 15 were still living. A blind clinical analysis was conducted primarily in terms of two of Shneidman's guiding concepts—perturbation and lethality—by means of a Meyerian "life chart" and a "psychological autopsy," respectively. Results indicated that four of the five individuals deemed to be most suicidal had, in fact, completed suicide, a chance probability of 1 out of 1,131. Shneidman concluded that some prodromal clues to these suicides were instability, trauma, and certain personality traits. The role of the "significant other" and the "burning out" of affect seemed prominent. He further concluded that a suicide in a 50-year-old person could be seen as a discernible part of a lifestyle, as well as a predictable outcome, by the time that person is 30 years of age—a precursor to Maris's (1981) notion of the *suicidal career*.

Psychological Testing

Shneidman became deeply involved in personality testing research in the early stages of his professional career. He was particularly interested in projective personality assessment and even invented his own test called the Make-A-Picture Story (MAPS). The MAPS test (Shneidman, 1949, 1952) was developed to assist the practitioner in arriving at differential diagnoses and lead to a deeper understanding of individual psychodynamics. The basic test material of the MAPS consists of 21 background pictures printed achromatically on thin cardboard and 67 figures and was used with adolescents and adults. Shneidman himself used this extensively (e.g., Shneidman, 1948a, 1948b); others (e.g., Heuvelman & Graybill, 1990; Nueringer & Orr, 1968) applied the MAPS test to various studies of psychopathology.

Shneidman's first study using MAPS analyzed the formal responses of 50 normal and 50 psychotic individuals to the MAPS test. These responses were compared on the basis of approximately 800 "signs," such as figure number, repetition, placement, selection, interaction signs, activity, meaning, chronology, background, and time. Of the approximately 800 "signs," 64 differentiated the normal and psychotic groups at the 10% level of confidence. On the basis of these "significant signs," Shneidman (1948a) concluded that schizophrenia can be extremely variable and that there is evidence of extreme interest in the self, social isolation, and an absence of being bounded by the dictates of reality. His research showed that individuals with schizophrenia overused symbols, inhibited and repressed aggression, had anxiety and fearfulness, and (among male patients) lacked identification with the male role and had a tendency to debase or degrade women.

In 1986, Shneidman gave the MAPS Test to 14 undergraduates who were studied intensively at the Harvard Psychological Clinic by Henry Murray and his colleagues during the years from 1959 to 1962. A protocol of a Harvard senior was presented to illustrate the use of the MAPS in drawing inferences about personality characteristics such as aggression, sociability, and achievement.

In terms of other personality assessment research, Shneidman and Farberow (1958) began to look at data from patients' responses to the Thematic Apperception Test (TAT) and how this assessment tool related to suicidality. They drafted the first report of the results of TAT data obtained from patients who either attempted or completed suicide and compared them with similar data obtained from nonsuicidal patients. They concluded that exclusive use of the TAT could not successfully discriminate suicidal versus nonsuicidal patients.

As we have discussed previously, Shneidman's theoretical work on psychological pain and suicide is one of his central and lasting contributions (Shneidman, 1996b). To this end, Shneidman developed the Psychological Pain Survey in an attempt to measure or quantify psychache (Shneidman, 1993). To create this assessment approach, he used the Method of Paired Comparisons, in which an incident, such as one from a Nazi concentration camp, is cited as an anchor point of extreme psychological pain and the suicidal person is asked to rate his or her own psychache compared with the incident (Shneidman, 1993, 1999). The suicidal person rates the psychological pain of a person in various stimulus pictures of suffering individuals on a Likert scale from 1 to 9. The individual then rates his or her own pain on the same scale using comparison rating as a psychological reference point.

Outgrowths of Shneidman's Theory and Research

Dozens of empirical studies have drawn directly from Shneidman's earlier theoretical and empirical work. For example, a considerable amount of empirical work has been done on suicide notes, as well as Shneidman's notions of psychache, the 10 commonalities of suicide, and the cubic model of suicide, to name but a few of Shneidman's ideas that have spawned lines of empirical inquiry.

Suicide notes continue to be a rich source of data on the psychology of suicide. For example, Leenaars has conducted a series of studies over the years using and extending various methodologies developed by Shneidman and Farberow (Leenaars, 1988a, 1989). Some more recent studies have continued to expand on ideas originally developed in Shneidman's early work in this area (e.g., Bauer et al., 1997; Black, 1993; Diamond, More, Hawkins, & Soucar, 1995; O'Connor & Leenaars, 2003).

An excellent example of recent empirical work inspired by Shneidman's theorizing in psychological pain comes from Dr. Israel Orbach and colleagues (Orbach, Mikulincer, Gilboa-Schechtman, & Sirota, 2003; Orbach, Mikulincer, Sirota, & Gilboa-Schechtman, 2003). These researchers have conducted a series of studies using factor analysis to study intensively the nature of psychological pain and how such pain differentiates suicidal patients from other clinical samples. Additional interest and empirical work using the psychache construct can be seen in other recent work. For example, Berlim et al. (2003) have examined the role of psychache in a sample of suicidal outpatients with mood disorders in Brazil, and Zimmerman (1995) studied psychache to determine whether it covaries with social welfare and suicide rates.

Various studies of commonalities across suicides have appeared throughout the literature. For example, although certain patterns of constructs in young adults' suicides may differ psychologically from older adult patterns, significant commonalities of suicide cut across the adult life span (Bauer et al., 1997; Leenaars, 1988a). However, Werth (1996) has directly challenged Shneidman's list of 10 commonalities and asserted that it is inherently biased against allowing for the possibility of rational suicide.

Jobes and colleagues (Jobes, Jacoby, Cimbolic, & Hustead, 1997) used a variety of ideas from Shneidman's work in their development of the Suicide Status Form (SSF) and a subsequent use of the SSF in a clinical approach called the Collaborative Assessment and Management of Suicidality (CAMS); refer to Jobes (2000) and Jobes and Drozd (2004). Indeed, Jobes and colleagues (2004) further studied qualitative phenomenological descriptions of suicidality as per written responses to incomplete sentence prompts about a suicidal patient's psychache, press, and perturbation. These researchers have shown that open-ended patient-written descriptors of these constructs can be reliably coded into meaningful content categories. Moreover, one recent clinical study of various psychological constructs has clearly shown that psychological pain was ranked by a sample of suicidal outpatients as the number one problem related to their suicidality (Jobes, 2003).

Shneidman is probably best known for his theorizing and clinical wisdom on suicidal patients. A closer examination of his extensive empirical work, however, reveals both groundbreaking methodologies and many findings that preceded more recent findings in the contemporary research literature. Perhaps even more valuable, his research and theories have sparked additional follow-up investigations in support of his work and have also led other researchers to challenge some of his ideas as well. Not to acknowledge the empirical researcher in Shneidman is to miss a critical component of what made his scholarly contributions so influential.

SHNEIDMAN'S PRACTICE CONTRIBUTIONS
RELATED TO COGNITION AND SUICIDE

A practicing clinician throughout his professional life, Shneidman has written extensively about clinical practice with suicidal patients and recounted numerous case examples throughout his writing. In examining his work, we again find that Shneidman does not specifically and directly emphasize a "cognitive therapy" approach with suicidal patients. When his work is examined through a cognitive lens, however, a great deal of his writing on clinical suicidology either directly or indirectly addresses and underscores cognitive aspects of suicidality. For example, more than 2 decades ago, he (1985) wrote,

> The main point of working with a lethally oriented person—in the give and take of talk, the advice, the interpretations, the listening—is to increase that individual's psychological sense of possible choices . . . with this in mind—and keeping in mind also the four psychological components of the suicidal state of mind (heightened inimicality, elevated perturbation, conspicuous constriction of intellectual focus, and the idea of cessation as the solution)—then a relatively simple formula for treatment can be stated. . . . Simply put, the way to save a highly suicidal person is to decrease the constriction, that is, to widen the range of possible thoughts and fantasies (*from* the dichotomous two—either one specific outcome or death—*to* at least three or more possibilities for an admittedly less-than-perfect solution), most importantly—without which the attempt to broaden constriction will not work—to decrease the individual's perturbation. (pp. 141–142)

In this quote, we see Shneidman's clear emphasis on working on the cognitive aspects of suicide; indeed, it seems to be quite a central aspect to his clinical approach. Across his writing on clinical practice with suicidal individuals, Shneidman has advocated a thoughtful, strategic, and incremental approach to persuading, convincing, inviting, entreating, and cajoling the patient to reconsider suicide. The goal is to help the patient to chart a possible new course of action for dealing with the psychological pain—from the necessity of death to the possibilities inherent in a reconsidered life. In our effort to elaborate on Shneidman's clinical contributions, we march our way through work related to the clinical applications of the 10 commonalities, the cubic model, psychotherapy maneuvers, as well as Shneidman's notion of pain-oriented psychotherapy, which he calls "anodyne therapy."

Clinical Responses to the 10 Commonalities

In relation to our earlier theoretical discussion of Shneidman's 10 commonalities of suicide, Shneidman (1985) noted the distinct clinical implications of this theoretical work. As he observed, the 10 commonali-

EXHIBIT 2.1
Shneidman's 10 Commonalities of Suicide

Commonality	Clinical response
1. Stimulus (unbearable pain):	*Reduce the pain.*
2. Stressor (frustrated psychological needs):	*Fill the frustrated needs.*
3. Purpose (to seek a solution):	*Provide a viable answer.*
4. Goal (cessation of consciousness):	*Indicate alternatives.*
5. Emotion (hopeless–helpless):	*Give transfusions of hope.*
6. Internal attitude (ambivalence):	*Play for time.*
7. Cognitive state (constriction):	*Increase the options.*
8. Interpersonal act (communication of intent):	*Listen to the cry, involve others.*
9. Action (egression):	*Block the exit.*
10. Consistency (with lifelong patterns):	*Invoke previous positive patterns of successful coping.*

ties (see Exhibit 2.1) have obvious and practical clinical implications for saving a life.

Shneidman (1980) observed that suicidal patients are invariably keen on *doing something*. Knowing this simple fact is critical to shaping clinical treatment with suicidal patients. In Shneidman's view, the clinical suicidologist should not be at all hesitant to go about doing a number of such "somethings" to avert a suicide. Clinically responding to the 10 commonalities listed earlier is very much in that spirit.

The Cubic Model and Clinical Intervention

The clinical application of the cubic model of suicide is a unique way of clinically understanding an acute and lethal psychological state (the 5–5–5 cubelet). In this regard, the clinical implications of this simple model are self-evident. Namely, when the clinician does virtually anything to help move a suicidal patient figuratively out of the corner cubelet of the model, then that patient is shifted in a significantly less dangerous psychological space. Clinically targeting and decreasing psychological pain (e.g., with talk therapy), orchestrating a reduction of felt presses (e.g., a change in job or a medical leave from college), and ameliorating perturbation (e.g., with medication or a calming influence) can be a significant and potentially life-saving clinical response (Shneidman, 1980; see also a case example by Jobes & Drozd, 2004).

Psychotherapeutic Maneuvers

In many of his writings, Shneidman has said that the suicidal patient demands (and should in turn receive) a different kind of clinical relationship. Indeed, as Shneidman (1985) himself said,

Working with a highly suicidal person demands a different kind of involvement. There may be an important conceptual difference between ordinary psychotherapy with individuals where dying or living is not *the* issue and psychotherapy with acutely suicidal persons as there is between ordinary psychotherapy and ordinary talk. (p. 141)

We want to underscore Shneidman's emphasis (within reason) of psychotherapeutically going the extra mile for the suicidal patient. He has vigorously argued for a strategic and incremental kind of clinical maneuvering. Indeed, in his book *The Suicidal Mind*, Shneidman (1996a) dedicated an entire chapter to discussing 24 psychotherapeutic maneuvers that the clinician can use to match clinical treatment to a suicidal patient's idiosyncratic frustrated psychological needs. Examples of these maneuvers include *establish*, *explain*, *arrange for*, *monitor*, and *explore*—to name but a handful. In this fashion, Shneidman made it clear that the suicidal patient gets fundamentally stuck in his or her psychological suffering, wherein cognitive constriction and perturbation come together to become the figurative lethal psychological noose closing around the neck of the patient. To appropriately respond, the clinician must respond decisively. In 1985, Shneidman said,

the way to save a person's life is to "do something." Those "somethings" include putting that information (that the person is in trouble with himself) into the stream of communication, letting others know about it, breaking what could be a fatal secret, talking to the person, talking to others, proffering help, getting loved ones interested and responsive, creating action around the person, showing response indicating concern, and, if possible, offering love. (pp. 142–143)

Again, at the risk of taking certain interpretive liberties to keep within the focus of this text, another way of understanding this aspect of Shneidman's clinical approach is to think of it as a version of cognitive restructuring and problem solving. With his overt emphasis on clinically addressing cognitive constriction–dichotomous thinking and active behavioral interventions, Shneidman can at times sound a bit like a cognitive–behavioral enthusiast. However, given that Shneidman is a protégé of personologist Henry Murray, there is no inconsistency here; this particular cognitive aspect of Shneidman's thinking is simply a part of a much larger psychological consideration of the whole (suicidal) person. The point is that Shneidman was among the first to argue for a fundamentally different kind of clinical approach when one encounters a suicidal patient. In this regard, he changed the thinking of his contemporaries and thereby influenced many other clinician–scholars who followed.

Pain-Oriented Psychotherapy

It is fitting to end our chapter with a discussion of Shneidman's (2001) relatively recent bottom-line thinking about psychotherapy with suicidal individuals. Specifically, we are referring to his concept of *anodyne therapy*. This approach to psychotherapy once again emphasizes Shneidman's keen interest in psychological needs and his primary preoccupation with psychological pain (i.e., psychache) as it pertains to suicidality. Shneidman (2001) summarized the essence of his approach as follows:

> I believe that the rule for saving a life in balance can, amazingly enough, be rather simply put: Reduce the inner pain. When that is done, then the inner-felt necessity to suicide becomes redefined, the mental pressure is lowered, and the person can choose to live. . . . I believe that, in large part, psychotherapy consists in helping the patient reconceptualize the can'ts, the won'ts, the absolutes, and the non-negotiables of the patient's present firmly held positions; to widen the stubbornly fixed blinders of present perceptions; to think the unthinkable. (p. 201)

The therapeutic cognitive restructuring and a strategic clinical effort to shift and change the thoughts and perceptions of the suicidal patient are obvious.

As described by Shneidman (2001), *anodyne* refers to "an agent (a benign individual acting as helper) that relieves pain" (p. 202). Moreover, Shneidman asserted that the goal of anodyne therapy is not necessarily the cure of mental disease; rather, the emphasis of this approach is on the soothing of the suicidal person's psychological pain. Although anodyne therapy recognizes the fundamental importance of frustrated psychological needs as part of the etiology of suicidality, the treatment is positively oriented in that "it seeks to liberate the individual from narrow, truncating, unhealthy, life-endangering views of the 'self'" (p. 202).

Given Shneidman's insistence that all suicides stem from intolerably felt psychache and the related pain source of unmet psychological needs, the clinician's role is simply to serve as an anodyne—a person who helps relieve felt pain. When clinicians position themselves in such a way that they address and respond to the essential psychological needs that are idiosyncratically distressing to their patients, then heightened perturbation will lessen, the need for escape may decrease, and patients may thus be in a position to choose to live. This notion essentially captures more than 50 years of Shneidman's clinical wisdom on how one best works clinically with a suicidal person.

CONCLUSION

Throughout this chapter, we have endeavored to reveal the considerable contributions of a completely original thinker, scholar, scientist, and clinician. Although we are obviously great admirers of Dr. Shneidman's work, we have nevertheless sought to present his contributions in theory, research, and practice in a balanced and objective manner. We have quoted his own words at length throughout this chapter to provide a window into the way he thinks and to give the reader a clearer sense of how Shneidman puts things— with his own sense of panache and his idiosyncratic style of writing. Shneidman loves ideas, words, and finding distinctive ways of saying important things. As the founder of modern-day suicidology, Shneidman's legacy is rich and has spurred a vibrant field that works to advance on many fronts including those considered here (i.e., theory, empirical science, and clinical practice). As noted throughout this chapter, even though Shneidman does not consider himself a cognitivist per se, this current volume on cognition and suicide would be notably incomplete without duly considering his cognition-related contributions. Indeed, much of his work directly bears on the topic at hand, and additional aspects of his work have further relevance and meaning when reexamined through a cognitive lens.

REFERENCES

Bauer, M. N., Leenaars, A. A., Berman, A. L., Jobes, D. A., Dixon, J. F., & Bibb, J. L. (1997). Late adulthood suicide: A life-span analysis of suicide notes. *Archives of Suicidology, 3,* 91–108.

Berlim, M. T., Mattevi, B. S., Pavanello, D. P., Caldieraro, M. A., Fleck, M. P., Wingate, L. R., & Joiner, T. E., Jr. (2003). Psychache and suicidality in adult mood disordered outpatients in Brazil. *Suicide and Life-Threatening Behavior, 33,* 242–248.

Black, S. T. (1993). Comparing genuine and simulated suicide notes: A new perspective. *Journal of Consulting and Clinical Psychology, 61,* 699–702.

Diamond, G. M., More, G. L., Hawkins, A. G., & Soucar, E. (1995). Comment on Black's (1993) article, "Comparing Genuine and Simulated Suicide Notes: A New Perspective." *Journal of Consulting and Clinical Psychology, 61,* 46–51.

Eisenthal, S., Farberow, N. L., & Shneidman, E. S. (1966). Follow-up of neuropsychiatric patients in suicide status. *Public Health Reports, 81,* 977–990.

Farberow, N. L., & Shneidman, E. S. (1955). Attempted, threatened, and completed suicide. *Journal of Abnormal Psychology, 50,* 230.

Farberow, N. L., Shneidman, E. S., & Neuringer, C. (1966). Case history and hospitalization factors in suicides of neuropsychiatric hospital patients. *Journal of Nervous and Mental Disease, 142,* 32–44.

Jobes, D. A. (2000). Collaborating to prevent suicide: A clinical-research perspective. *Suicide and Life-Threatening Behavior, 30,* 8–17.

Jobes, D. A. (2003, November). *Clinical care of suicidal outpatients in two Air Force life skills centers.* Keynote presentation at the 2nd Annual Department of Defense Suicide Prevention Conference, Quantico, Virginia.

Jobes, D. A., & Drozd, J. F. (2004). The CAMS approach to working with suicidal patients. *Journal of Contemporary Psychotherapy, 34,* 73–85.

Jobes, D. A., Jacoby, A. M., Cimbolic, P., & Hustead, L. A. T. (1997). The assessment and treatment of suicidal clients in a university counseling center. *Journal of Counseling Psychology*, *44*, 368–377.

Jobes, D. A., Nelson, K. N., Peterson, E. M., Pentiuc, D., Downing, V., Francini, K., & Kiernan, A. (2004). Describing suicidality: An investigation of qualitative SSF responses. *Suicide and Life-Threatening Behavior*, *34*, 99–112.

Joiner, T. E., Rudd, M. D., Rouleau, M. R., & Wagner, K. D. (2000). Parameters of suicidal crises vary as a function of previous suicide attempts in youth inpatients. *Journal of the American Academy of Child and Adolescent Psychiatry*, *39*, 876–880.

Heuvelman, L. R., & Graybill, D. (1990). Assessment of children's fantasies with the Make a Picture Story: Validity and norms. *Journal of Personality Assessment*, *55*, 578–592.

Leenaars, A. A. (1988a). *Suicide notes*. New York: Human Sciences Press.

Leenaars, A. A. (1988b). Are women's suicides really different from men's? *Women's Health*, *14*, 17–33.

Leenaars, A. A. (1989). Are young adults' suicides psychologically different from those of other adults? *Suicide and Life-Threatening Behavior*, *19*, 249–263.

Maris, R. W. (1981). *Pathways to suicide: A survey of self-destructive behaviors*. Baltimore, MD: Johns Hopkins University Press.

Murray, H. A. (1938). *Explorations in personality*. New York: Oxford University Press.

Neuringer, C., & Orr, S. G. (1968). Prediction of pathology from Make-A-Picture Story (MAPS) test figures. *Journal of Consulting and Clinical Psychology*, *32*, 491–493.

O'Connor, R. C., & Leenaars, A. A. (2003). A thematic comparison of suicide notes drawn from Northern Ireland and the United States. *Current Psychology*, *22*, 339–347.

Orbach I., Mikulincer, M., Gilboa-Schechtman, E., & Sirota, P. (2003). Mental pain and its relationship to suicidality and life meaning. *Suicide and Life-Threatening Behavior*, *33*, 231–241.

Orbach, I., Mikulincer, M., Sirota, P., & Gilboa-Schechtman, E. (2003). Mental pain: A multidimensional operationalization and definition. *Suicide and Life-Threatening Behavior*, *33*, 219–230.

Shneidman, E. S. (1948a). Schizophrenia and the MAPS test: A study of certain formal psycho-social aspects of fantasy production in schizophrenia as revealed by performance on the Make A Picture Story (MAPS) test. *Genetic Psychology Monographs*, *38*, 145–223.

Shneidman, E. S. (1948b). Some objective aspects of fantasy production in schizophrenia on the Make-a-Picture-Story (MAPS) Test. *American Psychologist*, *3*, 340.

Shneidman, E. S. (1949). Some comparisons among the Four Picture test, Thematic Apperception test, and Make a Picture Story test. *Rorschach Research Exchange*, *13*, 150–154.

Shneidman, E. S. (1952). Manual for the Make A Picture Story method. *Projective Techniques Monographs, 2*, 92.

Shneidman, E. S. (1959). The logic of suicide. In E. S. Shneidman & N. Farberow (Eds.), *Clues to suicide*. New York: McGraw-Hill.

Shneidman, E. S. (1971). Perturbation and lethality as precursors to suicide in a gifted group. *Life-Threatening Behavior, 1*, 23–45.

Shneidman, E. S. (1972). Can a young person write his own obituary? *Suicide and Life-Threatening Behavior, 2*, 262–267.

Shneidman, E. S. (1973). Suicide notes reconsidered. *Psychiatry: Journal for the Study of Interpersonal Processes, 36*, 379–394.

Shneidman, E. S. (1980). A possible classification of suicidal acts based on Murray's need system. *Suicide and Life-Threatening Behavior, 10*, 175–181.

Shneidman, E. S. (1984). Aphorisms of suicide and some implications for psychotherapy. *American Journal of Psychotherapy, 38*, 319–328.

Shneidman, E. S. (1985). *The definition of suicide*. New York: Wiley.

Shneidman, E. S. (1986). MAPS of the Harvard Yard. *Journal of Personality Assessment, 50*, 436–447.

Shneidman, E. S. (1987). A psychological approach to suicide. In G. R. VandenBos & B. K. Bryant (Eds.), *Cataclysms, crises, and catastrophes: Psychology in action* (pp. 147–183). Washington, DC: American Psychological Association.

Shneidman, E. S. (1991). A life in death. In C. E. Walker (Ed.), *The history of clinical psychology in autobiography* (pp. 225–292). Pacific Grove, CA: Brooks/Cole.

Shneidman, E. S. (1993). *Suicide as psychache: A clinical approach to self-destructive behavior*. Northvale, NJ: Aronson.

Shneidman, E. S., (1996a). *The suicidal mind*. New York: Oxford University Press.

Shneidman, E. S. (1996b). Suicide as psychache. In J. T. Maltsberger & M. J. Goldblatt (Eds.), *Essential papers on suicide. Essential papers in psychoanalysis* (pp. 633–638). Northvale, NJ: Aronson.

Shneidman, E. S. (1999). The psychological pain assessment scale. *Suicide and Life-Threatening Behavior, 24*, 287–294.

Shneidman, E. S. (2001). *Comprehending suicide: Landmarks in 20th century suicidology*. Washington, DC: American Psychological Association.

Shneidman, E. S., & Farberow, N. L. (Eds.). (1957a). *Clues to suicide*. New York: McGraw-Hill.

Shneidman, E. S., & Farberow, N. L. (1957b). Some comparisons between genuine and simulated suicide notes. *Journal of General Psychology, 56*, 251.

Shneidman, E. S., & Farberow, N. L. (1958). TAT heroes of suicidal and non-suicidal subjects. *Journal of Projective Techniques, 22*, 211–228.

Shneidman, E. S., & Farberow, N. L. (1960). A socio-psychological investigation of suicide. In H. P. David & J. C. Brengleman (Eds.), *Perspectives in personality research* (pp. 270–293). New York: Springer Publishing Company.

Terman, L. M. (1922). A new approach to the study of genius. *Psychological Review*, *29*, 310–318.

Terman, L. M., Sears, R. R., Cronbach, L. J., & Sears, P. (1922). *Terman Life Cycle Study of Children with High Ability, 1922–1986*. Archive of the Henry A. Murray Research Center of the Radcliffe Institute for Advanced Study, Harvard University, Cambridge, Massachusetts.

Werth, J. L. (1996). Can Shneidman's "ten commonalities of suicide" accommodate rational suicide? *Suicide and Life-Threatening Behavior*, *26*, 292–299.

Zimmerman, S. L. (1995). Psychache in context: States' spending for public welfare and their suicide rates. *Journal of Nervous and Mental Disease*, *183*, 425–434.

II

THEORETICAL SYSTEMS

3

COGNITIVE THERAPY, COGNITION, AND SUICIDAL BEHAVIOR

GREGORY K. BROWN, ELIZABETH JEGLIC,
GREGG R. HENRIQUES, AND AARON T. BECK

Cognitive theory has played an important role in the conceptualization, assessment, and prevention of suicide and attempted suicide (Rudd, Joiner, & Rajab, 2001). Aaron Beck's work in all three of these areas has led to the advancement of both the research and treatment of suicidal behavior. This chapter reviews the development of the cognitive model of suicide behavior, the nomenclature, the instruments used to assess suicide behavior, and a cognitive therapy intervention for suicide attempters.

DEVELOPMENT OF THE COGNITIVE MODEL FOR SUICIDE BEHAVIOR

Beck's cognitive theory specifies that the way people think about and interpret life events plays a causal role in their emotional and behavioral responses to those events (A. T. Beck, 1976). Cognitive theory arose from research on depressed patients, whose thoughts and images were found to be negatively biased in systematic and habitual ways (A. T. Beck, 1964). Clinically, Beck observed that depressed patients often have a negative view of themselves, the world, and the future. Beck subsequently labeled this cognitive style as the *negative cognitive triad* (A. T. Beck, 1967, 1970). The development of cognitive therapy for depressed individuals hinged on the identification of dysfunctional automatic thoughts and beliefs and the application of cognitive and behavioral strategies to develop more adaptive ways of thinking and behaving (A. T. Beck, Rush, Shaw, & Emery, 1979).

During the period of time when Beck and his colleagues were developing the cognitive theory of depression, they were also evaluating patients who were seeking treatment during a suicidal crisis. As with depressed patients, Beck observed that suicidal patients exhibited negative thoughts and dysfunctional beliefs. These clinical observations were used to develop an integrated cognitive theory of suicidal thoughts and behavior.

In 1975, Beck formulated a hopelessness theory of suicide based on his clinical experiences with 50 depressed suicidal patients. He reported that suicidal crises were consistently "related to the patients' conceptualization of their situation as untenable or hopeless" (A. T. Beck, Kovacs, & Weissman, 1975). He theorized that hopelessness was the catalytic agent in suicidal episodes and that suicidal behavior resulted when an individual was both hopeless and his or her reasoning was impaired. Beck argued that suicidal behavior was derived from specific cognitive distortions in which patients viewed their experiences negatively and they believed that their attempts to attain major goals would end in failure (A. T. Beck, Kovacs, & Weissman, 1975). At the time Beck was developing these ideas, there was much inconsistency in the terminology of suicidal behavior and little empirical research. Because such tools were essential if Beck was to test his theory, over the next several years he and his colleagues developed a wide array of techniques for assessing and measuring suicidal behavior.

DEVELOPMENT OF A CONSISTENT NOMENCLATURE FOR SUICIDAL BEHAVIOR

In 1958, Stengel and Cook published the monograph *Attempted Suicide* in which they defined a suicide attempt as "every act of self injury consciously aiming at self-destruction." However, Kreitman (1977) argued the patient's motivation to kill himself or herself would be extremely difficult to assess given that many patients are unable to provide a clear account of their intentions at the time of the self-damaging behavior. In other words, Kreitman maintained that patient self-reports of intent to kill oneself were unreliable. Thus, in an effort to provide a term that would suggest a behavioral analogue of suicide without taking into account the psychological motivation for the act, Kretiman grouped all forms of self-injurious behavior into one category and coined the term *parasuicide*. Parasuicide was defined as a nonfatal act in which an individual deliberately causes self-injury or ingests a substance in excess of any prescribed or generally recognized therapeutic dosage (Kreitman, Philip, Greer, & Bagley, 1969). Kreitman (1977) also noted that the recent work of Beck and his colleagues may enable more reliable assessments (i.e., intent and motivation) to be made in the future.

In 1970, the Center for the Study of Suicide Prevention of the National Institute of Mental Health convened a large conference that had a committee on classification chaired by Beck. The lack of consistent definitions of suicidal behavior across studies had led to confusion in the field, and the goal of this meeting was to achieve a consensus on widely used definitions involving suicide behavior. Subsequently, a classification scheme for suicidal behavior was constructed (A. T. Beck et al., 1973). According to this scheme, suicidal phenomena are described as completed suicides, suicide attempts, or suicide ideation. Each construct is categorically qualified by specific variables, that is, degree of intent, degree of lethality, and method (A. T. Beck et al., 1973).

Contrary to Kreitman's argument that suicidal intent could not be reliably assessed, Beck and colleagues (1973) maintained that a key variable in the three forms of suicidal behavior was the intent to die, especially when the behavior was nonlethal in nature. The group agreed that if the self-injurious behavior had no suicidal intent, then the diagnosis of "attempted suicide" would be contraindicated and the term "self-injurious behavior" would be used. Given that the definition of suicide attempt required an intent to commit suicide and potentially lethal self-injurious behavior, Beck and his group subsequently developed and validated measures for these variables: the Suicide Intent Scale and the Lethality Scales. These measures and their psychometric properties are described subsequently.

In an attempt to build on this nomenclature and further improve communication in the field, O'Carroll and colleagues (O'Carroll et al., 1996) provided definitions for commonly used terms in suicide research. Specifically, they defined a *suicide attempt* as "a potentially self-injurious behavior with a nonfatal outcome, for which there is evidence (either explicit or implicit) that the person intended at some (nonzero) level to kill himself/herself." *Suicide ideation* refers to "any self-reported thoughts of engaging in suicide-related behavior." Although this definition of a suicide attempt delineates the importance of an intent to kill oneself and of self-injurious behavior, sometimes it is difficult to determine whether an individual intended to kill oneself or whether an individual actually engaged in a self-injurious behavior. Consider, for example, an individual who reports that she "doesn't know why" she took the pills. As another example related to ambiguous behavior, consider a patient who states that he "started to drive on the wrong side of the road, but then decided he might hurt someone else, so he returned to his lane." Both of these instances are cases in which the intent and behavior are ambiguous.

Figure 3.1 is offered to specify clearly our current classification scheme. The two dimensions of suicidal intent and self-injurious behavior are categorized into definite, possible, or none. To accommodate the uncertainty that is observed in clinical treatment settings, the darker gray cells in Figure 3.1 illustrate the distinction between a "definite" and a "possible" suicide attempt. A definite suicide attempt is a self-injurious behavior with a nonfatal outcome for which there is clear evidence that the person intended to kill himself or herself. In such an instance, the patient has clearly initiated and completed a behavior that was engaged in with the purpose of killing him- or herself. A possible suicide attempt is uncertain or potential self-injurious behavior with a nonfatal outcome for which there is evidence (either explicit or implicit) that the person may have intended to kill himself or herself. In such instances, either the intent is ambiguous, the behavior was initiated but not completed, or both. Both the darker and lighter gray cells in Figure 3.1 indicate definite or possible intentional self-injurious behavior.

ASSESSMENT OF SUICIDE BEHAVIOR

Suicide Intent Scale

The Suicide Intent Scale (SIS; A. T. Beck, Schuyler, & Herman, 1974) is an interview-administered measure of the seriousness of the intent to commit suicide among patients who have actually attempted suicide. The SIS consists of 15 items that quantify an attempter's verbal and nonverbal behavior before and during the most recent suicide attempt. Each item is rated on an ordinal scale from 0 to 2 with the total score ranging from 0 to 30. The first part of the SIS (Items 1–8) covers objective circumstances that surround the suicide attempt and includes items on the preparation and manner of execution of the attempt, the setting, as well as prior cues the patient gave that could facilitate or hamper the discovery of the attempt. This part of the scale can be completed retrospectively for patients who have committed suicide (e.g., through review of medical records). The second part of the SIS (Items 9–15) covers the attempter's perceptions of the method's lethality, expectations about the possibility of rescue and intervention, the extent of premeditation, and the alleged purpose of the attempt. The interview takes about 10 minutes to administer. A self-report version of this scale, the Suicide Intent Questionnaire, is also available (Linehan, 1982).

Several studies have found that the first part of the SIS (Items 1–8) differentiated fatal and nonfatal suicide attempts (A. T. Beck, Schuyler, & Herman, 1974; R. W. Beck, Morris, & Beck, 1974). Total SIS scores differentiated repeat attempters from those who do not subsequently attempt suicide (R. W. Beck et al., 1974; Ojehagen, Regnell, & Traeskman-Bendz, 1991). Suicide attempters' reactions to their suicide attempt (glad to be alive, ambivalent, and wish they were dead) were predictive of eventual suicide, with

		Intentional Self-Injurious Behavior		
		Definite	Uncertain/ Potential	None
Suicide Intent	Definite	**Definite Suicide Attempt**	Possible Suicide Attempt	Suicide Ideation
	Uncertain	Possible Suicide Attempt	Possible Suicide Attempt	Possible Suicide Ideation
	None	Intentional Self-Injurious Behavior Without Suicide Intent	Possible/ Potential Self-Injurious Behavior Without Suicide Intent	

Figure 3.1. Classification of suicide attempts and self-injurious behavior.

those who wished they were dead committing suicide at a greater rate than those who were ambivalent or glad to be alive (Henriques, Wenzel, Beck, & Brown, in press). Two 10-year prospective studies have evaluated the predictive validity of the SIS for completed suicide for patients who were hospitalized after attempting suicide. In both studies, the SIS total scale does not predict completed suicide (A. T. Beck & Steer, 1989; Tejedor, Diaz, Castillon, & Pericay, 1999). However, one of these studies found that the Precautions subscale of the SIS was associated with an increased risk of suicide (A. T. Beck & Steer, 1989). In addition, inconsistent findings have been reported with respect to the predictive validity of the SIS for subsequent nonfatal suicide attempts (R. W. Beck et al., 1974; Tejedor et al., 1999). Although Beck and his colleagues (R. W. Beck et al., 1974) found that the SIS differentiated patients who subsequently reattempted suicide from patients who did not reattempt suicide within 1 year of discharge (N = 231), a more recent prospective study with a smaller sample size (N = 132) failed to replicate these findings (Tejedor et al., 1999).

Lethality Scales

The Lethality Scales (LS; A. T. Beck, Beck, & Kovacs, 1975) are interviewer-administered scales that measure the medical lethality of a suicide attempt on a scale from 0 (e.g., *fully conscious and alert*) to 10 (e.g., *death*). There are eight separate scales according to the method of the attempt (shooting, jumping, drug overdose, etc.). Ratings are based on an examination of the patient's physical condition on admission to the medical, surgical, or psychiatric service and are determined by a review of the medical charts and consultation with the attending physician.

In a recent study, the degree of intent to commit suicide and the severity of self-injury were examined in individuals ($N = 180$) who had recently attempted suicide (Brown, Henriques, Sosdjan, & Beck, 2004). This study found a minimal association between the degree of suicide intent and extent of medical lethality for patients who attempted suicide. For patients who had accurate expectations about the likelihood of dying from their attempt, however, the resulting degree of danger to their lives was proportional to the degree of suicide intent. These results supported the findings from a previous study with a similar sample of suicide attempters (A. T. Beck, Beck, & Kovacs, 1975). In addition, the Brown et al. (2004) study found a significant interaction between the accuracy of expectations and degree of suicide intent on the severity of the self-injury. Specifically, patients were more likely to make a lethal suicide attempt when they had both an accurate expectation of the lethality of the attempt and had a higher level of intent to commit suicide. These findings were obtained even when other risk factors for suicide (multiple suicide attempts, depression, hopelessness, and suicide ideation) were controlled.

As indicated by the A. T. Beck et al. (1973) and the O'Carroll et al. (1996) definitions of a suicide attempt, both suicide intent and the lethality of the self-injury behavior need to be assessed to identify suicide attempts. The Brown et al. (2004) study supported this definition and suggests that suicide intent and lethality are independent dimensions of suicide attempt behavior and that both of these characteristics require careful assessment for accurate identification of suicide attempters. The Brown et al. (2004) study supports the low validity of medical lethality as a measure of the seriousness of intent given that 52% of the patients in this study had inaccurate expectations of the lethality of their attempt. Including an independent assessment of suicide intent is important because the actual physical outcome of an act of self-injury may be greatly influenced by the means or methods that were available and may not be highly associated with suicide intent (Hawton, 2001).

Scale for Suicide Ideation

Although the SIS was developed to measure suicide intent for those who attempted suicide, the measurement of suicide ideation as an indicator of suicide risk among those who had not recently attempted suicide was proposed by A. T. Beck et al. (1973). Subsequently, A. T. Beck, Kovacs, and Weissman (1979) developed a clinical rating scale, the Scale for Suicide

Ideation (SSI). This measure was designed to quantify the severity of current suicidal intent by scaling various dimensions of self-destructive thoughts, plans, and expectations.

The SSI is a 21-item interviewer-administered rating scale that measures the current intensity of patients' specific attitudes, behaviors, and plans to commit suicide on the day of the interview. Each item consists of three options graded according to suicidal intensity on a 3-point scale ranging from 0 to 2. The ratings for the first 19 items are summed to yield a total score, ranging from 0 to 38. The SSI consists of five screening items. Three items assess the wish to live or the wish to die, and two items assess the desire to attempt suicide. If the respondent reports any active or passive desire to commit suicide, 14 additional items are administered. Individual items assess suicidal risk factors such as the duration and frequency of ideation, sense of control over making an attempt, number of deterrents, and amount of actual preparation for a contemplated attempt. Two additional items record incidence and frequency of previous suicide attempts. The SSI takes approximately 10 minutes to administer.

The SSI has been standardized with adult psychiatric patients in psychiatric inpatient (A. T. Beck, Steer, Kovacs, & Garrison, 1985) and outpatient settings (A. T. Beck, Brown, & Steer, 1997). In addition, the SSI has been used in a wide variety of settings such as primary care practices, emergency rooms, rehabilitation programs, and private practice. The SSI also has been administered to college students (Clum & Curtin, 1993; Clum & Yang, 1995), including African American college students (Blanton-Lacy, 1997; Molock, Kimbrough, Lacy, McClure, & Williams, 1994), as well as elderly clinical populations (Mireault & de Man, 1996).

The predictive validity of the SSI for completed suicide has been established for patients seeking outpatient psychiatric treatment (A. T. Beck, Brown, Steer, Dahlsgaard, & Grisham, 1999; Brown, Beck, Steer, & Grisham, 2000). Specifically, patients who scored in the higher risk category (i.e., SSI total score greater than 2) were approximately 7 times more likely to commit suicide than those who scored in the lower risk category (Brown et al., 2000). Although suicide ideation is a criterion for a major depressive episode in the *Diagnostic and Statistical Manual of Mental Disorders* (4th ed.; American Psychiatric Association, 1994), the Brown et al. (2000) study found that the presence of suicide ideation provides an independent estimate of the risk for suicide for psychiatric patients.

Studies have indicated that the Beck Hopelessness Scale, SIS, and SSI are reliable and valid assessment measures with a variety of patient populations and treatment settings. Predictive validity of these measures has also been established for completed suicide. Moreover, these scales assess the types of cognitions and behaviors that are potentially modifiable with psychiatric treatment. These measures may also be useful for screening and facilitating case management for individuals who are potentially at risk for suicide.

Beck Hopelessness Scale

Because the concept of hopelessness was central to Beck's theory, he developed the Beck Hopelessness Scale (BHS) in an effort to measure this construct (A. T. Beck, Weissman, Lester, & Trexler, 1974). The BHS is a self-report instrument that consists of 20 true–false statements designed to assess the extent of positive and negative beliefs about the future during the past week. Each of the 20 statements is scored 0 or 1. A total score is calculated by summing the pessimistic responses for each of the 20 items. The total BHS score ranges from 0 to 20.

The BHS has been established as an important risk factor for suicide in prospective studies of psychiatric patients in hospital and outpatient settings (A. T. Beck, Brown, Berchick, Stewart, & Steer, 1990; A. T. Beck, Brown, & Steer, 1989; Brown et al., 2000). For example, psychiatric patients who scored a 9 or above on the BHS were approximately 11 times more likely to commit suicide than patients who scored 8 or below (A. T. Beck et al., 1989). Research has found that patients whose hopelessness does not significantly change with psychiatric treatment may be more likely to commit suicide (Dahlsgaard, Beck, & Brown, 1998) and that stable levels of hopelessness in those patients with remitted depression were more predictive of suicide attempts than high levels of hopelessness at any one point (Young et al., 1996). In a study of hospitalized suicide attempters, Petrie, Chamberlain, and Clarke (1988) found that the BHS provided a unique estimate of subsequent suicide attempts.

In summary, Beck and colleagues have developed numerous assessment measures of suicidal behavior and worked to develop a clear and consistent nomenclature. More recently, Beck and colleagues have turned their attention to developing effective interventions for suicidal behaviors.

COGNITIVE THEORY AND THERAPY FOR SUICIDE ATTEMPTERS

Suicide Mode

In response to recent research developments, A. T. Beck (1996) refined his original model of cognitive therapy. His revised theory encompasses the concept of "modes" that serve as structural or organizational units containing schemas. Beck defines modes as interconnected networks of cognitive, affective, motivational, physiological, and behavioral schemas that are activated simultaneously by relevant internal and external events and orient the individual toward achieving some goal. Beck introduced the concept of modes to account for the diversity of symptoms observed in most psychiatric conditions.

Although A. T. Beck (1996) touched on a suicide mode, the characteristics were elaborated on by Rudd (2000) and Rudd et al. (2001). They postulated that when the suicide mode is activated, an individual experiences suicide-related cognitions, negative affect, physiological arousal, and the motivation or intent to engage in suicidal behavior (Rudd et al., 2001). Beck speculated that the repeated activation of a mode would subsequently lower the threshold for future activation. This speculation was developed by Rudd et al. (2001) in the context of suicidal behavior; they suggested that the suicide mode is more easily activated in individuals who have engaged in prior suicidal behavior. This suggests that easily accessible memories serve as a salient trigger for individuals with a history of suicidal behavior. This notion is supported by research suggesting that suicidal crises may occur more rapidly and intensely in multiple suicide attempters and that these crises are not related to negative life events (Joiner & Rudd, 2000). Furthermore, as the suicide mode becomes progressively more active, the capacity to wield cognitive control over suicidal urges should be minimized as with inhibitions against suicidal behavior.

This theoretical formulation served as the foundation for the development of a targeted intervention focused on the cognitive risk factors that have been shown to be related to suicidal behaviors and are modifiable using cognitive therapy. Beck, Brown, and colleagues have adapted cognitive therapy for individuals who have recently attempted suicide, and they are currently conducting several randomized controlled trials to assess the effectiveness of this approach. Preliminary results of our initial clinical trial with suicide attempters suggest that patients who received the short-term, targeted cognitive therapy intervention (plus enriched usual care) were significantly less likely to reattempt suicide during the follow-up period than patients who received enriched usual care alone.

A novel element of this short-term cognitive intervention is the focus on the proximal vulnerability factors preceding a suicide attempt. The patient's suicide ideation and suicidal behavior are the primary focus of treatment, in contrast to traditional psychiatric approaches that view suicidal behavior as a symptom of an underlying mental disorder (Berk, Henriques, Warman, Brown, & Beck, 2004; Henriques, Beck, & Brown, 2003). Specific psychological and social vulnerability factors such as hopelessness, poor problem solving, impaired impulse control, noncompliance with the health system, and social isolation are targeted rather than the treatment of depression and other psychiatric problems per se.

COGNITIVE THERAPY INTERVENTION FOR SUICIDE ATTEMPTERS

Individuals who attempt suicide represent one of the highest risk groups for committing suicide (Harris & Barraclough, 1997). Despite the evidence supporting suicide attempts as a major risk factor for suicide, there have been very randomized controlled trials that have been shown to be effective for reducing the suicidal behavior (Brown et al., 2005; Salkovskis, Atha, & Storer, 1990).

In a recent study, 120 patients who recently attempted suicide were recruited from the hospital emergency department (Brown et al., 2005). Averaging in their mid-30s, 61% of the participants were women, 60% Black, 35% White, and 5% Hispanic and other ethnicities. Most had attempted to kill themselves by drug overdosing (58%), with 17% by stabbing, 7% by jumping, and 4% by hanging, shooting, or drowning. Seventy-seven percent had major depression and 68% had a substance-use disorder.

After a clinical evaluation, each participant was randomly assigned to one of two conditions: cognitive therapy or usual care. Those in the cognitive therapy group were scheduled to receive 10 outpatient cognitive therapy sessions. Both groups were encouraged to receive usual care from clinicians in the community and were tracked by study case managers by mail and phone throughout the 18-month follow-up period. The case managers offered referrals to local mental health and drug abuse treatment and social services.

This study found that 24% of the individuals in the cognitive therapy condition and 42% of the individuals who received usual care made another suicide attempt. The most important finding was that patients who received the cognitive therapy intervention were 50% less likely to make a repeat suicide attempt during the 18-month follow-up period than those who did not receive cognitive therapy. Although the groups did not differ significantly in suicidal thoughts, those who received cognitive therapy scored better on measures of depression severity and hopelessness.

The following treatment was developed for suicide attempters; however, the concepts can also be adapted for use with patients experiencing suicidal ideation. The treatment comprises five main components: (a) cognitive therapy for depression, hopelessness, and suicide ideation; (b) problem-solving, with a focus on the problems that triggered the most recent attempt or suicidal ideation; (c) increasing patients' adaptive use of social support; (d) increasing patients' use of and compliance with adjunctive medical, substance abuse, and psychiatric and social interventions; and (e) identifying and decreasing suicidal ideation.

Research has shown that the vast majority of people who attempt suicide or experience suicidal ideation are feeling depressed, hopeless, or both (e.g., A. T. Beck, Kovacs, & Weissman, 1979; Brown, Beck, Steer, & Grisham, 2000). The general cognitive therapy principles used with suicidal individuals are based on standard cognitive therapy for depression. These include agenda setting, symptom monitoring, reviewing the presenting problem and goal setting, educating about the cognitive model, assigning and reviewing homework, periodically summarizing throughout the session, obtaining feedback, eliciting automatic thoughts, labeling emotions, identifying cognitive distortions, completing dysfunctional thought records, activity scheduling, using coping cards, and role-play techniques (see A. T. Beck, Rush, et al., 1979; J. S. Beck, 1995). In sum, the overarching focus of the therapy is the notion that the therapist is attempting to help patients transform their hopelessness into hope.

Individuals who attempt suicide have been found to have problem-solving deficits (Marx, Williams, & Claridge, 1992). As part of the intervention, patients are taught to identify the problems and stressful life events that preceded the suicide attempt, identify a wide range of solutions, and then develop strategies to work out and implement the steps necessary to accomplish these goals (Hawton & Kirk, 1989). This problem-solving technique helps patients identify clear links between their life problems and their suicidal thoughts and behaviors. Additionally, it assists patients in identifying their strengths and resources while teaching them a systemic method for overcoming their problems and enhancing their feelings of control and competency.

Low levels of perceived and actual social support are related to suicidal behavior (Fridell, Ojehagen, & Traeskman-Bendz, 1996). A major goal of therapy is to develop social resources for the patient. This includes scheduling pleasurable social activities and broadening the patients' network of social support. Whenever possible, family members are encouraged to participate in therapy. This could help the therapist determine whether the patient's perception of his or her social support system is real or distorted. Additionally, such meetings can help family members to recognize when the patient is at high risk for suicide and what to do if the patient is suicidal.

Many individuals who attempt suicide or experience suicidal ideation may also have concomitant medical, psychiatric, or substance abuse problems that could either exacerbate or maintain the distress experienced by the individual (A. T. Beck, Steer, & McElroy, 1982; Hughes & Kleespies, 2001). At the onset of each therapy appointment, therapists assess patients' compliance with their adjunctive regime. If compliance is an issue for the patient, then the therapist may use cognitive strategies such as the examination of negative beliefs and behaviors regarding compliance. Once these beliefs have been examined, maladaptive thoughts will be challenged and solutions will be generated to overcome the difficulties (Newman & Beck, 1999).

When working with patients who have attempted suicide or who are currently suicidal, it is important for the therapist to have a clear conceptualization of the events that preceded the attempt or ideation and the attempt itself. One way to accomplish this is by having patients "tell their story" (Ellis & Newman, 1996). Patients are asked to discuss the upsetting situation or event(s) that led to the suicide attempt. Next, patients are asked to identify the meaning of the event or the situation that led to the attempt. The therapist will assist the patient in developing more adaptive beliefs and responses to deal with upsetting events. An integral part of the therapy involves identifying and targeting suicidal cognitions. Patients will learn to recognize thinking patterns that lead to suicidal ideation and develop strategies targeting cognitive distortions such as addressing the advantages and disadvantages of suicide and listing reasons for living and dying.

Session Overview

Cognitive therapy for suicide attempters is designed as a 10-session protocol. The general session framework (early, middle, later) is presented in the following sections; however, the intervention is flexible and can be tailored to meet the requirements of the patient.

The key elements of the therapy will be illustrated using a patient that we call "Suzanne." Suzanne is a 34-year-old divorced woman. She is currently on disability because she is unable to work due to various health problems. She has a history of cocaine and alcohol abuse. Suzanne reports that she has been depressed as long as she can remember, and she has attempted suicide three times. The last suicide attempt took place the week before Suzanne attended therapy.

Early Sessions

The primary goals of the early sessions of treatment are (a) to engage the patient in treatment, (b) to orient the patient to the cognitive model, (c) to develop a safety plan with the patient, and (d) to develop a cognitive conceptualization of the suicide attempt.

Engaging the Patient in Treatment

Initial therapy sessions set the stage for the rest of the treatment by focusing on engaging the patient in treatment. Historically, it has been difficult to conduct therapy with suicidal individuals because only 20% to 40% of the patients who have attempted suicide have been compliant in attending outpatient psychiatric appointments following hospitalization (Kreitman, 1979; O'Brien, Holton, Hurren, Watt, & Hassanyeh, 1987). Therefore, the focus of the first few sessions should be on developing rapport with clients in an effort to engage them in therapy. Beck and his colleagues have developed several strategies for engaging a patient in treatment including having patients "tell their story" and being sensitive to cultural issues. Therapists are encouraged to take an active role in the process of engaging patients, which includes reminder phone calls, flexible scheduling, and the willingness to conduct therapy over the phone.

An important aspect of engaging the patient in treatment involves having patients tell their story, that is, describe in detail the incident(s) that preceded their suicide attempts. The goal of this exercise is to elicit the triggering problems, thoughts and feelings, and images that led up to the suicide attempt. Additionally, this is an opportunity for the therapist to display empathy toward the patient in an effort to further build rapport and engagement in therapy. For many patients, this is the first time they have the opportunity to talk about their suicide attempt, and although the experience can be cathartic for some, it can be difficult for others. Therapists should be cognizant that many patients may be reluctant to talk (or incapable of talking) about their suicide attempts for a variety of reasons, including avoidance of distressful emotions, shame about their behavior, and concealment or humiliation about the events that prompted the attempt.

Suzanne was reluctant to discuss her suicide attempt during the first session, but she reported that after talking to the therapist for a while, she felt "safe and more comfortable about opening up." She told the therapist that she had overdosed on her antidepressant medication the previous week after her boyfriend had broken up with her. She said that she had planned to marry this man and was completely shocked when he told her he wanted to end things, even though they had been arguing constantly for the past several weeks. Suzanne reported that after her boyfriend left, she began to feel hopeless. She thought "I am always going to be alone," "no one will ever love me," and "there is no point to going on with life." Suzanne then started drinking and using cocaine again, even though she had been sober for almost 2 years. At this point, Suzanne reported that she knew the only solution to her problems was to end her life. She then proceeded to the medicine cabinet and overdosed on her antidepressant medication. Her roommate found Suzanne unconscious on the bathroom floor. By hearing Suzanne "tell her story," the therapist was able to elicit some of the thoughts and feelings that preceded the suicide attempt, thus aiding in the development of the cognitive case conceptualization.

Orienting the Patient to the Cognitive Model

During the first several sessions of therapy, the patients are introduced to the cognitive model of psychotherapy. Patients are educated about the connection between thoughts, feelings, and behaviors and about the activation of suicidal modes. In addition, patients come to understand that the majority of learning in cognitive therapy takes place outside of the therapy session and that homework assignments are integral to success in therapy. Patients are also asked to read *Choosing to Live: How to Defeat Suicide Through Cognitive Therapy* (Ellis & Newman, 1996). This book is a self-help guide that illustrates an array of cognitive–behavioral techniques akin to those included in the intervention. Chapters of the book can be assigned as homework.

Developing a Safety Plan

Often when patients experience feelings of depression and hopelessness, they can get overwhelmed and are not capable of using adaptive coping strategies. Therefore, one of the first goals of therapy is for the therapist and patient to collaborate in the formation of a detailed crisis plan that can be implemented if the patient should find himself or herself in a future crisis situation. The crisis plan develops throughout the course of therapy as the patient learns new coping strategies. Initially, crisis plans include contacting emergency services. As the patient progresses through therapy, however, they can include the use of behavioral coping strategies such as going for a walk, calling a friend, or watching a funny movie. Other strategies that can be used in times of crisis are cognitive restructuring, the use of coping cards, relaxation techniques, increased use of social supports, and the use of a "hope kit." Crisis plans always include the telephone numbers of (a) social supports, (b) the therapist, (c) the psychiatric emergency room, and (d) other crisis hotlines that handle emergency calls.

While telling her story, Suzanne was able to identify the thoughts and feelings that preceded her suicide attempt. These included hopelessness, unlovability, and generally feeling overwhelmed. Together with her therapist, Suzanne came up with an emergency plan that she would use the next time she experienced these thoughts and feelings. According to her plan, when Suzanne started experiencing the thoughts and feelings that she associated with her suicide attempt, she would take a bath, call her mother, or go for a walk. If her feelings would not subside after doing those things, Suzanne wrote down the phone numbers for a crisis hotline, the emergency department, and the therapist's on-call number.

Developing a Cognitive Case Conceptualization of the Suicide Attempt

A fundamental element of the treatment is the identification of the precise automatic thoughts and core beliefs that led to the suicide attempt. As the patient tells the story of his or her suicide attempt, the therapist listens for the pertinent automatic thoughts and core beliefs. These are then integrated into an overall cognitive conceptualization of the suicide attempt, including but not limited to early childhood experiences, conditional beliefs and compensatory behavioral strategies, and the significant life events that led to the suicidal crisis (see A. T. Beck, Rush, et al., 1979). Consider Suzanne's case. She had been verbally and sexually abused by her stepfather as a child and had a history of two prior suicide attempts. During the previous month, she had been arguing constantly with her boyfriend, and he told her that he no longer wanted anything to do with her. Suzanne started thinking that she was all alone in the world and that no one loved her. Her feelings of hopelessness increased, and she became depressed. She did not return phone calls to her friends. Suzanne started drinking and using cocaine. She felt the pain of her existence was intolerable, and she overdosed on her prescription of imipramine. The cognitive case conceptualization of Suzanne's suicide attempt is presented in Figure 3.2. The conceptualization serves as a guide for the therapist in preparing interventions and can also be used to explain the

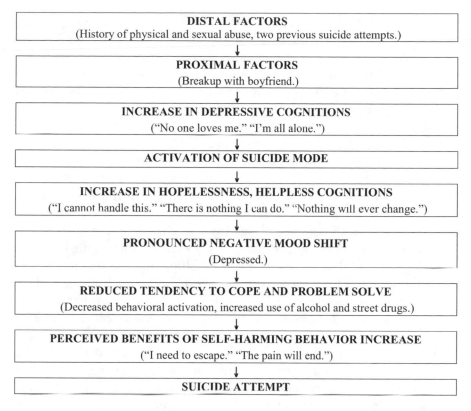

| DISTAL FACTORS |
| (History of physical and sexual abuse, two previous suicide attempts.) |

↓

| PROXIMAL FACTORS |
| (Breakup with boyfriend.) |

↓

| INCREASE IN DEPRESSIVE COGNITIONS |
| ("No one loves me." "I'm all alone.") |

↓

| ACTIVATION OF SUICIDE MODE |

↓

| INCREASE IN HOPELESSNESS, HELPLESS COGNITIONS |
| ("I cannot handle this." "There is nothing I can do." "Nothing will ever change.") |

↓

| PRONOUNCED NEGATIVE MOOD SHIFT |
| (Depressed.) |

↓

| REDUCED TENDENCY TO COPE AND PROBLEM SOLVE |
| (Decreased behavioral activation, increased use of alcohol and street drugs.) |

↓

| PERCEIVED BENEFITS OF SELF-HARMING BEHAVIOR INCREASE |
| ("I need to escape." "The pain will end.") |

↓

| SUICIDE ATTEMPT |

Figure 3.2. Conceptualization of suicidal behavior.

typical operation of the suicide mode to the patient. The conceptualization should be continually updated as new data are obtained during the course of treatment.

The Middle Phase (Sessions 4–7)

In the middle phase of therapy, suicidal behavior is targeted. This is accomplished by using cognitive restructuring techniques and behavior change. Strategies include the construction of coping cards, the creation of a hope kit, and learning behavioral coping skills.

Coping Cards

During this phase of treatment, the patient and therapist work together to identify core beliefs that are activated when the patient was or is feeling suicidal. After the fundamental core beliefs are uncovered, standard cognitive therapy techniques such as Socratic questioning, recognizing cognitive distortions, dysfunctional thought records, behavioral experiments, and role-plays are applied to generate an array of adaptive alternatives to each belief (see A. T. Beck, Rush, et al., 1979).

Each suicide-promoting core belief and set of alternative responses is placed on small wallet-sized coping cards. Coping cards are designed so that patients can easily carry them around, thus serving as an easily accessible way of jump-starting adaptive thinking during a suicidal crisis. Additionally, patients are encouraged to review the coping cards when they are not in crisis so that they are familiar with the skills in times of crisis.

Suzanne said that the coping cards were "her lifesaver." The majority of the middle therapy sessions were spent identifying the cognitions that led to the suicide attempt and then coming up with rational responses to those cognitions. One card that Suzanne reported she used frequently was what she called her "unlovability card." She said that she frequently had the thought that "no one loves me." However, in conjunction with her therapist she was able to come up with considerable evidence to challenge this belief including (a) the fact that her mother told her frequently how much she loved and cared for her, (b) that she had many friendships that she had maintained since childhood, (c) her friends call her frequently to see how she is doing and express concern for her well-being, and (d) she has a cat that loves her unconditionally. Suzanne made a coping card that on one side had the thought "no one loves me" and on the reverse side she printed the aforementioned evidence to challenge this thought. She said that she kept this card in her wallet and looked at it frequently even if she was not feeling suicidal. She said it helped her to feel better, and when she was feeling down, it helped remind her that her thoughts might not make sense.

Construction of a Hope Kit

Another activity that is undertaken in the middle phase of therapy is the construction of a hope kit. A hope kit consists of a container that holds mementos (photographs, letters, souvenirs) that serve as reminders of reasons to live. Patients are instructed to be as creative as possible when creating their hope kit, so that the end result is a powerful and personal reminder of their connection to life that can be used when feeling suicidal. We have found that patients report making their hope kits to be a highly rewarding experience that often leads them to discover reasons to live they had previously overlooked.

Suzanne was rather artistic and reported that she enjoyed this task. She found an old shoe box and decorated it using some of her favorite pictures. Inside she included pictures of her mother, her friends, and her cat. She also included the lyrics of her favorite song, a potpourri bag filled with her favorite scent, and a piece of her childhood blanket. Suzanne kept the hope box on her dresser, and it frequently reminded her of all the good things in her life.

Behavioral Coping Skills

A variety of behavioral coping strategies can be taught to patients to help them safely deal with suicidal thoughts and behaviors. These include distraction techniques such as reading, watching television or movies, talking to friends, counting backwards from 100, or physical exercise; creating intense physical sensations such as holding ice cubes, taking a hot or cold shower, or drinking hot tea (Linehan, 1993); self-soothing activities such as taking a hot bath, having a nice meal, or planning a night out with a friend; and relaxation techniques. Each behavioral skill that the patient finds helpful should be added to their crisis plan.

Suzanne compiled an "antisuicide" list in which she recorded activities that she found helpful to distract her when she was experiencing suicidal ideation. Some of these included going for a walk, calling her mother, taking a long bath, going to the library, making a date with a friend, smelling the flowers at the local grocery store, and putting an ice cube in her mouth.

Later Sessions (Sessions 8–10)

The major focus of the later sessions is the development of a relapse prevention task (RPT). Patients use the coping skills that they have developed while visualizing themselves in a future suicidal crisis. The premise of guided visual imagery is described to the patients, along with possible deleterious consequences (i.e., feeling distressed). The patients are asked to imagine a sequence of events that led up to the suicide attempt as well as the related thoughts and feelings that precipitated a suicidal crisis in the past. The patients then imagine themselves using their skills to cope successfully with each event leading up to the crisis. This gives the patient an opportunity to practice these newly acquired skills in a safe environment. This is also a good opportunity for the therapist to evaluate the patient's skills and decide whether termination is appropriate. When the therapist has confidence that the patient will be able to use his or her newly acquired skills to prevent future suicide attempts, termination is indicated. Therapy is generally not terminated until the patient performs the RPT effectively.

When working with suicidal patients, it is important to start the preparations for termination from the first session. Therapists should emphasize the brevity of the intervention and discuss how the treatment is designed to teach them a set of skills that will be helpful when and if a future suicidal crisis emerges. Additionally, patients should be encouraged to use mental health services and social supports. Patients are often offered booster sessions if they require additional help reviewing coping skills or in case of emergencies. Finally, many people that have attempted suicide will experience ideation or even suicide attempts again in the future. It should be emphasized that the possibility of relapse in the future does exist, and a plan should be put into place to help the patient cope with setbacks.

Suzanne was well prepared to complete the relapse prevention task. During the course of the therapy, she had developed a series of skills that could help her cope with a future suicidal crisis. Guided by her therapists, she was to walk through the events that led to her suicide attempt. She visualized her boyfriend breaking up with her, and she was able to reexperience the feelings of hopelessness that went along with that. She then visualized using her coping cards to get her through the crisis and reported that she would also call her mother to come over so that she would not be alone. She also saw herself asking her roommate to hold on to her medications until she felt safe and she was no longer in danger of using the medications for self-harm.

After she completed the first of the relapse prevention tasks, the therapist then presented Suzanne with a future scenario in which she had fallen in love with another man who also ended up breaking up with her. In this scenario, however, her mother was out of town and could not be reached by telephone. Again, Suzanne was able to visualize herself in the scenario, and she described the thoughts and feelings that she might have if she had just found out her boyfriend had left her and she couldn't find her mother. She said she would first try using her coping cards and her hope box, but that if those things did not work, she said she would try calling one of her close friends. The therapist then presented her with the scenario that she was also unable to reach any of her friends. Suzanne appeared slightly rattled by this prospect but was quickly able to problem solve a solution, and she visualized herself leaving the house and going for a walk to the phone booth on the corner of her street to call the crisis line for help. After the completion of the task, both Suzanne and her therapist felt confident that she now possessed the skills to handle a future crisis effectively.

CONCLUSION

For more than 3 decades, Beck and colleagues have been at the forefront of research on suicidal behaviors in the United States. This research program was sparked by the simple yet profound insight that hopeless cognitions play a crucial and integral role in the development of suicidal behaviors. During this period, empirically supported assessment measures have been generated and disseminated, and a consistent nomenclature for suicidal behavior has been developed. More recently, attention has turned to the development of a brief, focused intervention that directly targets suicidal behavior as the primary focus of the therapy. Specific cognitive and behavioral strategies derived from general principles of cognitive theory have been developed, which include a multistep crisis plan, a detailed cognitive conceptualization of the suicide attempt, coping cards, a hope kit, and cognitive rehearsal of coping skills as well as an assessment of treatment progress. It is our hope that these developments will be advanced and refined in the decades to come.

REFERENCES

American Psychiatric Association. (1994). *Diagnostic and statistical manual of mental disorders* (4th ed.). Washington, DC: American Psychiatric Association.

Beck, A. T. (1964). Thinking and depression: II. Theory and therapy. *Archives of General Psychiatry, 10,* 561–571.

Beck, A. T. (1967). *Depression.* New York: Harper and Row.

Beck, A. T. (1970). Cognitive therapy. Nature and relation to behavior therapy. *Behavior Therapy, 1,* 184–200.

Beck, A. T. (1976). *Cognitive therapy and the emotional disorders.* Oxford, England: International Universities Press.

Beck, A. T. (1996). Beyond belief: A theory of modes, personality, and psychopathology. In P. Salkovskis (Ed.), *Frontiers of cognitive therapy* (pp. 1–25). New York: Guilford Press.

Beck, A. T., Beck, R., & Kovacs, M. (1975). Classification of suicidal behaviors: I. Quantifying intent and medical lethality. *American Journal of Psychiatry, 132,* 285–287.

Beck, A. T., Brown, G. K., Berchick, R. J., Stewart, B. L., & Steer, R. A. (1990). Relationship between hopelessness and ultimate suicide: A replication with psychiatric outpatients. *American Journal of Psychiatry, 147,* 190–195.

Beck, A. T., Brown, G., & Steer, R. A. (1989). Prediction of eventual suicide in psychiatric inpatients by clinical rating of hopelessness. *Journal of Consulting and Clinical Psychology, 57,* 309–310.

Beck, A. T., Brown, G. K., & Steer, R. A. (1997). Psychometric characteristics of the Scale for Suicide Ideation with psychiatric outpatients. *Behavior Research and Therapy, 35,* 1039–1046.

Beck, A. T., Brown, G. K., Steer, R. A., Dahlsgaard, K. K., & Grisham, J. R. (1999). Suicide ideation at its worst point: A predictor of eventual suicide in psychiatric outpatients. *Suicide and Life-Threatening Behavior, 29,* 1–9.

Beck, A. T., Davis, J. H., Frederick, C. J., Perlin, S., Pokorny, A. D., Schulman, R. E., et al. (1973). In H. Resnik & B. Hathorne (Eds.), *Suicide prevention in the 70's* (pp. 7–12). Washington, DC: U.S. Government Printing Office.

Beck, A. T., Kovacs, M., & Weissman, A. (1975). Hopelessness and suicidal behavior: An overview. *Journal of the American Medical Association, 234,* 1146–1149.

Beck, A. T., Kovacs, M., & Weissman, A. (1979). Assessment of suicidal intention: The Scale for Suicide Ideation. *Journal of Consulting and Clinical Psychology, 47,* 343–352.

Beck, A. T., Rush, A. J., Shaw, B. F., & Emery, G. (1979). *Cognitive therapy of depression.* New York: Guilford Press.

Beck, A. T., Schuyler, D., & Herman, I. (1974). Development of suicidal intent scales. In T. Beck, H. L. P. Resnik, & D. J. Lettieri (Eds.), *The prediction of suicide.* Bowie, MD: Charles Press.

Beck, A. T., & Steer, R. A. (1989). Clinical predictors of eventual suicide: A five to ten year prospective study of suicide attempters. *Journal of Affective Disorders, 17,* 203–209.

Beck, A. T., Steer, R. A., Kovacs, M., & Garrison, B., (1985). Hopelessness and eventual suicide: A 10-year prospective study of patients hospitalized with suicidal ideation. *American Journal of Psychiatry, 142,* 559–563.

Beck, A. T., Steer, R. A., & McElroy, M. G. (1982). Relationships of hopelessness, depression, and previous suicide attempts to suicidal ideation in alcoholics. *Journal of Studies on Alcohol, 43,* 1042–1046.

Beck, A. T., Weissman, A., Lester, D., & Trexler, L. (1974). The measurement of pessimism: The hopelessness scale. *Journal of Consulting and Clinical Psychology, 42,* 861–865.

Beck, J. S. (1995). *Cognitive therapy: Basics and beyond.* New York: Guilford Press.

Beck, R. W., Morris, J. B., & Beck, A. T. (1974). Cross-validation of the Suicidal Intent Scale. *Psychological Reports, 34,* 445–446.

Berk, M., Henriques, G., Warman, D., Brown, G. K., & Beck, A. T. (2004). A cognitive therapy intervention for suicide attempters: An overview of the treatment and case examples. *Cognitive and Behavioral Practice, 11,* 265–277.

Blanton-Lacy, M. (1997). The validity of the Beck Depression Inventory, Scale for Suicide Ideation, and Hopelessness Scale in an African-American college population. *Dissertation Abstracts International, 58,* 409.

Brown, G. K., Beck, A. T., Steer, R. A., & Grisham, J. R. (2000). Risk factors for suicide in psychiatric outpatients: A 20-year prospective study. *Journal of Consulting and Clinical Psychology, 68,* 371–377.

Brown, G. K., Henriques, G. R., Sosdjan, D., & Beck, A. T. (2004). Suicide intent and accurate expectations of lethality: Predictors of medical lethality of suicide attempts. *Journal of Consulting and Clinical Psychology, 72,* 1170–1174.

Brown, G. K., TenHave, T., Henriques, G. R., Xie, S. X., Hollander, J. E., & Beck, A. T. (2005). Cognitive therapy for the prevention of suicide attempts: A randomized controlled trial. *Journal of the American Medical Association, 294,* 563–570.

Clum, G. A., & Curtin, L. (1993). Validity and reactivity of a system of self-monitoring suicide ideation. *Journal of Psychopathology and Behavioral Assessment, 15,* 375–385.

Clum, G. A., & Yang, B. (1995). Additional support for the reliability and validity of the Modified Scale for Suicide Ideation. *Psychological Assessment, 7,* 122–125.

Dahlsgaard, K. K., Beck, A. T., & Brown, G. K. (1998). Inadequate response to therapy as a predictor of suicide. *Suicide and Life-Threatening Behavior, 28,* 197–204.

Ellis, T. E., & Newman, C. F. (1996). *Choosing to live: How to defeat suicide through cognitive therapy.* Oakland, CA: New Harbinger.

Fridell, E. J., Ojehagen, A., & Traeskman-Bendz, L. (1996). A 5-year follow-up study of suicide attempts. *Acta Psychiatrica Scandinavica, 93,* 151–157.

Harris, E. C., & Barraclough, B. (1997). Suicide as an outcome for mental disorders: A meta-analysis. *British Journal of Psychiatry*, *170*, 205–228.

Hawton, K. (2001). Studying survivors of nearly lethal suicide attempts: An important strategy in suicide research. *Suicide and Life-Threatening Behavior*, *32*, 76–84.

Hawton, K., & Kirk, J. (1989). Problem-solving. In K. Hawton, P. Salkovskis, J. Kirk, & D. M. Clark (Eds.), *Cognitive behaviour therapy for psychiatric problems: A practical guide* (pp. 406–426). Oxford, England: Oxford University Press.

Henriques, G., Beck, A. T., & Brown, G. K. (2003). Cognitive therapy for adolescent and young adult suicide attempters. *American Behavioral Scientist*, *46*, 1258–1268.

Henriques, G., Wenzel, A., Beck, A. T., & Brown, G. K. (in press). Suicide attempters' reactions to the attempt as a predictor of eventual suicide. *American Journal of Psychiatry*.

Hughes, D., & Kleespies, P. (2001). Suicide in the medically ill. *Suicide and Life-Threatening Behavior*, *31*(Suppl.), 48–59.

Joiner, T. E., & Rudd, M. D. (2000). Intensity and duration of suicidal crisis vary as a function of previous suicide attempts and negative life events. *Journal of Consulting and Clinical Psychology*, *68*, 909–916.

Kreitman, N. (1977). *Parasuicide*. London: Wiley.

Kreitman, N. (1979). Reflections on the management of parasuicide. *British Journal of Psychiatry*, *135*, 275–277.

Kreitman, N., Philip, A. E., Greer, S., & Bagley, C. R. (1969). Parasuicide. *British Journal of Psychiatry*, *115*, 746–747.

Linehan, M. M. (1982). *Suicide Intent Scale: Self-Report Form*. Unpublished inventory, University of Washington, Seattle.

Linehan, M. M. (1993). *Skills training manual for treating borderline personality disorder*. New York: Guilford Press.

Marx, E. M., Williams, J. M. G., & Claridge, G. C. (1992). Depression and social problem solving. *Journal of Abnormal Psychology*, *101*, 78–86.

Mireault, M., & de Man, A. F. (1996). Suicidal ideation among the elderly: Personal variables, stress and social support. *Social Behavior & Personality*, *24*, 385–392.

Molock, S. D., Kimbrough, R., Lacy, M. B., McClure, K. P., & Williams, S. (1994). Suicidal behavior among African American college students: A preliminary study. *Journal of Black Psychology*, *20*, 234–251.

Newman, C. F., & Beck, A. T. (1999). *Cognitive therapy of rapid cycling bipolar affective disorder: Treatment manual*. Unpublished manuscript, University of Pennsylvania, Philadelphia.

O'Brien, G., Holton, A. R., Hurren, K., Watt, L., & Hassanyeh, F. (1987). Deliberate self-harm correlates of suicidal intent and depression. *Acta Psychiatrica Scandinavica*, *75*, 474–477.

O'Carroll, P. W., Berman, A. L., Maris, R. W., Moscicki, E. K., Tanney, B. L., & Silverman, M. M. (1996). Beyond the Tower of Babel: A nomenclature for suicidology. *Suicide and Life-Threatening Behavior*, *26*, 237–252.

Ojehagen, A., Regnell, G., & Traeskman-Bendz, L. (1991). Deliberate self-poisoning: Repeaters and nonrepeaters admitted to an intensive care unit. *Acta Psychiatrica Scandinavica, 84,* 266–271.

Petrie, K., Chamberlain, K., & Clarke, D. (1988). Psychological predictors of future suicidal behaviour in hospitalized suicide attempters. *British Journal of Clinical Psychology, 27,* 247–257.

Rudd, M. D. (2000). The suicidal mode: A cognitive–behavioral model of suicidality. *Suicide and Life-Threatening Behavior, 30,* 18–33.

Rudd, M. D., Joiner, T., & Rajab, M. H. (2001). *Treating suicidal behavior: An effective time limited approach.* New York: Guilford Press.

Salkovskis, P. M., Atha, C., & Storer, D. (1990). Cognitive–behavioural problem solving in the treatment of patients who repeatedly attempt suicide: A controlled trial. *British Journal of Psychiatry, 157,* 871–876.

Stengel, E., & Cook, N. (1958). *Attempted suicide.* London: Oxford University Press.

Tejedor, M. C., Diaz, A., Castillon, J. J., & Pericay, J. M. (1999). Attempted suicide: Repetition and survival—findings of a follow-up study. *Acta Psychiatrica Scandinavica, 100,* 205–211.

Young, M. A., Fogg, L. F., Scheftner, W., Fawcett, J., Akiskal, H., & Maser, J. (1996). Stable trait components of hopelessness: baseline and sensitivity to depression. *Journal of Abnormal Psychology, 105,* 155–165.

4

SUICIDE FROM THE PERSPECTIVE OF RATIONAL EMOTIVE BEHAVIOR THERAPY

ALBERT ELLIS AND THOMAS E. ELLIS

Suicide has been described as "the only really serious philosophical problem" (Camus, 1942/1955). It is therefore fitting that, as a fundamentally philosophical system, rational emotive behavior therapy (REBT) would speak specifically to the issues of suicide and suicidal behavior. However, REBT heretofore has been relatively quiet on suicide, with only a few papers devoted specifically to the topic. In this chapter, we discuss how suicide and suicidal behavior are conceptualized in REBT, as well as how suicidal patients might be helped through REBT interventions.

Recent years have seen an increase in discussions of suicidality from a cognitive perspective. For example, T. E. Ellis (1986) reviewed empirical findings regarding cognition and suicide and suggested possible directions for treatment in a generic cognitive therapy context and later authored a self-help book (T. E. Ellis & Newman, 1996). Linehan has conducted extensive research on suicidal individuals with borderline personality disorder and developed a form of cognitive–behavioral therapy (dialectical behavior therapy [DBT]) that is considered applicable to a broad range of suicidal patients (Linehan, 1993). Most recently, Rudd, Joiner, and Rajab (2001) described a comprehensive cognitive–behavioral approach to working with suicidal individuals using a problem-solving orientation.

Articles examining suicide specifically from an REBT perspective are much more limited in number. T. E. Ellis and Ratliff (1986) showed that "emotional responsibility" (the tendency to believe that one's difficulties are caused by circumstances rather than by one's perceptions) differentiated between suicidal and nonsuicidal depressed psychiatric inpatients. A. Ellis (1989) presented the case of a 27-year-old suicidal woman and showed how the use of REBT techniques such as unconditional acceptance can be helpful. Diekstra, Engels, and Methorst (1988) presented a theoretical approach to much the same issue, suggesting REBT as a possible form of crisis intervention for depressed individuals with suicidality. Woods and Muller (1988) administered the Irrational Beliefs Test to 207 psychotherapy patients and found that those who were suicidal tended to have more irrational thinking regarding helplessness and perfectionism. A subsequent study of undergraduate students showed that those with lower irrationality scores were less likely to view suicide as an appropriate response to a crisis situation (Woods, Silverman, Gentilini, Cunningham, & Grieger, 1992).

Although these works have begun to consider the relationship between suicidal behavior and REBT theory, this chapter is the first to propose a general REBT framework for understanding and intervening with suicidal individuals. We begin by showing how REBT conceptualizes suicide and related phenomena, followed by a discussion of the practical application of the theory to crisis intervention and therapy. This is followed by a detailed illustration of the treatment of a suicidal client using an REBT approach.

GENERAL REBT CONCEPTS APPLIED TO SUICIDALITY

The following section illustrates the application of REBT concepts to suicidal individuals.

"A–C Thinking" and Helplessness–Hopelessness

A. T. Beck and associates have shown how hopelessness plays a pivotal role in increasing suicide risk by mediating between depression and suicidality (Minkoff, Bergman, Beck, & Beck, 1973). However, the precise sources of hopelessness are less well understood. One likely influence is deficient problem-solving skills (see Reinecke, chap. 11, this volume). Various authors (e.g., Clum & Lerner, 1990) have shown that problem-solving deficiencies discriminate suicidal from nonsuicidal depressives and that training in problem-solving skills results in significant benefits. However, hopelessness may also be fueled through beliefs about sources of unhappiness and one's control (or lack of control) of those sources (T. E. Ellis & Ratliff, 1986).

The idea that people are made unhappy not by circumstances, but by their views of those circumstances, is central to the "A-B-C" model of REBT. In this model, "A" represents Activating events, "C" stands for emotional and behavioral Consequences, and "B" stands for the Beliefs and other cognitive processes that serve as mediators between the events and the responses. Although clients in general commonly believe that their "Cs" are directly caused by "As," suicidal individuals may be especially inclined to overlook the role that their own thinking ("B") plays in their upset. Because precipitating events (e.g., interpersonal losses) often are not alterable, a state of helplessness and hopelessness may result (this perspective is consistent with a substantial body of research showing an association between suicidality and the cognitive dimensions of self-efficacy and negative attributional style (Institute of Medicine, 2002). The realization that one can reduce negative emotions and modify dysfunctional behaviors by changing one's thinking can have an empowering effect that might be especially beneficial to suicidal individuals (T. E. Ellis & Newman, 1996).

Awfulizing and Low Frustration Tolerance

Perhaps no self-statement is more emblematic of the suicidal state than "I can't stand it." Taken to its extreme (as it sometimes is), this evaluation means, "This situation is so awful, either it will kill me or I shall kill myself." This mind-set can be divided into three components (which may or may not coexist): (a) "catastrophizing," wherein the severity and significance of the problem are exaggerated (e.g., "If I screw up my speech, it will be the end of the world."); (b) The individual underestimates his or her ability to tolerate the situation (e.g., "I would not be able to stand it if I had a panic attack at the mall."); and (c) "awfulizing," wherein a "true" catastrophe, such as a natural disaster, is construed as "awful" (e.g., "This experience was so bad, it should not or must not exist; it is too awful to bear, and I can never be happy again."). Although it is commonly recognized that the suicidal person's background and problem-solving deficits may produce an inordinate number and severity of bona fide problems in living (e.g., Linehan, 1993), the REBT framework adds the concept of low frustration tolerance (LFT). In other words, it is not just that the suicidal individual has many problems, but also that he or she believes that these problems are even greater than they are, should not exist, and are unbearable. This tendency has been recognized by Linehan (1993) in her discussion of helping people with borderline personality disorder to cultivate an attitude of mindful acceptance, as well as by Rudd et al. (2001) in their discussion of developing distress tolerance in suicidal patients.

Conditional Human Worth

A fundamental philosophical premise of REBT maintains that it is logically impossible to rate the worth of human beings in their totality (A. Ellis,

TABLE 4.1

Rational Emotive Behavior Therapy Model of Suicidal Behavior: Common
Activating Events, Beliefs, and Consequences

Activating events (A)	Beliefs (cognitive processes; B)	Emotional–behavioral consequences (C)
Interpersonal loss	"A–C" thinking	Despair
Achievement loss	Awfulizing	Desperation
Health loss	Catastrophizing	Self-disgust
Interpersonal conflict	Contingent self-worth	Suicidal ideation
Relationship failure	Low frustration tolerance	Suicidal impulses
Occupational failure	Negative self-rating	Self-harm behaviors
Social stressors	Hopelessness	Suicide

1973). REBT maintains that humans by nature tend to base their self-worth
on a variety of contingencies, including achievement, social acceptance, looks,
wealth, and good deeds. Clients in REBT are taught to reduce *self*-rating in
favor of rating *behaviors* in ways that will help them to achieve their goals.
The suicidal person not only bases his or her worth on external criteria but,
having fallen short of these standards, concludes that he or she has no reason
to live or is not worthy of living. As is illustrated in the case vignette that
appears later in the chapter, learning *unconditional self-acceptance* (USA) is a
fundamental aspect of conducting REBT with suicidal individuals.

THE A-B-C MODEL APPLIED TO SUICIDALITY

Table 4.1 shows the application of the three-component model of REBT
to suicidality. Here, the C (emotional and behavioral consequences) takes
the form of suicidal thoughts and behaviors (lethal or not), as well as related
feelings of desperation and despair (following Beck's lead, hopelessness is not
presented here as an emotion but as a negative appraisal of the future leading
to the emotion of despair; Beck, Rush, Shaw, & Emery, 1979).

Consistent with research in the area, the model shows that a variety of
activating events (As) are capable of setting the suicidal process into mo-
tion. Prominent among these are losses of various sorts, including interpersonal losses (e.g., divorce or death of loved ones) and achievement setbacks
(such as business failures). Medical illnesses and associated losses in physical
capabilities constitute another common situational trigger, particularly among
elderly individuals.

Obviously, not all people with these adverse events become suicidal.
REBT explains individual differences in emotional and behavioral responses
primarily through the mediational link at B (beliefs).

Common dysfunctional beliefs manifested by suicidal individuals include the following:

- My worth as a person depends on my achieving the things I strongly want to achieve and my being loved by people whose affection I very much want.
- If I fail at love or achievement, I am a worthless person and my life is therefore not worth living.
- I cannot stand life without the love that I crave.
- I can't bear being unhappy.
- I can't bear being sick or in pain.
- I must receive caring and support from others, even if I have to threaten suicide or injure myself to get it.
- Being miserable today means I will be miserable forever.
- I am a fundamentally unlucky and unfortunate person and therefore can't expect anything but unhappiness and misfortune in the future.
- Mistakes and failure are too shameful to bear.
- Life isn't worth living if I can't have what's important to me.
- I will be better off if I kill myself.
- My loved ones would be better off if I were dead.

REBT with suicidal individuals overlaps considerably with other cognitive–behavioral therapies. It is not indistinguishable, however (for a more detailed discussion of differences between REBT and other forms of cognitive–behavioral therapy [CBT], see A. Ellis & Dryden, 1997, 2001). REBT uniquely places philosophical issues at the center of the therapy, notably, values regarding health, happiness, adversity, and human worth. Specifically, REBT seeks not only to help clients learn to put their beliefs to the empirical test by examining the evidence for and against them but also to work toward profound philosophical changes. Thus, a client who believes that "Life should be fair and it's unbearable when it's not" is encouraged to shift to a more stoic philosophy maintaining that "I might *prefer* that life treat me fairly, but there is no reason why life *must* be fair, and I can certainly stand it when it isn't." The client who believes that a person's life is not worthwhile unless he or she achieves success and love is encouraged to adopt a more humanistic view that people's lives are not rateable in toto—one can refuse to condemn oneself for failure and can seek to enjoy life simply because one chooses to, not because one "deserves" happiness.

This stance provides a unique edge for clinicians working with clients in especially trying circumstances. Clients who are unemployed, convicted of crimes, socially isolated, disabled, suffering chronic pain, or otherwise experiencing multiple, severe adversities often tax the therapist's ability to resist being pulled into the client's bleak worldview, self-condemnation, hopelessness, and helplessness. REBT's philosophical stance of stoicism ("While I might not like adversity, it's not true that I can't stand it") and unconditional self-acceptance ("I may make mistakes or do bad things, but I never become a bad person who doesn't deserve to live") allows the therapist to challenge hopelessness and suicidality while empathizing and validating the reality of the client's life experiences. We further discuss the application of these philosophical principles in the chapter's case vignette.

PRINCIPLES OF CRISIS INTERVENTION

Writings on therapeutic interventions with suicidal clients often fail to make a crucial distinction between crisis intervention and psychotherapy. The purpose of crisis intervention is essentially to preserve life, that is, to stabilize the client as quickly as possible to prevent his or her responding to emotional distress by committing suicide or engaging in self-harm behavior. Crisis intervention generally does little to address vulnerability factors that contributed to the crisis in the first place, however, and failure to address these in therapy leaves the client vulnerable to future suicidal crises when thematically similar trigger events occur (see Rudd, chap. 16, this volume).

In the REBT framework, crisis intervention essentially refers to making changes at A (addressing situational and environmental triggers) and at C (reducing emotional urgency and inhibiting self-harm behaviors). As shown in Table 4.2, such changes are tailored to the client's specific situation. For example, for the individual distressed primarily about the breakup of an intimate relationship, conflict mediation can be highly effective in rapidly reducing emotional distress. For higher risk situations, hospitalization is another example of changing the A.

By the same token, effort can be focused directly on the emotional and behavioral consequences (C) themselves. Linehan's (1993) DBT model provides numerous interventions aimed at improving emotional and behavioral regulation, including a hierarchical approach that assigns self-harm behaviors top priority before any other therapeutic agenda items will be addressed. Additionally, DBT provides numerous tools for reducing negative emotionality, such as meditation and self-soothing exercises. It should be noted that suicidal individuals commonly receive psychotropic medications, another example of an intervention at C. When the acute crisis has been stabilized, it is possible then to turn attention to modifying cognitive factors at B.

PRINCIPLES OF THERAPY

As noted earlier, changes at A and C may reduce the urgency of a crisis but are unlikely to protect the client from suicidal crises when future adverse events occur. The client with a suicidal history who believes that she must be loved for life to be worth living is at risk of suicidal crises occurring whenever she experiences a significant rejection. The formerly suicidal executive who

TABLE 4.2

Rational Emotive and Behavior Therapy Model of Therapy With Suicidal Patients

Situation change (A)	Cognitive interventions (B)	Symptom reduction (C)
Conflict resolution	"B–C" thinking	Pharmacotherapy
Problem solving	Decatastrophizing	Coping skills training
Relationship enhancement	Performance (not self-) rating	Self-soothing
Social services	Unconditional self-acceptance	Distraction
Occupational enhancement	Unconditional other acceptance	techniques
Hospitalization	Unconditional life acceptance	Physical exercise
Activity enhancement		

believes that his worth is based on his achievements might rally when he obtains a new job but remains vulnerable should the company suddenly downsize or declare bankruptcy. It is not uncommon to read news reports of perfectionistic administrators or military officers who seem to be doing well in life, only to commit suicide when it is disclosed that they have falsified their record or are being investigated under suspicion of criminal conduct.

Because suicidal persons differ widely one from another (T. E. Ellis, 1988), therapy with suicidal clients needs to take into account the idiosyncracies of each individual's suicidality. The suicidal thoughts, behaviors, and motivations of the individual with borderline personality disorder differ significantly from those of the depressed widow, which, in turn, differ from those of the adolescent with substance abuse problems. In each case, the therapist must consider how each individual's mediational process at B gives a specific set of circumstances life-and-death meaning. Indeed, educating the client about this process and exploring for key beliefs becomes the starting point for the therapy once the suicidal crisis has been stabilized.

CASE VIGNETTE

"Frank" was a 55-year-old teacher, never married, whose partner of 10 years had recently left him because she would no longer put up with his constant severe depression. He had a history of migraine headaches, had painful rheumatoid arthritis, and had a long history of relating poorly to his supervisor and principals, who had kept him from becoming an assistant principal or principal himself. Frank had been in therapy on and off for 20 years and thought his therapists were "stupid" and "inefficient" because they were psychoanalytic and kept "harping on" his past. He refused to use antidepressants because he had had bad side effects from Prozac 8 years prior; he sedated himself when things got rough with marijuana, yoga, and meditation, all of which helped only temporarily.

At age 25, he was hospitalized for 1 week after he attempted suicide with borrowed sleeping pills after a previous partner had left him. He was so turned off by treatment he received at that time that he became more than ever devoted to pot, yoga, and meditation and became something of an "Eastern freak." This helped him a great deal, he reported, until he lost his latest woman friend and decided that she was right: He was too depressed for *any* woman to put up with.

Frank's father had been a school principal who was severely depressed all his life. His mother was first a secretary and then a homemaker, who was also very depressed. Both parents, however, were kind and helpful—he only resented the restrictions they placed on him when he rebelled against social rules and insisted on doing things his own independent way. Because after awhile they mainly let him do what he wanted, he bitterly resented several therapists who kept insisting that his parents abused and neglected him and that this was a main cause of his depression. He viewed these therapists as "psychoanalytic idiots" and kept seeing new ones.

Frank came to try me (A. E.) as a therapist largely because he attended my regular Friday night workshop several times and liked my no-nonsense approach. At this workshop, I interview two volunteer clients, whom I have usually never seen before. I give them a half-hour session of REBT, and then open the workshop to the members of the audience—about 80 or more people—to pose questions and make comments to the volunteer client and to me. A study that Debbie Joffe and I recently did (A. Ellis & Joffe, 2002) tends to show that most of the volunteer clients have little trouble being interviewed in public, benefited from the session, and would be willing to have more similar public sessions.

Frank enjoyed several of my Friday night workshops, participated himself in responding to the volunteer clients, and kept attending new workshops. He continued to see me because he said that I have a "no bullshit" approach to my clients that was "extremely refreshing" compared with his previous therapists. Maybe my approach would, at long last, help reduce his lifelong depression. What did he have to lose?

I could see right away that Frank probably had a severe personality disorder with strong depressive and suicidal tendencies. I specialize in treating clients with personality disorders, expect them to take a fairly long time to learn and apply REBT principles, and welcome the challenge of helping these difficult customers (DCs). So I was happy to take Frank on and delighted with his acceptance of my "no bullshit" approach.

Where to start? As usual, with potentially suicidal clients, I asked Frank whether he was seriously considering ending his life again, and, if so, whether he had a specific method of doing so. He assured me that this was not the case at present and said that if he changed his mind, he would definitely tell me. Two months later, after he had passed an examination for assistant principal for a third time but was turned down by a board of education director who interviewed him, Frank concluded that he would *never* get an assistant principal position and began to have suicidal thoughts—no definite plans but thoughts that being dead would be less painful than being alive.

Suicidal clients often have one main insistence that leads to their depression and hopelessness: "My worth as a person depends on my achieving the things I strongly want to achieve and my being loved by people that I deeply care for." Frank believed this with a vengeance. He *had* to get to be a school principal or an assistant principal and was worthless if he failed to do so. Because his life was only meaningful and enjoyable with this kind of achievement, it had to be meaningless and unenjoyable if he never had it. Proved!

To address this dysfunctional (and potentially deadly) idea, I first endeavored to help Frank achieve USA—to prefer but not absolutely need achievement and love and not to attach his worth as a person to failure. Conditional acceptance—respecting himself because he did well and won the approval of others wouldn't work. He had accomplished it several times, and it only temporarily allowed him to accept himself. Then he needed more achievement and more love.

Frank was intelligent and clearly saw that only unconditional acceptance was workable. He saw, during our first few sessions, that, at least in principle, he could accept himself unconditionally—whether or not he achieved a principalship and whether or not he was approved by a partner.

Frank saw this, but at first didn't believe it. He lightly (intermittently) saw the virtues of his having USA when he was depressed, but he believed that it was a utopian ideal that he—or anyone—couldn't really achieve. He could, he insisted, only partly experience it, largely because of his inborn tendency to be depressed and to be unable, after years of hard efforts with therapy, to stop damning himself and to stop whining about the rotten aspects of a world that he didn't control. Even when, under normal conditions, he could partly accept failure and rejection, under extreme conditions, try as he might, he couldn't accept them and felt depressed and hopeless.

This was fascinating, I thought, as I kept working with Frank. His own theory of his depressive state was remarkably close to my theory: (a) He had a severe personality disorder. (b) It was not merely socially learned or conditioned. (c) He could partly and lightly accept it and his tendency to excoriate himself and to awfulize about his life conditions, but he could not really and permanently do so. (d) Therefore, he was wise in resorting to relaxing and pleasurable distractions, such as pot, yoga, and meditation, which worked for a while. That was as far as he could go. One day, when he was older, less attractive, less competent, he might "rationally" end it all. If he couldn't stop his arthritic, migraine, and other pain, he might as well do so.

As Frank and I talked about living, dying, and suicide, I shared that his philosophy was not that different from my own, except that only extreme and untreatable physical pain would lead me to contemplate suicide. Mental and emotional pain, I would somehow conquer. He said that he appreciated my honesty but doubted that he could ever fully accept my mental and emotional antisuicidal philosophy, although he saw that it made "real sense." He did, however, agree to work on it.

We went back to helping Frank achieve unconditional self-acceptance. I got him to read Hayakawa's (1941) *Language in Action*, which in simple English presents Alfred Korzybski's view of humans rendering themselves "unsane" by overgeneralizing. Thus, they tell themselves, "I failed several times, and since I must always succeed to be worthwhile, I am a worthless failure with a capital F who will never be able to succeed." Korzybski and Hayakawa show that you can't be what you do because you are an ongoing person who does many "good" and "bad" things.

Using REBT with Frank, I forcefully and directively showed him that his strong preferences to achieve and be approved by a favored partner were great; but his grandiose insistence that he had to do so were unhealthily unrealistic and self-destructive. His "musturbating" led to his I-can't-ism; as soon as he insisted and fully believed "I can't do something"—can't play Ping-Pong, achieve at work, win at love, or anything else, he then made doing that thing almost impossible. Frank's "I *can't* give myself unconditional self-acceptance" made it almost impossible to do so.

Frank got it—and used it. Once he changed "I *can't* give myself unconditional self-acceptance," to "I *can* do it, even though it's very hard to do," he was on his way to doing it. He sometimes slipped back into "normal" conditional acceptance and had to work again to achieve unconditional self-acceptance, but at least he kept at it.

Meanwhile, we proceeded, Frank and I, to help him acquire *unconditional other acceptance* (UOA). This, too, was a hard nut for him to crack. He wasn't generally hostile to people at work or in his social relations, but he specifically was furious at his previous therapists, who *absolutely should not* have made him endlessly and futilely explore his past. "How could they be so stupid and iatrogenic? Incredible! Unforgivable!"

I showed Frank that I agreed with him that his past therapists were probably on the wrong track but that hardly made them, on the whole, stupid, rotten people. Nor were they entirely wrong because therapists sometimes help their clients by showing them the importance of past experiences and how to stop dwelling on them today. Frank refused to see it. He had continually told his therapists that they were wrong about him, and they completely refused to listen. How therapeutic was that?

Moreover, they were so wrong and so iatrogenic that they had practically driven him, once, to trying suicide. And that forced hospitalization, supposedly to "save" him, only provided medication and no therapy, and made him worse. They, his therapists, especially considering their profession, were "putrid people!" Let's not cavalierly let them off the hook! Well, maybe they were not *completely* rotten, but they so frequently acted badly that we can legitimately call them "bad people." To hell, then, with UOA!

It took me several more sessions to convince Frank that he could benefit considerably by adopting the REBT philosophy of UOA. Perhaps he was technically correct in rating his former therapists as bad therapists if it could be shown that they mainly harmed him and their other clients; but they still were not rotten people, because they obviously did some other beneficial deeds. Besides, what good would it do for him to rate them globally and to hate them violently? His hatred would make him obsessed with them, his enemies, and prevent him from helping himself. How idiotic!

I made this point several times to Frank, and it finally reached him. He especially didn't want to act idiotically because he was proud of his intelligence and was beginning to believe, by acquiring USA, that he couldn't be an idiot. Neither, therefore, could his former therapists, be idiots. Frank began deciding that they weren't "horrible idiots," even though they had "terribly harmed" him.

His acquiring USA and UOA helped Frank get on the ideological road to a key concept for suicidal individuals, *unconditional life acceptance* (ULA). With my help, he began to see life as including some very bad aspects—especially his tendency toward severe depression, his painful arthritis, and migraine headaches and his loss of two love relationships. Yet it was hardly *all* bad or terrible. He could still enjoy himself in several important ways. As a homework assignment, I had him list several of these ways, and his list included (a) thinking independently and against the conventional grain, (b) succeeding with some of his most difficult students, (c) teaching many of his students some of the main principles and practices of REBT, (d) listening to classical music and playing the piano, and (e) having a few close friendships with men and with women in whom he had no sexual interest.

Most of all, Frank appreciated and enjoyed his own use of REBT and his increasing use of USA, UOA, and ULA. As he got to practice these philosophies more thoroughly, despite some temporary setbacks, he decided to use them more with others and decided to become a school counselor. This would have more satisfactions and fewer headaches for him than being an assistant principal. He started to take counseling courses and pursue this new career.

I worked with Frank a year and a half, which is longer than I take with the great majority of my "nice neurotic" clients. I taught him a number of cognitive, emotive, and behavioral techniques that he could use on his own. Many of them I describe in detail in several of my other writings (A. Ellis, 1962/1994, 1999, 2001a, 2001b, 2002; A. Ellis & Blau, 1998; A. Ellis & Dryden, 1997; A. Ellis & Harper, 1961/1997). These include cognitive methods, such as disputing irrational beliefs, the use of rational coping statements, the use of cost–benefit analysis, the use of educational REBT self-help materials, modeling, and listening to recorded live sessions. Some of the emotional–experiential techniques I used with Frank in addition to USA,

UOA, and ULA, which are described in this chapter, included shame-attacking exercises, rational–emotive imagery, forceful coping statements, role-playing, humor, and dramatic stories and metaphors. Some of the REBT behavioral methods Frank used to help himself included risk-taking homework assignments, reinforcements for doing his homework, stimulus control, and relapse prevention methods (A. Ellis, 2001a, 2001b, 2002).

As Frank overcame his rage and self-downing, he also tried to better his life and tried to actualize and enjoy himself more. At this point, he had become intent on living instead of dying, so he decided to make the most of what he hoped would be a long life. He was taken with the ideas that Robert Harper and I suggested in the first edition of *A Guide to Rational Living* (A. Ellis & Harper, 1961/1997). We encouraged our clients to choose to devote themselves to a *vital absorbing interest* with which they could involve themselves for 20 or more years. He chose working for peace and following REBT's unconditional other acceptance philosophy and Tibetan Buddhist position of the Dalai Lama (Dalai Lama & Cutler, 1998). He became politically active and concentrated on teaching peace-loving attitudes to his students. Both of these vital absorbing interests gave him great pleasure and extra reasons for living. His political interest also helped him meet several peace-loving women, who might well accept him as a partner despite his depressive tendencies.

I only see Frank occasionally for therapy now when his self-therapy and Prozac don't seem to be working and when he thinks he could use a booster shot of REBT. He still comes regularly to my Friday night workshop, however, and speaks helpfully to the volunteer clients, thereby updating his use of REBT on himself and others. He highly rates his adeptness at helping others with REBT but does not highly rate his whole self or being for having this adeptness. In terms of Alfred Korzybski's techniques, he is a *person* who does good things but not a completely *good person*.

Were there any special reasons why my collaborative use of REBT with Frank worked well, despite his having a severe personality disorder, many years of depression, a long history of failing at important projects, being rejected by suitable partners, and years of ineffective previous therapy? Yes, I think there were several possible reasons the therapy succeeded.

1. Frank was thoroughly fed up with psychodynamic treatment and quite ready to take on REBT.
2. He was primed for therapy with me because of his favorable impression of my regular Friday night workshops.
3. Except for his age, 55, he largely fit the YAVIS type of client, who often succeeds at therapy, since he was Young (moderately), Active, Verbal, Intelligent, and Successful (moderately).
4. He really committed himself to using REBT, persisted at it despite some setbacks, and ultimately devoted himself to teach-

ing it to his friends, political associates, and students. He thereby heavily sank its teachings into his head and heart.

More germane to the focus of this book, why do I think that Frank's suicidality disappeared? In essence, I would suggest that the critical change was in his beliefs regarding what constituted acceptable and unacceptable conditions for living. When I first began working with him, Frank firmly believed that life was only worth living if he met certain prescribed standards (notably, regarding achievement and acceptance) and if life were reasonably free of hassles and discomfort. By working hard to replace his conditions for living with *unconditional* acceptance of himself and life's circumstances, he replaced a rigid (and therefore irrational) mind-set with a set of beliefs about himself and the world that was more reasonable, flexible, and appropriate to his circumstances. In addition (on a less philosophical and more practical level), by cultivating vitally absorbing activities, he changed his life in such a way as to satisfy better his still high, although no longer rigid and unrealistic, standards, thus making his life more "worth living."

SUMMARY AND CONCLUSIONS

Suicidality is one of the few truly life-or-death situations in psychotherapy, yet many therapeutic systems—including REBT—have been slow to speak specifically to how the theory explains suicidality and what therapeutic strategies can be derived from the theoretical framework to reduce suicide risk for vulnerable clients. This chapter has attempted to fill this void by extending REBT theory to suicidality and illustrated how REBT methods might be used to treat suicidal individuals.

Contributions have been even more lacking in the research arena. Almost no studies have been published examining the fundamental questions regarding REBT and suicidality. The foregoing, theoretically derived, formulation awaits testing, examining fundamental issues such as the following:

- What are the characteristics of suicidal individuals in terms of REBT theory, and how do they differ from other clients with similar diagnoses who are not suicidal? To what extent are such core REBT constructs as low frustration tolerance, demandingness, and contingent self-worth (vs. self-acceptance) implicated in suicidal ideation and suicidal behavior?
- In what ways, if any, should REBT be modified for suicidal clients, and do such modifications lead to improved outcomes relative to traditional REBT? Are such "standard" interventions as vigorous disputation and Socratic questioning any more or less beneficial for this population?

- Should REBT theory view all suicidal individuals essentially alike (i.e., as manifesting essentially similar irrational beliefs); if not, what are the subtypes and what are the implications for individualizing their treatment?
- Does modification of irrational thinking through REBT translate into a reduction in suicidal wishes, urges, and behaviors in most clients?
- Do REBT treatment strategies confer measurable advantages to treatment of suicidal individuals above and beyond other therapeutic approaches, including other cognitive–behavioral therapies? For example, does REBT's trademark emphasis on the development of high frustration tolerance and "emotional toughness" have particular promise for reducing the allure of suicide for an emotionally distressed person?

If one views suicidality, not only as a manifestation of psychopathology but also as a fundamentally philosophical issue, then it is reasonable to suggest that it might be helpful (or perhaps essential) to address philosophical issues directly, such as those regarding the meaning of suffering or the worth of a human being. The philosophical basis of REBT, as well as its general track record of efficacy (Solomon & Haaga, 1995), suggest that it is not unreasonable to predict that it will prove to be an efficacious approach to working with suicidal individuals.

REFERENCES

Beck, A. T., Rush, A. J., Shaw, B. F., & Emery, G. (1979). *Cognitive therapy of depression*. New York: Guilford Press.

Camus, A. (1955). The myth of Sisyphus and other essays (Justin O'Brien, trans.). New York: Random House. (Original work published 1942)

Clum, G. A., & Lerner, M. S. (1990). Treatment of suicide ideators: A problem-solving approach. *Behavior Therapy, 21*, 403–411.

Dalai Lama, B., & Cutler, H. C. (1998). *The art of happiness: A handbook for living*. New York: Riverhead.

Diekstra, R. F., Engels, G. I., & Methorst, G. J. (1988). Cognitive therapy of depression: A means of crisis intervention. *Crisis, 9*, 32–44.

Dryden, W., & Ellis, A. (2001). Rational emotive behavior therapy. In K. Dobson (Ed.), *Handbook of cognitive–behavioral therapies* (2nd ed., pp. 349–392). New York: Guilford Press.

Ellis, A. (1973). *Humanistic psychotherapy: The rational emotive approach*. New York: Julian Press.

Ellis, A. (1989). Using rational–emotive therapy (RET) as crisis intervention: A single session with a suicidal client. *Journal of Adlerian Theory, Research, and Practice, 45*, 75–81.

Ellis, A. (1994). *Reason and emotion in psychotherapy.* New York: Carol. (Original work published 1962)

Ellis, A. (1999). *How to be happy and remarkably less disturbable.* Atascadero, CA: Impact Press.

Ellis, A. (2001a). *Feeling better, getting better, and staying better.* Atascadero, CA: Impact Press.

Ellis, A. (2001b). *Overcoming destructive beliefs, feelings, and behaviors.* Amherst, NY: Prometheus Books.

Ellis, A. (2002). *Overcoming resistance: A rational emotive behavior therapy integrative approach.* New York: Springer Publishing Company.

Ellis, A., & Blau, T. (Eds.). (1998). *The Albert Ellis reader.* New York: Citadel Press.

Ellis, A., & Dryden, W. (1997). *The practice of rational emotive behavior therapy* (2nd ed.). New York: Springer Publishing Company.

Ellis, A., & Harper, R. (1997). *A guide to rational living.* North Hollywood, CA: Melving Powers. (Original work published 1961)

Ellis, A., & Joffe, D. (2002). A study of volunteer clients who experienced live sessions of rational emotive behavior therapy in front of a public audience. *Journal of Rational-Emotive and Cognitive-Behavior Therapy, 20,* 151–158.

Ellis, T. E. (1986). Toward a cognitive therapy for suicidal individuals. *Professional Psychology, 17,* 125–130.

Ellis, T. E. (1988). Classification of suicidal behavior: A review and step toward integration. *Suicide and Life-Threatening Behavior, 18,* 358–371.

Ellis, T. E., & Newman, C. F. (1996). *Choosing to live: How to defeat suicide through cognitive therapy.* Oakland, CA: New Harbinger.

Ellis, T. E., & Ratliff, K. (1986). Cognitive characteristics of suicidal and nonsuicidal psychiatric inpatients. *Cognitive Therapy and Research, 10,* 625–634.

Hayakawa, S. I. (1941). *Language in action.* New York: Harcourt Brace.

Institute of Medicine. (2002). Psychiatric and psychological factors. In S. K. Goldsmith, T. C. Pellmar, A. M. Kleinman, & W. E. Bunney (Eds.), *Reducing suicide: A national imperative* (pp. 69–119). Washington, DC: National Academies Press.

Linehan, M. M. (1993). *Cognitive–behavioral treatment of borderline personality disorder.* New York: Guilford Press.

Minkoff, K., Bergman, E., Beck, A. T., & Beck, R. (1973). Hopelessness, depression, and attempted suicide. *American Journal of Psychiatry, 130,* 455–459.

Rudd, M. D., Joiner, T. E., & Rajab, M. H. (2001). *Treating suicidal behavior.* New York: Guilford Press.

Solomon, A., & Haaga, D. A. (1995). Rational emotive behavior therapy research: What we know and what we need to know. *Journal of Rational-Emotive and Cognitive-Behavior Therapy, 13,* 179–191.

Woods, P. J., & Muller, G. E. (1988). The contemplation of suicide: Its relationship to irrational beliefs in a client sample and the implications for long range suicide prevention. *Journal of Rational-Emotive and Cognitive-Behavior Therapy, 6,* 236–258.

Woods, P. J., Silverman, E. S., Gentilini, J. M., Cunningham, D. K., & Grieger, R. M. (1992). Cognitive variables related to suicidal contemplation in adolescents with implications for long-range prevention. *Journal of Rational-Emotive and Cognitive-Behavior Therapy, 9,* 215–245.

5

LINEHAN'S THEORY OF SUICIDAL BEHAVIOR: THEORY, RESEARCH, AND DIALECTICAL BEHAVIOR THERAPY

MILTON Z. BROWN

Linehan's biosocial theory (1981, 1986, 1993) states that suicidal behavior is a learned method for coping with acute emotional suffering. Suicidal behavior is viewed as a skill deficit; that is, people are thought to seek death as the solution for their intense suffering because they can think of no other effective options. The theory has roots in social behaviorism (Staats, 1975) and radical behaviorism (Skinner, 1957/1992) and has been further shaped by emerging research.

Linehan's work through the years has focused prominently (although not exclusively) on borderline personality disorder (BPD). Suicidal ideation and behavior are often chronic in individuals with BPD, including recurrent suicide attempts and various forms of self-injury. Although Linehan's theory was originally developed to explain chronic suicidal behavior, it is also useful for understanding other dysfunctional behaviors in BPD, including nonsuicidal self-injury (e.g., Linehan, 1993). However, unique aspects of BPD and nonsuicidal self-injury are not reviewed here; the reader is referred to other sources that cover these topics more thoroughly (M. Z. Brown, 2002; M. Z. Brown, Comtois, & Linehan, 2002; Linehan, 1993). This chapter begins with a detailed description of Linehan's theory of suicide and discusses research relevant to the theory. Next, treatment strategies used in dialectical behavior therapy (DBT), which developed out of Linehan's theory of suicide, are discussed.

THE CAUSES OF SUICIDAL BEHAVIOR

Linehan's theory of suicide is based on the assumption that there are numerous causal pathways to dysfunctional behaviors. A behavioral analysis (i.e., functional analysis) is required to discover the specific controlling variables for specific suicidal acts for specific individuals. In this analysis, the causal variables to be considered include environmental factors, cognition, emotions, and overt behaviors. In some cases, cognition is a primary cause of suicidal behavior, and at other times, it has a minimal role. Although Linehan's theory allows for multiple causal pathways, it focuses on several common causal processes, especially emotion dysregulation. Situational factors are seen as having a prominent role in most cases even when cognitions and emotions are identified as important. It is not sufficient to explain dysfunctional behaviors simply in terms of internal experiences, because the origin of these experiences also must be explained (Baum & Heath, 1992). An exclusive focus on dysfunction inside the person risks ignoring a wide range of potentially important contextual factors in the onset and maintenance of suicidality. Cognition is symbolic activity that regulates behavior, not in an absolute way, but only in certain contexts. Therefore, it is crucial to understand the context in which thinking leads to problematic emotions and overt behaviors (Wilson, Hayes, & Gifford, 1996). Important environmental cues often trigger problematic cognitions, emotions, and behaviors. Like all other forms of human activity, cognitions are "not initiating causes," although they participate in overall causal relations. From a dialectical framework, events, including private and overt behaviors, can be both the cause and outcome of multiple complex events (Linehan, 1993).

Environmental Causes

Environmental events are important distal causes of suicidal behaviors. For example, from adverse childhood circumstances, individuals can acquire emotional responses, dysfunctional thought patterns, and dysfunctional behavioral repertoires (e.g., through classical conditioning, observational learning, and reinforcement). The suicidal person is the product of a biological vulnerability to emotion dysregulation and harmful childhood environments. Environmental events are also the first proximal cause in a chain of events, including dysfunctional thoughts, emotions, and behaviors, that result in specific suicidal actions. Neuropsychological evidence indicates that some stimulus events can activate emotions and emotional behaviors through pathways that bypass brain structures responsible for cognition (Gross, 1999). Conditioned emotions and overt behaviors can be elicited without awareness of the triggers (Bargh & Chartrand, 1999). Emotion-congruent cognition often follows emotional activation and behaviors that may be cued by the environment (Gilligan & Bower, 1984).

Adverse Events

Stressful life events lead to distressing emotions, depression (Jacobson, Martell, & Dimidjian, 2001), and suicidal behavior (Baumeister, 1990; Heikkinen, Aro, & Lonnqvist, 1993; Linehan & Shearin, 1988). Suicidal behaviors are associated with decreased socioeconomic status and high levels of interpersonal loss, conflict, separation, and divorce (Baumeister, 1990; Chiles, Strosahl, Cowden, Graham, & Linehan, 1986; Linehan, Chiles, Egan, Devine, & Laffaw, 1986; Maris, 1981; Rothberg & Jones, 1987; Welch & Linehan, 2002). Because chronically suicidal individuals both create and are controlled by aversive environments, they are often in a state of perpetual, unrelenting crisis. Lacking interpersonal and problem-solving skills, they are often passive about solving problems on their own and instead actively try to get others to solve their problems or regulate their emotions (Kehrer & Linehan, 1996; Linehan, Camper, Chiles, Strosahl, & Shearin, 1987; Pollock & Williams, 1998; Schotte & Clum, 1987). In addition, many suicidal people have strong fears of abandonment and seek excessive reassurance from others, and these same individuals sometimes seek excessive *negative* feedback from others (Joiner, 1995). These behaviors can frustrate or burn out friends, family, and therapists (Potthoff, Holahan, & Joiner, 1995). Furthermore, when suicidal individuals act in a hostile manner, others will likely respond by treating them in an unsupportive and hostile manner (e.g., Farberow, McKelligott, Cohn, & Darbonne, 1970).

Lack of Social Support

An absence of social support is associated with suicidality (Clum & Febbraro, 1994; Heikkinen et al., 1993; Linehan, 1986). Social support may be important in all types of suicidal behavior for several reasons. With an inattentive, hostile, or invalidating social network, or in the absence of a social network, a person's crisis may not be recognized, especially if the person does not clearly communicate his or her needs. Emotional support during the crisis, active assistance in reducing the stress, and suggestions of possible alternatives for solving the person's problems consequently are unavailable (Wagner, 1997). Also, suicidal individuals often experience themselves as "outsiders" and feel hopeless about securing satisfying relationships.

Some suicidal individuals fail to get adequate support or help from others because they consistently fail to communicate their emotional vulnerability clearly to others, including their therapists. This "apparent competence" probably results from individuals inhibiting their emotional experiences and expressions, even when such emotional expression is appropriate and expected, because during childhood their emotional displays, even when they were normal reactions, were punished and invalidated. Thus, the person may be experiencing inner turmoil while at the same time communicating (through words, manner, or both) apparent calmness and control.

Models for Suicidal Behavior

There is considerable evidence that suicidal behavior is prompted by awareness of the suicidal behavior of others. Observational learning can lead to the acquisition or strengthening of a wide range of dysfunctional and antisocial behaviors (Bandura, 1977). Exposure to suicidal models may be important in terms of acquisition of the suicidal response and development of outcome expectations. Suicidal models may have the greatest influence when a person is ambivalent about living. Media coverage of suicides, especially those of highly attractive or famous people, increases the probability of suicidal behavior of others (reviewed in Williams, 1997). Suicidal persons, more often than nonsuicidal persons, are linked socially with significant other persons who had previously been suicidal (Kreitman, Smith, & Tan, 1970).

The Role of Emotional Dysregulation

The final common pathway in nearly all suicidal behavior is acute emotional suffering—what Shneidman (1993) referred to as internal perturbation or *psychache*. Suicidal behavior is a solution for intolerable emotions when individuals know of no other effective options for coping. Numerous *escape theories* of suicide have been offered (e.g., Baumeister, 1990; Maris, 1992; Shneidman, 1992, 1993), most of which explain suicide as escape from depressive affect. Some theorists have also described avoidance and escape behaviors as important *causes* of depression (Jacobson et al., 2001). Suicide is the ultimate escape from problems in life, and suicide attempters expect death to bring relief from their painful emotions. Escape theories of suicide are compatible with radical behavioral theory, which explains suicidal behavior as resulting from rule-governed behavior when death is equated with relief from suffering (Hayes, 1992). In addition, nonfatal suicidal behavior relieves negative emotions for some individuals. For some, substance use (and overdose) becomes a way to "self-medicate" emotions and lower self-awareness. Some individuals experience relief when their suicidal behavior is effective at getting others to stop making demands (or stop other aversive behaviors) or getting them a reprieve from their stressful environments (e.g., when they are hospitalized). Often these individuals do not have a clear conscious intent to "manipulate" others and genuinely accept death as a way to end their pain, they have both motives simultaneously, or they are willing to have either solution. In any case, the relief of aversive emotions after suicidal behavior keeps the probability high that suicidal behavior will occur in the future as a coping response in similar situations.

Emotion dysregulation comprises several closely linked components: physiological activation, subjective experience (including valence and action urges), cognition, overt verbal and nonverbal expressions, and tendencies for dysfunctional overt action (Ekman & Davidson, 1994). Individuals who are highly sensitive or reactive to emotional stimuli and also unable to regulate emotions (e.g., distract or soothe) experience emotions that are intense, frequent, and prolonged. This emotion dysregulation is often pervasive across multiple emotions and across a wide range of situations, and impulsive and maladaptive behaviors (including suicidal behaviors and nonsuicidal self-injury) often occur in response to these emotions. Sometimes these behaviors are maladaptive attempts to change emotions; at other times, they are automatic mood-dependent responses to emotions. Although suicidal behaviors are not logically inevitable outcomes, paradigms of escape conditioning suggest that escape behaviors can become so well learned that they are automatic for some individuals when faced with extreme and uncontrollable emotional pain. Data support the idea that unconscious procedural knowledge and conscious processing occur in separate brain systems (e.g., Eichenbaum, 2003).

Emotion dysregulation may be particularly problematic for suicidal individuals because they have difficulty tolerating emotions. Linehan (1986, 1993) has speculated that chronically suicidal individuals, including those diagnosed with BPD, are "emotion-phobic" and chronically emotionally dysregulated—a difficult combination. They have low emotion tolerance because they have an exceptionally reactive physiological response system, have inadequate skills for coping with emotional pain, and often actively invalidate their emotions. They often feel ashamed to experience basic emotions such as sadness or anger. Because they invalidate and suppress their emotions, chronically dysregulated individuals vacillate between extremes of emotional experiencing and inhibition. By avoiding experiencing their emotions, they fail to learn that they can tolerate the emotions and that punishment will not follow their expression.

Suicidal individuals have typically experienced numerous childhood adversities, including harsh parenting, neglect, major losses, and other traumatic experiences (Twomey, Kaslow, & Croft, 2000; Wagner, 1997). Many persistently avoid grieving over these unfortunate circumstances, however. They become grief-phobic and seem unable to tolerate normal grieving, fearing that if they ever do cry, they will never stop. Their pathological grieving involves avoiding cues and reminders of the loss (Callahan & Burnette, 1989; Gauthier & Marshall, 1977). One study found that pathological grieving was associated with a high likelihood of suicidal ideation independent of depression (Prigerson et al., 1999). This process of inhibited grieving overlaps considerably with posttraumatic stress disorder (PTSD).

According to Linehan's theory, intolerance of negative emotion among chronically suicidal individuals is partly due to being raised in environments where emotional displays were punished, trivialized, and treated as pathological. In these invalidating environments, they learn that they should not cry or show anger or fear. In cases of sexual abuse, an adult may threaten punishment if the child becomes upset. Children in such circumstances learn to react to their emotions as others did—with criticism, contempt, anger, and sometimes physical violence. As adults, when such individuals feel emotional, they become upset for being upset, which results in a rapid escalation of emotion. Their attempts to suppress the emotion cycle are ultimately ineffective (Wegner, 1994).

Evidence for Emotion Dysregulation

A variety of studies provide empirical support for the hypothesis that negative emotion is a primary factor in suicidal behaviors. Suicidal individuals report highly distressing life events and high levels of aversive internal states both before suicidal behavior and in general (e.g., Rothberg & Jones, 1987). Suicide attempts and other forms of self-injury are often described as intentional efforts to escape distressing circumstances or to feel better (Bancroft, Skrimshire, & Simkins, 1976; Favazza & Conterio, 1989; Hawton, Cole, O'Grady, & Osborn, 1982; Kienhorst, De Wilde, Diekstra, & Wolters, 1995; Parker, 1981; Smith & Bloom, 1985; Williams, 1986). Analysis of the reasons given by suicidal individuals with BPD suggested that, overall, the intent of suicide attempts is to regulate emotions (M. Z. Brown, Comtois, & Linehan, 2002). Two psychophysiology studies support the claim that suicide is motivated by the expectation of emotion relief (Doron et al., 1998; Welch, 2003).

Evidence for emotion dysregulation comes from the vast literature showing that depression increases the risk of suicide ideation, attempted suicide, and completed suicide (e.g., Lewinsohn, Rohde, & Seeley, 1994). Depression comprises several primary emotions, such as sadness, shame, anxiety, irritability, and anger, all of which may drive suicidal behavior. This research has been reviewed elsewhere (M. Z. Brown, 2002). There is evidence that depressed mood and anxiety temporarily improve after a suicide attempt (Jones, Congiu, Stevenson, Strauss, & Frei, 1979; van Praag, 1985). Some individuals report feeling more calm and less depressed after their decision to commit suicide and before their attempt (e.g., Kienhorst et al., 1995; Shneidman, 1973, pp. 34–35).

Suicidal individuals often meet criteria for both anxiety disorders and clinical depression, both of which predict suicide attempts (e.g., Kessler, Borges, & Walters, 1999). Severe anxiety, agitation, and panic are common in the days and months before suicide (Busch, Clark, Fawcett, & Kravitz, 1993; Fawcett, Scheftner, Fogg, & Clark, 1990; Noyes, 1991; Warshaw, Dolan, & Keller, 2000). Individuals with comorbid anxiety and depressive disorders report more suicide ideation and behavior than those with depression or anxiety alone (Bakish, 1999; Noyes, 1991). However, a 20-year prospective study of 6,891 outpatients found that depression, but not anxiety, predicted eventual suicide (G. K. Brown, Beck, Steer, & Grisham, 2000).

Although anger predicts eventual suicide (Farmer & Creed, 1986; Romanov et al., 1994), anger toward others is not likely a primary cause of suicide in many cases. Anger may simply be a correlate of suicide, as suggested by Linehan's (1981) notion that suicidal individuals pass through stages; the ambivalent suicide attempter (early stage) often is angry and depressed, whereas a person is more likely to be apathetic and depressed soon before committing suicide. It may be the case that anger at oneself, but not toward others, leads to suicide (e.g., Farmer & Creed, 1986), or it may be that the role of anger in suicide varies, possibly distracting attention away from suicidal thoughts and feelings in some individuals. Two studies have found that chronically suicidal BPD individuals with *less* anger engage in *more* suicidal and self-injurious behaviors (M. Z. Brown, 2002; Heard & Linehan, 1991).

There is considerable evidence of biological anomalies that correspond to emotion dysregulation and suicidal behavior; this topic is beyond the scope of this chapter and is discussed elsewhere (Beauchaine, 2001; Gross, 1999; Williams, 1997).

Hopeless Thinking

The process of escaping emotional suffering with suicide involves hopeless thinking. According to hopelessness theory (Abramson, Metalsky, & Alloy, 1989), depression leads to suicidality because of extreme hopeless thinking. When individuals expect that intolerable emotions (and the situations that elicit them) will not ameliorate, they become depressed and view suicide as the only way to prevent further suffering. Measures of hopelessness have been found to predict strongly suicidal behavior (e.g., G. K. Brown et al., 2000), and hopelessness may account for the correlation between depression and suicidal behavior (e.g., Cole, 1988). It is important to know, however, which aspects of hopelessness are linked with suicidal behavior. Studies have found that suicide attempters do not excessively anticipate negative events in the future; rather, they anticipate few positive events and think of few reasons for living (MacLeod, Rose, & Williams, 1993; MacLeod & Tarbuck, 1994). Believing there are fewer reasons for living is associated with increased hopelessness and suicidality, and reasons for living may predict suicidality more strongly than global negative expectancies (Dean, Range, & Goggin, 1996; Strosahl, Chiles, & Linehan, 1992). In addition, the hopeless thinking of suicidal individuals may be based on their expected inability to tolerate future negative events rather than on expecting a high likelihood of negative events. One study found that emotional suffering predicted suicidal intent, planning, and action more strongly than hopelessness (Holden & Kroner, 2003). This hopeless and passive–withdrawn behavior may result from learned helplessness when emotional suffering persists despite one's best efforts (Abramson, Seligman, & Teasdale, 1978). In contrast, individuals strongly believe that suicide will effectively solve their problems in life.

Hopeless and all-or-nothing thinking is likely related to ineffective problem solving. Accumulating life stressors (including failure to obtain positive events) that fail to get solved increase hopeless thinking; hopeless thinking, in turn, can lead the individual to give up attempting to solve problems as they become increasingly overwhelmed.

Self-Invalidation and Shame

Linehan's biosocial theory states that emotion dysregulation and self-invalidation are interrelated problems that together lead to suicidal behavior. Self-invalidation involves experiences such as negative self-judgments, shame, self-contempt, self-directed anger, and low self-esteem. Suicidal individuals invalidate themselves when they blame and judge themselves harshly for their lack of control of behavior and emotions, and when they treat their normal responses as invalid. Self-invalidation also involves denying one's emotional vulnerability, and in doing so, individuals set unrealistically high or perfectionistic expectations and minimize the difficulty of solving problems. The inevitable failure that follows leads to more self-hatred and shame.

Suicidal individuals inhibit primary emotions that they experience as aversive and treat as invalid. In a similar way, shame may provide a motivation for suicide by invoking an urge to hide or escape from aversive self-awareness (cf. Baumeister, 1990). Suicide may be sought as the most complete and permanent way to hide from the shameful scrutiny of self and others, especially when individuals feel hopeless about changing their shameful qualities. Suicidal behavior and self-injury can also function as self-punishment—a form of self-invalidation. The person seeks to harm the self as one might desire to harm any hated person. Viewed as self-punishment, suicidal behavior can be understood as functioning to verify the strong belief that one is bad and deserves punishment. At a minimum, suicide becomes an acceptable option when believing one doesn't deserve to live.

Self-punishment may be understood in terms of self-verification theory (Swann, 1990). This theory states that individuals feel an aversive state of tension (or "disintegration anxiety") when fundamental beliefs about themselves or the world lack sufficient confirmation because humans have a basic need to make sense of the world. Similarly, cognitive dissonance theory postulates that inconsistencies between important cognitions (e.g., "I deserve to be punished" and "I have not been punished") create aversive affect, or *dissonance* (Festinger, 1957). Individuals take various habitual actions to restore their sense of predictability, familiarity, and control. Anxiety is expected to diminish when these basic beliefs get confirmed (e.g., after "deserved" punishment). Thus, individuals act consistent with their basic beliefs about themselves, or their self-concept (Aronson & Mettee, 1968). This theory also explains why people with negative self-concept seek and solicit negative feedback from others—to confirm their perceived negative qualities (Joiner, 1995).

Several converging lines of evidence show an association of negative self-conscious emotions to suicidal behavior. One study found that proneness to shame predicted suicide ideation independently from guilt-proneness (Hastings, Northman, & Tangney, 2000). Another study found that higher shame is associated with higher current and past suicide ideation when statistically controlling for age, gender, and current depression severity but that guilt shows almost no correlation with current suicide ideation (Lester, 1998). Strong negative self-perceptions have been linked to a history of suicidal behavior and suicide ideation (e.g., Crook, Raskin, & Davis, 1975). Suicide intent and lethality of suicidal behaviors have been found to correlate with self-criticism more strongly than depression (Fazaa & Page, 2003). Suicide attempters frequently feel like they are rejected, worthless, and failures (Bancroft et al., 1976; Bulik, Carpenter, Kupfer, & Frank, 1990; Hassan, 1995; Hawton, Cole, O'Grady, & Osborn, 1982). Perfectionism predicts suicidality above and beyond depression and hopelessness (Baumeister, 1990; Dean et al., 1996).

Among individuals with BPD who attempt suicide and engage in nonsuicidal self-injury, self-punishment was a common reason reported for doing both types of behaviors (51% vs. 59%, respectively); self-punishment was reported less often by those who only attempted suicide and more often by those who only engaged in nonsuicidal self-injury (M. Z. Brown et al., 2002). Suicidal individuals report high hostility toward themselves and others (Brittlebank et al., 1990; Ross & Heath, 2003; Vinoda, 1966), but most attribute their suicidal and self-injurious behavior to anger at self rather than anger at others (Bennum & Phil, 1983; Roy, 1978). Self-punishment may more often explain the suicidal behavior of chronically suicidal individuals (or those who meet criteria for BPD) than it explains the suicidal behavior of other individuals.

Several prospective studies suggest a link of negative self-concept to suicidal ideation (Kaplan & Pokorny, 1976) and suicide attempts (Lewinsohn et al., 1994). Negative self-concept predicted, independently of depression, both suicide attempts (Lewinsohn et al., 1994) and suicide (Beck & Stewart, 1989, cited in Weishaar & Beck, 1992). One prospective study of a BPD sample found that shame (self-report and nonverbal behaviors), more than other emotions, predicted subsequent suicide ideation and overt suicidal and nonsuicidal self-injury (M. Z. Brown, 2002). Similarly, hostility toward oneself is positively associated with suicide ideation (Goldney, Winefield, Saebel, Winefield, & Tiggemann, 1997) and the suicide intent of overdose (Farmer & Creed, 1986).

Problem Avoidance and Impaired Emotional Processing

Anger, contempt, and shame interfere with various ways in which suicidality might be resolved. High emotional dysregulation interferes with problem solving through cognitive dysregulation and problem avoidance. Shame, in particular, motivates concealing problems from therapists. Anger can interfere with the collaboration necessary for effective treatment. Anger, contempt, and shame may also interfere with emotional processing of fear and sadness and when individuals avoid fear and sadness cues. The biosocial theory proposes inhibition of grieving as a fundamental process contributing to the maintenance of suicidal behaviors in BPD. One study suggests that anger and contempt interfere with recovery from grieving (Bonanno & Keltner, 1997). Similarly, contempt can interfere with improvement in major depression (Ekman, Matsumoto, & Friesen, 1997). High levels of anger can also interfere with the treatment of PTSD by interfering with the processing of fear (Foa, Riggs, Massie, & Yarczower, 1995). In previous maladaptive environments, individuals have learned to cut off or invalidate their own primary emotional responses (often with other emotions modeled in the environment) as a means to regulate these emotions that they experience as intolerable. These individuals, however, continue to reexperience precipitating events that elicit similar emotional responses because they have not learned to process the emotional material effectively.

THE DISTAL CAUSES OF SUICIDAL BEHAVIORS: BIOLOGICAL–ENVIRONMENTAL TRANSACTIONS

Linehan (1993) explained the emergence of extreme emotionality, self-invalidation, and suicidal behavior according to learning principles, biological predispositions, and reciprocal influences between individuals and their environments over time. Initial biological vulnerabilities, caused by genetics, intrauterine development, or brain trauma, can make individuals prone to emotional reactions that are easily elicited, highly intense, and long-lasting. This high emotionality increases vulnerability to stressful life events, which can increase the risk of suicide by increasing emotionality further. Biologically based behavioral predispositions (e.g., temperament) can also lead to negative emotionality and suicidality through more indirect paths. These negative behavioral patterns can evoke negative reactions from others that in turn worsen the individual's problems regulating their emotions and behaviors; or they can cause the individual to enter dysfunctional situations (Scarr & McCartney, 1983). Within social learning theory, this is the principle of "reciprocal determinism": The environment and the individual adapt to and influence each other in a transactional process. Similarly, individuals may be adversely affected when their temperament is a "poor fit" with their environment (Chess & Thomas, 1986).

Some genetic influences can be powerful enough to overwhelm a benign environment, and some powerful environmental events can create dysfunction in most individuals despite large, preexisting individual personality differences. Generally, individuals who are more severely and chronically suicidal grew up in environments that were more severely and pervasively traumatic or invalidating. There is evidence that traumatic events and extreme environmental conditions can modify neural structures such as the limbic system, thus increasing emotional vulnerability (Dennenberg, 1981; Greenough, Black, & Wallace, 1987). When the limbic system gets overwhelmed through chronic and intense activation, individuals become sensitized to react intensely to emotional stimuli (i.e., "kindling"). This increased emotional vulnerability can increase the probability of future trauma and also further strain interpersonal relationships, in a perpetual cycle.

The Invalidating Environment

Linehan has explained suicidal behaviors according to principles of social learning theory. Self-invalidation develops when individuals learn to disregard, criticize, and punish themselves (and their emotions) from observing others who have invalidated them in these ways (Bandura & Kupers, 1964; Herbert, Gelfand, & Hartmann, 1969). Chronically suicidal individuals typically report chronic and pervasive invalidation from others during childhood, often involving communications that the individual's emotions and behaviors are invalid and that the individual is invalid as a person (i.e., rejection). The accuracy of an individual's communication of private experiences is rejected and many behaviors are attributed to negative characteristics such as manipulative intent, lack of motivation, negative attitude, or paranoia. Many normal behaviors or emotional responses are treated as trivial or pathological. Abuse is often the most damaging form of invalidation, especially when individuals are blamed for the abuse they receive (Wagner, 1997).

Invalidating families often expect behaviors beyond the child's capabilities, without helping the child learn new behaviors, and excessively punish negative behaviors. Excessive punishment creates an aversive environment for the child, which increases negative emotional behaviors and family conflict in a vicious cycle. Abusive environments also create self-hatred. Experiments demonstrate that innocent victims are often devalued and rejected, perhaps because we learn that people generally get what they deserve and that evil is punished (Lerner & Miller, 1978). Many studies find that suicide attempters report high rates of sexual, physical, and emotional abuse during childhood and adulthood (e.g., Twomey et al., 2000; Wagner, 1997), but data on other forms of invalidation are lacking.

Social Reinforcement of Dysfunctional Behaviors

Self-invalidation, self-punishment, suicidal behaviors, and self-injury are a class of behaviors that get reinforced by the reactions of other people (Bandura, 1977, p. 150). Suicide attempts (and communication) appear to be followed by large changes in the environment (often in ways desired by the suicidal person), which can reinforce suicidal behavior and create positive expectancies. Others may help the suicidal person or stop making demands (or stop other aversive behaviors). Abusive family members are less likely to deprecate or punish individuals (or are likely to stop such behaviors) when those individuals preemptively deprecate or punish themselves (e.g., "Since I'm going to hurt anyway, let me take control of it and get it over with"). When punishment from others seems inevitable, self-punishment may be the lesser of two evils.

Empirical investigations have shown that people generally reduce aversive behavior or increase affiliative behavior (e.g., reassurance) toward people who act ashamed or deprecate themselves (at least in the short-term; Keltner & Harker, 1998; Powers & Zuroff, 1988). In the long term, intense self-deprecation becomes aversive to others and could reinforce others' negative views about the person, justifying further abuse or rejection (Strack & Coyne, 1983). Individuals further self-deprecate or self-punish to stop the ensuing abuse or rejection, thus creating a vicious cycle. Such extreme reactions may be especially likely to develop when individuals have few other effective ways to influence their harsh or unresponsive environments. These behaviors may become exceptionally strong when others intermittently respond positively (or less negatively). Almost half of BPD suicide attempters report that they intend to influence others by attempting suicide and injuring themselves (M. Z. Brown et al., 2002).

Similarly, invalidating environments reinforce the escalation of other emotional behaviors. Coercive, hostile, and aggressive behaviors often function to end punishment or demands from others, usually by creating such aversive consequences for them persisting (Snyder, Edwards, McGraw, Kilgore, & Holton, 1994). At the same time, caregivers are not responsive to moderate expressive behaviors, which reinforces the extreme emotional behaviors.

According to social learning theory, self-punishment and self-destructive behaviors are maintained by their acquired capacity to alleviate thought-produced distress and to lessen external punishment (Bandura, 1977, p. 151). When people fail to meet their standards, they tend to engage in distressing self-critical thinking that often persists until reprimanded or punished. The punished person feels better because punishment from others tends to restore their favor. During the course of socialization, the sequence of transgression–distress–punishment–relief is repeatedly experienced and strengthened. Self-punishment and restitution have a similar function to restore relationships, reduce further threat, and relieve distress. Studies have shown how self-punitive behavior can develop by its self-protective and stress-reducing value (Stone & Hokanson, 1969). When adults could avoid painful shocks by giving themselves less intense shocks, they increased self-punitive responses and became less emotionally distressed. Through a process of escape conditioning, self-punishment that has been successful in averting anticipated threats can persist long after the threats have ceased to exist. Studies with animals document the persistence of anticipatory self-punishment (cited in Bandura, 1977, p. 151).

APPLICATION OF LINEHAN'S SUICIDE THEORY: DIALECTICAL BEHAVIOR THERAPY

DBT is a comprehensive, multimodal treatment that balances change strategies with acceptance strategies (Linehan, 1993). This balance is achieved by integrating cognitive–behavioral therapy (CBT) strategies with validation and mindfulness approaches within a dialectical framework. Linehan developed DBT after finding that standard CBT often was not effective with the chronically suicidal women she treated. Therefore, Linehan added acceptance strategies (validation and mindfulness) to the treatment along with dialectical strategies to help integrate these apparently opposing core strategies. DBT later evolved into a treatment for suicidal behavior (and intentional self-injury) in BPD and has accumulated substantial evidence for its efficacy (Linehan et al., 2005)

As its name suggests, dialectical philosophy is central to DBT. Within a dialectical framework reality is seen as continuous, dynamic, and holistic. Reality, from this perspective, is simultaneously both whole and consisting of bipolar opposites. Dialectical truth emerges by the process of combining (or synthesizing) elements from opposing positions (the *thesis* and *antithesis*). The primary dialectic in DBT is that of acceptance and change. A therapist may validate patients' perceptions that they are working as hard as they can and yet stress that at the same time they must work even harder to move past their suffering. The acceptance–change balance is modeled both in the treatment strategies of DBT as well as the behavioral skills taught in DBT, with change-based skills such as emotion regulation and interpersonal effectiveness being balanced by more acceptance-based skills such as mindfulness and distress tolerance. From a dialectical perspective, learning to accept is a change in itself, and working to change includes an acceptance of current capabilities.

The therapeutic relationship itself frequently involves the therapist and the patient on opposite poles of a dialectic, with the goal being to synthesize the opposing views. For example, a therapist's position may be that the patient's suicidal behavior is the problem, whereas the patient's position may be that this behavior is the solution. A potential synthesis of these positions may be that suicidal behavior is an effective short-term solution to a life of constant suffering. They can then work on learning more adaptive coping methods to promote a life worth living. Dialectics also involves increasing flexible thinking in place of extreme all-or-nothing thinking and behavior.

Structure and Stages of Treatment

DBT is a multimodal treatment consisting of individual behavior therapy, skills training, as-needed phone consultation, and a therapist consultation team. Individual therapy focuses primarily on managing crises, strengthening and generalization of skills, increasing motivation to act skillfully while decreasing the motivation for dysfunctional behaviors, and overall treatment coordination and planning. Skills training focuses primarily on the acquisition of DBT skills; phone consultation primarily targets short-term crisis management, generalization of skills, and repair of egregious breaks in the therapeutic relationship between sessions; the case consultation team functions to maintain therapist motivation and effectiveness. DBT is a team-based approach that emphasizes assisting and supporting therapists in treating this population.

DBT delineates treatment stages that correspond to stages of disorder, each one associated with its own targets and goals. Individuals in Stage I have multiple pervasive and serious problems and out-of-control behaviors. The goals of treatment in Stage I are primarily to help the patient achieve stability and behavioral control, especially stop suicidal and self-injurious behaviors; to reduce severe obstacles to a reasonable quality of life (e.g., homelessness and disabling Axis I disorders), and to acquire the necessary capabilities to achieve these goals.

Early in Stage I, it is important to assess for history of suicidal behavior and nonsuicidal self-injury, current suicide ideation and behavior, and the risk factors for suicidality (mentioned earlier). Environmental risk factors to assess are recent stressful events (especially interpersonal stressors), history of abuse and trauma, current social support, suicide models, and reinforcement for suicidal behavior. Cognitive risk factors to assess include suicide ideation, hopelessness, knowledge of how to solve problems effectively and influence others, rigid all-or-nothing thinking, perceived self-efficacy, and negative self-concept. Overt behavioral risk factors include social isolation, passivity, and substance use. Demographic suicide risk factors include age, sex, and race.

Individuals enter Stage II when they have stopped major dysfunctional behaviors, and the main goals of treatment are to reduce the effects of early trauma and to increase patients' capabilities to experience emotions effectively. In Stage III, treatment focuses on the resolution of residual problematic behaviors that interfere with achieving other personal goals. Self-respect and self-trust become the central focus.

Treatment Strategies

DBT treatment strategies fall into six broad categories: (a) problem solving, (b) validation, (c) dialectical strategies, (d) general change procedures, (e) communication strategies, and (f) case management strategies. In addition, DBT includes a number of specific behavioral treatment protocols covering suicidal behavior, crisis management, therapy-interfering behavior, relationship problem solving, and ancillary treatment issues.

Core Strategies: Validation and Problem Solving

Core strategies consist of the balanced use of validation and problem-solving strategies. Validation strategies require the therapist to recognize and communicate how the patient's responses make sense. Validation in DBT involves communicating explicitly (i.e., verbally) that patients' current responses make sense as well as acting as if the person makes sense (i.e., implicit validation). Validation in DBT focuses considerably on communicating how patients' responses make sense or are normal in terms of the current context, rather than in terms of their psychiatric disorder or learning history. Validation is thought to improve collaboration with problem solving, improve attendance, and reduce therapy-interfering behaviors.

Problem solving begins with a detailed behavioral analysis of specific instances of suicidal urges or actions to identify the "links" in the chain of events that lead to suicidality for particular patients in specific situations. These links may include environmental events (and contextual factors), thinking, emotions, action tendencies, and overt behaviors, as well as the function, or consequences, of the suicidal behavior. DBT therapists use Linehan's theory of suicidal behavior as hypotheses to guide the behavioral analyses. Specifically, they assess for emotion dysregulation, self-invalidation and shame, inhibited grieving (and other forms of emotion inhibition), crisis-generating behaviors, active passivity, and apparent competence. The goal of problem solving is the generation of effective solutions for crucial dysfunctional thoughts, emotions, and behaviors identified by the behavioral analyses, and the application of relevant change procedures (discussed subsequently). Because emotion dysregulation is a systemic response comprising closely linked subjective feelings, cognition, and expressive and action tendencies, working on dysfunctional emotions also often involves working on dysfunctional thinking. For example, a therapist working on dysfunctional shame would also likely work on self-invalidating thoughts (e.g., self-judgments and "shoulds") and hopeless thinking (e.g., never being accepted by others).

Communication Strategies

DBT therapists also balance acceptance and change through communication styles. The most common style is reciprocal, that is, being warm and responsive to the patient. Reciprocal communication is balanced by an irreverent communication style in which the therapist uses a matter-of-fact or confrontational manner, or humorous or off-the-wall comments, to get the patient's attention or get them "unstuck."

Dialectical Strategies

Dialectical strategies are woven into all therapy interactions. They include balancing acceptance and change throughout therapy and in every therapeutic exchange, primarily by balancing problem solving with validation and reciprocal communication with irreverence. Dialectical strategies also involve decreasing rigid thinking (i.e., nondialectical thinking) by highlighting the opposing sides to each issue while providing opportunities for reconciling the apparent contradictions. This is done with stories, metaphors, paradox, and ambiguity (when therapeutic) and by drawing attention to natural change.

Case Management

There are three case management strategies in DBT. First, DBT requires that therapists meet regularly with a consultation team because severely suicidal or out-of-control patients are rarely treated effectively by a single therapist. DBT also places emphasis on the therapist as a consultant to the patient. This strategy stems from the view that the therapist's role is primarily to teach the patient how to interact effectively with the environment, rather than to teach the environment how to interact effectively with the patient. However, the DBT therapist enters and directly intervenes in the patient's environment when necessary to protect the patient's life or to modify a situation beyond the patient's control, or when it is simply the humane thing to do.

Change Procedures

The purpose of change procedures in DBT is to modify the dysfunctional thoughts, emotions, and behaviors identified as problematic in the behavioral analyses. These strategies are adaptations of basic cognitive–behavioral techniques: contingency management, cognitive restructuring, exposure-based strategies, and skills training.

In Stage I of DBT, changing overt behaviors is the top target, and behavior change is expected to lead to cognitive and emotional change. In contrast to other models of treatment, it is not assumed that negative thoughts or behaviors must change for patients to stop suicidal behavior. DBT therapists target suicidal and self-injurious behaviors during the first session and work hard to elicit a commitment from the patient to stop engaging in these behaviors. For many patients, behavioral stability (which marks the end of Stage I treatment) is achieved by distress tolerance and self-management; their "quiet desperation" becomes a primary Stage II target.

The selection of change procedures is primarily determined by what is pragmatic for particular targeted links. If suicidal responses stem from a problem in the environment, the therapist may teach the patient problem-solving skills and coach him or her in resolving the situation in a nonsuicidal fashion. For other patients, formal or informal cognitive restructuring may be the most effective path for changing dysfunctional emotions and suicidal behaviors. Linehan has suggested that cognitive restructuring works primarily by teaching or motivating patients to initiate new overt behaviors from which they learn new (more functional) emotional and cognitive responses.

In DBT, cognitive restructuring often involves getting patients to generate opposite-to-emotion thoughts (to replace ineffective thoughts) without necessarily disputing dysfunctional thoughts head on. DBT therapists may also challenge cognitions directly (e.g., raise doubts that suicide will solve the patient's problems, maintaining that there is no evidence that things will be better for the patient after death). DBT therapists also decatastrophize fear and worry thoughts by modeling a "so what?" or accepting attitude, rather than working on verbally correcting estimates of the probabilities of feared events. In this way, cognitive restructuring in DBT is more similar to Ellis than to Beck because the aim is to "weave a web of logic" from which the patient cannot escape. DBT therapists also have patients vividly imagine their ultimate feared outcomes to rehearse how they would cope with such outcomes and desensitize to the images (cf. Borkovec, Alcaine, & Behar, 2004).

In DBT, cognitive modification of hopeless thinking involves inspiring hope through verbal cheerleading, generating and highlighting reasons for living, and believing wholeheartedly in patients' ultimate capabilities to succeed. Given that self-invalidation often maintains suicidal behavior, another commonly used cognitive intervention for suicidal behavior in DBT is teaching and reinforcing the patient's use of self-validation. The therapist teaches self-validation by communicating to the patient how her behaviors make sense in terms of her past, her biology, her current beliefs or feelings, or her current situations (how her behaviors are effective in some way or that they are normal responses to current events). The therapist then instructs the patient to counteract actively her negative judgments and unrealistic standards of acceptable behavior (i.e., perfectionistic "shoulds") by rehearsing self-validating statements (both in and out of sessions).

Another cognitive strategy used in DBT is contingency clarification. The therapist clarifies the effects of the patient's suicidal behavior on other people (including the therapist) and on reaching personal goals. By teaching the patient to notice the natural "if–then" relationships operating in the patient's life, the therapist hopes to increase the probability of adaptive behavior. The key idea is to motivate patients to block dysfunctional behaviors, including suicidal behaviors, and to instead engage in new, more adaptive behaviors. This "pros and cons" analysis can be applied in a crisis or to increase the odds the patient will adopt a non-suicidal approach to solving problems in future crises.

Methods for addressing cognition (and corresponding emotions and suicidal behaviors) more unique to DBT include mindfulness and opposite action. DBT therapists sometimes try to get their patients to relate to their thinking differently or focus attention away from dysfunctional thoughts, rather than change the content of thoughts. Mindfulness practice teaches patients to step back from and observe their thoughts (i.e., "thought defusion"), and acknowledge them as simply "thoughts passing through my mind" (i.e., "deliteralization") that do not need to be changed or acted on (cf. Hayes, Strosahl, & Wilson, 1999). Patients learn to discriminate facts and events from inferences and judgments. Therapists sometimes label hopeless or suicidal thoughts that arise in sessions as ineffective "avoidance thoughts" that are habit-responses to stress. In these situations, therapists highlight the thoughts and instruct the patient to refocus on the current therapy tasks and accompanying emotion rather than avoid a difficult discussion in therapy, which could reinforce the patient's hopeless–suicidal thinking. Mindfulness of negative judgments such as "I'm bad" can involve observing the thoughts or describing instead of judging (i.e., just sticking to the facts). Many patients who have chronic worry are emotion phobic and avoid experiencing the physical sensations associated with emotion (Borkovec et al., 2004). A helpful intervention for emotion-phobic patients is to have them focus away from negative thoughts and instead focus on the physical sensations of emotions that they avoid (this strategy provides non-reinforced exposure to emotions).

Opposite action can involve engaging in opposite thinking (as noted earlier) or acting as if the opposite thoughts are true. It involves assessing the action urges (i.e., what dysfunctional behaviors do they feel like doing when they experience the thought or emotion?) and acting opposite to them. Key assessment questions are the following: "What does the patient not do because of his or her dysfunctional thoughts and emotions?" and "What would the patient do if he or she didn't have these dysfunctional thoughts and emotions?" For example, patients working on shame who feel like using judgmental language and hiding can act as if they are not ashamed by not hiding (direct eye contact, assertive body language, clear matter-of-fact voice) while they describe (rather than judge) the things they feel ashamed of (i.e., those things that generate thoughts that they are "bad") and self-validate. The therapist's continued positive regard changes the patient's experience of being "bad" by disconfirming the patient's fears of rejection (Jacobson, 1989). It is important, however, to monitor and block subtle forms of avoidance during opposite action.

Patients can also practice doing things that they think they "don't deserve" to do. Patients working on perfectionism can practice intentionally doing things "half way" or "good enough" and accepting doing an imperfect job. Patients who are ashamed of feeling emotions such as anger or sadness can practice mindfully experiencing their sadness or anger rather than avoiding them. DBT therapists place a high value on "dragging out new behavior" in therapy sessions, including emotional experiencing, when dysfunctional thoughts and emotions arise.

Opposite action is similar to behavioral experiments used in cognitive therapy, except that in DBT the opposite behaviors are repeated (e.g., the person stays in the feared situation) until distress diminishes. Insight, which may occur after a brief or single opposite action, is not seen as sufficient in most cases. Opposite action typically involves exposure to emotion cues and blocking of avoidance. Thus, when a dysfunctional cognition is identified, one option is that the therapist can determine the cue that triggered the thought or emotion and expose the patient to the cue until his or her distress is reduced. Barlow (1988) theorized that exposure therapy is so effective because it reverses emotion action tendencies. Decades of research in social psychology on cognitive dissonance induction have shown that getting people to act in opposition to their attitudes (as long they believe they have freely chosen the behavior) is a powerful way to change beliefs and attitudes (e.g., Zimbardo & Leippe, 1991).

Opposite action (i.e., exposure therapy) is only used when the thoughts, emotions, and action urges are dysfunctional. For example, patients are not encouraged to act opposite to shame (i.e., engage in the behaviors they fear will lead to rejection from others) if they are likely to actually get rejected by others whom they care about. Opposite action is not encouraged if an ultimate feared catastrophe is actually likely to be true.

Linehan's treatment approach is based on the assumption that opposite action and exposure are some of the most powerful change strategies. They appear to be at least as effective as cognitive restructuring (CR) for treating depression, social phobia, generalized anxiety disorder, and panic and for changing negative cognitions (Borkovec, Newman, Pincus, & Lytle, 2002; Gortner, Gollan, Dobson, & Jacobson, 1998; Hope, Heimberg, & Bruch, 1995; Jacobson et al., 1996; Williams & Falbo, 1996). For some problems, opposite action and exposure may be more effective than CR (Dimidjian et al., 2004). For example, a review by Foa, Rothbaum, and Furr (2003) found that the exposure therapy for PTSD is often more effective than CR at treatment follow-up and that its effectiveness can be diminished when CR is added. Although DBT therapists frequently use cognitive restructuring, they tend to rely more on other change strategies such as problem solving, opposite action, and exposure.

CONCLUSION

Linehan's biosocial theory offers clinicians and researchers a model for understanding the onset and maintenance of suicidal behaviors. In turn, this model informs treatment. It is also useful for understanding characteristics of chronically suicidal individuals such as those meeting criteria for BPD. More data are clearly needed to test elements of the theory (e.g., emotion intolerance). Linehan has adapted the theory and the treatment to fit emerging empirical findings on suicidality, emotion dysregulation, and mechanisms of change. Promising research methodologies are being developed to facilitate this evolution.

REFERENCES

Abramson, L. Y., Metalsky, G. I., & Alloy, L. B. (1989). Hopelessness depression: A theory-based subtype of depression. *Psychological Review, 96*, 358–372.

Abramson, L. Y., Seligman, M. E. P., & Teasdale, J. D. (1978). Learned helplessness in humans: Critique and reformulation. *Journal of Abnormal Psychology, 87*, 49–74.

Aronson, E., & Mettee, D. R. (1968). Dishonest behavior as a function of differential levels of induced self-esteem. *Journal of Personality and Social Psychology, 9*, 121–127.

Bakish, D. (1999). The patient with comorbid depression and anxiety: The unmet need. *Journal of Clinical Psychiatry, 60*(Suppl. 6), 20–24.

Bancroft, J., Skrimshire, A., & Simkins, S. (1976). The reasons people give for taking overdoses. *British Journal of Psychiatry, 128*, 538–548.

Bandura, A. (1977). *Social learning theory.* Englewood Cliffs, NJ: Prentice Hall.

Bandura, A., & Kupers, C. J. (1964). The transmission of patterns of self-reinforcement through modeling. *Journal of Abnormal and Social Psychology, 69*, 1–9.

Bargh, J. A., & Chartrand, T. L. (1999). The unbearable automaticity of being. *American Psychologist, 54*, 462–479.

Barlow, D. H. (1988). *Anxiety and its disorders: The nature and treatment of anxiety and panic.* New York: Guilford Press.

Baum, W. M., & Heath, J. L. (1992). Behavioral explanations and intentional explanations in psychology. *American Psychologist, 47*, 1312–1317.

Baumeister, R. F. (1990). Suicide as escape from self. *Psychological Review, 97*, 90–113.

Beauchaine, T. (2001). Vagal tone, development, and Gray's motivational theory: Toward an integrated model of autonomic nervous system functioning in psychopathology. *Developmental Psychopathology, 13*, 183–214.

Beck, A. T., & Stewart, B. (1989). *The self-concept as a risk factor in people who kill themselves.* Unpublished manuscript.

Bennum, I., & Phil, M. (1983). Depression and hostility in self-mutilation. *Suicide and Life-Threatening Behavior, 13*, 71–84.

Bonanno, G. A., & Keltner, D. (1997). Facial expressions of emotion and the course of conjugal bereavement. *Journal of Abnormal Psychology, 106*, 126–137.

Borkovec, T. D., Alcaine, O., & Behar, E. (2004). Avoidance theory of worry and generalized anxiety disorder. In R. G. Heimberg, C. L. Turk, & D. S. Mennin (Eds.), *Generalized anxiety disorder: Advances in research and practice*. New York: Guilford Press.

Borkovec, T. D., Newman, M. G., Pincus, A. L., & Lytle, R. (2002). A component analysis of cognitive–behavioral therapy for generalized anxiety disorder and the role of interpersonal problems. *Journal of Consulting and Clinical Psychology, 70*, 288–298.

Brittlebank, A. D., Cole, A., Hassanyeh, F., Kenny, M., Simpson, D., & Scott, J. (1990). Hostility, hopelessness and deliberate self-harm: A prospective follow-up study. *Acta Psychiatrica Scandinavica, 81*, 280–283.

Brown, G. K., Beck, A. T., Steer, R. A., & Grisham, J. R. (2000). Risk factors for suicide in psychiatric outpatients: A 20-year prospective study. *Journal of Consulting and Clinical Psychology, 68*, 371–377.

Brown, M. Z. (2002). *The impact of negative emotions on the efficacy of treatment for chronic parasuicide in borderline personality disorder*. Doctoral dissertation, University of Washington, Seattle.

Brown, M. Z., Comtois, K. A., & Linehan, M. M. (2002). Reasons for suicide attempts and nonsuicidal self-injury in women with borderline personality disorder. *Journal of Abnormal Psychology, 111*, 198–202.

Bulik, C. M., Carpenter, L. L., Kupfer, D. J., & Frank, E. (1990). Features associated with suicide attempts in recurrent major depression. *Journal of Affective Disorders, 18*, 29–37.

Busch, K., Clark, D., Fawcett, J., & Kravitz, H. (1993). Clinical features of inpatient suicide. *Psychiatric Annals, 23*, 256–262.

Callahan, E., & Burnette, M. (1989). Intervention for pathological grieving. *The Behavior Therapist, 12*, 153–157.

Chess, S., & Thomas, A. (1986). *Temperament in clinical practice*. New York: Guilford Press.

Chiles, J. A., Strosahl, K., Cowden, L., Graham, R., & Linehan, M. M. (1986). The 24 hours before hospitalization: Factors related to suicide attempting. *Suicide and Life-Threatening Behavior, 16*, 335–342.

Clum, G. A., & Febbraro, G. A. (1994). Stress, social support, problem-solving appraisal/skills: Prediction of suicide severity within a college sample. *Journal of Psychopathology and Behavioral Assessment, 16*, 69–83.

Cole, D. A. (1988). Hopelessness, social desirability, depression, and parasuicide in two college student samples. *Journal of Consulting and Clinical Psychology, 42*, 861–865.

Crook, T., Raskin, A., & Davis, D. (1975). Factors associated with attempted suicide among hospitalized depressed patients. *Psychological Medicine, 5*, 381–388.

Dean, P. J., Range, L. M., & Goggin, W. C. (1996). The escape theory of suicide in college students: Testing a model that includes perfectionism. *Suicide and Life-Threatening Behavior, 26*, 181–186.

Dennenberg, V. H. (1981). Hemispheric laterality in animals and the effects of early experience. *Behavioral and Brain Sciences, 4,* 1–49.

Dimidjian, S., Hollon, S., Dobson, K., Schmaling, K., Kohlenberg, R., McGlinchey, J., et al. (2004, May). Behavioral activation, cognitive therapy, and antidepressant medication in the treatment of major depression: Methods and acute phase outcomes. Paper presented at the American Psychiatric Association, New York City, New York.

Doron, A., Stein, D., Levine, Y., Abramovitch, Y., Eilat, E., & Neuman, M. (1998). Physiological reactions to a suicide film: Suicide attempters, suicide ideators, and nonsuicidal patients. *Suicide and Life-Threatening Behavior, 28,* 309–314.

Eichenbaum, H. (2003). Memory systems. In M. Gallagher & R. J. Nelson (Eds.), *Handbook of psychology: Biological psychology* (Vol. 3, pp. 543–559). New York: Wiley.

Ekman, P., & Davidson, R. J. (1994). *The nature of emotion.* New York: Oxford University Press.

Ekman, P., Matsumoto, D., & Friesen, W. V. (1997). Facial expression in affective disorders. In P. Ekman & E. L. Rosenberg (Eds.), *What the face reveals: Basic and applied studies of spontaneous expression using the Facial Action Coding System* (pp. 331–341). New York: Oxford University Press.

Farberow, N. L., McKelligott, J., Cohen, S., & Darbonne, A. (1966). Suicide among patients with cardiorespiratory illnesses. *Journal of the American Medical Association, 195,* 422–428.

Farmer, R., & Creed, F. (1986). Hostility and deliberate self-poisoning. *British Journal of Medical Psychology, 59,* 311–316.

Favazza, A. R., & Conterio, K. (1989). Female habitual self-mutilators. *Acta Psychiatrica Scandinavica, 79,* 283–289.

Fawcett, J., Scheftner, W., Fogg, L., & Clark, D. (1990). Time-related predictors of suicide in major affective disorder. *American Journal of Psychiatry, 147,* 1189–1194.

Fazaa, F., & Page, S. (2003). Dependency and self-criticism as predictors of suicidal behavior. *Suicide and Life-Threatening Behavior, 33,* 172–185.

Festinger, L. (1957). *A theory of cognitive dissonance.* Stanford, CA: Stanford University Press.

Foa, E. B., Riggs, D. S., Massie, E. D., & Yarczower, M. (1995). The impact of fear activation and anger on the efficacy of exposure treatment for posttraumatic stress disorder. *Behavior Therapy, 26,* 487–499.

Foa, E. B., Rothbaum, B. O., & Furr, J. M. (2003). Augmenting exposure therapy with other CBT procedures. *Psychiatric Annals, 33,* 47–53.

Gauthier, J., & Marshall, W. (1977). Grief: A cognitive–behavioral analysis. *Cognitive Therapy and Research, 1,* 39–44.

Gilligan, S. G., & Bower, G. H. (1984). Cognitive consequences of emotional arousal. In C. E. Izard, J. Kagan, & R. B. Zajonc (Eds.), *Emotions, cognition, and behavior* (pp. 547–588). Cambridge, England: Cambridge University Press.

Goldney, R. D., Winefield, A., Saebel, J., Winefield, H., & Tiggemann, M. (1997). Anger, suicidal ideation, and attempted suicide. *Comprehensive Psychiatry, 38,* 264–268.

Gortner, E., Gollan, J., Dobson, K., & Jacobson, N. S. (1998). Cognitive–behavioral treatment for depression: Relapse prevention. *Journal of Consulting and Clinical Psychology, 66,* 377–384.

Greenough, W. T., Black, J. E., & Wallace, C. S. (1987). Experience and brain development. *Child Development, 58,* 539–559.

Gross, J. J. (1999). Emotion and emotion regulation. In L. Pervin & O. John (Eds.), *Handbook of personality: Theory and research* (pp. 525–552). New York: Guilford Press.

Hassan, R. (1995). *Suicide explained.* Victoria, Australia: Melbourne University Press.

Hastings, M. E., Northman, L. M., & Tangney, J. P. (2000). Shame, guilt, and suicide. In T. E. Joiner & M. D. Rudd. (Eds.), *Suicide science: Expanding the boundaries* (pp. 67–79). Boston: Kluwer Academic.

Hawton, K., Cole, D., O'Grady, J., & Osborn, M. (1982). Motivational aspects of deliberate self-poisoning in adolescents. *British Journal of Psychiatry, 141,* 286–291.

Hayes, S. C. (1992). Verbal relations, time and suicide. In S. C. Hayes & L. J. Hayes (Eds.), *Understanding verbal relations* (pp. 109–118). Reno, NV: Context Press.

Hayes, S. C., Strosahl, K. D., & Wilson, K. G. (1999). *Acceptance and commitment therapy: An experiential approach to behavior change.* New York: Guilford Press.

Heard, H. L., & Linehan, M. M. (1991, August). Predicting parasuicidal behavior in borderline clients. Poster presented at the meeting of the American Psychological Association, San Francisco.

Heikkinen, M., Aro, H., & Lonnqvist, J. (1993). Life events and social support in suicide. *Suicide and Life-Threatening Behavior, 23,* 343–358.

Herbert, E. W., Gelfand, D. M., & Hartmann, D. P. (1969). Imitation and self-esteem as determinants of self-critical behavior. *Child Development, 40,* 421–430.

Holden, R., & Kroner, D. (2003). Differentiating suicidal motivations and manifestations in a forensic sample. *Canadian Journal of Behavioural Science, 35,* 35–44.

Hope, D. A., Heimberg, R. G., & Bruch, M. A. (1995). Dismantling cognitive–behavioral group therapy for social phobia. *Behaviour Research & Therapy, 33,* 637–650.

Jacobson, N. S. (1989). The therapist–client relationship in cognitive behavior therapy: Implications for treating depression. *Journal of Cognitive Psychotherapy, 3,* 85–96.

Jacobson, N. S., Dobson, K., Truax, P., Addis, M., Koerner, K., Gollan, J., et al. (1996). A component analysis of cognitive–behavioral treatment for depression. *Journal of Consulting and Clinical Psychology, 64,* 295–304.

Jacobson, N. S., Martell, C. R., & Dimidjian, S. (2001). Behavioral activation treatment for depression: Returning to contextual roots. *Clinical Psychology: Science and Practice, 8,* 255–270.

Joiner, T. E. (1995). The price of soliciting and receiving negative feedback: Self-verification theory as a vulnerability to depression theory. *Journal of Abnormal Psychology, 104*, 364–372.

Jones, I. H., Congiu, L., Stevenson, J., Strauss, N., & Frei, D. Z. (1979). A biological approach to two forms of human self-injury. *Journal of Nervous and Mental Disease, 167*, 74–78.

Kaplan, H. B., & Pokorny, A. D. (1976). Self-derogation and suicide: I. Self-derogation as an antecedent of suicidal responses. *Social Science & Medicine, 10*, 113–118.

Kehrer, C., & Linehan, M. M. (1996). Interpersonal and emotional problem solving skills and parasuicide among women with borderline personality disorder. *Journal of Personality Disorders, 10*, 153–163.

Keltner, D., & Harker, L. (1998). The forms and functions of the nonverbal signal of shame. In P. Gilbert & B. Andrews (Eds.), *Shame: Interpersonal behavior, psychopathology, and culture* (pp. 78–98). New York: Oxford University Press.

Kessler, R., Borges, G., & Walters, E. (1999). Prevalence of and risk factors for lifetime suicide attempts in the national comorbidity survey. *Archives of General Psychiatry, 56*, 617–626.

Kienhorst, I. C. W. M., De Wilde, E. J., Diekstra, R. F. W., & Wolters, W. (1995). Adolescents' image of their suicide attempt. *American Academy of Child and Adolescent Psychiatry, 34*, 623–628.

Kreitman, N., Smith, P., & Tan, E. (1970). Attempted suicide as a language: An empirical study. *British Journal of Psychiatry, 116*, 465–473.

Lerner, M. J., & Miller, D. (1978). Just world research and the attribution process: Looking back and ahead. *Psychological Bulletin, 85*, 1030–1051.

Lester, D. (1998). The association of shame and guilt with suicidality. *Journal of Social Psychology, 138*, 535–536.

Lewinsohn, P. M., Rohde, P., & Seeley, J. R. (1994). Psychosocial risk factors for future adolescent suicide attempts. *Journal of Consulting and Clinical Psychology, 62*, 297–305.

Linehan, M. M. (1981). A social–behavioral analysis of suicide and parasuicide: Implications for clinical assessment and treatment. In H. G. Glazer & J. F. Clarkin (Eds.), *Depression: Behavioral and directive intervention strategies* (pp. 229–294). New York: Garland.

Linehan, M. M. (1986). Suicidal people: One population or two? *Annals of the New York Academy of Sciences, 487*, 16–33.

Linehan, M. M. (1993). *Cognitive–behavioral treatment of borderline personality disorder*. New York: Guilford Press.

Linehan, M. M., Camper, P., Chiles, J., Strosahl, K., & Shearin, E. (1987). Interpersonal problem solving and parasuicide. *Cognitive Therapy and Research, 11*, 1–12.

Linehan, M. M., Chiles, J., Egan, K., Devine, R., & Laffaw, J. (1986). Presenting problems of parasuicides versus suicide ideators and nonsuicidal psychiatric patients. *Journal of Consulting and Clinical Psychology, 54*, 880–881.

Linehan, M. M., Comtois, K. A., Murray, A. M., Brown, M. Z., Gallop, R. L., Heard, H. L., et al. (2005). *Two year randomized trial + follow-up of dialectical behavior therapy vs. treatment-by-experts for suicidal behaviors and borderline personality disorder*. Manuscript submitted for publication.

Linehan, M. M., & Shearin, E. (1988). Lethal stress: A social–behavioral model of suicidal behavior. In S. Fisher & J. Reason (Eds.), *Handbook of life stress, cognition, and health* (pp. 265–285). New York: Wiley.

MacLeod, A. K., Rose, G. S., & Williams, M. G. (1993). Components of hopelessness about the future in parasuicide. *Cognitive Therapy and Research, 17*, 441–455.

MacLeod, A. K., & Tarbuck, A. F. (1994). Explaining why negative events will happen to oneself: Parasuicides are pessimistic because they can't see any reason not to be. *British Journal of Clinical Psychology, 33*, 317–326.

Maris, R. (1981). *Pathways to suicide: A survey of self-destructive behaviors*. Baltimore: Johns Hopkins University Press.

Maris, R. (1992). How are suicides different? In R. W. Maris, A. L. Berman, J. T. Maltsberger, & R. I. Yufit (Eds.), *Assessment and prediction of suicide* (pp. 65–87). New York: Guilford Press.

Noyes, R. (1991). Suicide and panic disorder. *Journal of Affective Disorders, 22*, 1–11.

Parker, A. (1981). The meaning of attempted suicide to young parasuicides: A repertory grid study. *British Journal of Psychiatry, 139*, 306–312.

Pollock, L. R., & Williams, J. M. G. (1998). Problem solving and suicidal behavior. *Suicide and Life-Threatening Behavior, 28*, 375–387.

Potthoff, J. G., Holahan, C. J., & Joiner, T. E. (1995). Reassurance seeking, stress generation, and depressive symptoms: An integrative model. *Journal of Personality and Social Psychology, 68*, 664–670.

Powers, T. A., & Zuroff, D. C. (1988). Interpersonal consequences of overt self-criticism: A comparison with neutral and self-enhancing presentations of self. *Journal of Personality and Social Psychology, 54*, 1054–1062.

Prigerson, H. G., Bridge, J., Maciejewski, P. K., Beery, L. C., Rosenheck, R. A., Jacobs, S. C., et al. (1999). Influence of traumatic grief on suicidal ideation among young adults. *American Journal of Psychiatry, 156*, 1994–1995.

Romanov, K., Hatakka, M., Keskinen, E., Laaksonen, H., Kario, J., Rose, R. J., & Koskenvou, M. (1994). Self-reported hostility and suicidal acts, accidents, and accidental deaths: A prospective study of 21,443 adults aged 25 to 59. *Psychosomatic Medicine, 56*, 328–336.

Ross, S., & Heath, N. L. (2003). Two models of adolescent self-mutilation. *Suicide and Life-Threatening Behavior, 33*, 277–287.

Rothberg, J. M., & Jones, F. D. (1987). Suicide in the U.S. army: Epidemiological and periodic aspects. *Suicide and Life-Threatening Behavior, 17*, 119–132.

Roy, A. (1978). Self-mutilation. *British Journal of Medical Psychology, 51*, 201–203.

Scarr, S., & McCartney, K. (1983). How people make their own environments: A theory of genotype–environmental effects. *Child Development, 54*, 424–435.

Schotte, D. E., & Clum, G. A. (1987). Problem-solving skills in suicidal psychiatric patients. *Journal of Consulting and Clinical Psychology, 55,* 49–55.

Shneidman, E. S. (1973). *Voices of death.* London: Harper & Row.

Shneidman, E. S. (1992). A conspectus of the suicidal scenario. In R. W. Maris, A. L. Berman, J. T. Maltsberger, & R. I. Yufit (Eds.), *Assessment and prediction of suicide* (pp. 50–64). New York: Guilford Press.

Shneidman, E. S. (1993). *Suicide as psychache: A clinical approach to self-destructive behavior.* Northvale, NJ: Aronson.

Skinner, B. F. (1992). *Verbal behavior.* Acton, MA: Copley. (Original work published 1957)

Smith, G. W., & Bloom, I. (1985). A study in the personal meaning of suicide in the context of Baechler's typology. *Suicide and Life-Threatening Behavior, 15,* 3–13.

Snyder, J., Edwards, P., McGraw, K., Kilgore, K., & Holton, A. (1994). Escalation and reinforcement in mother–child conflict: Social processes associated with the development of physical aggression. *Development and Psychopathology, 6,* 305–321.

Staats, A. W. (1975). *Social behaviorism.* New York: Dorsey.

Stone, L. J., & Hokanson, J. E. (1969). Arousal reduction via self-punitive behavior. *Journal of Personality and Social Psychology, 12,* 72–79.

Strack, S., & Coyne, J. C. (1983). Social confirmation of dysphoria: Shared and private reactions to depression. *Journal of Personality and Social Psychology, 44,* 798–806.

Strosahl, K., Chiles, J. A., & Linehan, M. M. (1992). Prediction of suicide intent in hospitalized parasuicides: Reasons for living, hopelessness, and depression. *Comprehensive Psychiatry, 33,* 366–373.

Swann, W. B. (1990). To be known or to be adored: The interplay of self-enhancement and self-verification. In E. T. Higgins & R. M. Sorrentino (Eds.), *Handbook of motivation and cognition* (Vol. 2, pp. 408–448). New York: Guilford Press.

Twomey, H., Kaslow, N., & Croft, S. (2000). Childhood maltreatment, object relations, and suicidal behavior in women. *Psychoanalytic Psychology, 17,* 313–335.

van Praag, H. M. (1985). An empirical study on the cathartic effect of attempted suicide. *Psychiatry Research, 16,* 123–130.

Vinoda, K. (1966). Personality characteristics of attempted suicides. *British Journal of Psychiatry, 112,* 1143–1150.

Wagner, B. M. (1997). Family risk factors for child and adolescent suicidal behavior. *Psychological Bulletin, 121,* 246–298.

Warshaw, M. G., Dolan, R. T., & Keller, M. B. (2000). Suicidal behavior in patients with current or past panic disorder: Five years of prospective data from the Harvard/Brown anxiety research program. *American Journal of Psychiatry, 157,* 1876–1878.

Wegner, D. M. (1994). Ironic process of mental control. *Psychological Review, 101,* 34–52.

Weishaar, M. E., & Beck, A. T. (1992). Clinical and cognitive predictors of suicide. In R. W. Maris, A. L. Berman, J. T. Maltsberger, & R. I. Yufit (Eds.), *Assessment and prediction of suicide* (pp. 467–483). New York: Guilford Press.

Welch, S. S. (2003). *Patterns of emotion in response to parasuicide imagery in borderline personality disorder*. Unpublished doctoral dissertation, University of Washington, Seattle.

Welch, S. S., & Linehan, M. M. (2002). High-risk situations associated with parasuicide and drug use in borderline personality disorder. *Journal of Personality Disorders, 16,* 561–569.

Williams, J. M. G. (1986). Differences in reasons for taking overdoses in high and low hopelessness groups. *British Journal of Medical Psychology, 59,* 269–277.

Williams, J. M. G. (1997). *Cry of pain: Understanding suicide and self-harm*. London: Penguin Books.

Williams, S. L., & Falbo, J. (1996). Cognitive and performance-based treatments for panic attacks in people with varying degrees of agoraphobic disability. *Behaviour Research & Therapy, 34,* 253–264.

Wilson, K. G., Hayes, S. C., & Gifford, E. (1996). Cognition in behavior therapy: Agreements and differences. *Journal of Behavior Therapy and Experimental Psychiatry, 28,* 53–63.

Zimbardo, P. G., & Leippe, M. R. (1991). *The psychology of attitude change and social influence*. New York: McGraw-Hill.

6

SUICIDE AND THE INNER VOICE

LISA FIRESTONE

> George began "hearing" a voice inside, a male voice, not unlike his father's, saying emphatically, "Die, boy, die." He heard this voice as he increasingly felt tempted to jump in front of a train or truck or out of a window. He spent considerable time . . . working on his intense depressive feelings; his self-destructive impulses and behavior; his wish to die and rejoin his parents; his negative introjects, such as the voice. (Blatt, 2004, p. 19)

In this chapter, I first discuss separation theory, developed by Robert Firestone, with specific emphasis on how the theory explains cognitions and suicide. I describe how separation theory defines the self and antiself systems and explains the concept of the "voice" (R. W. Firestone, 1988, 1997a; R. W. Firestone, Firestone, & Catlett, 2002; R. W. Firestone, Firestone, & Catlett, 2003). I delineate the research, both clinical and empirical, that validated this theoretical perspective. My colleagues and I conducted this research while developing the *Firestone Assessment of Self-Destructive Thoughts* (FAST; R. W. Firestone & Firestone, 1996), an instrument to assess suicide risk (L. Firestone, 1991; R. W. Firestone & Firestone, 1998). I then discuss implications of this theoretical approach for clinical practice, including a treatment approach called voice therapy (R. W. Firestone, 1988, 1997a), to address this negative thought process. Finally, I provide a case example to illustrate these concepts and methods.

Voice therapy is similar in certain respects to cognitive therapy; however, there are a number of basic differences. The major differences among rational–emotive therapy, cognitive therapy, and voice therapy can be found in (a) the importance each system places on investigating the etiology of the client's disturbance, (b) the theory of personality on which the therapeutic methodology is based, (c) the techniques used to identify and correct dysfunctional thinking, and (d) the emphasis on emotion or affect. The therapist practicing voice therapy is concerned with the dynamic origins of the voice. Separation theory and voice therapy procedures are more deeply rooted in an integrated psychoanalytic–existential approach than in a cognitive–behavioral model. The theoretical focus is on understanding the psychodynamics of the client's functional disturbance in the present, and the methods are based on an underlying theory of personality that emphasizes a primary defensive process. R. W. Firestone (1988, 1997a) conceived of self-destructive or neurotic tendencies as the perpetuation of psychological defenses that originally had survival value but later predispose maladaptive responses and increase personal distress. The "voice" represents the end process of incorporating destructive attitudes into oneself; as such, it refers to an alien viewpoint that is an overlay on the personality functioning as a negative force in the direction of self-hatred and self-attacks.

Unlike cognitive therapy, voice therapy expressly discourages therapists from replacing self-critical thoughts with more realistic ones, focusing rather on the historic origins of the disturbance. Suicidal patients are helped to see that their self-destructive impulses stem from critical or hostile messages that were adopted from the parents and that the voice is in fact "alien" to their real self (Ellis, 2001, p. 137). The specialized techniques of voice therapy can be used as an adjunct to other approaches, including cognitive–behavioral therapy. The methods of voice therapy bring to the surface not only negative or dysfunctional cognitions but also the feelings associated with them. Identifying "automatic thoughts" in the presence of strong affect can provide the "hot emotional climate" necessary for changing core schemas.

THEORY

Separation theory (R. W. Firestone, 1997a) provides a framework for understanding the suicidal process. The theoretical approach, as it relates to suicide, focuses on internalized negative thought processes. There are three premises underlying this approach to suicide and self-destructive behavior (R. W. Firestone, 1997b). The first states that a division exists within each individual between the self system, which is life-affirming and goal-directed, and the antiself system, which is self-critical, self-hating, and, ultimately, suicidal. The second premise states that self-destructive thoughts exist on a continuum from mildly self-critical to suicidal. The third premise states that there is a corresponding continuum of self-destructive behaviors that are strongly influenced or controlled by these destructive thoughts, or "voices." The voice is defined as "an integrated system of negative thoughts and feelings, antithetical to the self and cynical toward others, that is at the core of maladaptive behavior" (R. W. Firestone, 1997b, p. 16). At its extreme, the voice encourages and triggers self-harm and suicidal behavior.

The Self and the Antiself Systems

Robert Firestone's concept of the "division of the mind" (Figure 6.1) is derived from the observation that people are divided between the self and the forces within them that oppose or attempt to destroy the self. Both the self system and the antiself system exist within the individual and develop independently; both are dynamic and continually evolving.

The self system is the innate personality of the individual, including the biological, temperamental, and genetic traits, along with the harmonious identification with early caretakers. Positive nurturing experiences with caretakers and other significant figures in the person's early life have a significant impact on the development of the self system. The positive traits and values of parents and other caretakers are easily assimilated into the personality through identification and imitation.

The antiself system can be conceptualized as the defensive element of the personality. The child develops defenses to deal with a multitude of interpersonal experiences that cause emotional pain and frustration, ranging from neglect, intrusiveness, and rejection to actual parental aggression. Even parents who have a great deal of love and concern for their offspring will cause them some degree of pain and frustration. Parents' ability to meet their children's needs adequately will be influenced by their own life experiences, the parenting they received, and the degree to which they have resolved these issues for themselves (Baumeister, Bratslavsky, Finkenauer, & Vohs, 2001; Fonagy et al., 1995; Main & Hesse, 1990; Main & Solomon, 1986; Sanders & Giolas, 1991; Siegel, 2001).

The Fantasy Bond

The fantasy bond (R. W. Firestone, 1985) is an imaginary connection with the primary caregiver that acts as the core defense against interpersonal pain and frustration, deprivation, rejection, and aggression. This defense is a process of parenting oneself internally in fantasy and externally by using objects and persons in the environment. This process of parenting oneself is made up of both the self-nourishing and the self-punishing components. Both of these take on a unique character, resulting from the incorporation and internalization of parental attitudes and responses in the process of growing up in a particular interpersonal environment (Firestone, 1997a). The self-nourishing component continues into adult life in the form of praising and coddling oneself; vanity; eating disorders; addiction to cigarettes, alcohol, and other drugs; compulsive masturbation; and an inward, self-feeding habitual style of sexual relating. The self-punishing component includes self-critical thoughts, guilt reactions, warnings, prohibitions, and attacks on self, which are all examples of the punitive aspect of parental introjects.

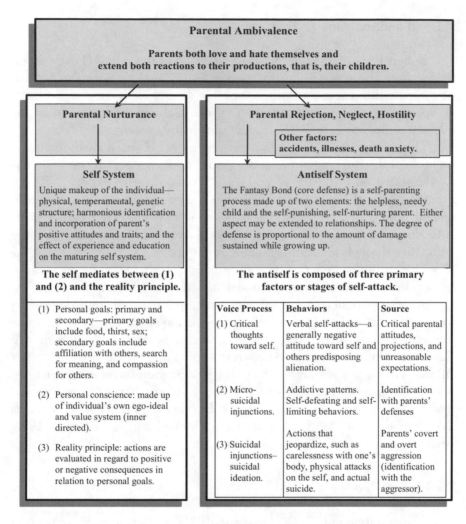

Figure 6.1. Division of the mind. Copyright © 2004 by The Glendon Association.

This conceptualization parallels that of Berne's (1961) transactional analysis (TA). The TA approach sees the person as being in either the child or parent state (similar to the self-parenting process described here) or the adult state (corresponding to the self system). In their relationships, many people act out either the childlike or parental aspects of the self-parenting process. Unlike Berne, Robert Firestone believes that people's tendencies to reenact these childish–parental elements in their current relationships are *not* manifestations of their attempts to achieve the gratification that was missing from the early environment. Rather, he believes that the person repeats the past and the self-parenting process to protect his or her defense system and psychological equilibrium.

Robert Firestone has observed that defenses that were originally formed to cope with interpersonal pain in the early environment become much more ingrained in the personality with the realization of death. Between ages 3 and 7, children begin to develop a concept of death and attempt to cope with the existential anxiety and dread through the defenses they developed early in life. Unfortunately, defenses cannot selectively cut off emotional pain without cutting off other feelings, leading to emotional deadness and serious deterioration in the quality of life. Being cut off from feeling for oneself and for one's life can contribute to suicidal behavior. The fantasy of suicide can provide a sense of triumph over death, that is, of taking control over one's destiny (Kaiser in Fierman, 1965; Maltsberger, 1999; Orbach, 2002).

The Voice

The voices or destructive thoughts act as a secondary line of defense protecting the core defense. As mentioned earlier, the "voice" can be defined as an integrated system of negative thoughts and attitudes, antithetical toward the self and suspicious and hostile toward others, that is at the core of maladaptive behavior. Voice attacks are sometimes experienced consciously, but more often than not are only partially conscious or even totally unconscious. These thoughts reach their most dangerous and life-threatening expression in suicidal behavior. Suicide can be conceptualized as a triumph of the antiself—the self-destructive aspect of the personality. The following is an excerpt from an interview with a woman who made a serious suicide attempt:

> Actually, I wanted to flee from these thoughts, not from the too heavy demands but from the many thoughts because they made me do what they wanted. I couldn't live with them any longer. I wanted to kind of kill them.

Our research (L. Firestone, 1991; R. W. Firestone, 1997a, 1997b) has described three levels or stages of self-destructiveness that people experience, each of which is associated with different behaviors and has different sources. The first level includes thoughts that lead to low self-esteem and inwardness. These thoughts run down the person, are cynical toward others, contribute to a self-denying posture, support tendencies to isolate oneself, and promote distrust of others and extreme self-hatred. These thoughts are important in relation to suicide because they contribute to several behaviors and lifestyles that have been shown by research to have a strong association with suicide risk. Self-denial and cynicism toward others lead to a lack of investment in life. It is easier for a person to kill oneself if he or she is less invested in life. Isolation is also a risk factor for suicide. The voices encouraging isolation are particularly dangerous, because our research has shown that isolation provides the environment in which these negative thoughts take more hold over the individual (R. W. Firestone et al., 2003). Isolation prohibits one from opening up to others and gaining a more rational evaluation of oneself and one's circumstances. An isolated lifestyle also deprives people of the compassion and caring they might receive from family or friends. Finally, this level includes extreme self-hating thoughts that cause a great deal of psychological distress and emotional pain, similar to Shneidman's (1993) concept of psychache and Baumeister and colleagues' (2001) descriptions of self-hate.

The second level of self-attacks includes thoughts that contribute to the cycle of addictions. These thoughts take two forms. First, they encourage, almost seduce, the person into engaging in the behavior. After the person has indulged, he or she berates himself or herself for having given in to the addiction. Often these self-attacks include vicious diatribes in which the person is beating him or herself up internally. However, these self-criticisms do not result in changing the addictive behavior. Instead, they lead to considerable pain and distress. In seeking relief, the person often engages again in the addictive behavior, thereby completing the cycle.

The source of these microsuicidal behaviors (R. W. Firestone & Seiden, 1987) that truncate or shorten a person's life seems to be in an identification with early caretakers. People imitate the defensive behavior of their parents, which includes the ways they soothed themselves. Considering the fact that there is a significant correlation between substance abuse and suicide (Lester, 2000), the processes of identification and imitation can be seen to play an important role in suicide risk.

The third level or stage of self-attack is the most serious and most relevant in relation to suicide. This level includes the following.

Thoughts of Being a Burden to Friends and Family

This feeling of being a burden is common in suicidal individuals and contributes to a sense of hopelessness, an affect that is an established risk factor for suicide (Beck, Steer, Beck, & Newman, 1993). The following excerpt is from an interview with a woman who made a serious suicide attempt.

> I then said to myself that I didn't want my children to end up with a disturbed mother and that they would have to come to see me in a psychiatric hospital, but that they should rather have no mother at all, then. I didn't want that my children or my relatives would have to suffer because I was nuts.

Feeling That Nothing Matters Anymore

Disconnecting from points of identity, not caring, or being unable to enjoy activities as one did in the past are important risk factors for suicide. It is easier to kill a self with whom one no longer feels identified. This type of disconnect, known as anhedonia, is also associated with suicide risk (Fawcett et al., 1990; Loas, Perot, Chignague, Trespalacios, & Delahousse, 2000; Oei et al., 1990; Orbach, 2003).

Thoughts Urging Self-Harm and Extreme Risk-Taking Behavior

These thoughts have an extremely agitated quality that is temporarily relieved when the person acts on them. This often develops into a cyclical pattern in which the agitated thoughts escalate, the person acts on injunctions to injure himself or herself, and subsequently experiences feelings of relief when the thoughts temporarily diminish or disappear.

Actual Thoughts About the Details of Suicide

Having a detailed plan increases risk, especially if the method planned is highly lethal and the time frame is short.

Thoughts Baiting the Person to Take His or Her Own Life

At this level, there is extreme thought constriction: "Do it or you are a coward." "It's the only thing you can do."

Richard Heckler's (1994) interviews with 50 people who made serious suicidal attempts led him to conceptualize a "suicidal trance," in which those thoughts take more and more control over a person's behavior. He described these baiting thoughts as those a person experiences just before taking his or her own life. For example,

> The reality for myself is almost constant pain and torment. The voices and visions, which are so commonly experienced, intrude and so disturb my everyday life. The voices are predominantly destructive, either rambling in alien tongues or screaming orders to carry out violent acts. They also persecute me by way of unwavering commentary and ridicule to deceive, derange, and force me into a world of crippling paranoia. Their commands are abrasive and all-encompassing and have resulted in periods of suicidal behavior and self-mutilation. I have run in front of speeding cars and severed arteries while feeling this compulsion to destroy my own life. (A patient with a history of suicide attempts, as reported by Jamison, 1999, pp. 119–120)

The thoughts at the third level drive behaviors that are highly self-destructive. The source of these thoughts seems to be identification with the aggressor, both the overt and covert aggression of the parent or primary caretakers. At times of stress when a parent "loses it" with the child, the child protects himself or herself by identifying with the powerful aggressor instead of with himself or herself as the helpless child. The child incorporates the parent's hostility toward him or her being expressed at that moment (Fairbairn, 1952; Ferenczi, 1933/1955). This incorporation represents an internalization of the parent at his or her worst, not as the parent was on average. The person may later unleash that anger against himself or herself. For example, an excerpt from the diary of a young woman who committed suicide included these thoughts:

I sit here with my untamed piano, untamed mind, untamed heart, with the music I only know, within myself. My mother is alive! Screaming viciously, laughing viciously, Jekyll and Hyde. Mommy Dearest. (L. Firestone, 2004)

A Developmental Perspective

Unfortunately, children have a stronger memory trace for negative events than for positive ones (Armony & LeDoux, 1997; Buchanan & Lovallo, 2001; Cahill, Roozendaal, & McGaugh, 1997). This propensity may stem from the fact that these experiences seem life-threatening, and therefore the intensity of focus is a survival mechanism. Also, many situations that may not seem significant to the adult may be very frightening to the child.

Under conditions of physical, emotional, or sexual abuse on the part of a primary caretaker or caretakers, the person to whom the child naturally turns for care also becomes the frightening or punishing agent, and the child typically fails to develop a secure attachment (Main & Solomon, 1986). Research has also found that parents who have unresolved trauma, even when they are not abusive, are prone to display frightened/frightening behavior with their children. This often results in the formation of a disorganized/ disoriented attachment with their infants (Hesse, Main, Abrams, & Rifkin, 2003). This is especially important during the first few years of life when the ability to regulate emotions is limited, and children are dependent on caretakers to provide this function for them. The lack of ability or skill to regulate affect is strongly associated with suicide risk (Linehan, 1993; Rudd, Joiner, & Rajab, 2001). Fear states aroused by these interactions can cause the brain to release certain toxins that actually change the structure of the brain and central nervous system, destroying cells and synapses that are responsible for the regulation of emotions and the development of compassion and empathy (Lyons-Ruth & Jacobvitz, 1999; Perry, 1997; Schore, 1994; Siegel, 1999; van der Kolk, McFarlane, & Weisaeth, 1996).

Dissociation

At these times of stress, children learn to depersonalize in an attempt to cope with the overwhelming emotions of fear, anxiety, and anger. The split within the personality develops when the child depersonalizes under the circumstances that threaten his or her "going on being" (Winnicott, 1958). Ironically, the child's desperate struggle to preserve intactness and wholeness produces fragmentation and disintegration.

This ability to dissociate is initially a survival mechanism but later leads to serious problems and can contribute to suicide risk (Briere & Runtz, 1987; Brown, Cohen, Johnson, & Smailes, 1999; Chu & Dill, 1990). Recent research with suicide attempters indicates that this type of dissociation may play a key role in the person acting on a suicidal impulse (Maltsberger, 2002; Orbach, 2002).

One has to be removed from oneself to kill oneself. Suicide is diametrically opposed to our animal instinct to survive at all costs. This excerpt from an interview with a woman who made a serious suicide attempt illustrates this point:

> *Patient:* And then I cut myself in the strategic places [wrist] and put the arm into water and watched the rings, which was pretty. I was more or less simply watching myself. In the previous months when I was feeling so low after the breakdown of the relationship with my boyfriend, I had often looked at myself from outside, like now while I was cutting myself.
>
> *Interviewer:* The way you tell it, it sounds as if you were separated from your feelings.
>
> *Patient:* Yes, completely.

Anna Freud (1966) contended that the mechanism of identification or introjection combines with imitation.

> To form one of the ego's most potent weapons in its dealings with external objects which arouse anxiety. (p. 110) . . . By impersonating the aggressor, assuming his attributes or imitating his aggression, the child transforms himself from the person threatened into the person who makes the threat. (p. 113)

It is painful for clients to realize how divided they are and to recognize that it may not be safe to trust their own thoughts. In essence, rather than facing the destructive enemy within, the client begins to believe that the antiself actually represents his or her own point of view.

Case Example

The following is an excerpt from an interview of a man in a Swiss psychiatric hospital 3 days after he made a serious suicide attempt:

> As time went past I became more and more isolated. In early summer I found that it got worse and worse. I began to forget things. In discussions with colleagues I had problems following the conversation. I have also a young girlfriend. And in addition I had become impotent. Of course, this led to additional worries. I started to think about my life. I simply had to say to myself that if now my colleagues and my girlfriend left me, then I had nothing left.
>
> Then I developed problems with sleep. Last Monday I had an appointment with a physician. And last Monday I simply said to myself "No." I was afraid that now everything would come out into the open. I was afraid that people would say that I had always lived on the expenses

of my friends and my girlfriend, and that in fact I had nothing of my own. I would then be called a scoundrel.

The patient stated that after having the thought "I should just go," he began his suicide attempt.

> So I fetched a knife and cut my blood vessels in the wrist. But I had to realize that this didn't work. So I got my axe out and chopped my hand off. I simply wanted to go. So I was lying there for several hours. I was slightly unconscious when the phone rang. I said to myself that I won't answer. After the fourth ring I still picked up the receiver.

In an earlier portion of this interview, the patient described aspects of the self system, that is, he revealed the fact that he loves skiing and hiking, activities he expected to be able to engage in more often when he retired. Instead, he found himself dominated by aspects of the antiself system, thoughts influencing him increasingly to isolate himself, and ruminations about his perceived deterioration in functioning. In this interview, the patient reported experiencing negative thoughts at the extreme end of the continuum: "I simply had to say to myself, 'if my colleagues and girlfriend leave me, I will have nothing, I would be called a scoundrel. I should just go.' "

Suicidal crises are fraught with ambivalence, an ambivalence that separation theory addresses directly: whether to live life as a fully vital human being who is feeling and experiencing life, or whether to deaden oneself, resort to addictive behaviors to cut off feeling, and, in essence, live a life that never reaches its full human potential. This ambivalence is clearly demonstrated in a later part of the patient's interview in which he describes ignoring the first three rings of the phone, but then, as he feels life returning, answering the phone—an act that saved his life.

RESEARCH

On the basis of Robert Firestone's theoretical approach, my colleagues and I felt it was logical that an assessment of individuals' self-destructive thoughts could be used to predict the likelihood of their engaging in self-destructive behavior. We also felt that an instrument of this type could aid a clinician in understanding his or her client, developing case conceptualization, and planning effective treatment. We developed the FAST (L. Firestone, 1991; R. W. Firestone & Firestone, 1996, 1998), a scale that is derived from 20 years of clinical experience and research into the self-attacking attitudes and negative parental introjects that drive self-destructive behavior. Items on the scale were drawn from clinical material obtained from Robert Firestone's 22-year longitudinal study of the "voice" (R. W. Firestone, 1986, 1997b). The items represented all 11 levels of the continuum of self-destructive thoughts (Exhibit 6.1).

The relationship between the voice process and self-destructive behaviors, including suicide, was empirically established by our research on the

EXHIBIT 6.1
Continuum of Negative Thought Patterns

Levels of increasing suicidal intention	Content of voice statements
Thoughts that lead to low self-esteem or inwardness (self-defeating thoughts):	
1. Self-depreciating thoughts of everyday life.	*You're incompetent, stupid. You're not very attractive. You're going to make a fool of yourself.*
2. Thoughts rationalizing self-denial; thoughts discouraging the person from engaging in pleasurable activities	*You're too young (old) and inexperienced to apply for this job. You're too shy to make any new friends. Why go on this trip? It'll be such a hassle. You'll save money by staying home.*
3. Cynical attitudes toward others, leading to alienation and distancing	*Why go out with her (him)? She's cold, unreliable; she'll reject you. She wouldn't go out with you anyway. You can't trust men (women).*
4. Thoughts influencing isolation; rationalizations for time alone but using time to become more negative toward oneself	*Just be by yourself. You're miserable company anyway; who'd want to be with you? Just stay in the background, out of view.*
5. Self-contempt; vicious self-abusive thoughts and accusations (accompanied by intense angry affect)	*You idiot! You bitch! You creep! You stupid shit! You don't deserve anything; you're worthless.*
Thoughts that support the cycle of addiction (addictions):	
6. Thoughts urging use of substances or food followed by self-criticisms (weakens inhibitions against self-destructive actions, while increasing guilt and self-recrimination following acting out)	*It's okay to do drugs, you'll be more relaxed. Go ahead and have a drink, you deserve it. (Later) You weak-willed jerk! You're nothing but a drugged-out, drunken freak.*
Thoughts that lead to suicide (self-annihilating thoughts):	
7. Thoughts contributing to a sense of hopelessness, urging withdrawal or removal of oneself completely from the lives of people closest	*See how bad you make your family (friends) feel. They'd be better off without you. It's the only decent thing to do—just stay away and stop bothering them.*
8. Thoughts influencing a person to give up priorities and favored activities (points of identity)	*What's the use? Your work doesn't matter any more. Why bother even trying? Nothing matters anyway.*
9. Injunctions to inflict self-harm at an action level; intense rage against self	*Why don't you just drive across the center divider? Just shove your hand under that power saw!*
10. Thoughts planning details of suicide (calm, rational, often obsessive, indicating complete loss of feeling for the self)	*You have to get hold of some pills, then go to a hotel, etc.*
11. Injunctions to carry out suicide plans; thoughts baiting the person to commit suicide (extreme thought constriction)	*You've thought about this long enough. Just get it over with.* *It's the only way out!*

Note. Any combination of the voice attacks listed above can lead to serious suicidal intent. Thoughts leading to isolation, ideation about removing oneself from people's lives, beliefs that one is a bad influence or has a destructive effect on others, voices urging one to give up special activities, vicious self-abusive thoughts accompanied by strong anger, voices urging self-injury, and a suicide attempt are all indications of high suicide potential or risk. Copyright © 1996 by The Glendon Association.

FAST. The original subject pool included 500 persons in outpatient psychotherapy. The criterion variable in the study, past suicide attempts, was established through both patient and therapist reports. A second study was undertaken with inpatient populations, drawn from the diagnostic categories found to have the highest risk of suicide: major depression, bipolar disorder, substance abuse, schizophrenia, personality disorders, and anxiety disorder. Participants were asked to endorse how frequently they experienced negative thoughts toward themselves (or "voices") on a 5-point Likert-type scale from 1 (*never*) to 5 (*almost always*). In addition, participants completed a battery of additional instruments covering diverse areas of self-destructiveness to provide construct validity for the 11 levels of the FAST.

Internal reliability consistency for the FAST was established using Cronbach's (1951) alpha. The internal consistency coefficients for the 11 levels of the FAST ranged from .76 to .91, with a median of .84. All exceeded acceptable measurement standards. The test–retest reliability for the FAST total score was .94.

The validity of the FAST was examined through content-related, construct-related, and criterion-related methods (L. Firestone, 1991; R. W. Firestone & Firestone, 1996). Content-related validity was established through three methods: (a) The statements were taken directly from self-destructive thoughts that people revealed, with the suicidal items coming from people with a past history of suicide attempts; (b) experts were used to identify the level the items best represented; and (c) the assumption that self-destructive thoughts exist on a continuum ranging from self-depreciation through suicidal injunctions was supported by a Guttman Scalogram Analysis (Gilpin & Hays, 1990). The hypothesized hierarchy of self-destructiveness was confirmed (Figure 6.2).

Construct validity of the 84 FAST items was examined using factor analysis. A three-factor solution was identified (R. W. Firestone & Firestone, 1996). Composite Factor 1 was labeled "Self-Defeating Composite" and consisted of Levels 1–5 on the continuum. Level 6 is Composite Factor 2 and was labeled the "Addictions Composite." Composite Factor 3 is made up of Levels 7–11 and was labeled the "Self-Annihilating Composite." These are the thoughts that represent the full spectrum of self-annihilation, from psychological suicide (Levels 7 and 8) to actual physical suicide (Levels 10 and 11).

A final composite, made up of 27 items, was empirically derived by summing those items that were found to have the most significant discriminatory power in distinguishing patients with current suicidal intent and was labeled the "Suicide Intent Composite." (This composite has been developed into a brief screener for suicide risk, the Firestone Assessment of Suicide Intent [FASI]; R. W. Firestone & Firestone, in press.)

Convergent and divergent validity methods supported the construct validity of the FAST. The highest correlations with the FAST were other measures of similar constructs, and there were highly negative correlations with tests of opposing constructs, such as positive self-regard. Criterion validity for the FAST was evaluated by comparing scores with the criterion variable (previous suicide attempts and current suicidal ideation). The FAST had higher correlations with this criterion variable than any of the preexisting suicide measures.

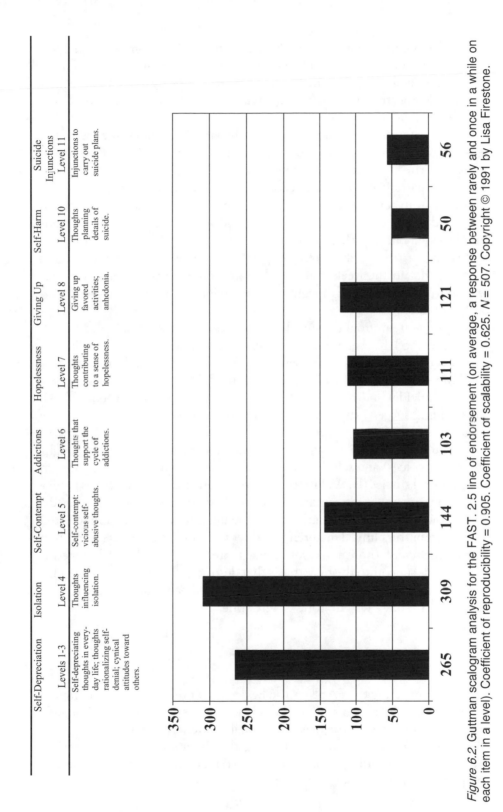

Figure 6.2. Guttman scalogram analysis for the FAST. 2.5 line of endorsement (on average, a response between rarely and once in a while on each item in a level). Coefficient of reproducibility = 0.905. Coefficient of scalability = 0.625. *N* = 507. Copyright © 1991 by Lisa Firestone.

Incremental validity was established using logistic regression analysis, confirming that the FAST adds significantly to our ability to discriminate those individuals who are at highest risk for suicide. Sensitivity and specificity were demonstrated, correctly classifying 95.8% of ideators and 89.2% of nonideators.

One interesting finding was how easily participants identified with the self-statements written in the second person, as though someone else were addressing the attack to them, rather than as "I" statements. On a number of occasions, participants reported recognizing their own styles of self-attack as they were filling out the test. Many participants had a physical reaction when they read statements with which they closely identified. Those reactions strengthened our hypothesis that items on the scale are related to internalized thought patterns that are only partly conscious. Moreover, therapists reported that in the weeks following the testing, clients brought up topics related to self-destructive thoughts and behavior that they had never previously discussed.

Sample items from the FAST can be seen in Exhibit 6.2.

The FAST has been translated into several languages, and ongoing research in other countries is in progress. Dr. Yasmin Farooqi in Pakistan translated the FAST into Urdu. She found that the FAST was able to distinguish between suicidal and nonsuicidal individuals in Pakistan (Farooqi, 2004). This finding suggests that self-destructive thought processes or voices may play a role in suicide across cultures.

The studies described suggest a connection between negative thought processes (voices) and self-destructive behavior and suicide. Participants in early clinical studies (R. W. Firestone, 1988) identified their voices as parental statements or as representative of overall attitudes they perceived as directed toward them in their early years. The items for the scale were selected directly from this clinical material. The fact that these statements were then able to distinguish those at risk for suicide more accurately than other instruments lends support to the hypothesis that destructive voices associated with self-destructive acts may well represent introjected parental attitudes (R. W. Firestone, 1986; R. W. Firestone & Firestone, 1998).

PRACTICE

Administering the FAST at the beginning of therapy allows therapists to assess where their clients fall on the continuum of self-destructive thoughts. It alerts the therapist to the negative thoughts clients are experiencing with the greatest degree of intensity, allowing the therapist to plan appropriate interventions. In addition, taking the FAST increases clients' awareness of their previously subconscious thoughts.

EXHIBIT 6.2
Sample Items From the FAST

1. You can't do anything right! You're disgusting!
2. You're a failure, a total failure!
3. Your future is hopeless; things will never get better.
4. You're a burden to your family. They'd be better off without you.
5. Look at the effort it takes to get through the day. Why go on?
6. The world is not a place that you can live in.
7. You better plan it, it's the only thing you can do. Kill yourself.
8. There's no place for you in this world. You don't belong to anyone! You don't belong anywhere! Just get yourself off the face of the earth!
9. There's a way out of this pain. Just end it.
10. Look, you're miserable every minute. There's no letup. Just end it.

Voice Therapy

Identifying the contents of the client's negative thought process is the first step in a three-step procedure in which the client and therapist collaborate in understanding the client's destructive ways of thinking. The process of verbalizing the voices can be approached in an intellectual manner, focusing on the cognitions, or in a more dramatic, cathartic method. In both methods, clients learn to expose their self-criticisms in the second person as "you" statements, as though they were another person verbalizing the thoughts about the client. This helps clients to begin to separate their own point of view from the hostile, alien point of view of the antiself. Prior to articulating voices, clients generally accept these negative thoughts as being true evaluations of themselves.

In the more abreactive approach, clients are encouraged to express the emotion behind the thoughts, to say the voices louder, or to say them in the tone they experienced them and to express the emotions behind them (which often are strong anger and sadness). The therapist might encourage the client to "say it louder," "really feel that," or "let go and blurt out anything that comes to mind." In early studies of the voice process, clients and participants frequently adopted this style of expression of their own volition. Putting their thoughts in the second person often led, in and of itself, to saying them with more intensity of feeling. Clients would start off with the thoughts they were aware of on the surface but arrived at much deeper material, core beliefs about self. Frequently they adopted the mannerisms or speech patterns of their parents, again supporting the contention that these thoughts are incorporated from early experiences within the family.

This emotional expression in many instances leads spontaneously to the second step in the voice therapy process, which involves developing insights into the sources of these negative thoughts. Statements such as "that's what my father used to say to me," or "that is the feeling I got from my mother," or "that was the atmosphere in our home," are often made by a participant or client after verbalizing the voice. The therapist can encourage this process by asking "Where do you think those thoughts came from?" "Where have you heard those before?" In voice therapy, the therapist refrains from interpreting to the client but instead helps elicit insight from the person. Insights are most powerful when they come from the client and when they are coupled with a full expression of feelings. When clients develop insight, they experience a sense of compassion for themselves and have a clearer sense of their true identities.

Another aspect of this step involves clients making connections between their voices and their current self-destructive behavior patterns. They explore what behaviors they are engaging in based on these ways of thinking. This process leads naturally to the third step.

The third step involves changing behaviors that are based on these self-destructive ways of thinking, thereby altering one's basic self-concept and core defenses. The corrective suggestions for behavioral change are arrived at through a collaboration between therapist and client and are designed to challenge clients' misconceptions about themselves. Collaborative interventions that effect changes in an individual's behavior are a necessary part of an effective therapeutic procedure. These suggestions are in line with the client's personal goals and ambitions. However, it is important to remember that acting on corrective suggestions always involves personal risk and feelings of increased vulnerability in clients, because they are breaking with psychological defenses that were originally necessary and that warded off painful emotions. It is important to prepare clients for the anxiety they are likely to experience when they implement suggestions that are counter to the dictates of the voice.

As a client acts against his or her voices, these destructive thoughts may become more intense, almost like a parent yelling at him or her to get back in line. If they can endure the anxiety and maintain the behavior change, however, the voice attacks become less intense and eventually fade into the background, almost like a parent who becomes tired of nagging. This does not imply that these voice attacks may not resurface, but, if they do, they will not have as much influence over the person's behavior.

Corrective suggestions may include the client engaging in positive goal-directed behaviors that his or her voice has been discouraging, such as asking someone out for a date or applying for a desired job. Other suggestions might include refraining from self-destructive behaviors that the voice is encouraging, such as substance abuse or risk-taking behavior. In either case, the goal is for the client to follow the suggestion, resist the voice attacks, go through the anxiety, and expand his or her boundaries and positive sense of self.

Application to Suicidal Clients

The most important first step in the therapy of an individual in suicidal crisis is to establish a strong therapeutic relationship, which includes trust.

The therapist must be able to communicate empathy and nonjudgment (Ellis, 2001). Establishing an effective therapeutic alliance may prove difficult and requires strong relational skills on the part of the therapist. Suicidal clients tend to evoke negative countertransference reactions in their therapists. They often make the therapist feel like getting rid of them, much as they want to get rid of themselves. Obviously, therapists must be aware of this reaction and try to see clients as they would be without the defended behaviors. A compassionate, caring stance toward suicidal clients is essential, because breakdowns in the treatment alliance can lead to disastrous outcomes. Research into clients' suicides during treatment indicates that the suicide often followed a break in the rapport (Maltsberger, Hendin, Haas, & Lipschitz, 2003).

It is important that therapists help clients identify their self-destructive thinking, especially as it applies to suicide. Often they have shared these thoughts with no one and were afraid they would be seen in a negative light if they did. Therapists can use their understanding of these thoughts to build rapport with clients. It is essential to help the client separate the thoughts or voices driving his or her hopelessness and desperation from a more realistic evaluation of himself or herself and his or her circumstances. This separation will lessen the probability that the client will act on these thoughts.

The therapist needs to support and strengthen aspects of the client's self system. With suicidal individuals in particular, the therapist needs to be finely attuned to any indication of activities or relationships that are meaningful to the client or offer a sense of relief or hope. The therapist can then encourage the client and support engagement in these activities or relationships. Corrective suggestions need to be focused on keeping the client alive. Therefore, the focus is toward reducing the level of self-destructive behavior in which the client is engaging.

Suggestions might include encouraging the client to spend time around caring others; supporting the pursuit of any activities that give the client energy or excitement; and encouraging the client to engage in acts of generosity, to spend time thinking of what he or she can do for others, thus helping him or her to develop a sense of meaning in his or her life. At the same time, there should be a focus on discouraging time spent alone, as well as substance use or other addictive behaviors. Helping clients recognize when they are attacking themselves is important in and of itself. It is also important to help them recognize their anger in situations rather than turning that anger against themselves. Therapists' statements, techniques, or suggestions that support the self system and the client's desire to live are potentially life saving.

Clinicians may be concerned that if a client recognizes hostile or suicidal thoughts toward the self, he or she will be more likely to act them out. Actually, the opposite seems to be true: becoming aware of partially conscious or even unconscious negative attitudes toward self and others allows greater mastery over one's behavior. Through the use of voice therapy techniques, these destructive introjects are brought to the surface and the person is able to see the various dimensions of the "enemy within." This allows the client to identify alien aspects of self and to understand their sources. Voice therapy empowers clients, helps them gain a degree of control over behaviors regulated by the antiself system, and increases their ability to resist acting out self-destructive tendencies. Depressed and suicidal clients in particular often become exhausted struggling against self-destructive thoughts. They may lack the means to develop an accurate view of themselves and their lives. Voice therapy can help them make the important distinction between their current negative view of self and an objective, compassionate point of view. Clients regain feeling for themselves and reconnect with themselves as a person, making suicide a less likely outcome.

Case Description and Analysis

"Fred" entered psychotherapy seeking marriage counseling for himself and his new wife, Mary. Although they had been married for almost a year, they had only recently begun living in the same city. They met when he was consulting with the company for which she worked. They continued their contact through e-mails, occasional phone calls, and an occasional rendezvous that typically lasted for only a weekend.

Previously married for 15 years, Fred had an amicable divorce with the mother of his 20-year-old daughter. Mary had also been married previously and had a son prior to her first marriage, who was now 18. Their difficulties began when they started to live together for the first time. It seemed that they argued over practical matters such as who did the dishes and how, and their fights were escalating.

Family Dynamics

Fred described a childhood filled with betrayal and abuse. He revealed that his mother would take the other children for an outing while leaving him at home, during which time he was invariably beaten by his father. He felt that his abusive childhood left him distrustful of women. Fred also described joining the Marine Corps, partially to escape his family. He was assigned to a unit in Vietnam, which proved to be a second source of trauma. Trained to conduct covert operations, he admitted committing many atrocities, for which he felt considerable guilt.

In discussing his relationship with women, he expressed ambivalence, on the one hand desiring love and closeness, yet on the other feeling manipulated and controlled. He felt that women generally used sex to control men and that men would be stronger if they "boycotted" all women. Fred described his prior marriage as friendly but asexual and distant.

Mary had a difficult childhood as well. She had been abandoned by her father early on, and her mother remarried when she was 16. At that point, her mother moved to another city with her new husband, leaving Mary behind. It was soon after this abandonment that Mary became pregnant with her son.

Fred stated that he wanted to get over his professed mistrust of women, to improve his increasingly depressed mood, and to process memories and feelings from his painful past, both as a child and in Vietnam. Fred denied any current suicidal ideation; however, he did admit that the thought occasionally crossed his mind. His overall demeanor was characterized by a self-effacing manner, and he often made negative comments about himself. Mary seemed to be uncomfortable with these remarks, but at times her manner toward Fred appeared to be quite critical in a way that fit in with his own self-attacks. Fred also disclosed that he felt intruded on by his wife's habit of "taking over their home" and her apparent need for control— to have everything "her way." Another strong feeling he experienced was a sense of claustrophobia, a feeling of being smothered by her desire to be with him constantly.

Memories began to emerge into Fred's conscious awareness, which often focused on gory situations in which he had participated in violent acts or inflicted bodily harm on another person. He expressed a great deal of remorse and pain about these violent behaviors. His guilt reactions were accompanied by self-recriminations. "Why should I be alive when I have done things like that?" He reported that he had been increasingly plagued by these feelings in recent weeks. He also was experiencing outbursts in which he acted out aggressive behaviors followed by extreme remorse. Fred admitted that his rage reactions tended to fluctuate between self-hatred and fury at Mary. Recently he had broken objects in their home during fights, and on one occasion he bit Mary's ear.

Fred's scores on the FAST can be seen in Figure 6.3.

Individual Voice Therapy Session With Fred

(Note: The following hypothetical session is an abridged version of what would likely take place over the course of three or four sessions. It has been condensed to illustrate better the steps in the therapeutic process.)

Therapist: Fred, you have said that you attack yourself a lot, and on the FAST you indicated some extremely self-hating thoughts and even thoughts of suicide. I was wondering if we could talk about that.

Fred: Yeah, filling out that test, I realized how familiar those thoughts are to me. I wouldn't have said I was suicidal, but I have a lot of thoughts like that. Like I would be better off dead, that nothing is going to work out for me, not now, not ever. That I am useless to other people, that people close to me would be better off without me.

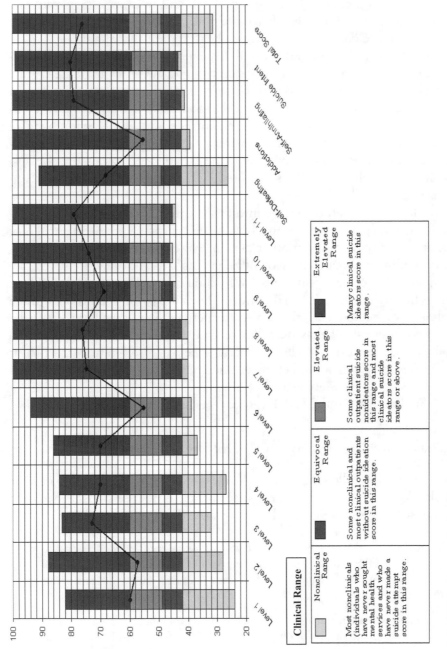

Figure 6.3. FAST T-score profile for Fred.

Therapist:	Fred, I want to try something with you. I want you to say those thoughts again, the ones you just told me. But instead of saying "I am useless," say it as though someone else were saying it to you, like "you're useless."
Fred:	Okay. *You're no good. You fail at everything you try. Stay away from people, leave them alone. No one wants you around. You're no good for anything. Do everyone a favor and die!* [Angrier and angrier, and then sadness]
Therapist:	It makes you sad.
Fred:	I can't believe the amount of anger behind those thoughts. I sounded like my father to myself as I said those things. He had that harsh tone in his voice toward me almost all the time. He was a very unhappy guy, and he saw me as the source of all of his problems. I was the target of his pain and misery. And my mother would leave me alone with him, just to let it happen. I was like the sacrificial lamb in our family. I absorbed his anger. Yet now I can see I unleash that same aggression toward myself. I don't need him to do it to me, I do it to myself. [*Sobs and cries*] I can't believe how much I do this to myself.
Therapist:	Like your father.
Fred:	It is like my worst nightmare to be like him. I hated him. And now when I see myself like him, when I act in ways that remind me of him, then I have the goods on myself. Then I really am bad, evil, dangerous to others. That's when I start thinking things like, "You should get away from other people, go off by yourself. You're unfit to be around other people." [*Pause*]
Therapist:	Just let the thoughts go.
Fred:	*You can't love anyone else. No one loves you. You're just filled with violence. No one is safe around you.* [Angrier] *You don't deserve to live. Everyone would be better off if you just died. Kill yourself, get yourself off of this earth.* [Louder and louder, crying painfully] [*Pause*]
Therapist:	That seems to be the final attack, that you should just get rid of yourself.
Fred:	Yeah, I can feel that really strong sometimes. But I had never realized that these were his feelings toward me. He wanted to get rid of me, first because I was what he saw as causing the problems and then because I think he was ashamed of beating me. Almost like he wanted to destroy the evidence of his crime.
Therapist:	Yes, it's almost like you are acting out his death wish for you.
Fred:	Yeah, it makes me angry. I don't want to do this to myself. I don't want to destroy myself every time I get angry. I need to get

a handle on my anger because when I act it out, then I am being him. That's my proof to myself that I am as bad as he is, that I deserve to die, because I am as evil as he was.

Therapist: You and I need to work together on strategies for dealing with your anger more effectively. We all get angry, anger is a natural reaction to frustration. But the power is in being able to control your anger, to let yourself feel it, accept the feeling, but then decide on what your behavior is going to be, behaving in a manner to accomplish what you want, to behave in accordance with your own morals.

Fred: Yeah, I would like to work on that. I try to suppress my rage, and then it builds up to a point where I explode. I want to learn to identify it and express it so I am not overwhelmed with it.

Therapist: So you try to hold back your anger, suppress it, and then it comes bursting out of you.

Fred: Yeah, and it's been getting worse since Mary has moved in. It has made me feel so pent up. Everything she does around the house makes me feel intruded on, messed with. So I feel the anger building, but I try to not feel it until the point where I feel like I am about to explode. Then the self-recriminations start. I think I am such a volatile guy.

Therapist: Could you say those thoughts as voices, as though someone else were saying them to you?

Fred: Can't you feel it building? You're going to hurt someone. You can't love anyone. You're just going to explode and hurt someone. You're a dangerous guy. People should get away from you. You're just like your father. That's why he punished you, you were a bad kid and now you're just like him. You think you can be any different, well you're not, you're just like me. [*Angrier and angrier, sadness and deep sobbing*] [*Pause*]

It makes me so angry. I feel like yelling back, "I'm not like you. I would never lay a hand on a helpless child. I loved my daughter. I was good to her. I didn't hurt her like you hurt me." I'm not like him. But when I get out of control with my anger, I have the goods on myself. I am like him at those moments and then I hate myself, just like I hated him. Sometimes his feelings are in me. I know I have to stop acting this way because then I really do hate myself.

Therapist: Breaking the identification with him is very important. You have to see his point of view as outside of you, not in you. Let's think about what you could do differently in your behavior that would help you break this connection. What are the voices you have before you have these outbursts? What's going on in your mind?

Fred: Well, usually something happens with Mary where I feel provoked. Like I'll come home and she has rearranged the furniture or she lets me know "our" plans for the weekend. Then I think to myself, *You weak piece of shit, you let her run the show, don't you? You can't let her treat you this way. You'd better put her in her place. This bitch is ruining your whole life. Are you going to let her get away with that, let her make a fool of you? You'd better make her listen. You'd better make her do things your way or you're nothing.*

Then I lash out and she starts to fight back, and it escalates. Finally I am so outraged that I can't even think. I just explode verbally and sometimes even physically. Then afterward it's like I annihilate myself. I tear myself apart and feel like I am the most poisonous, dangerous person and that I should just get out of here, that everyone would be better off if I were just dead.

Therapist: Where do you think those attacks come from?

Fred: That was my father's point of view, my mother's as well. You weren't really a man if you couldn't make your woman listen to you, if you were not in control. So now I act just like he did when I hear those voices.

Therapist: What could you do differently in the situation when you come home and Mary does something that annoys you? How could you handle it differently to go against these voices, to achieve your goal of being a nonviolent, nonthreatening guy, different from your father?

Fred: Well, I could just be aware that I'm provoked and maybe say it to her before the anger builds up.

Therapist: So when you start hearing the attacks on yourself and on Mary about the situation, you could recognize that you are attacking yourself, that these thoughts are not your point of view about the situation. Then you could just calmly tell her what you really feel about the situation.

Fred: Yeah, it sounds simple, but I know it would be a struggle to do that.

Therapist: If you stick to this plan and not let the thoughts get you enraged, then you will probably feel anxious, and initially the thoughts might get louder or more extreme. But if you go through the anxiety, the thoughts will fade into the background and you won't feel so compelled to act on them. Initially if you stay calm rather than yelling at her, the thoughts may get louder, call you a coward, or comment on how weak you are being. But if you stick with your calm mood, they will pass.

It would be hard, and it would make you anxious to act against those voices. The trick is to stick it out, not to give in to the voices, to starve the monster inside of you by not feeding it, not giving in to what it says. If you do this, not act out your aggression at those times when you are provoked, you will begin to feel stronger and develop more of a sense of yourself. You also might want to take some time to write down the thoughts if you have any during or after the situation in the second person, the way you have expressed them in the session today. On the other side of the page, write down a more realistic evaluation of yourself or Mary, a more compassionate view.

Fred: So I write down the thoughts rather than act on them.

Therapist: Exactly. Then bring them to our session next week and we can talk about them.

Fred: Okay, I'll try that. It would feel a lot better to me to get a handle on this anger.

Therapist: Next week let's talk about how this plan goes.

Fred: Sounds good. I know it will be hard and that sometimes Mary doesn't make it easy when she acts in certain ways. But for me the real strength would be in changing myself. This out of control, angry part of me definitely comes from my father. This has never been more clear to me than today. When I act like him I hate myself and I end up feeling suicidal. If I can break this connection to him, I think I could get some respect for myself and not feel like I need to kill myself to spare everyone from me.

Therapist: It's very important to separate yourself from this overlay of him on your personality and to start to get a real sense of your own identity.

Voice Therapy Research

Outcome research examining the efficacy of voice therapy is essential. Initial naturalistic studies are planned with therapists who have been trained in voice therapy methods. Randomized clinical trials of voice therapy also will be essential. The primary goal is to reduce the intensity and severity of negative thoughts the client is experiencing and reduce the self-destructive behaviors that result. A secondary goal is an increase in clients' sense of self and ability to make use of healthy coping strategies. Additional studies on the efficacy of voice therapy techniques as an adjunct to other treatment modalities also should be conducted.

CONCLUSION

To understand human behavior, we must explore the ways in which a fundamental ambivalence toward self compromises the desire to live, to act according to one's goals, wants, and priorities, to individuate, and to find personal meaning in life. In essence, people are torn between motives to actualize and to destroy themselves. Therefore, negative reactions against the self are an integral part of each person's psyche, ranging from critical attitudes and mild self-attacks to severe assaults on the self. These assaults include feelings and attitudes that predispose physical injury to the self and even complete obliteration of the self. Understanding this fundamental ambivalence toward self and the associated destructive thought processes can help us to conceptualize our suicidal clients, assess their risk, and intervene effectively to help resolve suicidal crises.

We believe that every person suffers some degree of pain growing up and has therefore internalized negative voices and possesses some potential for suicide. There are a multitude of factors that influence whether an individual ever reaches a suicidal crisis or actually takes suicidal actions; however, incorporated parental hostility seems to play a crucial role. We conceptualize suicide as representing the extreme end of a continuum of destructive mental processes that results in the ultimate annihilation of self. Clients who view suicide as the best solution are not basing their perceptions on rational thinking but on irrational, malevolent cognitive processes.

The ability of a scale made up of self-destructive thoughts or voices to assess suicide risk supports the contention that these thoughts are driving the suicidal process. The FAST provides a means for clinicians to better understand what is going on in the minds of their self-destructive clients. By identifying the areas where the client is experiencing the most intense destructive thoughts, clinicians can target their intervention more effectively to reduce the pain and desperation the client is experiencing. Clinicians can use the results of the FAST to facilitate the discussion of these thoughts in therapy, subject the thoughts to reality testing, and reduce the risk of the client acting on them.

Robert Firestone developed voice therapy as a cognitive–affective–behavioral therapeutic methodology that brings introjected hostile thoughts, with the accompanying negative affect, to consciousness, rendering them accessible for treatment. This technique facilitates the identification of the negative cognitions driving suicidal actions, which in turn helps clients to gain a measure of control over all aspects of their self-destructive or suicidal behaviors. Clients become aware that their distortions or negative perceptions of events, and not the events themselves, are the principal cause of their depression, perturbation, and hopelessness. They develop a greater understanding of themselves and how these self-destructive voices adversely affect their lives. Their sense of self is also strengthened, giving them a more realistic perspective on themselves and their circumstances, so that they can more effectively cope with adverse life events. This process helps clients expand their personal boundaries, develop a sense of meaning in life, and reduce the risk of self-destructive behavior, including suicide.

REFERENCES

Armony, J. L., & LeDoux, J. E. (1997). How the brain processes emotional information. *Annals of the New York Academy of Sciences, 821,* 259–270.

Baumeister, R. F., Bratslavsky, E., Finkenauer, C., & Vohs, K. D. (2001). Bad is stronger than good. *Review of General Psychology, 5,* 323–370.

Beck, A. T., Steer, R. A., Beck, J. S., & Newman, C. W. (1993). Hopelessness, depression, suicidal ideation, and clinical diagnosis of depression. *Suicide and Life-Threatening Behavior, 23,* 139–145.

Berne, E. (1961). *Transactional analysis in psychotherapy: A systematic individual and social psychiatry.* New York: Grove Press.

Blatt, S. J. (2004). *Experiences of depression: Theoretical, clinical, and research perspectives.* Washington, DC: American Psychological Association.

Briere, J., & Runtz, M. (1987). Post sexual abuse trauma: Data and implications for clinical practice. *Journal of Interpersonal Violence, 2,* 367–379.

Brown, J., Cohen, P., Johnson, J. G., & Smailes, E. M. (1999). Childhood abuse and neglect: Specificity and effects on adolescent and young adult depression and suicidality. *Journal of the American Academy of Child and Adolescent Psychiatry, 38,* 1490–1496.

Buchanan, T. W., & Lovallo, W. R. (2001). Enhanced memory for emotional material following stress-level cortisol treatment in humans. *Psychoneuroendocrinology, 26,* 307–317.

Cahill, L., Roozendaal, B., & McGaugh, J. A. (1997). The neurobiology of memory for aversive emotional events. In M. E. Bouton & M. S. Fanselow (Eds.), *Learning, motivation, and cognition* (pp. 369–384). Washington, DC: American Psychological Association.

Chu, J. A., & Dill, D. L. (1990). Dissociative symptoms in relation to childhood physical and sexual abuse. *American Journal of Psychiatry, 147,* 887–892.

Cronbach, L. J. (1951). Coefficient alpha and the internal structure of tests. *Psychometrika, 16,* 297–334.

Ellis, T. E. (2001). Psychotherapy with suicidal patients. In D. Lester (Ed.), *Suicide prevention: Resources for the millennium* (pp. 129–151). Philadelphia: Brunner-Routledge.

Fairbairn, W. R. D. (1952). *Psychoanalytic studies of the personality.* London: Routledge & Kegan Paul.

Farooqi, Y. (2004). Comparative study of suicide potential among Pakistani and American psychiatric patients. *Death Studies, 28,* 19–46.

Fawcett, J., Scheftner, W. A., Fogg, L., Clark, D. C., Young, M. A., Hedeker, D., et al. (1990). Time-related predictors of suicide in major affective disorder. *American Journal of Psychiatry, 147,* 1189–1194.

Ferenczi, S. (1955). Confusion of tongues between adults and the child. In M. Balint (Ed.), *Final contributions to the problems and methods of psycho-analysis* (pp. 156–167). New York: Basic Books. (Original work published 1933)

Fierman, L. B. (Ed.). (1965). *Effective psychotherapy: The contribution of Hellmuth Kaiser*. New York: Free Press.

Firestone, L. (1991). The Firestone Voice Scale for Self-Destructive Behavior: Investigating the scale's validity and reliability (Doctoral dissertation, California School of Professional Psychology, 1991). *Dissertation Abstracts International, 52*, 3338B.

Firestone, L. (2004). Separation theory and voice therapy methodology applied to the treatment of Katie: A diary-based retrospective case conceptualization and treatment approach. In D. Lester (Ed.), *Katie's diary: Unlocking the mystery of a suicide* (pp. 161–186). New York: Brunner-Routledge.

Firestone, R. W. (1985). *The fantasy bond: Structure of psychological defenses*. Santa Barbara, CA: Glendon Association.

Firestone, R. W. (1986). The "inner voice" and suicide. *Psychotherapy, 23*, 439–447.

Firestone, R. W. (1988). *Voice therapy: A psychotherapeutic approach to self-destructive behavior*. Santa Barbara, CA: Glendon Association.

Firestone, R. W. (1997a). *Combating destructive thought processes: Voice therapy and separation theory*. Thousand Oaks, CA: Sage.

Firestone, R. W. (1997b). *Suicide and the inner voice: Risk assessment, treatment, and case management*. Thousand Oaks, CA: Sage.

Firestone, R. W., & Firestone, L. (1996). *The Firestone assessment of self-destructive thoughts*. Santa Barbara, CA: Glendon Association.

Firestone, R. W., & Firestone, L. (1998). Voices in suicide: The relationship between self-destructive thought processes, maladaptive behavior, and self-destructive manifestations. *Death Studies, 22*, 411–443.

Firestone, R. W., & Firestone, L. (in press). *Firestone Assessment of Suicide Intent*. Santa Barbara, CA: Glendon Association.

Firestone, R. W., Firestone, L., & Catlett, J. (2002). *Conquer your critical inner voice: A revolutionary program to counter negative thoughts and live free from imagined limitations*. Oakland, CA: New Harbinger.

Firestone, R. W., Firestone, L., & Catlett, J. (2003). *Creating a life of meaning and compassion: The wisdom of psychotherapy*. Washington, DC: American Psychological Association.

Firestone, R. W., & Seiden, R. H. (1987). Microsuicide and suicidal threats of everyday life. *Psychotherapy, 24*, 31–39.

Fonagy, P., Steele, M., Steele, H., Leigh, T., Kennedy, R., Mattoon, G., et al. (1995). Attachment, the reflective self, and borderline states: The predictive specificity of the Adult Attachment Interview and pathological emotional development. In S. Goldberg, R. Muir, & J. Kerr (Eds.), *Attachment theory: Social, developmental, and clinical perspectives* (pp. 233–278). Hillsdale, NJ: Analytic Press.

Freud, A. (1966). *The ego and the mechanisms of defense* (Rev. ed.). Madison, CT: International Universities Press.

Gilpin, A., & Hays, R. D. (1990). Scalogram analysis program [Computer program]. Durham, NC: Duke University Press.

Heckler, R. A. (1994). *Waking up, alive: The descent, the suicide attempt, and the return to life*. New York: Ballantine Books.

Hesse, E., Main, M., Abrams, K. Y., & Rifkin, A. (2003). Unresolved states regarding loss or abuse can have "second-generation" effects: Disorganization, role inversion, and frightening ideation in the offspring of traumatized, non-maltreating parents. In M. F. Solomon & D. J. Siegel (Eds.), *Healing trauma: Attachment, mind, body, and brain* (pp. 57–106). New York: Norton.

Jamison, K. R. (1999). *Night falls fast: Understanding suicide*. New York: Vintage Books.

Lester, D. (2000). Alcoholism, substance abuse, and suicide. In R. W. Maris, A. L. Berman, & M. M. Silverman (Eds.), *Comprehensive textbook of suicidology* (pp. 357–375). New York: Guilford Press.

Linehan, M. M. (1993). *Cognitive–behavioral treatment of borderline personality disorder*. New York: Guilford Press.

Loas, G., Perot, J. M., Chignague, J. F., Trespalacios, H., & Delahousse, J. (2000). Parasuicide, anhedonia, and depression. *Comprehensive Psychiatry, 41*, 369–372.

Lyons-Ruth, K., & Jacobvitz, D. (1999). Attachment disorganization: Unresolved loss, relational violence, and lapses in behavioral and attentional strategies. In J. Cassidy & P. R. Shaver (Eds.), *Handbook of attachment: Theory, research, and clinical applications* (pp. 520–554). New York: Guilford Press.

Main, M., & Hesse, E. (1990). Parents' unresolved traumatic experiences are related to infant disorganized attachment status: Is frightened and/or frightening parental behavior the linking mechanism? In M. T. Greenberg, D. Cicchetti, & E. M. Cummings (Eds.), *Attachment in the preschool years: Theory, research, and intervention* (pp. 161–182). Chicago: University of Chicago Press.

Main, M., & Solomon, J. (1986). Discovery of an insecure-disorganized/disoriented attachment pattern. In T. B. Brazelton & M. W. Yogman (Eds.), *Affective development in infancy* (pp. 95–124). Norwood, NJ: Ablex.

Maltsberger, J. T. (1999). The psychodynamic understanding of suicide. In D. G. Jacobs (Ed.), *The Harvard Medical School guide to suicide assessment and intervention* (pp. 72–82). San Francisco: Jossey-Bass.

Maltsberger, J. T. (2002). *Affective states in suicide*. Paper presented at the 2nd Aeschi Conference, "Understanding and Interviewing the Suicidal Patient," Aeschi, Switzerland.

Maltsberger, J. T., Hendin, H., Haas, A. P., & Lipschitz, A. (2003). Determination of precipitating events in the suicide of psychiatric patients. *Suicide and Life-Threatening Behavior, 33*, 111–119.

Oei, T. I., Verhoeven, W. M., Westenberg, H. G., Zwart, F. M., & van Ree, J. M. (1990). Anhedonia, suicide ideation and dexamethasone nonsuppression in depressed patients. *Journal of Psychiatric Research, 24*, 25–35.

Orbach, I. (2002, March). *The role of dissociation and bodily experiences in self-destruction*. Paper presented at the 2nd Aeschi Conference, "Understanding and Interviewing the Suicidal Patient," Aeschi, Switzerland.

Orbach, I. (2003). Suicide and the suicidal body. *Suicide and Life-Threatening Behavior, 33*, 1–8.

Perry, B. D. (1997). Incubated in terror: Neurodevelopmental factors in the "cycle of violence." In J. D. Osofsky (Ed.), *Children in a violent society* (pp. 124–149). New York: Guilford Press.

Rudd, M. D., Joiner, T., & Rajab, M. H. (2001). *Treating suicidal behavior: An effective, time-limited approach.* New York: Guilford Press.

Sanders, B., & Giolas, M. H. (1991). Dissociation and childhood trauma in psychologically disturbed adolescents. *American Journal of Psychiatry, 148*, 50–54.

Schore, A. N. (1994). *Affect regulation and the origin of the self: The neurobiology of emotional development.* Hillsdale, NJ: Erlbaum.

Shneidman, E. S. (1993). *Suicide as psychache: A clinical approach to self-destructive behavior.* Northvale, NJ: Aronson.

Siegel, D. J. (1999). *The developing mind: Toward a neurobiology of interpersonal experience.* New York: Guilford Press.

Siegel, D. J. (2001). Toward an interpersonal neurobiology of the developing mind: Attachment relationships, "mindsight," and neural integration. *Infant Mental Health Journal, 22*, 67–94.

van der Kolk, B. A., McFarlane, A. C., & Weisaeth, L. (Eds.). (1996). *Traumatic stress: The effects of overwhelming experience on mind, body, and society.* New York: Guilford Press.

Winnicott, D. W. (1958). *Collected papers: Through paediatrics to psycho-analysis.* London: Tavistock.

7

TO BE OR NOT TO BE: PERSONAL CONSTRUCTIONS OF THE SUICIDAL CHOICE

ROBERT A. NEIMEYER AND DAVID A. WINTER

How can we understand the cognitive processes entailed in suicide, an apparently paradoxical behavior in which an individual engages in an act of self-annihilation? In a personal construct view, there is no single answer to this question because the cognitive factors that contribute to the suicidal choice are nearly as variegated as the meaning systems of the persons who engage in self-destructive behaviors. Our goal in this chapter is to situate a discussion of suicide in the broad context of personal construct psychology, a comprehensive theory originally outlined by George Kelly (1955) and elaborated by subsequent generations of construct theorists. We begin by reviewing the structure of the theory and its implications for factors that contribute to the suicidal choice, briefly noting research relevant to several of these factors. We then provide a synthesis of this wide-ranging overview, distilling three qualitatively distinct cognitive paths to suicide implied by this conceptualization and follow this with a more in-depth review of selected research relevant to these pathways. Finally, we describe an empirically supported personal construct approach to treatment, illustrating such therapy in a brief case study. We hope that doing so will underscore the relevance of cognitive features addressed by other contributors to this volume and will also suggest distinctive concepts and methods that can enhance our understanding of and response to the suicidal predicament.

SUICIDE AND SIGNIFICANCE:
A FRAMEWORK OF PERSONAL CONSTRUCT THEORY

Approaching the specific issue of suicide from the general framework of personal construct theory (PCT) confronts us with both prospects and problems. On one hand, the intent of construct theorists to offer a comprehensive psychological account of human behavior provides a trove of conceptual, methodological, and practical tools for approaching suicide in a multidimensional way, an approach that is compatible with the complexity of the phenomenon. On the other hand, the unusually broad scope of PCT, which encompasses domains as diverse as developmental psychology, political behavior, and organizational transition (Fransella, 2003), requires a judicious attention to those aspects of the theory that have the most direct relevance for understanding self-destructive behavior. We therefore begin by offering a selective summary of PCT's assumptive structure (see Neimeyer, 1987), noting the implications of several features of the theory for a cognitive model of suicide. Where possible, we attempt to ground these concepts in brief clinical vignettes and relevant research, reserving a fuller discussion of selected studies and a detailed clinical illustration for later in the chapter.

The Anticipatory Posture

Kelly's fundamental postulate about the nature of human beings was that they are essentially interpretive, always in the process of attributing meaning to their experience. Like incipient scientists who attempt to devise hypotheses that render events understandable and to some degree predictable, people experiment with the social world but do so in ways that are both informed and constrained by the structure of their personal theories. Stated differently, all behavior is ultimately *anticipatory*, in the sense that it represents a means of testing crucial predictions or dealing with anticipated threats to the integrity and viability of the individual's construct system. In this respect, suicidal people are no different from anyone else; the critical question is what prediction is motivating their self-destructive action and whether crucial revisions or extensions of their construct systems might bring to light other workable options. To address this question, it is helpful to consider several of the corollaries of personal construct theory, grouping them into those concerned with the construing process, the structure of knowing, and the social embeddedness of our meaning-making efforts.

The Construing Process

Construct theory's emphasis on anticipation presupposes that human beings display certain basic dispositions, among which is the "set" to perceive regularly recurring patterns in the flux of living. As Popper (1963, p. 48) argued, this search for regularity is "logically *a priori* to all observational experience," involving an attempt to construe the replicative, orderly themes in events. "Like a musician," Kelly (1955, p. 52) noted, a person "must phrase his experience in order to make sense of it. The phrases are distinguished events. . . . Within these limited segments, which are based on recurrent themes, man begins to discover the bases for likenesses and differences." Of course, people differ markedly in how they phrase or punctuate life events and in the themes they impute to them. For example, cognitive formulations such as Beck, Epstein, and Harrison's (1983) emphasize the extent to which depressed people vary in their orientation to *sociotropy* versus *autonomy*, organizing life experiences in terms of love and approval on the one hand or success and accomplishment on the other. Research on the personal construct systems of depressed inpatients supports and extends this formulation, suggesting that a monolithic construct system organized along either of these lines leaves such individuals vulnerable to a suicidal collapse of meaning when they experience significant rejection or failure (Baker, Barris, & Neimeyer, 1998).

Obviously, however, people not only devise distinctively different constructs for organizing their experience, but they also seek validation for them, optimally revising their constructions of events in light of subsequent outcomes. Kelly (1955) formulated this process in terms of an *experience cycle*, anchored in (a) initial anticipations of important events in which (b) the individual is passionately invested, leading to (c) encounter with the expected, feared, or hoped-for event, which (d) confirms or disconfirms the person's hypotheses, prompting (e) constructive revision of the person's system (Neimeyer, 1987). Suicidal crises can arise when this cycle of meaning making is impeded at any of several phases. For example, Ron was a notoriously autocratic businessman who was clearly invested in "calling the shots" in all important domains of his life, from his entrepreneurial ventures to his personal affairs. When his wife left him for another (less controlling) man, however, Ron was unable to contend with the massive invalidation this represented and revise his constructions of interpersonal relationships accordingly. His decisive and irrevocable suicidal act represented an ultimate bid to reassert control over a life that had become, for him, intolerably unmanageable. Self-destructive acts can arise at other points in the experience cycle as well, as when the individual loses any sense of investment in continued living or seeks to avert a fateful encounter with an event that portends imminent invalidation of crucial self-constructions.

Of course, attempted suicide itself can represent an event that can be understood in terms of the experience cycle. If, in keeping with the personal scientist model, suicidal behavior is viewed as an experiment, its outcome may validate or invalidate the individual's hypotheses. For example, the person who awakens from unconsciousness following an overdose taken with suicidal intent will be faced with not only invalidation of the anticipation of death but perhaps also with further validation of a view of the self as a failure who is not even capable of taking his or her life. The outcomes of such desperate experiments are equally important to understand in terms of their social implications, as significant others might have been anticipated to react to the individual's self-harm in particular ways. Sometimes a person's suicidal gestures can be construed as *hostile* acts, in Kelly's (1955) sense that they attempt to extort validational evidence for some critical construction (Stefan & Linder, 1985). For example, Aldridge (1998) has described how the self-harm of women who were psychiatric inpatients allowed them to validate constructions of staff as "unsympathetic, uncaring, and unable to help." In a cyclical process, the behavior of the staff in turn allowed them to validate constructions of the inpatients' actions as "deviant, illegitimate, and uncooperative." Alternatively, encountering an unanticipated supportive response from others can suggest more hopeful revisions of the suicidal individual's constructions of the social world, as in Joan's experience that, contrary to her expectations, "people have shown me that they do care." In other cases, however, the invalidation may feel devastating. For example, in marked contrast to Mary's anticipation that her husband would not get angry with her for attempting suicide, "he just bashed the shit out of me." Such consequences of an act of self-harm may be as crucial a focus of therapy for self-injury as are its antecedents.

Viewed from the "inside out," people's choices by definition make sense in terms of their own construct system. In formal terms, Kelly (1955, p. 64) referred to this principle as the *elaborative choice*: "A person chooses for himself that alternative . . . through which he anticipates the greater possibility for extension and definition of his system." Of course, the alternatives available in any given circumstance are themselves defined by the scope of the person's meaning system, so that highly *constricted* systems that envision few options for responding to a life crisis place the individual at greater risk for viewing suicide as the "only way out." This personal construct formulation is compatible both with Shneidman's (1996) discussion of the role of constriction in reinforcing the "tunnel vision" of the suicidal person and with cognitive approaches that emphasize the role of deficient problem solving in the suicidal choice (Ellis, 2004).

A particularly vexing problem can arise when, as Kelly (1955, p. 77) noted, "the variation in a person's construction system is limited by the permeability of [its superordinate] constructs." That is, core constructions of self and world that regulate a person's basic sense of identity can become so tight and unable to accommodate new experience that needed change is resisted. In the extreme case, an individual can become so hemmed in by her or his core identity constructs that death itself may seem preferable to forfeiting them. This predicament was illustrated poignantly by Stan, whose construing of himself as intellectually superior and self-reliant translated into an interpersonal aloofness and haughtiness that consistently eroded potentially close relationships. Stan's inability to reconcile the gnawing loneliness that resulted from his core sense of self left him living in a sharp state of emotional contradiction, a contradiction he resolved by ending his life. Significantly, Stan's suicide note read as an extended indictment of the shallow fools who could not understand or tolerate his greatness.

In the case of some "personality disordered" individuals, self-harm can also be integrated into their core sense of identity and, in this case, represent not so much a one-time response to crisis as a "way of life"—perhaps not one that would be attractive to most people but one that is at least familiar and predictable for the person concerned. To quote Fred, whose history of self-harm involved swallowing not only tablets but also an impressive array of other objects, ranging from razors to starter motors, "I don't really want to stop. It doesn't harm me. It's just part of me, going to hospital and getting better." In such cases, self-injury can provide an island of structure and predictability when the individual feels adrift in a sea of chaos. Such an analysis can be particularly applicable to some people with a history of abuse, who have become used to predicting their world in terms of a construct of *abusing* versus *being abused* and who may therefore resort to self-abuse at times when life feels unpredictable. Many psychotherapists have felt baffled when a client has arrived for therapy with signs of cutting after an experience that seemed to go particularly well. On reflection, it may become clear that the therapist's satisfaction was due to the client's beginning to entertain alternative constructions of crucial life events, perhaps a vision of relationships that did not need to be viewed in terms of abuse. However, for the client the prospect of dismantling old constructions may have provoked considerable *anxiety*, which was reduced by a return to the known world of self-harm. For example, Paul, who construed his life in terms of self-hatred, guilt, and punishment, graphically described his dislodgement from his core role in the context of a loving new relationship as a sense of "not knowing who I am." Self-injury, paradoxically, helped reestablish the contours of a more familiar world.

The Structure of Knowing

Implicit in the previous discussion of the construing process is that people devise personal theories as frameworks for interpreting experience and channeling their decisions and actions in the social world. Much of personal construct theory specifically addresses the structural features of these theories, which as Kelly (1955, p. 56) argued, are organized into "construction system[s] embracing ordinal relationships between constructs." In the ideal case, new experiences can be assimilated at concrete or subordinate levels of our construct systems, gradually prompting extension or revision of superordinate values and commitments. Something of the kind typically occurs, for example, when consistent encounters with novel food, customs, and ways of life in the course of extended travel to a foreign country begin to foster more abstract changes in one's outlook, worldview, and values. In some circumstances, however, new experiences can precipitate unsustainable *threat*, understood as imminent and comprehensive changes in one's "core role" or identity structures, and *guilt*, triggered by behaviors that are radically at variance with one's basic construction of self. In the worst case scenario, suicide can represent the most dramatic way of escaping from the resulting predicament, as when Tanya, a promising college soccer player, slid into an ultimately fatal depression following an experience of sexual assault at a team party. For her, the rape represented not only a radical assault on her body, but also on her sense of herself as a moral being, and death was preferable to struggling with the resulting self-condemnation.

At a more basic level, Kelly (1955) envisioned the individual constructs that comprise our systems of meaning as contrasts, establishing partly consensual, partly private distinctions that give constructs their unique significance. For example, Suzy, an accomplished young violinist, described herself as a "cynical idealist"—cynical since the collapse of her religious faith some years before but an idealist in her propensity to retreat into a fantasy world populated by the characters of C. S. Lewis and J. R. R. Tolkien. Her construing of her options in the social world was sharply dichotomous, presenting her with choices to be *emotionally controlled* versus *burdening others*, *lonely* versus *vulnerable*, and *out of contact* versus *rejected*. Not surprisingly, Suzy increasingly was drawn to resolve this dilemma by ending her life, precipitating repeated psychiatric hospitalizations (Neimeyer, 1993). A link between depressive fatalism and such dichotomous, "either–or" thinking has been theorized in cognitive therapy formulations (Beck, Rush, Shaw, & Emery, 1979) and empirically demonstrated in personal construct research using repertory grid technique (Hughes & Neimeyer, 1990).

Kelly (1955, p. 85) recognized that speaking of personal meanings as comprising a "system" can imply—wrongly—that they are systematic, in the sense of being "logic-tight and wholly internally consistent," when in fact, this is rarely the case. More commonly, our constructions of self and world are fraught with contradiction, and this multiplicity of meaning can be both boon and bane for the construing person. On one hand, a conception of oneself as a "community" of situated identities (Mair, 1977) can contribute to the richness of the "dialogical self" (Hermans, 2002), a self that can negotiate with itself and foster growth and change by respecting and selectively bridging its own internal complexity (Neimeyer, 2000). On the other hand, a person sometimes confronts traumatizing experiences that are acutely disorganizing, fragmenting systems of meaning that once provided a coherent self-narrative (Neimeyer, in press; Neimeyer et al., 2002). The disintegration of meaning systems has been traced by personal construct researchers studying such conditions as posttraumatic stress disorder (Sewell, 2003) and psychosis (Winter, 1992), both of which can be an instigating context for suicide.

The Self in Social Context

If one tried to catch the essence of construct theory in a phrase, it might be described as a psychology of personal meaning. With his emphasis on how "persons differ from one another in their construction of events," Kelly (1955, p. 55) made clear his commitment to the primacy of the personal. This ineluctable individuality is evident in every domain of human life, including the uniquely personal meanings that can be compressed into the specific method chosen to end that life. Approaching this issue empirically, Lester (1993) adapted Kelly's (1955; cf. Fransella, Bell, & Bannister, 2003) repertory grid procedure to assess the meanings that participants associated with eight methods for committing suicide: using handguns, hanging, overdose, poison, jumping from a bridge, car exhaust, drowning, and cutting an artery. Comparing and contrasting the methods, respondents generated an impressive range of constructs, including *private* versus *public, controlling it* versus *taking you by surprise, masculine* versus *feminine*, and so on. Lester found considerable consensus regarding some methods, with handguns construed as *violent* as opposed to *peaceful*, and cutting as *messy* versus *neat*. In contrast, hanging, poisoning, and jumping were viewed idiosyncratically by different respondents. Lester noted that grid technique could help clinicians assess the subjective similarities and significance of different means of self-destruction for life-threatening clients, and potentially help predict "method switching" among chronically suicidal individuals when access to a preferred means was blocked.

Counterbalancing construct theory's emphasis on personal meaning is its equally emphatic proposition that our construct systems are intricately bound up with those of other people, particularly in intimate relationships. For example, Kelly's (1955, p. 90) commonality corollary, which defines psychological similarity in terms of people's basic "construction of experience," has provided a starting point for numerous research programs on the development and breakdown of close relationships, both within the family (Feixas, 1992) and in broader friendship networks (Neimeyer, Brooks, & Baker, 1995).

Because we rely crucially on significant others for validation of our core constructions of self and world, the loss of such relationships is potentially devastating, especially if our dependencies are "undispersed" (Walker, 1997), leaving us vulnerable to total isolation if the person on whom we rely dies, leaves, or betrays our trust. This precipitant to suicide is illustrated by Sylvia Plath, who killed herself following the breakup of her marriage to fellow poet Ted Hughes. Plath had written in her journal that she could not "conceive of life without" her husband because "my whole being has grown and interwound so completely with Ted's that if anything were to happen to him, I do not see how I could live. I would either go mad, or kill myself" (Kukil, 2000, p. 274). Similarly, Rose, a client who had taken an overdose of medication and swallowed bleach, described how this was a reaction to her partner of 12 years telling her that he was going to leave her: "I couldn't believe it . . . he said he loved me, but now he felt nothing. I went crazy. The pain was too intense. I wanted just to close my eyes and go to sleep."

Finally, Kelly (1955) viewed "sociality," the construing of another person's construction processes, as central to interpersonal relationships. At the deepest levels, this entails the coconstruction of a role relationship in which two people seek to grasp one another's most essential sense of self and grant access to their own. Because the level of intimacy this implies leaves partners open to the threat of profound invalidation, people often defend against this possibility by disengaging from intimate relationships through narcissistic self-absorption, superficial manipulation, retreating from the social world, and other strategies that limit the inevitable risk of genuine role relationships (Leitner, 1995). The resulting inability to take other people's perspectives in this way may be a factor in finding one's social world chaotic or alienating. Again, this may have been the case with Sylvia Plath, who wrote in her journal that she did not put herself "in other people's minds and viscera . . . half enough" (Kukil, 2000, p. 92).

THE LIMITING CONDITIONS OF HUMAN LIFE: A KELLIAN SYNTHESIS

As the foregoing review suggests, personal construct theory offers a trove of concepts for construing the suicidal choice that together provide a comprehensive framework to guide both research and intervention. At the level of *cognitive process*, these encompass the suicidal individual's constricted and constraining ways of organizing and thematizing experience; anticipating and investing in the outcomes of behavioral "experiments" in the social world, including the outcomes of the self-destructive act itself; and contending with the validation or invalidation of his or her crucial constructions of self and world. At the level of *cognitive structure*, the theory offers a multidimensional portrayal of the dilemmas desperate individuals face as they view the world through sharply dichotomized constructs; the limitations imposed on self-change by impermeable core constructs of identity; and the anxious confrontation with an overwhelmingly unfamiliar world when their construct systems become disorganized or fail to accommodate essential experiences. Finally, at the level of *social cognition*, construct theory emphasizes both the importance of gaining access to the suicidal person's idiosyncratic meaning system, including the meanings associated with a particular self-destructive act; grasping the extent to which he or she is supported by or isolated from the sustaining validation of others; and understanding suicide as a potential response to the threat of profound devastation in core role relationships.

Drawing on several of these factors, Kelly (1961) attempted to formulate three basic pathways that led to the suicidal choice, a model that has been extended and refined by subsequent construct theorists (Neimeyer, 1984; Stefan & Von, 1985). These paths include suicide as a dedicated act, as a planned and deterministic form of self-harm, and as a more impulsive or chaotic act of self injury, each of which are reviewed subsequently. Although this suggests that there may be various routes to suicide, it also indicates that all such acts, like any other, are experiments by which the individual attempts a better anticipation of his or her world. In other words, suicide is a "validating act" for the individual concerned, and, rather than being illogical and incomprehensible, has a personal meaning that can be understood within the context of his or her construct system.

Suicide as a Dedicated Act

One of the rarer forms of suicide that Kelly described (1961, p. 259) is the "dedicated act," which is "designed to validate one's life, to extend its essential meaning rather than to terminate it" per se. In such suicides, ranging from that of the religious martyr to that of the kamikaze pilot, death is essentially a means by which the individual anticipates that cherished beliefs, which are perhaps under threat, will be elaborated and taken forward by others. Kelly illustrated this category with the death of Socrates, who chose to drink the hemlock offered him by the Athenian authorities rather than recant his socially disruptive philosophy. A more contemporary example is Ahmed al-Haznawi, one of the pilots who flew into the World Trade Center on September 11, 2001, who wrote in his "last will and testament" that "The time of humiliation and subjugation is over. It's time to kill Americans in their heartland. Lord I regard myself as a martyr for you to accept me as such" (Borger, 2002). Sentiments such as these reflect particular social constructions of suicide, and in this case also of murder, as an honorable act that often receives powerful consensual validation from a relevant political or religious community. Similarly, social constructions of suicide as a potentially noble act may help explain high suicide rates in some countries, such as Japan and Hungary. Nonfatal acts of self-harm may also sometimes be construed as virtuous. For example, in providing constructs for a repertory grid, Sarah said that the contrast to being *self-destructive* was to be *egotistical*, which for her was a less preferred option. It was small wonder that she had been referred for treatment of recurrent self-destructive behavior and that she declined such help.

Deterministic Self-Harm

Kelly differentiated suicide as a dedicated act from "mere suicide." This may occur under two circumstances, which he termed the "limiting conditions" of realism and indeterminacy and which have also been described as experiences of certainty or chaos (Stefan & Linder, 1985; Stefan & Von, 1985). The former is reflected in "deterministic suicide," in which "the course of events seems so obvious that there is no point in waiting around for the outcome" (Kelly, 1961, p. 260). As a depressed client, George, who marked his 50th birthday by taking 50 sleeping tablets, explained, "I can't see the point of being alive. . . . No romance, the kids couldn't care two monkeys, my relatives don't see me any more." Deterministic acts of self-destruction are often well planned and make use of highly lethal methods, posing significant challenges to intervention.

Chaotic Self-Harm

Chaotic suicide contrasts markedly with deterministic suicide in that it occurs when "everything seems so unpredictable that the only definite thing one can do is abandon the scene altogether" (Kelly, 1961, p. 260). Such unpredictability, from a personal construct theory perspective, would be associated with acute anxiety.

Chaotic suicide was vividly described by Antonin Artaud when he wrote that "If I commit suicide, it will not be to destroy myself but to put myself back together again. Suicide will be for me only one means of violently reconquering myself . . . of anticipating the unpredictable approaches of God. By suicide, I reintroduce my design in nature. I shall for the first time give things the shape of my will" (Hirschman, 1965). Similarly, in her last poem, "Edge," written in the week before her suicide, Sylvia Plath (1981) described the order and certainty that may be achieved by death. This poem commenced: "The woman is perfected. / Her dead / Body wears the smile of accomplishment . . . ." The perfection described in the poem contrasts with Plath's "profound terror of an inner chaos she constantly suppressed" (Stevenson, 1998, p. 101).

Kelly (1961) viewed suicidal acts as the ultimate expression of a process of constriction, the strategy, especially manifested in depression, in which a person deals with the chaos of "the apparent incompatibility of his construction systems" (Kelly, 1955, p. 477) by drawing in the boundaries of his or her world. It is interesting that Ted Hughes (1998, p. 75) also used the term in describing his wife's poems, and Plath (1971) herself vividly portrayed the process of constriction with her metaphor of being encased in a bell jar.

As Stefan and Linder (1985) described, a further process of construing may be particularly relevant to chaotic suicide. This is what Kelly (1955) termed the circumspection–preemption–control (CPC) cycle, which he viewed as the basis of decision making. In the circumspection phase, the individual considers all of the issues involved in a decision; in the preemption phase, he or she selects the most important of the issues, presented as a choice between two alternatives; and in the control phase, one of these alternatives is chosen. Foreshortening of the circumspection phase of the cycle may be characteristic of impulsive acts of self-harm. Describing one such act, John said,

> I was thinking about a person I worked with who cut himself and killed himself. I thought that if he can do it I can do it. . . . I ran to the kitchen, grabbed a knife and started cutting myself out of sheer desperation. I didn't have the guts to do anything more drastic, for example throwing myself on the train lines.

Although less often lethal, the impulsivity associated with such acts poses its own challenges to intervention.

In summary, a personal construct theory approach to suicide suggests that superficially similar self-destructive acts can arise as the outcomes of qualitatively different paths, ranging from the dedicated (and often socially validated) sacrifice of life for a higher principle or purpose (at least as viewed by the suicidal individual), to fatalistic and carefully planned decisions to end one's suffering, to more unpredictable responses to a sense of impending chaos. This suggests a similarly multifaceted approach to research and intervention, topics to which we now turn.

RESEARCH STUDIES

The foregoing formulation of precipitants to suicide is supported by an extensive research literature on the anticipatory sets, cognitive structures, and problem-solving deficits of self-destructive individuals (see S. Hughes & Neimeyer, 1990, for a detailed review). To extend the selective discussion of research noted earlier, we review in this section a few additional studies conducted from an explicit personal construct perspective to illustrate the theory's potentially unique contribution to suicide assessment. We begin with a focus on cognitive features that can be assessed through repertory grid technique (Fransella et al., 2003), which factor analytic research on depressed clients has demonstrated yields measures of negative self-construing and construct system structure that are clearly distinguishable from indices of cognitive distortion and depressive symptomatology that are the focus of most cognitive therapy studies (Neimeyer & Feixas, 1992). We then conclude by discussing a recent study of the efficacy of personal construct therapy for suicide, setting the stage for a more detailed consideration of this approach and an illustration of its use in an actual case.

Repertory Grid Assessment

Landfield (1976) conducted an early study of cognitive structure in suicidal patients, comparing high- and low-intent parasuicidal clients, suicide ideators, high and low-maladjustment psychotherapy clients, and nonpsychiatric control participants. Using a repertory grid measure that required respondents to compare and contrast significant figures in their lives (family members, work associates, etc.) to generate a set of personal constructs (e.g., *trustworthy* vs. *untrustworthy*; *emotional* vs. *controlled*), he then had respondents rate each figure on each construct to yield a matrix of responses that were analyzed to produce three measures. These included constriction in construct application (the number of times that neither construct pole is applied to the figures), concreteness of constructs, and degree of disorganization of the system, as indexed by the number of functionally independent (uncorrelated) construct clusters. As hypothesized, high-intent parasuicidal clients scored highest on each measure, suggesting a distinctive cognitive structure marked by constriction and loose organization.

A novel study by Parker (1981) shed light on how suicidal behavior can be chosen over other seemingly more viable alternatives by focusing on the personal meaning of various problem-solving strategies among self-poisoning patients. Parker's version of the repertory grid elicited constructs typically used by such patients to construe problem-solving behaviors such as taking an overdose, killing oneself, talking to the key person, and seeking professional help. A grid including nine representative constructs (e.g., *useless* vs. *effective*; *thought out* vs. *desperate*) and 11 means of conflict resolution was then administered to a second set of self-poisoning patients grouped according to their scores on a scale for suicide intent. Factor analysis of the results reflected clear differences in the two groups, such that the low-intent group viewed taking an overdose as quite distinct from actually killing oneself, associating it more with a desperate escape from tension, whereas suicide was viewed as harmful and attacking of the key person. In contrast, the high-intent group viewed suicide as a helpful method of expressing feelings. For both groups, talking to the key person implied an admission of blame, a form of invalidation that could be avoided through suicidal behavior. Thus, Parker's findings suggested a link between constricted problem-solving options and the personal meanings of different actions when viewed through the person's construct system.

In a rare prospective study of cognitive predictors of suicide risk, S. Hughes and Neimeyer (1993) assessed a large group of depressed inpatients using repertory grid measures of polarized construing (operationalized as the number of extreme responses on the construct scales), construct system differentiation or disorganization (using the Landfield method), constriction (defined as the number of indeterminate ratings in the grid), and self-negativity (reflecting the mean distance between self and ideal self ratings), along with conventional measures of hopelessness, problem-solving ability, and life-event stress. Four levels of subsequent suicide risk were then monitored through (a) daily ratings of suicide ideation, (b) time spent during hospitalization on 15-minute checks for staff-evaluated potential for self-injury, (c) time spent in one-on-one observation for extreme risk of suicide, and (d) actual parasuicidal behavior. As hypothesized, hopelessness in anticipating the future as assessed at intake predicted subsequent suicide ideation and both forms of suicide precautions, although not actual parasuicidal actions. Contrary to predictions, however, the constriction measure was inversely predictive of all levels of risk, suggesting that it might better be conceived as a measure of subjective uncertainty, with a shift toward greater certainty characterizing increased risk. Negative self-construing was predictive of risk at every level beyond ideation, as was impaired ability to generate alternative problem solutions. Among the most interesting findings was the emergence of a distinctive cognitive set at the highest levels of risk associated with one-on-one observation and parasuicidal acts, one marked by significant construct system disorganization and, in the case of self-injuring patients, highly polarized or dichotomous thinking. It is interesting that life-event stress played little role in predicting suicide risk at any level, suggesting the futility of relying only on objective risk factors that disregard the mind-set of the self-destructive individual.

Two further studies have examined the relationships between aspects of construing and suicidal tendencies. Investigating people who had attempted suicide, depressive people without a history of suicide attempts, and normal control participants, Dzamonja-Ignjatovic (1997) found that although there was no difference between the groups in construct system organization, there was greater difficulty in anticipating the future (as assessed by the number of midpoint ratings given in a grid to "the self in 5 years") in people characterized by depression and suicidal tendencies and of polarized construing in those who were either depressed or suicidal. In a study of people who had self-harmed, Winter et al. (2000) found that those with more severe symptoms viewed themselves and significant others more negatively and themselves as more similar to other people who self-harm; whereas those with greater hopelessness and suicidal ideation had a more constricted view of the self in the future (as in the Dzamonja-Ignjatovic [1997] study, using a measure of the number of midpoint ratings assigned to the future self).

THE EFFICACY OF PERSONAL
CONSTRUCT THERAPY FOR SUICIDE

The Winter et al. (2000) study also investigated the outcome of six-session personal construct therapy with clients presenting with deliberate self-harm, as described in greater detail subsequently. Serial assessments were conducted with clients offered hospital services following self-harm, who were allocated either to personal construct therapy or to a normal clinical practice control condition. The latter involved assessment by, and possible follow-up with, a mental health team. Participants in the intervention condition showed greater reduction in scores on the Beck Scale for Suicide Ideation, the Beck Hopelessness Scale, and the Beck Depression Inventory from pre- to posttherapy assessments than did those in the control condition. On the repertory grid, participants in the intervention condition showed a more favorable construing of their present and future selves and a greater reduction in perceived self-destructiveness and perception of being controlled than the comparison group at the second assessment. Their perceptions of the world and of themselves in the future also became less constricted, as reflected in a reduction in the number of midpoint ratings on the grid, than did those of participants in the normal practice condition. Posttreatment interviews with clients in the intervention condition indicated a high level of satisfaction with therapy.

There were no significant differences between the two conditions on the questionnaire measures at 6-month follow-up assessment, but there was considerable sample attrition at this point. At this assessment, however, participants in the intervention condition showed a greater increase in their perceived ability to make sense of their worlds and in favorable construing of their partners, now and in the future. Hospital records were also examined to trace further episodes of self-harm in the participants, finding that the differences between the two conditions were not statistically significant. As House, Owens, and Storer (1992) noted in their review of outcome research on interventions, this is not an unusual finding for clients who deliberately self-harm because no studies have shown the benefit of intervention on reducing repetition rates, even when measurable gains are made in other areas. Hawton et al. (1998) reached similar conclusions and suggested that further treatment approaches should be developed and large research trials conducted on interventions that have been shown in small trials to be of possible benefit. Personal construct therapy would appear to be one such intervention.

PERSONAL CONSTRUCT THERAPY FOR SELF-HARMING CLIENTS: THE THERAPEUTIC APPROACH

The numerous routes to self-harm suggest that if therapy is to be effective, these routes should be matched by a similar range of therapeutic options. Personal construct psychotherapy allows such an approach because it is technically eclectic, with the technique selected on the basis of a personal construct formulation of a particular client's problem.

Psychotherapy Intervention

A personal construct psychotherapy intervention for self-harm developed by Winter et al. (2000) is provided on a six-session renewable contract, commencing within a few weeks of the act of self-harm. In the first session, the meaning of this act for the client is explored by discussing its antecedents, anticipated outcomes, and the extent to which these were validated or invalidated by its actual outcomes. A principal aim of this session is to bind in words the nonverbal communication expressed in the act of self-harm. As Stefan and Linder (1985) indicated, this process of "encoding" may enable the client to view self-harm as a strategy that might be replaced by other alternatives. These authors noted that "if alternative reconstruction of the issues surrounding the suicidal act does not occur, the client may well attempt suicide again" (p. 204). In the first session, clients are also asked to consider how their significant others may have been affected by the act of self-harm and are invited to bring a significant other to the next session to explore how he or she actually construed the parasuicidal act, as well as alternative ways of achieving the anticipated outcomes of self-injury.

The third session usually commences with the presentation of a formulation of the client's difficulties, in some cases with the aid of results of a formal assessment procedure such as a repertory grid. The therapeutic strategies used in this and subsequent sessions are determined by the principal features of this formulation. For example, if the self-harm is judged to have occurred in the context of abnormally or persistently tight construing and a deterministic view of the world, techniques aimed at loosening construing are used. These may include brainstorming of alternative ways of construing and behaving, guided imagery, relaxation, discussion of dreams, the use of metaphor, free association, and the use of open-ended questions (cf. Neimeyer, 1988). If undispersed dependency appears to be a relevant issue, there is a focus on widening the network of relevant social support in response to various client needs. If the self-harm occurred in the context of chaotic and loose construing, tightening techniques are used. These include the use of formal assessment techniques; challenging inconsistencies in the client's construing; keeping diaries or self-monitoring charts; task assignments; asking clients to give summaries at the end of each session; and the use of closed questions (cf. Neimeyer, 1988). If a low degree of sociality appears to be a major component of the act, the therapeutic focus is on discussing the viewpoints of significant others, interacting with these others, and construing them in psychological terms. If self-harm appears to be the individual's way of life, attempts are made to develop an alternative core role with which self-harm is incompatible. If guilt is a major issue, therapy might focus on reconstruction of the client's sense of self. Whatever the formulation, therapy tends to include the facilitation of experimentation, especially with alternative ways of approaching situations that might in the past have led to self-harm. These individualized interventions occupy the remaining sessions.

CASE STUDY

Assessment

Sarah's attendance at a hospital accident and emergency department followed an incident in which she had put her children to bed and then taken an overdose of tranquilizers. This was not her first overdose, and, as on previous occasions, she said that she did not know why she had acted in this way. A personal construct diagnostic assessment indicated four factors that might have been relevant. A pretreatment repertory grid indicated that her construct system was very tightly organized, essentially consisting of a single dimension of construing, one concerned with self-destructiveness, that differentiated her view of herself from that of her ideal self and virtually all significant others. Moreover, her life seemed to be largely organized around drinking, with little structure apart from this. It appeared that she tended to foreshorten the CPC cycle (see the earlier section "Chaotic Self-Harm") and to act impulsively. Finally, her account of her marital relationship suggested that she and her husband, Fred, whom she saw as "nagging" her, had considerable difficulties in construing each other's view of the world.

Treatment

Following from this assessment, therapy initially included the use of loosening techniques, such as the brainstorming of various approaches to problems. An attempt was made to elaborate with her an alternative structure to her life, incorporating new leisure activities and a search for work, either paid or voluntary. This was coupled with experiments in controlling her drinking, such as having alternate days of abstinence and engaging in a detoxification program at home. Exercises were conducted in following the CPC cycle; for example, she was persuaded not to act immediately on an impulsive decision to emigrate but instead to consider the alternatives in therapy. There was also a focus on the couple's understanding of each other's construing. Although a conjoint therapy session was suggested, it was agreed to follow Sarah's preferred approach of the therapist having an individual session with Fred and, with his permission, feeding back to her details of their discussion. On being given feedback, Sarah commented that she had never known Fred to be so open, and her greater appreciation of his view of their relationship reinforced her commitment to change aspects of her behavior that were creating difficulties between them.

Toward the end of therapy, tightening techniques were used, including activity schedules, in an attempt to ensure that Sarah's construing was sufficiently well structured to enable her to cope with the world without therapy; and she was also instructed in relapse prevention strategies. The therapist found her to be very trusting of any suggestions that she made, and Sarah became quite attached to the therapist, whom she presented with a large basket of chocolates at the final session.

Posttreatment

When interviewed following therapy, Sarah said that she "found the therapist a great help, she helped me see a lot of things . . . made me very aware of things I needed to deal with, especially the drink. She was marvelous." The positive outcome of therapy was reflected in changes in her scores on several measures, presented in Table 7.1. This table also indicates that such changes were matched by those in her construing, as assessed by the repertory grid. The considerable reduction in the percentage of variance accounted for by the first component from principal component analysis of this grid indicated a loosening of her construing. There was also a reduction in the percentage of the variance accounted for by the construct *self-destructive* versus *not self-destructive*, suggesting that self-destructiveness was a less superordinate, or salient, concern for her. Distances between elements in the grid, where high distances indicate dissimilarity in construing of the two elements concerned, revealed that she came to construe herself as much more similar to her ideal self and much less like her stereotype of someone who would self-harm. She imagined that her husband came to see her as more similar to his ideal wife, and there was less idealization of how she had been prior to engaging in self-harm. Angular distances between elements and constructs indicated that she saw herself as less *self-destructive, controlled,* and *unable to make sense of anything* following therapy. The changes on some of these measures were less marked at 6-month follow-up assessment than immediately posttherapy, but on all measures there was still a considerable difference from her pretherapy position. In the 2 years following completion of therapy, Sarah had no further reported attempts at self-harm, although there have been subsequent overdoses. Perhaps the fairest assessment of her treatment experience, then, would be that this brief, six-session intervention produced a broad and relatively durable change in her construing of self and others, one that mitigated her self-injurious lifestyle for nearly 3 years. However, "booster" sessions or longer term treatment might have been indicated in her case to reduce the risk of subsequent relapse.

Summary and Conclusion

As one of the original wellsprings of cognitive psychotherapy, personal construct theory is characterized by a remarkably comprehensive theory of personality in which the meaning-making attempts of human beings are placed

TABLE 7.1
Changes in Sarah's Questionnaire and
Repertory Grid Scores Following Therapy

	Pretreatment	Posttreatment	Follow-up
Beck Depression Inventory	25	11	17
Beck Hopelessness Scale	7	2	3
Beck Scale for Suicide Ideation	3	1	0
Repertory grid:			
	% variances		
Component 1	90.19	68.02	69.08
Self-destructiveness	8.33	6.54	3.63
	Element distances		
Self—ideal self	1.46	0.57	0.73
Self—someone who would self-harm	0.56	1.54	1.72
Husband's view of her—his ideal wife	1.63	0.67	1.03
Self before self-harm—ideal self	0.00	1.13	1.07
	Element–construct pole distances		
Self—"self-destructive"	15.7	140.4	75.6
Self—"controlled"	24.1	145.9	117.3
Self—"can't make sense of anything"	24.1	141.1	84.4

on center stage. As applied to the specific problem of suicide, this perspective suggests that even self-destruction can be viewed as a meaningful act, one chosen to validate a core sense of self, to ward off potentially devastating invalidation in the face of an apparently deterministic future, or to abdicate a life that has become unpredictable and overwhelming. Likewise, less lethal forms of self-harm can be undertaken to secure their anticipated personal or interpersonal outcomes, in some cases becoming so thoroughly integrated into the person's self-construing that they become a way of life.

As we have emphasized throughout this chapter, this multidimensional conceptualization of self-destructive behavior implies a similarly multidimensional approach to case conceptualization and treatment. For example, although general cognitive processes such as hopelessness are indeed associated with enhanced risk of self-injury, personal construct research suggests that a number of other specific cognitive features such as ambiguity concerning the present and future self, constriction, disorganization of systems of personal meaning, and polarized or dichotomous thinking should be added to the list of predictors of higher levels of suicide risk. Accordingly, the use of distinctive assessment procedures such as repertory grid technique could prove clinically useful not only in identifying unique constellations of risk factors in a given case, but also in providing a relevant focus for treatment. Likewise, investigating the personal and interpersonal significance of a threatened or completed act of self-injury could prove clarifying to both client and therapist, and suggest which of several cognitive–behavioral or personal construct procedures (e.g., problem solving, thought records, loosening or tightening procedures, promoting sociality with critical others) are of greatest importance in treatment.

Similarly, we believe that the promising personal construct research reviewed here deserves replication and extension by other investigators. In particular, more work is needed to validate a multidimensional model of suicidal cognition, one that links structural vulnerabilities in the meaning systems of individuals (e.g., constriction, polarization, disorganization) with the cognitive processes to which they give rise or that, perhaps recursively, produce them (e.g., hopelessness, impaired problem solving, difficulties in taking the role of the other). Additional longitudinal designs that trace shifts in these cognitive structures or processes with increasing risk as well as over the course of successful therapy deserve high priority. We are encouraged by the empirical support that is accumulating for cognitive models of the suicidal choice and are optimistic that construct theory might make a distinctive contribution to the conceptualization, assessment, and treatment of the psychosocial circumstances that provide an instigating context for self-destructive behavior.

REFERENCES

Aldridge, D. (1998). *Suicide: The tragedy of hopelessness*. London: Jessica Kingsley.

Baker, K. D., Barris, B. P., & Neimeyer, R. A. (1998). Cognitive organization in sociotropic and autonomous inpatient depressives. *Journal of Cognitive Psychotherapy, 11*, 279–297.

Beck, A., Epstein, N., & Harrison, R. (1983). Cognitions, attitudes and personality dimensions in depression. *British Journal of Cognitive Psychotherapy, 1*, 1–16.

Beck, A., Rush, J., Shaw, B., & Emery, G. (1979). *Cognitive therapy of depression*. New York: Guilford Press.

Borger, J. (2002, April 16). Chilling, defiant: The video suicide message of a September 11 killer. *The Guardian*, p. 3.

Dzamonja-Ignjatovic, T. (1997). Suicide and depression from the personal construct perspective. In P. Denicolo & M. Pope (Eds.), *Sharing understanding and practice* (pp. 222–234). Farnborough, England: EPCA Publications.

Ellis, T. E. (2004). Thoughts of Katie: A cognitive perspective. In D. Lester (Ed.), *Katie's diary: Unlocking the mystery of a suicide* (pp. 81–96). New York: Brunner Routledge.

Feixas, G. (1992). Personal construct approaches to family therapy. In R. A. Neimeyer & G. J. Neimeyer (Eds.), *Advances in personal construct psychology* (Vol. 2, pp. 217–255). Greenwich, CT: JAI Press.

Fransella, F. (Ed.). (2003). *International handbook of personal construct psychology.* Chichester, England: Wiley.

Fransella, F., Bell, R., & Bannister, D. (2003). A *manual for repertory grid technique* (2nd ed.). Chichester, England: Wiley.

Hawton, K., Arensman, E., Townsend, E., Bremner, S., Feldman, E., Goldney, R., et al. (1998). Deliberate self harm: A systematic review of efficacy of psychosocial and pharmacological treatments in preventing repetition. *British Medical Journal, 3171,* 441–447.

Hermans, H. (2002). The person as a motivated storyteller. In R. A. Neimeyer & G. J. Neimeyer (Eds.), *Advances in personal construct psychology* (pp. 3–38). Westport, CT: Praeger.

Hirschman, J. (Ed.). (1965). *Antonin Artaud anthology.* San Francisco: City Lights.

House, A., Owens, D., & Storer, D. (1992). Psycho-social intervention following attempted suicide: Is there a case for better services? *International Review of Psychiatry, 4,* 15–22.

Hughes, S., & Neimeyer, R. A. (1990). A cognitive model of suicidal behavior. In D. Lester (Ed.), *Understanding suicide.* New York: Charles Press.

Hughes, S. L., & Neimeyer, R. A. (1993). Cognitive predictors of suicide risk among hospitalized psychiatric patients: A prospective study. *Death Studies, 17,* 103–124.

Hughes, T. (1998). *Birthday letters.* London: Faber & Faber.

Kelly, G. A. (1955). *The psychology of personal constructs.* New York: Norton.

Kelly, G. A. (1961). Theory and therapy in suicide: the personal construct point of view. In M. Farberow & E. Shneidman (Eds.), *The cry for help* (pp. 255–280). New York: McGraw-Hill.

Kukil, K. (Ed.). (2000). *The journals of Sylvia Plath 1950–1962.* London: Faber & Faber.

Landfield, A. (1976). A personal construct approach to suicidal behavior. In P. Slater (Ed.), *Explorations of intrapersonal space* (pp. 93–107). London: Wiley.

Leitner, L. (1995). Optimal therapeutic distance. In R. Neimeyer & M. J. Mahoney (Eds.), *Constructivism in psychotherapy* (pp. 357–369). Washington, DC: American Psychological Association.

Lester, D. (1993). How do people perceive the different methods for suicide? *Death Studies, 17,* 179–184.

Mair, J. M. M. (1977). The community of self. In D. Bannister (Ed.), *New perspectives in personal construct theory* (pp. 125–149). London: Academic Press.

Neimeyer, R. A. (1984). Toward a personal construct conceptualization of depression and suicide. In F. R. Epting & R. A. Neimeyer (Eds.), *Personal meanings of death* (pp. 41–88). New York: Hemisphere.

Neimeyer, R. A. (1987). An orientation to personal construct therapy. In R. A. Neimeyer & G. J. Neimeyer (Eds.), *Personal construct therapy casebook* (pp. 3–19). New York: Springer.

Neimeyer, R. A. (1988). Integrative directions in personal construct therapy. *International Journal of Personal Construct Psychology, 1,* 288–297.

Neimeyer, R. A. (1993). Constructivist approaches to the measurement of meaning. In G. J. Neimeyer (Ed.), *Constructivist assessment* (pp. 58–103). Newbury Park, CA: Sage.

Neimeyer, R. A. (2000). Narrative disruptions in the construction of self. In R. A. Neimeyer & J. Raskin (Eds.), *Constructions of disorder* (pp. 207–242). Washington, DC: American Psychological Association.

Neimeyer, R. A. (in press). Re-storying loss: Fostering growth in the posttraumatic narrative. In L. Calhoun & R. Tedeschi (Eds.), *Handbook of posttraumatic growth: Research and practice.* Mahwah, NJ: Erlbaum.

Neimeyer, R. A., Botella, L., Herrero, O., Figueras, S., Pacheco, M., & Werner-Wildner, L. A. (2002). The meaning of your absence. In J. Kauffman (Ed.), *Loss of the assumptive world* (pp. 31–47). New York: Brunner Routledge.

Neimeyer, R. A., Brooks, D. L., & Baker, K. D. (1995). Personal epistemologies and personal relationships. In B. Walker & D. Kalekin-Fishman (Eds.), *The construction of group realities* (pp. 127–159). Malabar, FL: Krieger.

Neimeyer, R. A., & Feixas, G. (1992). Cognitive assessment in depression. *European Journal of Psychological Assessment, 8*, pp. 47–56.

Parker, A. (1981). The meaning of attempted suicide to young parasuicides. *British Journal of Psychiatry, 139*, 306–312.

Plath, S. (1971). *The bell jar.* New York: Harper & Row.

Plath, S. (1981). *The collected poems.* London: Faber.

Popper, K. (1963). *Conjectures and refutations.* London: Routledge.

Sewell, K. (2003). An approach to post-traumatic stress. In F. Fransella (Ed.), *International handbook of personal construct psychology* (pp. 223–232). Chichester, England: Wiley.

Shneidman, E. S. (1996). *The suicidal mind.* Oxford, England: Oxford University Press.

Stefan, C., & Linder, H. B. (1985). Suicide, an experience of chaos or of fatalism: Perspectives from personal construct theory. In D. Bannister (Ed.), *Issues and approaches in personal construct theory* (pp. 183–209). London: Academic Press.

Stefan, C., & Von, J. (1985). Suicide. In E. Button (Ed.), *Personal construct theory and mental health* (pp. 132–152). London: Croom Helm.

Stevenson, K. (1998). *Bitter fame: A life of Sylvia Plath.* London: Penguin.

Walker, B. (1997). Shaking the kaleidoscope: Dispersion of dependency and its relationships. In. G. J. Neimeyer & R. A. Neimeyer (Eds.), *Advances in personal construct psychology* (Vol. 4, pp. 63–10). Greenwich, CT: JAI.

Winter, D. (1992). *Personal construct psychology in clinical practice.* London: Routledge.

Winter, D., Bhandari, S., Metcalfe, C., Riley, T., Sireling, L., Watson, S., et al. (2000). Deliberate and undeliberated self-harm. In J. W. Scheer (Ed.), *The person in society* (pp. 351–360). Giessen, Germany: Psychosozial-Verlag.

III

COGNITIVE ASPECTS
OF SUICIDALITY

8

THE ROLE OF OVERGENERAL MEMORY IN SUICIDALITY

J. MARK G. WILLIAMS, THORSTEN BARNHOFER,
CATHERINE CRANE, AND DANIELLE S. DUGGAN

It seems so obvious that it is easily missed. When individuals have deliberately harmed themselves, then are asked what were their reasons for doing so, the answers they give often overlap or are inconsistent, reflecting the complexity of motivation: "I wanted to die," "to escape for a while," "to show that I loved someone." Rarely does anyone have a single professed reason. Yet most common of all is: "The situation was so unbearable, I had to do something, and didn't know what else to do" (Williams, 1986). In a sense, this does not give a reason at all, yet it gets to the heart of the issue by naming three elements of which they are aware: the unbearability and unendurability of the current state of affairs (in their external and internal world), the sense of compulsion to act (a compulsion that may have built up slowly or rapidly), and the sense of there being no other option at that time.

In this statement is therefore contained much of the research agenda for psychological understandings of suicidality: How do people come to view their circumstances as unendurable? What underlies such a strong compulsion to escape? It is the third, the sense of having no options, that concerns

The preparation of this chapter was supported by the Wellcome Trust.

us in this chapter, however. To understand this, we need to look at what processes normally underlie a person's ability to navigate through everyday life fluently, to meet hassles and catastrophes effectively. We will look at memory; in particular, autobiographical memory. Autobiographical memory is the aspect of episodic memory that constitutes a person's life history, without which we would not be able to remember prior experiences or learn from them.

Collectively, autobiographical memories form a database that we refer to when we try to make judgments about ourselves, our abilities, our experiences, our relationships, and our achievements. As a reflection of our personal history, these memories are strongly related to our sense of self, and it is because of this that their recollection is often accompanied by strong emotions. Autobiographical memory is not static. The retrieval of autobiographical memories is a constructive process (Conway & Pleydell-Pearce, 2000). Here is something really important: The process may itself be subject to disturbances, and these disturbances are likely to have maladaptive effects on other cognitive functions. *It is not just whether we remember an event but the way we remember it that plays a role in how we deal with current challenges or how we make future plans.* Processes underlying deficits in autobiographical memory may therefore be implicated in a wide range of adaptive functions, and it is because of this that they may critically affect the likelihood that life crises will become suicidal crises.

The goal of this chapter is to describe how a particular deficit in autobiographical memory, that is, a deficit in its *specificity*, may be implicated in occurrence and escalation of suicidal crises. We present findings in suicidal patients as well as other groups of patients to explore the processes that underlie these memory deficits. We then look at how these processes may relate to psychological mechanisms leading to suicidal behavior. First, we introduce the phenomenon of overgeneral memory. Second, we address the issue of etiology. Third, we consider what cognitive mechanisms underlie the phenomenon and how they may stabilize into a trait feature of some individuals. Fourth, we outline the evidence for the consequences of this memory deficit. Finally, we draw out the clinical implications.

THE SPECIFICITY OF AUTOBIOGRAPHICAL MEMORY

Research considering autobiographical memory in suicidal patients began by investigating mood-congruent memory—whether patients who had recently taken an overdose had the same sort of biased memory as had been found in depressed patients. Patients who had recently taken an overdose were compared with nonpsychiatric hospital control participants and community control participants on a task, in which they were given positive (e.g., happy, safe, interested) or negative (e.g., angry, hurt, clumsy) cue words and asked to respond by giving a specific memory. Although a mood-congruency bias was found, the study also had a serendipitous finding (Williams & Broadbent, 1986). Unexpectedly, the task proved to be difficult for the parasuicidal patients in a particular way. Instead of producing a specific memory, they responded, on about half of the occasions, with a categoric memory, a memory that summarized a number of similar events (e.g., "when I used to walk the dog every morning").

An obvious explanation would have been that this finding was simply due to differences in general mental speed. Whereas both hospital groups were relatively slow on a semantic processing task (Baddeley, Emslie, & Nimmo-Smith, 1992), however, only the suicidal group showed the overgeneral memory (Williams & Broadbent, 1986). Furthermore, research found that overgeneral retrieval occurs across various types of memory cue, including activity cues (Williams, 1988) and is still apparent even when suicidal participants are given further explanation, practice items, and prompts to clarify their answers.

Subsequent research replicating these results has established that overgeneral memory is a reliable feature of cognition in suicidal patients (Pollock & Williams, 2001; Williams et al., 1996) and is also characteristic of depression (Kuyken & Brewin, 1995; Kuyken & Dalgleish, 1995; Moore, Watts, & Williams, 1988; Puffet, Jehin-Marchot, Timsit-Berthier, & Timsit, 1991). Overgenerality is not apparent in all emotional disorders, however, (e.g., generalized anxiety disorder: Burke & Mathews, 1992) and when present in anxiety disorders (other than posttraumatic stress disorder [PTSD]) appears to be accounted for by comorbid depression (Wessel, Meeren, Peeters, Arntz, & Merckelbach, 2001; Wilhelm, McNally, Baer, & Florin, 1997).

Although these results might lead one to suggest that high levels of depression might account for the occurrence of overgenerality in suicidal patients, the association between overgenerality and depression seems to be complex. A large number of studies have shown that level of overgenerality, unlike other memory deficits and biases associated with depression, does not correlate with severity of mood disturbance. Lack of correlation has been reported within groups of suicidal patients (e.g. Williams & Broadbent, 1986; Williams et al., 1996) as well as depressed patients (e.g. Kuyken & Brewin, 1995; Peeters, Wessel, Merckelbach, & Boon-Vermeeren, 2003). Although exceptions have been reported in studies with adolescents, in whom Swales, Williams, and Wood (2001) found a positive and Orbach, Lamb, Sternberg, Williams, and Dawud-Noursi (2001) a negative relation between severity of depressive symptoms and specificity, other studies with adolescents confirm that severity of depressed mood need not be associated with overgenerality of memory (de Decker, Hermans, Raes, & Eelen, 2003).

Even stronger support for the assumption that overgenerality is not dependent on current mood comes from studies that have examined suicidal and depressed patients following recovery. Williams and Dritschel (1988) showed that overgenerality remains in recovered suicidal patients. Brittlebank, Scott, Williams, and Ferrier (1993) and Peeters et al. (2003) found similar results in depressed patients followed-up over 7 months to recovery. Mackinger, Pachinger, Leibetseder, and Fartacek (2000) compared nondepressed women with and without a history of major depression and found formerly depressed women to retrieve less specific memories. If, as these findings would suggest, overgenerality is not related to current mood state, a question arises: Which factors are implicated in its development? Research suggests that one factor may be critically important: the experience of severe trauma.

OVERGENERAL MEMORY AND TRAUMA

Indications that overgeneral memory might be related to trauma first came from studies showing overgenerality in patients experiencing PTSD. McNally and coworkers reported overgenerality in traumatized Vietnam veterans with PTSD (McNally, Lasko, Macklin, & Pitman, 1995; McNally, Litz, Prassas, Shin, & Weathers, 1994). This study, however, used a matched control group that had suffered comparable trauma but had not developed PTSD. It therefore seems possible that rather than being caused by the trauma itself, overgeneral memory is related to how the trauma is (or is not) processed. This would be consistent with a study by Kuyken and Brewin (1995) comparing groups of depressed women with and without a history of childhood abuse. Although those women with a history of sexual abuse were significantly more overgeneral, the effect of abuse on memory was largely mediated by the intrusions and avoidance of the trauma-related material (as rated on the Impact of Event Scale; see also Brewin, Reynolds, & Tata, 1999). Other studies have not confirmed a link between overgeneral memory following trauma and the presence of intrusions and avoidance of the trauma, however (see, e.g., Henderson, Hargreaves, Gregory, & Williams, 2002; Hermans et al., 2004), so that the mechanism by which trauma affects later memory remains open.

Despite this uncertainty about mechanisms, many studies have confirmed the links between trauma (especially that which occurs during childhood) and later problems in being specific in recalling autobiographical events. This occurs even when a person is attempting to retrieve neutral or positive events (Dalgleish et al., 2003; de Decker et al., 2003; Henderson et al., 2002; Meesters, Merckelbach, Muris, & Wessel, 2000). The only deviations from this pattern of results are Wessel et al. (2001), which differed because of the overall low rates of childhood trauma in their sample, and Orbach et al. (2001), which assessed children who were victims or witnesses (or both) of family violence and found that overgeneral memory was related to level of depression rather than to whether the child had witnessed violence.

Why is this important? Because although we know that childhood trauma constitutes a significant risk factor for later suicidal behavior (for overviews on this subject, see Bagley, 1991; Kendall-Tackett, Williams, & Finkelhor, 2003), we do not know by what means this past adversity turns into current vulnerability. Recent research (Yang & Clum, 2000) suggests that this risk is conferred by detrimental effects of early trauma on cognitive functioning, especially problem-solving ability. As we elaborate later, overgeneral memory appears to be critically implicated in problem-solving deficits and lack of future specificity. Thus, for a subgroup of individuals, an overgeneral retrieval style acquired early on as a result of traumatic experiences may serve as a factor mediating risk for later suicidal behavior. It must be stressed, however, that not all individuals who develop an overgeneral retrieval style have experienced trauma and not all people who experience trauma end up with overgeneral retrieval. To understand how overgeneral memory might mediate risk for suicidal behavior in individuals with and without a history of trauma, we first look at processes underlying overgeneral retrieval and its maintenance as a habitual cognitive style.

MECHANISMS UNDERLYING OVERGENERALITY IN AUTOBIOGRAPHICAL MEMORY

The phenomenon of overgeneral retrieval has been explained within "descriptions theory" (Norman & Bobrow, 1979). According to this theory, the retrieval of an autobiographical memory is an iterative process "in which some information about the target item is used to construct a description of the item and this description is used in attempts to recover new fragments of information" (Williams & Hollan, 1981). Initially, a partial description derived from the memory cue is thought to provide an entry point into the memory with the "general description" acting as an index for the memory search. The iterative process is cycled through until the discrepancy between the retrieved descriptions and the verification criterion is minimized and the memory record could then be output.

Using this model of memory retrieval as a framework, early accounts (Williams & Dritschel, 1988) depicted overgeneral memory as resulting from premature truncation of the iterative search process. An underlying assumption of this explanation is that memories are stored in a hierarchy from general to specific events. It is important that individuals have some strategic control over how much of the memory hierarchy is searched to meet the requirements of the situations in which they find themselves. At times, all of us need to be generic in the information we retrieve (e.g., "how long does it normally take for me to get to the train station?"). On other occasions, we may need to retrieve specific exceptions to the general information (e.g., "I heard on the news there was a traffic delay on my usual route"). Effective problem solving means being able to bring together both general information and specific updates and form them into a coherent "subjective experience" long enough for the information that is relevant to the current task to be extracted. Williams and Dritschel (1992) suggested that suicidal patients are able to access the general information, the "intermediate descriptions" but get stuck at this level, stopping short of retrieving a specific example. It is this truncated search that is responsible for overgeneral memory responses.

Affective Gating

The *descriptions framework* has provided a useful approach for modeling the main processes underlying overgeneral retrieval, but theoretically and empirically based refinements to general models of autobiographical memory have offered important additional implications for understanding overgenerality. Among these is the conceptual distinction among various modes of retrieval. In their theory of autobiographical memory, Conway and Pleydell-Pearce (2000) differentiated between (a) generative retrieval, which involves the intentional, staged search referred to in descriptions theory, and (b) direct retrieval, a "bottom-up" process in which event-specific knowledge is directly activated by a cue and in which the spreading of the activation alone establishes a stable representation, experienced as a spontaneous memory. In generative retrieval, both verbal–analytical and sensory–perceptual processing codes are used (see similar suggestions by Burgess & Shallice, 1996), but during early stages of retrieval, more semantic code is involved whereas more sensory–perceptual code is used later in the process. This concurrence of verbal–analytic (top-down) retrieval processes and sensory–perceptual (bottom-up) reminding processes necessitates central coordination—a function we assume to be critical in the regulation of affect, especially for those who have undergone traumatic episodes in their past. We suggest that an overgeneral retrieval style could sometimes be the result of increased allocation of resources to the operation of such a coordinating mechanism or "gateway," to reduce the impact of potentially emotional material. One of the main purposes of this "affective gating" would be the regulation of emotions. In individuals with a history of traumatic childhood experiences, affective gating may initially prevent retrieval of specific memories and hence control the experience of negative affect associated with these.

Of great importance regarding the hypothesized role of this affect gating mechanism would be studies showing evidence of beneficial short-term effects of overgenerality on the experience of negative emotions. Until recently, there was no independent evidence for this. At a minimum, an affective gating theory requires that, at some point, a person who tends to retrieve memories more specifically would risk experiencing greater affective disturbance. Otherwise, there would be no negative reinforcement for overgeneral retrieval. Raes, Hermans, de Decker, Eelen, and Williams (2003) showed just such evidence. They found that individuals with a specific retrieval style had greater degrees of mood disturbance following a frustrating failure to solve a puzzle task than individuals with an overgeneral retrieval style.

An affective gating theory must also take account of the fact that, for some people, this method of affect regulation will not work. This may be the case in people who are hypersensitive to stressors or in situations when a trauma has been extremely intense, so that a cognitive gating mechanism fails. The result of such a failure in gating would be a combination of apparently "normal" memory but unstable affect. Research shows that such a pattern seems to be characteristic of some patients with a diagnosis of borderline personality disorder (Arntz, Meeren, & Wessel, 2002). Because of unstable affect, these patients often adopt alternative affect regulation strategies such as repeated self-harm or alcohol or drug use. Retrieval of specific autobiographical memories may have an indirect influence on these outcomes by destabilizing affect.

What are the implications of these proposed mechanisms for our understanding of suicidal behavior, and indeed for the association between suicidal behavior and overgenerality of autobiographical memory? One possibility is that there may exist different general pathways to suicidal behavior: one pathway being more driven by hopelessness and the other more strongly related to failures in affect-regulation. Although in hopelessness-driven suicidal behavior, a sense of entrapment would escalate to suicidality through repeated failures in solving problems and resulting hopelessness, affect-driven suicidal behavior may result from a fundamental failure of affect regulation and the intrusion of distressing memories, leading to a buildup of emotional tension that eventually results in use of self-harming behavior as a (maladaptive) coping strategy.

It is suggested that overgeneral memory has a different role to play in each case. In hopelessness-driven suicide, as we describe later in more detail, it is suggested that overgeneral memory contributes to the increased risk of a suicidal crisis by impairing problem solving and detailed future thinking, thus locking individuals in a state of helplessness. In this case, overgeneral memory functions to reduce emotional distress by avoiding specific recollections and experiential awareness of emotional events at the cost of impairments in adaptive cognitive processes, which profit from input of specific memories. In contrast, it is suggested that in individuals at risk for affect-regulation suicidal behavior, for example, patients with borderline personality disorder, the presence of specific memories may indicate a dysfunctional affective gating mechanism—direct retrievals (remindings) are dominating the picture. In these patients, the aversive effects of such specific and involuntary "remindings" outweigh the benefits or preclude the use of these memories in adaptive cognitive processes. Given the background of fundamental deficits in emotion regulation and the high prevalence of traumatic experiences seen in these patients, the presence of intrusive and distressing specific memories and their aversive effects may lead to immediate escalation of emotional symptoms. Paradoxically, in these patients, adoption of an overgeneral retrieval style might have adaptive effects, preventing emotional reactivity to autobiographical memories from leading to a buildup of tension (Startup et al., 2001). How can we tell when memory is serving the interests of our patients? We suggest that the important factor is whether a person has strategic control over the level of memory specificity. All people need access to both general and specific memory representation for smooth and skillful problem solving, but the important factor is the flexible use of and navigation through the entire memory hierarchy. Getting stuck either in overspecific memories or overgeneral memory is maladaptive.

Practically, the existence of different mechanisms would have important consequences for further research investigating relations between specificity of autobiographical memory and deliberate self-harm. Because the two pathways suggest diametrically opposed effects of overgenerality, studies not differentiating groups prone to different mechanisms, especially patients with hopelessness depression and borderline personality disorder, may be in danger of producing inconsistent results (see, e.g., Sidley, Calam, Wells, Hughes, & Whitaker, 1999).

Stabilization of an Overgeneral Retrieval Style

Once an overgeneral retrieval style has been adopted, it may be subject to influence from a range of factors. Most such factors exert their influence via reduction of processing capacities (e.g., renewed attempts to suppress traumatic memories may increase the utilization of processing resources by affect gating mechanisms). There are also findings, however, that strongly suggest the general style or mode of cognitive processing adopted by the individual may promote tendencies for overgeneral retrieval. In a small series of experiments, Watkins and Teasdale (Watkins & Teasdale, 2001; Watkins, Teasdale, & Williams, 2000) were able to show that adoption of a ruminative thinking style, especially in the form of abstract–analytical thinking, leads to maintenance of overgenerality. In their experiments, induction of a ruminative mode led participants with depression or dysthymia to retain an overgeneral retrieval style, whereas a distractive mode, induced by a focusing on detailed imagery, caused decreases in overgenerality. These findings suggest that in individuals prone to ruminative thinking, overgeneral retrieval may not so much be a consequence of affective gating but may be more closely related to the adoption of a processing style that encourages a general and abstract–thematic level of processing at the expense of sensory–perceptual processing.

Although these findings suggest that ruminative thinking may have a causal influence on overgeneral memory, it has also been argued that overgeneral memory may have a central role in the adoption and maintenance of a ruminative response style. How might this occur? Williams (1996) suggested that initial failure to access a specific event memory may result in further iterations of the memory search. If these searches also lead to the retrieval of general events and if this truncated search process occurs repeatedly, an elaboration and strengthening of associative connections between event categories will result. Thus, in future attempts at retrieval when an initial cue activates a general event description, this description will be more likely simply to activate other general event descriptions. Through this process (which Williams [1996] termed *mnemonic interlock*) overgeneral retrieval may actually encourage (and be encouraged by) ruminative self-focus.

Preliminary empirical support for the concept of mnemonic interlock has come from a study by Barnhofer, de Jong-Meyer, Kleinpass, and Nikesch (2002), in which depressed and control participants were given a think-aloud modification of the Autobiographical Memory Task (AMT) in which they were asked to verbalize all thoughts that came to mind during retrieval and holding of a specific event over a 2-minute period. Results showed that following an initial categoric memory, patients with depression tended to produce sequences of consecutive categoric memories referring to various events. Overgeneral memory thus may not only be encouraged by adoption of ruminative thinking but may be more inherently related to processes that encourage this thinking style.

With what result? Following stabilization of overgeneral memory, a network of general event descriptions exists. The retrieval of specific events in response to cues becomes increasingly difficult as the strong associations formed between categoric memories encourage horizontal spread of activation at the general event description level, rather than the vertical spread of activation from general event descriptions to specific memories. That is, people will tend to be "caught" in the tendency to retrieve overgeneral memories. By encouraging rumination and preventing output of specific memories necessary for other adaptive cognitive functions, these processes are likely to contribute to persistence of symptoms and—as we show—may under certain conditions be centrally implicated in the escalation of hopelessness and depression to suicidal crises.

THE CONSEQUENCES OF OVERGENERAL MEMORY RETRIEVAL

Research has found that overgeneral memory has a number of important consequences. First, it makes an episode of emotional disturbance more persistent. Second, it impairs interpersonal problem-solving ability. Third, it reduces a person's ability to imagine the future in a specific way. We consider each in turn, before considering how they may combine to make general hopelessness escalate into suicidal behavior (the "cry of pain," discussed subsequently).

Overgeneral Memory and Prolongation of Affective Disturbance

In the preceding sections, we have suggested that memory overgenerality may play an important role in the suicidal behavior of individuals who are depressed and hopeless about the future. Findings from a number of prospective studies suggest that one of the maladaptive effects of overgeneral memory is to delay recovery from affective disturbance and hence to prolong the period at which an individual is at high risk of self-harm arising from hopelessness. Brittlebank et al. (1993) measured specificity of autobiographical memory in a group of patients with depression and found that it significantly predicted outcome of the sample as assessed by the Hamilton Depression Rating Scale over a 7-month follow-up period. A later research study by Brewin et al. (1999) using the Beck Depression Inventory did not replicate this finding. However, a recent replication by Peeters et al. (2003) supported the original results from the Brittlebank et al. (1993) study, and additional studies have identified associations between overgenerality and prolongation of affective disturbance in a variety of psychiatric and somatic conditions (Dalgleish, Spinks, Yiend, & Kuyken, 2001; Harvey, Bryant, & Dang, 1998; Mackinger et al., 2004; Mackinger & Leitich, 2002; Mackinger, Loschin, & Leibetseder, 2000; Svaldi & Mackinger, 2003).

How could these effects be explained? As described earlier, affective disturbance may be maintained by the same ruminative processes implicated in the maintenance of an overgeneral retrieval style. Maintenance of affective disturbance may also arise more directly, however, as a consequence of disturbances or deficits in adaptive cognitive functions that rely on memory and related processes. One such function that is also of central importance in suicidality is problem solving.

Overgeneral Memory and Problem Solving

Empirical studies have consistently shown problem-solving deficits in suicidal patients (e.g., Linehan, Camper, Chiles, Strosahl, & Shearin, 1987; Orbach, Bar-Joseph, & Dror, 1990). These deficits are said to be particularly detrimental when they occur in the context of interpersonal problem solving. Marx, Williams, and Claridge (1992) suggested that because interpersonal problem solving is open-ended, specificity of autobiographical memory is of particular relevance for this task. The retrieval of specific memories provides more detailed accounts of prior relevant experiences and richer contextualized cues to guide the generation of possible problem solutions.

One of the earliest studies to examine this issue (Evans, Williams, O'Loughlin, & Howells, 1992) used the Means–End Problem Solving procedure (MEPS) by Platt and Spivack (1975), in which participants are asked to provide solutions to connect the beginning and end of interpersonal problem situations, and the Autobiographical Memory Task (AMT) to compare problem solving and autobiographical memory specificity in suicidal patients and hospital control participants. Results not only replicated previous studies, showing impaired interpersonal problem solving and retrieval of fewer specific memories in the suicidal group, but, more important, they showed a significant relationship between individuals' problem-solving effectiveness and their ability to call to mind specific memories, both in suicidal patients and in the sample as a whole. This finding has since been replicated in two other studies in suicidal patients, both in first-time attempters (Pollock & Williams, 2001) and in a larger sample of suicidal individuals with more enduring and severe mental health problems, including high numbers of multiple attempters (Sidley, Whitaker, Calam, & Wells, 1997). Parallel findings in acutely depressed patients (e.g. Goddard, Dritschel, & Burton, 1996, 1997) and the positive relationships found in the control groups used in the studies cited here speak to the general validity of the association between memory specificity and problem-solving performance.

The causal role of autobiographical memory specificity in determining interpersonal problem-solving ability has been supported by a recent experimental study. Williams et al. (in press, Study 4) induced general or specific retrieval by experimentally manipulating the level of overgenerality in memory and then measuring problem solving using the MEPS after each block of high- or low-specificity retrieval. Results showed that, as expected, individuals were less effective in problem solving following induction of generality and more effective following induction of specificity. With regard to the findings in clinical groups, this result suggests that the correlation found between specificity of autobiographical memory and interpersonal problem solving cannot be solely attributed to the effect of third variables such as a general lack of effort in cognitive tasks.

Overgeneral retrieval of autobiographical memories may play a central role in suicidal behavior by hindering successful problem solving and hence locking patients in a state of despair. First, a stable overgeneral retrieval style may act as an important diathesis, and, second, factors such as stressful life events may cause dynamic increases in overgenerality, possibly through increased rumination. Thus, in crisis situations, successful solutions to problems may become increasingly difficult to achieve and stress is likely to persist. Repeated failures lead the individual to believe that he or she has run out of coping options and will be unable to achieve desired goals. An important factor in determining further escalation is whether this belief is also projected into the future, causing the individual to develop a sense of hopelessness.

Autobiographical Memory and Future Thinking

Although deficits in autobiographical memory would not be expected to be directly related to hopelessness, they do play a role in future thinking in that they are related to the detail in which people are able to construct or imagine future events or plans. Empirical support for the association between specificity of autobiographical memories and future events comes from a series of empirical studies by Williams et al. (1996). In the first of these studies, suicidal patients and control participants were given cue words and asked to generate both specific autobiographical memories and specific future events. Suicidal patients produced less specific memories as well as less specific future scenarios, and specificity of both types of events was significantly correlated. Two further studies aimed to delineate the causal relation between these abilities by experimentally manipulating memory retrieval style. Retrieval was manipulated by instructing participants to use the cue words to retrieve either specific or categoric events (Study 2) or by giving participants either high or low imageable cues (Study 3) to induce specific or categoric retrieval styles. In the test phase of both experiments, participants were asked to produce events that might happen in the future. As predicted, participants who had been induced to be categoric in the memory retrieval phase tended to produce general events, whereas participants who had been induced to be specific came up with specific events, showing a causal influence of memory retrieval on specificity of future thinking.

Failure to generate *specific* future scenarios is likely to have an impact on the formation and implementation of future plans. Self-management theories, for example, have generally acknowledged that behavior change requires specific strategies for implementation to go beyond general intentions for change (see, e.g., Azjen's theory of reasoned action). A striking illustration of this is given by a study carried out by Hutchings and colleagues (Hutchings, Nash, Williams, & Nightingale, 1998). They were interested in how overgenerality in the memory of mothers whose children had been referred to a child guidance clinic affected the outcome for the child as he or she went through the treatment. In this study, 10 of the 26 mothers who participated did not attend even the first treatment session. It is interesting that these mothers had been significantly more overgeneral during initial testing than the mothers who started to attend treatment.

We suggest that lack of future specificity is likely to have detrimental effects on planning for the future and to discourage the realization of future plans. In suicidal crises, this may contribute to the maladaptive processes that lock individuals into their current state of despair. The association among overgeneral memory and the maintenance of depressive symptoms, impairments in problem solving, and vagueness in future-thinking suggest that overgenerality is at the basis of several processes contributing to situations in which the danger of suicidal behavior accumulates. How do these processes relate to general models of suicidal behavior?

THE CRY OF PAIN MODEL OF SUICIDE

Williams (1997, 2001) has suggested that suicidal behavior may be explained as a "cry of pain." Drawing on biological and cognitive perspec-

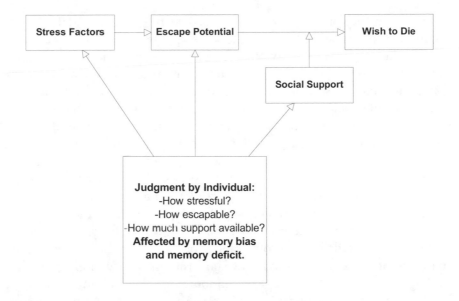

Figure 8.1. At important points in the causal pathway to suicidal behavior, a judgment by the individual allows scope for bias in estimates of the aversiveness of stress, its controllability, and how much social support is available. The judgment of escapability and available social support is affected by overgenerality in memory.

tives, this model describes suicidal behavior as a reaction to a situation in which the individual feels trapped and without any apparent opportunity for escape or rescue. Critical triggering situations include those in which individuals feel they have suffered a defeat central to their life, either as the result of external events such as the loss of relationships or loss of status or as the result of being unable to control inner turmoil. Animal models show that if animals are placed in situations in which they are both defeated and unable to escape (a situation described by Gilbert [1989] as "arrested flight"), they will show marked depressive behavior and may eventually die. In contrast, if escape is possible, defeat itself has few detrimental effects (Figure 8.1).

The cry of pain model assumes that psychobiological mechanisms analogous to those observed in animals may be activated by defeat and humiliation in humans. Two factors determine whether a sense of entrapment (a feeling of no escape) prevails. The first is escape potential, that is, whether the individual believes there is a chance to escape the situation. The second concerns rescue factors, whether the individual believes that he or she may be helped or saved from the situation by other people or circumstances. Suicidal behavior is seen as a response to a situation in which an individual feels defeated or humiliated and believes escape or rescue to be unlikely or impossible (for a preliminary test of the model, see O'Connor, 2003). Although activity, anger, and protest may prevail in early phases when escape potential is threatened but not eliminated, in most people, the risk of suicidal behavior is expected to increase with a growing sense of entrapment.

In the context of the cry of pain model, Williams and Pollock (2000, 2001) suggested that feelings of entrapment may arise from two main sources: deficits in problem solving and increased hopelessness for the future. Repeated unsuccessful attempts at problem solving will eventually lead individuals to believe that there is less and less opportunity for escape, and hopelessness, as a failure to expect positive changes in the future, reflects the fact that individuals expect increasingly fewer opportunities for rescue, that is, being helped by circumstances or others. As described earlier, specificity of autobiographical memory is, either directly or indirectly, related to both of these factors. Deficits in retrieving specific autobiographical memories contribute to judgments of inescapability, hindering successful problem solving by restricting detailed access to memories of potentially helpful prior positive or negative experiences and hence undermining motivation for problem solving. At the same time, implementation of problem-solving strategies is hindered by related deficits in constructing future scenarios. As problem solving repeatedly fails and ruminative processes and detachment ensue, expectancy for positive change is undermined—individuals will feel locked in, their hopelessness will increase, and they will judge both escape and rescue to be unlikely. The resulting feeling of entrapment will lead to suicidal ideation, and, if means are available, danger of suicidal behavior is high.

From this perspective, specificity of autobiographical memory is critically implicated in processes determining whether experiences of defeat lead to a suicidal crisis. It is important to note, however, that overgeneral memory may not only act as a proximal factor but that, in many people with an increased risk of suicide, it may be seen as a relatively stable diathesis acquired earlier in life. We have seen that overgeneral memory is related to depression and early childhood trauma, both of which are important risk factors for suicidal behavior. Research reviewed earlier shows that, once established, overgeneral memory remains a stable cognitive style in a high proportion of patients and may even be strengthened in a self-perpetuating interaction between rumination and categoric recall, leading to overelaboration of memory at the general event level. Thus, as a stable overgeneral retrieval style develops, ruminative thinking, problem-solving deficits, and lack of specificity in future thinking will be increasingly easy to trigger. As a result, the degree of objective stress required to trigger suicidal behavior is likely to decrease over time and escalation of cognitive processes leading to entrapment may be seen in response to seemingly less serious events. Such a development would parallel findings on episode sensitization in depression and is consistent with work by Joiner and Rudd (2000) showing suicidal ideation in people with multiple attempts to be associated less with stressful events than it is in those attempting suicide for the first time.

IMPLICATIONS FOR TREATMENT OF SUICIDAL PATIENTS

Treatment approaches to date have focused primarily on improving problem-solving abilities in suicidal patients. Although helpful in many cases, studies investigating these approaches have had mixed results (for an overview, see Hawton et al., 1998). This may be because the strategy of targeting problem-solving ability stops short of modifying the underlying causal processes that contribute to problem-solving deficits. Especially when an overgeneral retrieval style has been established, prevention of suicidal behavior will have to take into account processes related to this deficit: Rules for problem solving may not be applied when the patient is unable to access details of important experiences related to current problems.

Our research suggests that unless specificity of memory is assessed, an important vulnerability factor will remain unaddressed. This implies that clinicians become vigilant for those occasions when their patients are getting stuck in overgeneral accounts of their past. For example, patients may talk of times in the past when they "used to" go for walks with their partner, get bullied at school, have arguments with their mom, go out to parties. In such cases, it is easy to believe that one is hearing about the patients' past, but in fact one is only receiving an overgeneral summary. This is not the same as saying that the events never happened but simply that the way they are being retrieved, in summary form, is ultimately unhelpful for many patients. Summary memories do not assist patients in reconstruing the meaning of an event, they do not contain sufficient detail or hints for how to solve current interpersonal problems, and they exacerbate ruminative brooding. Is there any evidence that such overgenerality can be reduced in treatment?

Research in depression has shown that mindfulness-based cognitive therapy (Williams, Segal, Teasdale, & Soulsby, 2000), an approach teaching patients to cultivate moment-to-moment awareness, is successful in reducing overgenerality. Applying this approach to prevention of suicidal behavior may help patients to overcome detachment and experiential avoidance (e.g., by encouraging tolerance of all types of thoughts and memories and hence reducing the need for affective gating) and provide a basis on which problem solving may be improved. It remains to be seen whether such an approach is helpful in preventing suicidal behavior. Furthermore, research on specificity of autobiographical memory and interventions aimed at improving specificity may be beneficial in a domain for which effective interventions are urgently required.

REFERENCES

Arntz, A., Meeren, M., & Wessel, I. (2002). No evidence for overgeneral memories in borderline personality disorder. *Behaviour Research and Therapy, 40,* 1063–1068.

Baddeley, A. D., Emslie, H., & Nimmo-Smith, I. (1992). *The Speed and Capacity of Language Processing (SCOLP) test.* Bury St Edmunds, England: Thames Valley Test Company.

Bagley, C. (1991). The long-term psychological effects of child sexual abuse: A review of some British and Canadian studies of victims and their families. *Annals of Sex Research, 4,* 23–48.

Barnhofer, T., de Jong-Meyer, R., Kleinpass, A., & Nikesch, S. (2002). Specificity of autobiographical memories in depression: An analysis of retrieval processes in a think-aloud task. *British Journal of Clinical Psychology, 41,* 411–416.

Brewin, C. R., Reynolds, M., & Tata, P. (1999). Autobiographical memory processes and the course of depression. *Journal of Abnormal Psychology, 108,* 511–517.

Brittlebank, A. D., Scott, J., Williams, J. M. G., & Ferrier, I. N. (1993). Autobiographical memory in depression: State or trait marker? *British Journal of Psychiatry, 162,* 118–121.

Burgess, P. W., & Shallice, T. (1996). Confabulation and the control of recollection. *Memory, 4,* 359–411.

Burke, M., & Mathews, A. (1992). Autobiographical memory and clinical anxiety. *Cognition & Emotion, 6,* 23–35.

Conway, M. A., & Pleydell-Pearce, C. W. (2000). The construction of autobiographical memories in the self-memory system. *Psychological Review, 107,* 261–288.

Dalgleish, T., Spinks, H., Yiend, J., & Kuyken, W. (2001). Autobiographical memory style in Seasonal Affective Disorder and its relationship to future symptom remission. *Journal of Abnormal Psychology, 109,* 335–340.

Dalgleish, T., Tchanturia, K., Serpell, L., Herns, S., Yiend, J., de Silva, P., et al. (2003). Parental style and autobiographical memory in patients with eating disorders. *Emotion, 3,* 211–222.

de Decker, A., Hermans, D., Raes, F., & Eelen, P. (2003). Autobiographical memory specificity and trauma in inpatient adolescents. *Journal of Clinical Child and Adolescent Psychology, 32,* 22–31.

Evans, J., Williams, J. M. G., O'Loughlin, S., & Howells, K. (1992). Autobiographical memory and problem-solving strategies of parasuicide patients. *Psychological Medicine, 22,* 399–405.

Gilbert, P. (1989). *Human nature and suffering.* Hove and London: Erlbaum.

Goddard, L., Dritschel, B., & Burton, A. (1996). Role of autobiographical memory in social problem solving and depression. *Journal of Abnormal Psychology, 105,* 609–616.

Goddard, L., Dritschel, B., & Burton, A. (1997). Social problem solving and autobiographical memory in non-clinical depression. *British Journal of Clinical Psychology, 36,* 449–451.

Harvey, A. G., Bryant, R. A., & Dang, S. T. (1998). Autobiographical memory in acute stress disorder. *Journal of Consulting and Clinical Psychology, 66,* 500–506.

Hawton, K., Arensman, E., Townsend, E., Bremner, S., Feldman, E., Goldney, R., et al. (1998). Deliberate self-harm: Systematic review of efficacy of psychosocial and pharmacological treatments in preventing repetition. *British Medical Journal, 317*, 441–447.

Henderson, D., Hargreaves, I., Gregory, S., & Williams, J. M. G. (2002). Autobiographical memory and emotion in a non-clinical sample of women with and without a reported history of childhood sexual abuse. *British Journal of Clinical Psychology, 41*, 129–141.

Hermans, D., Van den Broeck, K., Belis, G., Raes, F., Pieters, G., & Eelen, P. (2004). Trauma and autobiographical memory specificity in depressed inpatients. *Behaviour Research & Therapy, 42*, 775–789.

Hutchings, J., Nash, S., Williams, J. M. G., & Nightingale, D. (1998). Parental autobiographical memory: Is this a helpful clinical measure in behavioural child management? *British Journal of Clinical Psychology, 37*, 303–312.

Joiner, T. E., & Rudd, M. D. (2000). Intensity and duration of suicidal crises vary as a function of previous suicide attempts and negative life events. *Journal of Consulting and Clinical Psychology, 68*, 909–916.

Kendall-Tackett, K. A., Williams, L. M., & Finkelhor, D. (2003). Impact of sexual abuse on children: A review and synthesis of recent empirical studies. *Psychological Bulletin, 113*, 164–180.

Kuyken, W., & Brewin, C. R. (1995). Autobiographical memory functioning in depression and reports of early abuse. *Journal of Abnormal Psychology, 104*, 585–591.

Kuyken, W., & Dalgleish, T. (1995). Autobiographical memory and depression. *British Journal of Clinical Psychology, 34*, 89–92.

Linehan, M. M., Camper, P., Chiles, J. A., Strosahl, K., & Shearin, E. (1987). Interpersonal problem solving and parasuicide. *Cognitive Therapy and Research, 11*, 1–12.

Mackinger, H. F., Leibetseder, M. M., Kunz-Dorfer, A., Fartacek, R., Whitworth, A. B., & Feldinger, F. (2004). Autobiographical memory predicts the course of depression during detoxification therapy in alcohol dependent men. *Journal of Affective Disorders, 78*, 61–65.

Mackinger, H. F., & Leitich, U. (2002). Tragen nicht-depressive Krebspatientinnen einen Depressionsmarker? [Do non-depressive female cancer patients carry a depression marker?]. *Verhaltenstherapie und Verhaltensmedizin, 23*, 75–89.

Mackinger, H. F., Loschin, G. G., & Leibetseder, M. M. (2000). Prediction of postnatal affective changes by autobiographical memories. *European Psychologist, 5*, 52–61.

Mackinger, H. F., Pachinger, M. M., Leibetseder, M. M., & Fartacek, R. R. (2000). Autobiographical memories in women remitted from major depression. *Journal of Abnormal Psychology, 109*, 331–334.

Marx, E. M., Williams, J. M. G., & Claridge, G. C. (1992). Depression and social-problem solving. *Journal of Abnormal Psychology, 101*, 78–86.

McNally, R. J., Lasko, N. B., Macklin, M. L., & Pitman, R. K. (1995). Autobiographical memory disturbance in combat-related posttraumatic stress disorder. *Behaviour Research & Therapy, 33*, 619–630.

McNally, R. J., Litz, B. T., Prassas, A., Shin, L. M., & Weathers, F. W. (1994). Emotional priming of autobiographical memory in post-traumatic stress disorder. *Cognition & Emotion, 8,* 351–367.

Meesters, C., Merckelbach, H., Muris, P., & Wessel, I. (2000). Autobiographical memory and trauma in adolescents. *Journal of Behavior Therapy and Experimental Psychiatry, 31,* 29–39.

Moore, R. G., Watts, F. N., & Williams, J. M. G. (1988). The specificity of personal memories in depression. *British Journal of Clinical Psychology, 27,* 275–276.

Norman, D. A., & Bobrow, D. G. (1979). Descriptions: An intermediate stage in memory retrieval. *Cognitive Psychology, 11,* 107–123.

O'Connor, R. C. (2003). Suicidal behaviour as a cry of pain: Test of a psychological model. *Archives of Suicide Research, 7,* 1–12.

Orbach, I., Bar-Joseph, H., & Dror, N. (1990). Styles of problem solving in suicidal individuals. *Suicide and Life-Threatening Behavior, 20,* 56–64.

Orbach, Y., Lamb, M. E., Sternberg, K. J., Williams, J. M. G., & Dawud-Noursi, S. (2001). The effect of being a victim or witness of family violence on the retrieval of autobiographical memories. *Child Abuse & Neglect, 25,* 1427–1437.

Peeters, F., Wessel, I., Merckelbach, H., & Boon-Vermeeren, M. (2003). Autobiographical memory specificity and the course of major depressive disorder. *Comprehensive Psychiatry, 43,* 344–350.

Platt, J. J., & Spivack, G. (1975). *Manual for the Means–Ends Problem Solving procedure.* Philadelphia: Department of Mental Health Services, Hahnemann Community Mental Health/Mental Retardation Center.

Pollock, L. R., & Williams, J. M. G. (2001). Effective problem solving in suicide attempters depends on specific autobiographical recall. *Suicide and Life-Threatening Behavior, 31,* 386–396.

Puffet, A., Jehin-Marchot, D., Timsit-Berthier, M., & Timsit, M. (1991). Autobiographical memory and major depressive states. *European Psychiatry, 7,* 141–145.

Raes, F., Hermans, D., de Decker, A., Eelen, P., & Williams, J. M. G. (2003). Autobiographical memory specificity and affect regulation: An experimental approach. *Emotion, 3,* 201–206.

Sidley, G. L., Calam, R., Wells, A., Hughes, T., & Whitaker, K. (1999). The prediction of parasuicide repetition in a high-risk group. *British Journal of Clinical Psychology, 38,* 375–386.

Sidley, G. L., Whitaker, K., Calam, R., & Wells, A. (1997). The relationship between problem-solving and autobiographical memory in parasuicide patients. *Behavioural and Cognitive Psychotherapy, 25,* 195–202.

Startup, M., Heard, H., Swales, M., Jones, B., Williams, J. M. G., & Jones, R. S. P. (2001). Autobiographical memory and parasuicide in borderline personality disorder. *British Journal of Clinical Psychology, 40,* 113–120.

Svaldi, J. J., & Mackinger, H. F. (2003). Obstructive sleep apnea syndrome: Autobiographical memory predicts the course of depressive affect after nCPAP therapy. *Scandinavian Journal of Psychology, 44,* 31–37.

Swales, M., Williams, J. M. G., & Wood, P. (2001). Specificity of autobiographical memory and mood disturbance in adolescents. *Cognition & Emotion, 15*, 321–331.

Watkins, E., & Teasdale, J. D. (2001). Rumination and overgeneral memory in depression: Effects of self-focus and analytic thinking. *Journal of Abnormal Psychology, 110*, 353–357.

Watkins, E., Teasdale, J. D., & Williams, R. M. (2000). Decentring and distraction reduce overgeneral autobiographical memory in depression. *Psychological Medicine, 30*, 911–920.

Wessel, I., Meeren, M., Peeters, F., Arntz, A., & Merckelbach, H. (2001). Correlates of autobiographical memory specificity: The role of depression, anxiety and childhood trauma. *Behaviour Research & Therapy, 39*, 409–421.

Wilhelm, S., McNally, R. J., Baer, L., & Florin, I. (1997). Autobiographical memory in obsessive-compulsive disorder. *British Journal of Clinical Psychology, 36*, 21–31.

Williams, J. M. G. (1986). Differences in reasons for taking overdoses in high and low hopelessness groups. *British Journal of Medical Psychology, 59*, 269–277.

Williams, J. M. G. (1988). General and specific autobiographical memory and emotional disturbance. In M. M. Gruneberg, P. Morris, & R. N. Sykes (Eds.), *Practical aspects of memory: Current research and issues* (pp. 295–300). Chichester, England: Wiley.

Williams, J. M. G. (1996). Depression and the specificity of autobiographical memory. In D. C. Rubin (Ed.), *Remembering our past: Studies in autobiographical memory* (pp. 244–267). Cambridge, England: Cambridge University Press.

Williams, J. M. G. (1997). *Cry of pain: Understanding suicide and self-harm.* Harmondsworth, England: Penguin.

Williams, J. M. G. (2001). *Suicide and attempted suicide.* London: Penguin.

Williams, J. M. G., & Broadbent, K. (1986). Autobiographical memory in suicide attempters. *Journal of Abnormal Psychology, 95*, 144–149.

Williams, J. M. G. & Dritschel, B. H. (1988). Emotional disturbance and the specificity of autobiographical memory. *Cognition and Emotion, 2*, 221–234.

Williams, J. M. G., Ellis, N. C., Tyers, C., Healy, H., Rose, G., & MacLeod, A. K. (1996). The specificity of autobiographical memory and imageability of the future. *Memory and Cognition, 24*, 116–125.

Williams, J. M. G., Healey, H., Chan, S., Crane, C., Barnhofer, T., Eade, J., et al. (in press). Retrieval of autobiographical memories: The mechanisms and consequences of truncated search. *Cognition and Emotion.*

Williams, M. D., & Hollan, J. D. (1981). Processes of retrieval from very long-term memory. *Cognitive Science, 5*, 87–119.

Williams, J. M. G., & Pollock, L. R. (2000). The psychology of suicidal behavior. In K. Hawton & K. van Heeringen (Eds.), *International handbook of suicide and attempted suicide* (pp. 79–90). Chichester, England: Wiley.

Williams, J. M. G., & Pollock, L. R. (2001). Psychological aspects of the suicidal process. In K. van Heeringen (Ed.), *Understanding suicidal behaviour* (pp. 76–93). Chichester, England: Wiley.

Williams, J. M. G., Segal, Z. V., Teasdale, J. D., & Soulsby, J. (2000). Mindfulness-based cognitive therapy reduces overgeneral autobiographical memory in formerly depressed patients. *Journal of Abnormal Psychology, 109,* 150–155.

Yang, B., & Clum, G. A. (2000). Childhood stress leads to later suicidality via its effect on cognitive functioning. *Suicide and Life-Threatening Behavior, 30,* 183–198.

9

THE BODY–MIND OF THE SUICIDAL PERSON

ISRAEL ORBACH

The thousands of studies carried out over the last 2 decades have accumulated a plethora of data aimed at understanding the causes for self-destruction. The theoretical, clinical, and empirical findings show that almost every type of stress, acute or minor, and any kind of pathology can be causally linked to suicide. Thus, the question of why some people choose to die by their own hands remains a mystery. Elsewhere (Orbach, 1994) I have suggested that, rather than positing what the solitary cause of suicide is, the question to be asked about suicide is *what makes suicide possible*. What processes enable some individuals, when under stress, to carry out the self-destructive act? My assumption is that there are certain facilitative factors that make the suicidal person act on his or her wish to die.

One of the facilitators of suicide is bodily dissociation, that is, a detachment from body senses. Bodily dissociation is usually accompanied by negative attitudes toward the body and lack of bodily protection or care. Such a state may become a facilitative process for the physical suicidal attack on the body when under stress. How do such facilitative processes develop? The literature suggests that bodily experiences are the first building blocks on the child's unique personality. Early care, which evolves around the body, shapes an individual's attitudes toward his or her own body. Consistent positive or negative bodily experiences in early to late childhood can turn into basic attitudes of life preservation or self-destruction. Such attitudes may then combine with internal and external stresses leading to effective coping or to suicidal behavior.

Early care, within this context, refers to the primary child–parent interactions, which encompass basic physical and emotional need fulfillment— the child's need to be touched, held, and enveloped. Early care is to be juxtaposed with touch deficiency, physical neglect, physical abuse, and trauma. Bodily experience is here defined in terms of sensation thresholds, awareness of bodily functions, and responsiveness to internal and external stimulation, physical anhedonia, and bodily detachment. Attitudes toward the body refer to perception, beliefs, feelings, and care for the body.

This chapter begins with a discussion of suicide facilitators, including the axis of the theory, dissociation. Next, I illustrate the extent to which early care affects development, particularly the development of self-preservation tendencies. These preliminary discussions lead into an elaboration of the negative early care, body experiences, and self-destruction hypothesis, including general empirical evidence, evidence provided by directly testing the hypothesis, and mediating processes that are involved in self-preservation and self-destruction. Finally, some recent neuropsychological theories that lend support to the notion of the suicidal body are presented. The main concept to be extrapolated from this chapter is how the "suicidal body" is formed, how it is experienced, and how the experience of the suicidal body facilitates suicide.

FACILITATING PROCESSES OF SUICIDE

As mentioned earlier, facilitators are not causes of suicide; however, they increase the probability of choosing suicide over other alternatives of coping with mental pain. Facilitators function to enhance the likelihood of suicide by assisting an individual to overcome the obstacles on the road to self-annihilation. Self-destructive behavior involves many internal and external constraints. Death may arouse fear and anxiety, its process is painful, and killing one's self bears social implications for both the victim and his or her survivors. All these may act as inhibitors and need to be confronted by and dealt with by the person who intends to commit suicide. The suicidal people use certain defense mechanisms to overcome inhibiting factors and to enable them to carry out the suicidal act despite the inhibiting forces.

A number of facilitators have been identified, including sociocultural norms, religious indoctrinations regarding the acceptability of the suicidal act, fantasies about death, a subjective attraction to death, and the availability of weapons to the contemplator of suicide (Orbach, 1997).

One of the most potent facilitators of suicidal behavior is related to the subject matter of this chapter—bodily dissociation. The body of the suicidal person is epitomized by bodily dissociation. Unusually high thresholds for physical sensation, a pervasive negative attitude toward the body, or active neglect toward bodily care and protection—characteristics of bodily dissociation—may potentially yield estrangement between the body and the self. This, in turn, facilitates the attack on the body. In the absence of the natural shield protecting the body, suicidal behavior may be carried out with greater ease than when self-preservation attitudes toward the body exist.

My contention is that the quality and degree of self-preservation and self-protection are extensions of one's early care experiences provided to one by others. An individual who was afforded positive early care, when subject to stress, will use a coping mechanism that takes into account self-preservation and protection. An individual with negative early care experiences is likely to disregard self-preservation when coping with stress, however, and instead resort to coping that involves dissociation and perhaps self-destruction.

Alienation from the body equals alienation from bodily attainments such as need satisfaction. Interactions between self and world, satisfaction of physical needs, and other such bodily experiences are hazy in a suicidal individual. Thus, individuals with suicidal bodies feel that in regard to ultimate detachment from the body, the gains outweigh the losses.

ROLE OF EARLY CARE AND BODY EXPERIENCES IN SELF-PRESERVATION

The caregiver–infant interaction has long been thought to be a critical determinant in the development of the child (Borenstein & Tamis-Le Mandu, 2001). Caregiving and mothering constitute an initial and all-encompassing ecology of infant development. Infants and caregivers engage in a continuous dyadic interaction to which both contribute, through which each alerts the other, and by which both are changed (Borenstein & Tamis-Le Mandu, 2001).

Many developmental processes ensue at the point of physical contact between mother and infant, including attachment, emotional regulation, promotion of language, and social understanding (Borenstein & Tamis-Le Mandu, 2001). Harlow and his colleagues (e.g., Harlow & Suomi, 1970) provided most convincing evidence for the importance of tactile stimulation in the infant's emotional and social development. Mother–infant physical contact is also the arena in which awareness of the body, self-love and care, bodily love and care, self-image, and self-protection begin to develop. Thus, physical care and physical contact may become life-preserving forces, whereas physical neglect may lead to the weakening of self- and life-preservation forces.

Tactile stimulation during early care has proved both life enhancing and vital in both animal and human babies. Kuhn and Schanberg (1998) have shown that maternal separation in pups, even for a very short time, produces a decrease in the growth enzyme ornithine decarboxylase. Schanberg and Field (1987) found that the decrease in the growth hormone is directly related to the lack of tactile stimulation in the form of mothers' licking of the pups. Tactile stimulation has also been shown to increase weight gain and caloric intake in premature babies (Helders, Cats, & Debast, 1989). In addition, Róiste and Bushnell (1996) found that infants treated with massage were quicker to feed, were discharged from the hospital earlier, and were judged to show more advanced cognitive development at 15 months.

The vital significance of early physical contact was demonstrated by the Kangaroo Mother Intervention technique (KMI), wherein a 24-hour skin-to-skin contact substituted for the incubator treatment of low-birth-weight babies. The physical-contact facet of this method has shown that tactile interaction can even prove lifesaving. When compared with the incubator, the KMI method proved equally effective in terms of survival, and in cases of serious illness, the KMI has often provided superior results (Sloan, Camacho, Rojas, & Stern, 1994).

Early positive touch can assist an infant in learning to regulate his or her own states of arousal. In line with this, infants treated with the KMI method show more organized sleep–wake cycles and higher thresholds to negative emotionality than did incubator babies (Feldman, Weller, Sirota, & Eidelman, 2002). Feldman et al. further studied the self-modulation of KMI babies versus incubator babies in a complex-task situation. The task demanded either that an infant allocate attention to stimuli that become increasingly complex or that an infant explore a toy for increasingly longer sessions. The researchers found that KMI babies were more efficient in modulating their arousal to suit the demands of the task at a given moment. The authors deduced that maternal proximity provides the basis for the development of the infants' stress tolerance, emotional regulation, and attention organization. These functions, vital to personality, learning, social actions, and self-preservation, are shaped very simply by maternal smile, touch, voice, body heat, skin texture, movement, physiological rhythms, and nursing. What unifies these multiple elements, say Feldman et al. (2002), is the mother's unique social and affective style.

Holding can help regulate emotional arousal and moderate affect in babies. Koester, Papousek, and Papousek (1989) suggested that in helping to moderate the overall levels of stimulation to which a baby is exposed, holding may potentially assist an infant in learning to regulate his or her own states of arousal. Babies who received enhanced contact with their mothers over a 3-month observation period reportedly smiled more and cried less than babies who received less contact (de Chateau, 1976). Positive touch and stimulation were found to enhance positive affect and attenuation in babies of depressed mothers (Pelaez-Nogueras, Field, Hossain, & Pickens, 1996).

Early tactile interaction is most prominently known to affect later social relationships, ranging from intimate to superficial, in the form of pervading attachment styles. Touching can communicate a wide range of emotions, including love and caring, sympathy, empathy, sense of security, as well as negative emotions (Stack, 2001).

Ainsworth, Blehar, Waters, and Wall (1978) found that patient and durable holding in infancy was positively correlated to the development of secure attachments in adulthood. Higher levels of physical contact and love are also related to secure positive attachments (Ainsworth et al., 1978). In fact, frequency and duration of touch are considered to be an index of the degree of attachment, maternal sensitivity, and responsiveness (Stack, 2001).

Anisfeld, Casper, Nozyce, and Cunningham (1990) reported that infants who were carried in soft carriers (more physical contact) were more secure in their behavior later in life than infants who were carried in infant seats (less physical contact). MacDonald (1987) and MacDonald and Parke (1984) found that child–father physical play was related later to better social adjustment and emotional security in the children. Koff, Rierdan, and Stubbs (1990) provided support to the assumption that parental physical care behavior can foster the child's positive body image and self-esteem.

Studies are suggesting that early care, especially positive touch interactions, play a central role in shaping the self-image of infants. Kruger (1989) specified that self-image depends on degrees of caressing and holding. Deficiencies in such positive touch may damage the self-image and body boundaries. Similarly, Gupta and Schork (1995) studied the relationships between body image and perception of physical touch in childhood among 173 adults. They reported a significant negative correlation between quality of early physical touch and body image later in life; that is, the more reported negative touch, the lower the body image and satisfaction from the body.

Thus far, empirical evidence has been provided to illustrate the importance of touch. We have also demonstrated that primary care has a long-lasting effect on multiple arenas of an individual's life, particularly through the formation of pervasive attachment styles. This suggests that physical care and contact have potentially life-preserving implications, whereas physical neglect may lead to the weakening of self and life-preserving forces. To be further explored are the mediating processes between early care and life preservation.

THEORETICAL EXPLANATIONS FOR THE ASSOCIATION BETWEEN PHYSICAL CARE AND LIFE PRESERVATION

Care and Taming of Self-Aggression

According to Anna Freud (1949), a baby is born into the world with internal aggression. In dealing with these innate aggressions, as well as the externally afflicted aggressions, self-protection and preservation are not naturally taken into account. It is the role of the primary caregiver to teach the infant to regulate its aggressions. At first, the primary caregiver must actively tame the infant's aggression. For example, a relaxed, gently restricting mother may tone down the aggressive urge. Ultimately, however, the infant will learn and internalize the primary caregiver and will modulate his or her own aggressions independently. If, however, interactions with a primary caregiver fail to teach the infant self-regulation, the infant will resort to self-punishment to resolve internal and external frustrations. Evidence to this effect is that individuals with a history of childhood neglect are likely to wage attacks on their own bodies when faced with frustration or stress. Such self-punitive behavior may even include self-biting and scratching (Grossman, 1991). Without appropriate care and aggression-taming in childhood, self-aggressive behavior may continue later in life (for empirical and clinical evidence, see Putnam & Stein, 1985; Kraemer & Clarke, 1990; Laufer, 1991).

Attunement to the Child's Needs

An infant is born with an amalgamation of internal urges and arousals. It is elementary for an infant to learn to associate physiological arousal with practical needs so that these urges may be fulfilled appropriately. This learning process unfolds in parallel to the caregiver's developing ability to discern and discriminate the needs of the infant. Fulfillment of needs does not only placate the newborn and convey empathy and understanding on behalf of the caregiver, it also provides the newborn with meaning, a method in the madness. Thus, for example, when food is offered in response to signals indicating nutritional need, the infant will develop an awareness of the distinct state of hunger as opposed to other internal tensions and needs. If, however, a mother's reaction is continually inappropriate, the child will come to conceptualize his or her body as confusing and unpredictable and to experience the body in a distorted way (see also Shapiro, 1991).

According to Bruch (1973), learning to differentiate inner-body functions and needs and recognizing them as being owned by one's self is essential to self-care and self-preservation. This presents a new perspective on the link between primary care and later self-care. According to this view, inefficient self-care is a natural extension of poor primary care because a critical learning period involving the association between physiological arousal, type of need, and the appropriate fulfillment of that need has been forsaken. Resonant of this theory are findings on the association patterns of individuals with eating disorders. It is interesting that the gastric activity of people with anorexia is not dissimilar from that of normal subjects. When questioned about their sensations of hunger, however, patients with anorexia reported that they felt nothing (Silverstone & Russell, 1967). Obese subjects were found to make similar mistakes in association between physiological arousal and nutritional need. In contrast to patients with anorexia who fail to discern internal hunger cues, obese patients failed to associate their satiation with cessation of food intake. Whereas subjects of normal weight use enteroceptive cues, subjects who are obese rely on external cues in their eating (Schachter, 1968).

Lack of attunement to bodily needs in infancy, eventuating in lack of awareness of bodily needs and bodily cues, not only hampers the development of a sense of self but may also be at the heart of a distorted perception of the body and a split between the sense of self and the body. These may serve as a basis for further detachment from the body, facilitating neglect and self-damaging behavior.

Learning Parental Attitudes Toward the Child's Body

According to Van der Velde (1985), the infant learns to associate need fulfillment with various facets of observable caretaking behavior. The child learns and imitates these behaviors so that he or she may use them when undertaking self-care. Furthermore, Van der Velde postulated that such learning heeds the pairing of need frustration and need satiation with environmental cues (diapering, caressing) of the primary caregiving experience. Eventually the infant even comes to link the posture and body language of the caregiver with the frustration or satiation of needs. This acquired behavior is further strengthened by the child's linguistic development. Parental physical caring behavior also fosters the child's body image and self-esteem that further enhance the child's motivation for self-preservation or self-destruction. Empirical evidence for this relationship was provided by Koff et al. (1990).

Greenspan (1979) focused mostly on the role of representational learning, beginning at 14 to 18 months, as a key process in the development of self-care, self-protection, and self-regulation. When a child becomes mobile, it is the parents' responsibility to take an active role as protectors against danger by setting examples for self-care, by setting limits to self-harm, as well as through proper instructions about dangers in the environment. Through these processes, children acquire standards of self-protection and self-care by learning to anticipate and avoid danger.

Touch and Regulation of Tensions

Tactile stimulation and touch help modulate the overall level of stimulation to which an infant is exposed (Koester et al., 1989). Allowing the infant to function on lower levels of arousal is beneficial for the development of thresholds and dispositions. Other researchers suggest a more direct link between touch and the regulation of physiological and behavioral patterns (e.g., Brazelton, 1990; Fogel, 1997). Touch itself can activate or sooth infants (see Stack, 2001). Most important, regulation by the primary caregiver may teach the infant to regulate his or her own states of arousal (Koester et al., 1989). In sum, early touch and physical contact from others is introjected as a direct or indirect measure of self-regulation, whereas its absence can interfere with the acquisition of self-regulation strategies.

Touch, Attachment, and Emotional Communication

The skin is a mirror of passions that reflects emotion and conveys meaning, says Stack (2001). The skin can convey psychological states by virtue of its ability to integrate neural, glandular, and mental changes related to emotions (Montague, 1986). Thus, "the pitch and timber of tactile communication are color, texture, and temperature" (Virel, quoted in Stack, 2001). Pines (1980) claimed that parent–child interactions and touch have the potential to set an emotional tone. Pines (1980) also suggested that bodily interactions constitute the main mode of parent–child communication. The child's nonverbal affect may find expression through the skin. The skin may weep and rage. The mother responds to the child's communication with appropriate body language.

Not only is emotional communication enhanced through bodily contact, so also is the parent–child attachment. Touch and physical contact are associated with loving care from the beginning of life to its end (Stack, 2001). High levels of physical contact and love are related to secure positive attachment (Ainsworth et al., 1978).

Hence, positive physical contact has not only a direct, local, and temporary positive effect, it also enhances a general positive emotional environment and positive attachments and interpersonal relationships between parents and child, with long-lasting effects that enhance positive and healthy growth and development.

Touch and Growth

We can view the relationship of physical contact, brain changes, and development from another perspective as well. As seen earlier, there is evidence that touch and physical contact have a direct impact on brain physiology in the form of an increase and decrease of enzymes and hormones. Lack of physical touch is related to a decrease in the enzyme ornithine decarboxylase. This enzyme is necessary for the infant's growth. Furthermore, brain opioid and oxytocin (hormone) are activated by various pleasurable prosocial activities including grooming, touch, and sexual interchanges. Such neurochemical changes in the brain may promote feelings of security and a sense of well-being in children as well as in adults (Panksepp, 1998).

From this biological perspective, physical contact can enhance positive physiological changes in the brain, which can affect one's general well-being, one's sense of enjoyment, and one's positive physical development.

EFFECTS OF NEGATIVE EARLY CARE
AND BODILY EXPERIENCES

The effects of abuse and neglect far outlive the period of maltreatment. It is interesting that deprivation of positive touch and subjection to abuse often result in similar long-term effects. Lewis, Solnit, Stark, Gabrielson, and Klatskin (1996) studied children who accidentally ingested poison and found that "maternal depletion" in the form of lack of care was present in all the cases in which the ingestions occurred. This factor was not characteristic of the control group. Green (1978) found that self-mutilating acts such as biting, cutting, self-burning, pulling out hair, bashing one's head against the wall, or attempting suicide are phenomena among abused and neglected children. Spitz (1965) demonstrated that absence of maternal care in institutionalized children is related to psychological maladjustment, stunted development, and physical deterioration. Furthermore, neglect that results from institutionalization is correlated to self-harm and high mortality. Similarly, abused teenagers were found to be substantially more suicidal than their nonabused counterparts, which indicated that early physical abuse may indeed affect self-destructive tendencies even many years following the cessation of the abuse (Bayatpour, Wells, & Holford, 1992; Goodwin, 1981). Kaplan, Asnis, Lipschitz, and Chorney (1995) produced similar results when investigating 251 adolescent inpatients. They found that three variables differentiated the suicidal from the nonsuicidal inpatients in this sample: physical abuse, depression, and dissociation. Field (1997) reported that children and adolescents hospitalized for psychiatric problems (depression, conduct disorder, and suicidal behavior) suffered from touch neglect or abuse during early childhood.

Longitudinal studies show that there is an association between inadequate mothering by depressed women and their children's behavior, brain activity, and stress responses. These changes reflect alterations in cortical activity, anatomic reactivity, and stress hormone secretion. These studies imply that the problem with inadequate mothering is that it surpasses the social learning environment and it permeates psychobiological and neural processes (see Ashman & Dawson, 2002).

THE NEGATIVE EARLY CARE AND
SELF-DESTRUCTION HYPOTHESIS

Even when the decision to end one's own life has been consolidated, the concept of maiming one's own body is heavily weighed. The logical extension of this is that individuals who hate or feel alienated from their bodies will find it easier to commit a self-destructive act. Moreover, such an individual, when exposed to stress or trauma, will become increasingly dissociated and detached from his or her body. Dissociation will domino into a distorted experience of one's surroundings, an effect that will reduce coping and increase mental anguish.

My hypothesis is that the link between early care and self-preservation is the molding of the suicidal body. *Suicidal body*, as a term, refers to the proposition that suicidal individuals experience their bodies in a different way from nonsuicidal individuals. The suicidal body is experienced as extraneous or foreign. Its inputs are foggy, its metacognitive representation is distorted and confusing, and its image is negative. The suicidal body results from early trauma, abuse, or neglect that encouraged or made necessary bodily dissociation. Negative or distorted beliefs may also be due to the internalized primary caregiver's attitudes toward the infant's body. Bodily dissociation and dejection, characteristic of the suicidal body, may be formed in the process of pervasively inappropriate, insensitive care. Overall, the suicidal body is formed by poor preservation of the infant during early care.

I (Orbach, 1994) described the progress of development of the dissociated personality and how dissociation may lead to suicide. Dissociation is born of intolerable circumstances in early life such as neglect, rejection, and physical abuse. In its seminal stage, it takes the form of a defense mechanism, whereby thresholds for pain and other senses are heightened to assuage the effects of the unpleasant conditions. Following prolonged use of dissociation as a defense mechanism, sensations are no longer simply filtered out, but rather an individual begins to experience numbness, detachment, insensitivity to pain, and estrangement toward the body. An individual who has developed full-fledged dissociation is highly suicide prone. Lowered sensitivity to physical pain as well as bodily estrangement facilitates carrying out the act of self-destruction. In addition, because dissociated individuals also experience lower sensitivity to physical pleasure, they often feel they have little to lose by complete bodily detachment or suicide.

The empirical data presented here touch on several aspects of the theoretical hypothesis presented earlier showing that (a) there is a triangular link between negative early care, bodily experience, and self-destruction; (b) suicidal individuals experience their bodies in a different way from nonsuicidal persons; (c) suicidal individuals show different attitudes and feelings toward their bodies; and (d) suicidal individuals have more negative memories about parental care and attitudes than nonsuicidal persons.

Negative Early Care–Bodily Experience–Self-Destruction

Salk (1985) found in a postmortem study that three factors significantly distinguished between adolescents who committed suicide compared with two control groups: (a) medical negligence during pregnancy; (b) chronic maternal illness; and (c) neonatal respiratory difficulties after birth. One of the interpretations Salk suggested is that medical neglect during pregnancy fostered maternal rejection even before the child was born and thereafter. Lester (1991) reported that experiences of early physical abuse and physical punishment in childhood were associated with increased suicide attempts in a sample of prison inmates who were found to have been carried longer in the womb and breast-fed for a shorter time. Early physical abuse was found to affect self-destruction even later in life (Bayatpour et al., 1992), because abused teenagers were far more suicidal than the nonabused teens.

I found (Orbach & Mikulincer, 1998) that suicidal adolescent inpatients compared with nonsuicidal inpatients and normal individuals received lower scores on self-report scales of body image feelings and attitudes, body care, body protection, and comfort in touch. These bodily aspects also correlated with physical anhedonia, depression, and suicidal tendencies as measured by various self-reports. It was further found in this study that there were significant correlations between attitudes toward the body feelings image, touch, protection, and care, on one hand, and perceived early care (parental bonding), self-esteem, and suicidal tendencies on the other hand.

The Suicidal Body as a Different Body Experience

Suicidal individuals exhibit significantly higher thresholds for sensation than do nonsuicidal people. Such has been demonstrated in a study that subjected suicidal and nonsuicidal youth to thermal pain stimulation. The participants could manipulate the temperature at will, although the pain induction procedure was automatically terminated at 50 degrees Centigrade (Orbach, Mikulincer, King, Cohen, & Stein, 1997). To measure the corresponding subjective body experience of participants, self-reports were administered on hopelessness, dissociation, suicidal tendencies, depression, and anxiety. The results indicated that suicidal subjects had significantly higher pain thresholds and tolerance when compared with the two control groups. This outcome persisted even after controlling motivation to participate, medication diagnosis, and length of hospitalization. Significant positive correlations were found between self-reported hopelessness, suicidal tendencies, severity of the suicidal behavior, and pain threshold and tolerance (Orbach et al., 1997).

Other physiological studies suggest that the unique bodily experience of suicidal individuals may be due to faster habituation to sensory stimuli. Spiegel (1969) and Thorell (1987) studied electrodermal activity and skin-conductance level responses to repeated tone stimuli in suicidal and nonsuicidal subjects. Lower responsivity indicated a faster habituation to acoustic stimuli. All these measures were lower in depressed suicidal patients compared with depressed nonsuicidal patients and nondepressed and healthy subjects. Edman, Asberg, Levander, and Schalling (1986), using a similar research paradigm, found that some of the suicidal patients who were electrodermally hyporesponsive committed suicide within a 1-year follow-up period. Fast habituation to noise can be interpreted as representing one form of bodily detachment from the environment. The preceding findings accord with our theoretical formulation of the role of bodily functions in suicidal individuals, demonstrating how these individuals tend to detach themselves from the environment by means of their altered bodily functions. Fast habituation and higher thresholds can both be interpreted as representing bodily detachment.

Orbach et al. (1996) sampled two groups subject to acute stress resulting from a suicide attempt or an accident. Each group was then measured for three personality variables that would lead to mounting stress: negative self-image, perceived life stress, and perceived life anxiety. Then the effect of mounting stress on tolerance for pain was measured in each acute-stress group (accident or suicide attempt). It is quite interesting that the effect of mounting stress on pain tolerance was reversed between the two groups. The suicidal group demonstrated a positive correlation between negative self-image, perceived life stress and anxiety, and tolerance for physical pain. The accident subjects, however, displayed a negative correlation between the three mounting stress variables and tolerance for pain. That is, mounting stress set off opposite mechanisms in each group. In the accident group, mounting stress lowered thresholds for external stimulation to enhance detection of harm and prevent further injury. In the suicide group, mounting inner stress raised thresholds for external stimulation, mobilizing defensive detachment and resulting in greater exposure to further harm and eventually self-destruction.

Different Attitudes and Feelings

The perception of and attitudes toward one's own body are never objective. There should, however, be a range of correspondence between the physical measures of one's body and the body perception of that individual. Even when this discrepancy works in an individual's favor, as is sometimes the case with people with narcissistic personality disorder, this perceptual disparity is considered problematic. Three body-related attitudes and perceptions have emerged in the empirical arena as distinguishing suicidal from nonsuicidal individuals. Suicidal youth exhibit a greater discrepancy between perceived body image and ideal body image, display greater negativity toward their body image, and have higher dissociative tendencies in relation to their bodies (Orbach, Lotem-Peleg, & Kedem, 1995). In fact, the higher the suicidal tendency, the larger the discrepancy between perceived and ideal body image, the stronger the negative feelings, and the higher the dissociative tendencies.

Body experience and body-related attitudes are mentioned here separately, although they often work together. Orbach, Stein, Shani-Sela, and Har-Even (2001) studied facets of body-related attitudes and bodily experiences adjacently to study their effects in suicidal and nonsuicidal subjects. The body-related attitudes studied were body-related feelings, body image, body protection, body care, and comfort in touch. The variables of bodily experiences examined were bodily dissociation, bodily apathy, and levels of physical self-control. Depression and anxiety were also accounted for. The suicidal group scored significantly lower on body related attitudes. In regard to bodily experiences, members of the suicidal group showed a diminished sense of control over their own bodies and higher bodily dissociation than did subjects in the control group. The comorbidity of certain body-related attitudes and bodily experiences found in individuals with suicidal tendencies might have considerable predictive value.

An additional correlation emerged between the body-related attitude of body protection and the body experience of dissociation in individuals with suicidal tendencies. One explanation of the nature of this correlation is that inability or unwillingness to protect the body combined with a sense of estrangement from bodily experiences will allow for, if not facilitate, suicidal tendencies.

The authors interpreted the findings through the contention that basic attitudes about life and death are interwoven with feelings, attitudes, and experiences of the body. Enjoyment in life is strongly linked to good feelings about the body and vice versa. Lack of enjoyment in life and death wishes are strongly associated with a hateful relationship and lack of comfort with the body.

Negative Memories of Parental Care

Negative early care can be understood not only methodologically but also through personal testimony. The stipulations of the negative early care hypothesis extend from poor primary care to mature suicidal behavior. Studies have revealed that suicidal persons tend to have negative memories of past parental care. In other words, there is an empirical correlation between perceived early care and suicidal behavior. de Jong (1992) found that suicidal college students rated their parents as less warm than their counterparts. Suicidal adolescents, characterized by suicidal ideation, also self-reported feelings of having been touch deprived (Field, 1997). Over a 10-year prospective study, Wagner and Cohen (1994) looked into the caretaking strategies of mothers. At the close of the century-long investigation period, the researchers concluded that the mothers of suicidal youngsters were comparatively lacking in quality and quantity of warmth. Very similar findings were reported in a study by Pearce, Martin, and Wood (1995) that examined the self-reports of 300 high school students on the history of positive and negative touch in the family. They found that the suicidal students reported far more negative touch (hitting, slapping) than positive touch (caressing, hugging) as well as more depression and violence. None of the suicidal students reported less negative touch (and depression and violence) compared with the nonsuicidal students.

Orbach et al. (in press) undertook the investigation of three precepts of the negative early care and self-destruction hypothesis: (a) that suicidal individuals experience their bodies in a way different from nonsuicidal individuals; (b) that suicidal individuals bear different attitudes toward their bodies than nonsuicidal individuals; (c) that suicidal individuals have more negative recollections of their primary care experiences. Both objective measures and self-report were used in the collection of data on bodily experiences. A tactile stimulator provided recordings of tactile sensitivity in suicidal and nonsuicidal individuals. The self-report of bodily experiences included accounts of physical anhedonia, bodily dissociation, anxiety about the body, and responses to various types of touch (tactile defensiveness). Data on the body-related attitudes of subjects were collected through self-report on body image, body care, body protection, and similar items. Lastly, perceived early care in the form of parental bonding, recollection of positive and negative touch, and history of maltreatment were measured in the subjects. Measures of depression, anxiety, severity of pathology, and suicidal tendencies were also included. The study comprised three groups of adolescent subjects: suicidal inpatients, nonsuicidal inpatients, and a nonclinical group.

The primary assumption, in accordance with the negative early care hypothesis, was that suicidal inpatients will show higher tactile thresholds, will self-report more negative body experiences, score low on body-attitude measurements, and have more negative recollections of parental care than the other two groups. With a few minor exceptions, all hypotheses were confirmed.

At this point, it is difficult to determine whether all people who were abused, neglected, or traumatized as children are at risk of suicide, nor can we say whether all suicidal people suffered from bodily maltreatment. At this stage, it is probably safe to state that the body–mind dynamics of the suicidal person described here represent at least a subtype of suicidal people.

SPECIFIC MEDIATING PROCESSES BETWEEN EARLY CARE AND SELF-DESTRUCTION

What are the specific mediating processes between early caretaking, body experiences, and attitudes and self-destructive behavior? Some mediating processes between early caretaking and self-neglect or lack of self-preservation were defined earlier, but now the purpose is to introduce some processes mediating actual suicidal behavior. The description and definition of these processes are based on several theoretical models dealing directly with suicide.

The Body as a Representation of Hateful Relationships

The self is not innate; it is shaped by relationships with objects environmental, inanimate, animate, and imaginary. By so purporting, Maltsberger (1993) chose an object relations approach to explaining the development of a self-destructive being. The pivotal characters in the active construction of the infant's self are introjected parental figures. Early development of the self necessitates integration and organization of various facets into a cohesive whole. In the case of poor parental support in the formation of the self, the child will develop a less cohesive self, making confusion and perhaps even disintegration more likely to occur. Formation of a stable, integrated self is crucial to distinguish the self from the "not self." Confusion between self and others allows an individual to internalize hated figures and to resolve external conflicts with them by harming his or her own body. In the case of suicidal individuals, the body may, for example, take on the form of a hateful relationship with a parent. In fact, oftentimes the desire to destroy oneself is motivated by an unconscious desire to destroy a parental figure. Maltsberger (1993) claimed that confusion of self and others, disturbances in self-representations, and intense anger mutually account for self-destruction. Confusion of self and others apparently legitimizes how hurting oneself equals victimizing another. In fact, it was found that the tendency to turn aggression and anger inward is highly associated with suicidal behavior (Apter, Orvaschel, Lask, Moses, & Tyano, 1989).

Depression and Distortion of the Experience of Physical Pain and Pleasure

Furman (1984) traced the origins of suicidal behavior to early sadomasochistic relationships with the caretakers. Such circumstances may result in the child's distorted perception and experience of pain and pleasure; that is, the child may come to experience pain as pleasure. Self-inflicted pain becomes a method to reduce the threat of external punishment. This process is also accompanied by a loss of bodily love. When such masochistic tendencies are coupled with depression or impulsivity, suicidal acting may take place.

Suicide and Dissociation

Several authors describe dissociative processes associated with suicidal behavior (e.g., Baumeister, 1990; Maltsberger, 1993; Orbach, 1994; Shneidman, 1980). Dissociation is a kind of mental avoidance or escape activity characterized by psychogenic amnesia; loss of personality identity; confusion; fragmentation; loss of control over thoughts, feelings, and actions; and depersonalization. Dissociation may also appear in the form of loss of touch with the body and body sensations (Vanderlinden, Van Dyck, Vanderyckan, Vertommen, & Jan Verkes, 1993).

As mentioned earlier, Orbach (1994) asserted that dissociation is born of intolerable circumstances in early life such as neglect, rejection, and physical abuse. Initially dissociation functions as a defense mechanism in the form of heightened thresholds. Later, after a pervasive use of dissociation in a defensive manner, thresholds become fixed at levels of numbness and detachment from bodily experiences, indiscriminant of whether they are pleasant or negative.

An endorsement for this interpretation is provided by a series of studies on pain analgesia in suicidal subjects reported earlier. In one self-report study on differences between self-mutilators diagnosed as patients with borderline personality disorder who do not feel pain during self-mutilation and those who do feel pain (Russ, Shearin, Clarkin, Harrison, & Hull, 1993), it was found that ratings of dissociation, trauma symptoms, suicide attempts, and childhood sexual abuse were higher in patients who did not experience pain during self-mutilation compared with their counterparts. Similarly, Orbach, Herman, Kedem, and Apter (1995) found that suicidal youngsters demonstrated higher levels of dissociative tendencies and that these were positively correlated with suicidal tendencies and negative feelings toward the body.

Body, Brain, and Emotions

Viewing the suicidal process from the perspective of the body is consistent with recent conceptualizations of neuropsychological functioning of the brain and body. According to Damasio, emotions and cognitions, as well as awareness of the world and the self, are all based on the body proper.

Damasio's (1994, 1999) basic contention is that cognition and emotion are embodied. Bodily processes such as visceral, muscular, and endocrine functions grant corporeality to the mind, feelings, emotions, and imagination. The human experience is constantly being generated by the interaction of the mind with bodily experiences. Emotional and cognitive activities are based on the brain's readings of what Damasio has defined as somatic markers. Certain bodily states are inherently ordained as pleasurable or painful. A loss of bodily senses, therefore, would result in the absence of emotion or distortion of emotions and cognitive experiences, including pain and pleasure, frustration and satiation, love and hate. All these affects cannot be experienced without the neural events that generate them in the brain.

Further support for Damasio's theory comes from Nuñez (1999) and Sheets-Johnstone (1999). According to these authors, the mind is fully embodied; that is, bodily grounded experiences are inherently part of every subject matter of the study of the mind. This stands contrary to the dualistic and functionalistic view, in which one sees cognition, for example, as abstract and separated from the nature of the body of the living human animal and the bodily experiences it sustains.

There is an appealing congruence between Damasio's contentions and the Negative Early Care and Self-Destruction Hypothesis. Drawing an analogy between the suicidal body and the physical body, and between the suicidal mind and emotions and cognitions of the mind, yields both support and further explanation of the interdependence between the suicidal body and mind. Juxtaposed to Damasio's theory, I have postulated in this chapter that the suicidal person's attempts do not immediately resort to dissecting ties between the suicidal body and suicidal mind as a first means to combat mental pain. Rather, the suicidal person's first defensive ploy is numbing the suicidal body and physical dissociation. Numbing the body means killing its vitality. When the anguish persists, the quintessentially flawed defense crumbles, leaving one last option of killing the lifeless body.

A BRIEF NOTE ABOUT TREATMENT IMPLICATIONS

One possible inference from the theory and data presented here is that increasing awareness of the body and its care, enhancement of a positive body image, and eliciting pleasant bodily experiences and increasing sensitivity to the senses may be instrumental in therapeutic work with suicidal individuals. Such therapeutic approaches to suicidal youngsters have been demonstrated in several therapeutic programs. Bradley and Rotheram-Borus (1990) constructed a program of suicide prevention based on raising sensitivity to bodily cues with suicidal adolescents. Field (1997) urged body massage with adolescents to decrease suicidal tendencies. MacLeod, Williams, and Linehan (1992) recommended the use of the various senses to improve one's mood and regulate negative emotions. Cash (1997) suggested the treatment of body image distortions in various types of self-destructive behavior. Viewing the body as an integral part of one's identity and well-being may prove to be a most beneficial approach in the treatment of suicidal behavior.

CONCLUSION

In conclusion, this chapter focuses on the body experience of suicidal individuals. Various body processes and bodily experiences have been implicated in the self-destructive behavior from clinical and empirical perspectives. These include early bodily care, body perceptions, feelings about the body, physical dissociation, and physical anhedonia. It is assumed that such processes can facilitate the physical attack on the body, inherent in the suicidal act. It is difficult to understand how an individual can attack his or her own body without the existence of such facilitators.

Many unanswered questions remain regarding the involvement of bodily processes and body-related attitudes and their relationship to the suicidal process. At what stage of the suicidal process do bodily manifestations come into play? Do the bodily processes constitute a stable characteristic of the suicidal person, or are they contextual? Do the bodily processes exist in all forms of suicidal behavior? To what degree are the bodily processes related to depression, and to what degree are they a function of the suicidal state of mind? Further research is needed to tackle these questions. Even at this stage, however, it is important to focus on the bodily processes involved in self-destructive behavior from a theoretical, empirical, and treatment perspective.

REFERENCES

Ainsworth, M. D. S., Blehar, M. C., Waters, E., & Wall, S. (1978). *Patterns of attachment: A psychological study of the Strange situation*. Hillsdale, NJ: Erlbaum.

Anisfeld, E., Casper, V., Nozyce, M., & Cunningham, N. (1990). Does infant-carrying promote attachment? An experimental study of the effects of increased physical contact on the development of attachment. *Child Development, 61,* 1617–1627.

Apter, A., Orvaschel, H., Lask, M., Moses, T., & Tyano, S. (1989). Psychiatric properties of the K-SADS-P in an Israeli adolescent psychiatric population. *Journal of the American Academy of Child and Adolescent Psychiatry, 28,* 61–65.

Ashman, S. B., & Dawson, G. (2002). Maternal depression, infant psychobiological development, and risk for depression. In S. H. Goodman & I. H. Gotlib (Eds.), *Children of depressed parents: Mechanisms of risk and implications for treatment* (pp. 37–58). Washington, DC: American Psychological Association.

Baumeister, R. F. (1990). Suicide as escape from self. *Psychological Review, 97,* 90–113.

Bayatpour, M., Wells, R. D., & Holford, S. (1992). Physical and sexual abuse as predictors of substance use and suicide among pregnant teenagers. *Journal of Adolescent Health, 13,* 128–132.

Borenstein, M. H., & Tamis-Le Mandu, C. S. (2001). Mother–infant interaction. In G. Bremner & A. Fogel (Eds.), *Blackwell handbook of infant development* (pp. 269–295). Oxford, England: Blackwell.

Bradley, J., & Rotheram-Borus, M. J. (1990). *Evaluation of imminent danger for suicide: A training manual*. Tulsa: University of Oklahoma Youth Services.

Brazelton, T. B. (1990). Touch as a touchstone: Summary of the round table. In K. E. Barnard & T. B. Brazelton (Eds.), *Touch: The foundation of experience* (Clinical Infant Reports, No. 4, pp. 561–566). Madison, WI: International Universities Press.

Bruch, H. (1973). *Eating disorders*. New York: Basic Books.

Cash, T. F. (1997). The treatment of body image disturbances. In J. K. Tompson (Ed.), *Body image, eating disorders, and obesity* (pp. 83–107). Washington, DC: American Psychological Association.

Damasio, A. R. (1994). *Descartes' error: Emotion, reason, and the human brain*. New York: Quill.

Damasio, A. R. (1999). *The feeling of what happens: Body and emotion in the making of self-consciousness*. London: Harcourt.

de Chateau, P. (1976). The influence of early contact on maternal and infant behavior on primiparae. *Birth and the Family Journal, 3*, 149–155.

de Jong, M. L. (1992). Attachment, individuation, and risk of suicide in late adolescence. *Journal of Youth and Adolescence, 21*, 357–373.

Edman, G., Asberg, M., Levander, S., & Schalling, D. (1986). Skin conductance habituation and cerebrospinal fluid 5-hydroxyinoleucetic acid in suicidal patients. *Archives of General Psychiatry, 43*, 586–592.

Feldman, R., Weller, A., Sirota, L., & Eidelman, A. I. (2002). Skin-to-skin contact (Kangaroo care) promotes self-regulation in premature infants: Sleep–wake cyclicity, arousal modulation, and sustained exploration. *Developmental Psychology, 38*, 194–207.

Field, T. M. (1997, December). *Touch therapies for adolescents with suicidal ideation.* Paper presented at a symposium, "Early Attachment in Infancy and Self-Destructive Behavior in Adulthood," Bar-Ilan University, Israel.

Fogel, A. (1997). *Infancy: Infant, family, and society.* St. Paul, MN: West.

Freud, A. (1949). Aggression in relation to emotional development. *The Psychoanalytic Study of the Child, 3*, 37–42.

Furman, E. (1984). Some difficulties in assessing depression and suicide in childhood. In H. S. Sudak, A. B. Ford, & N. B. Rushforth (Eds.), *Suicide in the young* (pp. 245–258). Boston: John Wright/PSG.

Goodwin, J. (1981). Suicide attempts in sexually abused victims and their mothers. *Child Abuse and Neglect, 5*, 217.

Green, A. H. (1978). Self-destructive behavior in battered children. *American Journal of Psychiatry, 135*, 579–581.

Greenspan, S. I. (1979). *Intelligence and adaptation.* New York: International Universities Press.

Grossman, W. I. (1991). Pain, aggression, fantasy, and concepts of sadomasochism. *Psychoanalytic Quarterly, 60*, 22–52.

Gupta, M. A., & Schork, N. J. (1995). Touch deprivation has an adverse affect on body image: Some preliminary findings. *International Journal of Eating Disorders, 17*, 185–189.

Harlow, H. F., & Suomi, S. J. (1970). The nature of love simplified. *American Psychologist, 25*, 161–168.

Helders, P. J. M, Cats, B. P., & Debast, S. (1989). Effect of a tactile stimulation/range-finding programme on the development of VLBW-neonates during the first year of life. *Child Care, Health and Development, 15*, 369–380.

Kaplan, M., Asnis, G. M., Lipschitz, D. S., & Chorney, P. (1995). Suicidal behavior and abuse in psychiatric outpatients. *Comprehensive Psychiatry, 36*, 229–235.

Koester, L. S., Papousek, H., & Papousek, M. (1989). Patterns of rhythmic stimulation by mothers with three-month-olds: A cross-modal comparison. *International Journal of Behavioral Development, 12*, 143–154.

Koff, E., Rierdan, J., & Stubbs, M. L. (1990). Gender, body image, and self-concept in early adolescence. *Journal of Early Adolescence, 10*, 56–68.

Kraemer, G. W., & Clarke, A. S. (1990). The behavior neurobiology of self-injurious behavior in rhesus monkeys. *Neuropsychopharmacological and Biological Psychiatry, 14,* 141–168.

Kruger, D. W. (1989). *Body self and psychological self: A developmental and clinical integration of disorders of the self.* New York: Brunner/Mazel.

Kuhn, C. M., & Schanberg, S. M. (1998). Responses to maternal separation: Mechanisms and mediators. *International Journal of Developmental Neuroscience, 16,* 261–270.

Laufer, M. E. (1991). Body image, sexuality, and the psychotic core. *International Journal of Psychoanalysis, 24,* 514–518.

Lester, D. (1991). Physical abuse and physical punishment as precursors of suicidal behavior. *Stress Medicine, 7,* 255–256.

Lewis, M., Solnit, A. J., Stark, M. H., Gabrielson, I. W., & Klatskin, E. H. (1996). An exploration study of accidental ingestion of poison in young children. *Journal of the American Academy of Child Psychiatry, 5,* 255–271.

MacDonald, K. (1987). Parent–child physical play with rejected, neglected, and popular boys. *Developmental Psychology, 23,* 705–711.

MacDonald, K., & Parke, R. D. (1984). Bridging the gap: Parent–child play interaction and peer interactive competence. *Child Development, 55,* 1265–1267.

MacLeod, A. K., Williams, J. M., & Linehan, M. M. (1992). New developments in the understanding and treatment of suicidal behavior. *Behavioral Psychotherapy, 20,* 193–218.

Maltsberger, J. T. (1993). Confusion of the body, the self, and others in suicidal states. In A. Leenaars, A. L. Berman, P. Cantor, R. E. Litman, & R.W. Maris (Eds.), *Suicidology: Essays in honor of Edwin Shneidman* (pp. 148–172). Northvale, NJ: Aronson.

Montague, A. (1986). *Touching: The human significance of the skin* (3rd ed.). New York: Harper & Row.

Nuñez, R. (1999). Could the future taste purple? Reclaiming mind, body, and cognition. In R. Nuñez & W. J. Freeman (Eds.), *Reclaiming cognition: The primacy of action, intention, and emotion* (pp. 41–60). Thorverton, England: Imprint Academic.

Orbach, I. (1994). Dissociation, physical pain, and suicide: A hypothesis. *Suicide and Life-Threatening Behavior, 24,* 68–79.

Orbach, I. (1997). A taxonomy of factors related to suicidal behavior. *Clinical Psychology: Science and Practice, 4,* 208–224.

Orbach, I., Gilboa-Schechtman, E., Sheffer, A., Meged, S., Har-Even, D., & Stein, D. (in press). Negative bodily self in suicide attempters. *Suicide and Life-Threatening Behavior.*

Orbach, I., Herman, L., Kedem, P., & Apter, A. (1995). Dissociation tendencies in suicidal adolescents. *Journal of Social and Clinical Psychology, 14,* 393–408.

Orbach, I., Lotem-Peleg, M., & Kedem, P. (1995). Attitudes towards the body in suicidal, depressed, and normal adolescents. *Suicide and Life-Threatening Behavior, 25,* 211–221.

Orbach, I., & Mikulincer, M. (1998). The Body Investment Scale: Construction and validation of a body investment scale. *Psychological Assessment, 10*, 415–425.

Orbach, I., Mikulincer, M., King, R., Cohen, D., & Stein, D. (1997). Threshold for tolerance of physical pain in suicidal and nonsuicidal adolescents. *Journal of Consulting and Clinical Psychology, 65*, 646–652.

Orbach, I., Stein, D., Palgi, Y., Asherov, J., Har-Even, D., & Elizur, A. (1996). Perception of physical pain in accident and suicide attempt patients: Self-preservation vs. self-destruction. *Journal of Psychiatric Research, 30*, 307–320.

Orbach, I., Stein, D., Shani-Sela, M., & Har-Even, D. (2001). Body attitudes and body experiences in suicidal adolescents. *Suicide and Life-Threatening Behavior, 31*, 237–249.

Panksepp, J. (1998). *Affective neuroscience: The foundation of human and animal emotions*. Oxford, England: Oxford University Press.

Pearce, C. M., Martin, M., & Wood, K. (1995). Significance of touch for perceptions of parenting and psychological adjustment among adolescents. *Journal of the American Academy of Child and Adolescent Psychiatry, 34*, 160–167.

Pelaez-Nogueras, M., Field, T. M., Hossain, Z., & Pickens, J. (1996). Depressed mothers' touching increases infants' positive affect and attention in still-face interactions. *Child Development, 67*, 1780–1792.

Pines, D. (1980). Skin communication: Early skin disorders and their effect on transference and countertransference. *International Journal of Psychoanalysis, 61*, 315–323.

Putnam, N., & Stein, M. (1985). Self-inflicted injuries in childhood. *Psychological Pediatrics, 24*, 514–518.

Róiste, A., & Bushnell, I. W. R. (1996). Tactile stimulation: Short- and long-term benefits for preterm infants. *British Journal of Developmental Psychology, 14*, 41–53.

Russ, M. J., Shearin, E. N., Clarkin, J. F., Harrison, K., & Hull, W. J. (1993). Subtypes of self-injurious patients with borderline personality disorder. *American Journal of Psychiatry, 150*, 1869–1871.

Salk, L. (1985). Relationship of maternal and prenatal condition to eventual adolescent suicide. *Lancet, 16*, 624–627.

Schachter, S. (1968). Obesity and eating. *Science, 161*, 751–756.

Schanberg, S. M., & Field, T. M. (1987). Sensory deprivation stress and supplemental stimulation in the rat pup and preterm human. *Child Development, 58*, 1431–1447.

Shapiro, S. (1991). Affect integration in psychoanalysis. *Bulletin of the Menninger Clinic, 55*, 363–374.

Sheets-Johnstone, M. (1999). Emotion and movement: A beginning empirical-phenomenological analysis of their relationships. *Journal of Consciousness Studies, 6*, 259–277.

Shneidman, E. S. (1980). *Voices of death*. New York: Harper & Row.

Silverstone, J. T., & Russell, G. F. M. (1967). Gastric hunger contraction in anorexia nervosa. *British Journal of Psychiatry, 113*, 257–263.

Sloan, N. L., Camacho, L. W., Rojas, E. P., & Stern, C. (1994). Kangaroo mother method: Randomized controlled trial of an alternative method of care for stabilized low birthweight infants. *Lancet*, *344*, 782–785.

Spiegel, D. (1969). Automatic reactivity in relation to the affective meaning of suicide. *Journal of Clinical Psychology*, *25*, 359–362.

Spitz, R. A. (1965). *The first year of life*. New York: International Universities Press.

Stack, D. M. (2001). The salience of touch and physical contact during infancy: Unraveling some of the mysteries of the somethetic sense. In G. Bremner & A. Fogel (Eds.), *Blackwell handbook of infant development* (pp. 351–378). Oxford, England: Blackwell.

Thorell, L. H. (1987). *Electrodermal activity in depressive patients: Its relationship to symptomatology, suicidal behavior, cortisol dysregulation, and clinical recovery*. Unpublished doctoral dissertation, Linkoping, Sweden: Linkoping University.

Vanderlinden, J., Van Dyck, R., Vanderyckan, W., Vertommen, H., & Jan Verkes, R. (1993). The Dissociation Questionnaire (DISQ): Development and characteristics of a new self-report questionnaire. *Clinical Psychology and Psychotherapy*, *1*, 21–27.

Van der Velde, C. D. (1985). Body image of one's self and of others: Developmental and clinical significance. *American Journal of Psychiatry*, *142*, 527–537.

Vinoda, K. S. (1966). Personality characteristics of attempted suicides. *British Journal of Psychiatry*, *112*, 1143–1150.

Wagner, B. M., & Cohen, P. (1994). Adolescent sibling differences in suicidal symptoms: The role of parent–child relationships. *Journal of Abnormal Child Psychiatry*, *22*, 321–336.

10

TRAIT PERFECTIONISM DIMENSIONS AND SUICIDAL BEHAVIOR

PAUL L. HEWITT, GORDON L. FLETT, SIMON B. SHERRY,
AND CARMEN CAELIAN

I have a good self, that loves skies, hills, ideas, tasty meals, bright colors. My demon would murder this self by demanding that it be a paragon, and saying it should run away if it is anything less. . . . I have this demon who wants me to run away screaming if I am going to be flawed, fallible. It wants me to think I'm so good I must be perfect. Or nothing. (Sylvia Plath, 1982, p. 176)

In this chapter, we provide evidence that perfectionism should be viewed as a vulnerability factor of importance in suicide and present a model of perfectionism and suicide that reflects the importance of interpersonal perfectionistic behavior. Our conceptual and empirical analysis is based on the hypotheses that (a) trait perfectionism dimensions are vulnerability factors linked directly with suicide and (b) trait perfectionism is linked indirectly with suicidal tendencies via its association with life stress and social disconnection. In subsequent sections of this chapter, we report results of research that investigates the link between perfectionism and suicide in a variety of populations. These findings highlight how socially prescribed perfectionism is a particularly robust factor in suicidality.

PERFECTIONISM AND SUICIDE

To grasp immediately a sense that perfectionism plays an important role in suicidal behavior, at least anecdotally, one has only to read case studies in the suicide literature of individuals who either made serious suicide attempts or who have actually committed suicide. The suicide literature, and especially the adolescent suicide literature, is replete with references to perfectionism as a relevant factor in the suicide process. As one example, Blatt (1995) described three extremely perfectionistic individuals (i.e., Vincent Foster, Alasdair Clayre, and Denny Hansen) who were highly accomplished and talented individuals who all committed suicide. These individuals appeared to derive little satisfaction from their achievements, did not experience a bolstering of self-esteem from their successes, and did not reduce their needs for future "perfect" accomplishments following failure. Similarly, many biographical and autobiographical materials point to well-known individuals who were described as extreme perfectionists who engaged in suicidal behavior. People in this category include authors such as Ernest Hemingway, Virginia Woolf, and Sylvia Plath and philosophers such as Ludwig Wittgenstein. Most recently, in 2003, well-known perfectionists such as Bernard Loiseau, David Kelly, and Leslie Cheung killed themselves. Loiseau was the chef from France who killed himself when his restaurant's rating was downgraded. Kelly was the British Ministry of Defence scientist who killed himself after allegedly revealing information to the media about the Iraqi weapons dossier. Cheung was the Asian superstar of films and records who leapt to his death from a hotel balcony. There certainly is little doubt that numerous factors contributed to these individuals' suicides; however, a common factor across these individuals' lives was a seemingly relentless pursuit of perfection.

In both the suicide literature and the biographical literature domains, two facets of perfectionistic behavior seem to be described as most relevant to suicidal behavior. These factors involve perfection that is demanded by oneself (e.g., Delisle, 1990; Mack, 1986; Shaffer, 1974) and perfection that is demanded for one by significant others (Baumeister, 1990; Delisle, 1990; Hayes & Sloat, 1989; Shafii, Carrigan, Whittinghill, & Derrick, 1985). For instance, Berman and Jobes (1991) suggested that rigid perfectionism is a risk factor especially when the perfectionist "is threatened with not achieving at self- or other-demanded levels of performance" (p. 129).

The two perfectionism factors described are essentially the same as two of the three dispositional dimensions of perfectionism we have described elsewhere in a different context (Hewitt & Flett, 1991). In general, we have conceptualized perfectionism as a construct that incorporates highly stable and independent dimensions involving both self-related and interpersonal components. For example, *self-oriented perfectionism* is a self-related dimension involving strong motivations for oneself to be perfect, holding unrealistic self-expectations, all or none thinking, and focusing on one's own flaws. On the other hand, *socially prescribed perfectionism* is an interpersonal dimension involving perceptions of one's need and ability to meet the standards and expectations imposed by others. It entails the belief that others, or society in general, have unrealistic standards and expectations for one's own behaviors and that others are highly evaluative and will be satisfied only when the unrealistic standards are met. Thus, socially prescribed perfectionism involves the perception that one is unable to meet unrealistic expectations and standards that others have for oneself.

MODELS INCORPORATING PERFECTIONISM AND SUICIDE

Although numerous authors over the years have implicated perfectionism as important (e.g., Hollender, 1965; Marks & Haller, 1977; Shaffer, 1974), several models of suicidal behavior have incorporated perfectionism more or less directly. For example, Baumeister's (1990) escape from the self model directly implicates perfectionism in his proposal that some suicide attempts (and related forms of self-destructive behavior) arise from a strong desire to escape from aversive self-awareness—that is, from the painful awareness of shortcomings and lack of success that the person attributes to himself or herself. Unrealistically high expectations from either the self or from others (i.e., perfectionism)—and therefore the probability of failing to meet these expectancies—play a central role in this model of suicide. Of particular importance is the discrepancy between impossibly high self or other expectations and a reality that falls short of those expectations.

Similarly, Orbach (1997) hypothesized that one of three distinct clusters associated with suicide involves perfectionism with attendant themes of depression, hopelessness, and shame. Self-destructive processes focus on intrapunitiveness and self-devaluation and this cluster is believed to be associated with a variety of stressors including negative reactions to loss, rejection, failure, and disappointment.

Finally, we (Hewitt & Flett, 1993a, 1993b, 2002) have described a model of perfectionism that involves the importance of stress and the presence of ego-involving stressors or failures in severe maladjustment including suicide potential. The pathway by which perfectionism can produce suicidal potential involves a model whereby perfectionistic behavior generates the frequency and enhances the aversiveness of stress, both of which can result in considering and attempting suicide. With respect to generating stressors, Hewitt and Flett (2002) proposed that perfectionism creates stress by setting up perfectionists to encounter frequent stressful failure because their expectations are so high that they are impossible to meet. Perfectionists also focus on the flaws in their performance rather than recognizing the aspects of their work that are well done, resulting in never experiencing satisfaction or self-rewards. Also, when they encounter failure, perfectionists tend not to alter their high standards to more realistic levels; rather they continue to attempt to perform to unrealistic levels and face future failure experiences. Because socially prescribed perfectionists do not have control over the expectations they are expected to meet, they continually encounter stressful experiences as they come up short time and time again.

Hewitt and Flett (2002) also proposed that perfectionism can interact with extant stress to lead to suicidal outcomes. Even if the stress is not generated by perfectionism itself, perfectionists are likely to react to stress in less adaptive ways than those who are not perfectionistic. Hewitt and Flett (2002) illustrated this point by noting that perfectionists tend to perceive stress as more aversive than nonperfectionists and to view failure experiences as evidence of their worthlessness as persons. They may also be at risk for a social form of hopelessness when they realize that they are unable to satisfy the perceived perfectionistic expectations of others. This alienation from others may make perfectionists more vulnerable to outcomes such as suicide (Hewitt & Flett, 1991, 2002).

The enhanced aversiveness of stressors may be especially pertinent when the type of stressful event is congruent with the perfectionism dimension in question. That is, *specific types of stressors* may interact with *specific dimensions of perfectionism* to produce increased suicidal behaviors. We have argued that if extant stressors (e.g., achievement vs. social stressors) are congruent with the particular perfectionism dimension that is elevated, the aversiveness of the stressful event will be increased and depression and suicide potential may ensue (Hewitt & Flett, 1993a, 2002; Oatley & Bolton, 1985). Because self-oriented perfectionism is a personality style that focuses on attainment of achievement standards as a primary concern, stressors reflecting achievement disruptions should be most likely to interact with self-oriented perfectionism to predict suicidal behavior. Socially prescribed perfectionism should interact with interpersonally related stressors in predicting suicide behavior because socially prescribed perfectionism involves interpersonal variables such as fear of negative evaluation, and need for approval and belonging.

EMPIRICAL RESEARCH ON PERFECTIONISM AND SUICIDAL BEHAVIOR

Although there are the long-standing references to perfectionism being relevant to suicide, research on the association has recently begun to increase. The research, as with most suicide research, can be separated into studies dealing with suicide ideation and those with suicide attempts. In the next section, we provide a review of this research supporting the importance of self-oriented and socially prescribed perfectionism. The first part of the next section focuses on research that has studied perfectionism dimensions and used suicide ideation as the main suicide outcome in clinical and nonclinical groups, and the second focuses on some research using suicide attempts as the outcome.

Suicide Ideation

The existing perfectionism research dealing with suicide ideation as the major outcome has focused on adults and has highlighted the primary importance of social pressures to be perfect in thinking about suicide. A brief review of this literature follows. To our knowledge, Hewitt, Flett, and Turnbull-Donovan (1992) conducted the first published study on suicide in which perfectionism was treated as a multidimensional personality construct. This study was conducted to determine whether the various dimensions were differentially related to suicide outcomes. A heterogeneous sample of 87 psychiatric patients completed the Multidimensional Perfectionism Scale (MPS; Hewitt & Flett, 1991; Hewitt, Flett, Turnbull-Donovan, & Mikail, 1991) along with measures of depression, hopelessness, suicidal ideation, and suicidal threat. The results indicated that socially prescribed perfectionism was correlated significantly with suicide ideation and suicide threat. Moreover, socially prescribed perfectionism accounted for unique variance in the suicide measures, even after removing variance caused by levels of depression and hopelessness ratings. This finding was particularly meaningful considering that depression and hopelessness are regarded as two of the best suicide predictors (Beck, Steer, Beck, & Newman, 1993; Beck, Steer, Kovacs, & Garrison, 1985; De Man, 1999; Lewinsohn, Rohde, & Seeley, 1996). Self- and other-oriented perfectionism were unrelated to suicidality in this study.

A subsequent study was conducted by Hewitt, Flett, and Weber (1994) in response to limitations in the Hewitt et al. (1992) study. Specifically, our first study must be interpreted with caution because of the use of a single-item measure of hopelessness and the use of the MMPI suicide ideation measure, which has been questioned in terms of its psychometric characteristics. As a result, Hewitt et al. (1994) examined perfectionism, depression, hopelessness, and suicide ideation in two samples consisting of 91 psychiatric patients and 160 university students, respectively. Participants completed the MPS, the Beck Depression Inventory (BDI; Beck, Steer, & Brown, 1987), the Beck Hopelessness Scale (BHS; Beck, Weissman, Lester, & Trexler, 1974), and the Scale for Suicide Ideation (SSI; Beck, Steer, & Ranieri, 1988). Analyses indicated that both self-oriented and socially prescribed perfectionism were correlated significantly with suicide ideation in the psychiatric sample. The psychiatric patients were subsequently divided into three groups (low, moderate, or high suicidal ideation) and then compared via analyses of variance. Analyses indicated that the moderate and high ideation groups had significantly higher levels of self-oriented and socially prescribed perfectionism than the low ideation group, and the medium and high groups did not differ from each other in levels of either dimension of perfectionism. A stepwise discriminant function analysis found that hopelessness distinguished the suicide ideation groups, followed by socially prescribed perfectionism, depression, and self-oriented perfectionism. Thus, both MPS dimensions contributed to the discrimination of groups when considered along with hopelessness and depression. A similar pattern of findings emerged when analyses were conducted on the data from the student sample, supporting the hypotheses that self-oriented perfectionism and socially prescribed perfectionism were both associated with suicide ideation and each contributed unique variance in the prediction of suicide ideation. Moreover, the fact that the findings were identical in clinical and nonclinical adult samples suggested that relationship between perfectionism and suicide ideation is robust.

Measures of trait perfectionism were incorporated into research by Dean, Range, and colleagues. They conducted a series of studies to test predictions from Baumeister's escape model of suicide discussed earlier using suicide ideation as their major outcome variable in nonclinical samples of college students. Dean and Range (1996) and Dean, Range, and Goggin (1996) had college students complete a battery of questionnaires, including the MPS and measures of life stress, depression, anxiety, reasons for living, hopelessness, and suicide ideation. Neither self- nor other-oriented perfectionism (requiring perfection of others) was correlated with suicide ideation; however, socially prescribed perfectionism was associated with suicide ideation and hopelessness and predicted unique variance in suicide ideation in one of the two studies (Dean et al., 1996). Furthermore, causal modeling highlighted an indirect relationship between socially prescribed perfectionism and suicide behaviors with significant paths from socially prescribed dimension to low reasons for living to suicidal behaviors in one study (Dean & Range, 1996) and from socially prescribed perfectionism to depression to hopelessness to reasons for living to suicide ideation in the second study (Dean et al., 1996).

Hamilton and Schweitzer (2000) obtained further support for the role of socially prescribed perfectionism in suicide ideation in a recent study involving more than 400 university students. Participants completed the General Health Questionnaire—28 (GHQ–28; Goldberg, 1988), a measure of psychological distress in several areas, and the Multidimensional Perfectionism Scale by Frost and colleagues (Frost, Marten, Lahart, & Rosenblate, 1990). This perfectionism measure is similar to the Hewitt and Flett (1991) version in that it conceptualizes perfectionism as a multidimensional trait. However, the Frost et al. (1990) measure assesses six dimensions of perfectionism, compared with three dimensions on the Hewitt and Flett (1991) measure, in addition to providing an overall perfectionism score. The six dimensions measured include personal standards, concern over mistakes, doubts about actions, parental criticism, parental expectations, and organization. According to Frost and colleagues (Frost, Heimberg, Holt, Mattia, & Neubauer, 1993), the concern about mistakes, parental expectations, and parental criticism dimensions are most closely related to socially prescribed perfectionism as defined by Hewitt and Flett (1991). In the Hamilton and Schweitzer (2000) study, participants who endorsed suicidal ideation had higher levels of over-

220   HEWITT ET AL.

all perfectionism than those who did not report suicidal thoughts. Furthermore, participants with higher levels of concern over mistakes and doubts about actions reported more suicidal ideation, indirectly supporting the general thesis that perfectionism is associated with suicide outcomes (also see Adkins & Parker, 1996; Chang, 1998).

A study by Enns, Cox, Sareen, and Freeman (2001) examined the relationship of perfectionism to suicidal ideation using both the Hewitt and Flett (1991) and Frost et al. (1990) MPS measures with a sample of 96 medical students. Consistent with Hamilton and Schweitzer (2000), these authors found that socially prescribed perfectionism, concern over mistakes, and doubts about actions were all associated with increased suicidal ideation among participants, suggesting once again that different dimensions of perfectionism are associated with thoughts of suicide.

Finally, in line with the studies just discussed, a recent longitudinal investigation of the link between perfectionism and suicidal ideation among university students indicated that only socially prescribed perfectionism was related to suicidal thoughts occurring over time (Hewitt, Caelian, Sherry, & Flett, 2005). In this study, the student sample was administered measures of perfectionism, depression, hopelessness, stress, and suicide ideation 4 months after their initial participation in the study. The findings of the study again underscored the importance of socially prescribed perfectionism as relevant in terms of predicting suicide ideation over time. As found in the other research cited earlier, the relevance of this perfectionism dimension is not due simply to overlap with either hopelessness or depression and suggests the importance of evaluating socially prescribed perfectionism in suicide risk.

The literature reviewed earlier supports the position that perfectionism is an important variable to consider in our efforts to understand better and to predict suicidal ideation among adults. Despite what has been learned in this area and the present serious concerns about rates of suicidal behavior among North American youth, research examining the link between perfectionism and suicide in this population is very limited. In the first of these studies, Hewitt, Newton, Flett, and Callander (1997) had a sample of 66 adolescent psychiatric inpatients complete a package of measures that included the Child–Adolescent Perfectionism Scale (CAPS; Flett, Hewitt, Boucher, Davidson, & Munro, 2003), the Suicide Ideation Questionnaire (SIQ; Reynolds, 1988), and Hopelessness Scale for Children (HSC; Kazdin, Rodgers, & Colbus, 1986). Note that the CAPS is an extension of our MPS for use with children and adolescents that includes measures of self-oriented and socially prescribed perfectionism. As with the majority of adult research, correlational analyses indicated that self-oriented perfectionism was not significantly related to suicidal ideation; however, socially prescribed perfectionism was strongly correlated with this outcome measure. Further analysis revealed that socially prescribed perfectionism accounted for unique variance in suicide ideation scores after controlling for the contribution of hopelessness.

Suicide Attempts

Because only a subset of those who contemplate suicide actually make a suicide attempt, it is important to examine levels of perfectionism in those who do and do not attempt suicide to determine whether perfectionism contributes to actual suicidal behavior in addition to suicidal ideation. The role of perfectionism in high-intent suicide attempts was explored in a study conducted with a sample of residentially treated alcoholic patients (Hewitt, Norton, Flett, Callender, & Cowan, 1998). The study included 39 inpatients with alcoholism who had made a serious suicide attempt and a matched group of 39 inpatients with alcoholism but no history of suicide attempts. The attempter group had at least one suicide attempt that was rated as moderate to high in lethality by clinicians. Participants in both groups completed the MPS, the BHS (Beck et al., 1974), 1-item global ratings of achievement hopelessness (i.e., My prospects for achieving my goals in the future are hopeless) and social hopelessness (i.e., I feel totally hopeless about my future social relationships), and the BDI (Beck, Steer, & Brown, 1987). Group comparisons via analyses of variance found that the two groups differed significantly on socially prescribed perfectionism, all three hopelessness measures, and depression. As expected, the attempter group had significantly higher levels on each of these variables. Next, a stepwise discriminant function analysis was conducted to determine the unique contribution of the variables. The four variables that entered the equation in order were depression, social hopelessness, socially prescribed perfectionism, and other-oriented perfectionism. The suicide attempter group was distinguished by higher levels of depression, social hopelessness, and socially prescribed perfectionism, and lower levels of other-oriented perfectionism (a finding with other-oriented perfectionism has not been obtained in other samples). To our knowledge, this is the only published study examining the role of perfectionism in suicidal attempts among adults, but its findings suggest that this is an area worthy of further investigation.

Two studies have been conducted on suicide attempts among youth. For example Boergers, Spirito, and Donaldson (1998) examined self-reported reasons for suicide attempts provided by 120 adolescents shortly after they presented to hospital following their attempts. The three motives for suicide reported most frequently were a wish to die, a desire to escape, and an attempt to obtain relief. Adolescents who endorsed a wish to die as the reason behind their attempts had higher levels of socially prescribed perfectionism compared with adolescents who reported less serious motives. Moreover, socially prescribed perfectionism predicted death as the primary reason offered for adolescent suicide attempts.

Likewise, Enns, Cox, and Inayatulla (2003) recently examined the relationship between personality variables and treatment outcome for adolescents hospitalized for suicidal ideation or behavior. Seventy-eight adolescents admitted to a psychiatric inpatient unit for suicidality completed measures of perfectionism, neuroticism, self-criticism, interpersonal dependency, depression, hopelessness, and suicidal ideation at the beginning and end of their inpatient treatment. At Time 1, socially prescribed perfectionism, neuroticism, self-criticism, and dependency were all associated with suicidal ideation, depression, and hopelessness scores. In regression analyses, only neuroticism was uniquely predictive of Time 2 suicide scores and readmission to hospital within the following year.

Finally, one additional study provides indirect evidence in support of the role of perfectionism in suicide risk. Donaldson, Spirito, and Farnett (2000) investigated the relationship between cognitive risk factors for suicide (i.e., perfectionism and depressive cognitions) and the hopelessness experienced by adolescents who attempted suicide. Sixty-eight adolescents presenting to a hospital following a suicide attempt completed the CAPS (Flett, Hewitt, et al., 2003), Depressive Experiences Questionnaire for Adolescents (DEQ-A; Blatt, Schaffer, Bers, & Quinlin, 1992), and the HSC (Kazdin et al., 1986). Correlational analyses indicated that socially prescribed perfectionism and self-criticism were associated with hopelessness. Furthermore, both of these risk factors contributed unique variance to the prediction of hopelessness after accounting for that contributed by prior suicide attempts. Although self-criticism accounted for more variance than did socially prescribed perfectionism in this analysis, both findings are important considering that prior suicide attempts are a strong predictor of future suicidality (e.g., Lewinsohn et al., 1996).

Collectively, the results outlined here indicate that there is a consistent association between socially prescribed perfectionism and suicidal ideation and suicide attempts. Furthermore, it is apparent that socially prescribed perfectionism contributes nonredundant information to the prediction of these suicidal behaviors, beyond that contributed by other demonstrated risk factors such as depression and hopelessness. The relationship between self-oriented perfectionism and suicide is less clear and may exist indirectly as a function of moderating factors that confer risk for suicide (e.g., stress).

PERFECTIONISM, LIFE STRESS, AND SUICIDE

As described earlier, we (Hewitt & Flett, 2002) described two ways in which perfectionism can result in suicidal ideation and suicide attempts. To our knowledge, research investigating mediational models of the perfectionism–stress–suicide link, whereby perfectionism generates stress, which then produces suicidal behavior, have not yet been published. Although there is some evidence that both self-oriented and socially prescribed perfectionism can generate stress (see Hewitt & Flett, 1993a), no work has been done that assesses the pathways among trait perfectionism, stress, and suicide outcomes. The only work that comes close to this was described by Dean and Range (1999) who, via structural equation modeling in a sample of 132 clinical outpatients, found a significant path from socially prescribed perfectionism to depression, depression to hopelessness, and hopelessness to suicide ideation. Although this mediation model did not test stress per se, it provides support for the proposition that socially prescribed perfectionism can mediate the link between predictors of suicide and subsequent suicidal behavior.

In terms of the moderational model proposed by Hewitt and Flett (2002), no studies have assessed whether specific perfectionism dimensions interact with specific stressors in predicting suicide outcomes; however, the results of Hewitt and colleagues (1994; Hewitt et al., 2005) provide some evidence that perfectionism interacts with extant stress to predict suicidality. As outlined earlier, Hewitt et al. (1994) administered measures of perfectionism, life stress, and suicide ideation to a sample of 160 university students. Both self-oriented and socially prescribed perfectionism interacted with the presence of life event stressors to predict increased suicide ideation. Similarly, in the Hewitt et al. (2003) longitudinal study, also described previously, we investigated whether perfectionists who experienced stress in the form of major life events or daily hassles would experience suicidal ideation over time. In this study, the stress measures administered at Time 2 covered the time period since the Time 1 administration of measures. Only socially prescribed perfectionism was associated with life stress 4 months from the initial assessment and only the socially prescribed dimension interacted with both the presence of major life stress and presence of daily hassles to predict future suicide ideation. These two studies provide support for the moderator model and suggest that perfectionistic individuals, by virtue of being either self-oriented or socially prescribed perfectionists, experience extant stress more aversively than others.

Some indirect evidence exists for the moderational model of perfectionism as it relates to hopelessness, a significant predictor of suicide. Chang and Rand (2000) examined the ability of the perfectionism–stress relationship to predict psychological symptoms and hopelessness 1 month in the future. Two hundred and fifteen college students completed measures of perfectionism and life stress at Time 1 and measures of psychological symptoms and hopelessness approximately 1 month later. Only socially prescribed perfectionism was associated with psychological symptoms and hopelessness experienced 1 month after the study begun. Additionally, socially prescribed perfectionism predicted unique variance in psychological symptoms and hopelessness at Time 2 and interacted with life stress to account for additional variance in these outcomes. More specifically, individuals high in socially prescribed perfectionism were likely to experience hopelessness only if they also encountered high levels of life stress. It is interesting that self-oriented perfectionism also accounted for unique variance in hopelessness scores at Time 2.

The possibility that hopelessness serves as a mediator or a moderator of the link between perfectionism and suicidality deserves further empirical attention. We have noted elsewhere that socially prescribed perfectionism has an inherent element of helplessness and hopelessness associated with it (e.g., Flett, Hewitt, Blankstein, & Koledin, 1991; Hewitt & Flett, 1991). Many socially prescribed perfectionists seem to be individuals who not only anticipate the possibility of negative events but also become quite certain that such events will indeed be experienced, and they lack a sense of personal efficacy to avoid experiencing these events (Hewitt & Flett, 2002). Other empirical research on hopelessness and the trait dimensions of perfectionism has shown that socially prescribed perfectionism is associated consistently with hopelessness in all of the studies that have tested this association, including research with adult psychiatric patients, adolescents, and university students (e.g., Chang & Rand, 2000; Dean & Range, 1996; Dean, Range, & Goggin, 1996; Hewitt et al., 1992, 1997, 1998; O'Connor & O'Connor, 2003; Ohtani & Sakurai, 1995). These unequivocal findings suggest that socially prescribed perfectionism is indeed an aspect of perfectionism associated with generalized hopelessness, and it is possible that hopelessness is a direct or indirect mediator of the link between socially prescribed perfectionism and suicidality.

Finally, it should be noted that one other study (Dean & Range, 1999) examined the association among perfectionism, life stress, and suicidality in a clinical sample of 132 outpatients and did not yield evidence in support of a moderational model. Unfortunately, this study used a measure of life stress that requires participants to assess the stressfulness of life events over a 2-year period, and it is questionable whether an accurate measure of stress was indeed obtained in this study.

Although existing research with this moderational model is limited, it does suggest that socially prescribed perfectionism may function as a risk factor for suicide when the perfectionist encounters stress. Socially prescribed perfectionism appears to be directly linked to suicide outcomes in addition to interacting with stress to lead to suicide. In contrast, self-oriented perfectionism most often does not relate directly to suicidal behavior but seems to have either a more complex relationship with suicide ideation in that it tends to be associated with suicide ideation in the presence of significant life stress or a less robust relationship with suicide overall.

Although the research and theorizing regarding the link between perfectionism and suicide involves either discrepancies (e.g., Baumeister, 1990) or stressful failures (Hewitt & Flett, 2002), there is another possible mechanism through which perfectionism may result in suicidal behavior and may be particularly relevant for social components of the perfectionism construct (Hewitt et al., 2003). This conceptualization focuses on interpersonal outcomes of perfectionism and builds on findings that perfectionism is associated with negative relationship outcomes such as problems with establishing and maintaining close relationships (Habke & Flynn, 2002). One way that perfectionism may influence suicide is by contributing to a sense of alienation and lack of belonging, perceived lack of social support, and hopelessness about future interpersonal outcomes (Baumeister & Leary, 1995; Hewitt et al., 1994, 1998). Certainly disconnection from or lack of integration with the social world have been discussed as relevant features of suicide (e.g., Durkheim, 1897/1951), and social isolation is a suicide predictor that becomes more powerful as age increases (Pearson, 2000). In terms of the interpersonal aspects of the perfectionism construct, the perfectionistic individual who experiences stressful failures and an inability to be perfect may eventually experience an inability to obtain approval and belonging, leading to a lack of social connection because of the inability to meet perceived demands from others or to maintain a "perfect" façade (Hewitt et al., 2003). If so, then variables such as social alienation, lack of belonging, and a sense of perceived hopelessness about future interpersonal outcomes should mediate the link between socially prescribed perfectionism and suicidality. In the next section, we provide a detailed discussion of a possible model of socially prescribed perfections, social disconnection, and suicide behavior.

PERFECTIONISM, SOCIAL DISCONNECTION, AND SUICIDAL BEHAVIOR

In the following sections, socially prescribed perfectionism is proposed as one interpersonal risk factor that confers vulnerability to suicide behaviors by depriving people of the benefits of social connection and by exposing them to the costs of social disconnection. We term this model the social disconnection model (SDM); its central components involve socially prescribed perfectionism, objective and subjective social disconnection, and both interpersonal hostility and sensitivity. The model is presented in Figure 10.1, and a detailed explanation of this model is presented here.

Four main relationships involving objective and subjective social disconnection are postulated as central components of the SDM. In the first, objective social disconnection (i.e., actual severed or impaired relationships) is proposed to mediate the link between socially prescribed perfectionism and suicidal behaviors (see Paths 1, 2, and 4 in Figure 10.1). In the second relationship, subjective social disconnection (i.e., the phenomenological experience of aloneness) is postulated to mediate the link between socially prescribed perfectionism and suicidal behaviors (see Paths 1, 3, and 5 in Figure 10.1). In the third relationship, interpersonal hostility (i.e., as anger, suspiciousness directed toward others) is postulated to mediate the link between socially prescribed perfectionism and objective social disconnection (see Paths 2, 2a, and 2b in Figure 10.1). Finally, in the fourth relationship, interpersonal sensitivity (i.e., evaluative fear and vigilance experienced around

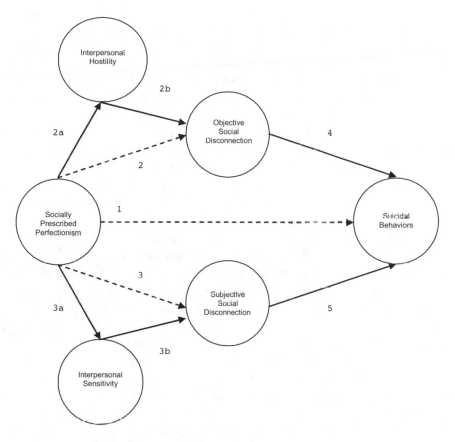

Figure 10.1. The social disconnection model: Objective social disconnection and subjective social disconnection as factors contributing to suicidal behaviors among socially prescribed perfectionists. Solid arrows represent direct effects; broken arrows represent mediated effects.

others) is proposed to mediate the link between socially prescribed perfectionism and subjective social disconnection (see Paths 3, 3a, and 3b in Figure 10.1). All of these factors should contribute to a profound sense of hopelessness about future interpersonal outcomes (i.e., social hopelessness). In the ensuing sections, the objective social disconnection portion of the SDM (i.e., the upper half of Figure 10.1) is discussed first and the subjective social disconnection portion of the SDM is discussed second (i.e., the lower half of Figure 10.1).

Socially Prescribed Perfectionism, Interpersonal Hostility, Objective Social Disconnection, and Suicidal Behavior

It is well known that interpersonal hostility and aggressiveness create difficulties in the development and maintenance of social relationships. Socially prescribed perfectionists are typified by their interpersonal hostility. For example, research using the interpersonal circumplex consistently demonstrates that socially prescribed perfectionists are located in the hostile dominant or hostile submissive quadrants (see Habke & Flynn, 2002). Also, several studies, adopting different methods and involving diverse populations, have yielded similar results (e.g., Habke & Flynn, 2002; Hewitt et al., 2003), suggesting that the connection between socially prescribed perfectionism and interpersonal hostility is reliable. In the SDM, interpersonal hostility is postulated as the "mechanism through which" (Baron & Kenny, 1986, p. 1173) socially prescribed perfectionism engenders objective social disconnection (see Paths 2, 2a, and 2b in Figure 10.1). To elaborate, the SDM proposes that the anger, suspicion, irritability, and resentment socially prescribed perfectionists direct toward others result in severed or impoverished kinship, friendship, and affiliative networks. Put differently, as a consequence of their interpersonal hostility, socially prescribed perfectionists are likely to become objectively disconnected from others. Estrangement, intimate relationship problems, lack of companionship, infrequent social contact, and inadequate received support are indicative of objective social disconnection. Although there is ample evidence to suggest that socially prescribed perfectionism breeds relationship-impairing interpersonal discord (e.g., Haring, Hewitt, & Flett, 2003; Hewitt, Flett, & Mikail, 1995), additional research is needed to establish a direct connection between socially prescribed perfectionism and objective social disconnection. Finally, leaving aside the question of how or why socially prescribed perfectionists generate objective social disconnection, the SDM postulates that socially prescribed perfectionists (a) produce objective social disconnection in their lives and (b) engage in suicidal behaviors amid such environmental conditions. Thus, the SDM is consistent with evidence linking indicators of objective social disconnection to suicidal behaviors (e.g., Barraclough, 1988; Gould, Fisher, Parides, Flory, & Shaffer, 1996).

Socially Prescribed Perfectionism, Interpersonal Sensitivity, Subjective Social Disconnection, and Suicidal Behaviors

In addition to interpersonal hostility, socially prescribed perfectionists are characterized by their interpersonal sensitivity (Hewitt & Flett, 1991). For instance, dependent attitudes are positively correlated with socially prescribed perfectionism in psychiatric patients and in university students (Sherry, Hewitt, Flett, & Harvey, 2003). Dependent attitudes involve basing self-worth on others' approval, requiring acceptance, needing admiration, craving nurturance, and pleasing others.

Recent research in our laboratory has obtained direct evidence of a link between trait socially prescribed perfectionism and trait interpersonal sensitivity. For instance, in one study, 227 university students completed a battery of measures that included the Multidimensional Perfectionism Scale and the Interpersonal Sensitivity Measure (Flett, Besser, Hewitt, & Velyvis, 2003). The Interpersonal Sensitivity Measure (IPSM) was developed by Boyce and Parker (1989) as a measure of vulnerability to depression. It consists of five factors, including interpersonal awareness, need for approval, timidity, fragile inner-self, and separation anxiety. Numerous studies with this measure have confirmed the role of interpersonal sensitivity in psychological distress. Our results confirmed that socially prescribed perfectionism is associated with total overall scores on the IPSM ($r = .34$, $p < .001$), and with subscale measures of heightened interpersonal awareness, fragile inner-self, and separation anxiety.

In the SDM, interpersonal sensitivity is postulated as the "mechanism through which" (Baron & Kenny, 1986, p. 1173) socially prescribed perfectionism engenders subjective social disconnection (see Paths 3, 3a, and 3b in Figure 10.1). To expand, the SDM proposes that the attachment insecurity, excessive neediness, and evaluative fear socially prescribed perfectionists experience around others bring about emotions, cognitions, and perceptions that signify rejection, alienation, and loneliness. Otherwise stated, as a result of their interpersonal sensitivity, socially prescribed perfectionists are likely to become subjectively disconnected from others. Feeling rejected or excluded by others, perceiving others as uncaring or unsupportive, and sensing a lack of emotional intimacy is indicative of subjective social disconnection. Theoretical reviews (e.g., Blankstein & Dunkley, 2002) and empirical studies (e.g., Flett, Hewitt, & DeRosa, 1996) have contributed to the general conclusion that socially prescribed perfectionism is implicated in the generation and the maintenance of subjective social disconnection. Lastly, again setting aside the issue of how or why socially prescribed perfectionists generate subjective social disconnection, the SDM postulates that socially prescribed perfectionists (a) produce subjective social disconnection in their lives and (b) engage in suicide behaviors during such phenomenological experiences. Thus, the SDM is congruent with research linking indicators of subjective social disconnection to suicidal behaviors (e.g., Groholt, Ekeberg, & Wichstrom, 2000; Heisel, Flett, & Besser, 2002).

The proposed model takes a decidedly interpersonal focus to the study of the perfectionism and suicide link and emphasizes the importance of socially prescribed perfectionistic behavior in some suicides and suicide attempts. Although it is possible that socially prescribed perfectionism can produce social disconnection through either main pathway, it is possible that socially prescribed perfectionism can produce both a perception of disconnection and actual disconnection. Whereas suicidal behavior can, of course, be produced by different personality (e.g., hopelessness) or environmental factors, other components of the perfectionism construct that involve interpersonal precursors or motivations, such as needs for respect, caring, and attention or powerful desires to be viewed as being perfect (see Hewitt et al., 2003) may also be involved in the negative impact of social disconnection.

Although life events have not been incorporated explicitly into the model displayed in Figure 10.1, it follows that negative interpersonal events should have substantial impact on socially prescribed perfectionists with an elevated sense of social disconnection. These vulnerable individuals may react with a profound sense of despair to interpersonal events that contribute to a sense of humiliation and public shame.

TREATMENT IMPLICATIONS

The interpersonal focus of the proposed model supports the importance of focusing on interpersonal facets of perfectionistic behavior. In fact, the clinical work of the first author places an emphasis not on the perfectionistic behavior itself (i.e., self-criticism, unrealistic expectations, etc.), but rather on the interpersonal precursors of the perfectionistic behavior. That is, an attempt is made to change the interpersonal and intrapersonal variables that are hypothesized to produce the perfectionistic behavior (see Hewitt & Flett, 2002). This involves focusing on interpersonal styles and needs, such as needs for approval, caring, or respect or needs to avoid abandonment, rejection, or feelings of irrelevance and humiliation that are all seen to drive the perfectionism. This is done using an interpersonal psychotherapeutic approach (Sullivan, 1953) that uses the therapeutic relationship as well as current and past relationships to facilitate change.

CONCLUSION

In this chapter, we have attempted to present some models of the often-noted presumed association between perfectionistic behavior and suicidality and provided a review of the extant research that has been done to address this empirical question. Overall, the findings are strongly suggestive that one interpersonal perfectionism dimension—socially prescribed perfectionism—is consistently and strongly associated with suicidal ideation and suicide attempts in both adult and adolescent clinical and nonclinical samples. The importance of this interpersonal perfectionism dimension is further developed by our description of a model of suicide that incorporates perfectionistic behavior and the resultant sense of alienation from the social world for individuals who have excessive levels of socially prescribed perfectionism. We are hopeful that this model will spawn future research that will be an aid in the understanding of the link between perfectionistic behavior and suicide.

Lastly, we are hopeful that this chapter will draw attention to the importance and uniqueness of perfectionistic behavior in the prediction of suicidal behavior. Just as both depression symptoms and hopelessness are assessed and used as factors in evaluating suicide risk, perhaps perfectionistic behavior should be strongly considered.

REFERENCES

Adkins, K. K., & Parker, W. (1996). Perfectionism and suicidal preoccupation. *Journal of Personality, 64*, 529–543.

Baron, R. M., & Kenny, D. A. (1986). The moderator–mediator variable distinction in social psychological research: Conceptual, strategic, and statistical considerations. *Journal of Personality and Social Psychology, 51*, 1173–1182.

Barraclough, B. (1988). International variation in the suicide rate of 15–24 year olds. *Social Psychiatry and Psychiatric Epidemiology, 23*, 75–84.

Baumeister, R. F. (1990). Suicide as escape from self. *Psychological Review, 97*, 90–113.

Baumeister, R., & Leary, M. (1995). The need to belong: Desire for interpersonal attachments as a fundamental human emotion. *Psychological Bulletin, 117*, 497–529.

Beck, A. T., Steer, R. A., Beck, J. S., & Newman, C. F. (1993). Hopelessness, depression, suicidal ideation, and clinical diagnosis of depression. *Suicide and Life-Threatening Behavior, 23*, 139–145.

Beck, A. T., Steer, R. A., & Brown, G. (1987). *Manual for the Beck Depression Inventory—II.* New York: Psychological Association.

Beck, A. T., Steer, R. A., Kovacs, M., & Garrison, B. (1985). Hopelessness and eventual suicide: A 10-year prospective study of patients hospitalized with suicide ideation. *American Journal of Psychiatry, 142*, 559–563.

Beck, A. T., Steer, R. A., & Ranieri, W. F. (1988). Scale for Suicide Ideation: Psychometric properties of a self-report version. *Journal of Clinical Psychology, 44*, 499–505.

Beck, A. T., Weissman, A., Lester, D., & Trexler, L. (1974). The measurement of pessimism: The Hopelessness Scale. *Journal of Consulting and Clinical Psychology, 42*, 861–865.

Berman, A. L., & Jobes, D. A. (1991). *Adolescent suicide: Assessment and intervention.* Washington, DC: American Psychological Association.

Blankstein, K., & Dunkley, D. (2002). Evaluative concerns, self-critical, and personal standards perfectionism: A structural equation model strategy. In G. L. Flett, L. Gordon, & P. L. Hewitt (Eds.), *Perfectionism: Theory, research, and treatment* (pp. 285–315). Washington, DC: American Psychological Association.

Blatt, S. J. (1995). The destructiveness of perfectionism: Implications for the treatment of depression. *American Psychologist, 50*, 1003–1020.

Blatt, S. J., Schaffer, C. E., Bers, S. A., & Quinlin, D. M. (1992). Psychometric properties of the Depressive Experiences Questionnaire for Adolescents. *Journal of Personality Assessment, 59*, 82–98.

Boergers, J., Spirito, A., & Donaldson, D. (1998). Reasons for adolescent suicide attempts: Associations with psychological functioning. *Journal of the American Academy of Child and Adolescent Psychiatry, 37,* 1287–1293.

Boyce, P., & Parker, G. (1989). Development of a scale to measure interpersonal sensitivity. *Australian and New Zealand Journal of Psychiatry, 23,* 341–351.

Chang, E. C. (1998). Cultural differences, perfectionism, and suicidal risk in a college population: Does social problem solving still matter? *Cognitive Therapy and Research, 22,* 237–254.

Chang, E. C., & Rand, K. L. (2000). Perfectionism as a predictor of subsequent adjustment: Evidence for a specific diathesis-stress mechanism among college students. *Journal of Counselling Psychology, 47,* 129–137.

Dean, P. J., & Range, L. M. (1996). The escape theory of suicide and perfectionism in college students. *Death Studies, 20,* 415–424.

Dean, P. J., & Range, L. M. (1999). Testing the escape theory of suicide in an outpatient clinical population. *Cognitive Therapy and Research, 23,* 561–572.

Dean, P. J., Range, L. M., & Goggin, W. C. (1996). The escape theory of suicide in college students: Testing a model that includes perfectionism. *Suicide and Life-Threatening Behavior, 26,* 181–186.

Delisle, J. R. (1990). The gifted adolescent at risk: Strategies and resources for suicide prevention among gifted youth. *Journal of Education of the Gifted, 13,* 212–228.

De Man, A. F. (1999). Correlates of suicide ideation in high school students: The importance of depression. *Journal of Genetic Psychology, 160,* 105–114.

Donaldson, D., Spirito, A., & Farnett, E. (2000). The role of perfectionism and depressive cognitions in understanding the hopelessness experienced by adolescent suicide attempters. *Child Psychiatry and Human Development, 31,* 99–111.

Durkheim, E. (1951). *Suicide: A study in sociology.* New York: Free Press. (Original work published 1897)

Enns, M. W., Cox, B. J., & Inayatulla, M. (2003). Personality predictors of outcome for adolescents hospitalized for suicidal ideation. *Journal of the American Academy of Child and Adolescent Psychiatry, 42,* 720–727.

Enns, M. W., Cox, B. J., Sareen, J., & Freeman, P. (2001). Adaptive and maladaptive perfectionism in medical students: A longitudinal investigation. *Medical Education, 35,* 1034–1042.

Flett, G. L., Besser, A., Hewitt, P. L., & Velyvis, V. (2003). *Dimensions of perfectionism, interpersonal sensitivity, and depression.* Manuscript in preparation.

Flett, G. L., Hewitt, P. L., Blankstein, K., & Koledin, S. (1991). Dimensions of perfectionism and irrational thinking. *Journal of Rational–Emotive and Cognitive Behavior Therapy, 9,* 185–201.

Flett, G. L., Hewitt, P. L., Boucher, D. J., Davidson, L. A., & Munro, Y. (2003). *The Child–Adolescent Perfectionism Scale: Development, validation, and association with maladjustment.* Manuscript submitted for publication.

Flett, G. L., Hewitt, P. L., & DeRosa, T. (1996). Dimensions of perfectionism, psychosocial adjustment, and social skills. *Personality and Individual Differences, 20,* 143–150.

Frost, R. O., Heimberg, R. G., Holt, C. S., Mattia, J. I., & Neubauer, A. L. (1993). A comparison of two measures of perfectionism. *Personality and Individual Differences, 14,* 119–126.

Frost, R. O., Marten, P., Lahart, C., & Rosenblate, R. (1990). The dimensions of perfectionism. *Cognitive Therapy and Research, 14,* 449–468.

Goldberg, D. (1988). *A user's guide to the General Health Questionnaire.* Windsor, Canada: NFER-Nelson.

Gould, M. S., Fisher, P., Parides, M., Flory, D., & Shaffer, D. (1996). Psychosocial risk factors of child and adolescent completed suicide. *Archives of General Psychiatry, 53,* 1155–1162.

Groholt, B., Ekeberg, O., & Wichstrom, L. (2000). Young suicide attempters: A comparison between a clinical and an epidemiological sample. *Journal of the American Academy of Child and Adolescent Psychiatry, 39,* 868–875.

Habke, M., & Flynn, C. (2002). Interpersonal aspects of trait perfectionism. In G. L. Flett & P. L. Hewitt (Eds.), *Perfectionism: Theory, research, and practice* (pp. 151–180). Washington, DC: American Psychological Association.

Hamilton, T. K., & Schweitzer, R. D. (2000). The cost of being perfect: Perfectionism and suicide ideation in university students. *Australian and New Zealand Journal of Psychiatry, 34,* 829–835.

Haring, M., Hewitt, P. L., & Flett, G. L. (2003). Perfectionism and quality of intimate relationships. *Journal of Marriage and the Family, 65,* 143–158.

Hayes, R. L., & Sloat, R. S. (1989). Gifted students at risk for suicide. *Roeper Review, 12,* 102–107.

Heisel, M., Flett, G. L., & Besser, A. (2002). Cognitive functioning and geriatric suicide ideation: Testing a mediational model [Special issue: Suicidal behaviors in older adults]. *American Journal of Geriatric Psychiatry, 10,* 428–436.

Hewitt, P. L., Caelian, C. F., Sherry, S. B., & Flett, G. L. (2005). *Perfectionism and the prediction of future suicidal ideation.* Manuscript in preparation.

Hewitt, P. L., & Flett, G. L. (1991). Perfectionism in the self and social contexts: Conceptualization, assessment, and association with psychopathology. *Journal of Personality and Social Psychology, 60,* 456–470.

Hewitt, P. L., & Flett, G. L. (1993a). Dimensions of perfectionism, daily stress, and depression: A test of the specific vulnerability hypothesis. *Journal of Abnormal Psychology, 102,* 58–65.

Hewitt, P. L., & Flett, G. L. (1993b). Perfectionism and goal orientation in impulsive and suicidal behavior. In W. McCown, M. Shure, & J. Johnson (Eds.), *The impulsive client: Theory, research, and treatment* (pp. 247–263). Arlington, VA: American Psychological Association.

Hewitt, P. L., & Flett, G. L. (2002). Perfectionism and stress processes in psychopathology. In G. L. Flett & P. L. Hewitt (Eds.), *Perfectionism: Theory, research, and treatment* (pp. 255–284). Washington, DC: American Psychological Association.

Hewitt, P. L., Flett, G. L., & Mikail, S. (1995). Perfectionism and relationship maladjustment in chronic pain patients and their spouses. *Journal of Family Psychology, 9,* 335–347.

Hewitt, P. L., Flett, G. L., Sherry, S. B., Habke, M., Parkin, M., Lam, R. W., et al. (2003). The interpersonal expression of perfectionism: Perfectionistic self-presentation and psychological distress. *Journal of Personality and Social Psychology, 84*, 1303–1325.

Hewitt, P. L., Flett, G. L., & Turnbull-Donovan, W. (1992). Perfectionism and suicide potential. *British Journal of Clinical Psychology, 31*, 181–190.

Hewitt, P. L., Flett, G. L., Turnbull-Donovan, W., & Mikail, S. (1991). The Multidimensional Perfectionism Scale: Reliability, validity, and psychometric properties in psychiatric samples. *Psychological Assessment, 3*, 464–468.

Hewitt, P. L., Flett, G. L., & Weber, C. (1994). Perfectionism, hopelessness, and suicide ideation. *Cognitive Therapy and Research, 18*, 439–460.

Hewitt, P. L., Newton, J., Flett, G. L., & Callander, L. (1997). Perfectionism and suicide ideation in adolescent psychiatric patients. *Journal of Abnormal Child Psychology, 25*, 95–101.

Hewitt, P. L., Norton, G. R., Flett, G. L., Callender, L., & Cowan, T. (1998). Dimensions of perfectionism, hopelessness, and attempted suicide in a sample of alcoholics. *Suicide and Life-Threatening Behavior, 28*, 395–406.

Hollender, M. H. (1965). Perfectionism. *Comprehensive Psychiatry, 6*, 94–103.

Kazdin, A., Rodgers, A., & Colbus, D. (1986). The Hopelessness Scale for Children: Psychometric characteristics and concurrent validity. *Journal of Consulting and Clinical Psychology, 54*, 241–245.

Lewinsohn, P., Rohde, P., & Seeley, J. (1996). Adolescent suicidal ideation and attempts: Prevalence, risk factors, and clinical implications. *Clinical Psychology: Science and Practice, 3*, 25–46.

Mack, J. (1986). Adolescent suicide: An architectural model. In G. Klerman (Ed.), *Suicide and depression among adolescents and young adults* (pp. 53–76). Washington, DC: American Psychiatric Press.

Marks, P. A., & Haller, D. L. (1977). Now I lay me down for keeps: A study of adolescent suicide attempts. *Journal of Clinical Psychology, 47*, 390–399.

Oatley, K., & Bolton, W. (1985). A social–cognitive theory of depression in reaction to life events. *Psychological Review, 92*, 372–388.

O'Connor, R. C., & O'Connor, D. B. (2003). Predicting hopelessness and psychological distress: The role of perfectionism and coping. *Journal of Counseling Psychology, 50*, 362–372.

Ohtani, Y., & Sakurai, S. (1995). Relationship of perfectionism to depression and hopelessness in college students. *Japanese Journal of Psychology, 66*, 41–47.

Orbach, I. (1997). A taxonomy of factors related to suicidal behavior. *Clinical Psychology: Science and Practice, 4*, 208–223.

Pearson, J. (2000). Suicidal behavior in later life: Research update. In R. W. Maris, S. S. Canetto, J. L. McIntosh, & M. M. Silverman (Eds.), *Review of suicidology* (pp. 202–225). New York: Guildford Press.

Plath, S. (1982). *The journals of Sylvia Plath*. New York: Dial Press.

Reynolds, W. M. (1988). *SIQ: Suicide Ideation Questionnaire*. Odessa, FL: PAR.

Shaffer, D. (1974). Suicide in childhood and early adolescence. *Journal of Child Psychology and Psychiatry, 15,* 275–291.

Shafii, M., Carrigan, S., Whittinghill, J. R., & Derrick, A. (1985). Psychological autopsy of completed suicide in children and adolescents. *American Journal of Psychiatry, 142,* 1061–1064.

Sherry, S. B., Hewitt, P. L., Flett, G. L., & Harvey, M. (2003). Perfectionism dimensions, perfectionistic attitudes, dependent attitudes, and depression in psychiatric patients and university students. *Journal of Counseling Psychology, 50,* 373–386.

Sullivan, H. S. (1953). *The interpersonal theory of psychiatry.* New York: Norton.

11

PROBLEM SOLVING: A CONCEPTUAL APPROACH TO SUICIDALITY AND PSYCHOTHERAPY

MARK A. REINECKE

As the chapters of this volume demonstrate, suicidality is multiply determined. Biological factors, personality characteristics, social and environmental variables, psychiatric history, and cognitive factors all appear to be associated with an increased risk of suicidal behavior. Variables from these domains are often associated and may, in some circumstances, transactionally influence one another. We are challenged, then, to understand the mechanisms by which these factors influence each other in contributing to risk for suicide.

In a similar manner, change in psychotherapy appears to be multiply determined. Patient characteristics, the quality of the therapeutic relationship, and the use of specific, theory-based therapeutic interventions all appear to be associated with clinical improvement. Insofar as psychotherapy involves the development of a "problem-oriented mind-set" and the selection of techniques to alleviate the patient's distress, psychotherapy itself may be thought of as an exercise in social problem solving. The patient and the therapist are confronted by a set of problems (in this case, the patient's suicidal ideations and the social, environmental, and intrapsychic factors that maintain them). Together they must identify the most central and salient components of the problem, develop a formulation, generate and evaluate alternative solutions, implement them, and evaluate their short- and long-term effects. We are challenged, then,

237

to understand the ways in which processes of rational problem solving inform the selection of therapeutic interventions by the therapist, and the patient's ability to use them to address difficulties in his or her life.

Cognitive factors, including deficits in problem solving, may serve as both proximal and distal risk factors for suicide. They may serve as general risk factors for psychopathology, concomitants of depression, and immediate predictors of suicidal behavior. Cognitive factors may, as such, play a central role in an individual's decision to attempt suicide. They function at the choice point at which an individual reflects on his or her life and predicament. By conceptualizing suicidality as an active, cognitive process—involving perception, choice, and decision—we direct our attention to the ways in which individuals understand their lives and the ways in which they use information to adapt to stressful life events. Suicide, from this perspective, is a choice made as a remedy for despair.

A number of cognitive factors appear to be associated with vulnerability for suicide. These include hopelessness, dysfunctional attitudes, cognitive rigidity, and cognitive distortions. Studies also indicate that deficits in problem solving are associated with both suicidal ideation and behavior (Chang, 1998; Clum & Febbraro, 2004; D'Zurilla, Chang, Nottingham, & Faccini, 1998; Linehan, Camper, Chiles, Strosahl, & Shearin, 1987; Rudd, Rajab, & Dahm, 1994; Schotte & Clum, 1982, 1987) and that treatments focusing on alleviating these deficits may reduce suicide risk (Gray & Otto, 2001; Joiner, Voelz, & Rudd, 2001; McLeavey, Daly, Ludgate, & Murray, 1994; Rudd et al., 1996; Salkovskis, Atha, & Storer, 1990). In this chapter, these literatures are reviewed from the perspective of an integrated model that addresses multiple predictors and pathways to suicide. The question is not *whether* social problem-solving deficits are associated with risk, but *how*. The goal is to develop a clearer understanding of possible relationships between problem-solving deficits and suicide, and how this may guide interventions to reduce suicide potential. I propose that deficits in problem-solving motivation and rational problem-solving skills may serve as proximal risk factors for suicide and that by improving problem-solving motivation and problem-solving skills, individuals may come to see their difficulties as surmountable. As problem-solving abilities increase, the risk of suicide declines. Moreover, we can view the process of psychotherapy as an exercise in rational problem solving. Experimental research on problem solving may inform our understanding of the ways in which clinicians conceptualize and address their patients' suicidal crises. The therapist, like the patient, implicitly or explicitly engages in a process of rational problem solving to address the patient's concerns.

METHODOLOGICAL CONSIDERATIONS

It is worth acknowledging that important conceptual and statistical impediments exist for testing cognitive diathesis–stress models of suicide.

The low base rate of completed suicide in the general population and psychometric limitations of existing assessment instruments limit our ability to test predictive models. Given the low base rate of completed suicide, sample sizes necessary to test multivariate predictive models are astronomically large. Moreover, the fact that a range of moderator variables may exist (as implied by the fact that suicide rates differ among various groups) suggests that there may be multiple pathways to suicide. Although research exists indicating that suicidal patients manifest deficits in social problem solving, a number of important issues remain unanswered. It is not clear, for example, whether social problem-solving deficits are a predictor of suicidality (or simply a concomitant), whether they make an independent and unique contribution to the prediction of suicide (or are simply a concomitant of depression), whether differences exist in associations between social problem solving and suicidal ideation and behavior, whether improvements in problem-solving skills over the course of psychotherapy mediate therapeutic improvement, and whether there are between-group differences in associations between problem solving and suicide (i.e., are there some individuals or groups for whom problem solving is associated with suicidal risk and others for whom it is not?). Low base rates of suicidal behavior and completed suicide in the general population make it difficult to answer many of these questions.

This difficulty is exacerbated by an inexact understanding of the ways in which identified vulnerability factors interact. Our models are poorly articulated, our measures are inexact, and we do not yet have a clear understanding of specific pathways to suicide. Moreover, many risk factors do not appear to be specific to suicide. Most individuals who are depressed, who experience feelings of hopelessness, who have a history of alcohol or substance abuse, who are impulsive, who have experienced suicidal ideation in the past, or who manifest problem-solving deficits do not commit suicide. Individual vulnerability factors, then, appear to be neither necessary nor sufficient to cause suicidal behavior. With this in mind, problem-solving deficits are best viewed as one of a constellation of factors that are associated with vulnerability for suicide and that may be a useful focus for clinical intervention. Given the lack of specificity of individual risk factors (including problem-solving deficits) and the low rate of completed suicide in the general population, research should be focused on individuals who have a history of suicidal ideations or attempts or who are at risk for suicide because of the presence of multiple risk factors.

PROBLEM SOLVING, COGNITION, AND SUICIDE

As noted, a range of social, environmental, biological, psychiatric, and cognitive factors appear to be associated with an increased risk of suicide ideation, gestures, and attempts. It has long been recognized that links exist between depression and suicide. An early review of follow-up studies by Guze and Robins (1970) suggested that the lifetime incidence of suicide among clinically depressed persons may be as high as 15%. More recent work suggests that the actual incidence may be lower (Bostwick & Pankratz, 2000; Inskip, Harris, & Barraclough, 1998), but the impact remains substantial. How can we understand this relationship? Beck (1967) proposed that depressed individuals manifest a range of negativistic thoughts about themselves, their worlds, and their future. A substantial body of research completed since that time supports descriptive aspects of the cognitive model of depression (Clark & Beck, 1999; Solomon & Haaga, 2003). Depressed individuals tend to view themselves as flawed or incapable and believe that others are rejecting or unsupportive. They tend, as a result, to believe that they do not possess the skills or resources to resolve their difficulties and view their future as hopeless. In an attempt to preserve what resources they retain, they tend to withdraw and to seek reassurance from others. Negativistic beliefs lead depressed individuals to perceive that they lack control over important events in their life, leading them to feel helpless. Yet how do these attitudes and beliefs lead the depressed individual to become suicidal?

Within this model, three specific beliefs are implicated in vulnerability for suicide. Suicidal individuals perceive that (a) their current predicament is intolerable, (b) they do not possess the skills or resources to resolve the problem, and (c) their future, as a consequence, is hopeless. There is substantial evidence that suicidal individuals view their problems as insoluble (Milnes, Owens, & Blenkiron, 2002) and that that they feel hopeless in the face of these difficulties (Beck, Brown, Berchick, Stewart, & Steer, 1990; Beck, Brown, & Steer, 1989; Beck, Steer, Kovacs, & Garrison, 1985). Problem-solving failures are believed to play a mediating role in the emergence of suicidal thoughts. As Shneidman (1985) stated, "The common stimulus in suicide is unendurable psychological pain" (p. 124), and the "common purpose is to seek a solution" (p. 129). It is a breakdown in the ability to "seek a solution" that, at least for some individuals, leads to suicidality.

It is proposed that a loss in an area of life that is seen as essential to one's sense of worth can lead an individual to experience emotional pain. This can take the form of depression, anxiety, anger, or resentment. If individuals view their predicament as unendurable and insurmountable, suicide becomes an option. Both components must be present—the situation must be seen as intolerable *and* unsolvable. Suicidal persons come to believe that their suicidal behavior will communicate their distress to others and so may effect a change in the environment, or that it will provide them with a sense of relief from their problems. From a problem-solving perspective, suicide reflects a breakdown in adaptive, rational problem solving. The suicidal individual is not able to generate, evaluate, and implement effective solutions and anticipates that his or her attempts will prove fruitless. Suicidality, as such, is believed to be characterized by deficits in both rational problem solving and problem-solving motivation.

D'Zurilla, Nezu, and Maydeu-Olivares (2004) suggested that social problem solving can be conceptualized as consisting of two processes—problem-solving orientation and rational problem-solving skill. Problem orientation is a motivational construct and includes individuals' awareness of problems, an appraisal of their personal competence for solving problems, and expectations about the effectiveness of problem-solving attempts. An individual with low problem-solving motivation may tend to view problem solving in a negative manner (i.e., "Nothing can help . . . it's pointless") and may doubt their ability or efficacy (i.e., "Why try? I can't pull this off"). They may, as a consequence, approach difficulties in an impulsive, careless, haphazard, or avoidant manner. Adaptive or rational problem solving, in contrast, refers to a constellation of competencies that underlie adaptive behavior. These include the ability to identify and define problems, generation of alternative solutions, evaluation of alternatives, solution implementation, and monitoring of solution effectiveness. Rational problem solving, then, is seen as an adaptive set of cognitive skills that are acquired over the course of development and that are used when confronted with problematic situations. Research indicates that both of these sets of variables—problem-solving motivation and rational problem-solving skill—may be implicated in depression and suicide.

Cognitive–behavioral therapy in general, and problem-solving interventions in particular, are directed toward alleviating specific maladaptive beliefs, developing cognitive and behavioral skills, reducing environmental stress, developing supports, and assisting patients to communicate their concerns to others more clearly and adaptively. They explicitly focus on assisting individuals to cope more effectively with problematic situations. The development and use of rational problem-solving skills, as such, may influence suicidality by alleviating stressors in the individual's life, developing adaptive skills that can be used in a range of situations, and providing the individual with perceptions of hope and personal efficacy.

PROBLEM SOLVING AND SUICIDE

An extensive body of research indicates that suicidal adults demonstrate deficits in social problem solving. Schotte and Clum (1982) proposed that associations exist among the occurrence of stressful life events, cognitive rigidity, rational problem solving, hopelessness, and suicidality. They suggested that individuals who are deficient in divergent thinking may experience difficulty coping with negative life events and may, as a result, experience feelings of hopelessness. These feelings of hopelessness, in turn, place them at risk for suicidal thoughts and behavior. This simple model, and elaborations of it, has served as a stimulus for research for more than 20 years.

In a study of 175 college students, Schotte and Clum (1982) found that those with suicidal ideation reported higher levels of stress, depression, and hopelessness than did those without suicidal ideation. Although the two groups did not differ with regard to cognitive flexibility, poor problem solvers who experienced high levels of stress were found to experience higher levels of suicidal thoughts than did other students. Consistent with cognitive diathesis–stress models, their findings suggest that problem-solving ability and life events may interact in contributing to vulnerability for suicidality, at least among college students.

These findings were replicated by Nezu (1986), who observed that depressed college students demonstrated lower levels of rational problem solving and reduced confidence in their problem-solving ability than did control participants. The following year, Schotte and Clum (1987) extended this line of investigation by proposing that it is not simply that suicidal individuals manifest cognitive rigidity, rendering them incapable of flexibly and adaptively responding to stressful life events, but they also manifest deficits in rational problem solving, which leads them to become hopeless and helpless. They observed that suicide ideators were able to generate less than half the number of potential solutions to interpersonal problems than did control participants. Moreover, they observed that people with suicidal ideation tended to focus on potentially negative outcomes of their attempts to solve their problems, thus inhibiting their attempts to implement solutions. These findings provided initial support for the notion that two related sets of variables—(a) rational problem-solving skills and (b) problem-solving orientation or motivation—may be implicated in risk for suicide. Links between social problem solving and suicide were also reported by Linehan et al. (1987) and Evans, Williams, O'Loughlin, and Howells (1992).

The question arises, might the relations observed among life events, problem solving, and suicide be mediated by yet another variable—level of depression? Several studies indicating that associations may exist between problem-solving deficits and depression support this possibility (Nezu & Ronan, 1988, Marx, Williams, & Claridge, 1992; Haaga, Fine, Terrill, Stewart, & Beck, 1993). Bonner and Rich (1988) addressed this issue by examining associations among problem-solving appraisal, life events, hopelessness, and depression in a sample of 186 college students. As anticipated, hopelessness was significantly correlated with both problem-solving appraisal ($r = .48, p < .05$) and depression ($r = .66, p < .05$) in their sample. The results of a multiple regression analysis indicated that problem-solving appraisal and stressful life events were independent predictors of hopelessness when level of depression was controlled. Once again, problem-solving appraisal and the occurrence of stressful life events appeared to interact in predicting level of hopelessness. Unfortunately, the authors did not include a measure of suicidal motivation. We cannot know from this study, then, whether life events and self-appraised problem-solving skill interact in predicting the occurrence of suicidal ideation when level of depression is controlled.

Orbach, Bar-Joseph, and Dror (1990) compared "qualitative aspects of problem solving" in a sample of 68 people, including individuals with suicidal ideation, individuals who had attempted suicide, and nonsuicidal psychiatric control participants. Results indicated that suicidal patients demonstrated less cognitive "versatility" and greater avoidance in their attempts to solve problems than did control participants. Their findings are congruent with other research in suggesting that motivational factors may influence the ways in which suicidal individuals respond to stressful life events.

Dixon, Heppner, and Anderson (1991) examined associations among life events, hopelessness, problem-solving appraisal—the perception of one's ability to solve problems—and suicidal ideation in two nonclinical samples of college students. They found that problem-solving appraisal was associated with both one's level of hopelessness and the severity of suicidal ideation and that suicidal ideation was predicted by both the occurrence of stressful life events and problem-solving appraisal.

In a prospective study, Priester and Clum (1993a) examined associations among self-appraised problem-solving ability, hopelessness, depression, and suicidal thoughts among college students who had experienced a negative life event (receiving a poor grade on an exam). Students who viewed themselves as poor problem solvers experienced higher levels of depression and hopelessness in response to the stressful life event than did their classmates. They did not, however, manifest higher levels of suicidal thoughts. These findings offer partial support for cognitive mediational models of suicide. The failure to observe an association between problem-solving appraisal and suicidal thoughts may have stemmed from the fact that there was little variance in severity of suicidal thoughts in the sample, reducing their ability to detect associations among the variables. The possibility exists as well that the life event examined (doing poorly on an exam) was not of sufficient intensity or personal importance to trigger suicidal thoughts.

Priester and Clum (1993b) also examined relations among problem-solving skills, life events, and suicidality in a sample of college students. They found that the ability to generate alternative solutions and the number of perceived negative consequences for solutions developed at an initial assessment predicted severity of suicidal thoughts in response to a later stressful life event. Problem-solving factors were found to interact with the occurrence of negative life events in predicting suicidal thoughts.

In a subsequent study of college students with chronic suicidal thoughts, Clum and Febbraro (1994) observed that global self-perceptions of problem-solving ability were associated with severity of suicidal ideation. Moreover, life events and perceived problem-solving ability interacted in predicting severity of suicidal ideation. As anticipated, students with low perceptions of problem-solving efficacy under conditions of high stress experienced the most severe suicidal thoughts.

Rudd et al. (1994) extended previous work by Schotte and Clum (1987) and Dixon et al. (1991) by examining associations among problem-solving appraisal, hopelessness, and suicidality in a sample of people with suicidal ideation and people who had attempted suicide. They found that both tended to view themselves as poor problem solvers. Moreover, problem-solving appraisal accounted for a significant percentage of the variance in both hopelessness and suicidality for both those with suicidal ideation and those who had attempted suicide. The correlation between problem-solving appraisal and hopelessness in this sample was .61 ($p < .0001$). Their findings are consistent with the view that self-evaluations of problem-solving ability are associated with severity of suicidal ideation and that problem-solving appraisals may mediate observed relationships among stressful life events, hopelessness, and suicide. It is possible, of course, that self-evaluations of problem-solving ability vary over time and that they may change in response to significant life events or changes in mood. Moreover, it is likely that additional variables mediate associations between the occurrence of stressful life events and suicide.

Although studies discussed thus far have examined relations among life events, problem-solving, hopelessness, and suicide among adults, similar findings have been reported in research with depressed and suicidal youth (Adams & Adams, 1993, 1996; Asarnow, Carlson, & Guthrie, 1987; Goldston et al., 2001; Rotheram-Borus, Trautman, Dopkins, & Shrout, 1990). Hawton, Kingsbury, Steinhardt, James, and Fagg (1999), for example, examined relations among mood, cognitive factors (including problem solving), and suicide in a sample of adolescents who had made a suicide attempt. Adolescents who made additional suicide attempts during the following year demonstrated poorer problem solving than did those without further attempts. The strength of the association between problem solving and suicide was reduced, however, when level of depression was controlled.

More recently, Reinecke, DuBois, and Schultz (2001) examined relations among problem solving, mood, and suicidal ideation in a sample of 105 adolescent inpatients. Negative problem orientation as well as avoidant and impulsive problem-solving style were associated with severity of depression and suicidal thoughts. Self-reported use of rational problem-solving strategies, as measured by the Social Problem-Solving Inventory—Revised (SPSI–R; D'Zurilla & Maydeu-Olivares, 1995), however, was not associated with level of depression or severity of suicidal thoughts. Structural equation modeling indicated that relationships between problem solving and suicide were mediated by the effects of problem solving on levels of depression and hopelessness. These findings suggest that the ability to maintain a positive attitude toward approaching problems may play an important role in depression and suicidality among adolescents. They are consistent as well with research indicating that depressed individuals may demonstrate biased or inaccurate appraisals of problems and of their ability to solve them. In short, the perception that "nothing will work" or "I can't solve it anyway" may lead adolescents to respond impulsively or to fail to attempt to solve their difficulties. This reduction in adaptive coping may, in turn, exacerbate their feelings of distress, leading to suicidality.

Taken together, these studies are consistent in suggesting that a motivational variable—problem-solving appraisal or orientation—may be an important predictor of hopelessness and suicidal thoughts among both adults and adolescents. Problem-solving appraisal is a potentially important construct insofar as it is similar in many ways to Bandura's (1977) concept of self-efficacy. It is not simply the ability to identify a problem and to flexibly generate and evaluate possible solutions that are implicated in suicide, it is one's confidence in one's own ability to effect a change in life.

Important questions, however, remain: Are perceptions of one's ability to solve problems—of one's sense of personal agency—stable over time? Do they vary with current mood? Are they situationally determined in the sense that they vary in response to specific, personally salient life events? Recent research has attempted to address these questions. Biggam and Power (1999), in a study of 61 incarcerated adolescents and young adults, observed that problem-solving ability may not be stable over time. Rather, it may be a state concomitant with depression and suicidal behavior. These findings are consistent with those of Ivanoff, Smyth, Grochowski, Jang, and Klein (1992) and Schotte, Cools, and Payvar (1990), who also suggested that trait problem-solving deficits may not be associated with vulnerability for depression.

Can we conclude, then, that problem-solving motivation and skills are a concomitant rather than a risk factor for suicide? Not at this point. Difficulties exist insofar as participants in several of these studies were drawn from the penal system, and many did not manifest a psychiatric illness at the time of participation. The possibility exists that pathways to suicide may differ among college students, psychiatric patients, and people in the penal system. Life events, coping skills, comorbid psychiatric illnesses, and the availability of social supports may also differ among groups. The use of cross-sectional designs also reduces our confidence in the conclusions drawn. That said, the results obtained in these studies are not consistent with a strong version of the Schotte and Clum (1982) model. Problem-solving skills are, most likely, not stable over time. Rather, an individual's ability to reflect on important problems may vary according to the situation and their mood. Insofar as mood appears to affect the encoding and retrieval of information and may be implicated in the activation of schemas, it is possible that mood may also affect problem-solving motivation and application of rational problem-solving skills.

Might problem solving be characterized by both trait and state components? A study by Young et al. (1996) suggests that there may be both state and trait components to scores on the Hopelessness Scale. Patients appear to manifest a relatively stable, "trait" level of hopelessness when they are not depressed, as well as an incremental, "state" increase in pessimism that accompanies the depressive episode. Patients' baseline or "trait" level of hopelessness was found to predict future suicide attempts, whereas the incremental increase and total score did not. It appears that patients who maintain a chronic, pessimistic outlook may be at higher risk for suicidal gestures and attempts than are patients who do not. The question, then, arises: Might rational problem solving and problem-solving motivation also be characterized by state and trait components? Might an individual demonstrate reasonably good problem-solving skills on a day-to-day basis yet experience difficulties solving problems in specific domains or when he or she is depressed or anxious? Are there relationships between "trait" levels of hopelessness and an individual's problem-solving motivation?

Research on social problem solving tends to focus on how depressed and suicidal individuals cope with immediate problems in their lives. As Reinecke et al. (2001) noted, however, self-report measures of problem solving might best be viewed as indices of perceived problem-solving efficacy. Ample research indicates that self-perceptions can be influenced by current mood. Moreover, evidence for the external validity of measures of problem solving, such as the Means-End Problem-Solving (MEPS) and the SPSI–R, is limited. These measures may or may not measure an individual's ability to cope with real-life, personally salient problems. Furthermore, scales such as these do not address how individuals cope with their negative moods. Suicidal individuals often wish to "feel better," not just resolve the problem that triggered their depression. The development and use of affect regulation skills, then, may be an important component of how an individual manages highly stressful life events (see Wagner & Zimmerman, chap. 13, this volume). Emotional, social, and instrumental problem-solving skills may be somewhat independent. Each is worthy of study.

Although it is not clear that problem-solving deficits are a stable predictor of suicidal behavior (Biggam & Power, 1999; Schotte et al., 1990), and relations among life events, problem solving, hopelessness, depression, and suicidality appear to be complex, problem-solving deficits can be an important focus in the treatment process (Lerner & Clum, 1990; Salkovskis, Atha, & Storer, 1990). Let us look, then, at how these findings have been used to guide the development of treatment programs for patients who are depressed and suicidal.

PROBLEM-SOLVING TREATMENTS

Problem-solving therapies were introduced during the early 1970s, and were based on early work by Thomas D'Zurilla and Marvin Goldfried on relationships between rational problem solving and social skills training. Problem-solving treatment protocols for a range of clinical problems have been developed during the intervening years and have stimulated a great deal of clinical interest (for reviews, see D'Zurilla & Nezu, 1999, 2001). These approaches are conceptually similar and may be seen as members of a family of cognitive–behavioral therapies for depression and suicide. Like other cognitive–behavioral therapies, they share a number of assumptions about human motivation, adaptation, development, and the nature of therapeutic change (Dobson & Dozois, 2001; Reinecke & Freeman, 2003). Manuals describing problem-solving therapies for depression and suicidal behavior have been developed (Hawton & Catalan, 1987; Nezu, Nezu, & Perri, 1989), and problem-solving techniques have been incorporated into several broader programs for treating suicidal patients (Linehan, 1993; Rudd, Joiner, & Rajab, 2001).

In practice, these approaches are active, problem focused, collaborative, strategic, and psychoeducational. Treatment begins by working with patients to identify a specific problem or concern and then to develop their motivation to address it directly. An attempt is made to understand patients' customary attitude toward problem solving and to assist them to develop a more positive problem-solving orientation. This may involve assisting them to accept that having problems is a normal part of life and is not to be avoided, to make adaptive attributions about possible causes for their difficulties, to reduce a tendency to magnify the significance of the problem, to develop a perception of personal efficacy and an expectation that the problem may be solvable, and to accept that a full solution may not be possible and that resolving the problem may require time and tenacity. As the individual develops a "positive problem-solving orientation," tendencies to avoid problems, withdraw from challenging situations, or to respond in an impulsive or careless manner are reduced.

As the patient's problem-solving motivation improves, interventions are introduced to develop their rational problem-solving skills. Patients are taught to approach problems in a relaxed manner. They next develop skills in problem identification—they are taught to recognize their most important concern as well as factors that may be maintaining it. An attempt is made to assist the patient to develop reasonable, realistic goals, as well as a clear and objective understanding of the nature of the problem and the steps that may be necessary to resolve it. Patients are encouraged to develop problem-focused goals (i.e., an understanding of the problem to be addressed) and emotion-focused goals (an understanding of how this problem makes them feel and how it affects their adjustment). This is followed by the development of skills in generating alternative solutions, evaluating their short- and long-term effectiveness, selecting the most effective solution, implementing it, and evaluating its effectiveness. These skills are typically taught through a combination of psychoeducational exercises, modeling, role-plays, and Socratic dialogue.

EFFICACY OF PROBLEM-SOLVING TREATMENTS
FOR SUICIDAL PATIENTS

A number of controlled outcome studies based on these approaches have been completed during recent years. Preliminary findings indicate that problem-solving therapy may be helpful in alleviating depression and in reducing suicidal risk (for reviews see D'Zurilla & Nezu, 1999, 2001; Hawton et al., 1998).

Gibbons, Butler, Urwin, and Gibbons (1978) conducted the first controlled study of problem-solving therapy with suicidal adults. Patients in the active treatment group received up to 3 months of problem-focused casework at home by a social worker. Participants in the control condition received "routine follow-up service." During the 12-month follow-up period, patients in both groups demonstrated equivalent levels of suicidal behavior (13.5% vs. 14.5%). It should be noted that of the 139 patients (of a total of 400) excluded from the study for various reasons, 36% made repeat suicide attempts during the follow-up period. Thus, it appears that both conditions may have been beneficial for this population, possibly with different mechanisms of effect.

Hawton et al. (1981) examined the effectiveness of brief problem-solving therapy for reducing suicidal behavior in a sample of 96 adolescents and adults who had been admitted to the hospital after making a suicide attempt, comparing treatment in the clinic to treatment delivered at the patient's home. During a 12-month follow-up period, patients in the two conditions showed equivalent outcomes, with 10.4% of patients in the home condition repeating suicidal behavior, compared with 14.6% of those in the clinic condition, a nonsignificant difference.

Hawton et al. (1987) conducted a study of older adolescents and adults who had been admitted to the hospital after a suicide attempt. After 12 months, participants who had received brief outpatient problem-solving therapy demonstrated a lower rate of repeat attempts than did patients who had been followed by a general practice physician (7.3% vs. 15.4%). This difference was not statistically significant, although it was found that two subgroups (women and patients with dyadic problems) did receive greater benefit from the treatment condition.

Lerner and Clum (1990) reported the results of a comparison of problem-solving therapy and supportive psychotherapy for treating suicidal adolescents and young adults ($N = 18$). Findings indicated that problem-solving therapy was more effective than supportive therapy in reducing levels of hopelessness, depression, and loneliness at 3-month follow-up. A significantly greater percentage of participants who had received problem-solving therapy demonstrated clinical improvement (defined as a 50% or greater reduction in severity of suicidal ideation, depression, and hopelessness) at follow-up than did patients receiving supportive psychotherapy (89% vs. 44%; $p < .05$).

Although problem-solving therapy appeared slightly more effective than supportive psychotherapy in reducing suicidal ideation, this difference was not statistically significant.

McLeavey et al. (1994) reported the results of a study of older adolescents and adults who had made a suicide attempt. Patients who received up to 6 weeks of interpersonal problem-solving training reported a lower rate of self-poisoning during the subsequent 12 months than did control participants who participated in brief problem-oriented counseling (10.5% vs. 25%). Although this difference did not reach statistical significance, the authors attributed this to a small sample size and the low base rate of suicidal behavior (characteristics of most of these studies). They also pointed out that 47% of the treatment group, compared with only 25% of the control group, reported a prior suicide attempt, underscoring the likely clinical significance of their results.

Salkovskis, Atha, and Storer (1990) conducted a study of 20 older adolescents and adults who had been referred for psychiatric care after a suicide attempt. Patients were randomly assigned to a cognitive–behavioral problem-solving treatment or to a "treatment as usual" control group. Participants who received problem-solving therapy demonstrated a lower rate of suicide attempts during the following 6 months than did control participants who were referred to a general practice physician (0% vs. 37.5%; $p < .05$). These effects tended, however, to decline with time. Although patients who received active treatment continued to make fewer suicide attempts than control participants during the subsequent 12 months (25% vs. 50%), this difference was not statistically significant. Nevertheless, their findings indicate that problem-solving therapy may be useful for reducing suicidal ideation, hopelessness, depression, and fatigue among suicide attempters and that it can be effective in reducing rates of repeat suicide attempts, at least in the short term.

More recently, van der Sande et al. (1997) conducted a relatively large study of patients who had been referred for psychiatric care after a suicide attempt ($n = 274$). Patients in the active treatment condition received inpatient care, followed by outpatient problem-solving therapy and emergency support. Participants in the control group received treatment as usual. During the 12-month follow-up period, there was no difference between groups with regard to rates of completed suicide or suicide attempts.

Taken together, these findings present a somewhat mixed picture. Evidence suggests that deficits in problem solving *may* serve as a vulnerability factor for suicidal thoughts and behavior. On one hand, we see studies with consistent findings of deficient problem-solving skills in suicidal individuals relative to comparison groups; on the other hand, treatment outcome studies often lack statistically significant differences in follow-up rates of suicidal behaviors between problem-solving therapies and comparison conditions. How might we account for this apparent discrepancy? Several issues appear pertinent:

1. As noted earlier, the outcome studies are typically studies with small samples, resulting in reduced statistical power to detect differences. This is especially a problem for low base rate phenomena such as suicidal behavior.
2. In a related issue, statistical differences versus clinical differences loom large. For example, most clinicians would welcome a treatment associated with a 10% repeat attempt rate versus 25%, as found by McLeavy et al. (1994), or 25% versus 50%, as found by Salkovskis et al. (1990), whether statistically significant or not.
3. Even in studies in which differences in suicidal ideation and behavior were nonsignificant, significant differences in favor of problem-solving training commonly have been observed on other relevant variables, such as depression and hopelessness (see Townsend et al., 2001, and Speckens & Hawton, 2005, for reviews). This is important insofar as studies comparing suicidal patients with either nonsuicidal psychiatric patients or nonclinical controls typically find that suicidal patients manifest deficits in rational problem solving or problem solving motivation. These deficits often are not apparent, however, after levels of hopelessness and depression are controlled. As many studies use a cross-sectional design, it is not clear whether problem solving deficits are a cause, consequence, or concomitant of depression, hopelessness, or suicide.
4. Although isolating problem-solving training as a stand-alone treatment may be necessary for research purposes, this would not be considered viable in most clinical settings. Suicidal patients typically exhibit more deficiencies than just problem-solving skills. They typically have comorbid Axis I or Axis II diagnoses (or both), as well as multiple environmental stressors. This complex picture suggests a need for multidimensional therapies, including medication and environmental interventions. In this sense, it is perhaps not surprising that brief problem-solving interventions alone show only modest effects. Thus, an important question to be addressed in future research is not whether problem-solving therapy is superior to treatment as usual but whether multidimensional treatment with problem-solving therapy is superior to the same treatment without it.
5. This question might be further expanded to consider what specific *types* of patients are most likely to benefit; although suicidal patients as a group may be characterized by deficient

problem-solving skills, it does not follow that all have the deficiency and would benefit from problem-solving training.

In this context, it appears appropriate to continue to attend to problem-solving training as a promising approach to working with suicidal individuals, although in need of further evaluation and refinement.

PSYCHOTHERAPY AS A FORM OF PROBLEM SOLVING

As we have seen, problem-solving therapies are based on the hypothesis that suicidality emerges when individuals do not believe they have the skills to resolve problems they view as insurmountable and unacceptable. Suicide, from this perspective, becomes an appealing option. Interventions based on this model can, in some circumstances, be effective in reducing patients' distress and in reducing the risk of further suicidal behavior. Yet might psychotherapy itself also be viewed as an exercise in problem solving? Patients typically (although not always) come to therapy with a desire to alleviate their distress. They seek behavioral, social, or emotional change and frequently feel unable to bring these changes about using their customary skills and approaches. The patient and the therapist then engage in a collaborative process of clarifying the nature of the patient's concerns, developing an understanding of their origins and of factors that may be maintaining them, and generating, evaluating, and implementing various interventions to alleviate their distress. If therapists are familiar with patient concerns, either through training or clinical experience, they can call on this knowledge base to develop a formulation of the patient's concerns as well as a therapeutic plan of action. When confronted by complex or unfamiliar problems, however, therapists cannot rely on prior knowledge or "templates" to guide their approach. Rather, they must rely on conceptual heuristics to develop a course of action.

When confronted by a complex clinical situation, therapists typically begin by implicitly or explicitly organizing their knowledge of the problem (Nezu, Nezu, Friedman, & Haynes, 1997; Nezu & Nezu, 1998). As Newell and Simon (1972) noted, problem solving may be viewed as a systematic process that begins with the clarification of the "problem space." As regards clinical practice with suicidal patients, this process involves clarifying one's understanding of the patient's current state, the desired goal or end state of the treatment, the available interventions that may bring about that end state, and the resources, constraints, and exigencies of the situation that will effect therapeutic progress. Therapeutic problems can be considered well understood if clear and explicit information is available on the four components. As is so often the case with suicidal patients, however, information may be missing on one or more of the components. Where information is missing, therapists must make an informed guess—they must draw on both their experience and their knowledge to develop a formulation of factors contributing to the patient's distress.

As Sternberg (1986) noted, problem solving may be viewed as a cycle in which the individual must recognize the problem, represent the problem mentally, develop a solution strategy, organize his or her knowledge about the problem, allocate resources to solve the problem, monitor progress, and evaluate the effectiveness of the solution. To be sure, not all individuals approach problem solving in a systematic, sequential manner such as this. Rather, the expert problem solver approaches the task at hand flexibly, stepping through each stage, repeating each as necessary, and cycling back to identify new problems as the initial problem is resolved.

Suicidal patients, however, do not tend to approach problems in this manner. Rather, they often are flummoxed by their predicament. They simply don't know what to do. They then turn to the therapist, an expert in resolving difficulties such as theirs, for a solution. Experts in any field, from bricklaying to neurosurgery, approach problems in a different way than do novices. Given their knowledge and expertise, experienced therapists attempt to identify missing information and to redefine the problem in ways that make a wider range of solutions available. Patients may, for example, become depressed and suicidal as the result of an abrupt break in a relationship. Their spouse has unexpectedly filed for divorce and moved out. They come to the therapist seeking advice as to how to make their spouse come back. The experienced therapist may help them to redefine the problem not as one of loss, but of dissatisfaction in the marriage; feelings of powerlessness, attachment insecurity, and dependency; a failure in social problem solving; or cognitive distortions and schemas that have been activated by a personally salient life event.

The expert therapist's understanding of the problem situation is better organized and more systematic than that of the patient. This allows the therapist to guide the patient to an awareness of underlying issues, mechanisms, or processes contributing to the problem. It is this understanding of underlying mechanisms and processes that allows the expert therapist to develop a broader range of possible solutions and to share these with the patient. Whereas friends and family members of the patient may offer simple advice designed to address the immediate, salient problem (e.g., "Just apologize to her," "Let's go to the club and get your mind off of this—Don't worry, she'll come back"), the experienced therapist is able to illuminate broader issues and underlying factors and to offer patients a clearer understanding of why these events have led them to become despondent and suicidal. Developing and sharing a rationale, however, is only the first step in the problem-solving process. Solution clarification—the identification of actions that may be taken to approach the goal or end state—must then begin.

When confronted with a complex problem (in any area), experts typically spend a greater amount of time gathering information about the problem and factors that may be maintaining it than do less experienced practitioners. By clarifying the nature of the problem, defining it, and representing it cognitively, the experienced clinician is better able to discriminate effective from ineffective courses of action. Effective representation of the problem allows the individual to identify a "viable path" to a solution (Pretz, Naples, & Sternberg, 2003, p. 26). When the therapist has a clear and parsimonious formulation of the patient's problem, the solutions quickly become evident. Experts are able to develop a more complete and sophisticated model of the problem than the patient. Moreover, their knowledge and experience allows them to focus on the most relevant information. They are less likely to be distracted by unimportant, albeit interesting, details of the problem.

How do expert therapists "narrow the field" and identify the most important components of the patient's problem? How do they recognize, define, and represent the problem? Quite often this is based on the therapist's working model or "schematic representation" of the patient's concerns—a therapist's theoretical orientation. For all therapists, regardless of orientation, two problem-solving processes are at play as they begin working with a patient. They clarify the specific nature of the problem, and they identify alternative courses of action to bring about a desired end state, given the exigencies of the patient's life. These processes are dependent on the therapist's knowledge and experience and are guided by implicit problem-solving heuristics. These heuristics, although based on experience and knowledge, can be problematic. As a number of authors have noted, our tendency to bring prior knowledge to bear when solving problems can introduce computational biases that, under some circumstances, can have negative consequences (Baron, 1998; Stanovich, 2003). Cognitive biases can occur when we make automatic inferences, supplementing our incomplete understanding of the current problem with declarative knowledge and linguistic and social information. Stanovich (2003) suggested that this can take four forms: (a) a tendency to supplement or "contextualize" the problem with as much prior knowledge as is available, even when the solution requires a "context-free" solution; (b) a tendency to "socialize" abstract problems, even when few social cues are available; (c) a tendency to perceive deliberate designs or motivations in situations that lack intentional design; and (d) a tendency toward narrative modes of thought.

These biases can lead therapists to adhere rigidly to a model or rationale and to fail to assimilate inconsistent information (it is always difficult to relinquish a cherished belief, particularly when this belief was quickly established); to identify and use an inappropriate analogue for a clinical problem (often by focusing on superficial similarities between the problems, rather than underlying principles or mediating processes); to adopt an overly positive or negative motivational set (e.g., making an overly optimistic or negative prognosis); to overestimate their own skill, expertise, or efficacy; to establish an inappropriate behavioral end state or goal; to misplace therapeutic priorities (e.g., by focusing too much on the details of therapeutic process and not enough on strategic direction), and to perceive relationships and meanings because they believe they are there, rather than because they exist. Therapists, like their patients, attempt to make sense of their experiences and to respond to problems in a sensible manner. Often, however, problem-solving processes can be influenced by emotion and by the biased heuristics we all use.

The experienced therapist attempts to redefine the suicidal patient's unsolvable and insurmountable problems in terms of simple, sensible concepts and goals that *are* attainable. The therapist then shares this rationale with the patient and encourages him or her to take action on the basis of that information. By reframing the problem (the four problem components), potential solutions often become apparent. By encouraging action, the therapist instills the suicidal patient with hope.

CONCLUSIONS

As we have seen, a body of evidence accumulated over the past 30 years indicates that deficits in rational problem solving, problem-solving motivation, and self-appraisals of problem-solving skill may be interlinked with negative life events, depression, hopelessness, suicide ideation, and suicidal behavior. Relationships among these variables appear to be complex and may vary over time. Although we do not yet have a full understanding of these associations or how they contribute to vulnerability for suicide, the outlines of a comprehensive, integrated psychosocial model of suicide are beginning to emerge. Moreover, preliminary evidence suggests that therapeutic interventions based on these models can be effective in improving the adjustment of suicidal patients and in reducing the risk of additional suicide attempts. Finally, the process of psychotherapy itself can be understood as an exercise in rational problem solving. By conceptualizing psychotherapy in this way— as an example of an "expert" working with a patient to define a problem systematically, identify goals, clarify strategies for achieving these goals, and address factors that may hinder or support these efforts—our attention is directed toward understanding factors that may facilitate therapeutic change and the social contexts and computational biases that frame and guide our thought.

Vygotsky (1962) proposed that all human learning and skill acquisition occurs through guided experience in a "zone of proximal development." Put simply, parents and teachers guide the development of children by providing them with experiences that are just beyond their current level of competence. An expert, in short, guides the development of an apprentice or novice by exposing that person to more sophisticated skills than he or she currently possesses. Through guided modeling and practice, the novice acquires these skills and becomes better able to accomplish tasks alone. So, too, with psychotherapy. The therapist may be seen as an expert, assisting patients to develop a meaningful and sophisticated understanding of their problems and to identify a course of action for addressing their concerns. By thinking of the therapist as an active problem solver, we are encouraged to identify irrational heuristics that may limit effective problem solving.

Problem solving, from this perspective, is not simply a conceptual model of psychotherapy. Rather, it is an extraordinarily broad and complex domain. As a colleague, Clifford Swensen, once quipped, "To have problems is to be human . . . if we didn't have any, we'd make some up." Problem solving, then, may be viewed as applied cognition—it is the ways in which cognitive processes are brought to bear to meet adaptive goals. It is inextricably linked with emotion, motivation, planning and executive function, attentional deployment, language, intellectual ability, behavioral skills and expertise, as well as social and environmental factors that define a problem and which place limits on potential solutions. The innocuous question, "what role do problem-solving deficits play in suicide?" on closer inspection, becomes quite complex. It is interesting that, as we reflect on this question, define our constructs, evaluate our evidence, and refine our models, the recursive, cyclical nature of the problem-solving process reemerges. As simple solutions to the initial problem are identified, we cycle back to recognize, define, and represent new and ever more challenging problems. To have problems is to be human.

REFERENCES

Adams, J., & Adams, M. (1993). Effects of a negative life event and negative perceived problem-solving alternatives on depression in adolescents: A prospective study. *Journal of Child Psychology and Psychiatry, 34,* 743–747.

Adams, J., & Adams, M. (1996). The association among negative life events, perceived problem solving alternatives, depression, and suicidal ideation in adolescent psychiatric patients. *Journal of Child Psychology and Psychiatry, 37,* 715–720.

Asarnow, J., Carlson, G., & Guthrie, D. (1987). Coping strategies, self-perceptions, hopelessness, and perceived family environments in depressed and suicidal children. *Journal of Consulting and Clinical Psychology, 55,* 361–366.

Bandura, A. (1977). Self-efficacy: Toward a unifying theory of behavioral change. *Psychological Review, 84,* 191–215.

Baron, J. (1998). *Judgment misguided: Intuition and error in public decision making.* New York: Oxford University Press.

Beck, A. (1967). *Depression: Clinical, experimental, and theoretical aspects.* New York: Harper & Row.

Beck, A., Brown, G., Berchick, R., Stewart, B., & Steer, R. (1990). Relationship between hopelessness and ultimate suicide: A replication with psychiatric outpatients. *American Journal of Psychiatry, 147,* 190–195.

Beck, A., Brown, G., & Steer, R. (1989). Prediction of eventual suicide in psychiatric inpatients by clinical ratings of hopelessness. *Journal of Consulting and Clinical Psychology, 57,* 309–310.

Beck, A., Steer, R., Kovacs, M., & Garrison, B. (1985). Hopelessness and eventual suicide: A 10-year prospective study of patients hospitalized with suicidal ideation. *American Journal of Psychiatry, 142,* 559–563.

Biggam, F., & Power, K. (1999). Suicidality and the state-trait debate on problem-solving deficits: A re-examination with incarcerated young offenders. *Archives of Suicide Research, 5,* 27–42.

Bonner, R., & Rich, A. (1988). Negative life stress, social problem-solving self-appraisal, and hopelessness: Implications for suicide research. *Cognitive Therapy and Research, 12,* 549–556.

Bostwick, J. M, & Pankratz, V. S. (2000). Affective disorders and suicide risk: A reexamination. *American Journal of Psychiatry, 157,* 1925–1932.

Chang, E. (1998). Cultural differences, perfectionism, and suicidal risk: Does problem solving still matter? *Cognitive Therapy and Research, 22,* 237–254.

Clark, D., & Beck, A. (1999). *Scientific foundations of cognitive theory and therapy of depression.* New York: Wiley.

Clum, G., & Febbraro, G. (1994). Stress, social support, and problem-solving appraisal/skills: Prediction of suicide severity within a college sample. *Journal of Psychopathology and Behavioural Assessment, 16,* 69–83.

Clum, G., & Febbraro, G. (2004). Social problem solving and suicide risk. In E. Chang, T. D'Zurilla, & C. Sanna (Eds.), *Social problem solving: Theory, research, and training* (pp. 67–82). Washington, DC: American Psychological Association.

Davidson, J., & Sternberg, R. (Eds.). (2003). *The psychology of problem solving.* Cambridge, England: Cambridge University Press.

Dixon, W., Heppner, P., & Anderson, W. (1991). Problem-solving appraisal, stress, hopelessness, and suicide ideation in a college population. *Journal of Counseling Psychology, 38,* 51–56.

Dobson, K., & Dozois, D. (2001). Historical and philosophical bases of the cognitive–behavioral therapies. In K. Dobson (Ed.), *Handbook of cognitive–behavioral therapies* (2nd ed., pp. 3–39). New York: Guilford Press.

D'Zurilla, T., Chang, E., Nottingham, E., & Faccini, L. (1998). Social problem-solving deficits and hopelessness, depression, and suicidal risk in college students and psychiatric inpatients. *Journal of Clinical Psychology, 54,* 1091–1107.

D'Zurilla, T., & Maydeu-Olivares, A. (1995). Conceptual and methodological issues in social problem-solving assessment. *Behavior Therapy, 26,* 409–432.

D'Zurilla, T., & Nezu, A. (1999). *Problem-solving therapy: A social competence approach to clinical intervention* (2nd ed.). New York: Springer Publishing Company.

D'Zurilla, T., & Nezu, A. (2001). Problem-solving therapies. In K. Dobson (Ed.), *Handbook of cognitive–behavioral therapies* (2nd ed., pp. 211–245). New York: Guilford Press.

D'Zurilla, T., Nezu, A., & Maydeu-Olivares, A. (2004). Social problem solving: Theory and assessment. In E. Chang, T. D'Zurilla, & C. Sanna (Eds.), *Social problem solving: Theory, research, and training* (pp. 11–27). Washington, DC: American Psychological Association.

Evans, J., Williams, J., O'Loughlin, S., & Howells, K. (1992). Autobiographical memory and problem-solving strategies of suicidal patients. *Psychological Medicine, 22*, 399–405.

Gibbons, J., Butler, J., Urwin, P., & Gibbons, J. (1978). Evaluation of a social work service for self-poisoning patients. *British Journal of Psychiatry, 133*, 111–118.

Goldston, D., Daniel, S., Reboussin, B., Reboussin, D., Frazier, P., & Harris, A. (2001). Cognitive risk factors and suicide attempts among formerly hospitalized adolescents: A prospective naturalistic study. *Journal of the American Academy of Child and Adolescent Psychiatry, 40*, 91–99.

Gray, S., & Otto, M. (2001). Psychosocial approaches to suicide prevention: Applications to patients with bipolar disorder. *Journal of Clinical Psychiatry, 62*(Suppl. 25), 56–64.

Guze, S., & Robins, E. (1970). Suicide and primary affective disorders. *British Journal of Psychiatry, 117*, 437–438.

Haaga, D., Fine, J., Terrill, D., Stewart, B., & Beck, A. (1993). Social problem-solving deficits, dependency, and depressive symptoms. *Cognitive Therapy and Research, 19*, 147–158.

Hawton, K., Arensman, E., Twonsend, E., Bremner, S., Feldman, E., Goldney, R., et al. (1998). Deliberate self-harm: A systematic review of the efficacy of psychosocial and pharmacological treatments in preventing repetition. *British Medical Journal, 317*, 441–447.

Hawton, K., Bancroft, J., Catalan, J., Kingston, B., Stedeford, A., & Welch, N. (1981). Domiciliary and out-patient treatment of self-poisoning patients by medical and non-medical staff. *Psychological Medicine, 11*, 169–177.

Hawton, K., & Catalan, J. (1982). *Attempted suicide: A practical guide to its nature and management.* Oxford, England: Oxford University Press.

Hawton, K., Kingsbury, S., Steinhardt, K., James, A., & Fagg, J. (1999). Repetition of deliberate self-harm by adolescents: The role of psychological factors. *Journal of Adolescence, 22*, 369–378.

Hawton, K., McKeown, S., Day, A., Martin, P., O'Connor, M., & Yule, J. (1987). Evaluation of out-patient counseling compared with general practitioner care following overdoses. *Psychological Medicine, 17*, 751–761.

Inskip, H. M., Harris, E. C., & Barraclough, B. (1998). Lifetime risk of suicide for affective disorder, alcoholism and schizophrenia. *British Journal of Psychiatry, 172*, 35–37.

Ivanoff, A., Smyth, N., Grochowski, S., Jang, S., & Klein, K. (1992). Problem solving and suicidality among prison inmates: Another look at state versus trait. *Journal of Consulting and Clinical Psychology, 60,* 970–973.

Joiner, T. E., Voelz, Z., & Rudd, M. (2001). For suicidal young adults with comorbid depressive and anxiety disorders, problem-solving treatment may be better than treatment as usual. *Professional Psychology: Research and Practice, 32,* 278–282.

Lerner, M., & Clum, G. (1990). Treatment of suicide ideators: A problem-solving approach. *Behavior Therapy, 21,* 403–411.

Linehan, M. (1993). *Cognitive–behavioral therapy of borderline personality disorder.* New York: Guilford Press.

Linehan, M., Camper, P., Chiles, J., Strosahl, K., & Shearin, E. (1987). Interpersonal problem solving and parasuicide. *Cognitive Therapy and Research, 11,* 1–12.

Marx, E., Williams, J., & Claridge, G. (1992). Depression and social problem solving. *Journal of Abnormal Psychology, 101,* 78–86.

McLeavey, B., Daly, R., Ludgate, J., & Murray, C. (1994). Interpersonal problem solving skills training in the treatment of self-poisoning patients. *Suicide and Life-Threatening Behavior, 24,* 382–394.

Milnes, D., Owens, D., & Blenkiron, P. (2002). Problems reported by self-harm patients: Perception, hopelessness, and suicidal intent. *Journal of Psychosomatic Research, 53,* 819–822.

Newell, A., & Simon, H. (1972). *Human problem solving.* Englewood Cliffs, NJ: Prentice-Hall.

Nezu, A. (1986). Cognitive appraisal of problem-solving effectiveness: Relation to depression and depressive symptoms. *Journal of Clinical Psychology, 42,* 42–48.

Nezu, A., & Nezu, C. (1998). Clinical decision making in everyday practice: The science in the art. *Cognitive and Behavioral Practice, 2*(1), 5–25.

Nezu, A., Nezu, C., Friedman, S., & Haynes, S. (1997). Case formulation in behavior therapy: Problem-solving and functional analytic strategies. In T. Eells (Ed.), *Handbook of psychotherapy case formulation* (pp. 368–401). New York: Guilford Press.

Nezu, A., Nezu, C., & Perri, M. (1989). *Problem-solving therapy for depression: Therapy, research, and clinical guidelines.* New York: Wiley.

Nezu, A., & Ronan, G. (1988). Social problem-solving as a moderator of stress-related depressive symptoms: A prospective analysis. *Journal of Counseling Psychology, 35,* 134–138.

Orbach, I., Bar-Joseph, H., & Dror, N. (1990). Styles of problem solving in suicidal individuals. *Suicide and Life-Threatening Behavior, 20,* 56–64.

Pretz, J., Naples, A., & Sternberg, R. (2003). Recognizing, defining, and representing problems. In J. Davidson & R. Sternberg (Eds.), *The psychology of problem solving* (pp. 3–30). Cambridge, England: Cambridge University Press.

Priester, M., & Clum, G. (1993a). Perceived problem-solving ability as a predictor of depression, hopelessness, and suicide ideation in a college population. *Journal of Counseling Psychology, 40,* 79–85.

Priester, M., & Clum, G. (1993b). The problem-solving diathesis in depression, hopelessness, and suicide ideation: A longitudinal analysis. *Journal of Psychopathology and Behavioral Assessment, 15,* 239–254.

Reinecke, M., DuBois, D., & Schultz, T. (2001). Social problem solving, mood, and suicidality among inpatient adolescents. *Cognitive Therapy and Research, 25,* 743–756.

Reinecke, M., & Freeman, A. (2003). Cognitive therapy. In A. Gurman & S. Messer (Eds.), *Essential psychotherapies: Theory and practice* (2nd ed., 224–271). New York: Guilford Press.

Rotheram-Borus, M., Trautman, P., Dopkins, S., & Shrout, P. (1990). Cognitive style and pleasant activities among female adolescent suicide attempters. *Journal of Consulting and Clinical Psychology, 58,* 554–561.

Rudd, M. D., Joiner, T. E., & Rajab, M. (2001). *Treating suicidal behavior: An effective, time-limited approach.* New York: Guilford Press.

Rudd, M. D., Rajab, H., & Dahm, P. (1994). Problem-solving appraisal in suicide ideators and attempters. *American Journal of Orthopsychiatry, 64,* 136–149.

Rudd, M. D., Rajab, H., Orman, D., Stulman, D., Joiner, T. E., & Dixon, W. (1996). Effectiveness of an outpatient problem-solving intervention targeting suicidal young adults: Preliminary results. *Journal of Consulting and Clinical Psychology, 64,* 179–190.

Salkovskis, P., Atha, C., & Storer, D. (1990). Cognitive–behavioural problem solving in the treatment of patients who repeatedly attempt suicide: A controlled trial. *British Journal of Psychiatry, 157,* 871–876.

Schotte, D., & Clum, G. (1982). Suicide ideation in a college population: A test of a model. *Journal of Consulting and Clinical Psychology, 50,* 690–696.

Schotte, D., & Clum, G. (1987). Problem-solving skills in suicidal psychiatric patients. *Journal of Consulting and Clinical Psychology, 55,* 49–55.

Schotte, D., Cools, J., & Payvar, S. (1990). Problem-solving deficits in suicidal patients: Trait vulnerability or state phenomenon? *Journal of Consulting and Clinical Psychology, 58,* 562–564.

Shneidman, E. (1985). *The definition of suicide.* New York: Wiley-Interscience.

Solomon, A., & Haaga, D. (2003). Cognitive theory and therapy of depression. In M. Reinecke & D. Clark (Eds.), *Cognitive therapy across the lifespan: Evidence and practice* (pp. 12–39). Cambridge, England: Cambridge University Press.

Speckens, A., & Hawton, K. (2005). Social problem solving in adolescents with suicidal behavior: A systematic review. *Journal of Suicide and Life-Threatening Behavior, 35,* 365–387.

Stanovich, K. (2003). The fundamental computational biases of human cognition: Heuristics that (sometimes) impair decision making and problem solving. In J. Davidson & R. Sternberg (Eds.), *The psychology of problem solving* (pp. 291–342). Cambridge, England: Cambridge University Press.

Sternberg, R. (1986). *Intelligence applied? Understanding and increasing your intellectual skills.* San Diego, CA: Harcourt Brace Jovanovich.

Townsend, E., Hawton, K., Altman, D. G., Arensman, E., Gunnell, D., Hazell, P., et al. (2001). The efficacy of problem-solving treatments after deliberate self-harm: Meta-analysis of randomized controlled trials with respect to depression, hopelessness, and improvement in problems. *Psychological Medicine, 31,* 979–988.

van der Sande, R., van Rooijen, E., Buskens, E., Allart, E., Hawton, K., van der Graaf, Y., & van Engeland, H. (1997). Intensive in-patient and community intervention versus routine care after attempted suicide: A randomized controlled intervention. *British Journal of Psychiatry, 171,* 35–41.

Vygotsky, L. (1962). *Thought and language.* Cambridge, MA: MIT Press.

Young, M., Fogg, L., Scheftner, W., Fawcett, J., Akiskal, H., & Maser, J. (1996). Stable trait components of hopelessness: Baseline and sensitivity to depression. *Journal of Abnormal Psychology, 105,* 155–165.

12

SUICIDE AND POSITIVE COGNITIONS: POSITIVE PSYCHOLOGY APPLIED TO THE UNDERSTANDING AND TREATMENT OF SUICIDAL BEHAVIOR

LARICKA R. WINGATE, ANDREA B. BURNS, KATHRYN H. GORDON,
MARISOL PEREZ, RHEEDA L. WALKER, FOLUSO M. WILLIAMS,
AND THOMAS E. JOINER JR.

Clinical psychology tends to focus on groups of individuals who are experiencing clinically significant distress, often due in part to, caused by, or exacerbated by maladaptive ways of coping with their environments. Psychologists study this side of human behavior with the noble intention of understanding psychopathology—learning to prevent and treat the experience of painful, maladaptive psychological conditions. This work is well respected, and the traditional model of clinical psychology serves a useful purpose; however, the model is incomplete without the study of the positive aspects of human behavior. Seligman and Csikszentmihalyi (2000) suggested that by adopting such a perspective, we are missing a substantial portion of human psychology, in that relatively few people will develop psychopathology in the course of their lives. This fact raises an important question: How do the majority of individuals successfully cope with life's stressors, while maintaining a sense of well-being? This question is the focus of positive psychology, an approach that emphasizes the positive aspects of the human experience: optimism, hope, faith, creativity, wisdom, and meaningful connection to others.

Positive psychology is defined as "the scientific study of ordinary human strength and virtues" (Sheldon & King, 2001, p. 216), and in many ways, it is a movement that facilitates psychology's gravitation toward sanguine elements of human life. Positive psychology focuses on creating and enhancing happiness in everyday living. Rather than investigating individual weaknesses, vulnerabilities, and mental illness, positive psychology promotes the understanding of human virtues and strengths such as creativity, hope, future, courage, and forgiveness. Snyder and Lopez (2002) suggested that psychologists studying positive psychology should ask the question, "What are the strengths that a person employs to be productive in life?" Seligman and Csikszentmihalyi (2000) summarized individual traits, which, along with other similar virtues, are the mantras of positive psychology. These traits include well-being, flow, and happiness, as well as group traits such as responsibility and altruism. Proponents of positive psychology are devoted to building and creating individual and collective strength—an approach that could enhance and complement the traditional study of pathology and problem behavior.

Suicidal behavior constitutes one possible target for interventions inspired by a positive psychology approach. Suicide refers to self-inflicted death, in which an individual makes an intentional, direct, and conscious effort to end his or her own life. Shneidman (1985) described the act of suicide as a flight from intolerable emotion, noting that in the absence of extreme despair and psychological pain, it is unlikely that people will choose suicide as a solution to their problems. More is currently known about suicide risk factors and vulnerabilities than is known about suicide buffers and resilience factors. For example, a search for suicide articles provided 4,272 articles on "suicide and risk" compared with 2,395 articles on "suicide and resilience or protective factors." Yet, from the standpoint of psychological intervention, it is the intersection of risk factors and protective factors for a particular individual that becomes important because risk factors increase whereas protective factors decrease the potential for suicidal behavior (see Blumenthal & Kupfer, 1988; Goldsmith, Pellmar, & Bunney, 2002; Silverman & Felner, 1995). Efforts to address the current bias in research toward suicide vulnerability (rather than well-being and resistance to suicidality) may therefore increase knowledge and contribute substantially to the field's understanding of suicidal behavior.

Suicide and related mental illness are conceptualized quite differently when viewed through the lens of positive psychology than when considered through a paradigm focused on weaknesses and abnormalities. Seligman and Csikszentmihalyi (2000) suggested that rather than a focus on despair itself, the aim of a positive psychological approach is to examine the strategies used to *overcome* the despair in the majority of the population who do not become suicidal. To gain a greater perspective on the suicidal person, positive psychology therefore potentially targets those people who do not engage in lethal suicidal behavior, despite the presence of numerous risk factors. That is, the positive psychology emphasis is on (a) those who suffer from multiple suicidogenic factors (e.g., recent stressor, history of suicide attempt, poor coping resources) and are at high risk (see Joiner, Walker, Rudd, & Jobes, 1999, for risk categorization) but do not consider suicide, (b) those who consider suicide but do not attempt, and (c) those who attempt suicide but do not complete the act.

Suicide continues to be a complex problem, the answers to which, in many respects, elude scientists and clinicians. Suicide research tends to be difficult to conduct because the actual base rate for completed suicides is relatively low, and as a result of the low base rate, the false positive error rate for short-term prediction is high. At best, the prediction rate is said to be approximately 30% (Maris, 2002). Additionally, suicidal people are often excluded in clinical research and epidemiological studies, and inconsistent nomenclature for labeling suicide creates challenges in labeling suicide-related death (Goldsmith et al., 2002). The difficulties in current suicide research warrant an alternative approach, and a positive perspective may be suitable. Working from a perspective that focuses on studying those who do not complete or even attempt suicide may expand the pool of potential research participants and make research in this arena more manageable, and likely more generalizable.

Solutions to help lessen the substantial problem of suicide may emerge through a positive psychology approach by focusing on people's individual and collective strengths. For example, some questions that a positive psychologist might pose regarding suicide are the following: "On what resources do those in therapy who say, 'I would never consider killing myself' or 'I've thought about it, but I could never kill myself,' rely?" and "What are the alternatives to suicidal behavior, and how might these alternatives become solutions that also create buffers for potentially suicidal people?" Posing such questions may help psychologists to understand some of the between-group differences in suicidal behavior that have been noted across the U.S. population. Epidemiologists, for instance, continue to be intrigued by the apparent resilience of African American women, who demonstrate unusually low suicide rates despite high odds for suicide (see Nisbet, 1996). Some speculate that African American resilience to suicide is founded in religious participation, strong social ties, and familial support. If the mechanisms of these protective factors could be more clearly understood, then others who are designated as "high risk" could potentially be empowered with this insight. Additionally, strategies that alleviate the hopelessness and helplessness that plague suicidal individuals suggest likely points of intervention. In "treating" suicidal behavior from a positive psychology perspective, one elicits hope in addition to creating positive interpersonal relationships.

Interventions that strategically elucidate individual "strengths" provide a foundation for challenging negative attitudes and developing a sense of autonomy and personal effectiveness. Because suicide risk factors fall into a number of domains (i.e., interpersonal, biological, psychological, etc.,), multifaceted preventive approaches may be most effective in reducing the incidence of suicide and suicidal behaviors.

Here we focus on positive psychology's relationship to suicide and attempt to forge a new dimension in suicide research. The chapter explores the relationships between optimism and suicide, as well as the relationship between health and suicide from a positive psychology perspective. We frame suicide in terms of Fredrickson's (2001) broaden-and-build theory of positive emotions and relate suicide to the positive concepts of effectiveness and belongingness. Finally, we apply self-determination theory to the understanding and treatment of suicidal behavior.

OPTIMISM AND SUICIDE

A key concept to positive psychology is optimism. An abundance of research exists relating low levels of optimism to psychopathology (Bulik, Wade, & Kendler, 2001; Day & Maltby, 2003; Symister & Friend, 2003). However, no direct research currently exists concerning the possible relation between optimism and suicidal behavior.

Optimism can be broadly defined as "an expectation that good things will happen" (Chang, 2001). Two distinct theoretical models encompass optimism: one that discusses optimism in terms of expectations (Carver & Scheier, 2001) and another that discusses optimism in terms of explanations (Gillham, Shatte, Reivich, & Seligman, 2001).

The expectancy model theorizes that humans use two kinds of feedback loops when determining our own behavior (Carver & Scheier, 2001). The first is a discrepancy-reducing loop in which one's behaviors are aimed at diminishing discrepancies between one's perception of the situation and one's goals. The intent is to have situational outcomes that bring one closer to one's goals. The second feedback loop is a discrepancy-enlarging loop in which there are situations that one wants to avoid, and the behaviors that one chooses are aimed at reducing the possibility of those situations occurring. Optimism's role in these feedback loops is with regard to confidence and doubt. An optimist will approach a situation with more confidence and will put more effort toward a discrepancy-reducing loop to attain an outcome that is more goal related. A pessimist, however, will perceive the wanted outcome as unattainable and therefore either will not put forth any effort or will disengage from the loop completely. An optimist will thus have more confidence and more motivation than a pessimist. According to this model, positive affect arises when behaviors are successful at diminishing discrepancies between one's perception of the situation and one's goals. An optimist, then, would have a better likelihood for and greater frequency of positive affect. In comparison, negative affect arises when the behaviors are unsuccessful at diminishing discrepancies between one's perception of the situation and one's goals. Depression, according to this model, results from doing poorly within a discrepancy-reducing loop. Anxiety, in contrast, results from doing poorly in a discrepancy-enlarging loop.

But what about suicide? How can this model explain suicidal behaviors? Furthermore, what does this model say about the connection between suicide and optimism? People who are not suicidal tend to fear death and have a discrepancy-enlarging loop regarding death. In other words, most people will engage in behaviors that seek to make death a less probable event. To reach the point of having a suicidal attempt or completion, suicidal individuals have to reduce the discrepancy-enlarging loop while slowly converting death into a discrepancy-reducing loop. Confidence in one's ability to commit suicide plays a key role in this behavioral system. As confidence increases, the discrepancy-reducing loop increases, making the goal of suicide more attainable and probable. Note that confidence previously was associated with optimism. This is not to suggest that suicidal individuals are optimists. Confidence and motivation are often descriptors applied to an optimistic individual, but they can be used to describe nonoptimistic individuals as well. When applied to an optimistic individual, confidence and motivation often refers to the ability to deal with life. When applied to a nonoptimist, or a suicidal person, the terms may refer to one's perceived ability and drive to end one's life. Not surprisingly, as discussed later in this section, research shows that suicidal individuals tend not to have a favorable view toward life (Wetzel, 1975). So according to the expectation model, individuals who have a discrepancy-reducing loop toward death and no discrepancy-enlarging loop toward death will be at risk for suicide. Intuitively, a discrepancy-reducing loop toward death is more related to a pessimistic view of life than an optimistic one. Optimism, according to this model, would therefore be expected to have a negative correlation with suicide.

The second theoretical model that could relate optimism and suicide is the explanatory model proposed by Seligman and colleagues (Buchanan & Seligman, 1995). This model states that explanations vary in three ways. First, the occurrence of negative life events is attributed to either internal or external causes. Second, the consequences of the negative life event are perceived as either stable or unstable. In other words, they will be viewed as either temporary or permanent. And third, the negative life event is attributed to either a global deficit or a situational deficit. In this model, optimism is defined in terms of how people explain past events in their lives. According to this model, people are optimistic when they attribute negative life events to temporary, specific, and external causes. Pessimists, however, attribute negative life events to permanent, pervasive, and internal causes. This model of pessimism is similar to the model for hopelessness depression, which suggests that certain interpretations that are made frequently can put individuals at risk for hopelessness depression (Abramson, Metalsky, & Alloy, 1989) and suicidal ideation. These interpretations are (a) that the causes of the negative life event are considered to be stable and global; (b) that negative interpretations about the self are inferred from the negative life event; and (c) that the consequences of the event are thought to be negative or catastrophic. Hopelessness (viewed here as similar to pessimism) has been supported by empirical research as having a central role in suicidal ideation (Bedrosian & Beck, 1979; Chioqueta & Stiles, 2003; Dyer & Kreitman, 1984; Minkoff, Bergman, Beck, & Beck, 1973; Nekanda-Trepka, Bishop, & Blackburn, 1983) and is arguably the best predictor overall of suicide completions in clinical populations (Steer, Kumar, & Beck, 1993). Thus, a pessimistic explanatory style would likely lead to depressive symptomatology, possibly including suicidal ideation. A significant amount of research supports this notion (Seligman, Schulman, DeRubeis, & Hollon, 1999; Ziegler & Hawley, 2001). As pessimism and negative thoughts about the future have been so strongly related to suicidality, optimism may be particularly relevant to the study and treatment of suicidality.

Although the literature thus supports a connection between a pessimistic outlook and psychopathology, there is also an abundant amount of literature to suggest that optimistic expectations promote psychological well-being. For example, multiple studies have found that among pregnant women, optimism prior to childbirth was predictive of fewer depressive symptoms after childbirth (Carver & Gaines, 1987) and fewer anxiety symptoms (Park, Moore, Turner, & Adler, 1997). Similar findings have been found for women who have abortions. Women who were more optimistic prior to the abortion had better postabortion adjustment (Major, Richards, Cooper, Cozzarelli, & Zubek, 1998). In another study assessing optimism in men diagnosed with prostate cancer, the more optimistic the men were, the less vulnerable they were to negative moods both during and after treatment (Johnson, 1996).

On the basis of the literature relating optimism to psychological well-being, one plausible inference might be that optimism serves as a buffer against suicide. Although there are no studies directly assessing the association between optimism and suicide, there are a few studies that yield promising results. Wetzel (1975) investigated the association between ratings of life and death across varying levels of suicide intent. He found that high-risk suicidal individuals tended to view life less favorably than nonsuicidal individuals and rated death more favorably than nonsuicidal individuals. In addition, varying levels of suicidal individuals differed in their views about life, but not about death. As suicide risk increased, life was viewed less favorably. This finding might generalize to optimism as well. In other words, as suicide risk increases, optimism decreases.

Findings of a second study suggest the importance of optimism in suicidality (Osman et al., 1998). These authors developed the Reason for Living Inventory for adolescents. After conducting exploratory factor analyses on a sample of 350 adolescents, Osman et al. (1998) found that the first factor to emerge was the future optimism factor. In addition, the future optimism scale was negatively and moderately correlated with suicidal ideation, threat, likelihood, hopelessness, and depression. Finally, both the high school nonsuicidal group and nonsuicidal psychiatric group endorsed significantly higher levels of future optimism than the suicidal psychiatric group. A third study investigated the relationship between negative cognitive style and suicidality (Abramson et al., 1998). The results suggested that those with a negative cognitive style or pessimistic explanatory style were significantly more likely than others to exhibit later suicidality, measured by both structured diagnostic interview and questionnaire self-report, during the prospective follow-up period. These findings, combined with the Osman et al. (1998) and Wetzel (1975) findings, suggest that level of optimism is a good indicator of suicidal risk, whereas less optimism is correlated with increased suicidal risk. Given the lack of research in this area and the association between optimism and suicidal risk, further research is warranted. In addition, future research should investigate whether increasing optimism during therapy serves as a preventative measure against suicide.

POSITIVE PSYCHOLOGY'S RELATION TO SUICIDE THROUGH HEALTH

The comorbidity of depressed mood and increased reports of physical complaints is well documented (Salovey, Rothman, Detweiler, & Steward, 2000). Although the factors associated with poor health are certainly not the only cause of suicide (because many people who are physically healthy die by suicide and the majority of people diagnosed with terminal illnesses do not attempt suicide), they are certainly related to depressed mood and may be an impetus for suicide (Wingate, Brown, & Joiner, 2004). Research shows that the risk for suicide is elevated among people with particular illnesses, including illnesses of the central nervous system, gastrointestinal system, genitourinary system, cancer, and autoimmune disorders. Of these people, those who commit the most suicides are those with cancer and neurological disorders (Goldblatt, 2000). Epidemiologic and prospective studies have examined and supported the association between cigarette smoking and suicide (Malone et al., 2003). Cigarette smoking is a risk factor for physical problems, including lung cancer, chronic obstructive pulmonary disease, coronary heart disease, and stroke (Hemenway, Solnick, & Colditz, 1993). It is also associated with mental health disorders, including major depression, schizophrenia, and alcoholism (Malone et al., 2003). Both physical illnesses and the previously mentioned mental disorders have been independently associated with suicide, and it is possible that cigarette smoking plays an important role in the relationship between disorders and suicide.

Suicidal behavior and its precursors could also be related to physical health in the opposite direction. Having feelings of depression or being in a poor emotional state could possibly lead to poor physical health. In fact, research on immunology serves to support the claim that negative mood states increase people's susceptibility to illness. In experimental studies in which participants' moods were manipulated, findings have suggested a causal influence of affective states on immune system functioning (Salovey et al., 2000). It has also been shown that when people are systematically exposed to a respiratory virus, those with a more negative mood at the time of the experiment developed a more severe illness in response to the virus than those who had a more positive mood (Cohen et al., 1995). An additional example of the relationship between mental state and poor health is the long-studied and consistent relationship between heart disease and depression. A review of the literature on depression and coronary heart disease found that a history of major depression, current depression symptoms, a diagnosis of clinical depression, and an increase in depressive symptoms with time predict coronary heart disease and mortality in people that did not have evidence of heart disease when they were assessed for depression (Carney & Freedland, 2003). Depression increases the likelihood that people who are otherwise healthy will develop heart disease and worsens the prognosis for people who already have heart disease (Glassman et al., 2003). The findings suggest the possibility that a poor emotional state can be a precursor to a poor physical state and vice versa. These processes may act in a cycle, so that poor mental health leads to poor physical health which leads to poorer mental health, and so on, thus promoting a chronic relation between poor health and poor emotional states (particularly those related to suicidal behavior).

Positive psychology may be the mechanism that can serve to interrupt this cycle or relationship between poor health and poor emotions. Research has shown that positive emotions can lead to increases in physical health. Positive emotional states are thought to be associated with healthier patterns of responding in both cardiovascular activity and the immune system (Salovey et al., 2000). Experimental studies have shown that when emotional state is manipulated in a positive direction, participants have greater immune system response (Salovey et al., 2000). Because poor health may be a risk factor for suicidal behavior, an increase in health may serve as a protective factor against suicide.

SUICIDE AND THE BROADEN-AND-BUILD THEORY OF POSITIVE EMOTIONS

The experience of a suicidal crisis is unquestionably characterized by profound negative emotions such as hopelessness and despair. Nonetheless, there is compelling reason to assert that although they almost certainly will not occur spontaneously until after the acute crisis is past, positive emotions can play a critical role in the treatment of suicidal behavior and in the prevention of future suicidal crises. This reasoning is based on Fredrickson's (2001) broaden-and-build theory of positive emotions. Fredrickson's theory holds that the experience of positive emotions leads to a cognitive and behavioral broadening in which an individual is able to conceive of and enact a greater and more varied repertoire of ideas and actions than she or he is capable of when experiencing a negative mood state. In turn, this broadening allows for the accruing and development of new personal resources, which are predicted to endure long past the end point of the positive emotional state (Fredrickson, 2001). When applied to the established treatments of suicidal behavior, this theory suggests that the occurrence of positive moods, with the associated broadening and openness predicted by the theory, could provide unique windows of opportunity for the teaching and development of new problem-solving and coping skills. These skills might then be drawn on when future negative moods or moments of suicidality strike (Joiner, Voelz, & Rudd, 2001).

Fredrickson's broaden-and-build theory contrasts the effects of positive emotions on human response styles with the theorized effects of negative emotions proposed by emotion theorists (e.g., Frijda, Kuipers, & Schure, 1989; Tooby & Cosmides, 1990). These theorists have proposed that the function of negative emotions, such as fear, anger, and disgust, is to elicit *specific action tendencies*. For example, fear produces the drive to escape, anger the drive to attack, disgust the drive to expel, and so on (Fredrickson, 2001). These specific action tendencies are presumed to have been established by virtue of being the evolutionarily adaptive response options to life-threatening situations (Tooby & Cosmides, 1990), and thus promote the survival of the species by efficiently narrowing an individual's momentary thought–action repertoire in such a way as to call to mind only particular behaviors (e.g., escape, attack, expel) in response to their triggering emotions (Fredrickson, 2001). In a less adaptive manner, however, it follows that when faced with the extreme sadness, hopelessness, and pain that can precipitate feelings of suicidality, the individual's available thought–action repertoire might be narrowed to the extent that escape through suicide is viewed as the only option.

In contrast, according to Fredrickson's model, positive emotions broaden, rather than constrict, the individual's thought–action repertoire. For example, joy creates the urge to play, to push limits, and to be creative; interest creates the drive to explore and take in new information; and contentment creates the urge to savor one's life circumstances (Fredrickson, 2001). This aspect of the broaden-and-build theory has received substantial empirical support, particularly through the research of Isen and colleagues (reviewed in Isen, 2000), who have demonstrated that people experiencing positive affect show more unusual, flexible, creative, and integrative thought patterns; are more open to information; and are more cognitively efficient.

It is important that this broadening effect of positive emotion is predicted to facilitate the acquisition and development of personal resources, including physical, social, intellectual, and psychological resources (Fredrickson, 2001). By opening the individual to new ideas, new skills, and new behaviors and by fostering the drives to play, share, explore, and so forth, positive emotions can lead to the development of skills, support networks, and coping mechanisms that endure long past the transient positive mood state itself. In other words, the experience of positive emotions can build a system of resiliency on which the individual can draw in the face of future negative mood states, including depressed or suicidal episodes. In turn, the development of such coping mechanisms can lead to better coping and associated improvements in general well-being and mood, leading to a positive spiral in which positive emotion and personal resources such as coping skills continuously build on one another. Fredrickson and Joiner (2002) provided some empirical support to this contention by demonstrating that in a sample of undergraduate students, assessed on two occasions separated by 5 weeks, initial positive affect predicted subsequent increases in broad-minded coping strategies, while at the same time initial broad-minded coping predicted subsequent increases in positive affect. Furthermore, Fredrickson and Joiner found that the increases in positive affect over time were partially mediated by changes in broad-minded coping, and vice versa. These results support the broaden-and-build theory's prediction of a positive spiral developing between positive emotion and personal resources.

On the basis of their specific findings, as well as the broaden-and-build theory in general, Fredrickson and Joiner (2002) noted that clinicians might be expected to bring about the greatest treatment effects by either deliberately inducing positive emotions in therapy (e.g., by asking patients to think about the best times in their lives) or timing interventions focused on skill-building to coincide with patients' natural experiences of positive moods. Patients' positive emotional states should render them more open to considering, learning, practicing, and implementing the skills presented in therapy, thus maximizing the likelihood of the patients' acquiring these skills and obtaining benefits from treatment.

It is entirely reasonable to question whether such a strategy is practical regarding the treatment of suicidal behavior because positive emotional states are extremely unlikely either to occur spontaneously or to be inducible in suicidal patients. To appreciate the manner in which the broaden-and-build principles might be applicable, it is necessary to distinguish between interventions for a suicidal crisis and more general treatment of suicidal behavior. Patients in a suicidal crisis state undoubtedly experience exclusively negative moods, during which their thought–action repertoires are expected to be constricted (Fredrickson, 2001; Joiner et al., 2001). However, the treatment of suicidality does not take place only in the context of acute crises but also in the more ongoing context of inpatient or outpatient therapy. In this broader context, the range of moods experienced by patients is broader, perhaps affording moments of positivity even to patients who are generally distressed (Joiner et al., 2001). It is these moments that may be capitalized on to maximize skill building and treatment effectiveness.

Such a possibility was investigated by Joiner and colleagues (2001). Consistent with the expectation that the extreme negative mood states associated with suicidality have the effect of narrowing patients' thought–action repertoires (Fredrickson, 2001), suicidality has been linked to deficits in problem-solving ability (Schotte & Clum, 1982; see also chap. 11, this volume). Furthermore, treatments of suicidal patients that focus on skill building and problem solving appear to be effective in reducing suicidal behavior (Rudd, Joiner, & Rajab, 2001) and suicidal ideation (Joiner et al., 2001). Incorporating the principles of the broaden-and-build theory, Joiner et al. (2001) predicted that the experience of positive emotion by adults undergoing treatment for suicidality should cause a broadening of patients' thought–action repertoires, which in turn should lead to greater utilization of important and therapeutic problem-solving skills and therefore to enhanced treatment response. They accordingly studied a group of suicidal adults in a military hospital, all of whom were participating in a treatment study for suicidal behavior. As predicted, they found that although all patients improved over the course of treatment, those participants who scored higher on a measure of positive affect and who thus were more prone to positive mood experiences had a tendency to demonstrate more positive gains in problem-solving attitudes and to improve regarding suicidal symptoms more than others (Joiner et al., 2001). What is more, they noted that the relationship between patients' positive affect and their improvement in suicidal symptoms was mediated by the changes in their problem-solving attitudes. This latter finding provides credence both to the previously noted finding that developing problem-solving skills is an important component of successful treatment of suicidality and to the broaden-and-build theory's prediction that positive emotion should facilitate the development of such skills and produce improvements in patients' general well-being via this mechanism. Thus, although positive emotion and suicidality seem to be contradictory concepts, it appears reasonable to expect that moments of positivity may occur, either spontaneously or through deliberate induction in therapy, even in generally suicidal clients and that these moments may provide important windows of opportunity for the development of curative resources, including problem-solving skills.

EFFECTIVENESS, BELONGINGNESS, AND SUICIDE

One of the tenets of the theory of positive psychology is that positive emotions and experiences that result in positive emotions have various salubrious effects on depressed clients. Positive emotions serve to broaden the repertoire of adaptive behaviors and foster skills that serve to decrease suicidal behavior. Two specific mechanisms may result in the decrease of suicidal behavior: the perception of one's self as being effective (the opposite of being a burden) and possessing a sense of belonging to a particular group. Both of these mechanisms can be regarded as protective factors against suicide; they are vehicles that can instill the positive emotions that serve to decrease the risk of suicide.

These mechanisms are described in Joiner's (in press) interpersonal–psychological theory of attempted and completed suicide. According to his theory, perceived burdensomeness and (lack of) belongingness are among necessary, but not sufficient, precursors to suicidality. When absent, these precursors actually serve as protective factors against suicide and can additionally be conceptualized as sources of positive emotions.

The first mechanism, the perception of effectiveness, can be conceptualized as the opposite of burdensomeness. Burdensomeness is the feeling that one is a burden, nuisance, or threat to loved ones and others in the environment. Burdensomeness is a source of intense psychological pain, and this fact is compatible with various theories of depression, such as the hopelessness theory of depression (Abramson et al., 1989; Abramson, Seligman, & Teasdale, 1978). More important, perceived burdensomeness may be one of the strongest sources of the desire to commit suicide. A number of studies have demonstrated the link between perceived burdensomeness and suicidality. In one study, raters were trained to evaluate suicide notes on the following dimensions: perceived burdensomeness; hopelessness; and generalized emotional pain (Joiner et al., 2002). Unknown to the raters, half of the notes were from individuals who attempted suicide and survived, and the other half were from individuals who died from completed suicide. In a regression analysis in which the predictors were controlled for each other, the notes from those who died by suicide contained more perceived burdensomeness than did notes from attempters. Additionally, no effects were found regarding hopelessness and emotional pain.

The predicted correlation between feeling burdensome to the family and suicidality was also found in a questionnaire study of college students (Brown, Dahlen, Mills, Rick, & Biblarz, 1999). Even when other variables, such as reproductive potential, were controlled, burdensomeness was notable as a unique and specific predictor of symptoms of suicidal behavior.

De Catanzaro (1995) conducted a survey regarding suicidal ideation, quality of family contacts, and reproductive behavior on several hundred community participants, as well as on five high-suicide-risk groups (e.g., general psychiatric patients, incarcerated psychiatric patients). It is interesting that, within each sample, perceived burdensomeness toward family and social isolation were especially correlated with suicidal ideation. It is important to note that these two variables match up to burdensomeness and (lack of) belongingness (cf. social isolation), two of the aspects in Joiner's (in press) theory of attempted and completed suicide.

If the evidence from the aforementioned research demonstrates that burdensomeness increases the risk of suicide, then the logical argument suggests the converse is also applicable: The feeling of effectiveness (i.e., not feeling that one is a burden) can decrease the risk of suicidality. There is empirical research to support this claim. In an effort to identify protective and risk factors that differentiated suicide attempters from those who had never made an attempt, Kaslow et al. (2002) studied abused African American women with low incomes. Self-efficacy, as well as effectiveness in obtaining material resources, were the protective factors found to be associated with nonattempters. In the current framework, these results could be regarded as suggesting that those who possess a general perception of effectiveness, as well as feeling that they are effective in providing material resources in particular, are buffered from feeling burdensome and thus are at relatively low risk for suicidality.

The perception that one is an effective, functioning, and valued member of the community can promote a variety of positive emotions. These positive emotions can function as a foundation on which to engage in various cognitions and behaviors that decrease suicidal behavior as well as its risk. The feelings of self-efficacy, efficiency, and a sense of usefulness in one's community can serve as a protective buffer to attempted or completed suicide.

A second important protective factor and mechanism for positive emotion is "belongingness." According to Baumeister and Leary (1995), the need to belong to valued groups or relationships is a commanding, pervasive, and fundamental human motivation. The authors have supported this view with a vast array of empirical evidence. According to Joiner's (in press) theory, this need is so powerful and encompassing that when it is satisfied, it can prevent suicide even when perceived burdensomeness is present. When this need is thwarted, however, numerous negative effects on health, adjustment, and well-being can occur, and these have been documented. More specifically, if one does not have a sense of belonging, the risk for suicide is increased. This view is consistent with Durkheim's (1951) theory of social integration, which posits that suicide occurs, in part, because of a failure of the individual to integrate into society.

A variety of studies support the view that belongingness is a protective factor against suicidal behavior. Thorlindsson and Bjarnason (1998) assessed suicidality and family and parental functioning in more than 4,000 high school students in Iceland. The authors concluded that those adolescents who were well integrated into their families thereby derived protection from suicide. The indices related to family integration (cf. belongingness) exercised stronger influence on suicidality than did indices related to parental functioning.

Various research data on social isolation indicate that nonmarried status is a demographic risk factor for suicide. National statistics indicate the following suicide rates in the United States in 1999: Divorced—32.7 per 100,000; widowed—19.7 per 100,000; single—17.8 per 100,000; married—10.6 per 100,000 (McIntosh, 2002). These statistics are consistent with the belief that belongingness (as indicated by married status) is a suicide buffer, whereas the absence of belongingness (as indicated by nonmarried status) is a risk for death by suicide. This is particularly evident with regard to divorce (which confers a threefold increase in risk relative to married status). On the basis of Joiner's (in press) theory, the notably and relatively high suicide rates among divorced people can be attributed to the fact that divorce can affect both basic feelings of effectiveness (e.g., feeling a failure as a spouse) and basic feelings of connectedness (losing social contact not only with a spouse but potentially with the spouse's family, with children, and with friends previously shared with the spouse).

There are various manifestations of belongingness, such as married status and integration within one's family. Having large numbers of children may also promote a sense of belongingness, and there is evidence that it protects against suicide. Over the course of a 15-year time period, Hoyer and Lund (1993) studied nearly 1 million women in Norway, and more than 1,000 women in the sample died by suicide. They reported that women with six or more children had one fifth the risk of death by suicide compared with other women. In a study of suicide and birth rates in Canada's provinces, Leenaars and Lester (1999) found a negative correlation between the suicide rate and the birth rate (as well as a positive correlation between the suicide rate and the divorce rate). The results of these studies suggest that having many children promotes an increased sense of belongingness and connectedness, which serves as a protective factor against suicide.

In sum, the feelings of effectiveness and belongingness are significant protective factors against suicide. According to Joiner's theory, even if people feel as if they are a burden to their community, they are protected from suicide if they have a sense of belongingness in that community. These feelings serve as vehicles in instilling the positive emotions that serve to expand the array of adaptive and beneficial cognitions and behaviors that decrease the risk of, desire for, and behavior of suicidality.

SELF-DETERMINATION THEORY: APPLICATION TO THE UNDERSTANDING AND TREATMENT OF SUICIDAL BEHAVIOR

Self-determination theory (SDT) is well suited for positive psychology's focus on what makes one's life meaningful. SDT posits that there are three innate human psychological needs: autonomy, relatedness, and competence. *Autonomy* is defined as effectively directing the course of one's own life. When the need for autonomy is neglected, individuals do not feel effective and responsible for their behaviors but instead feel that an external force is determining the course of their life (Ryan & Deci, 2000; cf. Abramson et al., 1989; Bandura, 1997). *Relatedness* embodies the fundamental human need for interpersonal connections (Baumeister & Leary, 1995). *Competence* refers to an individual's drive to master new skills and situations (Ryan & Deci, 2000). Ryan and Deci explained that when individuals have these essential needs met, they are "at their best, they are agentic and inspired, striving to learn; extend themselves; master new skills; and apply their talents responsibly." Furthermore, they suggested that this is "more normative than exceptional, suggesting some very positive and persistent features of human behavior." Important in the current context, they also call attention to situations in which these needs are obstructed: "the human spirit can be diminished or crushed, and individuals sometimes reject growth and responsibility" (Ryan & Deci, 2000).

Ryan and Deci (2000) proposed that when individuals have their psychological needs met in a situation, their behavior regarding that situation is self-determined. Ryan and Deci designed a continuum describing types of motivation that exist, varying on the level of self-determination of the behavior (see Ryan & Connell, 1989, for empirical support). The continuum ranges from complete lack of motivation (amotivation) to the most powerful type of motivation (intrinsic—engaging in an activity for personal satisfaction, interest, or enjoyment). Most behavior falls between the two extremes into the category of extrinsic motivation. Extrinsic motivation occurs when an individual is driven to behave based on some external reason, rather than solely for his or her own personal interest or satisfaction.

How does self-determination theory relate to the understanding and treatment of suicidal behavior? Based on Ryan and Deci's theorized psychological needs and continuum of motivation, Sheldon, Williams, and Joiner (2003) wrote a research-based approach to the application of SDT: *Self-Determination Theory in the Clinic*. The book serves as a guide to health care workers on how to motivate clients toward treatment adherence using SDT principles. As Sheldon et al. pointed out, SDT has a distinctive strength compared with previous schools of thought (e.g., humanistic psychology, behaviorism) in that it bears intuitive appeal and a 30-year accumulation of supporting research. Thus, SDT principles are attractive to both academic and applied psychologists.

How do current models of suicidal behavior fit into the self-determination framework? Rudd and colleagues (2001) highlighted the fact that existing data on suicide are relatively sparse and that available data have limited clinical relevance. They asserted that the general lack of integration between empirical findings and clinical application results in suboptimal treatment of the urgent condition of suicidality. Therefore, to achieve optimal clinical treatment of suicidality, a theoretical model should be consistent in both the cause of suicidal behavior and the treatment of suicidal behavior and should focus on dynamic variables that are accessible for change.

Joiner's (in press) interpersonal–psychological theory of suicide is of both clinical and theoretical relevance and focuses on dynamic factors of suicide. Joiner's theory, which is compatible with SDT principles, proposes three factors that are necessary for an individual to engage in serious suicidal behavior: (a) the acquired capability to enact lethal self-injury; (b) perceived burdensomeness (i.e., neglected autonomy and competence needs); and (c) lack of belongingness (i.e., neglected relatedness need). In light of Joiner's theory of suicidality, self-determination principles are applicable in two important ways for the treatment of suicidal clients: first, as motivation for adherence to therapy (Sheldon et al., 2003) and second, for actual alteration of the suicidal condition.

Regarding motivation to adhere to therapy, Sheldon et al. (2003) offered clinical techniques on how to facilitate motivation in clients through the nurturing of their psychological needs. The process of therapy itself may not be intrinsically rewarding to the client because it often involves confronting one's own maladaptive patterns of coping, skills deficits, and dysfunctional interpersonal relationships. Thus, the therapist's goal is to facilitate integrated extrinsic motivation or the adherence to therapy because it is in harmony with other needs (e.g., improving interpersonal relationships).

How can a therapist facilitate integrated motivation in suicidal patients? Sheldon et al. (2003) offered specific suggestions on how to motivate clients through supporting their chief psychological need for autonomy. Without a sense of autonomy, clients' achievement of competence in therapy (via skill building) likely will not be attributed to the clients themselves, but to the therapist. If clients achieve competence through skills learned in therapy and have had an active part in participating in the process, they are more likely to attribute the changes internally and thus more likely to maintain therapeutic changes. In contrast, if clients attribute their improvement solely to the therapist, they are more likely to return to old coping patterns once therapy has been terminated. Sheldon et al. (2003) proposed that fostering clients' autonomy results in taking ownership over the therapeutic process and therefore in feeling more intrinsically motivated to participate in the process. It is important that nurturing clients' psychological needs, particularly autonomy, is adaptable within all therapeutic frameworks.

Sheldon et al. (2003) suggested three specific therapeutic techniques for cultivating client autonomy: perspective taking, choice provision, and rationale provision. Perspective taking consists of the traditional concept of empathy in the therapeutic relationship. SDT posits that acknowledging clients' perspective respects their self: their feelings and their experiences. For example, if a suicidal client says "I am worthless," the autonomy-supportive response would be, "I understand that you feel worthless." This kind of statement achieves an expression of empathy from the therapist while not devaluing his or her opinion (as "You're not worthless, you are a great person" would; cf. self-verification theory, Giesler & Swann, 1999). Perspective taking also serves the function of giving the therapist credibility (therapists are supposed to be good listeners), showing that the therapist has the client's best interest in mind and allowing the client's perspective to be prioritized. If the client's needs determine the course of therapy, he or she is more likely to be invested and motivated in the process.

Choice provision consists of informing clients of available treatments for their specific diagnosis. For example, if a client presents with suicidal behavior, the therapist might offer that person the choice of empirically supported therapy (e.g., Rudd et al., 2001), psychotropic drugs, or a combination of both. According to SDT principles, if a client participates in the selection of a method of treatment, he or she is more likely to be internally motivated to adhere to it (as opposed to when a treatment is simply imposed on the client). This is likely because of the client's developing internal reasons for adhering to therapy (Sheldon et al., 2003).

Rationale provision comprises explaining why the therapist recommends the intervention methods for the client (e.g., "There is empirical support for cognitive–behavioral therapy in treating individuals who exhibit suicidal behavior"), along with the way the technique works (e.g., "through deconstructing the suicidal cognitive mode"; Rudd et al., 2001). Rationale provision is particularly important for autonomy support when there is only one frontline treatment for a particular disorder (e.g., medication for bipolar disorder). Rationale provision allows clients to feel that they are taking an active role in their treatment plan and in part of the decision-making process involved in their treatment.

SDT techniques have a twofold benefit with suicidal clients in that they not only motivate clients to internalize reasons for treatment adherence but also provide a safe arena to nurture needs which are often neglected in suicidal individuals (Joiner, in press). The therapy sessions can serve as an arena in which the clients' needs for autonomy (through choice and rationale provision), relatedness (through the therapeutic alliance), and competence (through skill building) are met. The goal of therapy is to teach clients that their needs can be met outside of therapy with the proper tools. Therefore, it is important to keep clients' basic needs in mind at all times within the selected treatment framework.

Rudd et al. (2001) provided a five-step treatment manual for suicidal behavior that is congruent with cognitive–behavioral and self-determination principles. The first step involves an initial interview and history, with the goal of determining the client's diagnosis(es) and assessing suicidal risk (see Joiner, Walker, Rudd, & Jobes, 1999). During this part of therapy, perspective taking is particularly important, so that clients feel their experience is being prioritized. As Sheldon et al. (2003) pointed out, the need for autonomy may come second to safety if it is determined that it is in the best interest of the client to be hospitalized. If the therapist comes to this decision, SDT principles such as rationale for hospitalization and sympathy for the client's concerns can still be used. Steps 2 and 3 involve the therapist providing information about the suicidal cognitive mode (see Rudd et al., 2001, for detailed explanation) and rationale for how the treatment works. Steps 4 and 5 involve the client and therapist working together to identify treatment goals and to target the three components of the therapy: symptom management, skill building, and personality development. The steps are not necessarily chronological but can and should be revisited throughout therapy using self-determination principles.

Self-determination principles are relevant to the understanding and treatment of suicidal behavior in two major ways. First, SDT can aid in internalization of motivation to attend and adhere to therapy. Second, suicidal clients often have their psychological needs for autonomy, competence, and relatedness neglected. Thus, understanding and specifically nurturing these needs may serve to teach clients how to direct the course of their own lives. Self-determination theory provides tools for therapists to enhance the therapeutic process and bring out the best qualities of the human experience.

CONCLUSION

Positive psychology is highly relevant to the understanding and treatment of suicidal behavior. Its focus on the study of human strengths and virtues provides a fruitful avenue for the study of protective and resiliency factors that can serve as a buffer against suicidal ideation and behaviors. The influence of positive psychology also seems to be extremely important in conceptualizing treatment for suicidal persons. Positive experiences including optimism, sound health, hope, creativity, and broadened thinking can play a vital role in helping to understand and alleviate suicidality.

This chapter considered the relationships among several concepts that relate the field of positive psychology to the study of suicide. The research on optimism supports a connection between a pessimistic outlook and psychopathology, as well as the promotion of psychological well-being through optimistic expectations. Studies on optimism and suicide suggest that level of optimism is a good indicator of suicidal risk. Health psychology research has shown that positive emotions can lead to increases in physical health. Positive psychology may be the mechanism that can serve to interrupt the cycle or relationship between poor health and poor emotions that may lead to suicidal behavior.

Fredrickson's (2001) broaden-and-build theory of positive emotions suggests that positive psychology may be a fruitful avenue for treatment of suicidal behavior in terms of using naturally occurring or induced states of positive emotion to introduce therapeutic concepts on which the client can later build. Expanding from Joiner's (in press) theory of suicidal behavior, the positive concepts of effectiveness and belongingness may be vital areas to focus on in the understanding and treatment of suicidal behavior. Finally, self-determination theory can aid in internalization of motivation to attend and adhere to therapy and in meeting the psychological needs for autonomy, competence, and relatedness in suicidal clients.

REFERENCES

Abramson, L. Y., Alloy, L. B., Hogan, H. E., Whitehouse, W. G., Cornette, M., Akhavan, S., & Chiara, A. (1998). Suicidality and cognitive vulnerability to depression among college students: A prospective study. *Journal of Adolescence*, *21*, 473–487.

Abramson, L. Y., Metalsky, G. I., & Alloy, L. B. (1989). Hopelessness depression: A theory-based subtype of depression. *Psychological Review*, *96*, 358–372.

Abramson, L. Y., Seligman, M. E. P., & Teasdale, J. (1978). Learned helplessness in humans: Critique and reformulation. *Journal of Abnormal Psychology*, *87*, 49–74.

Bandura, A. (1997). *Self-efficacy: The exercise of control*. New York: Freeman.

Baumeister, R. F., & Leary, M. R. (1995). The need to belong: Desire for interpersonal attachments as a fundamental human motivation. *Psychological Bulletin*, *117*, 497–529.

Bedrosian, R. C., & Beck, A. T. (1979). Cognitive aspects of suicidal behavior. *Suicide and Life-Threatening Behavior*, *2*, 87–96.

Blumenthal, S. J., & Kupfer, D. J. (1988). Overview of early detection and treatment strategies for suicidal behavior in young people. *Journal of Youth and Adolescence*, *17*, 1–23.

Brown, R. M., Dahlen, E., Mills, C., Rick, J., & Biblarz, A. (1999). Evaluation of an evolutionary model of self-preservation and self-destruction. *Suicide and Life-Threatening Behavior*, *29*, 58–71.

Buchanan, G. M., & Seligman, M. E. P. (1995). *Explanatory style*. Hillsdale, NJ: Erlbaum.

Bulik, C. M., Wade, T. D., & Kendler, K. S. (2001). Characteristics of monozygotic twins disconcordant for bulimia nervosa. *International Journal of Eating Disorders*, *29*, 1–10.

Carney, R. M., & Freedland, K. E. (2003). Depression, mortality, and medical morbidity in patients with coronary heart disease. *Biological Psychiatry*, *54*, 241–247.

Carver, C. S., & Gaines, J. G. (1987). Optimism, pessimism, and postpartum depression. *Cognitive Therapy and Research*, *11*, 449–462.

Carver, S. S., & Scheier, M. F. (2001). Optimism, pessimism, and self-regulation. In E. C. Chang (Ed.), *Optimism and pessimism: Implications for theory, research, and practice* (pp. 31–52). Washington, DC: American Psychological Association.

Chang, E. C. (2001). Introduction: Optimism and pessimism and moving beyond the most fundamental question. In E. C. Chang (Ed.), *Optimism and pessimism: Implications for theory, research, and practice* (pp. 3–13). Washington, DC: American Psychological Association.

Chioqueta, A. P., & Stiles, T. C. (2003). Suicide risk in outpatients with specific mood and anxiety disorders. *Crisis, 24,* 105–112.

Cohen, S., Doyle, W. J., Skoner, D. P., Fireman, P., Gwaltney, J. M., & Newsom, J. T. (1995). State and trait negative affect as predictors of objective and subjective symptoms of respiratory viral infections. *Journal of Personality and Social Psychology, 68,* 159–169.

Day, L., & Maltby, J. (2003). Belief in good luck and psychological well-being: The mediating role of optimism and irrational beliefs. *Journal of Psychology, 37,* 99–110.

de Catanzaro, D. (1991). Evolutionary limits to self-preservation. *Ethology and Sociobiology, 12,* 13–28.

de Catanzaro, D. (1995). Reproductive status, family interactions, and suicidal ideation: Surveys of the general public and high-risk groups. *Ethology and Sociobiology, 16,* 385–394.

Durkheim, E. (1951). *Suicide.* New York: Free Press.

Dyer, J. A., & Kreitman, N. (1984). Hopelessness, depression, and suicide intent in parasuicide. *British Journal of Psychiatry, 144,* 127–133.

Fredrickson, B. L. (2001). The role of positive emotions in positive psychology: The broaden-and-build theory of positive emotions. *American Psychologist, 56,* 218–226.

Fredrickson, B. L., & Joiner, T. (2002). Positive emotions trigger upward spirals toward emotional well-being. *Psychological Science, 13,* 172–175.

Frijda, N. H., Kuipers, P., & Shure, E. (1989). Relations among emotion, appraisal, and emotional action readiness. *Journal of Personality and Social Psychology, 57,* 212–228.

Giesler, R. B., & Swann, W. B., Jr. (1999). Striving for confirmation: The role of self-verification in depression. In T. E. Joiner & J. C. Coyne (Eds.), *The Interactional nature of depression* (pp. 189–218). Washington, DC: American Psychological Association.

Gillham, J. E., Shatte, A. J., Reivich, K. J., & Seligman, M. E. P. (2001). Optimism, pessimism, and explanatory style. In E. C. Chang (Ed.), *Optimism and pessimism: Implications for theory, research, and practice.* Washington, DC: American Psychological Association.

Glassman, A., Shapiro, P. A., Ford, D. E., Culpepper, L., Finkel, M. S., Swenson, J. R., et al. (2003). Cardiovascular health and depression. *Journal of Psychiatric Practice, 9,* 409–421.

Goldblatt, M. J. (2000). Physical illness and suicide. In R. W. Marris, A. L. Berman, & M. M. Silverman (Eds.), *Comprehensive textbook of suicidology* (pp. 342–356). New York: Guilford Press.

Goldsmith, S. K., Pellmar, T. C., & Bunney, W. E., for the Institute of Medicine. (2002). *Reducing suicide: A national imperative.* Washington, DC: The National Academy Press.

Hemenway, D., Solnick, S. J., & Colditz, G. A. (1993). Smoking and suicide among nurses. *American Journal of Public Health, 83,* 249–251.

Hoyer, G., & Lund, E. (1993). Suicide among women related to number of children in marriage. *Archives of General Psychiatry, 50,* 134–137.

Isen, A. M. (2000). Positive affect and decision making. In M. Lewis & J. M. Haviland-Jones (Eds.), *Handbook of emotions* (2nd ed., pp. 417–435). New York: Guilford Press.

Johnson, J. E. (1996). Coping with radiation therapy: Optimism and the effect of preparatory interventions. *Research in Nursing and Health, 19,* 3–12.

Joiner, T. E. (in press). *Why people die by suicide.* Cambridge, MA: Harvard University Press.

Joiner, T. E., Jr., Pettit, J. W., Perez, M., Burns, A. B., Gencoz, T., Gencoz, F., & Rudd, M. D. (2001). Can positive emotion influence problem-solving attitudes among suicidal adults? *Professional Psychology: Research and Practice, 32,* 507–512.

Joiner, T. E., Pettit, J. W., Walker, R. L., Voelz, Z. R., Cruz, J., Rudd, M. D., & Lester, D. (2002). Perceived burdensomeness and suicidality: Two studies on the suicide notes of those attempting and completing suicide. *Journal of Social and Clinical Psychology, 21,* 531–545.

Joiner, T. E., Jr., Voelz, Z. R., & Rudd, M. D. (2001). For suicidal young adults with comorbid depressive and anxiety disorders, problem-solving treatment may be better than treatment as usual. *Professional Psychology: Research and Practice, 32,* 278–282.

Joiner, T. E., Walker, R. L., Rudd, M. D., & Jobes, D. A. (1999). Scientizing and routinizing the assessment of suicidality in outpatient practice. *Professional Psychology: Research and Practice, 30,* 447–453.

Kaslow, N. J., Thompson, M. P., Okun, A., Price, A., Young, S., Bender, M., et al. (2002). Risk and protective factors for suicidal behavior in abused African American women. *Journal of Consulting and Clinical Psychology, 70,* 311–319.

Leenaars, A. A., & Lester, D. (1999). Domestic integration and suicide in the provinces of Canada. *Crisis, 20,* 59–63.

Major, B., Richards, C., Cooper, M. L., Cozzarelli, C., & Zubek, J. (1998). Personal resilience, cognitive appraisals, and coping: An integrative model of adjustment to abortion. *Journal of Personality and Social Psychology, 74,* 735–752.

Malone, K. M., Waternaux, C., Haas, G. L., Cooper, T. B., Li, S., & Mann, J. J. (2003). Cigarette smoking, suicidal behavior, and serotonin function in major psychiatric disorders. *American Journal of Psychiatry, 160,* 773–779.

McIntosh, J. L. (2002). *U.S.A. suicide statistics for the year 1999: Overheads and a presentation guide.* Washington, DC: American Association of Suicidology.

Minkoff, K., Bergman, E., & Beck, A. T. (1973). Hopelessness, depression, and attempted suicide. *American Journal of Psychiatry, 130*, 455–459.

Nekanda-Trepka, C. J. S., Bishop, S., & Blackburn, I. M. (1983). Hopelessness and depression. *British Journal of Clinical Psychiatry, 132*, 954–956.

Nisbet, P. A. (1996). Protective factors for suicidal Black females. *Suicide and Life-Threatening Behavior, 26*, 325–341.

Osman, A., Downs, W. R., Kopper, B. A., Barrios, F. X., Baker, M. T., & Osman, J. R. (1998). The reasons for living inventory for adolescents (RFL-A): Development and psychometric properties. *Journal of Clinical Psychology, 54*, 1063–1078.

Park, C. L., Moore, P. J., Turner, R. A., & Adler, N. E. (1997). The roles of constructive thinking and optimism in psychological and behavioral adjustment during pregnancy. *Journal of Personality and Social Psychology, 73*, 584–592.

Ryan, R. M., & Connell, J. P. (1989). Perceived locus of causality and internalization. *Journal of Personality and Social Psychology, 57*, 749–761.

Ryan, R. M., & Deci, E. L. (2000). Self-determination theory and the facilitation of intrinsic motivation, social development, and well-being. *American Psychologist, 55*, 68–78.

Rudd, M. D., Joiner, T., & Rajab, M. H. (2001). *Treating suicidal behavior: An effective time-limited approach.* New York: Guilford Press.

Salovey, P., Rothman, A. J., Detweiler, J. B., & Steward, W. T. (2000). Emotional states and physical health. *American Psychologist, 55*, 110–121.

Schotte, D., & Clum, G. (1982). Suicide ideation in a college population: A test of a model. *Journal of Consulting and Clinical Psychology, 46*, 690–696.

Seligman, M. E., & Csikszentmihalyi, M. (2000). Positive psychology: An introduction. *American Psychologist, 55*, 5–14.

Seligman, M. E. P., Schulman, P., DeRubeis, R. J., & Hollon, S. D. (1999, December 21). The prevention of depression and anxiety. *Prevention & Treatment, 2*, Article 0008a. Retrieved July 3, 2003, from http://journals.apa.org/prevention/volume2/pre0020008a.html

Sheldon, K. M., & King, L. (2001). Why positive psychology is necessary. *American Psychologist, 56*, 216–217.

Sheldon, K., Williams, G., & Joiner, T. E. (2003). *Self-determination theory in the clinic: Motivating physical and mental health.* New Haven, CT: Yale University Press.

Shneidman, E. S. (1985). *Definition of suicide.* New York: Wiley.

Snyder, C. R., & Lopez, S. J. (2002). *Handbook of positive psychology.* New York: Oxford University Press.

Steer, R. A., Kumar, G., & Beck, A. T. (1993). Hopelessness in adolescent psychiatric inpatients. *Psychological Reports, 72*, 559–564.

Symister, P., & Friend, R. (2003). The influence of social support and problematic support on optimism and depression on chronic illness: A prospective study evaluating self-esteem as a mediator. *Health Psychology, 22*, 123–129.

Thorlindsson, T., & Bjarnason, T. (1998). Modeling Durkheim on the micro level: A study of youth suicidality. *American Sociological Review*, *63*, 94–110.

Tooby, J., & Cosmides, L. (1990). The past explains the present: Emotional adaptations and the structure of ancestral environments. *Ethnology and Sociobiology*, *11*, 375–424.

Wetzel, R. D. (1975). Ratings of life and death and suicide intent. *Psychological Reports*, *37*, 879–885.

Wingate, L. R., Brown, J., & Joiner, T. E. (2004). *Suicide*. In A. J. Christensen, R. Martin, & J. Smyth (Eds.), *Encyclopedia of health psychology*. New York: Kluwer Academic.

Ziegler, D. L., & Hawley, J. L. (2001). Relation of irrational thinking and the pessimistic explanatory style. *Psychological Reports*, *88*, 483–488.

IV

SPECIAL TOPICS

13

DEVELOPMENTAL INFLUENCES ON SUICIDALITY AMONG ADOLESCENTS: COGNITIVE, EMOTIONAL, AND NEUROSCIENCE ASPECTS

BARRY M. WAGNER AND JOANNA H. ZIMMERMAN

In contrast to the extensive literature on cognitive influences on suicidal behaviors among adults, we know relatively little about the particular cognitive processes related to the development or maintenance of suicidal behaviors in children and adolescents. Clearly, a solid grasp of the state of the literature on cognitive factors is critical to develop optimal cognitive psychotherapy interventions for suicidal youth and preventive interventions for those at risk of suicidal behaviors. In this chapter, we seek to identify and describe the existing base of knowledge on cognitive factors of relevance to suicidal youth. In so doing, we intend to address the following questions: (a) What aspects of cognition already have a solid empirical base to support their use as targets of intervention? (b) Where are the biggest gaps in our knowledge, and in what specific areas is further investigation necessary?

We anchor our review within a developmental psychopathology framework, which—as described in more detail in the following section—holds that developmental processes are best understood by examining multiple, interdependent domains of functioning. In considering the role of cognition from within a self-regulatory framework, we incorporate two closely linked domains of functioning. First, we consider emotional processes, because the function of cognition in suicidal persons cannot be divorced from the emotional context in which cognition occurs. Second, we examine recent advances in cognitive neuroscience, because they may yield information that is critical to developing adequate models of the role of cognition.

DEVELOPMENTAL PSYCHOPATHOLOGY PERSPECTIVE

Several principles of the developmental psychopathology perspective are especially relevant to our discussion. First, as described by Cicchetti and Toth (1995), child and adolescent development can be conceptualized as a series of reorganizations at increasingly higher levels of complexity and differentiation. Such reorganization takes place within and across several domains, including socioemotional, biological, cognitive, linguistic, representational, and so on.

Second, developmental psychopathologists place an emphasis on the study of individual differences in young people, with a recognition that strengths and weaknesses manifest at earlier levels of development contribute to whether an individual will successfully manage the subsequent tasks of development (Cicchetti & Toth, 1998). This holds not only within specific domains, but also across domains, because the systems become increasingly integrated over time (thus, for example, emotional systems affect cognitive systems, biological systems affect both cognitive and emotional systems, and so forth).

Third, two properties of complex developmental systems are of relevance to our current discussion: multifinality and equifinality (Cicchetti & Rogosch, 1996). Multifinality holds that a given risk condition can lead to a diversity of outcomes, via its influence on various interconnected processes across development. For example, a disturbance in attachment relationships in early childhood may increase the likelihood of a variety of different conditions in later childhood and adolescence, including depression, suicidal behaviors, anxiety, aggression, and others. Predicting which negative outcome, if any, may result for a given child will require taking into account a host of relevant factors, including biological vulnerabilities, the quality of later parenting, the presence of ongoing stresses, school and neighborhood factors, and so forth. Equifinality holds that a particular outcome—a suicide attempt, for example—might be a common end point for youth traversing any of various developmental pathways.

How are these principles of developmental psychopathology relevant to our examination of cognitive influences on suicidal behaviors? First, it is well known that adolescence is a period of rapid reorganizations in all of the domains we have mentioned (biological, emotional, cognitive, etc.; Lerner et al., 1996). Although managing the simultaneous transitions poses a challenge to most adolescents, some are more vulnerable than others based on their developmental histories. The degree to which adolescents develop competently in the cognitive domain is in part dependent on how adequately they managed tasks in that domain earlier in development (Sroufe & Rutter, 1984). This underscores the importance of assessing trajectories of adjustment across development. Understanding the influence of the developmental course also requires knowledge of normative developmental shifts in relevant domains, such as the implications for mental health of increasing cognitive sophistication.

Second, the developmental approach points to the importance of considering the social context in which cognition takes place, including family, peer, school, and other contexts. For example, growing up with a depressed parent increases the risk of a child developing depression-prone cognitions (Zahn-Waxler & Kochanska, 1990). However, it is possible that those cognitions may fluctuate with context, so that they may be most intense when interacting with parents in the home but may be less influential when the adolescent is with peers. Moreover, positive experiences with peers may promote healthier cognitions, which could serve as a partial protective buffer against the negative effects of parental cognitions.

Third, researchers of adolescent cognition must seek to understand the ways in which changes in biological and emotional factors influence cognitive functioning. Emerging lines of work in neuroscience, for example, suggest very interesting questions to be posed regarding the links of brain maturation with both emotional and cognitive development during adolescence (Casey, Giedd, & Thomas, 2000; Keating, 2003); such work is reviewed in a later section of this chapter.

Fourth, the principles of multi- and equifinality suggest that researchers are not likely to uncover any one cognitive risk process that explains suicidal outcomes and that research seeking to identify universal risk factors common to all suicidal youth is likely to be a fruitless endeavor. Rather, it is likely that there are multiple risk pathways that researchers should strive to identify, along with factors that may protect youth from entering those pathways or that deflect youth who have entered those paths onto more benign developmental trajectories. In addition, the principle of equifinality teaches that the maladaptive cognitions of suicidal youth may be the end product of a variety of processes, whether they be family focused (a loss of hope of parental acceptance), emotion focused (a dissociative "walling off" to escape the emotional pain of biological vulnerabilities), a function of a difficult temperament style (a lack of cognitive control over impulsive self-destruction), or otherwise.

Cognition then, from a developmental psychopathology perspective, has an important place as one of several factors that may contribute jointly to successful or unsuccessful adaptation and self-regulation. Suicidal behavior can be viewed as one example of a self-regulatory failure involving mutual influences among factors in cognitive, biological, emotional, representational, social, and other realms.

COGNITIVE DEVELOPMENT AND MENTAL HEALTH

Even though most developmental psychologists do not adhere strictly to Piaget's (1972) cognitive developmental stage model, his general framework for adolescent cognitive development is still the most highly influential. Adolescence is heralded as the point marking the onset of formal operations, so that adolescents begin to perform abstract, complex mental operations and use systematic approaches to reasoning. Of greatest interest to the present discussion is the advent of metacognition and of hypothetical–deductive reasoning. In early adolescence, many youths begin with earnest to analyze their own thoughts, and in so doing they become aware of contradictions in their self-conceptions, which some may find disturbing (Harter, 1999). They project hypothetical scenarios into the future, they reanalyze the past, they compare their real selves (and others' selves) to ideal selves.

Although these are remarkable cognitive advances, they also carry potential liabilities for some at-risk youth (Damon & Hart, 1982). Certain depressive cognitions about the self, the other, and the future may be fully possible for the first time. The ability to project negative emotional states (such as feelings of rejection or loss) and negative scenarios into the future means that adolescents can envision a dark future with no escape. Perceptions and feelings of being less competent, less attractive, less lovable, and less honest than one's ideal can become a preoccupation in early to midadolescence, at which point adolescents are absorbed in a focus on their mental processes (Elkind, 1967). Young adolescents, who have not yet had the experiences that provide the capacity and skills for coping with these painful self-states, may seek to soothe or block them through escape tactics: avoidance, denial, or risk-taking behaviors (Baumeister, 1992).

NEUROSCIENCE CONTRIBUTIONS TO UNDERSTANDING COGNITIVE DEVELOPMENT

Recent research on the underlying brain mechanisms of self-regulation may inform work with suicidal youth. This research is most relevant if one considers suicidal behaviors alongside a multiplicity of risk behaviors that are elevated in the general population of postpubertal youth, including homicides, accidents, injuries, drug and alcohol abuse, unprotected or indiscriminate sex, and so forth (Grunbaum et al., 2002). A common link between these various risk behaviors is that they may all stem at least in part from insufficient cognitive self-regulation of both behavior and emotion. Regulating behavior involves the use of rules as a guide in choosing and sustaining actions, as well as the ability to hold in mind one's goals and to anticipate future consequences (Barkley, 1997). Behavior regulation also necessarily involves regulation of strong emotion, so that powerful, emotion-laden impulses and drives do not exert undue influences on behavior.

It has long been known that the cognitive processes associated with goal-directed behavior (working memory, planning, response inhibition, regulation of attention, etc.) continue to develop throughout adolescence (e.g., Keating & Bobbitt, 1978). Whereas the timing of increases in risk-taking behaviors and emotional intensity are linked to the timing of puberty, advances in cognitive control over emotion and behavior coincide with increasing age and experience. Thus there is a gap in early to midadolescence during which adolescents are prone to experiencing biologically driven, affect-laden motivations before they have the cognitive wherewithal to cope with them and so are prone to making poor, risky choices (Dahl, 2003). That adolescents are capable of making adult-level decisions has been shown in laboratory studies. The problem is that adolescents frequently are not yet capable of making reasoned decisions in the sorts of emotionally charged (i.e., "hot") situations that they encounter with peers on an everyday basis (Dahl, 2003). Over time, most adolescents gain the requisite experience to allow for cognitive control over emotional and behavioral impulses, but the lag between pubertal development and that period of increased regulatory control is the one that is fraught with the greatest potential for problem behaviors.

The various cognitive functions relevant to self-regulation, such as inhibiting impulses, planning and organizing, and allocating and directing attention, are typically conceptualized by temperament researchers as "effortful control" processes (Derryberry & Rothbart, 1988) and by neuropsychologists as "executive functions" (Posner & Rothbart, 2000). A growing body of work by neuroscientists has provided evidence that particular areas of the prefrontal cortex (PFC) are critical to these cognitive functions (Casey et al., 2000). Thus, any effort to understand the success and the difficulties adolescents have in self-regulation must necessarily give serious consideration to the course of development of the PFC.

Davidson and colleagues (Davidson, Jackson, & Kalin, 2000) have provided considerable evidence that the PFC plays a key role in the processing of emotion. Work from Davidson's lab has shown that asymmetries in electrical activation in the PFC are associated with characteristic patterns of temperament differences. Approach behaviors, certain types of positive affect, and quicker recovery from startle are associated with greater left PFC activity, and withdrawal, negative affect, and slower recovery from stress are associated with greater right PFC activation. Although it has long been known that lesions in the PFC are associated with poorer planning and organizational abilities, Davidson and associates have shown that lesions in the ventromedial PFC are associated with difficulty anticipating future positive or negative consequences. Davidson has interpreted these findings as implying that the PFC is associated with an affective working memory, that is, an ability to hold in mind positive and negative emotion even when the provoking stimuli are not present. Such processes would be critical in sustaining goal-directed behavior in the absence of immediate incentives.

Whereas it once was thought that brain development was functionally completed very early in development, research has now shown that this is not the case and that plasticity can occur across the life span. Indeed, there is a growing body of evidence that the brain structures necessary for effective cognitive control over behavior and emotion undergo considerable maturation and development during adolescence and into young adulthood. Specifically, research with nonhuman primates, pediatric neuroimaging studies, as well as human postmortem studies have all provided evidence that the PFC is one of the last brain regions to mature (Casey et al., 2000), with development and integration with other brain structures continuing well into adolescence and beyond. Yurgelin-Todd and associates (Baird et al., 1999) showed that when processing emotions, adolescents show greater brain activity in the amygdala and lower activity in the PFC compared with adults. The implication is that adolescents may be more likely to have "gut" responses to emotion and that the ability to use the higher order PFC functions to inhibit prepotent responses to strong emotions continues to mature into adulthood. Luna and colleagues (Luna et al., 2001) studied changes in brain activity associated with voluntary control over context-inappropriate behavior in children, adolescents, and young adults. They used neuroimaging techniques to show that among adolescents, the PFC was more active during tasks requiring voluntary behavioral control than in younger children but that integrated coordination between the PFC and other brain areas was most fully demonstrated by the young adults. These findings on increasing integration and coordination seem to represent the brain-systems equivalent of recent conceptions of cognitive development in adolescence, in which cognitive performance gains are thought to arise from newly emerging integrations of preexisting cognitive skills that increasingly come under voluntary control across time and experience (Keating, 2003).

Additional neuroscience findings point toward adolescence as a key developmental period for making gains in cognitive self-regulatory skills. There is an increase in frontal gray matter in preadolescence followed by plateaus during early and middle adolescence (Giedd et al., 1999). This increase is analogous to the overproduction of gray matter that occurs during fetal development and suggests that at the threshold of adolescence there may be a high potential for formation of new synaptic connections and neural pathways. During later adolescence and young adulthood, the level of cortical gray matter gradually decreases in a process often referred to as "pruning" (i.e., selective elimination of synapses that are not utilized; Giedd et al., 1999). Overall, because this appears to be the last point in development when there is an overproduction of gray matter, the findings suggest that adolescence may be a final critical period for developing brain wiring pathways that will remain stable into adulthood, a sort of ultimate "use it or lose it" opportunity to shape the wiring of functions involving the PFC. Presumably, if the adolescent is nurtured in an environment that promotes positive development of PFC functions, then the brain will acquire effective self-regulatory patterns that are long enduring. However, this hypothesis is speculative on several levels, including whether the increased gray matter does indeed represent a jump in the production of synapses and whether environmental influences can shape synaptogenesis in humans, as is apparently the case in rats (Bourgeois, Jastereboff, & Rakic, 1989).

Thus, the cognitive developmental and neuroscience findings reviewed in this section make it clear that the adolescent brain is still an immature one, particularly in terms of the capacity for effortful, cognitive self-regulation of emotion and behavior. Coupled with the major challenges posed by the biological and social transitions of early adolescence, this may go a long way toward explaining why early to midadolescence is associated with a jump in the rates of risky behaviors, including suicidal behaviors. The neuroscience findings are only suggestive, however, in terms of the implications for suicidal behaviors. A distinct body of literature that provides more direct evidence for the links of cognitive factors with suicidal behaviors is reviewed in the following sections. The work reviewed focuses on youth suicidal behaviors and ideation, not on completed suicide because little empirical evidence is available on cognition among youth who have completed suicide.

DEPRESSIVE SPECTRUM COGNITIONS

Researchers have demonstrated that suicidal youth tend to show certain negative cognitions with regard to their views of the self, world, and future that are similar to those associated with depressive states.

Perceptions of Self-Worth

Low self-esteem has consistently been linked to suicidal behavior (Yang & Clum, 1996). Adolescent suicide attempters are prone to viewing themselves as worthless and incompetent, a tendency demonstrated in both clinical (Overholser, Adams, Lehnert, & Brinkman, 1995) and nonclinical (Kienhorst, de Wilde, Van Den Bort, Diekstra, & Wolters, 1990) samples. Furthermore, it appears that more negative self-views are systematically related to greater suicidal intent, a larger number of self-destructive behaviors, and greater lethality of suicide attempts (Robbins & Alessi, 1985). There may be multiple ways in which lower self-esteem is linked to suicidal behaviors, and the processes have not been thoroughly explored. The suicidal behavior may represent a wish to destroy or lash out at a negative self, it may represent a way of relieving a perceived burden one places on others, or it may represent an indirect interpersonal plea for sympathy that the adolescent feels cannot be solicited more directly.

In addition to those possibilities, suicidal behaviors may represent a wish to escape from painful self-awareness. Baumeister (1992) described the suicidal state as a *cognitive deconstruction*, in which meaningful awareness is avoided because the emotions are too painful to bear. At the time of a self-destructive episode, many suicidal persons are detached from the future, including the possible negative consequences of their behaviors, and may be drawn to the thrill of risky behavior as an escape from ordinary self-awareness. Baumeister's description is not so different from that of dissociative states, which have also been found to pose a heightened risk of suicidal behaviors (Orbach, Kedem, Herman, & Apter, 1995; Putnam, 1997). In such states, painful memories are partitioned off as a means of self-protection. In so doing, however, it becomes much more difficult to construct meaningful self-narratives of the past, present, and future, and the lack of meaning may render one more susceptible to self-destructive behaviors.

The fact that impulsivity is a frequently cited characteristic of the adolescent suicide attempter (Askenazy et al., 2003; Spirito, Brown, Overholser, & Fritz, 1989) is also consistent with Baumeister's (1992) theory of the suicidal state, in that adolescents may be particularly unlikely to rein in behavior because of concerns with negative consequences to themselves or others. Indeed, adolescent suicide attempts are often impulsive and unplanned (Brown, Overholser, Spirito, & Fritz, 1991). Across a range of studies, adolescent attempters have been found to be more impulsive than high school students (Kashden, Fremouw, Callahan, & Franzen, 1993), medically ill adolescents (Slap, Vorters, Chaudhuri, & Centor, 1989), and psychiatric controls (Corder, Shorr, & Corder, 1974; Horesh, Gothelf, Ofek, Weizman, & Apter, 1999; Kashden et al., 1993; Kingsbury, Hawton, Steinhardt, & James, 1999). Even so, research suggests that suicidal youth are not uniformly characterized by poor impulse control (e.g., Patsiokas, Clum, & Luscomb, 1979). Instead, impulsivity may help define various subgroups of suicide attempters. For example, impulsive attempters may be less hopeless and less depressed than nonimpulsive attempters (Brown et al., 1991) but more likely to make another attempt (Spirito, Brown, et al., 1989). Also, impulsivity may be more strongly related to suicidality among male than female adolescents (Horesh et al., 1999).

Hopelessness

Hopelessness, and pessimistic beliefs about the future in general, has been consistently documented to be associated with suicidal behaviors in adults (e.g., Beck, Brown, Berchick, Stewart, & Steer, 1990). However, the findings with adolescents are less consistent (Yang & Clum, 1996). A number of researchers have found no evidence for a relationship between hopelessness and adolescent attempts when depression is taken into account, or that depression is a better predictor of suicidal symptoms than hopelessness (Boergers, Spirito, & Donaldson, 1998; Marciano & Kazdin, 1994; Rotheram-Borus & Trautman, 1988). However, other researchers have found that hopelessness is an important correlate of youth suicidal behavior even after controlling for depression (Nock & Kazdin, 2002), especially among girls (D. A. Cole, 1989; Spirito, Overholser, & Hart, 1991). Adolescents who have attempted suicide have reported greater hopelessness than a variety of comparison groups, including depressed, nonsuicidal youth and community control subjects (Beautrais, Joyce, & Mulder, 1999; Kienhorst, de Wilde, Diekstra, & Wolters, 1992; Spirito, Williams, Stark, & Hart, 1988). Hopelessness appears to increase the risk of attempted suicide among adolescents experiencing a major depressive episode (Dori & Overholser, 1999), and greater hopelessness in adolescence is associated with an increased risk of making more than one suicide attempt (Esposito, Spirito, Boergers, & Donaldson, 2003; Goldston et al., 2001).

Personal Control Over Events

Research indicates that suicidal adolescents may have distorted beliefs about personal control and responsibility. In general, attempters report a more external locus of control (i.e., believing that relevant outcomes are attributable to external forces beyond their control) than nondistressed youth (e.g., Beautrais et al., 1999), although not more than depressed, nonsuicidal adolescents (Kienhorst et al., 1992). Some work suggests that this tendency may reflect an underestimation, or at least a misjudgment, of the extent of one's personal control, compared with objective raters (Piquet & Wagner, 2003; Wilson et al., 1995). Other findings indicate that depressed youngsters who attempt suicide may overly blame themselves for negative life events (Joiner & Wagner, 1995; Rotheram-Borus, Trautman, Dopkins, & Shrout, 1990). Thus, adolescents who attempt suicide may tend to accept responsibility for situations over which they have no control, but at the same time they feel powerless to change stressful circumstances even when they may have played a role in causing them (Wilson et al., 1995). Distorted beliefs about responsibility and control may in turn contribute to hopelessness and despair (Abramson, Metalsky, & Alloy, 1989).

Negative Automatic Thoughts, Cognitive Schemas, and Attributional Style

Nock and Kazdin (2002) examined the association of negative automatic thoughts (i.e., cognitive distortions typically associated with depression) with suicidal ideation and attempts in a sample of 175 hospitalized children aged 6 to 13. Higher frequency of negative automatic thoughts was associated with higher suicidal ideation, a greater likelihood of a suicide attempt just prior to hospital admission, and higher suicidal intent. After controlling for depression, the relationships of negative automatic thoughts with the suicidal variables were attenuated, but they remained significant for suicidal ideation and suicide attempts. Frequency of automatic thoughts did not discriminate those who attempt suicide from those with suicidal ideation.

Regarding adolescents, researchers have found that those who attempt suicide and have elevated levels of depression are likely to have negative attributional styles for both positive and negative events (Rotheram-Borus et al., 1990; Summerville, Kaslow, Abbate, & Cronan, 1994). The evidence suggests that negative attributional style is not characteristic of adolescents who attempt suicide but are not depressed, however.

In related work, Reinecke and DuBois (2001) found in a sample of adolescent psychiatric inpatients that maladaptive, depression-related cognitive schemas (e.g., negative beliefs related to emotional deprivation, dependence, incompetence, etc.) were associated with higher suicidal ideation, even after controlling for stressful events and social support. The cognitive schemas mediated the association of daily stresses with suicidal ideation.

COPING AND EMOTION REGULATION

A number of researchers have viewed suicidal behavior as a sign of failed coping, that is, as a maladaptive response to overwhelming life stress (e.g., Simonds, McMahon, & Armstrong, 1991). Indeed, adolescent attempts are often preceded by periods of high and increasing levels of stress (e.g., Gispert, Davis, Marsh, & Wheeler, 1987) and are usually directly precipitated by undesirable life events (e.g., Beautrais, Joyce, & Mulder, 1997). Not surprisingly, then, investigators have studied a wide range of coping-related phenomena in an effort to identify specific coping difficulties that may characterize suicidal youths. The research findings can be grouped into three categories: (a) difficulties with problem solving, (b) overreliance on avoidant and other noneffortful coping responses, and (c) maladaptive styles of emotion regulation.

Deficits in Problem Solving

Empirical research has demonstrated clear linkages between problem-solving deficits and adolescent suicidal behavior (Curry, Miller, Waugh, & Anderson, 1992; Spirito, Overholser, & Stark, 1989; Yang & Clum, 1996). Compared with nonpsychiatric control groups, suicidal youths tend to think about problems in a less accurate manner, respond more emotionally to dilemmas, and begin the problem-solving process with a generally more avoidant stance. In addition, they may approach problems with low confidence in their ability to solve them (Clum & Febbraro, 1994; Hawton, Kingsbury, Steinhardt, James, & Fagg, 1999). Adolescents who attempt suicide tend to have difficulty generating, selecting, and implementing problem solutions, particularly when the problems are interpersonal in nature (Kingsbury et al., 1999; Rotheram-Borus et al., 1990; Sadowski & Kelley, 1993; Wilson et al., 1995). Moreover, the solutions they do propose may be maladaptive, that is, inappropriate or likely to exacerbate the stress (Wilson et al., 1995). Hawton and colleagues (1999) reported that adolescents who make repeated suicide attempts are less effective at solving interpersonal problems than single attempters, although the group difference was attributable to higher depression in the multiple attempters. In general, the bulk of the findings show problem-solving differences between suicidal youth versus nonpsychiatric control groups, but not versus psychiatric control subjects, leading to speculation that the problem-solving deficits may be descriptive of youths with psychopathology in general (Negron, Piacentini, Graae, Davies, & Shaffer, 1997) rather than of youths with suicidal problems in particular.

Orbach and colleagues (Orbach, Mikulincer, Blumenson, Mester, & Stein, 1999) examined the hypothesis that young suicidal persons perceive their families as holding them responsible for fixing problems that are beyond their ability to resolve, even as the true underlying family impasse is not acknowledged or addressed. Using a self-report measure, Orbach et al. found that adolescents who had attempted suicide were more likely than psychiatric or nondisturbed control subjects to report feeling unreasonable pressures and demands from parents, which they either perceive as vague or as involving unresolvable dilemmas.

Finally, research on adult and college-age samples suggests that those who attempt suicide may tend to focus rigidly on "cons," that is, the reasons why possible solutions may not be workable (Priester & Clum, 1993; Schotte & Clum, 1987). As suggested by Spirito, Overolser, and Stark (1989), the tendency to perceive negative consequences may discourage implementation of the few solutions adolescents who attempt suicide actually generate. Priester and Clum (1993) found this focus on cons to be a consistently important diathesis in their short-term longitudinal test of the diathesis–stress model of suicidal behavior (Schotte & Clum, 1982, 1987).

This rigidity regarding alternative solutions may be one sign of a larger cognitive rigidity among suicidal persons. Clinical accounts of cognitive inflexibility are supported by studies of adults (Patsiokas et al., 1979; Schotte & Clum, 1987) as well as adolescents (Fremouw, Callahan, & Kashden, 1993; Levenson & Neuringer, 1971) and children (e.g., Orbach, Rosenheim, & Hary, 1987). Although many studies have relied on simple cognitive tests (e.g., map reading; Levenson & Neuringer, 1971), others have found evidence for rigidity in tasks involving interpersonal problem solving as well (e.g., Priester & Clum, 1993).

Avoidant Coping

Much research literature on motivational and regulatory processes can be integrated into two main systems: a system oriented toward rewards and approach behaviors and one oriented around potential punishment and avoidance (Davidson et al., 2000; Derryberry & Reed, 1996). Research findings suggest that children tend to favor stylistically one regulatory system or the other. That is, some children tend to seek novelty and rewards, associate approach behaviors with positive emotions, and are typically optimistic. There are clear benefits to this style in many situations, but failure to attend to the threatening aspects of a dangerous situation can render one vulnerable to harm, and approach behaviors are problematic in circumstances that require inhibiting one's responses, especially among more highly emotionally reactive youth who characteristically respond with impulsive or aggressive approach behavior.

Other children attend to the potential for punishment and threat in situations and so are more avoidant, inhibited, and pessimistic (Kagan, 1994), as well as highly emotionally reactive (Rothbart & Ahadi, 1994). If children focus inflexibly on potential danger, they fail to redirect their attention to sources of emotional relief or to positive aspects of situations and thus are likely to experience ongoing distress and physiological arousal (Derryberry & Reed, 1994). Behaviorally, an inhibited child who avoids stressful challenges thereby denies him or herself opportunities to learn new coping skills and to develop self-perceptions of effectiveness at coping (Derryberry & Reed, 1996).

A number of research studies have indicated that people who attempt suicide tend to be characterized by an avoidant style. They often rely excessively on passive, avoidant coping methods, including social withdrawal, avoiding direct confrontation, and wishful thinking (Asarnow, Carlson, & Guthrie, 1987; Cohen-Sandler, Berman, & King, 1982; Josepho & Plutchik, 1994; Kingsbury et al., 1999; Rotheram-Borus et al., 1990; Spirito, Francis, Overholser, & Frank, 1996). Not only do they overutilize avoidant coping, they also underutilize appropriately assertive, active, socially engaged (i.e., approach) strategies to manage life stress, compared with matched psychiatric control subjects (Piquet & Wagner, 2003). An avoidant style is also consistent with literature cited earlier that people who attempt suicide tend to perceive that problem situations are beyond their ability to control.

Effortful Coping

As indicated in an earlier section of this chapter, temperament and neuroscience researchers have identified motivational systems that enable children to exert active control over regulatory tendencies such as approach and avoidance. The constructs of executive functioning (Barkley, 1996) and effortful control (Rothbart & Ahadi, 1994), although not mapping precisely onto one another, both reference processes in which individuals regulate their attentional and behavioral response tendencies. In general, effortful control under stressful circumstances implies a metacognitive monitoring process that allows for flexibly regulating attention and behavior in accord with situational demands. In the only published study to examine effortful versus automatic coping responses among suicidal youth, Piquet and Wagner (2003) found that people who attempt suicide were significantly less likely than psychiatric control subjects to employ approach coping responses that were effortful (e.g., communication aimed at problem solving), but were significantly more likely to make approach coping responses that were automatic (e.g., impulsive and aggressive behavior such as venting negative emotion and destructive action). This distinction within approach responses suggests that it is important to consider the effortful–automatic distinction when assessing coping among suicidal youth.

Maladaptive Emotion Regulation

The term *emotion regulation* generally refers to processes involved in coping with heightened levels of emotion (Kopp, 1989). Under certain conditions, patterns of emotion regulation may impair functioning and thus play a role in the development of psychopathology of various sorts (P. M. Cole, Michel, & Teti, 1994), including suicidal behavior (Zlotnick, Donaldson, Spirito, & Pearlstein, 1997). Managing emotions appears to be of great importance for suicidal youth because there is evidence that they experience intense negative emotions including anxiety, dysphoric affect, and aggression (Shaffer, Garland, Gould, Fisher, & Trautman, 1988), and youth who make repeated suicide attempts are reportedly more angry and dysphoric than those who make a single attempt (Gispert et al., 1987; Kotila & Lonnqvist, 1987; Stein, Apter, Ratzoni, Har-Even, & Avidan, 1998).

Studies of adolescent suicide attempters provide support for the notion that these youth often have difficulty regulating negative emotions, especially anger and sadness (Khan, 1987). In addition, one study comparing inpatients who had attempted suicide to those with suicidal ideation found evidence for greater difficulties modulating negative emotional states among those who had attempted suicide (Zlotnick et al., 1997). A number of writers have proposed that suicidal behavior can itself be a strategy for dealing with negative emotion. We have already mentioned that the suicide attempt can serve as a means of escape from emotional pain (Baumeister, 1992). Kienhorst and colleagues found that three-quarters of adolescent attempters reported that one reason for their attempt was to "stop feeling pain" (Kienhorst, de Wilde, Diekstra, & Wolters, 1995). Furthermore, several studies of the acute suicidal episode suggest that negative emotions may be temporarily reduced by suicidal behavior (Goldston et al., 1996; Negron et al., 1997). Thus, for some youth, suicidal behaviors may become a regularly used self-regulatory pattern for emptying emotional pain from cognitive awareness.

CONCLUSION

This review of cognitive influences on the development of suicidal symptoms during adolescence had two broad goals: (a) to document the current state of knowledge of cognitive factors and (b) to uncover the gaps in knowledge, with an eye toward important future research agendas in this area.

The review of findings indicates that a number of aspects of cognition are consistently associated with increased risk of suicidal behaviors. In particular, adolescents with suicidal behaviors tend to have lower self-esteem and higher hopelessness, to underestimate the controllability of negative events and blame themselves excessively for such events, to have negative attributional styles for positive and negative events, and to have negative cognitive schemas (e.g., deprivation, incompetence, etc.). In many instances, however, the findings were not significant once psychiatric symptoms—particularly depression—were taken into account. Thus, many of these cognitive characteristics are not unique to suicidal individuals, but seem instead to be common features of youth with psychiatric symptoms, including depression.

The developmental processes by which these factors influence one another remain to be elucidated. For example, depression in childhood or very early adolescence may lead to both suicidal ideation and negative cognitive characteristics, but alternate pathways and directions of effects are also plausible. Most of the research is cross-sectional or uses very short-term longitudinal designs. Further research on the developmental trajectories of cognition and psychopathology should help to clarify such processes. Nevertheless, the bulk of the evidence indicates that interventions should target specific cognitive problems such as self-concept (including self-worth), perceived control, negative attributional style, and other depression-related beliefs. In such intervention research, it will be important to investigate whether the interventions are useful with adolescents who are suicidal but are not depressed, because so many of the well-studied cognitive processes are linked to depression.

Research on coping has revealed that suicidal youths are more likely than nonpsychiatric control subjects to have problem-solving deficits and to be relatively inflexible with regard to generating alternative solutions to problems. Again, most of the research does not indicate significant problem-solving differences between suicidal adolescents and adolescents with other psychiatric disorders. Despite their lack of unique applicability to suicidal youth, problem-solving issues may still be part of a causal pathway resulting in suicidal symptoms, and the existing evidence indicates that interventions would do well to include a problem-solving training component.

Researchers have consistently found suicidal youth to use more avoidant coping styles, and less active, approach coping styles, than various control subjects, suggesting that interventions aimed at teaching more active coping might be beneficial. Nonetheless, drawing on Piquet and Wagner (2003), it is important to note that not all active coping strategies are equivalent in terms of salubrious effects; indeed, automatic approach coping appears to be associated with higher risk of suicidal symptoms. Thus, programs must be careful to increase selectively the use of effortful approach coping strategies, which seem to be lacking among suicidal youths. Most of the research conclusions on avoidant coping are based on findings from specific items on coping scales. It would be beneficial to attempt to replicate the research on avoidance coping using well-constructed and validated avoidance scales. Similarly, the work on effortful coping among suicidal adolescents should be replicated using a well-tested or validated measure of effortful versus automatic styles.

IMPLICATIONS FOR FUTURE RESEARCH

The literature tends to lack a developmental focus. It will be important to examine developmental trajectories of cognition during childhood that might lead to difficulties in early or midadolescence. Such work might examine a number of possible cognitive precursors to suicidal symptoms, including attributional style, depression-related beliefs, hopelessness, as well as cognitive control over attention and behavior. The construct of equifinality suggests that multiple developmental pathways may lead to any particular cognitive vulnerability to suicidal symptoms. Thus, researchers should not expect all suicidal youths to conform to any single developmental model of cognitive factors and should test multiple trajectories within a single study (which has not yet been done).

It would be helpful for researchers to examine the social context of cognition. For example, cognitions may vary depending on the setting of the adolescent (e.g., more negative attributions may be present with parents than with peers or at school), and specific cognitive challenges may or may not vary from one context to the next. Findings on this point would be very useful in targeting intervention programs toward specific deficits in specific settings.

Finally, research on the development of the adolescent brain has great promise as a line of inquiry that will shed light on the development of cognition. Additional research is needed on the question of whether changes in brain function—as indexed through brain imaging studies—are associated with the developmental course of cognitive self-control within the broader population of adolescents in general, and with suicidal youths in particular.

In addition, research is needed to test whether interventions that target cognitive self-regulation—that is, regulation of attention, emotion, and behavior—can result in structural or functional changes in the brain.

Research on the brain is providing a great boost for work in cognitive sciences in psychology more generally. Given the great urgency of the problem of youth suicidal behavior, advances in the brain sciences must be coupled with work on cognition to provide a solid grounding for developing preventive interventions for youth at risk for suicidal behaviors.

REFERENCES

Abramson, L. Y., Metalsky, G. I., & Alloy, L. B. (1989). Hopelessness depression: A theory-based subtype of depression. *Psychological Review, 96*, 358–372.

Asarnow, J. R., Carlson, G. A., & Guthrie, D. (1987). Coping strategies, self-perceptions, hopelessness, and perceived family environments in depressed and suicidal children. *Journal of Consulting and Clinical Psychology, 55*, 361–366.

Askenazy, F. L., Sorci, K., Benoit, M., Lestideau, K., Myquel, M., & Lecrubier, Y. (2003). Anxiety and impulsivity levels identify relevant subtypes in adolescents with at-risk behavior. *Journal of Affective Disorders, 74*, 219–227.

Baird, A. A., Gruber, S. A., Fein, D. A., Maas, L. C., Steingard, R. J., Renshaw, P. F., et al. (1999). Functional magnetic resonance imaging of facial affect recognition in children and adolescents. *Journal of the American Academy of Child and Adolescent Psychiatry, 38*, 195–199.

Barkley, R. A. (1996). Linkages between attention and executive functions. In G. R. Lyon & N. A. Krasnegor (Eds.), *Attention, memory, and executive function* (pp. 307–325). Baltimore: Paul H. Brookes.

Barkley, R. A. (1997). Attention-deficit/hyperactivity disorder: Self-regulation and time: Toward a more comprehensive theory. *Developmental and Behavioral Pediatrics, 18*, 271–279.

Baumeister, R. F. (1992). Suicide as escape from self. *Psychological Review, 97*, 90–113.

Beautrais, A. L., Joyce, P. R., & Mulder, R. T. (1997). Precipitating factors and life events in serious suicide attempts among youths aged 13 through 24 years. *Journal of the American Academy of Child and Adolescent Psychiatry, 36*, 1543–1551.

Beautrais, A. L., Joyce, P. R., & Mulder, R. T. (1999). Personality traits and cognitive styles as risk factors for serious suicide attempts among young people. *Suicide and Life-Threatening Behavior, 29*, 37–47.

Beck, A. T., Brown, M. S., Berchick, R. J., Stewart, B. L., & Steer, R. A. (1990). Relationship between hopelessness and ultimate suicide: A replication with psychiatric outpatients. *American Journal of Psychiatry, 147*, 190–195.

Boergers, J., Spirito, A., & Donaldson, D. (1998). Reasons for adolescent suicide attempts: Associations with psychological functioning. *Journal of the American Academy of Child and Adolescent Psychiatry, 37*, 1287–1293.

Bourgeois, J. P., Jastereboff, P. J., & Rakic, P. (1989). Synaptogenesis in visual cortex of normal and preterm monkeys: Evidence for intrinsic regulation of synaptic overproduction. *Proceedings of the National Academy of Sciences of the United States of America, 86,* 4297–4301.

Brown, L. K., Overholser, J., Spirito, A., & Fritz, G. K. (1991). The correlates of planning in adolescent suicide attempts. *Journal of the American Academy of Child and Adolescent Psychiatry, 30,* 95–99.

Casey, B. J., Giedd, J. N., & Thomas, K. M. (2000). Structural and functional brain development and its relation to cognitive development. *Biological Psychology, 54,* 241–257.

Cicchetti, D., & Rogosch, F. (1996). Equifinality and multifinality in developmental psychopathology. *Development and Psychopathology, 8,* 597–600.

Cicchetti, D., & Toth, S. L. (1995). Developmental psychopathology and disorders of affect. In D. Cicchetti & D. J. Cohen (Eds.), *Developmental psychopathology, Vol. 2: Risk, disorder, and adaptation* (pp. 369–429). New York: Wiley.

Cicchetti, D., & Toth, S. L. (1998). The development of depression in children and adolescents. *American Psychologist, 53,* 221–241.

Clum, G. A., & Febbraro, G. A. R. (1994). Stress, social support, and problem-solving appraisal/skills: Prediction of suicide severity within a college sample. *Journal of Psychopathology and Behavioral Assessment, 16,* 69–83.

Cohen-Sandler, R., Berman, A., & King, R. A. (1982). Life stress and symptomatology: Determinants of suicidal behavior in children. *Journal of the American Academy of Child Psychiatry, 21,* 178–186.

Cole, D. A. (1989). Psychopathology of adolescent suicide: Hopelessness, coping beliefs, and depression. *Journal of Abnormal Psychology, 98,* 248–255.

Cole, P. M., Michel, M. K., & Teti, L. O. (1994). The development of emotion regulation and dysregulation: A clinical perspective. *Monographs of the Society for Research in Child Development, 59,* 73–100.

Corder, B. F., Shorr, W., & Corder, R. F. (1974). A study of social and psychological characteristics of adolescent suicide attempters in an urban, disadvantaged area. *Adolescence, 9,* 1–5.

Curry, J. F., Miller, Y., Waugh, S., & Anderson, W. (1992). Coping responses in depressed, socially maladjusted, and suicidal adolescents. *Psychological Reports, 71,* 80–82.

Dahl, R. E. (2003, April). *The regulation of emotion and behavior in adolescence.* Paper presented at the Biennial Meetings of the Society for Research in Child Development, Tampa, FL.

Damon, W., & Hart, D. (1982). The development of self-understanding from infancy through adolescence. *Child Development, 53,* 841–864.

Davidson, R. J., Jackson, D. C., & Kalin, N. H. (2000). Emotion, plasticity, context, and regulation: Perspectives from affective neuroscience. *Psychological Bulletin, 126,* 890–909.

Derryberry, D., & Reed, M. A. (1994). Temperament and attention: Orienting toward and away from positive and negative signals. *Journal of Personality and Social Psychology, 66*, 1128–1139.

Derryberry, D., & Reed, M. A. (1996). Regulatory processes and the development of cognitive representations. *Development and Psychopathology, 8*, 215–234.

Derryberry, D., & Rothbart, M. K. (1988). Arousal, affect, and attention as components of temperament. *Journal of Personality and Social Psychology, 55*, 958–966.

Dori, G., & Overholser, J. (1999). Depression, hopelessness, and self-esteem: Accounting for suicidality in adolescent psychiatric inpatients. *Suicide and Life-Threatening Behavior, 29*, 309–318.

Elkind, D. (1967). Egocentrism in adolescence. *Child Development, 38*, 1025–1034.

Esposito, C., Spirito, A., Boergers, J., & Donaldson, D. (2003). Affective, behavioral, and cognitive functioning in adolescents with multiple suicide attempts. *Suicide and Life-Threatening Behavior, 33*, 389–399.

Fremouw, W., Callahan, T., & Kashden, J. (1993). Adolescent suicidal risk: Psychological problem solving and environmental factors. *Suicide and Life-Threatening Behavior, 23*, 46–54.

Giedd, J. N., Blumenthal, J., Jeffries, N. O., Castellanos, F. X., Liu, H., Zijdenbos, A., et al. (1999). Brain development during childhood and adolescence: A longitudinal MRI study. *Nature Neuroscience, 2*, 861–863.

Gispert, M., Davis, M. S., Marsh, L., & Wheeler, K. (1987). Predictive factors in repeated suicide attempts by adolescents. *Hospital and Community Psychiatry, 36*, 390–393.

Goldston, D. B., Daniel, S., Reboussin, D. M., Kelley, A., Ievers, C., & Bronstetter, R. (1996). First-time suicide attempters, repeat attempters, and previous attempters on an adolescent inpatient psychiatry unit. *Journal of the American Academy of Child and Adolescent Psychiatry, 35*, 631–639.

Goldston, D. B., Daniel, S., Reboussin, B. A., Reboussin, D., Frazier, P. H., & Harris, A. (2001). Cognitive risk factors and suicide attempts among formerly hospitalized adolescents: A prospective naturalistic study. *Journal of the American Academy of Child and Adolescent Psychiatry, 40*, 91–99.

Grunbaum, J. A., Kann, L., Kinchen, S. A., Williams, B., Ross, J. G., Lowry, R., et al. (2002). Youth Risk Behavior Surveillance—United States, 2001. *Morbidity and Mortality Weekly Report, 51*, 1–64.

Harter, S. (1999). *The construction of the self*. New York: Guilford Press.

Hawton, K., Kingsbury, S., Steinhardt, K., James, A., & Fagg, J. (1999). Repetition of deliberate self-harm by adolescents: The role of psychological factors. *Journal of Adolescence, 22*, 369–378.

Horesh, N., Gothelf, D., Ofek, H., Weizman, T., & Apter, A. (1999). Impulsivity as a correlate of suicidal behavior in adolescent psychiatric inpatients. *Crisis, 20*, 8–14.

Joiner, T. E., & Wagner, K. D. (1995). Attribution style and depression in children and adolescents: A meta-analytic review. *Clinical Psychology Review, 15*, 777–798.

Josepho, S., & Plutchik, R. (1994). Stress, coping, and suicide risk in psychiatric inpatients. *Suicide and Life-Threatening Behavior, 24*, 48–57.

Kagan, J. (1994). On the nature of emotion. In N. A. Fox (Ed.), The development of emotion regulation: Biological and behavioral considerations. *Monographs of the Society for Research in Child Development, 59*(Serial No. 240), 7–24.

Kashden, J., Fremouw, W. J., Callahan, T. S., & Franzen, M. D. (1993). Impulsivity in suicidal and nonsuicidal adolescents. *Journal of Abnormal Child Psychology, 21*, 339–353.

Keating, D. P. (2003, September). *Adolescent cognitive and brain development: The emergence of consciousness.* Paper presented at the New York Academy of Science Conference on Adolescent Brain Development, New York, NY.

Keating, D. P., & Bobbitt, B. L. (1978). Individual and developmental differences in cognitive processing components of mental ability. *Child Development, 49*, 155–167.

Khan, A. U. (1987). Heterogeneity of suicidal adolescents. *Journal of the American Academy of Child and Adolescent Psychiatry, 26*, 92–96.

Kienhorst, C. W. M., de Wilde, E. J., Diekstra, R. F. W., & Wolters, W. H. G. (1992). Differences between adolescent suicide attempters and depressed adolescents. *Acta Psychiatrica Scandinavica, 85*, 222–228.

Kienhorst, C. W. M., de Wilde, E. J., Diekstra, R. F. W., & Wolters, W. H. G. (1995). Adolescents' image of their suicide attempt. *Journal of the American Academy of Child and Adolescent Psychiatry, 34*, 623–628.

Kienhorst, C. W. M., de Wilde, E. J., Van Den Bort, J., Diekstra, R. F. W., & Wolters, W. H. G. (1990). Characteristics of suicide attempters in a population-based sample of Dutch adolescents. *British Journal of Psychiatry, 156*, 243–248.

Kingsbury, S., Hawton, K., Steinhardt, K., & James, A. (1999). Do adolescents who take overdoses have specific psychological characteristics? A comparative study with psychiatric and community controls. *Journal of the American Academy of Child and Adolescent Psychiatry, 38*, 1125–1131.

Kopp, C. B. (1989). Regulation of distress and negative emotions: A developmental view. *Developmental Psychology, 25*, 343–354.

Kotila, L., & Lonnqvist, J. (1987). Adolescents who make suicide attempts repeatedly. *Acta Psychiatrica Scandinavica, 76*, 386–393.

Lerner, R. M., Lerner, J. V., von Eye, A., Ostrom, C. W., Nitz, K., Talwar-Soni, R., et al. (1996). Continuity and discontinuity across the transition of early adolescence: A developmental contextual perspective. In J. A. Graber, J. Brooks-Gunn, & A. C. Petersen (Eds.), *Transitions through adolescence: Interpersonal domains and context* (pp. 3–22). Mahwah, NJ: Erlbaum.

Levenson, M., & Neuringer, C. (1971). Problem-solving behavior in suicidal adolescents. *Journal of Consulting and Clinical Psychology, 37*, 433–436.

Luna, B., Thulborn, K. R., Munoz, D. P., Merriam, E. P., Garver, K. E., Minshew, N. J., et al. (2001). Maturation of widely distributed brain function subserves cognitive development. *Neuroimage, 13*, 786–793.

Marciano, P. L., & Kazdin, A. E. (1994). Self-esteem, depression, hopelessness, and suicidal intent among psychiatrically disturbed inpatient children. *Journal of Clinical Child Psychology, 23*, 151–160.

Negron, R., Piacentini, J., Graae, F., Davies, M., & Shaffer, D. (1997). Microanalysis of adolescent suicide attempters and ideators during the acute suicidal episode. *Journal of the American Academy of Child and Adolescent Psychiatry, 36*, 1512–1519.

Nock, M. K., & Kazdin, A. E. (2002). Examination of affective, cognitive, and behavioral factors and suicide-related outcomes in children and young adolescents. *Journal of Clinical Child and Adolescent Psychology, 31*, 48–58.

Orbach, I., Kedem, P., Herman, I.., & Apter, A. (1995). Dissociative tendencies in suicidal, depressed, and normal adolescents. *Journal of Social and Clinical Psychology, 14*, 393–408.

Orbach, I., Mikulincer, M., Blumenson, R., Mester, R., & Stein, M. D. (1999). The subjective experience of problem irresolvability and suicidal behavior: Dynamics and measurement. *Suicide and Life-Threatening Behavior, 29*, 150–164.

Orbach, I., Rosenheim, E., & Hary, E. (1987). Some aspects of cognitive functioning in suicidal children. *Journal of the American Academy of Child and Adolescent Psychiatry, 26*, 181–185.

Overholser, J. C., Adams, D. M., Lehnert, K. L., & Brinkman, D. C. (1995). Self-esteem deficits and suicidal tendencies among adolescents. *Journal of the American Academy of Child and Adolescent Psychiatry, 34*, 919–928.

Patsiokas, A. T., Clum, G. A., & Luscomb, R. L. (1979). Cognitive characteristics of suicide attempters. *Journal of Consulting and Clinical Psychology, 47*, 478–484.

Piaget, J. (1972). Intellectual evolution from adolescence to adulthood. *Human Development, 15*, 1–12.

Piquet, M. L., & Wagner, B. M. (2003). Coping responses of adolescent suicide attempters and their relation to suicidal ideation across a 2-year follow-up: A preliminary study. *Suicide and Life-Threatening Behavior, 33*, 288–301.

Posner, M. I., & Rothbart, M. K. (2000). Developing mechanisms of self-regulation. *Development and Psychopathology, 12*, 427–441.

Priester, M. J., & Clum, G. A. (1993). The problem-solving diathesis in depression, hopelessness, and suicidal ideation: A longitudinal analysis. *Journal of Psychopathology and Behavioral Assessment, 15*, 239–254.

Putnam, F. W. (1997). *Dissociation in children and adolescents: A developmental perspective.* New York: Guilford Press.

Reinecke, M. A., & DuBois, D. L. (2001). Socioenvironmental and cognitive risk and resources: Relations to mood and suicidality among inpatient adolescents. *Journal of Cognitive Psychotherapy: An International Quarterly, 15*, 195–222.

Robbins, D. R., & Alessi, N. E. (1985). Depressive symptoms and suicidal behavior in adolescents. *American Journal of Psychiatry, 142*, 588–592.

Rothbart, M. K., & Ahadi, S. A. (1994). Temperament and the development of personality. *Journal of Abnormal Psychology, 103*, 55–66.

Rotheram-Borus, M. J., & Trautman, P. D. (1988). Hopelessness, depression, and suicidal intent among adolescent suicide attempters. *Journal of the American Academy of Child and Adolescent Psychiatry, 27,* 700–704.

Rotheram-Borus, M. J., Trautman, P. D., Dopkins, S. C., & Shrout, P. E. (1990). Cognitive style and pleasant activities among female adolescent suicide attempters. *Journal of Consulting and Clinical Psychology, 58,* 554–561.

Sadowski, C., & Kelley, M. L. (1993). Social problem solving in suicidal adolescents. *Journal of Consulting and Clinical Psychology, 61,* 121–127.

Schotte, D. E., & Clum, G. A. (1982). Suicidal ideation in a college population: A test of a model. *Journal of Consulting and Clinical Psychology, 50,* 690–696.

Schotte, D. E., & Clum, G. A. (1987). Problem-solving skills in suicidal psychiatric patients. *Journal of Consulting and Clinical Psychology, 55,* 49–54.

Shaffer, D., Garland, A., Gould, M., Fisher, P., & Trautman, P. (1988). Preventing teenage suicide: A critical review. *Journal of the American Academy of Child and Adolescent Psychiatry, 27,* 675–687.

Simonds, J. F., McMahon, T., & Armstrong, D. (1991). Young suicide attempters compared with a control group: Psychological, affective, and attitudinal variables. *Suicide and Life-Threatening Behavior, 21,* 134–151.

Slap, G. B., Vorters, D. F., Chaudhuri, S., & Centor, R. M. (1989). Risk factors for attempted suicide during adolescence. *Pediatrics, 84,* 762–772.

Spirito, A., Brown, L., Overholser, J., & Fritz, G. (1989). Attempted suicide in adolescence: A review and critique of the literature. *Clinical Psychology Review, 9,* 335–363.

Spirito, A., Francis, G., Overholser, J., & Frank, N. (1996). Coping, depression, and adolescent suicide attempts. *Journal of Clinical Child Psychology, 25,* 147–155.

Spirito, A., Overholser, J., & Hart, K. (1991). Cognitive characteristics of adolescent suicide attempters. *Journal of the American Academy of Child and Adolescent Psychiatry, 30,* 604–608.

Spirito, A., Overholser, J., & Stark, L. J. (1989). Common problems and coping strategies, II: Findings with adolescent suicide attempters. *Journal of Abnormal Child Psychology, 17,* 213–221.

Spirito, A., Williams, C. A., Stark, L. J., & Hart, K. J. (1988). The hopelessness scale for children: Psychometric properties with normal and emotionally disturbed adolescents. *Journal of Abnormal Child Psychology, 16,* 445–458.

Sroufe, L. A., & Rutter, C. M. (1984). The domain of developmental psychopathology. *Child Development, 55,* 17–29.

Stein, D., Apter, A., Ratzoni, G., Har-Even, D., & Avidan, G. (1998). Association between multiple suicide attempts and negative affect in adolescents. *Journal of the American Academy of Child and Adolescent Psychiatry, 37,* 488–494.

Summerville, M. B., Kaslow, N. J., Abbate, M. F., & Cronan, S. (1994). Psychopathology, family functioning, and cognitive style in urban adolescents with suicide attempts. *Journal of Abnormal Child Psychology, 22,* 221–235.

Wilson, K. G., Stelzer, J., Bergman, J. N., Kral, M. J., Inayatullah, M., & Elliott, C. A. (1995). Problem solving, stress, and coping in adolescent suicide attempts. *Suicide and Life-Threatening Behavior, 25*, 241–252.

Yang, B., & Clum, G. A. (1996). Effects of early negative life experiences on cognitive functioning and risk for suicide. *Clinical Psychology Review, 16*, 177–185.

Zahn-Waxler, C., & Kochanska, G. (1990). The origins of guilt. In R. Thompson (Ed.), *Nebraska symposium on motivation, Vol. 36: Social-emotional development* (pp. 183–258). Lincoln: University of Nebraska Press.

Zlotnick, C., Donaldson, D., Spirito, A., & Pearlstein, T. (1997). Affect regulation and suicide attempts in adolescent inpatients. *Journal of the American Academy of Child and Adolescent Psychiatry, 36*, 793–798.

14

SUICIDE AND COGNITION IN SCHIZOPHRENIA

ZAFFER IQBAL AND MAX BIRCHWOOD

Advances in the psychosocial and pharmacological approaches to the management of schizophrenia have not eliminated the heightened risk of suicide. The importance of targeting dysfunctional thinking in young, vulnerable individuals in the initial years of their illness to limit or prevent likely social, psychological, and mental deterioration is argued to be the crucial factor. This chapter aims to outline a cognitive–psychosocial model of suicidal ideation and risk and will detail recent research suggesting depression is the archetypal variable that precedes cognitions of distress, hopelessness, and suicidal intent in schizophrenia. Recent interventions for first-episode psychosis and other treatments are also outlined, and the potential for delivery within a clinical setting and future research areas is discussed.

INTRODUCTION

Suicide is regarded as one of the most intractable problems in the mental health field at the present time, the greatest risk occurring for those patients diagnosed as experiencing schizophrenia (Sartorius et al., 1987). Within schizophrenia and psychosis, moderate to severe depression and hopelessness precede suicidal ideation and intent (Birchwood, Iqbal, Chadwick, & Trower, 2000). The data for suicide hide much higher figures for attempted suicide (25%–30%), and in our recent study (Birchwood et al., 2000), the 1-year prevalence of at least moderate depression, suicidal ideation, or hopelessness was 61%, with higher figures for first episodes. Verdoux et al. (2001) reported a figure of 11.3% for suicidal behavior in first episodes alone, suggesting higher risk early in the trajectory of a psychotic illness. Although it continues to be difficult to predict who will eventually kill themselves using known demographic factors (Birchwood & Iqbal, 1998; Pokorny, 1993; Verdoux et al., 2001), it is clear that depression (Saarinen, Lehtonen, & Lonnqvist, 1999), hopelessness (Drake, Gates, Cotton, & Whittaker, 1985), and suicidal thinking (Young et al., 1998) are established precursors.

Persons with schizophrenia experience more lifetime depression than those without (Kreyenbuhl, Kelly, & Conley, 2002), and depression is an established precursor to future suicide (Addington & Addington, 1992; Aguilar et al., 2003; Drake & Cotton, 1986; Schwartz & Cohen, 2001). We therefore propose that the assessment of depressive symptoms, particularly in the context of hopelessness, within the various stages of the schizophrenic illness trajectory (e.g., prodromal, acute, remission, and postpsychotic) may well identify an established and clinically valuable precursor to suicidal intent and completion.

DEPRESSION IN SCHIZOPHRENIA

Depression in the context of a schizophrenic illness has been studied since the days of Kraepelin (1896) and Bleuler (1950), but the confused nosological status of depression in schizophrenia has impeded both therapeutic and theoretical development (Birchwood & Iqbal, 1998) and centers on the link established between depression and positive symptoms (Birchwood & Chadwick, 1997; Jones et al., 1994; Leff, Tress, & Edwards, 1988). This suggests that depression is intrinsic to psychosis but subordinate to the positive symptoms and that they "run the same course" during treatment (Leff, 1990). The term *intrinsic* suggests that the depression is an essential aspect of the syndrome of positive symptoms of schizophrenia. As such, depressive symptoms should be discernible at one or more stages during the course of an acute psychotic episode. Powerful evidence is available from the literature in support of the intrinsic depression theory. It is argued that a relationship between positive symptoms and depression is upheld by studies in which depression has been observed before (Hirsch & Jolley, 1989), during (Knights & Hirsch, 1981), and following (i.e., "postpsychotic depression"; McGlashan & Carpenter, 1976) the onset of acute psychosis. However, the notion of nonaffective psychosis centers on the differentiation between positive symptoms and depression during the acute phase, yet the evidence that depression occurs concomitantly with positive symptoms and recedes in line with their remission (Birchwood, Iqbal, et al., 2000; Leff, 1990) does not concord with this rationale. Here we argue that deciphering the interplay between depression and the schizophrenic process is the key to a conundrum that will ultimately provide clinicians with predictive tools to chart future hopelessness and suicidal intent.

Depressive symptoms are evident during acute psychosis, including the prodromal period prior to first onset or relapse, which may well explain the powerful empirical support available for the intrinsic theory (Hirsch, 1982). In addition, the presence of depression at this phase of the illness is supported by the hierarchical theories of symptom development (e.g. Foulds & Bedford, 1975). Although depression is not advocated as a diagnostic symptom in the *Diagnostic and Statistical Manual of Mental Disorders* (4th ed.; *DSM–IV*; American Psychiatric Association, 1994) or the International Classification of Diseases (10th ed.; World Health Organization, ICD–10) considerable evidence exists arguing that depression is an integral component of acute pathology. Three major areas of research have informed this issue: factor analytical studies of schizophrenic pathology; relapse prevention work in which the genesis of acute illness from the prodrome is meticulously charted, and cognitive–behavior therapy (CBT) approaches to the acute (and drug-resistant) positive symptoms of voices and delusions. We discuss each in the sections that follow, before turning to implications for CBT of persons with schizophrenia.

Depression as a Constituent of Acute Schizophrenia: Evidence From Factor Analytical Studies

The major factor analytical studies of the previous decade have reported the robust finding that depression constitutes a significant symptom group of both acute schizophrenic and psychotic disorders (Bottlender, Strauss, & Moeller, 2000; Kay & Sevy, 1990; Lindenmayer, Grochowski, & Hyman, 1995). For example, McGorry, Bell, Dudgeon, and Jackson (1998) provided powerful evidence to support this supposition in a sample of acute, first-episode patients. The authors examined the dimensional structure of each patient's schizophrenia, diagnosed with the third revised edition of the *Diagnostic and Statistical Manual of Mental Disorders* (3rd ed., rev.; *DSM–III–R*; American Psychiatric Association, 1987), using a broad multidiagnostic instrument assessing 92 core symptoms. Their results clearly revealed a four-factor solution: negative symptoms, positive symptoms, mania, and depression. A similar four-factor solution was obtained by van Os, Gilvarry, et al.'s (1999) factor analysis of the items scores (for 706 patients with chronic psychosis) across the 65 items composing the Comprehensive Psychopathological Rating Scale. We argue that this research is only controversial in that amendments have yet to be made to the major diagnostic manuals, although regular advancements in the study of psychotic pathology have always been integral to progression in the field of schizophrenia.

Depression as a Precursor to Relapse: Evidence From Relapse Prevention Studies

The emergence of dysphoric and depressive symptoms during relapse has been widely reported and is seen as a key predictor of acute onset (for a review, see Birchwood, Iqbal, & Upthegrove, 2005) and is nearly always part of the prodrome (Jackson, McGorry, & McKenzie, 1994). For example, McCandless-Glimcher et al. (1986) reported that 73% of relapses were preceded by a prodromal period of dysphoric and neurotic symptoms within a month of relapse. The relapse prevention literature suggests two stages in the relapse process: dysphoria, which includes anxiety, restlessness, and the blunting of drives, followed by low-level psychotic pathology, such as suspiciousness, ideas of reference, and so on. It has been argued that strong features of the prodrome include "loss of control," "fear of going crazy," and "puzzlement about objective experience" (Hirsch & Jolley, 1989)—key components of psychological distress.

Depression as a Psychological Reaction to Psychosis: Evidence From the CBT Literature

Voices and Depression

Although auditory hallucinations are a core feature of the diagnosis of schizophrenia (Jablensky et al., 1992), the experience of voices alone does not always result in the patient recognizing the need for clinical treatment or engaging in help-seeking behavior (van Os, Verdoux, et al., 1999). We argue that it is distress associated with such hallucinations that gives rise to the beliefs underpinning the need for treatment in the individual. The cognitive model of auditory hallucination was developed by Birchwood and Chadwick (1997) and emphasized the experience of "voices" as a key distressing and personal context to the person hearing voices. Many patients experience distressing voices that insult them and issue commands, whereas others hear voices that are warm and reassuring, leading to feelings of comfort and amusement (Chadwick & Birchwood, 1994). These experiences will have an impact on the subsequent behavior and reactions from the patient; some shout abuse and resist, whereas others comply without question (Beck-Sander, Birchwood, & Chadwick, 1997). It is clear that these variations in distress and reactions to voices raise the question of how the content and form of the voice, and the person's cognitive, behavioral, and affective responses are linked.

In a study of 70 patients who heard voices (Birchwood & Chadwick, 1997), using new scales of beliefs about voices (Chadwick & Birchwood,

1995), it was found that (a) beliefs rather than content governed the response and (b) the high rate of depression in this sample (60%) was directly attributable to the belief in the power of voices and not to voice frequency, loudness, or content. This work was independently replicated (Close & Garety, 1998), and in a subsequent study, it was found that these appraisals largely governed individuals' response to commands, rather than the command itself (Beck-Sander et al., 1997). This perspective seeks to understand the *maintenance* of distress and problem behavior and is not a causal model of auditory hallucinations.

Thus, auditory hallucinations in psychosis often contain critical evaluations of the individual who hears voices (e.g., attacks on the individual's self-worth), but the role and impact of such evaluations remain unclear. Previous research has shown that what people who hear voices experience with their dominant voice is a mirror of their social relationships in general (Birchwood, Meaden, Trower, Gilbert, & Plaistow, 2000). The more an individual feels subordinate to others in general, the more subordinate he or she feels to the dominant voice and the more powerful the voice seems. Moreover, experiences of feeling low in rank to both voices and others are associated with depression. However, although illuminating of possible power issues in the experience of voices, the direction of the relationship among psychosis, depression, and feeling subordinate is unclear.

Birchwood, Meaden, et al. (2000) found that more than 50% of people who hear voices were "severely depressed" and more than 75% reported that they were "highly distressed" by this hallucinatory experience. The authors proposed three models to elucidate the possible mechanisms to explain the production of depression and distress because of voices (see Figure 14.1). The first suggests that depression is primary and a core symptom of psychosis, which reduces the patient's tolerance of his or her voices and thus generates greater distress. The second argues that severity of the voice (e.g., frequency, loudness, delusions about voices) will lead to greater distress and depression. The third model, based on our research on the cognitive model of "voices" (Birchwood & Chadwick, 1997), argues that cognitive schemas governing interpersonal relationships are activated when the individual tries to make sense of his or her voices and that it is these schemas that, fundamentally, drive the distress about voices and associated depression.

Gilbert et al. (2002) tested the validity of these models in a sample of 125 patients with schizophrenia. Patients rated the power of their most dominant voice and how inferior or superior they felt in comparison to their voice. They also similarly rated their perception of their relative power and status in comparison to other people in their social world. The authors report that beliefs about being subordinate to voices and of the capacity of voices to shame the person were significantly associated with feelings of subordination and marginalization in wider social relationships. Moreover, covariance structure modeling rejected Models 1 and 2, but the data were consistent with

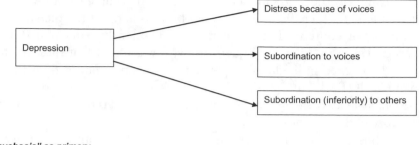

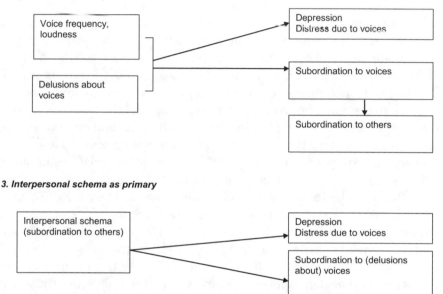

Figure 14.1. Three models of distress arising from voices.

Model 3, suggesting that the appraisal of social power and rank are primary, organizing schemas underlying the appraisal of voice power and the distress to which the voices give rise. In other words, social rank or "group fit" and social power variables are seen as primary and lead to the appraisal of voice power, distress, and depression.

Postpsychotic Depression (PPD)

Although we have described here the controversy surrounding the relationships between depression and acute psychotic symptoms, postpsychotic depression (PPD), however, is recognized in ICD–10 and *DSM–IV* as a de novo phenomenon occurring largely outside the acute episode and is regarded as a response to psychosis. However, the diagnostic criteria for PPD in ICD–10 require the presence of at least one psychotic symptom and, in *DSM–IV* a temporal link with the immediately preceding acute psychotic episode; recent studies have cast doubt on both prerequisites (Birchwood, Iqbal, et al., 2000; Bressan, Chaves, Pilowsky, Shirakawa, & Mari, 2003). We argue that depression during the acute episode and following remission (PPD) precedes hopelessness and suicidal intent. It is important to acknowledge the difficulties inherent with the assessment of PPD and, at the same time, to provide a possible elucidation for why such controversy exists as to its exegesis. For example, unraveling PPD onset following remission from a relapse is dependent on frequent and regular follow-up during which it will emerge whether increases in the severity of psychotic symptoms are evident (relapse) or not (PPD).

Our previous research has established that vulnerability to PPD is predicted by the appraisals individuals make of their psychosis, in particular, the psychological threat it carries to their future roles, goals, and identity (Birchwood, Iqbal, et al., 2000; Iqbal, Birchwood, Chadwick, & Trower, 2000). This work has pointed clearly to the appraisal of the life event as being of primary importance, particularly when the event involves loss (e.g., of a cherished goal) and is further appraised as humiliating (e.g., a challenge to a person's social status) and entrapping (in which escape is thwarted). This is grounded in "social ranking" theory from ethology (Gilbert, 1992; Price, Sloman, Gardner, Gilbert, & Rohde, 1994) and sees the onset of psychosis as a life event, focusing on the way patients appraise the threat it poses. These data were the first to show that it is possible to identify prospectively who develops PPD by reference to cognitive appraisal (vulnerability) variables and that first-episode patients appear to be particularly at risk.

In conclusion, we support the notion that PPD is embedded in the realities of a psychotic illness, and it is the beliefs or appraisals about psychosis and their impact on social ranking and group fit made by those who experience it that are important (Birchwood & Iqbal, 1998; Rooke & Birchwood, 1998) and lead to depression, distress, and ultimately suicidal behavior.

Depression and Persecution

There can be little doubt that the experience of voices and delusions is often immensely distressing. Freeman, Garety, and Kuipers (2001) documented the level of depression among a group of people with persecutory delusions and reported that more than 80% were at least moderately depressed on the Beck Depression Inventory with a mean score of 23. The same sample reported that 75% were anxious, and the mean delusional distress score was 8 (out of 10).

In a similar vein, the problems of social anxiety and social avoidance in the context of active psychotic symptoms may be traced directly to the symptoms themselves. Patients with persecutory delusions often deal with the perceived threat to their well-being through avoidance of high-risk social encounters; in cognitive therapy, this is one of a class of "safety behaviors" that function to reduce threat (Freeman et al., 2001). Social disengagement can also be traced to the content of command hallucinations that can directly undermine trust in others (Beck-Sander et al., 1997). Many studies also report correlations between negative symptoms, particularly alogia and affective flattening, and social disengagement (Chapman et al., 1998). The therapeutic implications of this pathway to emotional disorder lie in the treatment of core psychotic symptoms.

Depression as a Developmental Phenomenon

Birth cohort (e.g., Isohanni et al., 1998) and retrospective studies (Jones et al., 1993) reveal that first-episode psychosis is often preceded by social difficulty and emotional disorder as well as low-level "psychotic" experience stretching back into early adolescence (Poulton et al., 2000). These childhood antecedents of a developing psychosis will unfold in a social environment, and there is now considerable evidence that social factors influence morbidity and outcome, for example, urban living, particularly deprivation (Pedersen & Mortensen, 2001; van Os, Hanssen, Bak, Bijl, & Vollebergh, 2003), membership of marginalized social groups (Bhugra et al., 1997), the impact of migration (Bhugra, 2000), and the (favorable) correlates of "developing nation" status (Harrison et al., 2001). The unfolding antecedents of psychosis will also affect "normal" social and psychological development leading perhaps to low self-esteem, difficulty in establishing relationships, and susceptibility to stress. The science of developmental psychopathology (Rutter, 2000) shows that continuity exists between adolescent and adult disorder, including depression and risk of suicide (Fombonne, Wostear, Cooper, Harrington, & Rutter, 2001), which occurs in a dimensional rather than a categorical way, influenced by the social and familial context (Rutter, 2000). There is also considerable discontinuity between adolescent and adult emotional functioning. For example, Andrews and Brown (1995) showed that positive life events in late adolescence can serve to restore a disturbed developmental trajectory back to within normal limits. The domains of emotional functioning also interact; for example, social anxiety increases the developmental risk of adolescent depression (Stein et al., 2001). A strong case can be made that the variance in comorbid emotional disorder in psychosis is a product in part of these unfolding, disturbed, developmental pathways triggered by life events and social risk factors against the background of the psychosis diathesis (see Birchwood, 2003).

Childhood trauma and problems of parental attachment can predispose to adult depression (Brown, Bifulco, Veiel, & Andrews, 1990). There is evidence of a high rate of traumatic histories in people with psychosis, including sexual abuse (Greenfield, Strakowski, Tohen, Batson, & Kolbrener, 1994), unwanted pregnancy (Myhrman, Rantakallio, Isohanni, Jones, & Partanen, 1996), and dysfunctional parental attachment (Parker, Johnston, & Hawyard, 1988; Tienari, 1994). Such traumatic histories may also render patients prone to PPD and other emotional disorders (Iqbal, Birchwood, Hemsley, Jackson, & Morris, 2004). In posttraumatic stress disorder, traumatic responses to violent crime have been shown to be more likely in those who have a history of childhood trauma and who appraise the event as more personally threatening (Andrews, Brewin, Rose, & Kirk, 2000). These histories and developmental anomalies have been hypothesized to influence cognitive schemas that govern the processing of self and social information (Birchwood, Meaden, et al., 2000; Garety, Kuipers, Fowler, Freeman, & Bebbington, 2001). Such schemas have been observed to be active in the emotional response to psychosis in the way in which the individual appraises the interpersonal significance of the voice (i.e., of power and omnipotence: Birchwood, Meaden, et al., 2000) and also in the distress and persistence of voices in young adolescents (Escher, Romme, Buiks, Delespaul, & van Os, 2002).

This pathway to emotional disorder following the first episode of positive psychosis symptoms may therefore arise because of developmental disturbance leading to (a) dysfunctional cognitive schemas that affect adaptation to psychosis and its symptoms and (b) adolescent emotional disorder that shows continuity into adulthood. The therapeutic implications of this pathway lie in the focus on disturbances in "normal" developmental processes in adolescence and their continuity with emerging psychopathology with a particular therapeutic focus on dysfunctional schemas of self and others.

IMPLICATIONS FOR COGNITIVE THERAPY

The development of CBT to combat drug-resistant psychotic symptoms such as voices and delusions has required the elaboration of the psychological mechanisms underpinning these symptoms and their impact on the individual. Indeed, CBT has also been used during acute psychosis as a complementary and efficacious supplement to drug-treatment alone (Drury, Birchwood, Cochrane, & MacMillan, 1996). In the context of this brief review, the major implications from the CBT literature center on the psychological reaction of the individual to auditory hallucinations or delusions (or both), be they individual drug-resistant symptoms or part of the acute psychosis.

The major premise behind viewing voices from a cognitive perspective is that these are activating events to which the individual gives meaning and experiences leading to emotional and behavioral reactions (Chadwick & Birchwood, 1994). This approach suggests that distress caused by voices is a result of the beliefs held about auditory hallucinations and not just their presence. The rationale is that emotion and coping behavior are indeed connected to such hallucinations. A secondary assumption is that beliefs are not direct interpretations of voice content. Both of these hypotheses are supported by robust empirical evidence (see Chadwick, Birchwood, & Trower,

1996, for a review). Whether the voices are engaged or resisted can be discerned by the individual's beliefs about voices, specifically, whether the voices were benevolent or malevolent, respectively. The association between voices that are deemed to be malevolent and powerful and depression is well established (Birchwood, Meaden, et al., 2000), and this is particularly so for command hallucinations (Gilbert et al., 2002). In two studies of more than 200 patients with auditory hallucinations, we have shown that 40% were at least moderately depressed. This depression was strongly linked to patients' appraisal of voice power and entrapment.

The cognitive model of delusions (see Garety & Freeman, 1999, for a review) has at its center the concept that patients suffer distress, anxiety, and ultimately depression because of the impact of these symptoms on individuals' self-concept, their relationship with others, and how they perceive their future. Indeed, as many as four out of five patients with delusions will suffer from concurrent depression, as confirmed in the recent study by Freeman et al. (2001), who found that 56% of patients with persecutory delusions had moderate or severe depression and a further 24% had mild depression.

It is interesting that randomized controlled trials of CBT appear to have uniquely failed to have an impact on depression, although their efficacy in the treatment of voices and delusions is well established (Birchwood, Iqbal, Jackson, & Hardy, 2004). Table 14.1 lists randomized clinical trials of CBT for psychosis, noting whether each measured depression or distress linked to delusions. The trials included are all of those in the Pilling et al. (2002) review, plus four reported since 2002. The Cognitively Oriented Psychotherapy for Early Psychosis (COPE) trial of Jackson et al. (2001) is included because it incorporates many of the elements listed in Table 14.1 and includes an explicit focus on comorbidity. These trials have shown a decisive impact on psychotic symptoms (Pilling et al., 2002) with an effect size of 0.6 rising to 0.93 at follow-up (Gould, Mueser, Bolton, Mays, & Goff, 2001). Twelve trials are included; nine of these measured depression as a secondary outcome. Four measured distress, using either the Psychotic Symptom Rating Scales (PSYRATS; Haddock et al., 1999), which includes distress subscales, namely Durham et al. (2003) and Lewis et al. (2002), or the Personal Questionnaire Rating Scale Technique (PQRST; Brett-Jones, Garety, & Hemsley, 1987), namely Garety et al. (1994) and Kuipers et al. (1997). In no study was distress separately analyzed (PSYRATS uses the distress scale to compile total scores for hallucinations or delusions).

Overall, three of the nine studies measuring depression reported an improvement in depression score attributed to CBT (Drury et al., 1996; Garety, Kuipers, Fowler, Chamberlain, & Dunn, 1994; Sensky et al., 2000; Turkington, Kingdon, & Turner, 2002). All of these were secondary measures taken at the end of treatment, suggesting that the impact of the CBT on psychotic symptoms was also responsible for a decrease in the depressed affect associated with them. Two studies described a longer term improvement in depression at the 9-month follow-up (Drury et al., 1996; Sensky et al., 2000). In the Drury et al. (1996) study, this may have reflected the attempt to challenge secondary appraisals of psychosis (e.g., loss, shame) that informed their CBT program. Additionally, Tarrier, Kinney, McCarthy, and Wittkowski (2001) reported an improvement in mood following the alleviation of positive symptoms at the end of treatment.

In summary, three of the nine trials measuring depression reported that a reduction in the targeted psychotic symptoms was associated with a reduction in depression (and in one case, mood improvement; Tarrier et al., 2001) at the end of therapy. The mean effect size of those studies reporting a significant effect was 0.28 compared with the effect size of 0.65 (all studies) for psychotic symptoms, with more gains with time (EF = 0.93; Gould et al., 2001). Of the four studies measuring delusional distress, one (Durham et al., 2003) reported a reduction in the severity of delusions on the PSYRATS (distress scale aggregated in the delusions scale score) and another (Kuipers et al., 1998) reported an improvement in delusional distress (on PQRST) only at follow-up. Considering the high level of depression and distress associated with positive symptoms and the scale of the impact of CBT on the positive symptoms, it is surprising that the impact of CBT on depression occurred only in a minority of studies and with low effect size. These results call into question the assumption that easing distress and depression in psychosis will follow from the treatment of positive symptoms alone.

A COGNITIVE FRAMEWORK OF SUICIDAL INTENT

The link among psychosis-related events, particularly compulsory admission, and among events such as unemployment and later depression, point to the conclusion that depression in schizophrenia is rooted in the "objective" realities of the illness, many of which were identified in Rooke and Birchwood (1998) and other studies. In this sense, these events are analogous to the life events identified as causal in unipolar depression; however, analyses point to patients' appraisals as presenting a further independent contribution.

It is proposed therefore that it is the events that punctuate a long-term difficulty such as psychosis (e.g., compulsory admission, persistent voices, loss of job) that are appraised as signifying loss and entrapment and confirm the absence of a way forward with respect to core roles, relationships, or autonomy. Such events are likely to be ego involving because autonomy and success in social roles and personal goals (Oatley & Bolton, 1985) are highly prized in Western culture. Such events may also confirm a disbelief in the individual's ability to reaffirm a sense of identity and belonging (Price et al., 1994) and encourage engulfment in, and internalization of, the "schizophrenic" identity as a defensive maneuver (Birchwood, Mason, MacMillan, & Healy, 1993). Schizophrenia is perhaps unique in its capacity to limit

TABLE 14.1

Randomized Controlled Trials of Cognitive Therapy for Psychosis

Study	Inclusion criteria	CBT procedure	Control procedure	Follow-up	Results	Depression measure used	Does therapy alleviate depression better than control?		Effect size	Distress from symptoms targeted and measured?
							CBT end	Follow-up		
Rector et al. (2003)	DSM–IV diagnosis of schizophrenia or schizoaffective disorder, persistent +ve and –ve symptoms for 6 months assessed; nonorganic or concurrent substance abuse; no past treatment with behavioral or CB	n = 24; 6 months: engagement and assessment, education of cognitive model, coping skills, psychoeducation with normalization, relapse prevention Targets +ve and –ve symptoms; guided discovery, behavioral self-monitoring and cognitive strategies	Enriched treatment as usual (n = 18)	Posttreatment and 6 months	Significant clinical effects seen for +ve, –ve and overall symptoms for CBT group but no difference between groups at post treatment CBT showed significant reduction in –ve symptoms at follow-up	BDI	No	No	n/a	No
Durham et al. (2003)	ICD–10 and DSM–IV diagnosis of psychosis, schizophrenia, schizoaffective, or delusional disorder; Age 16 to 65, known to psychiatric services, experiencing positive symptoms and stabilized on antipsychotics for 6 months	n = 22; 9-month treatment phase over 20 sessions: engagement, education, therapeutic alliance, formulation, problem list, normalization, coping strategies, relaxation training, and problem solving	1. Supportive psychotherapy (n = 23) 2. Treatment as usual (n = 21)	Baseline, 3 months	Modest treatment effects reported at follow-up; CBT led to greater improvement in overall symptom severity; no treatment effects found for auditory hallucinations	n/a	n/a	n/a	n/a	PSYRATS; no treatment effect for hallucinations, but reduction in severity of delusions from CBT & SPT combined

Study	Population	Intervention groups	Assessment	Outcome	Depression measure				
McGorry et al. (2002)*	First prodromal episode ultra-high-risk group, age 14 to 30 years, highly symptomatic and moderately disabled by symptoms	Specific Preventive Intervention (SPI; n = 31): low-dose risperidone for 6 months and modified CBT (targets: stress management, depression, –ve and +ve symptoms, comorbidities)	Needs Based Intervention (NBI; n = 28)	Baseline, 6 months, 12 months	No significant difference between SPI and NBI; progression to acute psychosis at 6-month follow-up NNT = 4:1	Hamilton Rating Scale for Depression	No	No	n/a	No
Lewis et al. (2002)*	Early psychosis, nonorganic or primary substance misuse; DSM–IV schizophrenia or related disorder	(n = 101) CBT for 5 weeks: engagement, education, problem list generation, intervention, monitoring	1. (n = 106) supportive counseling 2. (n = 102) routine care alone	Baseline, 2, 3, 4, 5, 6 weeks	Trend for CBT group to improve fastest up to Week 5, but difference not maintained	n/a	n/a	n/a	n/a	PSYRATS; no difference seen in rate of change between treated and routine care groups on delusions and hallucinations scales
Turkington et al. (2002)	ICD–10 diagnosis of schizophrenia, age 18 to 65, nonorganic or primary substance misuse	CBT (n = 257): assessment, engagement, case formulations, symptom management, adherence, working with core beliefs, and relapse prevention; 6 sessions	treatment as usual (n = 165)	Assessed 9 months after therapy ended	CBT superior in lowering symptoms and promoting insight; higher attrition in treatment as usual group	Montgomery–Asberg Depress on Rating Scale	Yes	n/a	0.29	No
Jackson et al. (2001)*	FEP, 16 to 30 years, nonorganic or primary substance misuse; DSM–III–R schizophrenia or related disorder	Cognitive oriented psychotherapy (n = 44): engagement, assessment, adaptation and comorbidity targeted; 21 sessions (mean)	1. Refused CBT and treatment as usual in FEP service (n = 21) 2. No CBT or FEP service: (n = 15)	Baseline, treatment end, 12 months	All end-of-treatment differences were sustained over 12 months on the BPRS, SANS, QoL, and I/So	BDI	No	No	n/a	No

continues

TABLE 14.1 (Continued)

Study	Inclusion criteria	CBT procedure	Control procedure	Follow-up	Results	Depression measure used	Does therapy alleviate depression better than control?		Effect size	Distress from symptoms targeted and measured?
							CBT end	Follow-up		
Tarrier et al. (2001)	DSM–III–R diagnosis of schizophrenia and related disorders, age18 to 65, nonorganic or primary, substance misuse	CBT: coping strategy enhancements, problem solving, cognitive–behavioral relapse prevention; 20 sessions (n = 24)	1. Supportive counseling and routine care (n = 21) 2. Routine care (n = 27)	Assessed at baseline, 3 months, follow-up	Hallucination and delusions showed improvement with CB; no effect on affective symptoms	BDI	No	n/a	n/a	No
Sensky et al. (2000)	DSM–IV and ICD–10 diagnosis of schizophrenia, age 16 to 60, not primary substance misuse	CBT (n = 46): normalizing, collaborative critical analysis of beliefs, reattribution, coping strategies, guided discovery—9 months	Befriending (n = 44)	Baseline, 9 months, 9 months follow-up	Both interventions resulted in significant reductions in symptoms; CBT continued to improve at 9 months	Montgomery–Asberg Depression Rating Scale	Yes	Yes	0.21	CBT aimed to reduce distress and disability but no measurement of distress used
Bradshaw (2000)	DSM–IV criteria for schizophrenia, age 18 to 60 years, nonorganic or primary substance abuse	Day treatment program (n = 8) and CBT: Weekly over 3 years: (n = 7) engagement and education, behavioral treatment and cognitive treatment	Day treatment program	Assessed at end of 3-year treatment	Both groups showed improvement in psychosocial functioning but effect greater in the CBT group	n/a	n/a	n/a	n/a	No

Study	Diagnosis	Intervention	Control	Assessment times	Results					
Kuipers et al. (1997); Garety et al. (1997); Kuipers et al. (1998)	Schizophrenia or related disorder; nonorganic or primary substance misuse	CBT (n = 28) for 9 months, improving, coping strategies, developing a shared model, modifying beliefs and dysfunctional schema, management of social disability and relapse	Routine care (n = 32)	Baseline, 3, 6, 9, and 18 months	Only BPRS showed significant improvement for CBT group; cognitive flexibility regarding delusions predicted good outcome; improvement maintained at 9 months after therapy	BDI	No	No	n/a	Personal questionnaires: measure conviction, preoccupation and distress with delusions and hallucinations; no change seen in scores post CBT but significant improvement reported at 18-month follow-up for delusions

Note. BDI = Beck Depression Inventory; *DSM–III–R* = *Diagnostic and Statistical Manual of Mental Disorders* (3rd ed., rev.); CBT = cognitive–behavioral therapy; ICD = International Classification of Diseases; PAS = Psychiatric Assessment Scale; BPRS = Brief Psychiatric Rating Scale; CSE = Coping Strategies Enhancement; FEP = First Episode of Psychosis; I/So = Insight/Symptoms; QoL = Quality of Life; SANS = Scale for the Assessment of Negative Symptoms; +ve = positive; –ve = negative; *First-episode or prodromal (high risk) patients.

achievement in personal (e.g., work) and interpersonal domains and is a life event or difficulty that reduces options and sources of value sufficient in itself to trigger depression in the context of a cognitive vulnerability.

A theoretical model of depression and suicide, which may link depression and hopelessness on one hand and suicide on the other, is presented by Gilbert (1992) and suggests that the depressed and suicidal individuals perceive themselves as humiliated by shattering life events and entrapped. Brown, Harris, and Hepworth's (1995) finding was that humiliation and entrapment were of greater importance in provoking depression than experiences of loss or danger alone. A similar approach is postulated by Baumeister (1990), who proposed an "escape theory" of suicide, in which the individual is argued to hold unrealistically high expectations and, following the experience of bad outcomes, builds internal attributions for these outcomes thus making self-awareness painful. Hence, the individual ends up deriving a self-evaluation that is inadequate, incompetent, unattractive, or guilty (hence procreating negative affect). Baumeister suggested that the person tries to prevent self-awareness and emotion by escaping into a disinhibited and irrational state of mind called *cognitive deconstruction*. Suicide finally emerges as an escalation of the person's wish to escape from life's problems and their implications for the self.

We conclude that depression, hopelessness, and suicidal ideation during and immediately following an episode of acute psychosis are necessary but not sufficient conditions for parasuicide and suicide and demonstrate that suicide is not always a rational decision but often occurs in the context of a distressed mental state. The presence of these psychological vulnerabilities, we believe, supports a cognitive framework for depression and suicide in schizophrenia. Our recent study of 110 patients with schizophrenia followed up for 12 months subsequent to an acute episode of psychosis suggests a sound rationale for pursuing this stratagem. The need for treatment is further underlined by a 20% increase in depression scores at 4, 8, or 12 months compared with the point of discharge from hospital (recovery). The targeting of these aforementioned precursors would be essential. To develop an effective intervention, we also need a theoretical model of depression and suicide to understand the role of these risk variables. We argue that patients' appraisals of the meaning of their psychosis and its symptoms would provide such a backdrop.

We have proposed that distress arising from psychotic symptoms and the "comorbid" emotional dysfunctions will arise from pathways that are not driven by positive symptoms or primary psychotic experience alone. Indeed, when considering the prevalence of suicidal ideation during psychotic and nonpsychotic phases of the illness, suicide risk is observed more frequently during nonpsychotic periods (Birchwood & Iqbal, 1998). "Standard" CBT, with the aim of trying to target delusions and voice activity directly, will not address all of these pathways and will therefore fail to treat emotional dysfunction including the psychological factors influencing the perception of threat and distress from supposed persecutors (Birchwood, 2003). Moreover, this framework suggests that it may be possible to reduce distress and behavior arising from psychosis, without changing the core psychotic experience. For example, in our recent work with command hallucinations (Byrne, Trower, Birchwood, Meaden, & Nelson, 2003, and subsequently in this chapter), we demonstrated that by focusing on the patient's appraisal of the power and omnipotence of voices, this itself reduced depression and despair and compliance with the voices' commands, but it did not lead to a decrease in the frequency of hallucinations per se or a change in recorded positive symptoms. This position is consistent with the empirical evidence about the nature of delusions, which suggest they lie on continua and that they are not qualitatively distinct from similar beliefs held by people in the community (Delespaul, deVries, & van Os, 2002) and vary along dimensions of conviction, preoccupation, distress, and behavioral elaboration (Garety & Hemsley, 1988; Johns & van Os, 2001), which are subject to fluctuation on a day-to day basis (Myin-Germeys, van Os, Schwartz, Stone, & Delespaul, 2001).

Returning to the theme of this section, we believe the time has come to shift attention from CBT as a quasi-neuroleptic, to CBT as a therapy to relieve distress associated with psychotic experience and the "comorbid" emotional dysfunctions, of which reduction of distress and depression and thus suicidal intent is central. CBT has, we believe, a distinctive role to play in relieving distress, which is more in keeping with its natural roots in emotional dysfunction. Our recent trial of command hallucinations (Trower et al., 2004) with an adapted form of cognitive therapy designed to reduce distress and voice activity and a trial design that predicts reductions in distress without predicting reductions in symptoms are, we believe, possible clinical frameworks to target and treat these most intractable of difficulties for the person with psychosis.

CONCLUSION

The onset of suicidal intent and behavior in schizophrenia can be traced through the emergence of distress and depression leading to hopelessness and escape from "self." The difficulties arising from the clinical management and prediction of future suicide are due to several "entrenched" factors, namely, the diagnostic inflexibility that requires a differentiation between affective and nonaffective psychosis, the problems surrounding the definitions of PPD, and the evidence that positive symptoms during the prodrome, acute stage, and prior to relapse are invariably underpinned by distress, dysphoria, and depression.

We postulate that suicide onset is underpinned by the individual's cognitive appraisals of the symptoms and his or her experience of integrating psychosis and have provided evidence of these processes for patients with auditory hallucinations and for postpsychotic patients for whom the psychosis can be viewed as a catastrophic life event. Evidence from ethology suggests that the process of social "down ranking" and beliefs of persecution fuel the distress and hopelessness the individual experiences. Childhood risk factors affecting the developmental trajectories may also play a part in further burdening the patient, although this is a somewhat neglected area of research.

Trials of cognitive therapy have, in the main, failed to address the emotional dysfunction that is frequently observed throughout the schizophrenia trajectory by focusing on symptom reduction. Thus, cognitive therapy, which is uniquely positioned to target symptoms of distress and depression, has gained the role of a quasi-neuroleptic in the treatment of psychosis. It is only by refocusing the clinical targets of such therapeutic trails on to the clinical markers of depression and distress—precursors to hopelessness and suicide—that we may develop effective treatments for these devastating outcomes.

REFERENCES

Addington, D., & Addington, J. (1992). Attempted suicide and depression in schizophrenia. *Acta Psychiatrica Scandinavica*, 85, 288–291.

Aguilar, E. J., Leal, C., Acosta, F. J., Cejas, M. R., Fernandez, L., & Gracia, R. (2003). A psychopathological study of a group of schizophrenic patients after attempting suicide. Are there two different clinical subtypes? *European Psychiatry*, 18, 190–192.

Andrews, B., Brewin, C. R., Rose, S., & Kirk, M. (2000). Predicting PTSD symptoms in victims of violent crime: The role of shame, anger, and childhood abuse. *Journal of Abnormal Psychology*, 109, 69–73.

Andrews, B., & Brown, G. W. (1995). Stability and change in low self-esteem: The role of psychosocial factors. *Psychological Medicine*, 25, 23–31.

Baumeister, R. F. (1990). Suicide as escape from self. *Psychological Review*, 97, 90–113.

Beck-Sander, A., Birchwood, M., & Chadwick, P. D. (1997). Acting on command hallucinations: A cognitive approach. *British Journal of Clinical Psychology*, 36, 139–148.

Bhugra, D. (2000). Migration and schizophrenia. *Acta Psychiatrica Scandinavica Supplement*, 102, 68–73.

Bhugra, D., Leff, J., Mallett, R., Der, G., Corridan, B., & Rudge, S. (1997). Incidence and outcome of schizophrenia in whites, African-Caribbeans and Asians in London. *Psychological Medicine*, 27, 791–798.

Birchwood, M. (2003). Pathways to emotional dysfunction in first-episode psychosis. *British Journal of Psychiatry*, 182, 373–375.

Birchwood, M., & Chadwick, P. D. (1997). The omnipotence of voices III: testing the validity of the cognitive model. *Psychological Medicine*, 27, 1345–1353.

Birchwood, M. J., & Iqbal, Z. (1998). Depression and suicidal thinking in psychosis: A cognitive approach. In T. Wykes, N. Tarrier, & S. Lewis (Eds.), *Outcomes and innovation in psychological management of schizophrenia* (pp. 81–100). Chichester, England: Wiley.

Birchwood, M., Iqbal, Z., Chadwick, P., & Trower, P. (2000). Cognitive approach to depression and suicidal thinking in psychosis I. Ontogeny of post-psychotic depression. *British Journal of Psychiatry, 177*, 516–521.

Birchwood, M., Iqbal, Z., Jackson, C., & Hardy, K. (2004). Cognitive therapy and emotional dysfunction in early psychosis. In J. Gleeson & P. D. McGorry (Eds.), *Psychological interventions in early psychosis: A practical treatment handbook.* Chichester, England: Wiley.

Birchwood, M., Iqbal, Z., & Upthegrove, R. (2005). Psychological pathways to depression in schizophrenia: Studies in acute psychosis, post psychotic depression and auditory hallucinations. *European Archives of Psychiatry & Clinical Neuroscience, 255*, 202–212.

Birchwood, M., Mason, R., MacMillan, F., & Healy, J. (1993). Depression, demoralisation and control over psychotic illness: A comparison of depressed and non-depressed patients with a chronic psychosis. *Psychological Medicine, 23*, 387–395.

Birchwood, M., Meaden, A., Trower, P., Gilbert, P., & Plaistow, J. (2000). The power and omnipotence of voices: Subordination and entrapment by voices and significant others. *Psychological Medicine, 30*, 337–344.

Bleuler, E. (1950). *Dementia praecox or the group of schizophrenias* (J. Zinkin, Trans.). New York: International Universities Press. (Original work published 1911)

Bottlender, R., Strauss, A., & Moeller, H. J. (2000). Prevalence and background factors of depression in first admitted schizophrenic patients. *Acta Psychiatrica Scandinavica, 101*, 153–160.

Bradshaw, W. (2000). Integrating cognitive–behavioral psychotherapy for persons with schizophrenia into a psychiatric rehabilitation program: Results of a 3-year trial. *Community Mental Health Journal, 36*, 491–500.

Bressan, R. A., Chaves, A. C., Pilowsky, L. S., Shirakawa, I., & Mari, J. J. (2003). Depressive episodes in stable schizophrenia: Critical evaluation of the *DSM–IV* and ICD–10 diagnostic criteria. *Psychiatry Research, 117*, 47–56.

Brett-Jones, J., Garety, P. A., & Hemsley, D. (1987). Measuring delusional experiences: A method and its application. *British Journal of Clinical Psychology, 26*, 257–265.

Brown, G. W., Bifulco, A., Veiel, H. O., & Andrews, B. (1990). Self-esteem and depression. II. Social correlates of self-esteem. *Social Psychiatry and Psychiatric Epidemiology, 25*, 225–234.

Brown, G. W., Harris, T. O., & Hepworth, C. (1995). Loss humiliation and entrapment among women developing depression: A patient and non-patient comparison. *Psychological Medicine, 25*, 7–21.

Byrne, S., Trower, P., Birchwood, M., Meaden, A., & Nelson, A. (2003). Command hallucinations: Cognitive theory, therapy, and research. *Journal of Cognitive Psychotherapy, 17*, 67–84.

Chadwick, P. D., & Birchwood, M. (1994). Challenging the omnipotence of voices: A cognitive approach to auditory hallucinations. *British Journal of Psychiatry, 164,* 190–201.

Chadwick, P. D., & Birchwood, M. (1995). The omnipotence of voices II: The Beliefs about Voices Questionnaire. *British Journal of Psychiatry, 166,* 773–776.

Chadwick, P. D., Birchwood, M., & Trower, P. (1996). *Cognitive therapy for delusions voices and paranoia.* Chichester, England: Wiley.

Chapman, M., Hutton, S., Duncan, L.-J., Puri, B. K., Joyce, E. M., & Barnes, T. R. E. (1998). Core negative symptoms and social functioning: West London first-episode schizophrenia study. *Schizophrenia Research, 29,* 193–194.

Close, H., & Garety, P. (1998). Cognitive assessment of voices: Further developments in understanding the emotional impact of voices. *British Journal of Clinical Psychology, 37,* 173–188.

Delespaul, P., deVries, M., & van Os, J. (2002). Determinants of occurrence and recovery from hallucinations in daily life. *Social Psychiatry and Psychiatric Epidemiology, 37,* 97–104.

Drake, T., & Cotton, T. (1986). Suicide among schizophrenics: A comparison of attempted and completed suicides. *British Journal of Psychiatry, 149,* 784–787.

Drake, R., Gates, C., Cotton, P., & Whittaker, A. (1985). Suicide amongst schizophrenics: Who is at risk? *Journal of Nervous and Mental Disease, 172,* 613–617.

Drury, V., Birchwood, M., Cochrane, R., & MacMillan, F. (1996). Cognitive therapy and recovery from acute psychosis: A controlled trial I: Impact on psychotic symptoms. *British Journal of Psychiatry, 169,* 593–601.

Durham, R. C., Guthrie, M., Morton, R. V., Reid, D. A., Treliving, L. R., Fowler, D., & Macdonald, R. R. (2003). Tayside-Fife clinical trial of cognitive–behavioural therapy for medication-resistant psychotic symptoms: Results to 3-month follow up. *British Journal of Psychiatry, 182,* 303–311.

Escher, S., Romme, M., Buiks, A., Delespaul, P., & van Os, J. (2002). Independent course of childhood auditory hallucinations: A sequential 3-year follow up study. *British Journal of Psychiatry, 181*(Suppl. 143), 10–18.

Fombonne, E., Wostear, G., Cooper, V., Harrington, R., & Rutter, M. (2001). The Maudsley long-term follow-up of child and adolescent depression. 1. Psychiatric outcomes in adulthood. *British Journal of Psychiatry, 179,* 210–217.

Foulds, G. A., & Bedford, A. (1975). Hierarchy of classes of personal illness. *Psychological Medicine, 5,* 181–192.

Freeman, D., Garety, P. A., & Kuipers, E. (2001). Persecutory delusions: Developing the understanding of belief maintenance and emotional distress. *Psychological Medicine, 31,* 1293–1306.

Garety, P. A., & Freeman, D. (1999). Cognitive approaches to delusions: A critical review of theories and evidence. *British Journal of Clinical Psychology, 38,* 113–154.

Garety, P., & Hemsley, D. (1988). Characteristics of delusional experience. *European Archives of Psychiatry and Neurological Sciences, 236,* 294–298.

Garety, P. A., Kuipers, E., Fowler, D., Chamberlain, F., & Dunn, G. (1994). Cognitive behavioural therapy for drug resistant psychosis. *British Journal of Medical Psychology, 67,* 259–271.

Garety, P. A., Kuipers, E., Fowler, D., Freeman, D., & Bebbington, P. E. (2001). A cognitive model of the positive symptoms of psychosis. *Psychological Medicine, 31,* 189–195.

Gilbert, P. (1992). *Depression: The evolution of powerlessness.* Hove, England: Erlbaum.

Gilbert, P., Birchwood, M., Gilbert, J., Trower, P., Hay, J., Murray, B., et al. (2002). An exploration of evolved mental mechanisms for dominant and subordinate behaviour in relation to auditory hallucinations in schizophrenia and critical thoughts in depression. *Psychological Medicine, 31,* 1117–1127.

Gould, R. A., Mueser, K. T., Bolton, E., Mays, V., & Goff, D. (2001). Cognitive therapy for psychosis in schizophrenia: An effect size analysis. *Schizophrenia Research, 48,* 335–342.

Greenfield, S. F., Strakowski, S. M., Tohen, M., Batson, S. C., & Kolbrener, M. L. (1994). Childhood abuse in first-episode psychosis. *British Journal of Psychiatry, 164,* 831–834.

Haddock, G., Tarrier, N., Morrison, A. P., Hopkins, R., Drake, R., & Lewis, S. (1999). A pilot study evaluating the effectiveness of individual inpatient cognitive–behavioural therapy in early psychosis. *Social Psychiatry and Psychiatric Epidemiology, 34,* 254–258.

Harrison, G., Hopper, K., Craig, T., Laska, E., Siegel, C., Wanderling, J., et al. (2001). Recovery from psychotic illness: A 15- and 25-year international follow-up study. *British Journal of Psychiatry, 178,* 506–517.

Hirsch, S. R. (1982). Depression "revealed" in schizophrenia. *British Journal of Psychiatry, 140,* 421–424.

Hirsch, S. R., & Jolley, A. G. (1989). The dysphoric syndrome in schizophrenia and its implications for relapse. *British Journal of Psychiatry, 155,* (Suppl. 5), 46–50.

Iqbal, Z., Birchwood, M., Chadwick, P., & Trower, P. (2000). A cognitive approach to depression and suicidal thinking in psychosis II: Testing the validity of a social ranking model. *British Journal of Psychiatry, 177,* 522–528.

Iqbal, Z., Birchwood, M., Hemsley, D., Jackson, C., & Morris, E. (2004). Autobiographical memory and postpsychotic depression in first-episode psychosis. *British Journal of Clinical Psychology, 43,* 97–104.

Isohanni, I., Jarvelin, M. R., Nieminen, P., Jones, P., Rantakallio, P., Jokelainen, J., et al. (1998). School performance as a predictor of psychiatric hospitalization in adult life. A 28-year follow-up in the Northern Finland 1966 Birth Cohort. *Psychological Medicine, 28,* 967–974.

Jablensky, A., Sartorius, N., Ernberg, G., Anker, M., Korten, A., Cooper, J. E., et al. (1992). Schizophrenia: Manifestations, incidence and course in different cultures: A World Health Organization ten-country study. *Psychological Medicine, 20,* 97.

Jackson, H., McGorry, P., Henry, L., Edwards, J., Hulbert, C., Harrigan, S., et al. (2001). Cognitively orientated psychotherapy for early psychosis (COPE): A 1-year follow-up. *British Journal of Clinical Psychology, 40,* 57–70.

Jackson, H. J., McGorry, P., & McKenzie, D. (1994). The reliability of *DSM–III* prodomal symptoms in first episode psychotic patients. *Acta Psychiatrica Scandinavica, 90,* 375–378.

Johns, L. C., & van Os, J. (2001). The continuity of psychotic experiences in the general population. *Clinical Psychology Review, 21,* 1125–1141.

Jones, J. S., Stein, D. J., Stanley, B., Guido, J. R., Winchell, R., & Stanley, M. (1994). Negative and depressive symptoms in suicidal schizophrenics. *Acta Psychiatrica Scandinavica, 89,* 81–88.

Jones, P. B., Bebbington, P. E., Foerster, A., Lewis, S. W., Murray, R. M., Russell, A., et al. (1993). Premorbid social underachievement in schizophrenia: Results from the Camberwell collaborative psychosis study. *British Journal of Psychiatry, 162,* 65–71.

Kay, S. R., & Sevy, S. (1990). Pyramidical model of schizophrenia. *Schizophrenia Bulletin, 16,* 537–545.

Knights, A., & Hirsch, S. R. (1981). "Revealed" depression and drug treatment for schizophrenia. *Archives of General Psychiatry, 38,* 806–811.

Kraepelin, E. (1896). *Psychiatrie, 5th Aufl.* Leipzig, Germany: Barth.

Kreyenbuhl, J. A., Kelly, D. L., & Conley, R. R. (2002). Circumstances of suicide among individuals with schizophrenia. *Schizophrenia Research, 58,* 253–261.

Kuipers, E., Fowler, D., Garety, P., Chisholm, D., Freeman, G., Dunn, G., et al. (1998). London-East Anglia randomised controlled trial of cognitively behavioural therapy for psychosis III: Follow-up and economic evaluation at 18 months. *British Journal of Psychiatry, 173,* 61–68.

Leff, J. P. (1990). Depressive symptoms in the course of schizophrenia. In L. E. DeLisi (Ed.), *Depression in schizophrenia.* Washington, DC: American Psychiatric Press.

Leff, J.P., Tress, A., & Edwards, B. (1988). The clinical course of depressive symptoms in schizophrenia. *Schizophrenia Research, 1,* 25–30.

Lewis, S., Tarrier, N., Haddock, G., Bentall, R., Kinderman, P., Kingdon, D., et al. (2002). Randomised controlled trial of cognitive–behavioural therapy in early schizophrenia: Acute-phase outcomes. *British Journal of Psychiatry, 181*(Suppl. 43), 91–97

Lindenmayer, J. P., Grochowski, S., & Hyman, R. B. (1995). Five factor model of schizophrenia: Replication across samples. *Schizophrenia Research, 14,* 229–234.

McCandless-Glimcher, L., McKnight, S., Hamera, E., Smith, B. L., Peterson, K. A., & Plumlee, A. A. (1986). Use of symptoms by schizophrenics to regulate and monitor their illness. *Hospital and Community Psychiatry, 37,* 929–933.

McGlashen, T. H., & Carpenter, W. T. (1976). An investigation of the postpsychotic depressive syndrome. *American Journal of Psychiatry, 133,* 14–19.

McGorry, P. D., Bell, R. C., Dudgeon, P. L., & Jackson, H. J. (1998). The dimensional structure of first episode psychosis: An exploratory factor analysis. *Psychological Medicine, 28,* 935–947.

Myhrman, A., Rantakallio, P., Isohanni, M., Jones, P., & Partanen, U. (1996). Unwantedness of a pregnancy and schizophrenia in the child. *British Journal of Psychiatry, 169,* 637–640.

Myin-Germeys, I., van Os, J., Schwartz, J. E., Stone, A. A., & Delespaul, P. A. (2001). Emotional reactivity to daily life stress in psychosis. *Archives of General Psychiatry, 58,* 1137–1144.

Oatley, K., & Bolton, W. (1985). A social theory of depression in reaction to life events. *Psychological Review, 92,* 372–388.

Parker, G., Johnston, P., & Hayward, L. (1988). Prediction of schizophrenic relapse using the parental bonding instrument. *Australian and New Zealand Journal of Psychiatry, 22,* 283–292.

Pedersen, C. B., & Mortensen, P. B. (2001). Evidence of a dose–response relationship between urbanicity during upbringing and schizophrenia risk. *Archives of General Psychiatry, 58,* 1039–1046.

Pilling, S., Bebbington, P., Kuipers, E., Garety, P., Geddes, J., Orbach, G., & Morgan, C. (2002). Psychological treatments in schizophrenia: II. Meta-analyses of randomized controlled trials of social skills training and cognitive remediation. *Psychological Medicine, 32,* 783–791.

Pokorny, A. (1993). Predictors of suicide in psychiatric patients. *Archives of General Psychiatry, 40,* 249–253.

Poulton, R., Caspi, A., Moffitt, T. E., Cannon, M., Murray, R., & Harrington, H. (2000). Children's self-reported psychotic symptoms and adult schizophreniform disorder—A 15-year longitudinal study. *Archives of General Psychiatry, 57,* 1053–1058.

Price, J., Sloman, L., Gardner, R., Gilbert, P., & Rohde, P. (1994). The social competition hypothesis of depression. *British Journal of Psychiatry, 164,* 309–315.

Rector, N. A., Seeman, M. V., & Segal, Z. V. (2003). Cognitive therapy for schizophrenia: A preliminary randomised controlled trial. *Schizophrenia Research, 63,* 1–11.

Rooke, O., & Birchwood, M. (1998). Loss humiliation and entrapment as appraisals of schizophrenic illness: A prospective study of depressed and non-depressed patients. *British Journal of Clinical Psychology, 37,* 259–268.

Rutter, M. (2000). Risks and outcomes in developmental psychopathology. *British Journal of Psychiatry, 177,* 569.

Saarinen, P. I., Lehtonen, J., & Lonnqvist, J. (1999). Suicide risk in schizophrenia: An analysis of 17 consecutive suicides. *Schizophrenia Bulletin, 25,* 533–542.

Sartorius, N., Jablensky, A., Ernberg, G., Leff, J., Korten, A., & Gulbinat, W. H. (1987). Course of schizophrenia in different countries: Some results of a WHO international comparative 5-year follow-up study. In H. Hafner, W. F. Gattaz, & W. Janzarik (Eds.), *Search for the causes of schizophrenia* (pp. 107–113). New York: Springer-Verlag.

Schwartz, R. C., & Cohen, B. N. (2001). Psychosocial correlates of suicidal intent among patients with schizophrenia. *Comprehensive Psychiatry, 42,* 118–123.

Sensky, T., Turkington, D., Kingdon, D., Scott, J. L., Scott, J., Siddle, R., et al. (2000). A randomised controlled trial of cognitive–behavioural therapy for persistent symptoms in schizophrenia resistant to medication. *Archives of General Psychiatry, 57,* 165–172.

Stein, M. B., Fuetsch, M., Muller, N., Hofler, M., Lieb, R., & Wittchen, H. U. (2001). Social anxiety disorder and the risk of depression: A prospective community study of adolescents and young adults. *Archives of General Psychiatry, 58,* 251–256.

Tarrier, N., Beckett, R., Harwood, S., & Baker, A. (1993). A Trial of two cognitive–behavioural methods of treating drug-resistant residual psychotic symptoms in schizophrenic patients I: Outcome. *British Journal of Psychiatry, 162,* 524–532.

Tarrier, N., Kinney, C., McCarthy, E., & Wittkowski, A. (2001). Are some types of psychotic symptoms more responsive to cognitive behaviour therapy? *Behavioural and Cognitive Psychotherapy, 29,* 45–55.

Tienari, P. (1994). Interaction between genetic vulnerability and family environment: The Finnish adoptive family study of schizophrenia. *Acta Psychiatrica Scandinavica, 84,* 460–465.

Trower, P., Birchwood, M., Meaden, A., Byrne, S., Nelson, A., & Ross, K. (2004). Cognitive therapy for command hallucinations: Randomised controlled trial. *British Journal of Psychiatry, 184,* 312–320.

Turkington, D., Kingdon, D., & Turner, T. (2002). Effectiveness of a brief cognitive–behavioural therapy intervention in the treatment of schizophrenia. *British Journal of Psychiatry, 180,* 523–527.

van Os, J., Gilvarry, C., Bale, R., Van Horn, E., Tattan, T., White, I., & Murray, R. (1999). A comparison of the utility of dimensional and categorical representations of psychosis. *Psychological Medicine, 29,* 595–606.

van Os, J., Hanssen, M., Bak, M., Bijl, R. V., & Vollebergh, W. (2003). Do urbanicity and familial liability coparticipate in causing psychosis? *American Journal of Psychiatry, 160,* 477–482.

van Os, J., Verdoux, H., Maurice-Tison, S., Gay, B., Liraud, F., Salamon, R., & Bourgeois, M. (1999). Self-reported psychosis like symptoms and the continuum of psychosis. *Social Psychiatry and Psychiatric Epidemiology, 34,* 459–463.

Verdoux, H., Liraud, F., Gonzales, B., Assens, F., Abalan, F., & Van Os, J. (2001). Predictors and outcome characteristics associated with suicidal behaviour in early psychosis: A two-year follow-up of first admitted subjects. *Acta Psychiatrica Scandinavica, 103,* 347–354.

Young, A. S., Nuechterlain, K. H., Mintz, J., Ventura, J., Gitlin, M., & Liberman, R. P. (1998). Suicidal ideation and suicide attempts in recent-onset schizophrenia. *Schizophrenia Bulletin, 24,* 629–634.

15

TRAUMA AND SUICIDE: A CONSTRUCTIVE NARRATIVE PERSPECTIVE

DONALD MEICHENBAUM

Just like our patients who come to see us, I have a story to tell. The "story" begins in 1964 during my graduate training to become a clinical psychologist. It was my first summer at the Veteran's Administration Hospital, and one of my first assigned patients committed suicide. I felt like "I had failed" and I questioned whether I had chosen the correct occupation. During the postmortem psychological autopsy in which the staff and I attempted to analyze the presence of prior risk and protective factors, my fellow students and supervisor attempted to console me. They observed,

"It wasn't your fault!"
"Patient suicide comes with the territory of helping in the mental health field."
"Suicide is so rare an event that we cannot predict it. All we can do is assess for the risk of suicide."

Over time, I came to learn that my clinical experience was not that unique. As Bongar (2002) has observed, one in six clinical graduate students will experience a patient's suicide, and one in three will have a patient who

333

attempts suicide at some point during his or her clinical training. Moreover, with clinical experience the incidence of patient suicide does not greatly diminish. A practicing clinical psychologist will average five suicidal patients per month. One in two psychiatrists and one in seven psychologists reports losing a patient to suicide.

The challenge of identifying patients who are at risk is complicated by the finding that up to one third of the general population has suicidal thoughts at some point in their lives (Bongar, 2002). Yet the base rate of suicide is only 12 per 100,000 per year in the general population, rising to 60 per 100,000 in a psychiatric population (Bongar, 2002).

Now, some 40 years later, the clinical challenge of working with patients who are suicidal still weighs on me. As a clinician in private practice, as a clinical supervisor, as a consultant to psychiatric facilities, and now as research director for an Institute to Treat Victims of Violence (see http://www.melissainstitute.org), I have had my share of patients who have committed suicide. The most recent incident was a patient of a clinical graduate student whom I was supervising on her very first case. The patient committed suicide over the Christmas holidays.

In reviewing my clinical notes from these several suicidal patients and the consultations that I have conducted over the course of my years of clinical work, the one thing that they all had in common was a history of victimization, including combat exposure (my first clinical case), sexual abuse, and surviving the Holocaust. The patients who committed suicide ranged in age from adolescence to elderly, had varied ethnic backgrounds, and included both sexes.

The connection between trauma and suicide was further highlighted when I was asked by Dr. William Foote and his treatment team to consult for the Society of Northern Renewal, which was established in July 2002 to address the clinical needs of native Inuit people in the newest Canadian province of Nunavit (formerly the Northwest Territories). Beyond the stressors that come with dislocation, economic deprivation, social isolation, disruption of traditional cultural patterns, the demoralizing effects of social problems (e.g., poverty, substandard living, overcrowding), and substance abuse, a subgroup of the aboriginal people also experienced a prolonged period of victimization. Over a period of 6 years in the 1980s, in three native communities, a now self-confessed male pedophile school teacher, who was appointed by the government, sexually abused 85 male youths. One of the consequences of this victimization experience is the very high rate of suicide among the Inuit, especially among the cohort of abused male youth. Inuit people are twice as likely to commit suicide compared with other native populations and 4 times as likely to engage in self-destructive behaviors. This subgroup of victimized male youth has the highest completion rate of suicide attempts (some 38% of attempters). For comparison purposes, the suicide rate among female Inuit is 32 per 100,000 and 119 per 100,000 for male Inuit; for the cohort of abused young men age 15 to 29, the suicide rate is 200 per 100,000. In addition, there is a high rate of domestic violence, depression, and substance abuse.

Although I recognize that not all suicide attempters have a history of victimization, this chapter reflects my continual struggle to better understand the relationship between trauma exposure, when it indeed occurs, and suicide. Given that up to 50% of psychiatric patients have a history of victimization (Meichenbaum, 1994), the need to better understand the role that victimization plays in patient prognosis is critical.

The research literature is replete with findings of the co-occurrence of suicidal ideation and suicidal behaviors being associated with victimization, including combat veterans, especially those with combat guilt (Hendin, 1992; Hendin & Haas, 1991; Lindy, Green, & Grace, 1994); refugees with a history of exposure to severe trauma (Ferrada-Noli, 1996; Ferrada-Noli, Asberg, Ormstad, Lundin, & Sandborn, 1998); African American women who have a history of childhood maltreatment (Kingree, 2000); inner-city women who have been subjected to partner abuse (Thompson, Kaslow, Kingree, Puett, & Thompson, 1999); and methadone maintenance patients, especially women who have a history of rape and men who have witnessed a violent death (Brown, 1995). In fact, among abused women, some 49% to 66% have a history of suicide attempts and about one in four or five rape survivors will actively consider suicide at some point following the attack (Young & Clum, 1996). Kilpatrick and his colleagues (1985) have noted that suicidal ideation and self-injurious behaviors are often correlates of criminal victimization. Adolescent suicide attempters are also more likely to have been sexually and physically abused (National Research Council, 1993). As Evans, Hawton, and Rodhan (2004) have observed, "There is considerable evidence for a strong and direct association between sexual abuse and suicidal phenomenon" (p. 970). This finding takes on particular significance when considering that the rates of child sexual abuse (15% of women and 7% of men) appear comparable in Europe, Latin America, Australia, New Zealand, and North America (Gorey & Leslie, 1997).

The relationship between victimization and suicide is likely mediated by the level of depression. Although posttraumatic stress disorder (PTSD) is the psychiatric disorder most commonly associated with exposure to traumatic incidents, a number of studies have demonstrated that major depression is even more prevalent among trauma survivors (Gold, 2004). For example, childhood trauma has been found to predict the onset of major depression (DeMarco, 2000). In many studies, depression and PTSD co-occur, providing a likely pathway to suicidal phenomena.

PTSD and depression are not the only comorbid psychiatric disorders that co-occur with suicidal ideation and suicidal behaviors, however. In fact, individuals with comorbid psychiatric disorders are identified in 70% to 80% of all completed suicides. Mood disorders, anxiety disorders, personality disorders, dissociative identity disorder, and substance abuse disorders have all been found to be related to suicidal behaviors (Herman, 1997; Kessler, 2000; Kluft, 1996; Linehan, 1997; Rudd, Dahm, & Rajab, 1993). Moreover, PTSD often co-occurs with these various psychiatric comorbid disorders. As Ullmann and Brecklin (2002) reported, the combination of stressful life events, depression, and substance abuse disorder increased the likelihood of suicide in a national sample of women who have a history of having been sexually assaulted.

If the risk of suicide is particularly high among people who have been victimized and who have posttraumatic stress disorder and depression, what accounts for this relationship and what are the implications for treatment? Perhaps another way to frame this question is to consider how one might "make" a chronic PTSD patient. If a victimizing "bad" experience happened to you or to a loved one, such as the terrorist events of September 11, 2001, or some other victimizing experience during childhood, consider what you would have to do and think, or *not* do and *not* think, to develop chronic, persistent, intractable PTSD and related psychiatric difficulties, including self-injurious behaviors. If we can figure out the formula that contributes to PTSD, depression, and accompanying suicidal behaviors, then we can consider the treatment implications.

Some hints as to "how to make" an individual with chronic PTSD come from the burgeoning literature on cognitions and PTSD (Brewin & Holmes, 2003; Dalgleish, 2004; Ehlers & Clark, 2000; Meichenbaum, 1994, 2002; Meichenbaum & Fitzpatrick, 1993; Meichenbaum & Fong, 1993). This literature highlights that an individual's maladaptive appraisals of the trauma and its aftermath and the accompanying "catastrophic" cognitive style predict later PTSD. The individual's exaggerated probability of future negative consequences occurring and the adverse effects of these events are prognostic indicators of chronicity of PTSD and adaptive difficulties (Ehlers, Mayou, & Bryant, 1998; Engelhard, van den Hout, Arntz, & McNally, 2002). When this negative cognitive style is further accompanied by feelings of anger, shame, guilt, and hopelessness, then PTSD is more likely to occur (Andrews, Brewin, Rose, & Kirk, 2000). The presence of an avoidant cognitive style that results in impaired processing of trauma-related memories and the failure to recall positive coping memories result in more persistent chronic disorders (Harvey & Bryant, 1999). The persistence of such adaptive difficulties is further exacerbated by complicated grief reactions, especially when a loved one has died a violent death (Gray, Prigerson, & Litz, 2004). Exhibit 15.1 summarizes these findings in the form of a formula (the "Dirty Dozen") for the development of chronic, persistent PTSD and accompanying adaptive difficulties.

An analysis of the research literature suggests that victimized individuals *construct an emotionally charged narrative* to make sense of what happened and in an attempt to adjust to the losses that accompany victimization. Thomas (2003) characterized this narrative as a form of "inner conversations," in

EXHIBIT 15.1
A Formula for Chronic, Persistent Posttraumatic Stress Disorder (PTSD)

1. Experience PTSD and comorbid psychiatric disorders, especially depression.
2. Selectively focus on ongoing threats and vulnerability.
3. Engage in maladaptive appraisals of trauma and its aftermath.
4. Engage in "catastrophic" thinking.
5. Exaggerate the probability of future negative consequences occurring and the adverse effects of these events.
6. Ruminate about the ongoing negative implications of the trauma experience.
7. Suppress feelings and thoughts of the traumatic event.
8. Engage in cognitive and behavioral avoidance and safety behaviors that impair the processing of trauma-related memories and that maintain the condition. Fail to become socially reengaged.
9. Fail to recall positive coping memories or what one did to "survive" or what one was able to accomplish "in spite of" victimization.
10. Have accompanying unresolved feelings of anger, shame, guilt, humiliation, frustration, being slighted, and being abandoned.
11. Experience complicated grief and fail to engage in "grief work" that honors loved ones who were lost.
12. Encounter or inadvertently create a stressful environment that is unsupportive and that dismisses (fails to validate) and rejects (offers "moving on" statements) and that secondarily revictimizes.

the tradition of the social psychologist George Herbert Mead, who highlighted the manner in which individuals carry on "inner conversations" with themselves. Exactly what is the likely content of the victimized individual's narrative or the nature of his or her "inner conversations"?

In other words, if something traumatic happened to you, what would you have to say to yourself and to others, what would you have to do and *not* do to develop chronic PTSD that would increase your likelihood of engaging in suicidal behaviors?

As summarized in Exhibit 15.2 and in Appendix 15.1, it is proposed that for individuals to develop persistent PTSD, they need to

1. engage in conversations with themselves and with others that selectively focus on ongoing threats and vulnerabilities;
2. suppress feelings and thoughts about the traumatic events and engage in avoidance and safety behaviors that inadvertently maintain and exacerbate their condition;
3. ruminate about the continuing negative implications of trauma exposure; and
4. encounter a social environment that is unsupportive, rejecting, dismissive, and perhaps revictimizing.

When these "inner conversations" and behaviors that maintain and exacerbate persistent PTSD are accompanied by feelings of helplessness and hopelessness (e.g., "I feel trapped." "I can't handle it anymore." "It's too hard to keep going." "I'll never get over this." "I have to escape the pain."), the

EXHIBIT 15.2
What You Need to Do (and Not Do) to Develop Persistent Posttraumatic Stress Disorder (PTSD): A Constructive Narrative Perspective

Engage in self-focused cognitions that have a "victim" theme
1. See self as being continually vulnerable.
2. See self as being mentally defeated.
3. Dwell on negative implications.
4. Be preoccupied with others' views.
5. Imagine and ruminate about what might have happened ("near miss experience").

Hold beliefs
1. Changes are permanent.
2. World is unsafe, unpredictable, untrustworthy.
3. Hold a negative view of the future.
4. Life has lost its meaning.

Blame
1. Others with accompanying anger.
2. Self with accompanying guilt, shame, humiliation.

Engage in comparisons
1. Self versus others.
2. Before versus now.
3. Now versus what might have been.

Things to do
1. Be continually hypervigilant.
2. Be avoidant—cognitive level: suppress unwanted thoughts, dissociate, engage in "undoing" behaviors.
3. Be avoidant—behavioral level: avoid reminders, use substances, withdraw, abandon normal routines, engage in avoidant safety behaviors.
4. Ruminate and engage in contra-factual thinking.
5. Engage in delaying change behaviors.
6. Fail to resolve and share trauma story ("keep secrets").
7. Put self at risk for revictimization.

What *not* to do
1. Not believe that anything positive could result from trauma experience.
2. Fail to retrieve or accept data of positive self-identity.
3. Fail to seek social support.
4. Experience negative, unsupportive environments (indifference, criticism, "moving on" statements).
5. Fail to use faith and religion as a means of coping.

risk of suicide is increased by some 20% to 60%, depending on the form of abuse and victimization (Meichenbaum, 1994; Rudd, Joiner, & Rajab, 2002). The cumulative impact of engaging in such "inner conversations" and constructing such a narrative is that the effects of the trauma and the accompanying loss are seen as unending, unrelenting, inevitable, and intolerable. Suicide may be viewed as the only means of escape.

Let us now turn to the implications of this constructive narrative perspective for treatment and prevention.

EXHIBIT 15.3

Treatment Implications and Procedures of a Constructive Narrative
Perspective of Persistent Posttraumatic Stress Disorder (PTSD)

1. Develop a supportive, empowering *therapeutic alliance.*
2. Conduct *assessment interview* and use related measures.
3. Provide *rationale* for treatment plan.
4. Ensure *patients' safety* and *address disturbing symptoms.*
5. *Educate* patients and significant others.
6. Teach specific *coping skills* and *build in generalization-enhancing procedures.*
7. Help patients *change beliefs about implications* of experiencing PTSD and associated symptoms.
8. Reconsider *anything positive* that resulted from the experience.
9. Address issues of *guilt, shame, humiliation, anger.*
10. *"Uncouple"* traumatic memories from disabling affect.
11. Help patients *put into words* (or some other form of expression) what happened.
12. Process and *transform emotional pain*—help patients find meaning and make a "gift" of their experience to others.
13. Help patients *distinguish* "then and there" from "here and now," not overgeneralize danger.
14. Help patients *retell their stories* and share the *"rest of their stories."* Retrieve "positive identities." (Use imaginal reliving procedures.)
15. Help patients *spot triggers* and *reduce unhelpful avoidant safety behaviors.*
16. Have patients engage in *graduated in vivo behavioral experiments.*
17. Help patients *Reclaim* their lives and former selves.
18. Ensure patients *take credit* for changes—self-attributional efforts and self-mastery.
19. Help patients avoid *revictimization.*
20. Build in *relapse prevention procedures.*
21. Put patients in a *"consultative"* role in which they describe and discuss what they learned and what they can teach others.

IMPLICATIONS FOR TREATMENT FROM A CONSTRUCTIVE NARRATIVE PERSPECTIVE

To help patients to (a) "refashion" their narratives so they are more coherent and growth promoting; (b) reduce their emotional reactivity and increase their tolerance for trauma-related memories, emotions, and reminders; (c) become more "in charge" of how they use traumatic material; (d) selectively share experiences with supportive others to overcome any sense of estrangement, self-consciousness, and feelings of shame and guilt, the following treatment steps (summarized in Exhibit 15.3) are proposed.

1. The therapist needs to create and maintain a supportive, compassionate, caring, genuine, empathic, nonjudgmental, empowering *therapeutic alliance* so that patients feel both safe and comfortable to share the details and impact of their exposure to traumatic experiences. The therapist needs to provide a setting in which the patients can practice telling and retelling their stories with full intensity at their own pace. The

therapist needs to continually monitor the quality of the alliance over the course of therapy.

2. The therapist needs to conduct an *assessment interview* to determine the nature of patients' memories for traumatic events and their appraisal processes of their feelings, actions, symptoms, and the accompanying implications. Ehlers and Clark (2000) observed that the initial narrative accounts of individuals who have been victimized tend to be journalistic in nature—that is, brief, skeletal, fact-oriented, and without much emotional depth. In a safe therapeutic environment, patients can come to tell and retell their stories. As part of the assessment process, the therapist needs to ensure that patients also tell "the rest of the story" of what they did to survive and how they coped both with the traumatic events and the aftermath. As a result of the therapy process, patients need to appreciate that trauma is only one part of their lives, rather than the defining aspect.

    More specifically, the therapist needs to determine the following:

    - Are the patients' memories muddled and confused, fragmentary and disjointed, with memory gaps?
    - Do the patients' memories of traumatic events have a "here and now" quality primed with sensory and motoric features that are distressing?
    - What are patients' "hot spots" (worst moments, most painful memories)?
    - What are patients' beliefs and expectations (implications) of experiencing their distressing symptoms and their aftermath?
    - What are the patients' coping efforts? Are patients inadvertently making the situation worse and contributing to persistent PTSD?
    - What is most distressing since the traumatic event and how have the patients coped with this (e.g., addressing issues of secondary victimization)?

3. The therapist needs to provide patients with a *rationale for the treatment* and solicit patient feedback. For example, the therapist can use metaphors—disorganized cupboard or puzzle that needs rearranging, a wound that needs care, and so forth—to convey the need to reorganize and reframe traumatic memories. Creating a trauma narrative alone is not sufficient to improve psychological or physical health, but it is also essential to *integrate* thoughts and feelings about the traumatic events into a consistent and meaningful experience.

4. The therapist needs to ensure that patients are *safe* from the risk of further victimization and that any immediate disturb-

ing symptoms (e.g., hyperarousal, nightmares, dissociative and suicidal behaviors) are addressed.

5. The therapist needs to *educate* patients (and significant others) about the nature and impact of trauma and about the reactions (symptoms) that are the hallmark of the condition. Help patients better understand the distinctive characteristics of traumatic memories and the role of "triggers" and help patients reframe PTSD symptoms and accompanying comorbid sequelae as the "wisdom of the body," "survival behaviors," and as "coping efforts." Patients may be "stuck" using coping techniques such as dissociation that worked in the past but are overgeneralized now. There is also a need to educate patients about any myths concerning the trauma experience (e.g., about rape, child sexual abuse) and incorporate corrective information into traumatic memories.

6. *Teach specific coping skills* to deal with hyperarousal, intrusive ideation, dissociative behaviors, avoidance behaviors, and the like. The therapist needs to follow generalization guidelines when teaching coping skills such as acceptance and tolerance, self-regulation, problem solving, and the like (see Meichenbaum, 2002)

7. The therapist needs to help patients *change their problematic beliefs* about the implications of experiencing PTSD and associated symptoms. This involves helping to validate and normalize the patients' reactions and help them accept, tolerate, and cope with intense emotions, and using situational and developmental analyses to help patients better appreciate their adaptive efforts and their survival attempts. Collaboratively, the therapist and patient should examine the "impact," "toll," and "emotional price" of using these specific forms of coping and what more adaptive ways could be used. Finally, the therapist should engage patients in self-monitoring activities to increase early awareness of triggers and distressing symptoms to reduce the influence on daily activities.

8. The therapist needs to help patients reconsider whether *anything "positive"* could have resulted from the trauma experience and, moreover, to reflect on what they have done to "cope." The therapist should highlight data of "strengths" and "resilience" or what patients have been able to accomplish "in spite of" the trauma and work with patients so that they accept such data as "evidence" to unfreeze their beliefs about themselves, the world, and the future.

9. The therapist needs to help patients *alter patients' sense of responsibility, guilt, shame, and humiliation* that may accompany

victimization experience. There is a need to attend to feelings and beliefs maintaining shame, guilt, and anger, in addition to fear and anxiety (see Kubany & Manke, 1995; Smucker, Grunet, & Weis, 2003).

10. In a related fashion, help patients *"uncouple" traumatic memories from disabling affect and maladaptive behaviors* and educate patients on how their current behaviors such as ruminations, self-hatred, self-berating, avoidance, thought suppression, use of substances, persistent anger, and the like, inadvertently make the situation worse. Help patients appreciate the "If– then rules" that they implicitly hold that contribute to the maintenance of maladaptive behaviors (e.g., "If I talk about the traumatic events, I will lose total control"). Help patients access these beliefs and then test them, both in the therapy session and in vivo by means of gradual exposure and approximation. Help patients learn ways to break the "vicious cycle" of appraisals, feelings, thoughts, behaviors, and resultant consequences.

11. The therapist needs to help patients in a culturally sensitive fashion to *put into words,* or into some other form of expression, what happened and its impact and the implications. A number of therapeutic procedures have been developed to achieve this goal, including cognitive rescripting procedures as per Resick and Schnicke (1993); direct therapy exposure as per Foa and Rothbaum (1998); and imagery rescripting as per Smucker and Niederee (1995). By doing so, patients can contextualize their memories, develop useful insights, identify and discuss hot spots, begin to develop a sense of control, and learn that they can survive, not fall apart, nor "go crazy," in the retelling of the trauma experience.

12. The therapist needs to help patients organize, elaborate, integrate, and *process their traumatic memories* into a coherent narrative that fosters a sense of meaning and nurtures hope. Help patients fit their "trauma narratives" into their broader life histories, so that the traumatic events become part of their general life perspective, namely, "a slice of life" and not the whole story. Help patients come to terms with the losses and transform their emotional pain into something positive that can come from their experiences. Help patients find meaning, make a "gift" of their experiences, and use "spiritual" and religious practices, if congruent with their beliefs.

13. The therapist needs to help patients *change their beliefs about current and ongoing threats,* learning to discriminate between "then and there" and "here and now"; not overgeneralize the

degree of ongoing threat and danger. Help patients view trauma as a discrete, time-limited event that is not indicative of the world being globally threatening.

14. The therapist needs to help patients *retell their stories* by means of imaginal reliving, including their thoughts, feelings, and behaviors, as well as the reactions of others, and consider any accompanying problematic beliefs (see Smucker et al., 2003). Have patients consider how the traumatic events challenged their cherished beliefs of invulnerability, of a just and trusting world and a sense of self-worth. Where indicated, address the patients' feelings of abandonment, estrangement, inadequacy, and despair. Ask about the "rest of the story" of survival skills and strengths. Help patients retrieve and accept "positive identities."

15. The therapist needs to help patients *spot triggers* (both internal and external) and develop more adaptive coping behaviors and come to recognize that their so-called safety avoidant behaviors may inadvertently contribute to persistent PTSD. Assist patients in reducing unhelpful behavioral and cognitive strategies (e.g., use of substances to escape emotional pain; avoidant behaviors to control rage). Help them reclaim their lives and assume normal behavioral routines.

16. The therapist needs to help patients engage in *in vivo exposure and personal behavioral experiments* in a graduated fashion to test out their beliefs. Help patients emotionally accept that the traumatic event is in the past. Help patients examine their "What if . . . " thinking should possible events occur and "What is the worst thing that could happen?" The therapist helps patients put these thoughts in the form of predictions that are testable and learn how to use other cognitive restructuring procedures. Ensure that the patients have coping skills, plans, and backup plans to undertake personal experiments (often with the initial assistance of others).

17. The therapist needs to help patients *"reclaim" their lives and former selves*. Help patients connect with strengths, use social supports, help others, and reintegrate into their communities. The therapist should foster a "sense of possibilities" and the therapist can use the "language of becoming" that further nurtures hope.

18. The therapist needs to ensure that patients *"take credit" for changes that they have achieved*. The therapist needs to ask "what" and "how" questions and help patients develop a sense of personal efficacy and agency and enhance feelings of self-mastery.

19. The therapist needs to ensure that patients have skills to *avoid revictimization* experiences. Consider lessons learned and develop behavioral and interpersonal strategies to control perceived threats and reduce the risk of revictimization.
20. The therapist needs to build into the treatment regimen *relapse prevention procedures* (i.e., ways to anticipate and cope with possible lapses and anniversary effects).
21. The therapist needs to put patients in a *"consultative role"* so that they have an opportunity to describe and discuss what they have learned and how they specifically plan to implement what they have learned, even in the face of potential barriers and obstacles. Help patients get to the point where they could now teach others what they have learned. Revisit the collaboratively generated therapeutic goal statements and examine how patients have been able to achieve these goals and what is the "unfinished business" (e.g., use a personal journey metaphor).

These treatment steps, especially when combined with the assessment and therapeutic suggestions offered by Bongar (2002); Ellis and Newman (1996); Joiner, Walker, Rudd, and Jobes (1998); Linehan (1997, 1999); Meichenbaum (1994); Rudd and Joiner (1998); and M. D. Rudd et al. (2002), provide the clinician with the tools to address the needs of traumatized suicidal patients. Elsewhere (Meichenbaum, 2005), I have discussed standards of care for suicidal patients.

After some 40 years of clinical experience, I have a sense that I more fully understand the pathway from trauma exposure to suicidal behavior. A constructive narrative perspective that focuses on the emotionally laden "conversations" that victimized individuals have with themselves and with others and the accompanying behavioral scripts they engage provides a useful conceptualization. The practical implications of the constructive narrative perspective are summarized in Exhibit 15.3. The implementation of these therapeutic guidelines gives hope that future chapters of my story will have happy endings.

APPENDIX 15.1:
A CONSTRUCTIVE NARRATIVE PERSPECTIVE ON CHRONIC POSTTRAUMATIC STRESS DISORDER (PTSD)

For a victimized individual to develop chronic and persistent PTSD that increases the likelihood of suicide ideation and suicidal behavior, he or she would have to engage in the following self-talk and talk to others, and do the following behaviors:

Engage in self-focused cognitions that have a "victim" theme.

1. See oneself (and significant others) as *victim(s), permanently changed.* Representative statements:

   "I feel trapped by time—a prisoner of the past."

   "I am stuck in the past."

   "I can't shake the memory."

   "I'm soiled goods."

   "My body is ruined."

2. See oneself as being *mentally defeated* (feeling a loss of psychological autonomy) and experience the emotional pain as *intolerable.* Representative statements:

   "I don't feel human anymore."

   "I'm detached—like a spectator watching my life go by."

   "I have no control over anything."

   "I am in a state of continual confusion."

   "The emotional pain is unbearable. I can't stand it any longer."

3. Dwell on the negative implications of reactions (symptoms) resulting from exposure to traumatic events. See symptoms as signs of emotional and moral weakness. Representative statements:

   "This is not normal. I can't control my reactions."

   "I am just going downhill."

   "If I react like that, I am unstable. I'm going mad."

   "I am on a psychic tightrope and a psychological wreck."

   "I shut down emotionally. I am brain dead."

4. Be *preoccupied* that others will view oneself (and significant others) as "victims," "flawed," "permanently damaged." Representative statements:

   "Others can see I am a victim."

   "Others are ashamed of me now."

   "They think I'm too weak to cope on my own."

   "I am changed in a fundamental way."

Hold specific beliefs regarding trauma and the world.

5. Believe that trauma has brought about a *negative* and *permanent* change in the self and reduced the likelihood of achieving life's goals. Representative statements:

   "I deserve the bad things that happen to me."

   "I'll never be able to relate to people again."

   "I am undeserving of respect and undesirable to everyone."

   "I am too weak (incapable, ineffective, unable, helpless) to protect myself (my loved ones)."

> "I am a walking target."

6. Believe that the world is unsafe and unpredictable and that people are untrustworthy. Representative statements:
> "Nowhere is safe. The world is an extremely dangerous place."
> "I can't trust my own instincts anymore."
> "I can't rely on other people."
> "All men are alike. You can't trust them."
> "I don't want the other kids out of my sight."

7. Reflect a *negative view* of the *future* and have low expectations that things will (or can) change or improve (magnify the probability of future negative events). Representative statements:
> "I am very, very anxious about the future."
> "The worst is yet to come."
> "There is no hope."
> "I'm doomed!"
> "I'm futureless."

8. Maintain that life has lost or has little or no *meaning* (existential and spiritual despair). Representative statements:
> "Life is pointless."
> "My life's goals are no longer important."
> "Our life now has a dark cloud over it."
> "My life is destroyed."
> "I lost my faith in God. How could He allow this tragedy to happen?"
> "I don't care if I live or die. Nothing matters!"
> "Others will be better off without me."

Engage in extrapunitive narrative plotting.

9. Focus on others who are *blameworthy*, with accompanying anger and preoccupation with revenge, leading to slower recovery from PTSD (Cahill, Rauch, Hembree, & Foa, 2003; Delahanty et al., 1997). Representative statements:
> "I have been betrayed."
> "I will get even, even if it is the last thing I do."
> "I won't rest until there is justice."
> "My anger is palpable."
> "I am furious with God for letting this happen."

10. Focus on *blaming oneself* with accompanying guilt, shame, and humiliation. (In victims of violent crime, *shame* is a predictor of later PTSD.) (Andrews et al., 2000; Resick & Schninke, 1993.)
> "I failed to protect her."

"Think of the lowest thing in the world and whatever it is, I am lower."

"I am a gullible person, so weak and stupid."

"I am deserving of this pain. What do you pay when someone dies because of you? You pay with your own life."

"People will wonder what kind of family we are because we allowed this to happen."

"I don't deserve to live."

Engage in unfavorable negative comparisons.

11. Continually *compare self to others*. Representative statements:

    "I should be over this by now. Look at her."

    "How did she recover without any help, yet I need as much help as I can get?"

    "I blame myself for not being able to get back to normal."

12. Ruminate about how life was *before* the traumatic events versus how things are *now*. Maintain a rose-colored view of the past.

    "I can't connect with my former self."

    "Life will never be the same again."

    "I just keep wishing that life would go back to the way it was last year."

13. Ruminate about how life is now versus how life might have been if the traumatic events had *not occurred*.

    "I will never have grandchildren."

    "My child will never know his father."

    "The little boys will forget what she was like."

    "Where would she be now?"

    "Her friends have gone on with their lives."

14. Imagine and ruminate about what traumatic event *might have* occurred—continually reflect on a "near-miss experience" and what this portends for the future.

    "I keep wondering what they could have done to us. They are still out there."

    "Do you have any idea how close we were to X?"

    "It could have been us."

    "I can't get out of my mind how she must have suffered."

Engage in cognitive and behavioral trauma-maintaining activities (what to do to maintain persistent PTSD).

15. Be continually *hypervigilant* (readily triggered by reminders) and engage in *safety behaviors* even when unwarranted (e.g.,

always sit by the exit, carry a gun, etc.). Representative statements:

> "I have to be on the lookout all the time."
>
> "I stopped my normal routine. I have to check all the time."
>
> "I can't be around anything that reminds me of what happened."
>
> "Those reminders open old wounds."
>
> "My emotional alarm clock goes off when I least expect it to."

16. Engage in *deliberate avoidant behaviors* at the *cognitive level,* such as suppressing unwanted thoughts, dissociation, and engage in "undoing" behaviors. Representative statements:

> "I avoid thinking about it."
>
> "I try to push it out of mind, not think about it, but it doesn't work."
>
> "Maybe it wasn't rape? He didn't have a weapon, and he didn't physically harm me."
>
> "I keep imagining ways I could have defended myself."

17. Engage in *avoidant behaviors* such as avoidance of trauma reminders, use of alcohol or drugs to control anxiety, social withdrawal from others, abandonment of normal activities, and the adoption of safety behaviors that prevent or minimize exposure to trauma-related reminders and negative outcomes. Representative statements:

> "I keep busy (use distractions) so I don't have to think or feel."
>
> "I have to stay away from everyone or I will lose control."
>
> "I have become a social pariah."
>
> "I self-medicate."
>
> "I drink my pain away. It is the only way I can escape."

18. Engage in *rumination* and *contra-factual thinking* or *"what if"* *thinking.* Replay over and over again how this could have been prevented. Representative statements:

> "Only if . . . " "If only I had . . . "
>
> "Why me?" "Why did this have to happen to my loved one?" "Why now?"
>
> "If I do X, then Y will happen." "If I don't do X, then Z will happen."

19. Engage in *delaying change behaviors.* Representative statements:

> "I will change only when . . . "
>
> "Once I get (do) . . . I will then begin to . . . "
>
> "Once the insurance funds come in I will begin . . . "

20. *Fail to share and resolve traumatic account.* Fail to self-disclose and fail to seek social supports. Rather, keep the traumatic event a "secret," do not work through the event, fail to resolve, so the "story" remains fragmentary, disjointed, disconnected from the past, poorly elaborated and disorganized. As Ehlers and Clark (2000) observed, such traumatic memories are subject to "perceptual priming," mainly sensory and motoric aspects in which the worst moments stand out. Traumatic memories are poorly elaborated and poorly integrated into existing autobiographical memories (see Iqbal and Birchwood, chap. 14, this volume; Williams et al., chap. 8, this volume). Representative statements:

> "I can't share what happened with anyone. They won't understand."
> "I am sick of my secrets."
> "There is no closure."
> "I have difficulty making sense of what happened."
> "I feel like I can't let go of the memory."
> "There is no beginning, middle, and especially, no end in sight."

21. Put self at continuing *risk for revictimization* (Logan, Walker, Cole, & Leukefeld, 2002).

What not to do to maintain persistent PTSD.

22. Do not believe that anything positive will come from this traumatic event nor that one can become "strengthened" as a result of trauma experience.

23. Fail to retrieve any data of prior mastery experiences or signs of resilience. When such instances are pointed out, dismiss such "positive" data and do not take the data as "evidence" to unfreeze "negative" beliefs about self, the world, or the future.

24. Fail to seek social supports. Feel abandoned, alienated, and alone.

25. Encounter a negative social unsupportive environment of indifference, criticism, and "moving on" statements. (This is particularly true for women. See Tarrier & Humphreys, 2003.)

26. Do not understand or appreciate the role of one's faith or religion as a means of coping.

REFERENCES

Andrews, B., Brewin, C. R., Rose, S., & Kirk, M. (2000). Predicting PTSD in victims of violent crime: The role of shame, anger and blame. *Journal of Abnormal Psychology, 109,* 69–73.

Bongar, B. (2002). *The suicidal patient: Clinical and legal standards of care* (2nd ed.). Washington, DC: American Psychological Association.

Brewin, C. R., & Holmes, E. A. (2003). Psychological theories of posttraumatic stress disorder. *Clinical Psychology Review, 23*, 339–376.

Brown, L. S. (1995). Posttraumatic stress disorder among inner city methadone maintenance patients. *Journal of Substance Abuse Treatment, 12*, 253–257.

Cahill, S. P., Rauch, S. A., Hembree, E. A., & Foa, E. B. (2003). Effects of cognitive–behavioral treatment for PTSD on anger. *Journal of Cognitive Psychotherapy, 17*, 113–131.

Dalgleish, T. (2004). Cognitive approaches to posttraumatic stress disorder: The evolution of multirepresentational theorizing. *Psychological Bulletin, 130*, 228–260.

Delahanty, D. L., Herberman, H. B., Craig, K. J., Hayward, M. C., Fullerton, C. S., Ursano, R. J., & Baum, A. (1997). Acute and chronic distress and posttraumatic stress disorder as a function of responsibility for serious motor vehicle accidents. *Journal of Consulting and Clinical Psychology, 65*, 560–567.

DeMarco, R. R. (2000). The epidemiology of major depression: Implication of occurrence, recurrence and stress in a Canadian community sample. *Canadian Journal of Psychiatry, 92*, 214–219.

Ehlers, A., & Clark, D. M. (2000). A cognitive model of posttraumatic stress disorder. *Behavior Research and Therapy, 38*, 319–345.

Ehlers, A., Mayou, R. A., & Bryant, B. (1998). Psychological predictors of chronic PTSD after motor vehicle accidents. *Journal of Abnormal Psychology, 107*, 508–519.

Ellis, T. E., & Newman, C. F. (1996). *Choosing to live: How to defeat suicide through cognitive therapy*. Oakland, CA: New Harbinger.

Engelhard, I. M., van den Hout, M. A., Arntz, A., & McNally, R. J. (2002). A longitudinal study of "intrusion-based reasoning" and posttraumatic stress disorder disaster. *Behaviour Research and Therapy, 40*, 1415–1424.

Evans, E., Hawton, K., & Rodhan, K. (2004). Factors associated with suicidal phenomenon in adolescents: A systematic review of population-based studies. *Clinical Psychology Review, 24*, 957–979.

Ferruda-Noli, M. (1996). Cultural bias in suicidal behavior among refugees with posttraumatic stress disorder. *Nordic Journal of Psychiatry, 50*, 185–191.

Ferruda-Noli, M., Asberg, M., Ormstad, K., Lundin, T., & Sandborn, E. (1998). Suicidal behavior after severe trauma. Part I. PTSD diagnosis, psychiatric comorbidity and assessments of suicidal behavior. *Journal of Traumatic Stress, 11*, 103–112.

Foa, E. B., & Rothbaum, B. O. (1998). *Treating the trauma of rape: Cognitive behavioral therapy for PTSD*. New York: Guilford Press.

Gold, S. N. (2004). The relevance of trauma to general clinical practice. *Psychotherapy: Theory, Research and Practice, 41*, 363–373.

Gorey, K. M., & Leslie, D. R. (1997). The prevalence of child sexual abuse: Integrative review and adjustment for potential response and measurement biases. *Child Abuse and Neglect, 21,* 391–398.

Gray, M. J., Prigerson, M. G., & Litz, B. T. (2004). Conceptual and definitional issues in complicated grief. In B. T. Litz (Ed.), *Early intervention for trauma and traumatic loss* (pp. 65–86). New York: Guilford Press.

Harvey, A. G., & Bryant, R. A. (1999). A two-year prospective evaluation of the relationship between acute stress disorder and posttraumatic stress disorder. *Journal of Consulting and Clinical Psychology, 67,* 985–988.

Hendin, H. (1992). PTSD and risk of suicide. *American Journal of Psychiatry, 149,* 143.

Hendin, H., & Haas, A. P. (1991). Suicide and guilt as manifestations of PTSD: Vietnam combat veterans. *American Journal of Psychiatry, 148,* 586–591.

Herman, J. (1997). *Trauma and recovery* (2nd ed.). New York: Basic Books.

Joiner, T. E., Walker, R. L., Rudd, M. D., & Jobes, D. A. (1998). Scientizing and routinizing the assessment of suicidality in outpatient practice. *Professional Psychology: Research and Practice, 30,* 447–453.

Kessler, B. C. (2000). Posttraumatic stress disorder: The burden to the individual and to society. *Journal of Clinical Psychiatry, 61,* 4–14.

Kilpatrick, D. G., Best, C. L., Veronen, L. J., Amick, A. E., Villeponteaux, L. A., & Ruff, G. A. (1985). Mental health correlates of criminal victimization: A random community survey. *Journal of Consulting and Clinical Psychology, 53,* 866–873.

Kingree, J. B. (2000). Childhood maltreatment, PTSD and suicidal behavior among African American females. *Journal of Interpersonal Violence, 15,* 3–15.

Kleespies, P. M., & Dettmer, E. L. (2000). An evidence-based approach to evaluating and managing suicidal emergencies. *Journal of Clinical Psychology, 56,* 1109–1130.

Kluft, R. P. (1996). Dissociative identity disorder. In K. L. Michelson & J. Ray (Eds.), *Handbook of dissociation: Theoretical empirical and clinical perspectives* (pp. 337–366). New York: Plenum Press.

Kubany, E. C., & Manke, F. P. (1995). Cognitive therapy for trauma-related guilt: Conceptual bases and treatment outcomes. *Cognitive and Behavioral Practice, 1,* 27–62.

Lindy, J. D., Green, B. L., & Grace, M. C. (1994). The comorbidity of posttraumatic stress disorder and suicidality in Vietnam veterans. *Suicide and Life-Threatening Behavior, 24,* 58–67.

Linehan, M. M. (1997). Behavioral treatment of suicidal behaviors. In D. M. Stoff & J. J. Mann (Eds.), *The neurobiology of suicidal behavior* (pp. 302–328). New York: Annals of the New York Academy of Sciences.

Linehan, M. M. (1999). Standard protocol for assessing and treating suicidal behaviors for patients in treatment. In D. G. Jacobs (Ed.), *The Harvard Medical School guide to suicide assessment and intervention* (pp. 146–187). San Francisco: Jossey-Bass.

Logan, T. K., Walker, R., Cole, J., & Leukefeld, C. (2002). Victimization and substance abuse among women: Contributing factors, interventions and implication. *Review of General Psychology, 6,* 325–397.

Meichenbaum, D. (1994). *Treating post-traumatic stress disorder: A handbook and practice manual for therapy.* Chichester, England: Wiley.

Meichenbaum, D. (2002). *Treatment of individuals with anger-control problems and aggressive behaviors: A clinical handbook.* Clearwater, FL: Institute Press.

Meichenbaum, D. (2005). 30 years of working with suicidal patients: Lessons learned. *Canadian Psychologist, 46,* 64–72.

Meichenbaum, D., & Fitzpatrick, D. (1993). A constructive narrative perspective on stress and coping: Stress inoculation application. In L. Goldberger & S. Breznitz (Eds.), *Handbook of stress: Theoretical and clinical aspects* (2nd ed.). New York Free Press.

Meichenbaum, D., & Fong, G. (1993). How individuals control their own minds: A constructive narrative perspective. In D. M. Wegner & J. W. Pennebaker (Eds.), *Handbook of mental control* (pp. 473–490). New York: Prentice Hall.

National Research Council. (1993). *Understanding child abuse and neglect.* Washington, DC: National Academy Press.

Resick, P. A., & Schnicke, M. K. (1993). *Cognitive processing therapy for rape victims: A treatment manual.* Newbury Park, CA: Sage.

Rudd, M. D., Dahm, P. F., & Rajab, H. M. (1993). Diagnostic comorbidity in persons with suicidal ideation and behavior. *American Journal of Psychiatry, 150,* 928–934.

Rudd, M. D., & Joiner, T. E. (1998). The assessment, management, and treatment of suicidality: Towards clinically informed and balanced standards of care. *Clinical Psychology: Science and Practice, 5,* 135–150.

Rudd, M. D., Joiner, T. E., & Rajab, M. H. (2002). *A time-limited approach to treating suicidal behavior.* New York: Guilford Press.

Smucker, M. P., Grunet, B. K., & Weis, J. M. (2003). Posttraumatic stress disorder: A new algorithm treatment model. In R. L. Leahy (Ed.), *Overcoming roadblocks in cognitive therapy practice* (pp. 175–194). New York: Guilford Press.

Smucker, M. R., & Niederee, J. (1995). Treating incest-related PTSD and pathogenic schemas through imaginal exposure and rescripting. *Cognitive and Behavioral Practice, 1,* 63–92.

Tarrier, N., & Humphreys, A. L. (2003). PTSD and the social support of the interpersonal environment: The development of social cognitive behavior therapy. *Journal of Cognitive Psychotherapy, 17,* 187–198.

Thomas, P. M. (2003). Protection, dissociation, and internal roles: Modeling and treating effects of child abuse. *Review of General Psychology, 7,* 364–380.

Thompson, M. P., Kaslow, N., Kingree, J. B., Puett, R., & Thompson, N. J. (1999). Partner abuse and posttraumatic stress disorder as risk factors for suicide attempts in a sample of low-income, inner-city women. *Journal of Traumatic Stress*, *12*, 59–72.

Ullman, S. E., & Brecklin, L. R. (2002). Sexual assault history and suicidal behavior in a national sample of women. *Suicide and Life-Threatening Behavior*, *32*, 117–130.

Young, B., & Clum, G. A. (1996). Effects of early negative experiences on cognitive functioning and risk for suicide; A review. *Clinical Psychology Review*, *16*, 177–195.

16

FLUID VULNERABILITY THEORY: A COGNITIVE APPROACH TO UNDERSTANDING THE PROCESS OF ACUTE AND CHRONIC SUICIDE RISK

M. DAVID RUDD

It is now well accepted that the assessment, management, and treatment of suicidality in clinical practice is one of the most challenging and stressful tasks for any clinician (Jobes, 1995). The literature in suicidology routinely differentiates among treatment, treatment outcome, and risk assessment (e.g., Rudd, Joiner, & Rajab, 2000), with no clear theoretical link across the three areas. Additionally, there has been limited work addressing content versus process issues in each area specific to suicide risk assessment. The current theory being offered focuses specifically on the risk assessment *process*, not treatment outcome. Furthermore, its focus is not on the specific content of risk assessment (i.e., what questions to ask across what content domains). A considerable amount is known about the *content* of risk assessment (e.g., Rudd et al., 2000). This is a fairly significant departure from the routine in suicidology, but it is one I believe to be important for a number of reasons that are emphasized in this chapter.

Empirically grounded risk assessment models have emerged over the past several years, proving to be both effective and efficient in clinical practice (e.g., Joiner, Walker, Rudd, & Jobes, 1999; Rudd et al., 2000). Most of these models have emphasized the need to evaluate and respond to identifiable risk and protective factors (e.g., Clark & Fawcett, 1992; Hirschfeld & Russell, 1997; Joiner et al., 1999). Among the more commonly targeted risk factor domains are previous suicidal behavior, current suicidal symptoms, precipitant stressors, associated clinical symptoms, impulsivity, and self-control. Protective factors have routinely included social support among family and friends and previous or current treatment involvement, along with the efficacy of previous treatment efforts. Although these assessment models have led to useful clinical heuristics, they have not been driven by coherent theory—theory characterized by clearly defined constructs that lead to specific, testable hypotheses and ultimately help advance the science of clinical suicidology. Rather, the traditional approach to risk assessment has been to categorize or otherwise organize empirically supported risk factors and apply them to clinical practice, regardless of whether there was any underlying theory that would tie findings together in a meaningful way. In some ways, this approach neglects critical process issues to risk assessment, the most important of which is an understanding of the relationship between acute suicidal states and those that endure or recur over longer periods of time. This is one area of significant need in clinical suicidology, that is, theory that is specific to the variable nature of acute suicide risk and relates it to potential enduring risk over time.

There is a host of questions that beg attention. How can the emergence, persistence, resolution, and, ultimately, reemergence of suicide risk over time for a given individual be explained? How can the clinician understand the relationship between those who only think about suicide, those who make a single attempt, and those who make multiple suicide attempts over a lifetime? What is distinctive about a single specific episode of suicidality? How does one episode relate to subsequent episodes? Does one episode set the stage for subsequent episodes? If so, what is the mechanism of action? Another way of framing these questions is to address distinctions among those with suicidal ideation, those who make a single suicide attempt, and those who make multiple attempts (e.g., Rudd, Joiner, & Rajab, 1995). In other words, how is someone who makes a single attempt different from someone who makes multiple attempts? Why do some people with suicidal ideation and some who make single attempts go on to make multiple attempts, and why do some not? An emerging literature addresses what appears to be the distinctive nature and characteristics of those with multiple attempts, and this needs to be considered and integrated into the broader risk assessment literature (e.g., Rudd et al., 1995).

In some respects, this is a new kind of theory, one specific to the process of acute and chronic suicide risk, a theory grounded in identified fundamental assumptions and tied to broader models for understanding and treating suicidality. There is little debate that a considerable number of theoretical approaches exist for understanding suicidality, including philosophical, psychiatric, psychodynamic, sociological, sociocultural, and psychological (e.g., Rudd, 2004). What seems to be missing, however, is theory that is specific to the process of risk, theory that attempts to understand and explain the parameters of suicidal crises, both the intensity and duration of a single suicidal episode and how it relates to subsequent or multiple episodes. What is needed is theory that helps with questions such as the following: How does an episode of risk emerge? How long does it last? How intense or severe is it? What's the nature or course of recovery? Is the episode related to subsequent episodes? Is there a difference in the *process* of risk for different patients? Do those who attempt suicide multiple times become suicidal under different conditions and recover more slowly than those with only a single attempt? If so, what are the characteristic features of this process? Is it possible to identify process *types*, such as short- versus long-interval subsequent attempts? Needless to say, answers to these questions would prove invaluable in day-to-day clinical decision making. These are the kinds of questions clinicians ask with increasing frequency. How long will the suicidal state last? When acute risk resolves, should I worry or does it generate vulnerability for subsequent episodes? What steps can be taken to reduce risk effectively over both the short and long term?

Recent discussions about possible warning signs for suicide helped underscore the problem in the clinical practice of risk assessment (e.g., Rudd, 2003). Ultimately, warning signs are very different from risk factors, both conceptually and in terms of immediate and longer term clinical decision making. There is a temporal aspect to warning signs that convey the notion of imminent risk—that something will happen in the next few minutes or hours. For the most part, risk factors have no identified time constraint. A quick review of the literature reveals that research tying risk factors to suicidality often do so over long periods of time, with the minimum being at least 12 months (e.g., Joiner et al., 1999) and the maximum several decades. How, then, do extant findings relate to episodes of imminent risk? This is a question of considerable importance but one with no empirical data to respond. What is needed is research that looks at risk over very brief periods of time that are of particular salience for the clinical encounter, periods of an hour, a day, or a week. What is also needed is theory to drive this new line of research, focusing on the process of risk over the short and longer term. It is probably fair to say that clinicians have a good and ever-improving idea of what questions to ask in the immediate clinical setting and what clinical markers to look for and address. Clinical practice steadily improves, as science helps identify which factors are correlated to risk. In contrast, it is difficult to say that much is known about the process of risk, that is, how long an acute episode might last for a given patient, what specific factors are associated with longer duration suicidal crises or those of greater intensity, or what patients' risk status might be when the acute episode resolves. Resolution of an acute episode certainly does not resolve long-term or chronic risk. Understanding the nature of enduring or chronic risk is of critical importance in clinical practice. Being able to recognize and respond in effective fashion to chronic risk is vital to safe and effective practice.

FLUID VULNERABILITY THEORY: FUNDAMENTAL ASSUMPTIONS

Fluid vulnerability theory (FVT) is a way to understand the process of suicide risk, over both the short and longer term. It is a theory embedded in cognitive theory and therapy and the idea of the *suicidal mode*. I have discussed the notion of the suicidal mode at length elsewhere and do not repeat all the details here, but it is important to understand that the two ideas are very much complementary and interwoven (Rudd et al., 2000). Here I provide the necessary overview of the suicidal mode to ground FVT effectively. FVT is a way of understanding the onset of episodes of risk, that is, *acute activation of the suicidal mode*. Episodes of risk can be conceptualized as suicidal states, with some identifiable aspects that remit and others that endure over time, sometimes for long periods. It helps answer questions such as why people become suicidal, how long they will stay suicidal, how severe an episode will be, and whether there is high probability for another episode. At the most fundamental level, FVT is guided by the assumption that *suicidal episodes are time limited*. That is, they do not last an indeterminant period but endure for as long as the suicidal mode is active. In other words, the characteristic features of an individual's suicidal mode (i.e., suicidal belief system, physiological–affective symptoms, and associated behaviors and motivations) provide information on which to formulate hypotheses about the following: susceptibility to an episode of suicidality, likely triggers (i.e., precipitants), duration of an episode, and potential for future episodes (i.e., risk for chronic suicidality). In short, FVT hypothesizes that the state of suicidality, the factors that triggered the episode, and those that contribute to its severity and duration are fluid in nature and duration. That is, an individual's vulnerability to suicide is variable but nonetheless identifiable and quantifiable. A patient can be suicidal on Tuesday (i.e., an activated suicidal mode) and at low risk on Wednesday if the mode is effectively deactivated.

A few quick points about the suicidal mode need to be made here to provide the necessary foundation. First, the suicidal mode has four components or domains: the suicidal belief (cognitive) system, the affective system, the physiological system, and the behavioral (motivational) system. The four systems work in synchrony when triggered by either an internal (e.g., thought, feeling, image) or external precipitant (e.g., the loss of a relationship). The possibility of internal triggering provides a means to understand biological vulnerability, but more about that later. The end result is a suicidal episode or state that is characterized by specific or *core* cognitive themes (i.e., unlovability, helplessness, poor distress tolerance, and perceived burdensomeness), acute dysphoria and related physiological arousal (i.e., Axis I symptomatology), and associated death-related behaviors. As discussed in more detail later, these themes can each be tied to specific core beliefs, underlying assumptions, and related automatic thoughts (i.e., consistent with Beck's three levels of cognition; Alford & Beck, 1997). First, however, I briefly examine the suicidal mode (the reader is referred to Rudd et al. [2000] for a full and detailed description).

Beck (1996) recently offered a refinement of his original cognitive therapy model in response to a growing body of empirical studies and theoretical discourse that highlighted a number of shortcomings in efforts to explain more complex theoretical constructs and related interactions and then experimentally validate them (e.g., Haaga, Dyck, & Ernst, 1991). The model is consistent with the axioms noted earlier and builds on the concept of schemas and simple linear schema processing in a number of important ways. The theory is built around the concept of the *mode*, the structural or organizational unit that contains schemas. Beck (1996) defined modes as "specific suborganizations within the personality organization [that] incorporate the relevant components of the basic systems of personality: cognitive (or information processing), affective, behavioral, and motivational" (p. 4). He went on to note that, consistent with the original theory, each system is composed of structures identified as *schemas* (e.g., affective schemas, cognitive schemas, behavioral schemas, and motivational schemas). Beck integrated the physiological system as separate but noted its unique and significant contribution to the overall functioning of the mode. Of particular importance to the concept of the mode is the previously noted issue of reciprocal determinism and synchrony of action. Beck (1996) described the mode as an "integrated cognitive–affective–behavioral network [that] produces a synchronous response to external demands and provides a mechanism for implementing internal dictates and goals" (p. 4).

The *cognitive system* is described as involving all aspects of information processing including selection of data, attentional process (i.e., meaning assignment and meaning making), memory, and subsequent recall. Incorporated within this system is the notion of the *cognitive triad*, integrating beliefs regarding self, others, and the future. For our discussion of the *suicidal mode*, the representative cognitive triad, along with the associated conditional assumptions, rules, and compensatory strategies, is referred to as the *suicidal belief system* (SBS). Consistent with Alford and Beck's (1997) Axiom 6, three levels of cognition are assumed, with the majority of therapeutic efforts targeting the more conscious levels. This does not negate, however, the importance of preconscious and metacognitive processing. Additionally, it provides a means of integrating research and theory on implicit learning and tacit knowledge (e.g., Dowd & Courchaine, 1996).

The *affective system* produces emotional and affective experience. Beck (1996) noted the importance of the affective system, emphasizing its role in reinforcing adaptive behavior, through the experience of both positive and negative affect (Beck, Emery, & Greenberg, 1985). This makes both conceptual and logical sense. He went on to state that negative affective experiences serve to *focus the attention* of individuals on circumstances or situational contexts that are not in our best interest or serve *to diminish [us] in some way* (1996, p. 5). As a result, a negative valence is created for that event, situation, or experience, increasing sensitivity of the mode to being triggered or activated in the future under comparable circumstances. This helps explain low threshold for activation for some suicidal patients, as well as generalization across similar but not entirely identical situations or circumstances. For multiple attempters, then, they would not only have a lower *activation threshold* but also a broader range of internal and external triggers.

Finally, the *motivational and behavioral systems* allow for autonomic activation or deactivation of the individual for response. Although Beck noted that the motivational and behavioral systems are, for the most part, automatic in activation, they can be consciously controlled under some conditions. The *physiological system* comprises the physiological symptomatology accompanying the mode. For a *threat mode*, for example, this would include autonomic arousal, along with motor and sensory system activation. This would serve to orient the individual for action such as *fight or flight*. The synchronous and simultaneous interaction of multiple systems, and potential cognitive misinterpretation during a threat mode, leads to escalation and expansion of physical symptoms (e.g., perception of threat from panic symptoms such as "*I'm having a heart attack*"). Again, each system comprises structures or *schemas* specific to that system. Accordingly, the suicidal belief system comprises beliefs or schemas within each of the identified systems (i.e., affective schemas, behavioral schemas, and motivational schemas).

In short, FVT provides a means to understand the onset of an episode of acute suicidality, how one episode relates to another, how long the episode might last, and how severe it might be across each of the four mode domains. FVT essentially explains the *process* of suicidality, that is, why some people make a suicide attempt and never experience another episode and why another might make multiple attempts that span 20 to 30 years, some with brief intervals and others with very long intervals between attempts. Consistent with Litman's (1991) notion of the *suicide zone*, FVT predicts that suicide risk is time limited, that imminent risk cannot endure beyond periods of heightened arousal (i.e., activation across all four mode domains). This is not to say that chronic suicidality does not exist; it certainly does, but it is best understood as recurrent (and discrete) periods of imminent risk rather than enduring risk over time. In addition, susceptibility to subsequent attempts can be understood as a function of vulnerability to activation of the suicidal mode or *triggering*, susceptibility that extends across all domains:

- cognitive susceptibility (to include impaired problem solving, a lack of cognitive flexibility or cognitive rigidity, cognitive distortions inherent to the suicidal belief system, etc.);
- biological susceptibility (i.e., physiological and affective symptoms); and
- behavioral susceptibility (e.g., deficient skills that cut across a broad range of areas, such as interpersonal, self-soothing, and general emotion regulation).

As mentioned earlier, FVT is guided by a number of fundamental assumptions. The foundational assumption is that suicidal episodes are time limited. A second assumption is that baseline risk varies from individual to individual. Everyone has a baseline risk level, a threshold value at which the suicidal mode is activated, a value that is set in accordance with susceptibility across each domain just mentioned. It is important to understand that this threshold value varies for each individual. For some it may be so high that the suicidal mode is unlikely ever to be activated. In other words, it may be that for some people, there are no conditions under which they would ever consider suicide. Take for example the fact that under some of the most extreme and harsh conditions (e.g., prisoners of war), certain individuals would never consider suicide an option. In this case, the suicidal belief system is characterized by thoughts such as *I would never kill myself under any conditions* or core beliefs such as *life is too precious ever to consider suicide*. For others, however, the threshold value for activation is very low, with minimal stressors, physiological–affective symptoms, or limited skills, triggering a cascade of suicidal thoughts that tend to cluster around four primary themes: *I'm worthless and don't deserve to live* (core belief of unlovability), *I can't fix this problem and should just die* (core belief of helplessness), *I'd rather die than feel this way* (core belief of poor distress tolerance, i.e., negative emotion is intolerable), or *everyone would be better off if I were dead* (core belief of perceived burdensomeness). As suggested here, there are four primary core belief themes that are revealed in expressed automatic thoughts: unlovability, helplessness, poor distress tolerance, and perceived burdensomeness. I am suggesting here that these core beliefs are potentially quite different from those routinely associated with depression and are specific to suicidality (i.e., cognitive content specificity).

Regardless of relative value across each domain of the suicidal mode, FVT predicts that everyone has a baseline risk level that is determined by historical and developmental factors. That baseline risk level predicts ease of activation or why someone might become suicidal under a given set of conditions. In short, vulnerability can be understood as a function across each domain: cognitive, affective, physiological, and behavioral. As a patient improves in one area, vulnerability to subsequent episodes would be reduced. However, it is critical to keep in mind that an extremely low threshold for activation in any given area would essentially undermine or limit progress in another. For example, marked improvement in depressive symptoms and related physiological arousal could be undercut by easily activated depressive or suicidal schemas. This is generally consistent with the old adage that depressed patients can be at heightened suicide risk after neurovegetative symptoms have remitted.

From a cognitive perspective, the suicidal belief system helps determine this baseline risk. In other words, those with high versus low baseline risk levels would be characterized by very different cognitive content (i.e., again consistent with the notion of cognitive content specificity). It is likely that those experiencing chronic suicidality and making multiple attempts would endorse automatic thoughts representative of core beliefs across more themes than those who make single attempts, have suicidal ideation, or are depressed. From a cognitive theory standpoint, this is one way of understanding the importance of historical factors in most risk assessment models. For example, most risk models have incorporated the importance of historical factors such as previous attempts (e.g., Clark & Fawcett, 1992; Rudd et al., 1995), and previous psychiatric diagnoses (e.g., Tanney, 1992). The argument here is that those historical factors are characterized by cognitive content and variability exists across those that are highly vulnerable (i.e., those with high baseline risk) and those that are resilient (i.e., low baseline risk). This is not to minimize the importance of biological vulnerability but rather to emphasize that previous or multiple episodes of a mood disorder have associated cognitive content. That is, there is impact on the suicidal belief system, incorporating beliefs relevant to both self and others.

The third assumption in FVT states that after resolution of an acute episode an individual returns to his or her baseline risk level. This is important because baseline risk varies so much from individual to individual, as suggested earlier. If the clinician is working with a patient who has high baseline risk (i.e., the suicidal mode and acute episodes are easily triggered), resolution of an acute episode may not necessarily mean that risk has resolved to any significant degree. Accordingly, the fourth assumption in FVT states that those who make multiple attempts (i.e., two or more genuine suicide attempts) have higher baseline risk levels. In other words, of all identifiable groups, those individuals with multiple attempts are at greatest chronic risk. In short, repeated suicidal states have resulted in a suicidal mode that is easily triggered, with activation occurring across any of the four domains (i.e., internal and external triggering).

Several investigators have found that those with multiple attempts are at significantly higher enduring risk relative to those who make single attempts and those who have suicidal ideations (Clark & Fawcett, 1992; Rudd et al., 1996). In accordance with this assumption, FVT predicts that those who make multiple attempts would be characterized by suicidal belief systems that have the greatest breadth and depth of beliefs across the four themes identified earlier. It is also hypothesized that these individuals would be characterized by the most severe symptoms (i.e., physiological and affective systems) and related behavioral deficits (e.g., emotion regulation and interpersonal skills). As noted earlier, emerging data support these hypotheses (Clark & Fawcett, 1992; Rudd et al., 1995).

The fifth assumption in FVT states that suicide risk is elevated by aggravating factors, which essentially are precipitant stressors (either internal or external) that cut across the four domains of the suicidal mode. This period of aggravation is time limited in nature. It is important to remember, consistent with what was noted previously, that precipitant stressors can be *internal or external* and cut across the four domains of the suicidal mode. More specifically, a patient with a recurrent major depressive disorder can have the suicidal mode triggered by a reemergence of depressive symptoms. A patient with poor interpersonal skills can have an episode triggered by an argument with a close friend. What is important is the notion of *synchrony of action*, that is, once the mode is activated, all domains or subsystems are involved. Consistent with cognitive theory, the suicidal belief system is evident and potentially amenable to change during periods of activation. Accordingly, activation is critical to treatment progress and success.

The sixth assumption in FVT holds that the severity of the suicidal episode is dependent on the interaction between baseline risk and the severity of the aggravating factors. Again, it is important to recall that baseline risk is essentially the individual's susceptibility to having the suicidal mode triggered, with the suicidal belief system being a critical component in that it is expressed via suicidal thoughts, intent, and related behaviors that prepare for or facilitate a suicidal act. Consistent with previously articulated assumptions about the suicidal mode, the central pathway for suicidality is cognition, the private meaning assigned by the individual for experiences (Rudd et al., 2000). Again, the notion of synchrony of action is important. For example, if the precipitant is a reemergence of depressive symptoms, it is the *interpretation* of this reemergence that is critical (e.g., "It's hopeless; I'll never recover."). Activation of the suicidal mode is dependent on maladaptive meaning constructed and assigned regarding the self, the environmental context, and the future, that is, the suicidal belief system across the four themes referenced earlier. Consistent with this notion of synchrony of action of the suicidal mode, aggravating factors include not only the suicidal belief system, but also the affective, physiological, and behavioral components.

As previously noted, most risk models are categorical in nature, incorporating clinical symptoms of one sort or another. This is one way to understand aggravating factors. What current clinical factors contribute to the patient's risk status? What is the patient thinking? What is the patient feeling emotionally and physiologically? What behavior does the patient manifest? Of importance, the seventh FVT assumption states that risk is elevated by aggravating factors for only limited periods of time, such as a few hours, days, or weeks. This is a consequence of the suicidal mode. In short, the body cannot maintain arousal at the highest levels for indefinite periods of time, and, accordingly, risk will naturally resolve to some degree. Even if arousal is diminished to a minimal degree, it may well be enough to move the patient from imminent risk. Again, this process is always accompanied by cognition, that is, the suicidal belief system. For example, limited reductions in arousal might lead to thoughts such as, "Maybe I can tolerate this feeling, I don't need to kill myself," countering the core belief themes of helplessness and poor distress tolerance. However, improved symptoms do not always translate to lower risk if the suicidal belief system is active (e.g., "Depression will always be a part of my life, I might as well kill myself").

In accordance with what was just discussed, the eighth and final FVT assumption states that acute risk resolves when aggravating factors are effectively targeted. In short, you treat the aggravating factors, not baseline (enduring) factors, during periods of crisis and acute risk. Although this undoubtedly has impact on enduring factors (e.g., cognitive susceptibility), the primary targets are current symptoms (cognitive, affective, and physiological) and behaviors. If those are effectively targeted, then acute risk will resolve. As noted previously, however, risk only returns to baseline level. With reference to the questions previously posed, this is how FVT explains the duration of the suicidal episode. It will last only as long as it takes to treat the aggravating factors effectively. When periods of acute risk endure, it is because the aggravating factors are not effectively targeted. Part of the problem may well be that they are not all identified or recognized by the clinician. As noted before, the suicidal mode has four component parts, and although the suicidal belief system is central, all need to be targeted to resolve a suicidal episode.

CLINICAL IMPLICATIONS: DIFFERENTIATING ACUTE AND CHRONIC RISK

What are the implications of explaining the process of risk by using fluid vulnerability theory? There are a number of important consequences. First, it should be clear from the assumptions listed in this chapter that variable baseline risk means that even when some patients recover from a crisis, they can still be at relatively high risk, with vulnerability that manifests itself across multiple domains. Accordingly, we need to differentiate between acute and chronic risk for patients. In other words, all patients have a chronic risk level (i.e., baseline risk). As noted earlier, it is believed that baseline risk for multiple attempters is relatively high.

The implications for clinical practice are considerable. The primary implication is that clinicians need to monitor and record chronic risk factors (more enduring characterological aspects) in addition to acute risk. For some patients, resolution of an acute suicidal crisis does not mean that suicide risk is low. To the contrary, suicide risk may have only been reduced in marginal fashion. What the clinician needs to do is to make routine the assessment of acute and chronic risk, differentiating the two in all relevant clinical entries. For example, after a patient is discharged from an inpatient unit, risk is certainly not fully resolved after the acute crisis precipitating admission has been targeted. What continues to be of concern are the more enduring and chronic aspects of the individual's case, what I would argue are the component parts of the suicidal mode.

In any event, the clinician needs to note and characterize acute risk carefully at discharge by describing the aggravating factors that were treated across each domain. Similarly, the clinician needs to note that many areas, if not the majority, were not effectively treated in a short inpatient stay. These are the chronic or static factors noted before, comprising the patient's baseline or chronic risk level. For some, such as multiple attempters, this can be fairly high, regardless of effective and efficient treatment. Differentiating chronic and acute risk translates to understanding each suicidal mode component and articulating the patient's vulnerability across each.

A clinical example illustrates best the need to differentiate acute and chronic risk. Let us consider two patients with identical presentations except for a few historical or static factors. For example, say both suffered from a recurrent major depressive problem, were occasionally abusing alcohol, experiencing specific suicidal thoughts with no intent, and had access to a supportive and caring family. One, however, had made four previous and potentially lethal suicide attempts over the past 5 years and the other had no previous suicide attempts. We certainly would be struggling for ways to differentiate their risk status. Although the acute episodes might look very much the same, FVT tells us that after successful treatment of the aggravating factors (across each domain of the suicidal mode), these two patients would return to very different baseline risk levels. The patient with multiple attempts would return to a relatively high level of risk, characterized by a suicidal mode that is easily triggered by a range of stressors both internal and external (across all four domains) and a suicidal belief system likely cutting across all four content themes noted earlier.

For a chronically suicidal patient, it is likely that the suicidal belief system will still be active, even during periods of reduced arousal, emotional upset, and relative behavioral stability. In contrast, the other patient might well return to a baseline risk level that is characterized as minimal or even nonexistent. The patient's suicidal belief system might include a thought such as, "I'll never do that again, life is always worth living" (which could represent modification of an underlying core belief about the value of life, individual worth, and lovability). This is one way of understanding why some patients make a single attempt and fully recover, never to make another attempt, whereas others go on to make many more. In struggling to differentiate the patient's risk levels, we need to focus on the process of risk for each. How does risk emerge, resolve, and reemerge? Despite the resolution of acute factors for the person with multiple suicide attempts, the chronic problems persist. In many ways, this notion is similar to what Maris (1981) referred to as "suicidal careers."

I recommend that all clinicians get into the habit of differentiating between acute and chronic risk in every clinical entry for a suicidal patient. This can be accomplished by simply segmenting the risk assessment section into these two categories. I also suggest discussing vulnerability for each domain of the suicidal mode. In addition to a more precise understanding of risk status, it conveys clearly and cogently that risk is a complex construct, one that is not particularly well understood or empirically supported at present. It also makes it clear that there are elements of treatment that are enduring and long term for every suicidal patient, regardless of the pressures of managed care. It can also be argued that such a distinction allows for a more realistic informed consent process, with it incumbent on the clinician to differentiate acute and chronic elements of the patient's suicidality and how those affect the treatment process, content, and duration of care. If our understanding of a patient's suicidality is more precise, it is arguable that our treatment and management activities will be more efficient and effective.

IMPLICATIONS FOR FUTURE RESEARCH

Fluid vulnerability theory has clear implications for all those engaging in research on suicidality. As noted earlier, most (if not all) risk assessment models incorporate risk factors that are derived from empirical research using time frames that are simply inconsistent with risk time frames that are routine in clinical practice. Most clinicians make decisions that involve periods that vary from a few hours to days to weeks. As noted earlier, research on risk factors for suicide uses periods that vary from a year to decades (see Rudd et al., 2000, for review). What is desperately needed are studies that ask and help answer some simple clinical questions. For example, how long does a suicidal state last? How do I know the crisis is over? Are there differences in the duration and severity of suicidal states for multiple attempters?

The fundamental assumptions of FVT will help drive specific hypotheses about risk over acute and chronic time frames. Fluid vulnerability theory should help inform research on clinically relevant risk periods. More specifically, it will help us offer specific hypotheses about how easily a suicidal episode might be triggered, how long it might last, and the likelihood of another episode after recovery. FVT also will help us identify and differentiate high and low risk groups in accordance with the depth and breadth of suicide relevant cognitions (i.e., the suicidal belief system), affective and physiological symptoms, and behavioral deficits. At present, this kind of research is in its infancy. We are just now in the process of differentiating those who make multiple attempts from those who make single attempts and those with suicidal ideation (e.g., Rudd et al., 1995). The next step is to advance some of the early work on the parameters of suicidal crises (e.g., Rudd et al., 2000). In particular, we need to track suicidal crises longitudinally, looking at resolution and reactivation over longer periods. Of importance are questions about crisis resolution. Do symptoms remit in clusters or individually? Are some symptoms potentially protective (i.e., the observation of increased risk following remission of neurovegetative symptoms)? What about latent cognitive vulnerability following a suicidal crisis? In other words, do some hopelessness themes endure following crisis resolution? If so, are they significant risk factors? These are but a few questions that surface as important. It is hoped that FVT and the suicidal mode will provide a theoretical foundation that cuts across risk assessment and treatment, providing needed infrastructure for more fruitful scientific study.

REFERENCES

Alford, B. A., & Beck, A. T. (1997). *The integrative power of cognitive therapy*. New York: Guilford Press.

Beck, A. T. (1996). Beyond belief: A theory of modes, personality, and psychopathology. In P. Salkovskis (Ed.), *Frontiers of cognitive therapy* (pp. 1–25). New York: Guilford Press.

Beck, A. T., Emery, G., & Greenberg, R. L (1985). *Anxiety disorders and phobias: A cognitive perspective*. New York: Guilford Press.

Clark, D. C., & Fawcett, J. (1992). Review of empirical risk factors for evaluation of the suicidal patient. In B. Bongar (Ed.), *Suicide guidelines for assessment, management, and treatment* (pp. 16–48). New York: Oxford University Press.

Dowd, E. T., & Courchaine, K. E. (1996). Implicit learning, tacit knowledge, and implications for stasis and change in cognitive psychotherapy. *Journal of Cognitive Psychotherapy, 10*, 163–180.

Haaga, D. A., Dyck, M. J., & Ernst, D. (1991). Empirical status of cognitive theory of depression. *Pyschological Bulletin, 110*, 215–236.

Hirschfeld, R. M., & Russell, J. M. (1997). Assessment and treatment of suicidal patients. *New England Journal of Medicine, 337*, 910–915.

Jobes, D. A. (1995). The challenge and promise of clinical suicidology. *Suicide and Life-Threatening Behavior, 25*, 437–449.

Joiner, T. E., Walker, R. L., Rudd, M. D., & Jobes, D. A. (1999). Scientizing and routinizing the assessment of suicidality in outpatient practice. *Professional Psychology: Research and Practice, 30*, 447–453.

Litman, R. E. (1991). Predicting and preventing hospital and clinic suicides. *Suicide and Life-Threatening Behavior, 21*, 56–73.

Maris, R. W. (1981). *Pathways to suicide: A survey of self-destructive behaviors*. Baltimore: Johns Hopkins University Press.

Rudd, M. D. (2003). Warning signs for suicide? *Suicide and Life-Threatening Behavior*, *33*, 99–100.

Rudd, M. D. (2004). Cognitive therapy for suicidality: An integrative, comprehensive, and practical approach to conceptualization. *Journal of Contemporary Psychotherapy*, *34*, 59–72.

Rudd, M. D., Joiner, T. E., & Rajab, M. H. (1995). Help negation after acute suicidal crisis. *Journal of Consulting and Clinical Psychology*, *6*, 499–503.

Rudd, M. D., Joiner, T. E., & Rajab, M. H. (2000). *Treating suicidal behavior*. New York: Guilford Press.

Tanney, B. L. (1992). Mental disorders, psychiatric patients, and suicide. In R. W. Maris, A. L. Berman, J. T. Maltsberger, & R. Yuht (Eds.), *Assessment and prediction of suicide* (pp. 277–320). New York: Guilford Press.

EPILOGUE:
WHAT HAVE WE LEARNED ABOUT COGNITION AND SUICIDE AND WHAT MORE DO WE NEED TO KNOW?

THOMAS E. ELLIS

It is the privilege of the editor of a volume such as this to work with some of the most accomplished people in the field and to be among the first to see what they are currently thinking and what they are doing to further advance knowledge of the subject. However, it is the burden of the editor to attempt to bring coherence to a diversity of perspectives in such a way that the reader can best assimilate the information and use it to inform his or her practice or scholarly activity.

The contributors to this volume are to be commended for significantly advancing our understanding of the cognitive aspects of suicide; at the same time, I know that all would agree that this is only a beginning and that numerous unanswered questions remain. How are we to make sense of all of this, particularly in terms of what we can do to help suicidal people and perhaps even to prevent people from becoming suicidal in the first place? We clearly have pieces of the puzzle—is it possible to begin to bring them together into a coherent picture of suicide and its treatment?

In one sense, the answer is no—it is akin to setting out to bring impressionist, realist, and postmodern art together into some sort of amalgamated painting. The perspectives are too different; the unique vision offered by each would be lost. It is, however, certainly possible to consider which insights each offers in our quest to better understand human experience. It is with this mind-set that we approach the challenging task of reviewing in a few pages the contents of this wide-ranging collection of cognitive perspectives on suicide. In the pages that follow, I attempt to articulate what we know from the work of the volume's contributors and where gaps in our knowledge remain. I begin with some general observations and then move on to consider the body of knowledge on cognition and suicide from the standpoint of three major aspects of psychopathology: description, explanation, and amelioration.

WHAT HAVE WE LEARNED (IN GENERAL)?

Considering theoretical and research developments in the area of cognition and suicide in toto, we can now say with some confidence that "being suicidal" is not merely the result of having one or another psychological disorder or having a more severe case of a psychological disorder, be it depression, schizophrenia, or a personality disorder. Suicidal people are *cognitively different*, compared with people who may share the same diagnosis and symptom severity but are not suicidal. Various ways in which they differ are detailed within this book and include hopelessness (chap. 3), certain dysfunctional beliefs (chap. 4), overgeneral memory (chap. 8), perfectionism (chap. 10), and problem-solving deficits (chap. 11), among others.

Nor, apparently, is suicidality merely a crisis state, which anyone would enter if stressed severely enough. Indeed, specific cognitive diatheses have been identified that seem to set the stage for suicidality in vulnerable individuals (e.g., Schotte & Clum, 1987). This framework contrasts with early models of suicide intervention, still prominent today, wherein discussions about helping suicidal people are dominated by guidelines on assessing, monitoring, and resolving suicidal crises but contain relatively little on targeting the underlying vulnerabilities that set the stage for the suicidal response in the first place (see Williams, Barnhofer, Crane, & Duggan, chap. 8, this volume, for an excellent example of such a vulnerability). Some of these vulnerabilities have traitlike qualities, although the question of state-dependence remains a legitimate one (e.g., J. B. Ellis & Range, 1989).

In the same vein, and in contrast to what is often implied in suicide intervention guidelines, we are beginning to realize that it is not appropriate simply to revert to "therapy as usual" once a patient's suicidal crisis has been resolved. We now have a better understanding of cognitive diatheses that must be addressed lest suicidality recur during the next schema-relevant stressful life event (see Rudd, chap. 16, this volume, for a detailed discussion of recurrent suicidality).

Perhaps the most exciting general finding is that many of these cognitive vulnerabilities can be modified in therapy. Examples include dysfunctional attitudes and beliefs (chaps. 3 and 4), pessimism–optimism (chap. 12), overgeneral autobiographical recall (chap. 8), problem-solving skills (chap.

11), and perfectionism (chap. 10). Although we cannot assume that such cognitive changes will necessarily translate into reduced suicidal ideation and behavior, some early findings have produced support for such a model. Linehan's outcomes studies have shown great promise in this regard (see chap. 5). Equally impressive is a recent study (described by Brown and associates in chap. 3) showing that suicide attempters receiving 10 sessions of cognitive therapy were 50% less likely to make a repeat attempt over an 18-month follow-up period compared with similar patients receiving treatment as usual (Brown et al., 2005). Nonetheless, the lion's share of work remains to be done in this area, that is, outcome research testing various cognitive interventions and examining mechanisms accounting for changes in suicidality. However, it does seem reasonable to predict (as I speculated nearly 20 years ago; T. E. Ellis, 1986) that therapies tailored to the cognitive vulnerabilities of individuals who are suicidal might provide patients with previously unavailable alternatives that would potentially make suicidal ideation and behavior irrelevant.

We now turn to specific areas of investigation.

WHAT HAVE WE LEARNED (SPECIFICALLY)?

Description

Although common sense tells us that people who are suicidal surely must think differently from other people about themselves and the world, it was Shneidman's acute observational skills and gift for narrative description that produced the first in-depth description of what specifically was "different." Cognitive constriction. Rigidity. Black-and-white thinking. Characteristics that clinicians soon become aware of when attempting to help suicidal individuals and that first saw empirical support through Neuringer's important studies in the 1960s and 1970s (see chap. 1, this volume). These characteristics were consistent with Shneidman's conceptualization of suicide as an act of desperation in response to intractable emotional pain, which he later was to dub *psychache* (Shneidman, 1993). The depiction of the suicidal individual as experiencing a state of unbearable psychic pain, combined with cognitive characteristics causing him or her to feel trapped, took much of the mystery out of what was previously seen by many as a senseless act. What was less clear was why only some distressed people entered this state, and most did not.

It remained for Aaron Beck to identify a major difference between suicidal and nonsuicidal individuals with depression. Conventional wisdom suggests that suicidality necessarily occurs after depression passes a certain level of severity. However, clinical observation tells us otherwise: Even severely depressed individuals do not always become suicidal. Indeed, although the mortality rate of people with major depression is high (once thought to approach 15%, but probably closer to 5% to 6%; Inskip, Harris, & Barraclough, 1998), the overwhelming majority of depressed people do not die by suicide. We now know that a key mediator of the relationship between depression severity and suicidality is *hopelessness* (e.g., Minkoff, Bergman, Beck, & Beck, 1973). Although questions remain regarding trait versus state issues and generalizability across diagnostic and age groups (Abramson, Alloy, & Hogan, 2000), the hopelessness construct stands as one of the most valuable contributions to date in understanding the suicidal state and developing focused cognitive therapy interventions.

The introduction of the notion of a *suicidal mode* by Beck (see chap. 3, this volume) and further elaboration by Rudd (see Rudd, chap. 16, this volume; Rudd, Joiner, & Rajab, 2000) have extended the cognitive model beyond the description of thought *content* to a better understanding of the activation of a multisystem cognitive–affective–behavioral–motivational state of suicidality. This, combined with the schema construct, enables an individualized understanding of what specifically meaningful life events might trigger the suicidal state and what sorts of cognitive vulnerabilities (beliefs, attitudes, distortions, etc.) might be targeted in therapy to reduce the risk of future suicidal episodes. As discussed later, whether the predicted benefits of such interventions will actually follow is a separate question.

The influential rational–emotive behavior therapy (REBT) system of Albert Ellis (chap. 4) has been relatively silent on the issue of suicide until now. Although in great need of research scrutiny (e.g., T. E. Ellis & Ratliff, 1986), the REBT approach brings a potentially valuable philosophical component to the table. What topics can be more important in therapy with a suicidal individual than questions such as the worth of a human being, the true meaning of "awful," needs versus wishes, and whether a person can "stand" adversity? REBT therapists are comfortable in all of these arenas; it is to be hoped that the future holds increased application and testing of the REBT model with suicidal populations.

However promising traditional cognitive models such as Beck's and Ellis's might be, it can be argued by those with a constructivist orientation that they are less than complete (although Ellis argues strongly that REBT itself qualifies as a contructivist approach: A. Ellis, 1998). Two areas of development, constructivism and the emotional regulation model, either challenge or complement these models, depending on one's point of view. Constructivist theorists take issue with the notion that suicidal people "distort reality" and need help making perceptions and beliefs more "accurate" (see chaps. 7 and 15). Here, suicidality is described not so much as the result of an individual's distorted processing of life events as the outcome of a process of "meaning creation," wherein the individual behaves in a way consistent with his or her personal theory of self and world. Implications for therapeutic intervention are significant and discussed subsequently.

In contrast to these more cognitively oriented models is a collection of theories that paint a much more affectively laden picture. Most prominent among these is the dialectical behavior therapy (DBT) of Marsha Linehan, who made *emotional dysregulation* the cornerstone (although DBT's development has centered primarily on patients with borderline personality disorder, it seems clear that its usage is not narrowly limited to that population). Here, the suicidal individual is viewed as someone who is overwhelmed by an overreactive nervous system and an inadequate repertoire of coping resources (notably, the emotional reactivity is thought to have largely neurobiological origins, rather than being derived from primarily cognitive processes). Making matters worse, because of the process of "invalidation," the individual not only engages in ineffective coping behaviors but also engages in self-criticism that exacerbates the emotional distress that he or she is already experiencing.

The contributions of Firestone (chap. 6) and Orbach (chap. 9) also take an affectively oriented approach. Whereas Orbach's focus is a bit narrower (more specific to the body experience of the suicidal individual), both paint a poignant picture of self-loathing. An intimate and revealing depiction of the suicidal person's inner world emerges (especially evident in items for the two respective assessment instruments), deepening our understanding of, and empathy for, people for whom suicide becomes alluring.

Two other contributions deserve mention in this discussion of perspectives on describing suicidality. One is Joiner and associates' notion of "perceived burdensomeness" (Joiner, Pettit, & Walker, 2002). On the basis of cognitive–evolutionary theory, burdensomeness is an intuitively appealing and clinically useful construct with promising preliminary research support. The other emanates from acceptance and commitment therapy (ACT), a therapeutic approach based on relational frame theory (Hayes, Strosahl, & Wilson, 1999; ACT is generally not conceptualized as a cognitive therapy and was therefore not included in this book, although it probably should have been). ACT views *experiential avoidance* (a strategic pattern of avoiding negative thoughts and emotions) as a central aspect of psychopathology and suicide as its ultimate expression (see Hayes, Wilson, Gifford, Follette, & Strosahl, 1996, for a full discussion). Cultivating *acceptance* (willingness to experience thoughts, feelings, and situations fully) is viewed as a key to developing alternatives to suicide and achieving valued goals in life (Hayes, Follette, & Linehan, 2004).

Despite these important advances, significant gaps remain in the effort to produce a satisfactory cognitive description of suicidal phenomena. At this point, we have only an assortment of interesting although disconnected findings about various cognitive features of suicidal individuals. How do they fit together? How do the various vulnerabilities (e.g., perfectionism, impaired problem solving, body dissatisfaction, overgeneral recall) relate to one another? Do they tend to co-occur within a given individual, or might they represent different varieties of suicidality? What is the relationship between these cognitive characteristics and clinical (*Diagnostic and Statistical Manual of Mental Disorders*) diagnosis? Are the various cognitive deficits associated with specific diagnoses, or do they define suicidality across diagnoses?

This question of possible subtypes of suicidality (see T. E. Ellis, 1988) is crucial. In this vein, McCullough (2000) maintains that people with chronic depression are characterized by distinct differences in their levels of cognitive development and has developed a specific treatment that has shown great promise with this population (Keller et al., 2000). Might subtypes similarly exist among suicidal individuals? If so, how do they differ and what are the associated treatment implications?

Etiology

Next arises the question, having observed these cognitive features that characterize suicidal individuals, what can we say about why and how they occur? What are the respective roles of genetics, prenatal environments, early learning experiences, trauma, and societal influences? Furthermore, how can we extend what we know about the etiology of cognitive vulnerabilities to the treatment and prevention arenas? Consistent with the notion of *equifinality* discussed by Wagner and Zimmerman in chapter 13, we know that a single etiological explanation is unlikely; pathways to suicidality (cognitive and otherwise) may be very different, for example, in schizophrenia (chap. 14) and PTSD (chap. 15). Indeed, is it even possible to specify a finite number of pathways to suicide?

These questions, of course, implicate the entire field of suicidology and so extend beyond the scope of this book. Nonetheless, it seems safe to say that, although differing in their respective areas of focus and emphasis, all of the perspectives offered in this volume are consistent with a complex, biopsychosocial etiology. This is particularly evident in Linehan's DBT model (Linehan, 1993), which draws on research on biological and genetic influences on emotional dysregulation, combined with developmental influences, to produce the cognitive and behavioral phenomena that we observe in suicidal individuals.

One prominent pathway evident in this book comprises early learning experiences, notably in the context of the parent–child relationship. Here, we see overlap in research findings regarding self-oriented perfectionism, body image, the "inner critic," and the development of adaptive coping with social problems and negative affect. Indeed, looking across the perspectives presented in this book, one can begin to develop an "inventory" of necessary developmental tasks necessary to buffer an individual from future suicidality. These might include the following:

- realistic self-expectations (Hewitt);
- capacity for self-nurturance (Firestone);
- acceptance of shortcomings (A. Ellis);
- tolerance of adversity (A. Ellis);
- coping with negative affect (Linehan);
- attitude of respect and concern for the body (Orbach);
- adaptive views (schemas) concerning self, world, and the future (Beck); or
- effective problem orientation and systematic problem solving (Reinecke).

Another promising pathway is suggested by the sizable body of work regarding overgeneral memory, problem-solving deficits, and hopelessness. The connection between hopelessness and suicidality has been well documented (e.g., Weishaar & Beck, 1992) and has direct relevance to targeted interventions in cognitive therapy (see chap. 3). Although numerous studies have linked deficient problem solving with suicidality (see chap. 11), origins of these deficits are less clear. However, Williams and colleagues (chap. 8) observed that effective problem solving requires access to well-elaborated memories of prior, similar situations. The fact that suicidal individuals have been consistently shown to exhibit overgeneral memory (chap. 8, this volume; Williams, Teasdale, Segal, & Soulsby, 2000) suggests a possible etiological pathway. The origins of this memory characteristic are less clear; however, recent studies showing improvement in memory function following mindfulness-based cognitive therapy suggest that this may be more a learned than "hardwired" characteristic (Williams et al., 2000).

Despite these advances, gaps in our knowledge are considerable. For example, although most models assume biological influences, specific genetic, biochemical, and neurobiological factors contributing to these cognitive characteristics, if they exist, are practically unexplored. Early childhood influences are hypothesized both in attachment-oriented models such as Firestone's (chap. 6) and social learning models such as Linehan's (chap. 5). Some empirical support for these hypotheses exists (e.g., Lewinsohn, Rohde, & Seeley, 1996; Yang & Clum, 2000), yet many questions remain. For example, it is now generally recognized that traumatic stress has long-term, neurobiological effects on the brain (e.g., Heim & Nemeroff, 1999). What might this mean in terms of the functioning of memory, future development of problem-solving skills, and so forth?

Treatment

True to the pattern for psychotherapy in general, the development of treatment strategies for suicidal patients has outpaced their validation via empirically supported theories of etiology and rigorous outcome studies. However, it can be said that cognitive–behavioral approaches to suicidal patients are, to a greater extent than most other psychotherapies, tailored to the characteristic needs of the patient population, that is, the kinds of cognitive vulnerabilities discussed in this book. The field is still in its infancy in terms of controlled clinical research, but early findings show clear promise. These fall into two general categories: treatments for specific cognitive vulnerabilities and comprehensive therapeutic systems.

As detailed elsewhere in this volume, it has been shown that specific cognitive vulnerabilities of suicidal individuals can be modified. Prominent among these is impaired problem solving. As described by Reinecke in chapter 11, not only has deficient problem solving been consistently found in suicidal individuals, it is now clear that it is possible to improve problem-solving skills and related symptoms through specific, focused interventions (e.g., McLeavey, Daly, Ludgate, & Murray, 1994). Evidence exists suggesting that perfectionism (chap. 10) can be modified as well (e.g., Kutlesa, 2003), although it is too soon to tell whether these findings can be generalized to suicidal individuals. Finally, as mentioned earlier, Williams et al. (2000) have shown improvement in overgeneral autobiographic memory following a form of cognitive therapy utilizing mindfulness meditation techniques. This is especially interesting given the increasing visibility of mindfulness and acceptance techniques, part of what Hayes (2004) referred to as a developing "third wave" of cognitive and behavioral therapies.

Among comprehensive therapy systems, the best known and tested regarding suicidal behaviors is Linehan's DBT (see chap. 5). In focusing initially on borderline personality disorder (Linehan, 1993), Linehan's approach evolved along lines almost tailor-made to address multiple vulnerabilities of suicidal individuals: emotional dysregulation, ineffective problem solving, impulsivity, impaired interpersonal relationships. Equally important is DBT's recognition of the importance of the dialectical tension between change and acceptance (discussed later). Linehan also set a new standard in conducting rigorously designed randomized clinical trials with suicidal patients. Although it is clear that DBT is not a panacea, these studies have shown consistently positive outcomes and have immeasurably advanced the clinical science of the suicidal patient.

Aaron Beck, often referred to as the father of cognitive therapy, has produced or stimulated an enormous amount of clinical research on a wide range of conditions, including depression, various anxiety disorders, personality disorders, substance use disorders, bipolar illness, and anger problems. Most of these are structured, manual-based therapies based on specific cognitive models of the respective disorders. It is interesting that, although Beck has written authoritatively about suicide for many years, it is only recently that he and his associates have produced and begun evaluation of a treatment specifically designed for suicidal patients (see chap. 3). Preliminary results show significantly reduced suicide attempts in patients who received the treatment.

These two therapy systems, although different in a variety of ways, share two notable characteristics: (a) They both focus explicitly on suicidal ideation and behavior as treatment targets, unlike traditional psychotherapeutic approaches that focus on the psychological disorder, which is viewed as the chief source of the suicidality; and (b) Each has produced at least preliminary results in randomized clinical trials indicating that an intervention designed to remedy theory-based cognitive vulnerabilities actually reduced suicidal target behaviors and hence can be assumed to have reduced suicide risk. In other words, not only is it possible to modify these cognitive vulnerabilities, but such modifications do, in fact, translate into reduced suicide risk. This may seem like a rather minimal outcome expectation (therapy designed for suicidal patients actually makes them less suicidal!), but it is a remarkably rare finding given the current state of the art and science (see Linehan's foreword to this volume) and should therefore be recognized for the psychotherapeutic milestone that it is.

Finally, voice therapy (chap. 6) deserves mention as a therapy system of particular relevance to facilitating cognitive change in suicidal individuals. Voice therapy does not enjoy the same degree of research support as the foregoing therapies and is not generally mentioned in discussions of the various cognitive–behavioral therapies. However, its value lies in what it teaches us about self-loathing and the cognitive–affective interface. It is commonly observed in cognitive therapies, from Beck's cognitive therapy to A. Ellis's REBT, that "hot cognitions," central to meaningful work in therapy, are generally inaccessible in absence of emotional activation. Voice therapy offers valuable insights into what suicidal people are thinking and feeling while in the suicidal state (à la Beck's *suicidal mode*), as well as how to activate and modify these cognitive–affective networks in therapy. It therefore merits further evaluation.

These great strides notwithstanding, those who seek to develop efficacious, empirically supported cognitive approaches to treating suicidal patients still face enormous challenges. The gaps in our knowledge of the treatment of suicidal patients are sizable. Many of these have been discussed competently elsewhere (e.g., Linehan, 2000; Rudd et al., 2000) and so will not be discussed here. Instead, I list here questions that have arisen for me during the course of editing this volume, many from the perspective of a clinician wondering how I might apply this knowledge to my next suicidal patient:

Should case conceptualization and treatment planning be driven primarily by diagnosis, cognitive characteristics, some combination, or other considerations?

Will one "suicide therapy" ultimately suffice in the treatment of suicidal individuals, are several varieties needed, or can what we are learning about suicidal cognition perhaps be seamlessly integrated into other therapies, cognitive or otherwise?

What are the "varieties" of suicidal individuals and what are the implications for treatment planning (T. E. Ellis, 1988)? Would a dimensional approach be more useful for treatment purposes than a typology? If so, what are the relevant dimensions?

How should a competent cognitive–behavioral assessment be conducted? What assessment instruments should be used to assess the range of cognitive vulnerabilities and set the stage for treatment planning?

What is the ideal balance between cognitive and behavioral interventions? To what extent should the clinician focus on teaching skills (e.g., problem solving), addressing processing deficits (e.g., overgeneral memory), or modifying cognitive structures (e.g., maladaptive schemas)? If this is a matter of individual treatment planning, see the previous item.

What are the most potent "active ingredients" in treatment? Does it even make sense to use "surgical" interventions to target specific cognitive liabilities, or is it possible that "common" relationship factors such as the therapeutic alliance merit greater attention (Messer & Wampold, 2002; Norcross, 2002)?

What of the mixed message regarding change and acceptance? Implicit in the notion of "cognitive vulnerabilities" lies the assumption that such vulnerabilities need to be "corrected"; but to what extent should emphasis be placed on helping the patient to learn to accept himself or herself "warts and all," as well as accepting aspects of life that are contrary to one's wishes but are not likely to change?

These and many other questions remain. However, the authors of the foregoing chapters have made invaluable contributions in advancing our knowledge of cognition and suicide. Many of us entered this field because we were mystified by what could possibly be going on in a person's mind to allow self-destruction to become an option. Unanswered questions notwithstanding, the issues are perhaps a bit less mysterious now than before. Future researchers, therapy practitioners, and, most important, persons at risk for suicide, are all beneficiaries of the work within this volume.

REFERENCES

Abramson, L. Y., Alloy, L. B., & Hogan, M. E. (2000). The hopelessness theory of suicidality. In T. E. Joiner & M. D. Rudd (Eds.), *Suicide science: Expanding the boundaries* (pp. 17–32). New York: Kluwer Academic/Plenum.

Barlow, D. H., Allen, L. B., & Choate, M. L. (2004). Toward a unified treatment for emotional disorders. *Behavior Therapy, 35,* 205–230.

Brown, G. K., TenHave, T., Henriques, G. R., Xie, S. X., Hollander, J. E., & Beck, A. T. (2005). Cognitive therapy for the prevention of suicide attempts: A randomized controlled trial. *Journal of the American Medical Association, 294,* 563–570.

Ellis, A. (1998). How rational emotive behavior therapy belongs in the constructivist camp. In M. F. Hoyt (Ed.), *Handbook of constructive therapies: Innovative approaches from leading practitioners* (pp. 83–99). San Francisco: Jossey-Bass.

Ellis, J. B., & Range, L. M. (1989). Does mood affect reasons for living? Yes. *Journal of Cognitive Psychotherapy, 3,* 223–232.

Ellis, T. E. (1986). Toward a cognitive therapy for suicidal individuals. *Professional Psychology: Research and Practice, 17,* 125–130.

Ellis, T. E. (1988). Classification of self-destructive behavior: A review and step toward integration. *Suicide and Life-Threatening Behavior, 18,* 358–371.

Ellis, T. E., & Ratliff, K. (1986). Cognitive characteristics of suicidal and nonsuicidal psychiatric inpatients. *Cognitive Therapy and Research, 10,* 625–634.

Hayes, S. C. (2004). Acceptance and commitment therapy, relational frame theory, and the third wave of behavioral and cognitive therapies. *Behavior Therapy, 35,* 639–665.

Hayes, S. C., Follette, V. M., & Linehan, M. M. (Eds.). (2004). *Mindfulness and acceptance: Expanding the cognitive–behavioral tradition.* New York: Guilford Press.

Hayes, S. C., Strosahl, K., & Wilson, K. G. (1999). *Acceptance and commitment therapy: An experiential approach to behavior change.* New York: Guilford Press.

Hayes, S. C., Wilson, K. G., Gifford, E. V., Follette, V. M., & Strosahl, K. (1996). Emotional avoidance and behavioral disorders: A functional dimensional approach to diagnosis and treatment. *Journal of Consulting and Clinical Psychology, 64,* 1152–1168.

Heim, C., & Nemeroff, C. B. (1999). The impact of early adverse experiences on brain systems involved in the pathophysiology of anxiety and affective disorders. *Biological Psychiatry, 46,* 1509–1522.

Inskip, H. M., Harris, E. C., & Barraclough, B. (1998). Lifetime risk of suicide for affective disorder, alcoholism, and schizophrenia. *British Journal of Psychiatry, 172,* 35–37.

Joiner, T. E., Pettit, J. W., & Walker, R. L. (2002). Perceived burdensomeness and suicidality: Two studies on the suicide notes of those attempting and those completing suicide. *Journal of Social and Clinical Psychology, 21,* 531–545.

Keller, M. B., McCullough, J. P., Klein, D. N., Arnow, B., Dunner, D. L., Gelenberg, A. J., et al. (2000). A comparison of nefazodone, the cognitive behavioral–analysis system of psychotherapy, and their combination for the treatment of chronic depression. *New England Journal of Medicine, 342,* 1462–1470.

Kutlesa, N. (2003). A group intervention with university students who experience difficulties with perfectionism. *Dissertation Abstracts International Section A: Humanities & Social Sciences, 64,* 398.

Lewinsohn, P. M., Rohde, P., & Seeley, J. R. (1996). Adolescent suicidal ideation and attempts: Prevalence, risk factors, and clinical implications. *Clinical Psychology: Science and Practice, 3,* 25–46.

Linehan, M. M. (1993). *Cognitive–behavioral treatment of borderline personality disorder*. New York: Guilford.

Linehan, M. M. (2000). Behavioral treatments of suicidal behaviors: Definitional obfuscation and treatment outcomes. In R. W. Maris, S. S. Canetto, J. L. McIntosh, & M. M. Silverman (Eds.), *Review of suicidology* (pp. 84–111). New York: Guilford.

McCullough, J. P. (2000). *Treatment for chronic depression*. New York: Guilford.

McLeavey, B. C., Daly, R. J., Ludgate, J. W., & Murray, C. M. (1994). Interpersonal problem-solving skills training in the treatment of self-poisoning patients. *Suicide and Life-Threatening Behavior, 24*, 382–394.

Messer, S. B., & Wampold, B. E. (2002). Let's face facts: Common factors are more potent than specific therapy ingredients. *Clinical Psychology: Science & Practice, 9*, 21–25.

Minkoff, K., Bergman, E., Beck, A. T., & Beck, R. (1973). Hopelessness, depression, and attempted suicide. *American Journal of Psychiatry, 130*, 455–459.

Norcross, J. C. (Ed.). (2002). *Psychotherapy relationships that work: Therapist contributions and responsiveness to patients*. Oxford, England: Oxford University Press.

Rudd, M. D., Joiner, T. E., & Rajab, M. H. (2000). *Treating suicidal behavior*. New York: Guilford Press.

Schotte, D. E., & Clum, G. A. (1987). Problem-solving skills in suicidal psychiatric patients. *Journal of Consulting and Clinical Psychology, 55*, 49–54.

Shneidman, E. (1993). *Suicide as psychache: A clinical approach to self-destructive behavior*. Northvale, NJ: Aronson.

Weishaar, M. E., & Beck, A. T. (1992). Hopelessness and suicide. *International Review of Psychiatry, 4*, 177–184.

Williams, J. M. G., Teasdale, J. D., Segal, Z. V., & Soulsby, J. (2000). Mindfulness-based cognitive therapy reduces overgeneral autobiographical memory in formerly depressed patients. *Journal of Abnormal Psychology, 109*, 150–155.

Yang, B., & Clum, G. A. (2000). Childhood stress leads to later suicidality via its effect on cognitive functioning. *Suicide and Life-Threatening Behavior, 30*, 183–198.

AUTHOR INDEX

Numbers in italics refer to listings in the references.

Brown, J., 126, *144*, 237, *283*
Brown, L. K., 294, *303, 307*
Brown, L. S., 335, *350*
Brown, M. S., 295, *302*
Brown, M. Z., 6, 91–110, *111, 115*
Brown, R. M., 272, *279*
Brown, Y., xv, *xvi*
Bruch, H., 198, *210*
Bruch, M. A., 109, *113*
Bryant, B., 336, *350*
Bryant, R. A., 182, *188*, 336, *351*
Buchanan, G. M., 265, *279*
Buchanan, T. W., 126, *144*
Buchholtz-Hansen, P. E., xiv, xvi
Buiks, A., 317, *328*
Bulik, C. M., 99, *111*, 264, *279*
Bunney, W. E., 262, *281*
Burgess, P. W., 178, *188*
Burke, M., 175, *188*
Burnette, M., 95, *111*
Burns, A. B., 261–279, *281*
Burton, A., 183, *188*
Busch, K., 96, *111*
Bushnell, I. W. R., 196, *213*
Buskens, E., *260*
Butler, J., *257*
Byrne, S., 325, *327, 332*

Caelian, C. F., xv, 215–231, *233*
Cahill, L., 126, *144*
Cahill, S. P., 346, *350*
Calam, R., 180, *190*
Caldieraro, M. A., *46*
Callahan, E., 95, *111*
Callahan, T. S., 294, 297, *304, 305*
Callander, L., 221, *234*
Camacho, L. W., 196, *214*
Camper, P., 93, *114*, 182, *189*, 238, 242, *258*
Camus, A., 75, *88*
Cannon, M., *331*
Carlson, G. A., 244, *255*, 298, *302*
Carney, R. M., 268, *279*
Carpenter, L. L., 99, *111*
Carpenter, W. T., 310, *330*
Carrigan, S., 216, *235*
Carver, C. S., 266, *279*
Carver, S. S., 264, *279*
Casey, B. J., 289, 291, 292, *303*
Cash, T. F., *210*
Casper, V., 197, *210*
Caspi, A., *331*
Castellanos, F. X., *304*

Castillon, J. J., 57, *74*
Catalan, J., 247, *257*
Catlett, J., 119, *145*
Cats, B. P., 196, *211*
Cejas, M. R., *326*
Centor, R. M., 294, *307*
Chadwick, P., 310, 315, *327, 329*
Chadwick, P. D., 310, 312–313, 317–318, *326, 327, 328*
Chamberlain, F., 318, *328*
Chamberlain, K., 60, *74*
Chan, S., *191*
Chang, E., 238, *256*
Chang, E. C., 221, 224, 225, 232, 264, *280*
Chapman, M., 316, *328*
Chartrand, T. L., 93, *110*
Chaudhuri, S., 294, *307*
Chaves, A. C., 315, *327*
Chess, S., 101, *111*
Chiara, A., *279*
Chignague, J. F., 124, *146*
Chiles, J. A., 93, 97, *111, 114, 116*, 182, *189*, 238, 242, *258*
Chioqueta, A. P., 266, *280*
Chisholm, D., *330*
Choate, M. L., *378*
Chorney, P., 201, *211*
Chu, J. A., 126, *144*
Cicchetti, D., 268, *303*
Cimbolic, P., 41, *47*
Claridge, G., 242, *258*
Claridge, G. C., 63, *73*, 182, *189*
Clark, D., 96, *111*, 240, *256*
Clark, D. C., 96, *112, 144*, 356, 362, 363, *367*
Clark, D. M., 336, 340, 349, *350*
Clarke, A. S., 198, *212*
Clarke, D., 60, *74*
Clarkin, J. F., 208, *213*
Close, H., 313, *328*
Clum, G. A., 59, *72*, 76, *88*, 93, *111, 116*, 177, *192*, 238, 241, 242, 243, 244, 245, 246, 248, *256, 258, 259, 271*, *282*, 293, 294, 295, 296, 297, *303*, 306, *307, 308*, 335, *353*, 370, 375, *380*
Cochrane, R., *328*
Cohen, B. N., 310, *331*
Cohen, D., 203, *213*
Cohen, P., 126, *144*, 205, *214*
Cohen, S., 268, *280*
Cohen-Sandler, R., 298, *303*

Cohn, S., 93, *112*
Colbus, D., 221, *234*
Colditz, G. A., 267, *281*
Cole, A., *111*
Cole, D., 96, 99, *113*
Cole, D. A., 97, *111, 295, 303*
Cole, J., 349, *352*
Cole, P. M., 299, *303*
Comtois, K. A., 91, 96, *111, 115*
Conely, R. R., 310, *330*
Congiu, L., *114*
Connell, J. P., 275, *282*
Conterio, K., 96, *112*
Conway, M. A., 174, 178, *188*
Cook, N., *74*
Cools, J., 245, 246, *259*
Cooper, J. E., *329*
Cooper, M. L., 266, *281*
Cooper, T. B., *281*
Cooper, V., 316, *328*
Corder, B. F., 294, *303*
Corder, R. F., 294, *303*
Cornette, M., *279*
Corridan, B., *326*
Cosmides, L., 269, *283*
Cotton, P., 310, *328*
Cotton, T., 310, *328*
Courchaine, K. E., 360, *367*
Cowan, T., *234*
Cowden, L., 93, *111*
Cox, B. J., 221, 222, *232*
Coyne, J. C., 102, *116*
Cozzarelli, C., 266, *281*
Craig, K. J., *350*
Craig, T., *329*
Crane, C., xv, 173–187, *191, 370*
Creed, F., 97, 99, *112*
Croft, S., 95, *116*
Cronan, S., 296, *307*
Cronbach, L. J., 38, *49, 130, 144*
Crook, T., 99, *111*
Cruz, J., *281*
Csikszentmihalyi, M., 261, 262, *282*
Culpepper, L., *280*
Cumming, C., xv, *xvi*
Cunningham, D. K., 76, *90*
Cunningham, N., 197, *210*
Curry, J. F., 296, *303*
Curtin, L., 59, *72*
Cutler, H. C., 86, *88*

Dahl, R. E., 291, *303*

Dahlen, E., 272, *279*
Dahlsgaard, K. K., 59, 60, *71, 72*
Dahm, P. F., 238, 244, 259, 336, *352*
Dalai Lama, B., 86, *88*
Dalgleish, T., 175, 176, 182, *188, 189, 336, 350*
Daly, R., 238, *258*
Daly, R. J., 376, *380*
Damasio, A. R., 208, 209, *210*
Damon, W., 290, *303*
Dang, S. T., 182, *188*
Daniel, S., 257, *304*
Darbonne, A., 93, *112*
Davidson, J., *256*
Davidson, L. A., 221, *232*
Davidson, R. J., 95, 100, *112, 291, 298, 303*
Davies, M., 297, *306*
Davis, D., 99, *111*
Davis, J. H., *71*
Davis, M. S., 296, *304*
Dawson, G., 201, *210*
Dawud-Noursi, S., 175, *190*
Day, A., *257*
Day, L., 264, *280*
Dean, P. J., 97, 99, *111, 220, 224, 225, 232*
Debast, S., 196, *211*
de Catanzaro, D., 272, *280*
de Chateau, P., 196, *211*
Deci, E. L., 275, *282*
de Decker, A., 175, 176, 179, *188, 190*
de Jong, M. L., 205, *211*
Delahanty, D. L., 346, *350*
Delahousse, J., 124, *146*
Delespaul, P., 317, 325, *328, 330*
Delisle, J. R., 216, *232*
de Man, A. F., 59, *73, 219, 232*
DeMarco, R. R., 335, *350*
Dennenberg, V. H., 101, *112*
Der, G., *326*
DeRosa, T., 229, *232*
Derrick, A., 216, *235*
Derryberry, D., 291, *298zz, 304*
DeRubeis, R. J., 266, *282*
de Silva, P., *188*
Dettmer, E. L., *351*
Detweiler, J. B., 237, 238, *282*
Devine, R., 93, *114*
deVries, M., 325, *328*
de Wilde, E. J., 96, *114, 295, 299, 305*
Diamond, G. M., 41, *46*
Diaz, A., 57, *74*

Ferrier, I. N., 176, *188*
Ferruda-Noli, M., 335, *350*
Festinger, L., 98, *112*
Field, T. M., 196, 201, 205, 209, *211, 213*
Fierman, L. B., 123, *145*
Figueras, S., *169*
Fine, J., 242, *257*
Finkel, M. S., *280*
Finkelhor, D., 177, *189*
Finkenauer, C., 121, *144*
Fireman, P., *280*
Firestone, L., xv, 6, 119–143, *145*
Firestone, R. W., 120, 121, 123, 124, 128, 130, 132, *145*
Fisher, P., 228, *233,* 299, *307*
Fitzpatrick, D., 336, *352*
Fleck, M. P., 46
Flett, G. L., xv, 6, 215–231, 216, 217, 218, 219, 220, 221, 223, 224, 225, 228, 229, 230, *232, 233, 234, 235*
Florin, I., 175, *191*
Flory, D., 228, *233*
Flynn, C., 226, 228, *233*
Foa, E. B., 100, 107, 109, *112,* 342, *350*
Foerster, A., *330*
Fogel, A., 199, *211*
Fogg, L. F., 60, *74,* 96, *112, 144,* 260
Follette, V. M., 373, *379*
Fombonne, E., 316, *328*
Fonagy, P., 121, *145*
Fong, G., 336, *352*
Ford, D. E., *280*
Foulds, G. A., 311, *328*
Fowler, D., 317, 318, *328, 329, 330*
Francini, K., 47
Francis, G., 298, *307*
Frank, E., 99, *111*
Frank, N., 298, *307*
Fransella, F., 150, 155, 159, *168*
Franzen, M. D., 294, *305*
Frazier, P., *257*
Frederick, C. J., 71
Fredrickson, B. L., 264, 269, 270, 271, 278, *280*
Freedland, K. E., 268, *279*
Freeman, A., 247, *259*
Freeman, D., 315, 316, 317, 318, *328, 329*
Freeman, G., *330*
Freeman, P., 221, *232*
Frei, D. Z., *114*
Fremouw, W. J., 294, 297, *304, 305*
Freud, A., 127, *145,* 197, *211*

Fridell, E. J., 63, *72*
Friedman, S., 251, *258*
Friend, R., 264, *282*
Friesen, W., *112*
Frijda, N. H., 269, *280*
Fritz, G. K., 294, 303, *307*
Frost, R. O., 220, 221, *233*
Fuetsch, M., *331*
Fullerton, C. S., *350*
Furman, E., 207, *211*
Furr, J. M., 109, *112*

Gabrielson, I. W., 201, *212*
Gaines, J. G., 266, *279*
Gallop, R. J., *115*
Gardner, R., 315, *331*
Garety, P. A., 313, 315, 316, 317, 318, 325, 327, 328, 329, 330, *331*
Garland, A., 299, *307*
Garrison, B., 59, *72,* 219, *231,* 240, *256*
Garver, K. E., *305*
Gates, C., 310, *328*
Gauthier, J., 95, *112*
Gay, B., *332*
Geddes, J., *331*
Gelenberg, A. J., 374, *379*
Gelfand, D. M., 101, *113*
Gencoz, F., *281*
Gencoz, T., *281*
Gentilini, J. M., 76, *90*
Gibbons, J., 248, *257*
Giedd, J. N., 289, 292, 293, *303, 304*
Giesler, R. B., 277, *280*
Gifford, E., 92, *117*
Gifford, E. V., 373, *379*
Gilbert, J., *329*
Gilbert, P., 185, *188,* 313, 315, 318, 324, 327, 328, 329, *331*
Gilboa-Schechtman, E., 41, *47, 212*
Gillham, J. E., 264, *280*
Gilligan, S. G., 93, *112*
Gilpin, A., 130, *146*
Gilvarry, C., *332*
Giolas, M. H., 121, *147*
Gispert, M., 296, 299, *304*
Gitlin, M., 310, *332*
Glassman, A., 268, *280*
Glaudin, V., xiv, *xvi*
Goddard, L., 183, *188*
Goff, D., 318, *329*
Goggin, W. C., 97, 99, *111,* 220, 225, *232*
Gold, S. N., 335, *350*

Goldberg, D., 220, *233*
Goldblatt, M. J., 267, *280*
Goldfried, M., *246–247*
Goldney, R., *168, 188, 257*
Goldney, R. D., 99, *113*
Goldsmith, S. K., 262, 263, *281*
Goldston, D. B., 244, *257, 295, 299, 304*
Gollan, J., 109, *113*
Gonzales, B., *332*
Goodwin, J., 201, *211*
Gordon, K., *261–279*
Gorey, K. M., *351*
Gortner, E., 109, *113*
Gothelf, D., 294, *304*
Gould, M. S., 228, *233, 299, 307*
Gould, R. A., 318, 319, *329*
Graae, F., *297, 306*
Grace, M. C., *335, 351*
Gracia, R., *326*
Graham, R., 93, *111*
Gray, M. J., 336, *351*
Gray, S., 238, *257*
Graybill, D., 39, *47*
Green, A. H., 201, *211*
Green, B. L., 335, *351*
Greenberg, R. L., 360, *367*
Greenfield, S. F., 316, *329*
Greenough, W. T., 101, *113*
Greenspan, S. I., 199, *211*
Greer, S., 55, *73*
Gregory, S., 176, *189*
Grieger, R. M., 76, *90*
Grisham, J. R., 59, 62, *71, 72, 97, 111*
Grochowski, S., 245, *258, 311, 330*
Groholt, B., 229, *233*
Gross, J. J., 93, 97, *113*
Grossman, W. I., 198, *211*
Gruber, S. A., *302*
Grunbaum, J. A., 290, *304*
Grunet, B. K., 342, *352*
Guido, J. R., *330*
Gulbinat, W. H., *331*
Gunnell, D., *260*
Gupta, M. A., 197, *211*
Guthrie, D., 244, *255, 298, 302*
Guthrie, M., *328*
Guze, S., 240, *257*
Gwaltney, J. M., *280*

Haaga, D. A., 88, *89, 240, 242, 257, 259, 359, 367*
Haas, A. P., *146, 335, 351*

Haas, G. L., *281*
Habke, M., 226, 228, *233, 234*
Haddock, G., 318, *329*
Haller, D. L., 217, *234*
Hamera, E., *330*
Hamilton, T. K., 220, 221, *233*
Hanssen, M., 316, *332*
Hardy, K., 318, *327*
Har-Even, D., 204, *212, 213, 299, 307*
Hargreaves, I., 176, *189*
Haring, M., 228, *233*
Harker, L., 102, *114*
Harlow, H. F., 195, *211*
Harper, R., 85, *89*
Harrigan, S., *329*
Harrington, H., *331*
Harrington, R., 316, *328*
Harris, A., *257*
Harris, E. C., 61, *73, 240, 257, 372, 379*
Harris, T. O., 324, *327*
Harrison, G., 316, *329*
Harrison, K., 208, *213*
Harrison, R., 151, *167*
Hart, D., 290, *303*
Hart, K. J., 295, *307*
Harter, S., 290, *304*
Hartmann, D. P., 101, *113*
Harvey, 228
Harvey, A. G., 182, *188, 336, 351*
Harvey, M., *235*
Hary, E., *297, 306*
Hassan, R., 99, *113*
Hassanyeh, F., 64, *73, 111*
Hastings, M. E., 99, *113*
Hatakka, M., *115*
Hawkins, A. G., 41, *46*
Hawley, J. L., 266, *283*
Hawton, K., 58, 63, *73, 96, 99, 113, 162, 168, 187, 188, 244, 247, 248, 250, 257, 259, 260, 294, 297, 304, 305, 335, 350*
Hay, J., *329*
Hayakawa, S. I., *89*
Hayes, R. L., 216, *233*
Hayes, S. C., 92, 94, 108, *113, 117, 373, 376, 379*
Haynes, S., 251, *258*
Hays, R. D., 130, *146*
Hayward, L., 316, *331*
Hayward, M. C., *350*
Hazell, P., *260*
Healey, H., *191*

Healy, H., *191*
Healy, J., 319, *327*
Heard, H., *190*
Heard, H. L., xvi, 97, *113*, *115*
Heath, J. L., 92, *110*
Heath, N. L., 99, *115*
Heckler, R. A., 125, *146*
Hedeker, D., *144*
Heikkinen, M., 93, *113*
Heim, C., 375, *379*
Heimberg, R. G., 109, *113*, 220, *233*
Heisel, M., 229, *233*
Helders, P. J. M., 196, *211*
Hembree, E. A., *350*
Hemenway, D., 267, *281*
Hemsley, D., 317, 318, 325, *327*, *328*, *329*
Henderson, D., 176, *189*
Hendin, H., *146*, 335, *351*
Henriques, G. R., xv, 53–70, *72*, *73*, 378–379
Henry, L., *329*
Heppner, P., 243, 244, *256*
Hepworth, C., 324, *327*
Herberman, H. B., *350*
Herbert, E. W., 101, *113*
Herman, I., 56, *71*
Herman, J., 336, *351*
Herman, L., 208, *212*, 294, *306*
Hermans, D., 175, 176, 179, *188*, *189*, *190*
Hermans, H., 154, *168*
Herns, S., *188*
Herrero, O., *169*
Hesse, E., 121, 126, *146*
Heuvelman, L. R., 39, *47*
Hewitt, P. L., xv, 6, 215–231, 216, 217, 218, 219, 220, 221, 223, 224, 225, 228, 229, 230, *232*, *233*, *234*, *235*
Hirsch, S. R., 310, 311, 312, *329*, *330*
Hirschfeld, R. M., 356, *367*
Hirschman, J., 158, *168*
Hofler, M., *331*
Hogan, H. E., *279*
Hogan, M. E., 372, *378*
Hokanson, J. E., 103, *116*
Holahan, C. J., 93, *115*
Holden, R., 97, *113*
Holford, S., 201, *210*
Hollan, J. D., 177, *191*
Hollander, J. E., *72*, 378–379
Hollender, M. H., 217, *234*
Hollon, S. D., *112*, 266, *282*

Holmes, E. A., 336, *350*
Holt, C. S., 220, *233*
Holton, A., 102, *116*
Holton, A. R., 64, *73*
Hope, D. A., 109, *113*
Hopkins, R., *329*
Hopper, K., *329*
Horesh, N., 294, *304*
Hossain, Z., 196, *213*
House, A., 162, *168*
Howells, K., 182, *188*, 242, *257*
Hoyer, G., 274, *281*
Hughes, D., 63, *73*
Hughes, S., 154, 159, 160, *168*
Hughes, S. L., *168*
Hughes, T., 158, *168*, 180, *190*
Hulbert, C., *329*
Hull, W. J., 208, *213*
Humphreys, A. L., 349, *352*
Hurren, K., 64, *73*
Hustead, L. A. T., 41, *47*
Hutchings, J., 184, *189*
Hutton, S., *328*
Hyman, R. B., 311, *330*

Ievers, C., *304*
Inayatulla, M., 222, *232*
Inayatullah, M., *308*
Inskip, H. M., 240, *257*, 372, *379*
Institute of Medicine, 77, 89
Iqbal, Z., 7, 309–326, *327*, *329*
Isen, A. M., 269, *281*
Isohanni, I., 316, *329*
Isohanni, M., 316, *330*
Ivanoff, A., 245, *258*

Jablensky, A., 312, *329*, *331*
Jackson, C., 317, 318, *327*, *329*
Jackson, D. C., 291, *303*
Jackson, H. J., 311, 312, 318, 321, *329*, *330*
Jacobs, S. C., *115*
Jacobson, N. S., 93, 94, 108, 109, *113*
Jacobvitz, D., 126, *146*
Jacoby, A. M., 41, *47*
James, 294, 297, 298
James, A., 244, *257*, 294, 297, *304*, *305*
James, P., xv, *xvi*
Jamison, K. R., 125, *146*
Jang, S., 245, *258*
Jan Verkes, R., 207, *214*
Jarvelin, M. R., *329*
Jastereboff, P. J., 293, *303*

Morrison, A. P., 329
Mortensen, P. B., 316, 331
Morton, R. V., 328
Moscicki, E. K., 73
Moses, T., 207, 210
Mueser, K. T., 318, 329
Mulder, R. T., 295, 296, 302
Muller, G. E., 89–90
Muller, N., 331
Munoz, D. P., 305
Munro, Y., 221, 232
Muris, P., 176, 190
Murray, A. M., 115
Murray, B., 329
Murray, C., 238, 258
Murray, C. M., 376, 380
Murray, H. A., 35, 47
Murray, R., 331, 332
Murray, R. M., 330
Myhrman, A., 316, 330
Myin-Germeys, I., 325, 330
Myquel, M., 302

Naples, A., 253, 258
Nash, S., 184, 189
National Research Council, 352
Negron, R., 297, 299, 306
Neimeyer, R. A., xv, 6, 16, 27, 149–167, 167, 168, 169
Nekanda-Trepka, C. J. S., 266, 282
Nelson, A., 325, 327, 332
Nelson, K. N., 5, 15, 29–46, 47
Nemeroff, C. B., 375, 379
Neubauer, A. L., 220, 233
Neuman, M., 112
Neuringer, C., 16, 18, 27, 28, 39, 46, 47, 297, 305
Newell, A., 251, 258
Newman, C. F., 63, 65, 72, 73, 75, 77, 89, 219, 231, 344, 350
Newman, C. W., 124, 144
Newman, M. G., 109, 111
Newsom, J. T., 280
Newton, J., 221, 234
Nezu, A., 241, 242, 247, 248, 251, 257, 258
Nezu, C., 247, 251, 258
Niederee, J., 342, 352
Nieminen, P., 329
Nightingale, D., 184, 189
Nikesch, S., 181, 188
Nimmo-Smith, I., 175, 188

Nisbet, P. A., 263, 282
Nitz, K., 305
Nock, M. K., 295, 306
Norcross, J. C., 378, 380
Norman, D. A., 177, 190
Northman, L. M., 99, 113
Norton, G. R., 234
Nottingham, E., 238, 256
Noyes, R., 96, 97, 115
Nozyce, M., 197, 210
Nuechterlain, K. H., 310, 332
Nuñez, R., 208, 212

Oatley, K., 218, 234, 319, 330
O'Brien, G., 64, 73
O'Carroll, P. W., 55, 58, 73
O'Connor, D. B., 225, 234
O'Connor, M., 257
O'Connor, R. C., 41, 47, 185, 190, 225, 234
Oei, T. I., 124, 146
Ofek, H., 294, 304
O'Grady, J., 96, 99, 113
Ohtani, Y., 225, 234
Ojehagen, A., 56, 63, 72, 74
Okun, A., 281
O'Loughlin, S., 182, 188, 242, 257
Orbach, G., 331
Orbach, I., xv, 7, 41, 47, 123, 124, 127, 146, 147, 176, 182, 190, 193–210, 203, 204, 208, 212, 213, 217, 234, 243, 258, 294, 297, 306
Orbach, Y., 175, 190
Orman, D., 259
Ormstad, K., 335, 350
Orr, S. G., 39, 47
Orvaschel, H., 207, 210
Osborn, M., 96, 99, 113
Osman, A., 237, 282
Osman, J. R., 282
Ostrom, C. W., 305
Otto, M., 238, 257
Overholser, J. C., 293, 294, 295, 296, 298, 303, 304, 306, 307
Owens, D., 162, 168, 240, 258

Pacheco, M., 169
Pachinger, M. M., 176, 189
Page, S., 99, 112
Palgi, Y., 213
Pankratz, V. S., 240, 256
Papousek, H., 196, 211
Papousek, M., 196, 211

Parides, M., 228, *233*
Park, C. L., 266, *282*
Parke, R. D., 197, *212*
Parker, A., 96, *115*, 160, *169*
Parker, G., 222, 229, *232*, 316, *331*
Parker, W., 221, *231*
Parkin, M., *234*
Partanen, U., 316, *330*
Patsiokas, A. T., 294, 297, *306*
Pavanello, D. P., *46*
Payvar, S., 245, 246, *259*
Pearce, C. M., 200, 205, *213*
Pearlstein, T., 299, *308*
Pearson, J., 226, *234*
Pederson, C. B., 316, *331*
Peeters, F., 175, 176, 182, *190, 191*
Pelaez-Nogueras, M., 196, *213*
Pellmar, T. C., 262, *281*
Pentiuc, D., *47*
Perez, M., 261–279, *281*
Pericay, J. M., 57, *74*
Perlin, S., *71*
Perot, J. M., 124, *146*
Perri, M., 247, *258*
Perry, B. D., 126, *147*
Peterson, E. M., *47*
Peterson, K. A., *330*
Petric, K., 60, *74*
Pettit, J. W., *281, 373, 379*
Phil, M., 99, *110*
Philip, A. E., 55, *73*
Piacentini, J., 297, *306*
Piaget, J., 290, *306*
Pickens, J., 196, *213*
Pieters, G., *189*
Pilling, S., 318, *331*
Pilowsky, L. S., 315, *327*
Pincus, A. L., 109, *111*
Pines, D., 200, *213*
Piquet, M. L., 295, 298, 299, 301, *306*
Pitman, R. K., 176, *189*
Plaistow, J., 313, *327*
Plath, S., 158, *169, 234*
Platt, J. J., 182, *190*
Pleydell-Pearce, C. W., 174, 178, *188*
Plumee, A. A., *330*
Plutchik, R., 298, *305*
Pokorny, A. D., *71*, 99, *114, 331*
Pollock, L. R., 93, *115*, 175, 183, 186, *190, 191, 192*
Poorly, 310
Popper, K., *169*

Posner, M. I., 291, *306*
Potthoff, J. G., 93, *115*
Poulton, R., 316, *331*
Power, K., 245, 246, *256*
Powers, T. A., 102, *115*
Prassas, A., 176, *190*
Pretz, J., 253, *258*
Price, A., *281*
Price, J., 315, 319, *331*
Priester, M. G., 243, *258, 259*, 297, *306*
Prigerson, H. G., 95, *115*
Prigerson, M. G., 336, *351*
Puett, R., 335, *352–353*
Puffet, A., 175, *190*
Putnam, F. W., 294, *306*
Putnam, N., 198, *213*

Quinlin, D. M., 223, *231*

Rabung, S., 13, *27*
Raes, F., 175, 179, *188, 189, 190*
Rajab, H., 238, 244, *259*
Rajab, M. H., 53, *74, 75, 77*, 89, 126, *147*, 247, *259*, 271, *282*, 336, *352, 355, 356, 368, 372, 380*
Rakic, P., 293, *303*
Rand, K. L., 224, *225, 232*
Range, L. M., 97, 99, *111*, 220, 224, 225, *232, 370, 379*
Ranieri, W. F., 219, *231*
Rantakallio, P., 316, *329, 330*
Raskin, A., 99, *111*
Raskin, J. D., 16, *27*
Ratliff, K., 76, *89, 372, 379*
Ratzoni, G., 299, *307*
Rauch, S. A., *350*
Reboussin, B., *257*
Reboussin, D. M., 257, *304*
Rector, 320
Reed, M. A., 298zz, *304*
Regnell, G., 56, *74*
Reid, D. A., *328*
Reinecke, M. A., 6, 76, 237–255, *259*, 296, *306*
Reivich, K. J., 264, *280*
Renshaw, P. F., *302*
Resick, P. A., 342, 346, *352*
Reynolds, M., 176, *188*
Reynolds, W. M., 221, *234*
Rich, A., 242, *256*
Richards, C., 266, *281*
Rick, J., 272, *279*

Rierdan, J., 197, *211*
Rifkin, A., 126, *146*
Riggs, D. S., 100, *112*
Riley, T., *169*
Robbins, D. R., 293, *306*
Robin, R. S., xv, *xvi*
Robins, E., 240, *257*
Rodgers, A., 221, *234*
Rodhan, K., 335, *350*
Rogosch, 268
Rohde, P., 96, 99, *114*, 219, *234*, 315, *331*, 375, *379*
Róiste, A., 196, *213*
Rojas, E. P., 196, *214*
Romanov, K., 97, *115*
Romme, M., 317, *328*
Ronan, G., 242, *258*
Rooke, O., 315, *331*
Roozendaal, B., 126, *144*
Rose, G., *191*
Rose, G. S., 97, *115*
Rose, R. J., *115*
Rose, S., 317, *326*, 336, *349*
Rosenblate, R., 220, 221, *233*
Rosenheck, R. A., *115*
Rosenheim, E., 297, *306*
Ross, J. G., *304*
Ross, K., *332*
Ross, S., 99, *115*
Rothbart, M. K., 291, 298, 299, *304*, *306*
Rothbaum, B. O., 109, *112*, 342, *350*
Rothberg, J. M., 93, 96, *115*
Rotheram-Borus, M. J., 209, *210*, 244, *259*, 295, 296, 297, 298, *307*
Rothman, A. J., 237, 238, *282*
Rouleau, M. R., 38, *47*
Roy, A., 99, *115*
Rudd, M. D., 7, 17, *28*, 38, *47*, 53, 61, *73*, *74*, 75, 77, 89, 126, *147*, 186, *189*, 238, 244, 247, *258*, *259*, 263, 269, 271, 275, 277, 278, 281, *282*, 336, 338, 344, *351*, *352*, 355–367, 356, *367*, 368, 372, 377, *380*
Rudge, S., *326*
Ruff, G. A., *351*
Runtz, M., 126, *144*
Rush, A. J., 54, 63, 66, 67, *71*, 78, 88
Rush, J., 154, *167*
Russ, M. J., 208, *213*
Russell, A., *330*
Russell, G. F. M., 198, *213*
Russell, J. M., 356, *367*

Rutter, C. M., 289, *307*
Rutter, M., 316, *328*, *331*
Ryan, R. M., 275, *282*

Saarinen, P. I., *331*
Sadowski, C., 297, *307*
Saebel, J., 99, *113*
Sakinofsky, I., xv, *xvi*
Sakurai, S., 225, *234*
Salamon, R., *332*
Salk, L., 202, *213*
Salkovskis, P. M., 62, 74, 238, 246, 249, 250, *259*
Salovey, P., 237, 238, *282*
Sandborn, E., 335, *350*
Sanders, B., 121, *147*
Sardine, 310
Sareen, J., 221, *232*
Sartorius, N., 309, *329*, *331*
Sayler, M. E., *xv*
Scarr, S., 100, *115*
Schachter, S., 199, *213*
Schaffer, C. E., 223, *231*
Schalling, D., 203, *211*
Schanberg, S. M., 195, 196, *212*, *213*
Scheftner, W., 60, *74*, 260
Scheftner, W. A., 96, *112*, *144*
Scheier, M. F., 264, *279*
Schmaling, K., *112*
Schnicke, M. K., 342, 346, *352*
Schore, A. N., 126, *147*
Schork, N. J., 197, *211*
Schotte, D. E., 93, *116*, 238, 241, 242, 244, 245, 246, *259*, 271, *282*, 297, *307*, 370, *380*
Schulman, P., 266, *282*
Schulman, R. E., *71*
Schultz, T., 244, 246, *259*
Schuyler, D., 56, *71*
Schwartz, J. E., 325, *330*
Schwartz, R. C., 310, *331*
Schweitzer, R. D., 220, 221, *233*
Scott, J., *111*, 176, *188*, *331*
Scott, J. L., *331*
Sears, P., 38, *49*
Sears, R. R., 38, *49*
Seeley, J. R., 96, 99, *114*, 219, *234*, 375, *379*
Segal, Z. V., 187, *192*, 375, *380*
Seiden, R. H., 124, *145*
Seligman, M. E. P., 98, *110*, 261, 262, 264, 265, 266, 272, *279*, *280*, *282*
Sensky, T., 318, 319, 322, *331*

Wostear, G., 316, *328*

Xie, S. X., *72*, 378–379

Yang, B., 59, *72*, 177, *192*, 293, 295, 296,
    308, 375, 380
Yarczower, M., 100, *112*
Yiend, J., 182, *188*
Young, A. S., 310, *332*
Young, B., 335, *353*
Young, M. A., 60, *74, 144,* 245, 260
Young, S., *281*
Yule, J., *257*

Zahn-Waxler, C., 289, *308*
Ziegler, D. L., 266, *283*
Zijdenbos, A., *304*
Zimbardo, P. G., 109, *117*
Zimmerman, J. H., xv, 7, 287–302
Zimmerman, S. L., 41, *49*
Zlotnick, C., 299, *308*
Zubek, J., 266, *281*
Zuroff, D. C., 102, *115*
Zwart, F. M., *146*

SUBJECT INDEX

environmental causes and, 92–94
problem avoidance and, 100
research supporting, 96–97, 376
self–invalidation and, 98–99
blaming, 346–347
body–mind. *See* suicidal body
borderline personality disorder (BPD), 91, 96, 99, 102. *See also* dialectical behavior therapy
BPD. *See* borderline personality disorder
brain development, 291–293
broaden-and-build theory, 268–271
burdensomeness. *See* perceived burdensomeness

CAMS. *See* Collaborative Assessment and Management of Suicidality
catastrophizing, 77, 78, 336
causal processes, 92–100
CBT. *See* cognitive–behavioral therapies
change
acceptance and, 376
procedures in DBT and, 106–109
"chaotic suicide," 158–159
Cheung, Leslie, 216
Child–Adolescent Perfectionism Scale (CAPS), 221
children, 25–26. *See also* adolescent suicidality; developmental influences; early care
choice provision, 276, 277
cigarette smoking, 267–268
circumspection–preemption–control cycle, 159
classification of behaviors, 56, 57
clinical interventions, 375–378
Beck and, 62–63, 376–377
cognitive therapy and, 61–70
construct theory and, 162–164
overgeneral memory and, 370, 376
perfectionism and, 230, 371, 376
personal construct therapy and, 161–162
positive psychology and, 270–271, 275–278
posttraumatic stress disorder and, 339–344
problem-solving deficits and, 63, 107, 370, 376
problem solving model and, 246–247
rational emotive behavior therapy and, 80–87

schizophrenia and, 317–319
Shneidman's model and, 42–45
voice therapy and, 132–142
clinical populations, 4. *See also* borderline personality disorder; schizophrenia
cognitive–affective–behavioral network, 143, 359–360
cognitive–behavioral therapies (CBTs), 3
dialectical behavior therapy and, 103
introduction of, 13–14
voice therapy and, 120
cognitive constriction. *See also* problem-solving deficits
construct theory and, 152, 158, 160–161
Shneidman's work on, 33, 34–35, 36, 42, 152, 371
cognitive deconstruction, 294, 324
cognitive diatheses, 370
crisis intervention and, 80
identification of, 6, 370
therapy and, 370–371, 376
cognitive diathesis–stress model, 7, 238–239
cognitive features in suicidality, 370, 373–374. *See also* cognitive constriction; commonalities of suicide; dysfunctional beliefs; hopelessness; overgeneral memory; perfectionism; problem-solving deficits
etiology of, 374–375
Neuringer's research and, 16–17, 22–23
cognitive model
assessment and, 56–60
concept of modes and, 60–61, 372
development of, 53–54, 60–61
nomenclature and, 54–56
orientation of patient to, 65
therapeutic intervention and, 61–70
cognitive restructuring, 107
cognitive schemas, 295, 296, 313
cognitive suicidology
roots of, 15–18
cognitive system, 359–360
cognitive therapy
components of, 62–64
early sessions, 64–67
general principles for, 62–63
later sessions and, 69–70
middle phase of, 67–69
protocol for, 64
for psychosis, 317–319, 320–323
studies on effectiveness of, 62

voice therapy and, 119–120
cognitive triad, 359–360
cognitive vulnerability, 21–22. *See also* fluid vulnerability theory
Collaborative Assessment and Management of Suicidality (CAMS), 41
commonalities of suicide
    clinical intervention and, 42–43
    recent studies on, 41
    Shneidman's theory and, 33–34, 42–43
communication strategies
    cognitive therapy and, 63, 64–65
    in DBT, 105
competence, 93–94, 275, 276. *See also* effectiveness
    adolescent cognitions and, 293–294
completed suicide
    assessment measures and, 59
    comorbid psychiatric disorders and, 335–336
    low base rate of, 239
    research on predictors of, 37–39
    as term, 55
conceptualization of suicidal behavior, 66–67
constructive narrative approach
    development of posttraumatic stress disorder and, 336–338
    trauma exposure and, 334–336, 337
    treatment implications of, 339–344
constructivist therapy, 6, 372
construct theory. *See* constructive narrative approach; personal construct theory
construing process, 151–153, 158–159, 161
contingency clarification, 107–108
control over events, and adolescents, 295
coping. *See also* problem-solving model
    constructive narrative approach and, 340, 343
    crisis plan strategies and, 65–66
    emotion regulation and, 269–270, 296–300
    positive psychology and, 269–270
coping cards, 67–68
core identity, 152–153, 154
crisis intervention
    positive emotions and, 270–271
    in REBT framework, 80
crisis plan, 65–66
"cry of pain" model, 184–187
cubic model of suicide, 35–36, 43

DBT. *See* dialectical behavior therapy

"dedicated act," suicide as, 157
delusions
    auditory hallucinations and, 312–314, 317–318
    persecutory, 315–316, 318
depression, 362, 371–372
    adolescent suicidality and, 293–296
    auditory hallucinations and, 312–314
    cognitive therapy and, 62–63, 317–319
    construct theory and, 151, 158
    development of cognitive model and, 53–54
    emotional dysregulation and, 96–97
    masochistic tendencies and, 207
    optimism and, 264–265
    overgeneral memory and, 175–176, 182
    perfectionism and, 219, 220
    pharmacotherapy and, *xiv*
    physical health and, 267–268
    posttraumatic stress disorder and, 335
    problem-solving deficits and, 240–246
    REBT and, 81–82
    in schizophrenia, 310–317, 319–321
descriptions theory, 177, 178
detailed planning, 125
"deterministic suicide," 158
developmental influences, 7, 287–302, 374–375. *See also* early care
    adolescent cognition and, 290
    biosocial theory and, 92, 94, 95–96, 101
    childhood trauma and, 176–177
    cognitive vulnerability and, 21–22
    depression and, 289, 316–317
    mental health and, 290
    neuroscience research and, 290–293, 298–299
    parental cognitions and, 199, 289
    self-preservation role of early care and, 195–200
    separation theory and, 121–123, 125–126, 132
developmental psychopathology, 288–290
dialectical behavior therapy (DBT), 17–18, 103–109, 373, 374, 376. *See also* biosocial theory
    crisis intervention and, 80
    stages of treatment in, 104
    strategies in, 105–109
dialectical strategies, 106
"dialogical self," 154
dichotomous thinking, 7, 154
    Neuringer and, 25, 26

Shneidman and, 34–35, 42
disconnection, 124
discrepancy-reducing loop, 264–265
dissociation, 126–127, 193, 195
    adolescent suicidality and, 294
    suicidal body and, 193, 195, 202, 207–208
dissonance, 98
dysfunctional behaviors
    constructive narrative approach and, 342
    social reinforcement of, 102–103
dysfunctional beliefs
    biosocial theory and, 98–99
    constructive narrative approach and, 341–343
    FVT and, 361, 363, 365–366
    posttraumatic stress disorder and, 341–342, 346
    problem solving model and, 239–241
    REBT and, 78–80
    therapy and, 370

early care. *See also* developmental influences
    defined, 194
    effects of negative experiences and, 201
    mediating processes and, 206–209
    negative memories of, 205–206
    role in self-preservation, 195–200
    self-destruction hypothesis and, 201–206
    treatment implications and, 209–210
effectiveness, 271–274. *See also* competence
effortful coping, 298–299
elaborative choice, 152
emergency plan. *See* crisis plan
emotional dysregulation, 92, 94–97, 373, 374. *See also* hopelessness; psychache
    adolescents and, 299–300
    affective gating and, 178–180
    emotion regulation as term and, 299
    problem-solving deficits and, 100, 271, 296–297
    research on, 96–97
    separation theory and, 126
emotions. *See also* emotional dysregulation
    brain development and, 291–293
    effects of negative emotions and, 269
    positive psychology and, 268–271
    suicidal body and, 208–209
environmental causes. *See also* adverse life events; stress

invalidation and, 101
    Linehan's theory and, 92–94, 100–103
equifinality, 288, 289, 374
escape theories, 94, 324. *See also* emotional dysregulation
expectancy theory, and optimism, 264–265, 266
experience cycle, 151–152
experiential avoidance, 373
explanation, 5
    optimism and, 265–266
exposure therapy. *See* opposite action
extreme risk-taking, 125

family environment, 101, 297. *See also* developmental influences; early care; environmental causes; isolation; perceived burdensomeness
fantasy bond, 121–123
Farberow, Norman, 29–30, 31, 36, 37, 40
Farooqi, Yasmin, 132
Firestone Assessment of Self-Destructive Thoughts (FAST), 119, 138, 143
    research on, 128–132
fluid vulnerability theory (FVT)
    assumptions in, 358–364
    clinical implications of, 364–366
    research implications of, 366–367
    risk assessment and, 355–358
follow-up period. *See also* fluid vulnerability theory
    cognitive therapy and, 62
    FVT and, 364–366
    personal construct therapy and, 165
Foote, William, 334
frustration tolerance. *See* low frustration tolerance
FVT. *See* fluid vulnerability theory (FVT)

grieving, avoidance of, 95, 100
growth
    and touch, 200
Guide to Rational Living (A. Ellis & Harper), 86

Harper, R., 86
Al-Haznawi, Ahmed, 157
helplessness, 76–77. *See also* hopelessness
Hemingway, Ernest, 216
historical factors
    and baseline risk, 361
"hope kit," 66, 68

hopelessness. *See also* emotional
    dysregulation
    "A-B-C" model and, 76–77, 78
    adolescents and, 294–295
    assessment of, 60
    biosocial theory and, 97–98
    concept of, 17, 54, 372
    dialectical behavior therapy and, 107
    overgenerality and, 179–180, 183–184
    perfectionism and, 217–218, 219, 225
    pessimism and, 266
    positive psychchology and, 263–264
    problem-solving orientation and, 241–
        246
hypervigilance, 347–348

impulsivity, 294
individual idiosyncracies, 81
infants. *See* developmental influences; early
    care
innate psychological needs, 274–277
"inner conversations," 336–338. *See also* con-
    structive narrative approach
Institute to Treat Victims of Violence, 334
intellectually gifted persons
    suicide among, 38–39
intent
    assessment of, 54–55, 56–57
    lethality and, 58
    psychosis and, 319, 324–325
interpersonal hostility, 227–228
interpersonal–psychological theory, 271–
    274, 276
interpersonal sensitivity, 227–228
interventions. *See* clinical interventions
intimate relationships, 155–156
invalidation. *See* self-invalidation
Irrational Beliefs Test, 76
isolation, 123–124

Kelly, George, 15–16
Korzybski, Alfred, 84, 86

LASPC. *See* Los Angeles Suicide Prevention
    Center
lethality
    assessment of, 55, 57–58
    low self-esteem and, 293
    Shneidman's research and, 39
Lethality Scales (LS), 55, 57–58
logic of suicide, 32–33
Loiseau, Bernard, 216

loosening techniques, 164
Los Angeles County Coroner's Office, 37
Los Angeles Suicide Prevention Center
    (LASPC), 30
low frustration tolerance (LFT), 77
low self-esteem
    in adolescents, 293–294
LS. *See* Lethality Scales

Make-A-Picture Story (MAPS) test, 39–40
MAPS test. *See* Make-A-Picture Story
    (MAPS) test
married status, 274
martyrdom, 157
masochistic tendencies, 207
medication
    as crisis intervention, 80
    suicide recurrence and, *xiv*
mental health professionals
    chronic suicidality and, 355–358
    suicide of a patient and, 4, 333–334
mental hospital patients, 38
mentalism, 30–31
mind, division of, 121, 122
mindfulness meditation, 108, 376
mnemonic interlock, 181
moderational model, 224–225
modes, concept of. *See* suicidal mode
money therapy, 26–27
motivational system, 264–265, 291, 298–
    299, 360. *See also* belongingness;
    problem-solving orientation; self-
    determination theory
multifinality, 288, 289
Murray, Henry, 35, 44

need fulfillment
    in early care, 198–199
    self-determination approach and, 274–
        277
negative cognitive triad, 54, 202–203
negative early care, 201–206
negative thought processes. *See* self-destruc-
    tive thoughts
Neuringer, Charles
    interview with, 18–27
    roots of cognitive suicidology and, 16–
        17, 18
neurobiological factors, 7, 291–293, 373, 375
neuropsychology
    adolescent cognition and, 289, 291–293
    suicidal body and, 208–209

nomenclature, 54–56, 57
not caring, 124

object relations, and self-destruction, 207
opposite action, 108–109
optimism, 264–267, 370
overgeneral memory, 6, 173–187
    affective gating and, 178–180
    childhood trauma and, 176–177
    consequences of, 181–184
    etiology and, 375
    interventions and, 370, 376
    mechanisms underlying, 177–181
    stabilization of, 180–181

pain, psychological. See psychache
pain-oriented psychotherapy. See anodyne
    therapy
parasuicide
    as term, 54–55
parental cognitions, 199, 289
parent–child attachment, 200, 316–317
PCT. See personal construct theory
perceived burdensomeness, 124, 272–273,
    276, 373
perfectionism, 98, 108–109
    interventions and, 230, 371, 376
    models of, 217–218
    moderational model and, 224–225
    research on, 218–223
    role in suicide behavior, 215–217
    self-oreinted vs. socially prescribed,
    218–223
    social disconnection model and, 226–
    230
    suicidal ideation and, 219–221
persecutory delusions, 315–316, 318
personal construct theory (PCT), 149, 150–
    156
    anticipatory posture and, 150
    clinical interventions and, 162–164
    construing process and, 151–153, 158–
    159, 160–162
    pathways to suicidal choice and, 156–
    159
    research studies and, 159–161
    self in social context and, 155–156
    structure of knowing and, 153–155
personality assessment, 39–40
personality disorder, 82–87
personal meaning, 155, 346
personal strengths

resilience and, 262–264, 341
resource building and, 271
trauma and, 341
perspective taking, 276–277
perturbation, 30, 35, 39, 42
pessimism. See optimism; positive psychol-
    ogy
PFC. See prefrontal cortex
philosophical issues, 79–80
physical abuse. See negative early care; post-
    traumatic stress disorder; victimiza-
    tion and suicidality
physical health
    and positive psychology, 267–268
physiological system, 360
Plath, Sylvia, 156, 158, 215, 216
popular myths, 24
positive psychology, 261–279
    belongingness and, 271–272, 273–274
    broaden-and-build theory and, 268–271
    defined, 262
    effectiveness and, 271–273
    optimism and, 264–267
    physical health and, 267–268
    posttraumatic stress disorder and, 341–
    342
    self-determination theory and, 274–277
postpsychotic depression (PPD), 314–315
posttraumatic stress disorder (PTSD), 7, 95,
    176, 317, 333–349
    chronic, 344–349
    formula for, 337
    "inner conversations" and, 336–338,
    344–349
    treatment of, 339–344
postvention
    as term, 30
prefrontal cortex (PFC), 291–293
press, 35
problem-solving deficits. See also problem
    solving model
    adolescents and, 296–297
    construct theory and, 152
    DBT and, 105
    emotional dysregulation and, 100, 271,
    296–297
    etiology of, 375
    interventions and, 63, 107, 370, 376
    multiple risk factors and, 239
    overgeneral memory and, 177, 182–183,
    186
    repertory grid assessment and, 160

suicidality and, 6, 20–21, 98
  therapy as problem solving and, 251–254

problem-solving model, 237–255. *See also* problem-solving deficits
  dysfunctional beliefs and, 239–241
  efficacy of treatments and, 248–251
  hopelessness and, 241–246
  methodology and, 238–239
  treatments and, 246–247, 251–254

problem-solving orientation
  hopelessness and, 241–245
  interventions and, 247
  therapy as problem solving and, 251–254

psychache. *See also* emotional dysregulation
  anodyne therapy and, 44–45
  assessment of, 40
  as construct, 31
  cubic model of suicide and, 35
  problem-solving deficits and, 240
  recent empirical work on, 41
  as term, 15, 30
  voice therapy and, 124

psychoanalytic approach. *See* voice therapy

psychological autopsy, 39
  as term, 30

Psychological Pain Survey, 40

psychological testing, 39–40. *See also* assessment

psychotherapy. *See also* problem solving model
  crisis intervention and, 80
  personal construct therapy and, 163–164
  as problem solving, 251–253
  REBT and, 80–81, 81–87
  Shneidman and, 43–44

Rational emotive behavior therapy (REBT), 75–88, 372
  clinical interventions and, 80–87
  research and, 87–88, 372
  theory and, 76–80
  voice therapy and, 119–120

rationale provision, 276, 277

rational problem-solving skills, 241, 247

reasons for living, 97

Reasons for Living (RFL) Inventory, 17, 267

REBT framework. *See* rational emotive behavior therapy

"reciprocal determinism," 100–101

recurrent suicidality. *See also* fluid vulnerability theory
  baseline risk and, 362–363
  cognitive diatheses and, 370
  pharmacotherapy and, *xiv*

relapse prevention task (RPT), 69–70

relapse process, 312

relatedness, 275, 276. *See also* belongingness

relational frame theory. *See* acceptance and commitment therapy

repertory grid assessment, 160–161, 164, 166

research, 4, 6–7
  on assessment, 56–60
  on cognitive characteristics, 16–17, 22–23
  on depression in schizophrenia, 310–317
  efficacy of problem-solving therapy and, 248–251
  emotional dysregulation and, 96–97
  on the FAST, 128–132
  fluid vulnerability theory and, 366–367
  future research questions, 369–378
  negative early care hypothesis and, 201–206
  on perfectionism, 218–223
  personal construct theory and, 159–161
  on predictors of completed suicide, 37–39
  rational emotive behavior therapy and, 87–88
  by Shneidman, 36–41
  voice therapy and, 128–132

resilience
  vs. risk, 262–263
  strengths and, 263–264, 341

responsibility, beliefs about
  adolescents and, 295, 297
  posttraumatic stress disorder and, 341–342

RFL Inventory. *See* Reasons for Living (RFL) Inventory

risk factors. *See* suicide risk

RPT. *See* relapse prevention task

ruminative thinking style, 180–181

safety plan. *See* crisis plan

Satcher, David, 4

SBS. *See* suicidal belief system

Scale for Suicide Ideation (SSI), 58–59

schizophrenia, 7

triggers, 343, 361, 363

unconditional life acceptance (ULA), 85
unconditional other acceptance (UOA), 84–85
unconditional self-acceptance (USA), 78, 79–80, 83–85

validation, 105
victimization and suicidality, 334–335. *See also* posttraumatic stress disorder
vital absorbing interest, 86
voices. *See* auditory hallucination

voice therapy, 6, 133–134, 377
   case study in, 136–142
   clinical interventions and, 132–142
   concept of voice and, 119, 120
   FAST research and, 128–132
   outcome research and, 142
   separation theory and, 119, 120–128
vulnerability factors. *See* cognitive diatheses; fluid vulnerability theory

warning signs, 357–358. *See also* suicide risk
Wittgenstein, Ludwig, 216
Woolf, Virginia, 216

ABOUT THE EDITOR

Thomas E. Ellis, PsyD, is a professor of psychology at Marshall University in Huntington, West Virginia. He earned his bachelor's degree in psychology at the University of Texas at Austin in 1974 and his doctor of psychology degree at Baylor University in 1978. He completed his predoctoral internship at the West Virginia University School of Medicine, Charleston Division. He is a fellow of the American Psychological Association (APA; Society of Clinical Psychology and Psychotherapy divisions) and diplomate of the American Board of Professional Psychology (behavioral psychology). He is a founding fellow of the Academy of Cognitive Therapy and an associate fellow of the Albert Ellis Institute. He has published numerous journal articles and book chapters in the area of cognition and suicide. He is coauthor (with W. Fremouw and M. DePerczel) of *Suicide Risk: Assessment and Response Guidelines* (1990) and (with C. Newman) of *Choosing to Live: How to Defeat Suicide Through Cognitive Therapy* (1996). He is a consulting editor for *Suicide and Life-Threatening Behavior* and the *Journal of Rational–Emotive and Cognitive–Behavioral Therapy*. His research and scholarly work pertaining to suicidal individuals has focused on various cognitive characteristics, classification issues, and cognitive therapy interventions. His current research focuses on relationships among health beliefs, health risk behaviors, and suicide risk. He is the former director of the Clinical Division of the American Association of Suicidology. In addition, he is a member of the APA, the Association of Behavioral and Cognitive Therapies, and the International Academy for Suicide Research. He lives in Huntington, West Virginia, with his wife and two children.